EDUCATIONAL PSYCHOLOGY OF THE GIFTED

EDUCATIONAL PSYCHOLOGY OF THE GIFTED

Joe Khatena

1807 1982
175 YEARS OF PUBLISHING

JOHN WILEY & SONS
New York • Chichester • Brisbane • Toronto • Singapore

Library of Congress Cataloging in Publication Data:

Khatena, Joe.
    Educational psychology of the gifted.

    Includes bibliographical references and index.
        1. Gifted children—Education.   2. Gifted chil-
dren—Psychology.   3. Educational psychology.
I. Title.
LC3993.2.K52   371.95   81-11452
ISBN 0-471-05078-4   AACR2

Printed in the United States of America

10 9 8 7 6 5 4 3 2 1

PREFACE

This book is about the nature and nurture of the gifted, their intellectual and creative development, the problems they face, the guidance they need, and the special opportunities that have become available to them. It also discusses the support agents that are available today as well as the advances that can be expected to make a real difference in education of the gifted in the future. The rather limited conception of giftedness as a superior intelligence quotient (IQ) has given way in recent years to the six U.S. Office of Education categories of giftedness, namely, general intellectual ability, creative or productive thinking, specific academic aptitude, leadership ability, visual and performing arts ability, and psychomotor ability. Each of these receive careful attention early in the book.

To formulate constructs of intellectual functioning and to develop measures based on them is a formidable task. Of major importance in this search was the expanded conception of intelligence—from unitary to multidimensional—achieved by British and American factor analysts, which culminated in the three-dimensional model of the structure of intellect. All of this provided the rationale for the development of identification procedures and, relative to the structure of intellect, the theoretical basis for recognition of a variety of abilities and ways to educe them. A significant feature of the structure of intellect model is the inclusion of divergent thinking (or creative thinking) and the related areas of intellectual functioning for which measures became available in the early 1960s. Although the measurement of achievement presents little difficulty, approaches at identifying talent in the visual and performing arts, as well as in the leadership and psychomotor domains are, by comparison, less well defined and more challenging. The issues relating to these talents are discussed in depth.

The past few years have not been easy for the gifted and creative movements and, at times, their relationship has been questioned. A fruitful attempt to resolve this problem traces the origins of the two movements to humanistic psychology. This perspective is a directional one and is, therefore, dealt with in the opening chapter. The chapter on creative imagination imagery is original and unique. A discussion of developmental aspects of the intellect and creativity as continuous and discontinuous adds yet another significant contribution to knowledge about the gifted. Drawing from developmental stage theory, general systems, and sociocultural variables, the reader is given further understanding about the factors affecting the gifted as they grow up. In addition, fresh viewpoints concerning guidance of the gifted enhance the contents of the book; especially pertinent are the discussions on the constructs of developmental guidance, on creativity, and on stress and its mastery—subjects hitherto not handled by other texts on the gifted. Problems of special groups are viewed as arising from underachievement—used in the broadest sense of the word to encompass not only academic underachievement but also underachievement as it relates to developmental stages, femininity, and cultural diversity. Other features of note in the book are the extension of the concept of acceleration to include accelerative enrichment, the emphasis on process approaches as providing a rationale for the development of intellect and design in the curriculum, and the special factors of motivation that affect the gifted. Much of the chapter on differential models covers both the current endeavors of providing special opportunities for the gifted and the ways to evaluate them. The chapter on all kinds of support agents at all major levels provides up-to-date information that will be found most useful to the educator of the gifted. The book ends by highlighting the main thrust and issues of each chapter with forward-looking comments on where education of the gifted is headed.

Generally, the issues presented in the book are both multidimensional and complex. Nonetheless, they have to be faced, and a dialogue must emerge if we are to begin to make progress in our approaches to understand the gifted and to provide opportunities for them. The explosion of knowledge in recent years on the gifted must remind us that we can no longer be restricted to traditional education sources for answers to the many problems that confront us. We have to draw from a multiplicity of sources if we are to begin to have perspective about giftedness. Such areas as general systems, creativity, developmental stage theory, and sociocultural and survival research dimensions of human functioning are but a few of the numerous resources available to us. Furthermore, our understanding must extend itself both into the past and the future to find meaning for the present and to give the directions so badly needed to step forth to the frontiers of thought and practice—and beyond.

These are some of the matters given significant focus in the book and can be expected to establish the *raison d'etre* of gifted education in at least the next decade or so. We have hardly begun to tease the potentials that the gifted possess, just as we have barely scratched the surface on how we may strive to do for them. The book should have special attractiveness to inquiring educators and their fellow professionals who are interested or engaged in gifted education. To read the book is not to find ready-made recipes or blueprints for tryouts, but rather to acquire the necessary perceptions that should begin to put teachers of the gifted in command of the constructs of the field so that individualized plans in gifted education can be generated now and in the future. The challenge is to strive to become the best among educators of the gifted.

I would like to acknowledge with gratitude the sustained guidance of John C. Gowan, which facilitated the writing of this book, and the suggestions of E. Paul Torrance, which enhanced it. Each one, in a different way and without deliberately planning to do so, meaningfully prepared me for the task. In addition, let me thank Joan Wolf, University of Utah, and George Sheperd, University of Oregon, for their valuable reviews of the manuscript. I would also like to express my appreciation to Nelly Khatena, my wife, who confirmed the need for such a book and, with patience and encouragement, supported its advance to completion.

Joe Khatena

CONTENTS

1

HISTORICAL PERSPECTIVES

OVERVIEW

This chapter deals with some of the major influences attending the development of the gifted movement. Advances in thought on the gifted are perceived in terms of the gifted and the creative movements whose origins are rooted in humanism. The various strands in the development of thought that are important for the gifted are examined. These include a broad humanism that respects individual differences and finds expression in the measurement of intelligence, gifted children and creativity, and the power of the human mind as revealed through the scientific thrusts of parapsychology. Twelve research milestones that are significant to advances in thought on the gifted are identified. Further, research on intelligence and creativity and their relationship are discussed and characteristics unique to the intellectually able and creative receive attention and comment.

CHAPTER OUTLINE

Introduction
Origins of Gifted and Creative Movements
Research Milestones
Some Measurement and Educational Implications
Developmental Aspects of the Gifted
Gifted Children Have Problems
Intellectually and Creatively Gifted Children
    Terman and High-IQ Children
    Intelligence and Creativity

> *Be the catalyst of the mystery and magic of existence, for in the creativity of your child may lie a magnificient future for all.*[1]

INTRODUCTION

It is remarkable how often in the history of civilization we discover the existence of something long before we find the proper use for it. Perhaps the best example is Albert Einstein's discovery of $E = mc^2$, but there are many other illustrations, one of which is the subject of gifted children. When first brought to light by Lewis M. Terman's researchers in the early years of this century, the intellectually gifted were considered somewhat of a genetic curiosity. What we now know is that intellectually gifted children form the best current identifiable source of potential verbal creativity, and talented children, the best current identifiable source of potential nonverbal creativity. Indeed, we are interested in gifted and talented children nowadays for precisely this reason, and not because they form some special elite. It is the creative potential of the gifted and talented that excites us and that removes the issue from some kind of educational frill to the central question of whether our society can maximize creative performance in its adults soon enough to avoid disaster. Because not all gifted or talented children reach this actualization, the task for teachers, parents, and others is to be found in the answer to the question: What kinds of parental, educational, and other interventions will promote the maximization of creativity in such children?

Yet, if we are to do what we must to bring this about, we have to keep in mind that there are varieties of giftedness—intellectual and talent resources that differ markedly from those of the general population. Identification of the gifted is only the first of a number of interrelated concerns. The immediate question that springs to mind is: What do we do for the gifted now that we have begun to know who they are? It may appear that their education is of primary concern and, by and large, this must be true; so we busy ourselves planning for their formal education and deciding on suitable curriculum content and the best methodology to implement it. This is not to say that the effectiveness and significance of informal education can be omitted from consideration; to some extent, its admission as a facet of formal learning may be a key direction. The keen recognition that the gifted are highly individualistic and even idiosyncratic in their learning needs and

[1]Khatena, 1978c, p. 116.

HISTORICAL PERSPECTIVES

styles must ensure a greater use of individualized learning approaches, ranging from teacher control to student control over learning. Creative learning must receive the prominence it deserves, for in it lies intellectual and talent growth. Ferment can only preface the occurrence of eminence.

The influence of environmental factors on development and the factors that hinder or facilitate giftedness must also be of concern. To think of giftedness as only those unique attributes possessed by an individual is an incomplete concept. One must take into account interactive sociocultural and economic conditions that have so much to do with the emergence of talent. It was once thought that gifted individuals were less likely to have problems than their nongifted peers, but it is now recognized that the gifted, too, have problems and are also in need of guidance. The task of nurturing the gifted is complex. What once appeared to be the responsibility of the educator must now become the concern of all. This responsibility is manifesting itself in more deliberate parental involvement, both personally and publically; in legislation that is being widely enacted in the United States; and in the efforts of national, regional, and local groups who champion and even provide opportunities for the gifted. Hopefully, all this is prologue to universal educational opportunities for the gifted and their teachers—opportunities propelled by public and private support.

Historically, the serious inception of the gifted movement began with the efforts of Terman in the early years of this century. For many years, study of the gifted was dominated by Terman's work—particularly the basic concepts of giftedness derived from measures he had developed, namely, his construction and use of the *Stanford-Binet* and his *Genetic Studies of Genius*. The latter is a monumental five-volume longitudinal study by Terman and his associates of 1,528 gifted urban children in California who were followed from kindergarten through high school and, then, on through midlife (e.g., Terman, 1925; Terman & Oden, 1959). Terman refers to the discovery and encouragement of exceptional talent in the concluding remarks of his valedictory address (1954):

> . . . to identify the internal and external factors that help or hinder the fruition of exceptional talent, and to measure the extent of their influences, are surely among the major problems of our time. These problems are not new; their existence has been recognized by countless men from Plato to Francis Galton. What is new is the general awareness of them caused by the manpower shortage of scientists, engineers, moral leaders, statesmen, scholars and teachers that the country must have if it is to survive in a threatened world. (p. 41)

Contributions to thought on the gifted have come to us from many sources and those by Bayley and Oden (1955), Birch (1954), Brandwein (1955), Brown and Johnson (1952), Gowan (1955), Hollingworth (1926), and Witty (1951), are among the most thoughtful (Bish, 1975). There is no doubt today that one of the most significant and germane contributions to the advances in thought came from J. P. Guilford's structure of intellect model, first presented in his presidential address at the American Psychological Association (APA) in 1950. For the first time in the history of the testing movement a theoretical model was designed that (1) emphasized a variety of abilities that included divergent production or creative thinking and (2) regarded the activity of the intellect in an informational and problem-solving setting. The excitement generated in the subject of creativity and its cultivation found expression in Alex F. Osborn's *Applied Imagination* in 1963, followed soon after by the founding of the Buffalo Creative Problem-Solving Institute, and in the several Utah conferences organized by Calvin W. Taylor during 1955–1957.

In 1957, the Russians successfully launched sputnik, which Bish (1975) refers to as a 184-pound ball in space that ''caught the attention of more Americans than the blast of the H-bomb and had also stung their national pride'' (p. 282). So Americans blamed the education system and the common theme was that mathematics and science had been downgraded and that insufficient attention had been given to upgrading the scholarship of the ablest students (Bish, 1975, p. 283). This dissatisfaction found focus in the call for curriculum reforms by the Physical Science Study Group headed by J. R. Zacharias of MIT, the School Mathematics Group directed by E. G. Begle of Stanford University, and others—all of which later led to a hardening up of the curriculum in science and mathematics for gifted students. The government's response to sputnik was the passage of the National Defense Education Act in 1957. Following in its wake were (1) the first National Education Association (NEA) Invitational Conference on the Academically Talented Pupil held in February 1958; (2) the publication of the conference report, which sold out 8,000 copies in three months; and (3) the establishment of the three-year Academically Talented Project with Charles E. Bish as its director. The project's goal was to prepare the teacher through publication, conference, and consultation to better serve the needs of the gifted and talented—and all these aims were successfully acomplished.

Advances in psychology over the past 40 years have contributed to an expanded concept of giftedness. In recent years, information from psychometrics, personality, human development, learning, and guidance research has persuaded us to think afresh about giftedness and how this quality potential in individuals can best be cultivated for their good and the good of the communities of which they are members.

Several papers (Khatena, 1976c, 1977d, 1978g) have discussed some important advances in thought on the gifted with special focus on conceptions of intelligence that move from the unitary and global to the multiple and complex; on approaches at identification that lie within a continuum of formal to less formal procedures, which have roots in good measurement theory and practice;

on educational facilitation that relates itself to theoretical constructs of the accelerative-developmental process; on an increasing awareness of the significance of creativity in the expansion of giftedness; and on a realization that gifted people have problems and need guidance.

ORIGINS OF GIFTED AND CREATIVE MOVEMENTS

The gifted child movement initiated by Terman's studies in the 1920s and the creativity movement launched by Guilford's structure of intellect, E. P. Torrance's work (e.g., 1962a, 1965c) and the efforts of a number of other scholars in the 1950s and 1960s have enchanced our understanding of giftedness enormously. Gowan (1978a) perceives that these two movements, if we are to understand them, cannot be regarded as separate and independent disciplines. He suggests that these movements are only two of several that can be appropriately and meaningfully subsumed under the heading of humanistic psychology and that can be traced to William James, his colleagues and their students—notably John Dewey, Erik Erikson, Arnold Gesell, G. S. Hall, Joseph Jastrow, F. Kuhlman, D. W. MacKinnon, William McDougall, W. R. Rhine, and Lewis M. Terman. A chart prepared by Gowan (Figure 1) illustrates the interrelatedness of these and other contributors to seven areas of development that are pertinent to humanistic psychology and that have influenced thought on the gifted today. The seven areas are (1) a broad humanism, (2) measurement, (3) intelligence, (4) gifted children, (5) creativity, (6) development, and (7) parapsychology.

Here, in brief, are Gowan's comments about each of these areas (1978a, pp. 2–4):

Humanism finds the individual of intrinsic value with potential for development, process, and becoming and with rights, irrespective of sex and ethnic group. To this may be added the value of individual differences and the prizing of the idiosyncratic talents of the exceptional person.

Measurement relates, first, to the recognition of individual differences and the prizing of their worth, next, to the belief that different talents can be measured, are of value to society, and should be cultivated.

Intelligence and *Gifted Children* point to a relationship between high intelligence and gifted children that is characterized by changing views of intelligence—from unifactor to multifactor conceptions; from regarding gifted children not as abnormal geniuses, but as a pool for potential creativity; and from a mechanistic concept of intelligence, consisting of cognition and memory, to a concept of intelligence that emphasizes transformations, implications, and a more creative consciousness.

Creativity is a phenomenon that has moved from a religious to a psychological concept, from an unknown to a turn-on variable, from connectedness to

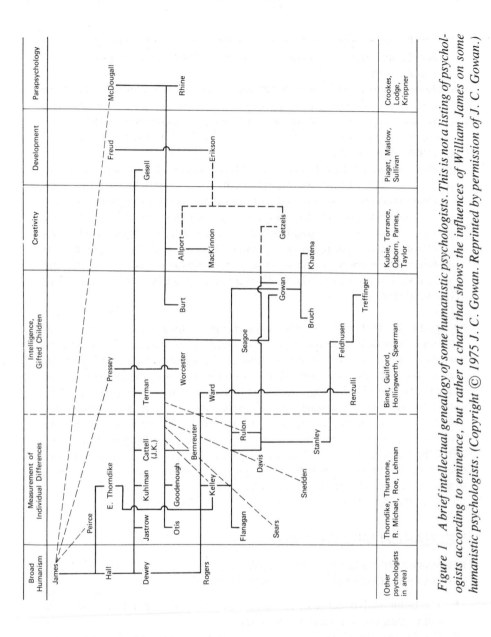

Figure 1   A brief intellectual genealogy of some humanistic psychologists. This is not a listing of psychologists according to eminence, but rather a chart that shows the influences of William James on some humanistic psychologists. (Copyright © 1975 J. C. Gowan. Reprinted by permission of J. C. Gowan.)

psychological openness, from a neurotic trait to an early dividend of mental health, and from a curiosity to an end in itself or a correlate of self-actualization.

Development is an aspect that shows change from continuous growth concepts to discontinuous developmental concepts; from separate views of development to fused views of concurrent development of psychomotor, affective, and cognitive processes; and from tests that do not measure developmental process to those that do.

Parapsychology is an aspect that has gone from quacks, spooks, and psychics to scientific investigation of the unknown; from unverifiable reports to an examination of physical effects; from superstitious epiphenomena to a niche in humanistic psychology demanded by modern views of the power of man's mind, such as (but not limited to) creativity, biofeedback, self-actualization, peak experience, dream analysis, and the like; and from folklore to a belief that all phenomena, of whatever kind, are natural and that we can account for them although we may not be in possession of all knowledge.

Keating (1978), in a review of the expanded proceeding of the Seventh Annual Hyman Blumberg Symposium (Stanley, George & Solano, 1977), commends Gowan on a valiant attempt at clarification of the terms used to describe the ablest. But, he suggests that Gowan's placement of gifted-creative child movements more in the humanistic than in the scientific camp is bound to provoke many interesting arguments. However, there appears to be no need for concern over such placement because, for the most part, the thrusts within the larger gestalt of humanism (as described by Gowan) have been scientific. Besides, there has been no other similar substantial effort to give coherence to this ever-expanding area of knowledge on the gifted. Acknowledgment must be given to the significance of Gowan's contributions that, at one and the same time, show the interrelationships among the scholars and the advancement of their ideas.

RESEARCH MILESTONES

In attempting to explain pertinent contributions to advances in thoughts relative to this subject, Gowan selects 12 significant research milestones:

1. The factor analytic advance of the structure of intellect and its identification and curriculum-intervention correlates.
2. The Terman and Oden (1959) midlife follow-up study of their gifted group that provided, among other information, evidence of the increase of mental age through age 50.

3. The importance of predisposing guidance and the trainability of scientific talent (Brandwein, 1955).
4. The direct influence of socioeconomic class on personality differences that hitherto were attributed to intelligence (Bonsall & Stefflre, 1955).
5. The identification-procedures research of Pegnato and Birch (1959), which shows that both the efficiency and effectiveness of various identification measures are less than has been assumed.
6. The development of creativity in children and the attempts to measure effects of this development by the *Torrance Tests of Creative Thinking* (Torrance, 1972a).
7. The use of the structure of intellect for curriculum development in the classroom (e.g., Meeker, 1969; F. E. Williams, 1971a).
8. The interrelationship between creativity and intelligence (Getzels & Jackson, 1962; Torrance, 1962a) and the issue of dimensionality (e.g., Khatena, 1971c; Treffinger & Poggio, 1972).
9. The work of Goldberg and Passow (1959) at De Witt Clinton High School in New York City that showed underachievers required assistance with learning skills and identification with a supportive teacher.
10. The study of facilitation of mathematically precocious youth through educational acceleration longitudinally (e.g., Stanley, Keating, & Fox, 1974).
11. The developmental theories of Erik Erikson and Jean Piaget fused by Gowan into the periodic developmental stages theory with its implications for creative development (Gowan, 1972, 1974).
12. The progression of identification procedures from *Stanford-Binet* to biographical information measures (e.g., Ellison, James, Fox, & Taylor, 1971; Khatena & Torrance, 1976a, 1976b; Schaefer, 1970).

SOME MEASUREMENT AND EDUCATIONAL IMPLICATIONS

Although there are still some issues to resolve on certain aspects of the validity of Guilford's tests—relative to the structure of intellect for instance—there is no doubt that his model is the most comprehensive explanation of intellectual abilities and their significant educational implications. These have been, and are still being, explored by his associates (e.g., Meeker, 1979) and others (e.g., Gray & Young, 1975). Discussing this question, Torrance (1970) points out that, in England, the Education Act of 1944 shows recognition of multiple talent (abstract, mechanical, concrete-practical), and he cites Guilford's structure of intellect and C. W. Taylor's multitalent model of giftedness, which is based on world-of-work needs that specify talent areas as they relate to academic ability, creative-productive abilities, evaluation, planning, forecasting, and communication. C. W. Taylor (1978) emphasizes that basic research has shown the existence of many different kinds of talents, not just one academic ability or general intelligence. Typical group intelligence tests, he says, attempt to measure no more than eight talents—less than one tenth of those now known, that is, nine tenths of currently measureable talents are not covered by intelligence tests.

These advances in thought on the intellect have led to expansion of the field of measurement. When this relates to measures of creativity and intelligence, there is the problem of dimensionality or convergent-discriminant validation (Campbell & Fiske, 1959), for example, where measures of the construct creativity are expected to yield high intercorrelations with other creativity measures (convergent validation) and low intercorrelations with measures of a different construct (discriminant validation), such as intelligence (Treffinger & Poggio, 1972). On the one hand, measures of intelligence were not found to identify high creatives (e.g., Getzels & Jackson, 1962) or to correlate highly with talented achievements outside the classroom (Wallach & Wing, 1969); on the other hand, IQ measures were found to yield substantial correlations with divergent-production tests (Guilford & Hoepfner, 1966) and creativity measures, like the *Torrance Tests of Creative Thinking* (Torrance, 1966, 1974b), were found to correlate substantially with intelligence and could serve as alternate measures of general intelligence (Wallach, 1968). There is still lack of agreement concerning these issues (Feldhusen, Treffinger, van Mondfrans, & Ferris, 1971; Guilford, 1971; Thorndike, 1966; Wallach & Kogan, 1965; Williams & Fleming, 1969); this, in fact, has prevented the emergence of a commonly accepted construct of creativity.

Terman's studies of the gifted did not take into account the socioeconomic variable as an influence on personality differences, but Gowan has indicated the importance of this dimension as a milestone in the development of the gifted-creative movements. This led Torrance, for instance, to suggest that the identification process of talent should take into account the positive talents of culturally disadvantaged children—for which he and his associates attempted to develop nontest measures that would tap the hidden giftedness of these children (Torrance, 1973, 1977b)—as well as plan for the construction of special programs designed to satisfy these needs (Torrance, 1977b).

On the matter of educational-intervention procedures, a federal government report (Marland, 1972a) identified learning opportunities provided for gifted and talented children that can be categorized under enrichment (curriculum and physical surroundings), methods of instruction, psychological climates conducive to learning, administrative arrangements to facilitate learning, and acceleration or advanced placement.

Over the past 20 years, renewed emphasis on process learning as a significant agent of educational facilitation has left its mark on our attempts to provide more effective schooling. Bruner (1961) advocated generic learning as a means of leaping over the barrier of specific event and specific information to thinking—

generic learning involves the grasp of a principle that allows the recognition of new problems one encounters as exemplars of old principles mastered. C. R. Rogers (1969), in a discussion of the facilitation of significant learning, stresses the nurture of the process of discovery, whereby learning how to learn and involvement in a process of change become the primary aims of education. A more recent expression of these directions (with the gifted and talented in mind) can be found in "The Enrichment Triad Model" (Renzulli 1979a). The model presents three levels of enrichment, namely, General Exploratory Activities (Type I), Group Training Activities (Type II), and Individual and Small Group Investigations of Real Problems (Type III), with the first two types of enrichment appropriate for all learners and Type III enrichment considered appropriate mainly for gifted students. Whereas Types I and II enrichment deal with strategies for expanding student interests and developing thinking and feeling processes (acting as logical input and support systems), Type III enrichment consists of activities that require actual investigation of real problems by using appropriate methods of inquiry.

The development of the structure of intellect model by Guilford initiated several approaches to educational facilitation. Mary N. Meeker is primarily responsible for the production of workbook materials that aim at developing numerous abilities identified by the Guilfordian model, namely, cognition, memory, convergent production, divergent production, and evaluation (Meeker, Sexton, & Richardson, 1970). Recognition of the volatile nature of creativity in learning has led to the production of training rationale and materials by Khatena (1978c), Renzulli (1973), Torrance & Myers (1970), F. E. Williams (1971a), and others to encourage the use of the creative potential in the classroom. The F. E. Williams model gives some importance to the affective domain, and Khatena (1978b) discusses the interactive effects of emotion and intellect in the realm of the creative imagination. Creative problem-solving approaches to learning provide yet other important models for productive education, most important of which are the materials developed by Osborn (1963), Parnes, Noller, and Biondi (1977), Torrance and Myers (1970), Feldhusen and his associates [e.g., Feldhusen & Treffinger (1977), W. J. J. Gordon (1961), and Prince (1968)].

DEVELOPMENTAL ASPECTS OF THE GIFTED

A starting point from which to examine the developmental characteristics of gifted children is the evidence from the Terman longitudinal study (reported in five volumes) of 1,528 gifted urban children in California who were followed from kindergarten through high school and, then, on through midlife. Extrapolating from these findings, it can be said that gifted children as they grow up to be adults generally maintain their intellectual superiority and versatility, emotional stability, social-adjustment capabilities, and educational achievement (Terman & Oden, 1959).

With the use of the *Torrance Tests of Creative Thinking* to study developmental patterns of creative thinking abilities in the United States and abroad has come some interesting thoughts on the creative development of children. Torrance (1967b) focuses on what is called the fourth-grade slump or drop in creative thinking abilities; this concept is based on the assumption that development of creative thinking abilities is continuous, that is, creative thinking abilities are expected to increase with age. Some of Torrance's later thoughts on the subject (Torrance, 1978a) reiterate his position that, although intelligence is less likely to be affected by stimulation, creative thinking abilities are affected by stimulation and show significant increments. This conception of continuous growth is closely related to measurement research.

Gowan—drawing on Sigmund Freud, Jean Piaget, and Erik Erikson, and others—considers development to occur in discrete stages. He groups these into three major periods (infancy, youth, and adulthood), during each of which the individual passes through three developmental stages, but each time at a higher level. He states that this is an important happening in nature and that in human life it is related to a transformation of energy called *periodicity,* which "occurs when the same pattern of events is seen to run through higher development as has been contained in a corresponding pattern from a lower sequence" (Gowan, 1971, p. 158). Two of his concepts with essential implications for the gifted are escalation and dysplasia (Gowan, 1974). By analogy he defines escalation as the jump from one riser to the next on a staircase consisting of five interrelated aspects: discontinuity, succession, emergence (the debut of new powers), differentiation, and integration. Dysplasia, he explains, occurs when one aspect of the psyche (e.g., the affective) continues to escalate although another aspect (e.g., the cognitive) becomes arrested at a given stage—a condition that porduces block, or *anomie,* and eventual neurosis.

GIFTED CHILDREN HAVE PROBLEMS

There is an increased awareness that highly gifted children also have problems as they grow up. Oden (1968) assessed the relationships of vocational achievement and genius. She compared 100 most successful and least successful men geniuses and found that the most successful men come from families that have higher socioeconomic status and give more encouragement to succeed. They also ranked higher as adolescents in volitional, intellectual, moral, and social traits, and they had more self-confidence, perseverence, and integration toward goals. In addition, although scholastic achievement had been similar for both groups in grade school, half of the successful men had graduated from college. The men geniuses were also found to be more prone to emotional and social difficulties.

The concern that most of these problems are culture bound and arise from the negative attitudes of our society toward creative, disadvantaged, physically handicapped, emotionally disturbed, and underachieving gifted individuals has been expressed by many prominent thinkers (e.g., Barron, 1963; Gallagher, 1975; Getzels & Jackson, 1962; Gowan & Bruch, 1971; Khatena, 1973g; Krippner, 1967; Kubie, 1958; Torrance, 1962a, 1965a, 1970).

Many problems that gifted children face stem from the conflicts they have with people who are around them—between a gifted child and a single person, or several people, or the representatives of education, government, social organizations, and the like. Torrance convincingly argues that many of the problems people encounter have to do with damming or distorting the creative energies (e.g., Torrance, 1962a). This applies as well to gifted children who are often dominated by the inner forces of their creativity. These forces sometimes make them do things beyond their control, acts that are in conflict with traditional modes of behavior and that call for adjustments. Effecting these adjustments satisfactorily leads gifted children to mental health and productivity, otherwise repression occurs with consequent personality problems, and possible breakdown or mental ill health. In addition, interest has risen in approaches to needed adjustment or constructive behavior (Torrance, 1965a), and the realization has developed that the gifted child, too, needs guidance, both in the areas of personal development and career plans (Gowan, 1978a; Torrance, 1976a; Zaffrann & Colangelo, 1977).

INTELLECTUALLY AND CREATIVELY GIFTED CHILDREN

Sustained research evidence about gifted children has come from two major sources. First, there are the studies that have used IQ as the main criterion for identification of the intellectually gifted, which stem from Terman's longitudinal studies of 1,528 gifted children begun in 1921 and still in progress with the assistance of his associates. Second, there are the studies that have used creative thinking abilities as the main criterion for the identification of the creatively gifted, which stem from the studies of Joy P. Guilford, E. Paul Torrance, and others like Frank Barron, Jacob W. Getzels, John C. Gowan, Philip W. Jackson, Joe Khatena, Donald W. MacKinnon, Calvin W. Taylor, Michael A. Wallach, and Cliff W. Wing.

TERMAN AND HIGH-IQ CHILDREN

Terman became interested in the gifted after he read two reports, one by Francis Galton and the other by Alfred Binet. While at Clark University, Terman's studies of mental tests and precocious children led to a doctoral dissertation that explored the intellectual processes of seven of the brightest and seven of the dullest boys selected from a large city school. The study, he explained, did not contribute as much to science as it did to his future thinking.

In 1921, with a grant from the Commonwealth Fund of New York City, Terman undertook to locate 1,000 subjects of IQ 140 or higher. Thus, his study of highly gifted children began (Terman & Oden, 1959). His gifted group came from schoolchildren in California, and the sole criterion for selecting his sample was IQ—as measured by the *Stanford-Binet* 1916 revision or the *Terman Concept Mastery Test* (1916)—relative to the top 1% of the school population selected for the purpose.

To establish a pool from which he could select gfifted children, Terman followed a two-step procedure for the identification of gifted children in kindergarten, primary grades, and high school and a three-step procedure for children in grades 3 to 8. Each classroom teacher was asked to nominate the first-, second-, and third-brightest child and the youngest in the class. A group intelligence test was then administered to all nominated children in grades 3 to 8. The children who showed promise were administered the *Stanford-Binet*. Because there was no group test suitable for these levels at the time, nominated children in kindergarten and the first two primary grades were administered only the *Stanford-Binet*. At the high school level, children were tested by the *Terman Concept Mastery Test*. The group finally identified as gifted comprised 851 boys and 671 girls and with some additions made in 1928 numbered 1,528 subjects. The mean IQ on the *Stanford-Binet* was 151 and on the *Terman Concept Mastery Test* 142.6.

From this group of identified gifted children, additional information regarding characteristics was obtained. Evidence from the three follow-up studies presented by Terman and his associates in *Genetic Studies of Genius* concerning the intellectually gifted as they grew up to midlife provides the following portrait (Burks, Jensen, & Terman, 1930; Terman & Oden, 1947, 1959):

Intellectually gifted children were born of intellectually and physically superior parents, and either because of better endowment or physical care or both, are as a group slightly superior to the general population in health and physique and tend to remain so. They generally maintained their relative intellectual superiority at least through adolescence at which time or soon after girls more often than boys showed a drop in IQ. Their children showed regression towards the mean on traits measured.

As a group they were not intellectually one-sided, emotionally unstable or lacking of social adaptability and other types of maladjustments. In fact they showed themselves to be superior on traits of emotional stability and social adjustment though to a less marked degree on intellectual and volitional traits. Their personal adjustments and emotional stability continued to be good as expected with below-normal incidence of serious personality problems, insanity, delinquency, alcoholism and homosexuality.

Incidence of marriage was about equal to that of the general population of Americans with normal sexual adjustment and few marital failures in their lives.

To the age of 35, they showed a higher mortality rate than the general population though the death rate after 35 years for them was lower. Their health ratings were in the main good, and physically they were above average.

Further, they were found to be either normal or superior in social-intelligence ratings, social interests, and play activities, averaging much better than the general population in practically every personality trait.

In educational achievement they were well in advance of their age mates but often found in grades two or three years below their level of curriculum attainment. When they received rapid promotion they were found equal or superior to gifted non-accelerates in health and general adjustment, did better school work and had greater success in later careers. Those with above 170 IQ were more accelerated in school and received better grades and more schooling.

They continued to achieve well through high school with almost no occurrence of failure in school subjects, and with nearly three quarters of the total marks earned by girls and half of those earned by boys being A grades. In their senior year they averaged above the 90th percentile on the Iowa High School Content Examination. Though this superiority continued into college there were many who lost interest and showed records of mediocre performance. However, educationally they were superior with about 70 percent graduating from college (a third of whom achieved academic distinction), 63 percent going to graduate school (67 percent men and 60 percent women), and 17 percent (14 percent men and 4 percent women) graduating with doctoral degrees.

In summing up the findings on the characteristics of the initial sample Terman and Oden observe that:

The deviation of gifted children from the generality is in the upward direction for nearly all traits; there is no law of compensation whereby the intellectual superiority of the gifted is offset by inferiorities along non-intellectual lines; the amount of upward deviation of the gifted is not the same for all traits; and the uneveness of abilities is no greater for gifted than for average children, but is different in direction—whereas the gifted are at their best in the "thought" subjects, average children are at their best in subjects that make the least demands upon the formation and manipulation of concepts. (1959, pp. 15–16)

Terman and Oden also point to the wide range of variability that exists within their sample group on every trait investigated, cautioning that descriptions of the gifted in terms of the typical, although useful as a basis for generalization, should not blind us to the fact that gifted children, far from falling into a single pattern, represent an almost infinite variety of patterns.

Terman was aware of, and concerned about, the fact that some of his gifted group were highly successful, whereas others were not. He observed (1) that intelligence, although an important determiner of success, was not the sole one, determiner and (2) that motivational factors had a lot to do with success (Terman, 1954). In attempting to identify the nonintellectual factors that influenced life success among the men in the gifted group, Terman and Oden (1947) had three judges, working independently, examine the records (from 1922 to 1940) of 730 men who were 25 years old or older and rate each one of them on life success, based on the extent to which a subject had made use of his superior intellectual ability—little weight was given to earned income. Two groups of 150 each were rated either highest or lowest for success. These were identified as the *A* and *C* groups respectively, and they were compared on about 200 items of information, obtained from childhood onward, to find out how they differed.

During the elementary school years the two groups were almost equally successful; however, differences in achievement and scholarship in favor of the *A's* became evident as they passed into high school. By the end of high school, the gap was marked. Terman found that these differences were not due to extracurricular activities or intelligence, but to family background. Interesting differences between *A's* and *C's* were found in childhood data on their emotional stability, social adjustments, and various traits of personality—generally in favor of the *A's*. Further, in 1940, it was found that *A's* and *C's* differed most widely on "persistence in the accomplishment of ends" and "integration toward goals" as contrasted with "drifting," "self-confidence," and "freedom from inferiority feelings" (Terman & Oden, 1947, pp. 349–352). The greatest contrast between the *A's* and *C's* was in drive to achieve and in all-round mental and social adjustment.

In 1959, Terman and Oden followed up their investigation with another study (by means of a biographical data blank), that explored what constitutes life success for gifted men and women. Its final question read, "From your point of view, what constitutes success in life?"

The replies showed a wide range of variability and lack of agreement. However, Terman and Oden placed the most frequently given definitions of life success as perceived by intellectually gifted people into five categories (1959, p. 152):

1. *Realization of goals, vocational satisfaction, a sense of achievement.*
2. *A happy marriage and home life, bringing up a family satisfactorily.*

3. *Adequate income for comfortable living (but this was mentioned by only 20 percent of women).*
4. *Contributing to knowledge or welfare of mankind, helping others, leaving the world a better place.*
5. *Peace of mind, well-adjusted, adaptability, emotional maturity.*

Terman and Oden observed that many people considered happiness, contentment, emotional maturity, and integrity as the most important achievements in life. Success was not necessarily limited to occupational advancement, but had much to do with heroic sacrifices, uncommon judgment in handling the little things of daily life, countless acts of kindness, loyal friendships, and the conscientious discharge of social and civic responsibility.

There is no doubt that Terman's seminal work prepared the way for thought and research on the gifted. He made unique contributions to our understanding of intellectually gifted people and what we can expect of them, both by the construction of IQ measures for their identification and by substantial and comprehensive longitudinal evidence that described their behaviors and achievements from childhood to midlife. In these respects, he is to date unrivaled by anyone. However, the *Genetic Studies of Genius* is not without flaws, among which are those relative to the sampling of ability for identification, the sampling of subjects, and related variables.

Because Terman chose to select his subjects on the IQ criterion, it is appropriate to consider his findings about the gifted, particularly as relevant to the population of high-IQ people, but not necessarily as relevant to all gifted people. The *Stanford-Binet* is known to favor the highly verbal subject, this automatically disqualifies many nonverbal and low socioeconomic gifted students from participating. In addition, it should be recognized that although IQ is a valuable global, one-dimensional model of intelligence, it does not tell us enough about the specific abilities of the child (Edwards, 1971; Gowan, 1978a; Stanley, 1974). Hence, we do not have proper data about children with high ability, especially in music and drawing where their relationship with abstract intelligence is only slightly above zero (Carrol, 1940, p. 205).

On the matter of sample subjects, those Terman selected as gifted cannot really be considered as representative of the gifted American population; at best, they may be considered representative of urban Californians who attended large or medium-sized public schools. Terman's sample included a strong Jewish component in the gifted child population, which was out of all proportion to the total population of Californians at the time. Further, the schools that were chosen were predominantly white, which meant that students in black schools were omitted from selection. Ideally, the *Stanford-Binet* or the *Terman Concept Mastery Test* should have been administered to all Californians to identify those who would qualify as gifted. Of course, this would have been prohibitive in terms of money and time. Relative to the location of his study, the next best thing would have been for Terman to select randomly from the total number of school-going Californians (because of their accessibility) a manageable number of subjects and administer to them the measures of IQ for the purpose of identifying the gifted. However, he chose to do the initial screening by means of teacher nominations, and, from what we are told by research about the unreliability of such teacher judgment, many gifted children must have been eliminated from the chance of participation right from the start.

In addition to these variables, Terman, as he later realized, should have depended on school records rather than on the teacher to identify the brightest children in the class for his initial screening process. Once children had been identified as gifted and selected for Terman's study, the fact that they were called genius must have had a positive influence on them (they must have been treated more respectfully both at home and in school); the full extent of such influence cannot be known. Although Terman recognized the importance of nonintellective factors, like will and motivation to life success, in his *A* and *C* studies (Terman & Oden, 1947), he paid nearly no attention to socioeconomic variables—an omission that can be traced back to sampling bias and the selection procedure used to determine his gifted group. In all fairness to him, the adverse efforts of socioeconomic influences were not well known then. Further, Terman omitted study of the interactive effects of heredity and environment and paid little heed to even an intuitive perception of the influence of creativity and self-actualization on life success. Finally, the *Genetic Studies of Genius* is a work that is descriptive and factual rather than speculative and theoretical and there is no attempt to generate hypotheses.

INTELLIGENCE AND CREATIVITY

The selection of gifted students in the Terman studies was done solely on the basis of general intelligence as defined by IQ and as measured by the *Stanford-Binet* or the *Terman Concept Mastery Test*. Of course, at the time when the Terman studies began in 1921, there were no effective intellectual measures that could yield a better index of superior abilities than IQ as measured by a test such as the *Stanford-Binet*. At the first Minnesota Conference on Gifted Children, it was pointed out that Terman's proposed genius or near-genius category challenged educators, sociologists, and psychologists to produce, if they could, "another concept as effective as the IQ for delimiting of a group of talent to include the most successful students, the best achievers in the academic world, and, as he [Terman] believed, in the world of human relationships and human endeavor generally" (Miles, 1960, p. 51).

The assumption underlying the validity of a prestigious individual measure of intelligence, like the Stanford-Binet or a Wechsler scale, as the sole criterion for identifying the gifted went unchallenged (Torrance, 1962a). If any dissent was heard, it related to the measurement of special talents, for instance, in art, music, and drama (Gallagher, 1966). Some very pertinent questions were asked about the content validity of IQ measures as adequate identifiers of all kinds of giftedness. For one thing, Spearman (1927) brought to our notice that, in addition to general mental ability (or g), there were specific abilities in human mental functioning; others, like Guilford (1950) and Thurstone (1924), were telling us that we should be looking at an intellect that comprised many abilities rather than a single general mental ability. These conceptions and others relating to the intellect are more fully described in Chapter 2. However, it is important to note that following Guilford's presidential address at the APA in 1950 on the subject of the structure of intellect—which presented the intellect as a complex three-dimensional model of abilities (comprising mental operations related to cognition, memory, convergent thinking, divergent thinking, and evaluation)—many questions were brought into focus through investigations, especially the ones that attempted to differentiate other mental functioning than those tested by IQ measures. For instance, IQ measures were found to be deficient in items that called for divergent or creative thinking. It was not that Terman was unaware of the existence of this dimension of mental functioning—as can be seen in two of his tests constructed for his first study of seven bright and seven stupid boys, namely, tests for inventiveness and imagination and "insight"—but his conceptions of both tended to border closer to convergent-thinking operations.

The most obvious emphasis of IQ measures was on cognition, memory, and convergent thinking. C. W. Taylor holds that intelligence is a concept created by Western culture that stresses important Western values. He maintains that tests of intelligence in our culture "essentially concerned themselves with how fast relatively unimportant problems can be solved without making errors [whereas in another culture] intelligence might be a measure more in terms of how adequately important problems can be solved making all the errors necessary and without regard for time" (1959, p. 54).

Guilford (1950) had remarked that, (1) if we were to study the domain of creativity, we need to look far beyond the boundaries of IQ nad (2) the conception that "creative talent is to be accounted for in terms of high intelligence or IQ . . . is not only inadequate but has been largely responsible for lack of progress in the understanding of creative people" (p. 454). His predictions that correlations of scores on intelligence and creativity tests would be moderate or low, that the highly intelligent could probably not be highly creative, and that the highly creative could probably not be highly intelligent sparked a series of studies in the 1960s whose findings tended to support these predictions.

The well-known Getzels and Jackson study (1962) was one attempt to look at the relationship of creativity and intelligence as well as at a number of other variables that related to these two areas. Getzels and Jackson administered

18

creativity tests to 533 students (292 boys and 241 girls) whose average IQ was 130; they depended on school records for intelligence test scores as derived from the *Henmon-Nelson Tests of Mental Ability, Stanford-Binet,* and, to a lesser extent, the *Wechsler Intelligence Scale for Children (WISC)*. Using this information, they selected the top 20% on creativity tests and the top 20% on IQ tests (matched for sex and age), excluding those students who were in the top 20% on both measures of intelligence and creativity. Comparing the performance of 24 highly creative and 28 highly intelligent students on total scholastic achievement, they found that, although there was a difference of 23 IQ points between the high-creative group and the high-IQ group, both groups performed equally well on scholastic achievement. This led them to conclude that creativity was just as important as, if not more important than, intelligence for scholastic achievement.

They also found relatively low correlations between IQ and performance tests that required the use of creative thinking abilities; they attributed this to the high-mean-IQ bias of their sample. They qualified this by stating that similar findings were obtained with less extreme groups. Torrance, in eight partial replications of this study, arrived at similar conclusions about the relationship of intelligence and creativity. His findings led him to conclude that the selection of the top 20% on IQ measures would exclude 70% of the top 20% on creativity measures, implying that correlations between intelligence and creativity are low and that creativity tests identify the gifted better than intelligence tests (Torrance, 1962a). Although these findings were considered a breakthrough in our understanding of the intelligence-creativity distinction by some, they were not so considered by others, like McNemar (1964) and Wallach (1970). For instance, among the deficiencies of the Getzels and Jackson (1962) study are (1) the failure of the authors to administer a single intelligence test to all subjects at the time creativity tests were administered and, therefore, to control for the variance introduced by use of old information derived from multiple-test data records; (2) the exclusion from their study of the top 20% of subjects on creativity and intelligence measures; and (3) the failure to report basic correlations between creativity, intelligence, and achievement. This last deficiency led McNemar (1964) to observe that, using the "high-blind logic" of the authors, we could deduce that the high-IQ and high-creative groups did equally well in school achievement despite an unreported difference of 23 points in creativity scores. He cited the corroborating evidence of Yamamoto's (1964) replication of the Getzels and Jackson (1962) study.

Some of these disagreements concerning the intelligence-creativity distinction can be traced to the more basic problem of validation of creativity measures with actual creativity, which is prized by our society. McNemar (1964), in "Lost: Our intelligence? Why?", expresses concern over the changing emphasis placed on IQ that resulted from factor analytic research. He concludes that general intelligence has not been lost in the trend to test more and more abilities; it was merely creativity tests to 533 students (292 boys and 241 girls) whose average IQ was 130; they depended on school records for intelligence test scores as derived from the *Henmon-Nelson Tests of Mental Ability, Stanford-Binet,* and, to a lesser extent, the *Wechsler Intelligence Scale for Children (WISC)*. Using this information, they selected the top 20% on creativity tests and the top 20% on IQ tests (matched for sex and age), excluding those students who were in the top 20% on both measures of intelligence and creativity. Comparing the performance of 24 highly creative and 28 highly intelligent students on total scholastic achievement, they found that, although there was a difference of 23 IQ points between the high-creative group and the high-IQ group, both groups performed equally well on scholastic achievement. This led them to conclude that creativity was just as important as, if not more important than, intelligence for scholastic achievement.

They also found relatively low correlations between IQ and performance tests that required the use of creative thinking abilities; they attributed this to the high-mean-IQ bias of their sample. They qualified this by stating that similar findings were obtained with less extreme groups. Torrance, in eight partial replications of this study, arrived at similar conclusions about the relationship of intelligence and creativity. His findings led him to conclude that the selection of the top 20% on IQ measures would exclude 70% of the top 20% on creativity measures, implying that correlations between intelligence and creativity are low and that creativity tests identify the gifted better than intelligence tests (Torrance, 1962a). Although these findings were considered a breakthrough in our understanding of the intelligence-creativity distinction by some, they were not so considered by others, like McNemar (1964) and Wallach (1970). For instance, among the deficiencies of the Getzels and Jackson (1962) study are (1) the failure of the authors to administer a single intelligence test to all subjects at the time creativity tests were administered and, therefore, to control for the variance introduced by use of old information derived from multiple-test data records; (2) the exclusion from their study of the top 20% of subjects on creativity and intelligence measures; and (3) the failure to report basic correlations between creativity, intelligence, and achievement. This last deficiency led McNemar (1964) to observe that, using the "high-blind logic" of the authors, we could deduce that the high-IQ and high-creative groups did equally well in school achievement despite an unreported difference of 23 points in creativity scores. He cited the corroborating evidence of Yamamoto's (1964) replication of the Getzels and Jackson (1962) study.

Some of these disagreements concerning the intelligence-creativity distinction can be traced to the more basic problem of validation of creativity measures with actual creativity, which is prized by our society. McNemar (1964), in "Lost: Our intelligence? Why?", expresses concern over the changing emphasis placed on IQ that resulted from factor analytic research. He concludes that general intelligence has not been lost in the trend to test more and more abilities; it was merely

Table 1 Personality Traits of Fifth Grade Boys and Girls Scoring High and Low in Intelligence and Creativity

Intelligence: High	Creativity			
	High		Low	
	Boys	Girls	Boys	Girls
	Acute degree of interpersonal sensitivity	Strong powers of integration and structuring in combination with ability to range freely and imaginatively with rich affect and enthusiastic involvement	Overriding concern with academic success	Rather mechanical use of academic achievement as means of attaining status and success with impression that such achievement has more the meaning of reducing pain than increasing pleasure
	Sharp awareness of own identity and integrity in midst of adults and peers	Come to grips with these and more controlled ways of functioning	Strong desire for academic excellence	To get this achievement, may work long hours at their studies for fear of criticism
	Sense of warmth, but sense of objectivity in relations with others	Display social awareness and sensitivity to emotional expression in others	Sense of competition with peers or siblings for status in eyes of adults	Affectively, hold themselves carefully within bounds relative to their own expression and their perceptions of others
	Earnestness and seriousness in matters concerning human beings		Intellective success perceived as critically important determinant of their standing with significant adults	Inhibit themselves emotionally to do well in school
	Maturity coupled with tolerance for being boylike—a simultaneous awareness of adult and peer group frames of reference and capacity to remain in contact with both		Preoccupied with how such adults view them	
			Narrowing down and rigidifying of intellective behavior as consequence of their so sedulous pursuit of success	
			Exceptionally low levels of general and test anxiety	
			High defensiveness suggesting presence of coping mechanisms for adequate handling of failure stresses in pursuit of success	

Give the impression of being engaged in battle against others and/or themselves	React negatively to school pressure	Simple avoidance or giving up, of resignations to a sour fate relative to academic activities	Try to deal with poor intellectual performance
Sensitivity to and therefore anger over own inadequacies	Anger and resentment toward school setting, regressive listlessness and/or mischief in response to academic demands	Blustering hyperactivity	Do not seem to know how to cope successfully with academic tasks and at least resort to imitating surface behaviors that reflect successful coping by others (e.g., trying to appear assertive, and being neat in one's work)
Angry lashing out at the world and supersensitivity to signs of rejection from others	Social shyness and withdrawal prominent	Basic sense of bewilderment, tend to seek comfort by some means or other (e.g., through melting into peer group, through protection from sympathetic adults, or through mischief)	Fear and depression over academic failure present at worst
Confidence appears shattered	Free and even wild imaginings—possibly more extreme because tinged with rebelliousness and even revealed in strongly nurturant adult environment that invokes no sanctions of academic failure and success		Frustration over academic work leads to use of relatively infantile defenses (e.g., being cruel and vengeful toward children who are weak, being passive and unresponsive in classroom, or developing psychosomatic complaints)
Engaged in various defensive and constructive maneuvers aimed at establishing self-worth			
Magnitudes of forces involved in these battles great because of their articulated sensitivities			
Detailed exploration of what other people think of them			
Introspective exploration of themselves, artistic ability			

Intelligence

Low

Source: M. A. Wallach and N. Kogan, Modes of Thinking in Young Children, pp. 269–285. Copyright © 1965 by Holt, Rinehart & Winston. Reprinted by permission of Holt, Rinehart & Winston.

misplaced by the expectation that factor analyses would identify those factors that, when and if measured, would be socially useful. On the matter of creativity-research findings, he observes that (1) creativity tests do not yield high correlations with IQ whose uncurtailed scatter would be bivariate normal; (2) if suitable criteria measures of literary, architectural, or scientific creativity are available, the relationship between IQ and creativity, as shown by a scattergram, is be triangular in shape; therefore, at the high-IQ levels, a wide range of creativity exists, whereas as this goes down to average and low IQ levels, the scatter for creativity is less and less; and (3) having a high IQ does not guarantee creativity, whereas having a low IQ means creativity is impossible.

Wallach (1970), in his appraisal of the study of the relationship between creativity and intelligence, comes to the conclusion that (1) the kind of creativity measures used in a study like that of Getzels and Jackson (1962) show much higher relations than were earlier reported (e.g., Hassan & Butcher, 1966) and (2) these creativity measures do no better than measure general intelligence. This is consistent with the issues raised by Wallach and Kogan (1965), who make a case against the *Torrance Tests of Creative Thinking* and for the instruments that they constructed to measure creative thinking abilities (about which more will be said in Chapter 2).

Finally, Anastasi and Schaefer (1971) also make the point that it is erroneous to regard intelligence and creativity as independent and distinct entities. They state that, generally, intelligence and creativity test scores correlate with each other almost as highly as individual intelligence and creativity scores correlate with each other.

Wallach and Wing (1969) explore the creativity-intelligence problem and make it quite clear that the intelligence measure, although predicting academic success, is useless for predicting talented accomplishments outside the classroom. These need measures that elicit ideational productivity and uniqueness of ideas: Wallach and Wing that ''alternative bases for talent identification are essential, and a set of substantive guidelines as to what sorts of alternatives are needed'' (1969, p. 130).

An interesting attempt to bring into focus the relationship of intelligence and creativity was a study by Wallach and Kogan (1965). The subjects, 151 fifth-grade pupils (70 boys and 81 girls), were administered both intelligence and creativity tests. The subjects were classified as intelligent and creative above or below the median so that there were four groups: high intelligent/high creative, high intelligent/low creative, low intelligent/high creative, and low intelligent/low creative. In this way, Wallach and Kogan presented a model that brought into sharp focus the interactive effects of both dimensions of intellectual abilities. They, then, defined the behaviors of each of these four groups (see Table 1).

Newland (1976) suggests (1) that an analysis of a comparable grade level relative to different socioeconomic levels would add further meaning to the study and (2) that a longitudinal study of similar dimensions would also be appropriate. Perhaps a study of these interactive elements relative to different ethnic groups that begins at earlier grade levels and goes up to the senior high school grades and that includes those from rural as well as urban communities would provide even more valuable evidence.

Intelligence measures do not set out to appraise a person's ability to be creative, imaginative, inventive, and original. Hence, when administered to groups, these measures will only pick out those who have the ability to memorize; to generalize and evaluate; to give a single solution to a problem; to show understanding of factual information and meaning of words; and to comprehend certain kinds of verbal and numerical relationships that call for single right answers. People who do thinking beyond these dimensions are, therefore, incorrectly assessed and often appear to be less bright or gifted than they really are. If we want to identify producers of knowledge as well as conservers of knowledge, we need to heed the caution that the IQ is not a universal measure of giftedness.

The well-known Getzels and Jackson studies of adolescents (1958, 1960, 1961) differentiate between the highly creative and the highly intelligent in grades 7 through 12. These studies found that:

- Highly creative and highly intelligent adolescents were equally superior on achievement tests, in spite of a difference of 23 mean IQ points.
- Teachers considered high-IQ adolescents more desirable students than their high-creative peers.
- High creatives showed a predisposition to take greater risks, to be independent, and to enjoy the uncertainty of the unknown.
- High creatives were better able to produce new forms and to venture combining elements that usually appear to be independent and dissimilar than were high-IQ adolescents.
- More high-IQ adolescents preferred conventional occupations, such as medicine, law, engineering, and so on, whereas high-creative adolescents preferred unconventional occupations, such as those relative to invention, writing, and so on.

Getzels and Jackson (1961) interviewed parents of both groups of adolescents. They found that, when compared to parents of high-IQ adolescents, parents of high-creative adolescents:

- Did not appear to make much mention of their experiences of financial troubles.
- Were less inclined to convey their present feelings of personal insecurity, whether real or imagined.
- Were less conscious and alert to their children's academic achievement.
- Were less critical of the school and their children.

• Expressed greater concern for their child's values, interests, enthusiasms, and openness to experience.

CREATIVE INDIVIDUALS

In a paper (C. W. Taylor, 1958) presented at two conferences [the Fifth American Society for Child Development (ASCD) Research Institute—Eastern Section, Washington, D.C., and the Second Minnesota Conference on Gifted Children], C. W. Taylor stressed the importance of reconsidering the significance of the IQ measure as the only index of the gifted individual. He indicated that any legitimate concept of giftedness would have to include the existence of nonintelligence intellectual characteristics and that the IQ measure does not do an adequate job of identifying creative talent:

> *In factor analysis studies by many research workers across the country, the factors which get at the ability to sense problem areas, to be flexible, and to produce new and original ideas tend to be* unrelated *or to have only low relations with the types of tests entering into our current measures of intelligence. Getzels and Jackson, in the College of Education at the University of Chicago, as well as Torrance, in the Bureau of Educational Research at Minnesota, have reported that if an IQ test is used to select top level talent, about 70 percent of the persons who have the highest 20 percent of the scores on a creativity test battery will be missed. (Or stated otherwise, more cases with high creativity scores are missed than are identified by using an IQ test to locate creative talent). C. W. Taylor, 1958, p. 174)*

He points to the findings of three University of Utah Research Conferences on Creativity that have emphasized the need (1) for a broad approach to the identification of creative talent, somewhat in contrast to the identification of the so-called gifted by means of *a single measuring device* such as an IQ and (2) for nonintelligence intellectual characteristics to be included in the search for the creative individual.

Elsewhere in the same paper, C. W. Taylor draws from his own research and that of others, like Guilford, Barron, Getzels and Jackson, to identify some of the more salient intellectual and personality characteristics of creative individuals:

> *• originality • redefinition • adaptive flexibility • spontaneous flexibility • associational fluency • expressional fluency • word fluency • ideational fluency • elaboration • ability to sense problems • capacity to be puzzled • the power to reject superficial explanations of one's own as well as of others • ability to sense ambiguities • effective questioning ability • ability to manipulate, restructure and rework ideas • ability and tendency to strive for more*

comprehensive answers or solutions or products • capacity to work intermit-
tently across long periods of time at the conscious or below the conscious
level • to be more observant (seeing both what others do and what they do not)
• to place high value on truthful reporting and testifying of their observations •
to have the ability to make them explicit • to make richer syntheses and note
their impulses more • curiosity or inquiringness of mind • liking to think •
liking to manipulate and toy with ideas • intellectual persistence/need for
recognition for achievement • need for variety • need for autonomy • need for
preference for complex order and for challenges therein • tolerance of am-
biguity • resistance to closing up and crystallizing things prematurely coupled
with a strong need for ultimate closure • need for mastery of a problem •
insatiability for intellectual ordering, and a need to improve upon currently
accepted orders and systems • high energy with vast work output through
disciplined work habits is usually found • willingness to take greater and more
long range risks for greater gain • tendency to accumulate an overabundance
of raw stuff plus a willingness ultimately to discard some of it in forming final
products • an intense esthetic and moral commitment to their work • a much
greater variety of occupational choices • greater interest in and awareness of
unconventional careers • sense that their views are not the predominant ones
of what success in adult life is • willing to be nonconforming and consequently
to be in the small minority • more devoted to autonomy • more self-sufficient •
more independent in judgment • more open to the irrational in themselves •
more stable • more capable of taking greater risks in the hope for greater
gains • more feminine in interests and characteristics (especially in awareness
of one's impulses) • more dominant and self-assertive • more complex as a
person • more self-accepting, more resourceful and adventurous (bohemian) •
more controlling of their own behavior by self-concepts • more emotionally
sensitive • more introverted and bold (1958)

The psychologist who probably has done more work than anyone else in the
area of developing measures of creativity is Torrance (1966, 1974b). His numerous contributions have helped us understand creative children and what we
can do for them so that they may realize their potential fully (1962a, 1965c,
1972a). Torrance (1975a) indicates the great importance of parental, teacher, and
societal influences on the development of a child's creative behaviors. He
suggests that to know what characteristics parents and teachers encourage and
discourage would help us understand and predict the behavior of children under
their guidance; In addition, to know the characteristics children consider ideal
would help us predict their creative achievements more accurately: "Such information would provide useful clues for helping people achieve their potentialities
and helping teachers modify their behavior to facilitate creative growth among

children'' (1975a, p. 130). The rest of the paper summarizes some of the work Torrance has done over 15 years in developing the *Ideal Pupil Checklist,* which is of particular interest. This checklist was developed from a survey of over 50 empirical studies that attempted to differentiate the personality characteristics of a group of highly productive creative people from a similar group of less creative people. According to this checklist, the most salient characteristics of creative people are the following (1975a, p. 138–139):

Adventurous, testing limits
Asking questions about puzzling things, wants to know
Attempting difficult tasks
Becoming preoccupied with tasks
Courageous in convictions
Curious, searching
Determined, unflinching
Feeling/expressing emotions strongly
Emotionally aware/sensitive
Energetic, virtuous
Guessing, hypothesizing
Independent in judgment
Independent in thinking
Industrious, busy
Intuitive, insightful
Liking to work alone
Never bored, always interested
Persistent, persevering
Preferring complex tasks
Regressing occasionally, may be playful, childlike, etc.
Remembers well
Self-assertive
Self-confident
Self-starting, initiating
Self-sufficient
Sense of beauty
Sense of humor
Sincere, earnest
Striving for distant goals
Thorough, exhaustive
Truthful even when it hurts
Unwilling to accept things on mere say-so
Visionary, idealistic
Willing to take risks

LONGITUDINAL STUDIES OF CREATIVE BEHAVIOR

What appears to be one of the first longitudinal studies on creative behavior, which was conducted by Torrance (1972b), is of special interest. In presenting evidence of the predictive validity of the *Torrance Tests of Creative Thinking* (1966, 1974b), Torrance differentiates between short-range (1 week to 9 months) and long-range (5 to 12 years) predictive validity.

Short-Range Prediction

Of the short-range predictive validity studies of immediate relevance are those done by Weisberg and Springer (1961) and Torrance (1963). The first study was of 32 intellectually gifted (high-IQ) fourth-grade children. It showed that the highly creative children when compared with the others in the group reflected more creative self-acceptance, greater self-awareness, an internal locus of evaluation that allowed for greater independence from environmental influences, and greater readiness to respond emotionally to the environment. That is, these creative preadolescents behaved more sensitively and more independently than less creative but equally intelligent children. The second study investigated some of the social-interaction behaviors of highly creative children, 25 each from grades 2 to 6. Each class was divided into five subgroups on the basis of their scores on the *Torrance Tests of Creative Thinking*. Children were required to discover intended and unintended uses of a box of science toys; observation was focused on techniques used by the groups to control its most creative members. The findings showed that: the highly creative children made outstanding contributions, despite obvious pressure exercised by groups to reduce their production and originality; although most of the creative members (68%) produced more ideas than other group members, few (24%) were credited by the others with making the most valuable contribution to the success of the groups; the creatives counteracted group pressures by being compliant, by showing counter aggression, by indomitable persistence, by apparently ignoring criticism, by showing silence and apathy, by inconsistent performance, and by filling in the gaps when others faltered (Torrance, 1972b, pp. 237–238).

Long-Range Prediction

Two of several of the long-range prediction studies are of special relevance. One, by Witt, began in 1965 and extended over a period of 6 years (1971). This study was of 16 highly creative disadvantaged children in grades 2 to 4 from a ghetto school in New Haven, Connecticut; 12 of these children were also in an out-of-school program designed to develop their creative strengths. The other, a major study by Torrance (1972b), spanned a period of either 7 or 12 years (1959–1971) and involved 392 students, the total enrollment of those attending the University of Minnesota High School in grades 7 to 12.

The findings of the Witt study showed that of the 12 children attending an out-of-school program, 10 revealed superior creative talent. They achieved high-level performance, receiving awards in one or more of the art forms (music, art, drama) and winning competitions in citywide contests, science and arts camps, and the like. They also won scholarships to excellent private schools for study under outstanding teachers in music, art, and other fields. Out of the 10 children, 3 children also demonstrated superior verbal creativity in science and other areas as indicated by similar honors they attained (Torrance, 1972b, p. 244).

The seven-year follow-up of Torrance's (1972b) major long-range prediction of the original 69 students in the 1960 class found significant relationship between their scores on the *Torrance Tests of Creative Thinking* and their achievements:

Poems, stories, songs written
Poems, stories, songs published
Books written
Books published
Radio and television scripts or performances
Original research designs developed
Philosophy of life changed
In-service training for co-workers created
Original changes in work situation suggested
Research grants received
Business enterprises initiated
Patentable devices invented
Literary awards or prizes received for creative writing, musical composition, art, and so on

The 12-year follow-up study of 236 students (out of the original group of 393) was conducted in 1971 when the subjects were between 25 and 31 years old. Torrance reports that the findings give some credence to the belief that the creative achievements of women are less predictable than those of men; that the creativity measures (*Torrance Tests of Creative Thinking)* used were consistently better predictors of women's adult creative achievement than the measure of intelligence used (*Lorge-Thorndike Intelligence Tests*); and that, although originality was a good predictor of quantity and quality of creative achievements as well as creative aspirations of students in grades 9 through 12, it did not predict the same for those in grades 7 and 8. Torrance attributes this last finding to a variety of complex factors, including: a slump in the subjects' creative thinking abilities, which was expected to occur; the fact that a large proportion of these subjects at the time of the follow-up testing were either in military service, still in college, or had undergone a period of rebellion and exploration and only recently regained an achievement orientation to life but had neither attended college nor sought success through other routes. Torrance (1972b) concludes:

> Although the subjects of the 12-year predictive validity study were fairly advantaged and most of them had ample opportunities and freedom to develop their creative abilities, the results do indicate that creativity tests administered during the high school years can predict real-life adult creative achievements. It is doubtful that such favorable results would be found for a population severely limited in opportunity and/or freedom. The subjects of this study now range from 25 to 31 years, and we do not know whether these results will continue to hold up at the end of another 12 years. An examination of the clues provided by the detailed responses of the subjects, however, suggests that the creative achievement differences between the more creative and less creative subjects are likely to widen as time elapses. (Pp. 250-251)

STUDIES ON CREATIVE PERCEPTIONS

A study by Khatena (1977c) on creative perceptions as they are related to components of the creative personality and as they are measured by the *Khatena-Torrance Creative Perception Inventory* (Khatena & Torrance, 1976a, 1976b) summarizes the findings of a number of investigations (Khatena, 1977b, pp. 521-523):

1. *People who perceive themselves as high creatives are experimentally and power oriented, have less need for structure and possess relatively high intuition.*
2. *On the matter of past experiences, highly gifted adolescent girls who perceived themselves as creative regularly read news magazines and other non-required reading materials, watched television news and special reports frequently, enjoyed courses in the sciences, music or art and were active in dramatic and musical groups, liked their teachers and generally felt that their high school education was adequate, dated more infrequently than their less creative peers in high school and going steady at an older age, not close to another and did not discuss intimate and/or important matters with her, did not often suffer "attacks of conscience" when they felt that they had done wrong by the standards of society, church or parent, and did not want to become more socially acceptable or better prepared as a responsible family member, daydreamed a lot, felt downcast, dejected and sensitive to criticism, brooded over the meaning of life to a greater extent, and overtly expressed anger toward friends and tried to get even when someone close hurt or upset them.*
   Creative adolescent boys, however, disliked school and their teachers, did fewer hours of homework, had teachers who were not very successful in

arousing academic interests, disliked physical education courses and seldom engaged in team sports and physical activities, did not particularly like science, enjoyed discussion courses often questioning teachers about subject matter; were regarded as radical or unconventional often wanting to be alone to pursue their own thoughts and their own interests, had parents of high educational income and occupational levels who were less strict, critical, or punitive, generally allowing them greater freedom than parents of less creative peers, and where this was not the case creative boys would express anger, and they did participate in church, religious, or charitable organizations' activities.

3. *When adults perceived themselves as creative, they tended to be more verbally original and imaginative.*

4. *Teachers who perceived themselves as high creatives were low value-centered and low creatives were high value-centered, where value-centeredness was the extent to which judged by behavior that was based on subjective approval or disapproval.*

CONCLUSIONS

The early efforts to find appropriate means for the identification of the intellectually gifted bore fruit in the development of IQ tests and in the study of characteristics of gifted persons over many years. Added meaning was given to this by the attempts of many educators, in school settings especially, to do something for such students. These efforts must not be mistaken for a broad sweep all over the country to provide special opportunities for all gifted children, which even to this day has not been realized. Rather, these efforts were the sporadic attempts of inspired and dedicated professionals who saw the importance of assisting the academic acceleration of these students but who received very little, if any, support. The impetus for advances in thought on the gifted came from several directions that today have converted what were largely individually inspired efforts to federal and national thrusts for the educational enhancement of the gifted. Subsumed under humanism are those influences that have broadened our perspectives and horizons that relate to special students. Therefore, we no longer look on giftedness within the narrow confines of IQ. Rather, we see giftedness as multidimensional and inclusive of all kinds of abilities and talents so that we regard creativity as subject to enhancement by means of educational intervention through which the gifted can be prepared to be productive, so that understanding creative development of the individual can better prepare us to provide those facilitative agents for the most productive interaction among the creativity peaks in the developmental cycles of gifted students, so that gifted students can receive and benefit from guidance, so that socioeconomic factors can be given proper attention in the screening procedures

30

that are designed to provide special opportunities, and so that we can derive from the new force of parapsychology fresh dimension and significance in educational planning for the gifted.

Terman and his associates engaged in sustained research of a single large California group of gifted students relative to their abilities, behavior, development, and fortunes and followed them through midlife. Creativity research began in earnest in the 1960s and, unlike the Terman studies, derived its information from many investigators using various groups of subjects of different ages and ethnic origins living all over the United States. The data obtained were generated by a multiplicity of techniques, ranging from the historical to the experimental. One major outcome has been to provide overwhelming supportive evidence to earlier thought and research that IQ measures identified only one kind of giftedness and that other measures are needed to measure special abilities and talent in a number of different areas of giftedness. Generally, measures for these many kinds of giftedness were not really available at the time—some are not yet available in effective form even today. However, in the 1960s, the attention of many researchers began to be occupied by the development of instruments to measure creative potential. The great strides that have been made to accomplish the production of reliable and valid measures still leave some issues unsettled.

The observation that 70% of the top 20% of subjects ranked on creativity tests are missed by IQ tests—drawn from the research evidence of Getzels and Jackson (1962) and Torrance (1962a)—suggests that IQ measures are in themselves not adequate as the sole criterion for identifying giftedness. The same may be said of creativity measures, which do not, in fact, identify the conservers of knowledge at the upper levels of IQ. This phenomenon seems to be more a function of measurement than of intellectual potential. If we are to accept Guilford's structure of intellect model, either kind of measure should contain items that require the use of the mental operations of cognition, memory, convergent and divergent thinking, and evaluation for any kind of approximate identification of intellectual functioning. A fuller treatment of the different dimensions of intellect and their implications will be found in Chapters 2 and 3. There is an increasing tendency to move away from a unidimensional to a multidimensional index of intellectual functioning. In particular, if we want to know about the function of specific abilities with which IQ measures do not attempt to deal, we must go to those measures that do deal with the functions of specific abilities. Only in this way can we derive reasonably appropriate clues concerning the identification of talent, for instance, in the areas of mechanical aptitude, mathematics, music, and art. Of course, we do know that more of the Spearman g is required for mathematics than for art and that IQ measures give us a better prediction of mathematical ability; but an appropriate special-abilities test will more accurately differentiate between those who can handle the symbol systems of the area at an exceptional level from those who cannot. This is not to say that we do have available measures for all special abilities; especially lacking, for instance, are good measures in music and art. However, for music and art, measures of creativity may be helpful in differentiating between those who can develop great skill and are conservers of the disciplines and those who can generate new skills and compose and innovate within the disciplines. Further treatment of this topic will be handled in Chapters 2 and 3, where theoretical formulations of giftedness and their measurement correlates will be discussed.

Finally, evidence derived from longitudinal research about high creatives as measured by the *Torrance Tests of Creative Thinking*, although of great value, may have somewhat limited generalizability because of unrepresentative sampling. Except for the short-range prediction studies and the long-range 6-year prediction study by Witt (1971), only the two major long-range studies by Torrance explored the relationship between creative achievements and the *Torrance Tests of Creative Thinking* administered to subjects who were not necessarily high creatives. Besides, except for Torrance's (1972b) 12-year study, the number of subjects in each of the other studies was small, ranging from 16 to 46. However, barely 22 years have elapsed since the construction of the Torrance measures, and a significant first step has been taken to find out more about creative and (to a lesser extent) about highly creative individuals longitudinally.

2

MANY
KINDS
OF
GIFTEDNESS

OVERVIEW

In this chapter, various definitions of the gifted are given and comments are made on these definitions. The early conception of a highly gifted person as one with a high level of general intelligence has been replaced by an expanded concept of giftedness that includes children who show themselves to be superior in at least one of the ability categories defined by the U.S. Office of Education (USOE), namely, creative or productive thinking, specific academic aptitude, leadership ability, visual and performing arts ability, and (although now a discontinued category) psychomotor ability. Two basic views that regard intelligence as a general or global mental capacity or as a culture and experience-bound construct are presented. The various theoretical orientations of intellectual functioning that are discussed show that early univariate models as the sole criterion for identifying the gifted gave way to accomodate multivariate models, the most comprehensive of which is the structure of intellect. One component of the structure of intellect is divergent production, or creativity. Creativity, as yet another viable dimension of giftedness, is also discussed. Other categories of giftedness—specific academic aptitude, leadership ability, visual and performing arts ability, and psychomotor abilities—receive attention as well. Appropriate comment is made where these categories relate to the models of intellectual ability.

CHAPTER OUTLINE

Introduction
Six Categories of Giftedness

INTRODUCTION

It is not uncommon to hear people talk about the exceptional person as gifted, as if there were no difference between one gifted person and another. *Webster's* (1962) defines gifted as, "having a natural ability or aptitude; talented"; when we look up the definition of talented, we find it to be "having talent; gifted"— the implications are (1) that giftedness is inherited and (2) that gifted and talented are synonymous terms. When used in the medieval sense, to be gifted is to provide evidence of accomplishment in some creative endeavor; this, in turn, is supposed

MANY KINDS OF GIFTEDNESS

to predict further accomplishments—there is no concept of potential to accomplish included. Giftedness is culture bound, not easily recognized as such (Gallagher, 1975), and highly dependent on societial needs (Newland, 1976)—all this adds further dimension to attempts at definition.

There are two important approaches of looking at giftedness: (1) relating giftedness to the universe of exceptional and extraordinary characteristics or qualities of the individual, either acquired through inheritance (avoiding the controversy of nature versus nurture) or as a result of the interaction of inheritance and environment; and (2) seeing giftedness as determined by the needs and biases of the cultural group of which the individual is a member. Newland (1976) attempts to give some coherence and clarity to the word gifted and finds it necessary to redefine gifted in terms of societial needs. Thus, a society would have to determine how many individuals were needed to carry out high-level operations and differentiate the essential characteristics required for these operations so that schools could locate such individuals to prepare them for their respective roles in society. Gallagher's (1975) comment about this subject as an unresolved issue is significant:

If our definition of gifted changes as the values of our society change, what will the definition look like in 1985? What values will be downgraded and what values more highly regarded? (P. 27)

Let us remember the important observation by Benedict (1935) that culture shapes man, but, although more slowly, man shapes culture as well. No definition of the gifted is adequate if it does not regard the interactive nature of individual excellence and societial needs and requirements.

In attempting to define gifted, we must first recognize the complexity of the term not only for its denotative meanings but also for its connotative meanings. The term giftedness is multidimensional, acquiring its many meanings from various fields of inquiry. Of particular relevance (as we shall see later in the chapter) are the changing conceptions of intelligence when different emphasis is placed on general mental ability (or g). General mental ability is conceived by some as dominant in a hierarchical structure of human abilities, by others the very existence of g is denied, as in the cube model of the structure of intellect.

Burt (1962) cites Leta Hollingworth and Lewis M. Terman as examples of those who accept Francis Galton's assumption that potential achievement is primarily determined by an individual's allowance of general ability and who base their definitions of the gifted on IQ, as assessed by tests of intelligence. A gifted person according to the Terman research and practice possesses an IQ of 130 and above. It is interesting to note that giftedness based on the *Stanford-Binet* IQ fluctuated between 150 and 110, depending on who defined it, where in the country a need was found to indentify giftedness, and for what project the identification was needed.

Definitions of gifted that included more than IQ stemmed from the early work of L. L. Thurstone on primary mental abilities and the more recent work of J. P. Guilford expressed in his structure of intellect model. The multivariate conception of intellect goes beyond intellectual ability and admits abilities to excel in music, in the creative arts, and in the psychomotor areas. It is more appropriately termed talent. An eclectic point of view recognizes the all-round gifted and those specially gifted (Burt, 1962). It identifies those highly intelligent people of IQ 125 and above as gifted and those of average and above average in academic ability but also endowed with poetic, musical, artistic, or mechanical ability as talented. This way of looking at the gifted does not present the kind of problem that the term academically talented does. Newland (1976) suggests that academically talented is a euphemism to avoid disturbing connotations of mental superiority, which explicitly anchors itself in intelligence testing (p. 10). Newland also suggests that the terms talent and talented have been inaccurately used to categorize individuals demonstrating superior skill—high levels of skill do not necessarily demand high levels of cognitive functioning (p. 24). He makes a sharp and useful distinction between gifted and talented when he proposes:

> *those children who anticipated superior social contribution as primarily a function of their superior conceptualization capacity be regarded as gifted and that those whose promise is not primarily so based be regarded as talented. (p. 24)*

Paul Witty proposed a broad definition of the term gifted:

> *The gifted or talented child is one who shows consistently remarkable performance in any worthwhile line of endeavor. (Henry, 1958, p. 19)*

Cutts and Mosely (1957), sensitive to the problem of using IQ alone to identify the gifted—because it does not make allowances for character, motivation, art or music talent, leadership, or the like—consider Witty's proposed definition as wise, whereas Newland questions the validity of a definition that would depend on demonstrated achievement for identification and the debatable nature of "worthwhile endeavor."

Here we have an approach to define giftedness in terms of performance and a commentary that would regard this approach as weak relative to the need to identify potential. There is, in any case, a certain looseness in the definition that contributes to ambiguity rather than clarity. It is not enough to make the point that we need to recognize that people can be gifted in a variety of ways but that the variety of giftedness needs to be more carefully specified in operational terms.

In attempting to bring together the many and varied definitions of the term gifted, the USOE sponsored a series of conferences held in Washington, D.C., which were attended by many of the leading exponents in the field of the gifted (Marland, 1972a). From these conferences there emerged a broadened concept of the superior child who is called gifted and talented. Such a child can be identified by professionally qualified persons as one with outstanding abilities capable of high performance and demonstrated achievement in any one of six areas, namely, general intellectual ability, creative or productive thinking, specific academic aptitude, leadership ability, visual and performing arts ability, and psychomotor abilities. The last category has been discontinued but still deserves attention.

Thus, we have official recognition of the complex nature of giftedness and an acceptance of a theoretical orientation that subscribes to a general intelligence as well as the importance of creative or productive thinking. The inclusion of specific academic aptitude, leadership ability, visual performing arts ability, and psychomotor ability recognizes both the complexity and multiplicity of giftedness, whose roots can be traced to a variety of sources—of which models of intellectual structure are but one, group dynamics are another, and artistic creation in the domain of rational-emotive interaction yet a third. The USOE's attempt to delineate giftedness as multiple is a very significant step forward. In its insistence that attention be paid to these categories of giftedness in planning for educational intervention for the purpose of obtaining funds that have now become available, a transition was made from the dark ages to modern times.

However, Renzulli (1979b) considers that the USOE definition, although useful, fails to include nonintellective or motivational factors; presents categories of giftedness that are by nature nonparallel (i.e., specific aptitude and visual performing arts call attention to performance, whereas the remaining four categories call attention to process that can be applied to performance); and is subject to misinterpretation and misuse by practioners. He attempts to get around these and related problems by proposing a definition of gifted that includes the three interactive areas of abilities, creativity, and task commitment in what he calls the revolving door concept: students are defined as gifted relative to specific projects they undertake and to their productivity and commitment to these projects. This definition may be expedient—even attractive—in that it moves away from identifying potential superiority as the continued development toward increasing levels of excellence, regardless of commitment to identifying giftedness by means of results—subjects must perform, that is, produce within a framework of time. However, Renzulli's definition shows that some careful rethinking and operationalizing of the USOE categories of giftedness, designed to develop appropriate screening procedures, appear necessary. His approach also points to the importance of motivational and creativity factors that can make all the difference between mediocrity and excellence and that must be given due attention in identification of the highly able.

SIX CATEGORIES OF GIFTEDNESS
GENERAL INTELLECTUAL ABILITY

It has been the custom to identify gifted children, especially as related to schooling, in terms of their intelligence as defined by IQ. Often the labeling of the child is done with a finality, without the full realization that IQ is nothing more than an index of the child's performance on a particular test and, at best, a predictor of academic achievement. This leads to a few words on intelligence, how people regard it, and some of the consequences relative to positions taken on intelligence.

Two Views on Intelligence

Simmons (1968) explains that the difficulty in formulating a single psychological approach to intelligence lies with the fact that psychologists tend to divide into one of two camps. In the main, psychologists look on intelligence (1) either as a thing that has real existence in the brain—something innate that sets limits to how people experience and the way they behave, a capacity transmitted by heredity in the same manner as physiological characteristics— or (2) as a synthetic construct that explains the great variety of human behaviors, which are highly dependent on experience and knowledge for their manifestation, and that is defined by its culture or subculture.

Intelligence as Innate

Those who assume that intelligence is innate and global attempt to measure true intelligence, that is, intelligence free from cultural contamination—what is commonly known as culture fair. Testing procedures are standardized to control for culture and situational differences. It is assumed that intelligence is real and constant over time and that deviations or declines in intelligence are pathological, for instance, in brain damage and anxiety. Measures of intelligence tend to encapsulate the knowledge of an individual in IQ and ignore important behaviors (such as verbal and motor behaviors, reaction time to success and failure, reaction to time press, and the like) that are observable during test taking and that would give valuable information about the individual that would go beyond the assigned IQ number index. In practice, the intelligence test does very little beyond predicting academic success; it is probably only a general measure of academic achievement that is not much different from a school achievement test (except in degree of specificity) or a general aptitude test.

Intelligence as Construct

Psychologists who take the construct view regard intelligence, not as a single function, not as something fixed or predetermined, but as culture and experience bound. They develop measures of specific abilities and regard variation in per-

MANY KINDS OF GIFTEDNESS

formance as the result of prior learning and experience. More attention is paid to what the individual says and does during the testing session and this information is most likely incorporated in the appraisal of the individual. Deviations in intellectual functioning of the tested individual are attributed to external and environmental influences and, hence, regarded as potentially controllable. Further, decline in intellectual functioning over time is attributed to changing conditions in the life, interests, and values of the individual, especially as they relate to test taking.

Changing Concepts of Intelligence

Guilford (1967) makes the point that tests have been developed ahead of an understanding of what they measure and that the definition of intelligence is far from settled. Common to the two views of intelligence described is the fact that intelligence is an intangible and abstract phenomenon. At best, it manifests itself in behaviors of the individual. What a test does is to sample some behaviors to derive evidence of intelligence. However, the lack of agreement on what behaviors constitute intelligence and the related problems of instrumentation have contributed to the difficulties of reaching a general consensus regarding theoretical formulations of intelligence. Mainly, however, tests of intelligence that go beyond the appraisal of intelligence as sensory and motor functions or mental traits have moved from a univariate approach giving a single score to a multivariate approach giving multiple scores.

Terman and the Stanford-Binet

Although Binet's scale was relatively neglected in France, it caught the interest of American psychologists and was soon applied to the study of mental retardates and normal children—the first American to use Binet's scale was Goddard (1908, 1911), who translated the 1908 version of the Binet scale into English (1908). However, both Alfred Binet and Henry H. Goddard used the scales for either average or mentally retarded children. Unlike them, Terman and his associates at Stanford University in 1916 revised and adapted the Binet scale for white Americans and modestly called their revision, the *Stanford-Binet* (Terman, 1916). Two other revisions of the *Stanford-Binet* followed: one in 1937 that consisted of two forms of the test (L and M) and the other in 1960 that essentially combined and refined the 1937 L and M forms and updated the measure (Terman & Merrill, 1937, 1960).

The first two revisions of the scale attempted to measure the intellectual performance of children from age 3 to young adulthood (or age 16) so that an individual's intellectual performance on the test was determined by comparison with the standards of performance for normal children of different ages. As in the Binet scale, the Terman 1916 scale expressed the scores obtained on the test in terms of mental age. Therefore, persons would be thought of as normal if they could do the test items persons of their age normally did, as retarded if they could only do those items done by younger persons, or as superior if they exceeded the performance of persons of their own age. Terman has defined mental age (MA) as the degree of general mental ability possessed by the average child of corresponding chronological age. The conversion of MA to IQ, the idea for which has been attributed to Wilhelm Stern, was included in the 1937 and 1960 revisions of the *Stanford-Binet*.

Wechsler and Intelligence

David Wechsler conceives intelligence as comprised of intellectual abilities; nonintellective forces, like drive, energy, impulsiveness, will, persistence, and the like; and temperament variables, such as interest and achievement, which are functions of the total personality. Like Binet, Wechsler, too, subscribes to the concept of general intelligence, which he is careful to point out is not synonymous with intellectual abilities, whereas he believes that general intelligence is some kind of mental energy that enters into all human behavior in some way or other and that intellectual abilities reflect that potential through a person's performance on tests.

It is some expression of an individual's personality in a global sense that can appropriately be called general intelligence, a potential energy whose nature is not known but whose use is for the good of society. General intelligence allows individuals to cope effectively with their environment and inferences about the nature of general intelligence may be drawn from the "intelligent" behavior of an individual in activities that require reasoning, abstract thinking, seeing appropriate relations among things, drawing inferences, understanding words literally and figuratively, problem solving, and the like.

A variety of abilities manifest themselves through this capacity, which Wechsler calls global. Such intellectual abilities may be defined and measured with a good degree of precision. Scores obtained for performance on tests related to the measure of these abilities serve to indicate the kind and level of intellectual ability a person may possess, and a person's global capacity or general intelligence may be inferred from this.

Univariate Approach to Intelligence

Binet and Intelligence

Early in this century a Frenchman, Alfred Binet, was commissioned by his government to discover some way of identifying children who could benefit from schooling and those who could not. As a scientist, he relied heavily on empirical data to assist him on his task: he felt that theory was important insofar as it provided direction to the empiricism that must follow. Nowhere in his writings does he formally state a clearly defined theory of intelligence. He recognizes that intellectual competency has to be identified by means of high complex mental processes without specifically defining these processes. Because this was difficult to do and until it became feasible, Binet felt some measure of general intelligence would be superior because it would reflect the operation of these higher complex mental processes.

Binet admitted the existence of multiple abilities as a unitary function that permeated all of behavior, which he called general intelligence. His search for a measure of general intelligence, facilitated by Théodore Simon, led to the construction of a developmental scale that would tell how well children could understand, reason, and judge; how adaptable and persistent they could be; and the extent to which they could apply self-criticism (Binet & Simon, 1905). This led to the brilliant idea that, if children could do the tasks relative to the abilities being measured that other children of their own age could do, they would be of average intelligence. For example, 6-year-olds who did the tasks that 6-year-old children could do, would have an MA of 6 years, in other words, they would be of average intelligence; if children were 6 years old and could do the tasks done by 7-year-olds, they would have an MA of 7 years, in other words, they would be brighter than children of their own age group. These theoretical notions about the nature of intelligence led Wechsler formally to define intelligence as "the aggregate or global capacity of the individual to act purposefully, to think rationally and to deal effectively with his environment" (1966, p. 7).

Although Wechsler's theoretical notions about the nature of intelligence are not completely implemented in the tests he consequently constructed, he does focus attention on the operation of nonintellective and temperament factors in the intellectual functioning of an individual that, taken as a whole, relate to the global capacity concept of intelligence. And he does indicate that, generally, intelligence may only be inferred from measures of a person's intellectual abilities.

Wechsler was the first to publish an individual test of intelligence for adults; later he extended the concepts involved in the construction of a test downward, to include youth and children. His tests now comprise the *Wechsler Adult Intelligence Scale (WAIS)* (1955); the *Wechsler Intelligence Scale for Children (WISC)*, prepared as a downward extension of the original *Wechsler-Bellevue Scale* (1939) and designed for use with children whose chronological ages range from 5 to 15 years—now revised as the *WISC-R* (1974) for children from 6 through 16½ years old; and the *Wechsler Preschool and Primary Scale of Intelligence* (1967), designed to test children whose ages range from 4 to 6½ years. All scales contain verbal and performance subscales that yield a verbal IQ, a performance IQ, and a full-scale or composite IQ.

Mental Age and IQ
Mental age is a term first coined by Binet to represent different degrees or levels

of intelligence as measured by his test. The measure assembled a series of intellectual tasks of varying difficulty for different age groups. There are six intellectual tasks at each level of the test. Successful performance on each task gives a credit of 2 months, with a maximum credit of 12 months obtainable per level. An MA is a score expressed in months and years that is derived by adding the number-of-months credit obtained by successful performance of the tasks at each level to the number-of-months credit before the level at which the subject gets all items correct, which is known as the basal age. For example, John, a child of 6 years, passes all six tests at year VII, five tests at year VIII, three tests at year IX, and one test at year X. He has a basal age of 6 years and is awarded a credit of 72 months to which is added $12 + 10 + 6 + 2$ months for a total of 102 months, which represents his MA.

An MA can, then, be converted into an IQ. The formula proposed by Terman (now obsolete) was

$$IQ = \frac{MA}{CA} \times 100$$

Wechsler explains that chronological age (CA) should not be thought of in literal terms as the life age (CA) of an individual at the time of testing, but in terms of the IQ formula. That is, like MA, CA is just a score that the examiner assumes individuals of a given age would attain if their ability were exactly the same as that of the average individual who has the same life age. This makes test scores in MA and CA identical units. That is, if individuals 8 years old were average 8-year-olds, their CA would also be 8 years. Wechsler suggests that it would be more appropriate to state the old IQ formula as

$$IQ = \frac{\text{Attained or actual score}}{\text{Expected mean score for age}}$$

and defines IQ as the ratio between a particular score obtained by a person on a measure of intelligence and the score in identical units obtained by an average individual of the same life age.

In the example, John's MA is 102 months and his life age (CA) is 72 months. To obtain his IQ, enter this information in the formula thus:

$$IQ = \frac{102}{72} \times 100 = 141.6 \text{ or } 142$$

Wechsler suggests that the value of an IQ is that it gives us a way of defining relative intelligence, tells us how bright persons are as compared to those of their own age, and remains relatively constant throughout life. However, the method

MANY KINDS OF GIFTEDNESS

of calculating IQ described above is inadequate because, depending on the age at which individuals are tested, they may obtain different IQs, even though their relative brightness remains the same. Further, intellectual growth does not proceed by equal amounts throughout its development—children's IQs tend to fall off as they grew older and progressively decline until ultimate arrest of growth. For these and other related reasons, psychologists have felt that the IQ as a measure of intelligence should be abandoned altogether. Wechsler points out that there was nothing intrinsically wrong with the IQ concept, but rather with the method by which IQ was calculated.

Deviation IQ

An IQ was first derived by dividing MA by CA and multiplying by 100 so that a child 5 years old with an MA of 6 would have an IQ of 120. This process was used to compute IQ values in the 1916 and 1937 revisions of the *Stanford-Binet* as well. However, an IQ obtained in this way did not allow for a comparison of one IQ with another at a specific age level or with IQs of different age levels. To get around this problem, the procedure used to compute standard scores was used to compute IQs. The IQs obtained in this way are called deviation IQs and are actually standard scores derived from an assumed mean of 100 and a standard deviation (SD) of 16 (on the *Stanford-Binet,* 1960 revision scale) or 15 (on the Wechsler scales). Of course, deviation IQs have been computed and are presented in tables found in test manuals. Thus, deviation IQ values are given for each age level 2 through 18 in the 1960 revision of the *Stanford-Binet* as are the values of each age level 4 through 75 and above, depending on which of the Wechsler scales is used. The average, or mean, IQ on the *Stanford-Binet* is 100, with an SD of 16. This indicates that, for persons to be considered highly intelligent, their IQs must be at least about two SDs above the mean (i.e., 100 + 2(16) = 132). On the Wechsler sclaes, because the SD is 15, persons must have IQs of at least 130 to be considered highly intelligent.

In this way, the inadequacies of the earlier method of computing IQ are avoided, so that an IQ indicates relative ability at different ages and remains (except for chance errors) the same from one age to another, provided no change in ability occurs. That is, John's deviation IQ of, say, 130 at age 10 can be compared with his deviation IQ at age 12 or John's deviation IQ can be compared to Donna's deviation IQ of, say, 140 at age 10 or at another age. The formula for deviation IQ is

$$\text{Deviation IQ} = (\text{IQ}_x - \text{IQ}_m)\, K + 100$$

where

$$\text{IQ}_x = \frac{\text{MA}}{\text{CA}} \times 100$$

SIX CATEGORIES OF GIFTEDNESS

IQ_m = mean IQ for age considered according to 1937 scale

$$K = \frac{16}{\sigma} (\text{assumed } \sigma \div \sigma \text{ for age considered according to 1937 scale})$$

Constancy or Stability of IQ

Wechsler (1965) indicates that constancy of IQ is a basic assumption of all scales of intelligence. If a measure of intelligence is to have practical value, both for purposes of prediction and diagnosis, it must assume and eventually demonstrate that IQ remains invariant over a considerable period of time. Without this assumption, no permanent scheme of classifying intelligence is possible. If they are close to the means, IQs tend to remain constant. That is, those individuals identified as having average intelligence will generally show little, if any, difference in IQ at various age levels. However, IQs that are one to two SDs above or below the mean tend to show more fluctuations at different age levels. That is, if an individual obtained an IQ of 130 at age 10, we can expect that person to obtain an IQ of between 135 and 140 or between 120 and 125 at age 12. It must be realized, however, that IQ differences relate to the scores obtained on a test and not to differences in true intelligence, the nature of which we do not really know and can only infer from test performance. Wechsler points out that depending on the age at which an individual is tested, the IQ may vary although the subject's relative brightness remains unchanged.

Bayley (1949) suggests that test results in the first two years of life tend to be inconsistent, that there is an increase in the predictive power of intelligence tests between the ages of 2 and 6 years, and that, after the age of 6, test scores tend to be relatively stable for most individuals. The study also reports that average changes in IQ tend to be about 5 points, although individual variations can be as much as 30 points from one testing to the next. Extreme changes in IQ scores are not unusual, for instance when very highly gifted individuals are tested at different age levels.

The constancy of IQ relates to measures used and the unchanging nature of the individual's capacity. Much of the problem hinges on the reliability of the measures used and the scores they give. Where equivalent or alternate forms of tests are used, the problem hinges on the sameness of the two measuring instruments. And, because the constancy of IQ is determined by repeated administrations of a test at different age levels, variations in IQ may be due to instrument discrepencies. Another important consideration is that of other exraneous variables that affect an individual during and between testing sessions. However, it must be remembered that, if changes in IQ do occur, they are changes in test scores and not of the level of intelligence, which, by definition, is independent of age.

Multivariate Approach to Intelligence

Once factor analysis became available to researchers interested in understanding the nature and measurement of intelligence, there emerged the conception of intelligence as multivariate rather than univariate. Factor analysis is a statistical technique that uses correlation coefficients to discover psychological functions that are basic to test performance and, in terms of intelligence, are used to differentiate fundamental intellectual abilities. By a complicated process of intercorrelating scores achieved on a number of tests by a group of people, certain common elements, or attributes, among the tests are identified. Each cluster, called a factor, is, then, given a name for the ability required to do the several related tests. Some tests, for instance, require the memorizing of lines, and the factor identified is visual memory; other tests may require the manipulation of numbers, and a numerical factor would then be identified. Factor scores tell how much of a certain attribute a person may have, whereas scores on a test tell how well a person has done on the test (Guilford, 1967). Identification of these elements, or attributes, through factor analyses makes it possible to theorize about the structure of intelligence. Factor analyses facilitated the development of several multivariate theories of intelligence: the two-factor theory, the hierarchical theory, the multifactor theory and the structure of intellect.

Two-Factor Theory of Intelligence
Spearman (1927) was one of the first to use factor analysis in psychology to explain the nature of intelligence. Using a simple factor analysis model, Spearman derived evidence that led him to believe that intelligence is composed of two factors in the main: (1) a general factor, or mental energy, that enters into all intellectual activity and is possessed by everyone in varying degrees—he labeled this factor $g;$ and (2) a large number of specific factors that are highly relevant to particular tasks that he labeled s. Spearman makes the point that, unlike the theory of general intelligence, the two-factor theory provides a satisfactory explanation of the tendency for all abilities to show not only overlap to some extent but also considerable unevenness. He suggests that g stands for the general mental energy that is a part of an individual's natural endowment, and he compares the s factors to a great many mechanisms, or engines, capable of being set in motion by this energy. Whereas s factors much depend on the influences of education and training, $g,$ being innate and ineducable, does not. Much of his theory of intelligence can be traced to his three famous neogenetic principles of cognition, namely, apprehension of experiences, eduction of relations, and eduction of correlates.

Hierarchical Models
Both Sir Cyril Burt and P. E. Vernon were followers of Spearman and firmly subscribed to the concept of g, although they gave more attention to group factors. They felt that the best way to explain the discovery of new factors was through a hierarchical model that would put the factors in some kind of logical

interrelationship, ranging from a general factor through group factors to specific factors.

The Burt Model. Burt's conception of intelligence (1949), which applied to the whole of the human mind, distinguished between abilities that were intellectual in nature—symbolized by Spearman's *g* factor—and practical, or behavioral in nature—which included psychomotor, mechanical, and spatial abilities. He placed these factors in a hierarchical order with each higher level factor subdividing into two immediately lower in a series of successive dichotomies. The first dichotomy emerges from the head of the hierarchy, the human mind, as the *relations* level (*g* level) and the *practical* level. These dichotomize to the next lower level, the *associations* level, which again subdivides into the levels of *perception* and *sensation* (Figure 2).

The Vernon Model. Vernon (1951) also conceived intelligence in terms of an hierarchical model headed by *g,* which subdivides into two sets of major group factors, namely, verbal-educational (*v:ed*) and kinesthetic-motor (*k:m*) factors. The latter is equivalent to Burt's practical factor. The major group factors subdivide into minor factors: *v:ed* subdivides into verbal, numerical, and educational factors; *k:m* subdivides into practical, spatial, mechanical, and physical factors. These, then, divide still further into specific factors (Figure 3).

According to Vernon (1960), intelligence corresponds to the general level of complexity and flexibility of a person's schemata accumulated during a lifetime, the acquisition of which is limited by innate ability. Further, the emergence of

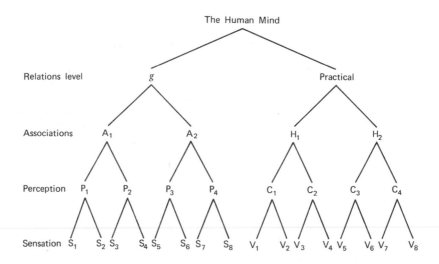

Figure 2   Burt's hierarchical model. (Burt, 1949. Copyright © 1949 British Journal of Educational Psychology. Reprinted by permission of the British Journal of Educational Psychology.)

MANY KINDS OF GIFTEDNESS

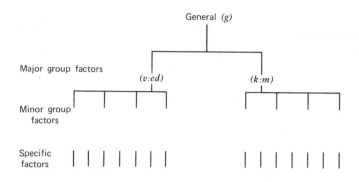

General *(g)*

Major group factors

(v:ed)   *(k:m)*

Minor group factors

Specific factors

Figure 3   Vernon's hierarchical model. (Vernon, 1951. Copyright © 1950 John Wiley & Sons, Inc. Reprinted by permission of John Wiley & Sons, Inc.)

higher order schemata is dependent on the acquisition of specific perceptual schemata so that the higher the level of schemata the more of the *g* factor it will contain. Vernon maintains that the complexity and flexibility of schemata are contingent on a stimulating environment.

Multifactor Theory of Intelligence

Thurstone and the Primary Mental Abilities. Thurstone (1924) conceived intelligence as operating at four major levels of trial and error, ranging from overt trial and error (at the least intelligent level) through perceptual trial and error and ideational trial and error to the conceptual (the most intelligent level). Intelligence at the least intelligent level operates as overt behavior of the trial-and-error-type. At the next level, perceptual trial-and-error intelligence, individuals may experience mentally an experience they would otherwise achieve by contact experience. Percepts are imaginal for the most part, and, when their sensory cues are dropped, corresponding ideas remain. At the ideational level of intelligence, experience can be anticipated without direct encounter. Thurstone illustrates the difference between perceptual and ideational intelligence by the situation of a certain street that is to be avoided before overt experience takes place. If a person should have an impulse to walk along this street and remembers that it is under construction, perceptual intelligence alone would allow the person to walk the street until a street-closed sign is seen, whereas ideational intelligence will help the person anticipate the situation well in advance.

The highest level of intelligence is conceptual intelligence, where trial and error is carried on among quite crude, loosely organized, tentative, and incomplete actions or concepts. It is the conceptual level of intelligence with which Thurstone concerns himself when he attempts to measure intelligent behavior.

By using factor analyses to manipulate test results, he discovered that certain groupings of these tests occurred with no presence of *g* and a limited number of elementary factors (Thurstone, 1938). This led him to conceive intelligence as consisting of about a dozen or so group factors that he called primary mental abilities. The most important of these he labeled verbal (V), number (N), spatial relations (S), word fluency (W), memory (M), and reasoning (R). He constructed the *Chicago Tests of Primary Mental Abilities* based on these factors. He did find that the primary factors related to each other—as a result of further work with these tests—and he explains this relationship as a function of a second-order factor.

Guilford and the Structure of Intellect. Guilford (1967) was dissatisfied with the various models that evolved from factor analysis and, following extensive research in measurement, conceived the structure of intellect model. This is a comprehensive extension of the multifactor theory that takes the form of a three-dimensional, or cube, model. It consists of five kinds of mental *operations* (cognition, memory, divergent production, convergent production, and evaluation), four kinds of *contents* (figural, symbolic, semantic, and behavioral), and six kinds of informational forms or *products* (units, classes, relations, systems, transformations, and implications), making a total of 120 possible intellectual abilities—each different from the rest by its unique combination of the mental operation, content, and product used (Figure 4).

OPERATION. The major kinds of intellectual activities involved in the processing of raw materials of information by a person. Briefly, the operation of *cognition* is knowing and, in terms of information-processing psychology, a matter of coding or constructing items of information; the operation of *memory* relates to the storing (or fixing) in the brain of information; the operations of *divergent* and *convergent production* are both similar—each depends on retrieval of information from storage—and significantly different—in divergent production, the situation is more or less open concerning when a number of different or alternative productions are logically possible and may occur, but, in convergent production, the given information is so restrictive that only one response is fully acceptable; the operation of *evaluation* involves comparison and judgment relative to certain criteria.

CONTENT. Broad classes of information in terms of their substantive nature. *Figural* (visual, auditory, and kinesthetic) content relates to concrete forms of information perceived or recalled as images; *symbolic* content relates to information in the form of denotative signs that in themselves have no significance (such as letters, numbers, and words) when the things for which they stand are not considered; *semantic* content relates to information that is meaningful and may occur in the form of words or pictures; and *behavioral* content relates to essentially nonverbal information that involves the attitudes, needs, desires, moods,

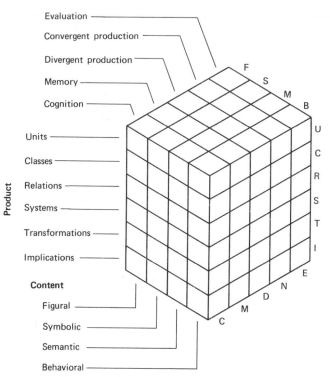

Figure 4 The structure of intellect. (Guilford, 1967. Copyright © 1967 McGraw-Hill. Reprinted by permission of McGraw-Hill Book Company.)

intentions, perceptions, thoughts, and the like, that occur in human interactions.

PRODUCT. The forms that information take when a person processes it. In brief: *units* are things taken as wholes and without analysis; it is through their various combinations that the remaining five product forms are derived; *classes* are three or more units of information that are categorized or grouped together by virtue of their common properties; *relations* are associated units of information that are meaningfully connected; *systems* are organized sets of units of information that are complexes of interrelated or interacting parts; *transformations* are changes in information or in its functioning that involve redefinition, revisions, or modifications; and *implications* are extrapolations of information that take the form of expectancies, predictions, or known or suspected consequences.

CREATIVE OR PRODUCTIVE THINKING

Until recently, the main method of identifying gifted children was by means of their general intellectual ability. Thought concerning general mental ability expanded through the years to conceive of this ability as a multifaceted phenomenon rather than a unitary one. This reached its prime articulation in the structure of intellect model (Guilford, 1950, 1967), which suggested that individuals could show themselves to be gifted in many different ways. Of particular importance and relevance is the focus Guilford gave to divergent thinking abilities within the operations face of his cube model, which is sometimes (less precisely although more inclusively) referred to as creativity.

Theory of Creativity

Creativity is recognized as a very complex concept (e.g., Gowan, 1972; Roweton, 1973; Torrance, 1974a) and, in terms of its measurement correlates, a great source of apprehension. Considerable lack of agreement over the definition of creativity exists (Torda, 1970) because, through usage, the term has become associated with various aspects of creative behavior and mental functioning that range along a cognitive-emotive continuum. This has been further complicated by the great number of different definitions concerning its energy source—depending on which of the several existing theoretical models of human functioning serves as the frame of reference.

Gowan's Theoretical Classification

Gowan (1972) has classified creativity theory along a rational-psychedelic continuum as follows:

Creativity as cognitive, rational, and semantic. This classification places creativity within the realm of problem-solving and hearkens back to the studies of leaders, such as S. J. Parnes, J. P. Guilford, and others, who were interested in creativity as a component of intellect.

Creativity as personal and environmental relative to child-rearing practices. The concern here is more heavily weighted toward personality correlates that hinge on originality, energy, and, in particular, self-concept.

Creativity as a high degree of mental health. Studies with this orientation were produced by figures such as A. H. Maslow and his school; they emphasize openness to experience and antiauthoritarian influences.

Creativity as Freudian. Sigmund Freud spoke of creativity as the sublimation of the sexual urge, which is a source of artistic activity and the main source of cultural energy, compensation, and the collective unconscious. From this base has sprung the candid neo-Freudian view that the oedipal crisis, which occurs during the narcissistic stage, is the genesis of creative functioning. A variation of this theme views creative accomplishments as sublimations of aggressive, phallic, or incestuous desires and, hence, as refinements of basic drives and primary processes. The preconscious is viewed as the source of creativity, and its development is considered central.

Creativity as Psychedelic. This classification traces the connections among creativity and hypnotism, extrasensory perception, and other paranormal aspects, such as precognition.

Much of what Gowan says about creativity and the way we draw on it is related to opening up the preconscious and bringing that material to the conscious level. He intimates that this activity is both governable and ungovernable and that there is both an open sesame that can be called on at will and a latent creative force that bubbles to the surface of its own volition.

Roweton's Theoretical Classification

Roweton's efforts (1973) suggested six theoretical approaches to the interpretation of creative behavior: definitional, behavioristic, dispositional, humanistic, psychoanalytic, and operational. The psychoanalytic, humanistic, and operational approaches are quite similar to Gowan's Freudian, mental health, and cognitive classifications respectively. The dispositional approach is similar to Gowan's cognitive and mental health categories.

According to Roweton, the definitional approach attempts to conceptualize what creativity is, and, although not easily subjected to empirical verification, it often provides experimental psychologists with a rich source of testable hypotheses. The behavioristic approach to creativity leans heavily on association and reinforcement theories with some attention given to the effects of incubation and transfer. This perspective is also of value—it lends itself to a more parsimonious expression of what we mean by creativity because it is based on observable behaviors and performances. Although inferences are not always easy to draw or deductions easy to make, the data are at least concrete.

Definition of Creativity

Because the understanding of the term creativity is dependent on its theoretical source, its definition has to be thought of in an appropriate context. Lack of agreement concerning definition of this term can be traced not only to the many different ways people can be creative but also to the fact that explanations of these behaviors derive meaning in part from referential theoretical models. Hence, there is need to describe and define operationally the particular abilities that people possess.

Among the many cogent earlier definitions relative to creative thinking as a *process* is thinking by analogy (Ribot, 1906); the initiative to break away from the usual sequence of thought into an altogether different pattern of thought (R. M. Simpson, 1922); the process of seeing relationships with both conscious and subconscious processes operating for the eduction of relations and correlates (Spearman, 1930); and, more recently, the distinction between cogito, or the ability to shake and throw things together, and intelligo, or the ability to choose and discriminate among many possibilities for synthesizing and binding together elements in original ways (Barchillon, 1961).

At no other time in the history of measurement have we had so many attempts to operationalize creativity for its scientific identification. Among the definitions of creativity that have led to the production of measures of creativity are: intellectual operations relative to divergent thinking, transformation, and redefinition; abilities set in motion by a sensitivity to problems (Guilford, 1967); the process of sensing gaps or disturbing missing elements, forming hypotheses concerning them, testing these hypotheses, communicating the results, and possibly modifying and retesting the hypotheses (Torrance, 1962a); the ability to generate or produce within some criterion of relevance many cognitive associates, many of which are unique (Wallach & Kogan, 1965); and the power of the imagination to break away from a perceptual set to restructure anew ideas, thoughts, and feelings into novel and meaningful associative bonds (Khatena & Torrance, 1973). To these may be added the definition of creativity operationalized as personality dimensions, products, process, and press (Rhodes, 1961).

Divergent-Production Abilities

Guilford's definition of intelligence as a systematic collection of abilities or functions for processing different kinds of information in different ways relative to content and product places creative thinking within the realm of intelligence and, in terms of the structure of intellect model, this is especially related to the divergent-production area of abilities (Guilford, 1975). He defines divergent production as a set of factors or intellectual abilities that pertain primarily to information retrieval, the testing of which calls for varied responses to each test item: testees of divergent production are required to produce their own answers and not choose from alternatives given to them.

Of special relevance to creative thinking are abilities having to do with fluency, flexibility, originality, and elaboration.

Fluency. This is an ability concerned with the ready flow of ideas relating to all divergent-production tests and, particularly, refers to three traditional kinds of tests in the semantic category that have parallel abilities in the figural and other content areas, namely, ideational fluency (divergent production of meaningful units or DMU), associational fluency (divergent production of meaningful relations or DMR), and expressional fluency (divergent production of meaningful systems DMS).

Flexibility. This ability involves what has been called spontaneous flexibility, which has to do with changes in direction of thinking when not instructed or required to do so, and adaptive flexibility, which involves changes in direction of thinking to solve problems.

Originality. The ability to produce responses that are statistically rare in the population, remotely related, and clever.

Elaboration. The ability to fill out ideas with details.

Creative Thinking Abilities

Guilford (1967) attempts to measure creative thinking, in the main, by way of the operation category of divergent production and the product category of transformation; either or both need to be involved in the thinking episode and are the source of novel ideas. He uses a test format that generally requires a person to respond to many stimuli, each of which sets out to measure a specific ability that at one and the same time calls for the interactive involvement of thinking operation, content, and product. Torrance (1974b) takes quite a different approach, he attempts to measure divergent thinking through the presentation of several complex tasks designed to trigger the expression of several creative thinking abilities. Like Guilford, he gives major roles to fluency, flexibility, originality, and elaboration (Torrance, 1974b). Torrance and Ball's (1980) streamlined scoring and interpretive manual relative to the Torrance figural tests has identified 5 norm-referenced measures, namely, fluency, originality, abstractness of titles, elaboration, and resistence to premature closure. In addition 13 criterion-referenced measures are identified:

Expression of feeling/emotion in drawings/titles
Articulateness in telling a story; context, environment
Movement/action (running, dancing, flying, falling, etc.)
Expressiveness of titles
Combination of two or more incomplete figures
Combination of two or more repeated figures
Unusual visual perspective (as seen from above, below, etc.)
Internal visual perspective (inside, cross-section, etc.)
Extending/breaking boundaries
Humor in titles/captions/drawings
Richness of imagery (variety, vividness, strength, etc.)
Colorfulness of imagery (excitingness, earthiness, etc.)
Fantasy (figures in myths, fables, fairy tales, science fiction, etc.)

Torrance's definition of creativity "as a process of becoming sensitive to problems, deficiencies; gaps in knowledge, missing elements, disharmonies, and so on; identifying the difficult; searching for solutions, making guesses or formulating hypotheses about the deficiencies; testing and retesting these hypotheses and possibly modifying and retesting them; and finally communicating the results"

(Torrance, 1974b, p. 8) is central to his measures of creative mental functioning. He annotates the definition in terms of strong human needs:

If we sense some incompleteness or disharmony, tension is aroused. We are uncomfortable and want to relieve the tension. Since learned ways of behaving are inadequate, we begin trying to avoid the commonplace and obvious (but incorrect) solutions by investigating, diagnosing, manipulating, and making guesses or estimates. Until the guesses or hypotheses have been tested, modified, and retested, we are still uncomfortable. The tension is unrelieved, however, until we tell somebody of our discovery. (Torrance, 1974b, p. 8).

Measures of divergent thinking and creative thinking abilities will be dealt with in Chapter 3.

SPECIFIC ACADEMIC APTITUDE

Gifted children may also be identified by their superior capacity to perform well in one or more academic school subjects that relate to the areas of language, mathematics, science, and social studies. In terms of the several models of intelligence, specific academic aptitude would relate, for instance, to the specific verbal educational abilities of Vernon's hierarchical model or the symbolic and semantic dimensions of Guilford's structure of intellect model. In terms of the Vernon model, the mental energy at work is g, whereas in Guilford's model, there would be the five thinking operations: cognition, memory, convergent thinking, divergent thinking, and evaluation. Of the two models, Guilford's tends to be highly operational, in that not only are the mental operations and content with which they work defined but also the product form to be processed and the eventual form it takes (namely, units, classes, relations, systems, transformations, and implications) is defined. In this way, we have at least $2 \times 5 \times 6$ (or 60) intellectual abilities that may be involved in the learning of academic subjects.

If by specific academic aptitude is meant the potential to do better in certain subject areas than in others, then, measures of intellectual abilities, generally, and the subtests of these measures, specifically, may be used to predict aptitude. However, if by specific academic aptitude is meant performance in the academic subject areas, then, the direct method of evaluating scores obtained, for example, in language or mathematics, should be the approach. Hence, to determine the academic subjects in which a child may have leanings toward excellence, it would be appropriate to administer tests relevant to the academic subjects that attempt to measure the capacity to do the subjects and not just measure knowledge of the subject content. In language, for example, such capacity may be identified in terms of understanding language that is factual, emotive, tonal, and

MANY KINDS OF GIFTEDNESS

intentional; the use of language that involves analogy; the use of language as it relates to productive thinking and evaluation; and the like. Briefly, what should be looked for is the ability to handle the symbolic and semantic systems of language. In mathematics, the aim should be to test for capacity to use the symbolic and semantic systems of numbers and may involve children's exhibition of their ability to handle number sets, probability, deductive and inductive thinking, and the like.

Measures are available to test for achievement levels in the several academic subject areas on the basis of scores that can be interpolated into specific academic aptitude. Where a measure of academic aptitude is available, this may also be used. Such measures will be dealt with in Chapter 3.

LEADERSHIP ABILITY

Ability that facilitates the handling and the representing of people as well as the initiating of events and situations on their behalf is what may be called leadership. Such ability requires a person to be bright, to have understanding of people, to know the mechanics of behavior in groups, to be aware of strategies of individual and group management, to have a sensitivity to changes, and to possess the creativity to handle the dynamics of human behavior, interaction, and change. Leadership ability draws its energy from intellectual and connotative sources of human functioning.

The structure of intellect model at present offers one good explanation of this dimension of giftedness. Of particular relevance is the behavioral component of the model. Behavioral content relates essentially to nonverbal information that involves the attitudes, needs, desires, moods, intentions, perceptions, thoughts, and the like, that occur in human interactions. The behavioral component of intellect along with the other two dimensions of intellectual functioning, namely, the five mental operations (cognition, memory, covergent thinking, divergent thinking, and evaluation) and the six products (units, classes, relations, systems, transformations, and implications) offer a reasonably good model for the assessment of abilities that make for leadership roles.

However, leadership studies over the years have revealed that ability of an individual is one of several dimensions; other dimensons relate to the group of which the individual is a member—the task at hand or the situation prevalent, motivational and reinforcement variables of the relationships, and interaction effects—each has an important part to play. Unlike the other five categories of giftedness, the attributes of leadership cannot be considered entirely personal. Leadership ability is not something inherited although certain ability predispositions appear to be present; rather, it appears to be emergent depending on the sociocultural group context as it is activated by specific situations. Leadership has been defined, for instance, as the interaction of both personality traits and situations (Fiedler, 1964); as a complex social phenomena, part personal but also part social (Gowan & Demos, 1962); as a product of functional relationship to specific individuals in specific situations (Knickerbocker, 1948); or as an emergent phenomenon created through interaction of leaders and followers, where an individual's status in a group is a joint function of his or her personality, the particular group setting, and the perception of the followers (Mann, 1959).

Research evidence (e.g., Fiedler, 1964; Stogdill, 1974) is not without contradiction, but, in the main, the current view favors the concept of leadership as emergent within the context of individual-group-situation interactions. One early theory on the subject regards the leader as a "Great Man," someone endowed with outstanding characteristics that impel him to direct the affairs of others; another, the times theory, defines leadership in terms of a social situation where a leader is needed for a particular task at a particular time. Leadership as effective influence (Gibb, 1947) is seen as arising out of interactions of the individual and the social situation so that the group allows for the expression of this ability. In such a circumstance, the influence exerted by the individual must be voluntarily accepted by the group so that there is shared direction before it can become effective. Where the influence is one of domination, the acceptance of leadership is with resentment. There is also the case where the influence is symbolic so that the leader is in a position of leadership without influence on the voluntary acceptance or domination of his or her leadership.

The trait-theory approach requires the identification of qualities or characteristics of an individual deemed to be related to leadership. However, a review of this approach (Gibb, 1947; Mann, 1959; Stogdill, 1948) indicated that, in itself, it is insufficient; a trait or pattern of traits had to be considered in the context of situations for them to have relevance, especially because situations differed radically one from another and the qualities needed for different situations varied accordingly.

This prepared the way for an interaction theory of leadership. Approaches include studies of personality variables that related leadership behavior to such attributes as intelligence and formal education, extroversion, assertiveness, and social maturity, which were found to be important (e.g., Fleishman, 1973; McGrath & Altman, 1966), although interpersonal sensitivity to interaction approaches of leadership was also recognized (e.g., Fiedler, 1967; Mann, 1959; Stogdill, 1974). Among interaction theoretical approaches, two are of special relevance: (1) interaction-expectation theory—of which expectation-reinforcement theory of role attainment (Stogdill, 1959), the path-goal theory of leadership (Evans, 1970), and motivational theory (House & Dessler, 1974) are three versions—and (2) contingency theory (Fiedler, 1964). An interaction-expectation theory of leadership includes three basic components: action, interaction, and sentiments—the increase in one is accompanied by a proportionate

MANY KINDS OF GIFTEDNESS

increase in the other two. The leader's role is one that is concerned with originating interaction and maintaining its structure until there is fulfillment of the group expectation, initiating organized paths that are perceived by followers as leading toward rewarding goals, and increasing the motivation of followers to perform by means of leader guidance, direction, support, and rewards.

Contingency theoretical models generally assume that no universally good leader exists and that there are a variety of leadership styles, whose effectiveness varies according to particular situations (Chemers & Rice, 1974). The most widely accepted contingency model of leadership is the one Fiedler developed (1964), where the effectiveness of leadership performance depends on the leader's motivational pattern, which is contingent on situational favorableness.

Three important ingredients of situational favorableness are acceptance of the leader by the followers; a clear outline by the leader of the task and the procedures for completing it that are accurately perceived by the followers; and the power of the leader to reward or punish followers. A leader posesses certain attributes that are stable and enduring, whose relevance is determined by situations. However, although manifestations of these attributes may appear to change with changes in a situation, the attributes themselves—which are more organized toward group activity and are central to the individual relatively—do not change.

What we have learned from theory and research about leadership suggests that a number of important variables have to be taken into account when leadership is to be identified. These variables, in the main, relate to the personal qualities of the individual leader in the context of the dynamics of the group, and they are energized into expression by their interactive relationship in different situations relative to the task at hand, the perceived goals and rewards, or the punishment of followers. All in all, leadership is a complex of many variables, which is succintly summarized by Stogdill's extensive review of the research and theory on the subject:

> The findings suggest that leadership is not a matter of passive status, or of the mere possession of some combination of traits. It appears rather to be a working relationship among members of a group, in which the leader acquires status through active participation and demonstration of his capacity for carrying cooperative tasks through to completion. Significant aspects of this capacity for organizing and expediting cooperative effort appear to be intelligence, alertness to the needs and motives of others, and insight into situations, further reinforced by such habits as responsibility, initiative, persistence, and self-confidence. (1974, p. 65)

VISUAL AND PERFORMING ARTS ABILITY

Ability in visual and performing arts is more appropriately considered as ability in one or more of the areas in the fine arts, not some single ability that necessarily enters into all activities defined as visual and performing arts. By visual arts we mean drawing, painting, sculpturing, designing, composing music in written form, and all other related forms of art whose products can be observed; by performing arts we mean music, dance, oratory, drama, and all other related forms of art that require performance.

Abilities that are required for superior production or performance are not easily measurable; few, if any, good and adequate psychological measures are available at present for this purpose. Although there are a number of measures available for musical abilities, they are generally regarded as incomplete indentifiers or as technically inadequate (Lehman, 1968). Measures of art abilities are fewer and are even less appropriate as identifiers of talent; measures of dramatic abilities, as such are almost nonexistent. That is why we may have to rely heavily on the observable behavior and product of individuals to determine potential talent in the visual and performing arts when psychometry cannot help us.

Intelligence has been recognized as having some relevance for the visual and performing arts. Changing conceptions of intelligence have not left these specialized areas of talent altogether unaffected. The measurement movement in music, for instance, reflects some of this: some test constructors tend to reflect a g factor in their measures (e.g., Kwalwasser & Dykema, 1930; Wing, 1961), whereas others tend to reflect the multiabilities model (e.g., E. Gordon, 1965; Seashore, Lewis, & Saetveit, 1960). Generally, however, those individuals who show themselves to have extraordinary talent in the arts tend to be highly gifted intellectually (e.g., Passow, Goldberg, Tannenbaum, & French, 1955) although they may not necessarily show this on an IQ test.

Another aspect of importance in thinking is the symbolic system that is acquired and used by individuals in these special fields of talent. The symbolic system of verbal language is generally not the major system used for communication in the visual and performing arts. Musical notation provides the basis for the communication of music (although some have attempted to substitute a number system for it, for instance, in the Far East and Southeast Asia). Nonverbal systems are the substitute for the verbal in the visual arts and dance, unlike oratory and drama, which are dependent on the verbal language system for communication—although dance, acting, and oratory also make use of body language in performance.

Imagery (visual, auditory, and kinesthetic—to mention three of several sense-modality image correlates) is an important component of thinking and expression in the visual and performing arts. In the various theoretical models of intellect, imagery lies in the nonverbal domain. Its role in art, music, dance, and acting is significant because imagery overcomes the barriers of intermediary symbolic systems to present to the individual visions that eventually find themselves expressed in one art form or another. A detailed discussion of imagery, right-brain-hemisphere processing, imagination, as well as their projections in creative behavior will appear in Chapter 4.

Common to all these art forms is creativity, a processing and energizing agent that differs in degree of operation, depending on the form of art used. On the subject of creativity and the visual arts Guilford (1968) focuses attention on the importance of three divergent production abilities in the figural dimension of the structure of intellect: fluency, flexibility, and elaboration. Communication of meaning in the visual arts is done in nonverbal ways and often involves these three divergent thinking abilities. Fluency in the figural information area is broken down into ideational fluency (or the ability to generate many ideas), analogy fluency (or the ability to produce many analogues), and expressional fluency (or the ability to organize figural information as systems rapidly). Two kinds of abilities relate to a shift in thinking from one class to another: spontaneous flexibility indicates automatic shifts in thinking; adaptive flexibility indicates shifts in thinking owing to the need for different solutions to a single problem. Guilford considers elaboration very important to art when, early in a creative production, a general schema, motif, or plan develops that is psychologically a system to which details are added as the system becomes distinct.

Other abilities that also have importance and relevance for creative artistic production are the ability to visualize changes in figural information (transformation ability outside the divergent-production category), the ability to evaluate one's own total production of an art object, and ability in the behavioral category as this relates to the translation of semantic or behavioral information to figural information.

Lowenfeld and Brittain (1964) discuss the creative and mental growth of talented children as related to art and identify five major characteristics. The first is fluency of imagination and expression, that is, ideas spontaneously flow and imagery expands with the creative process as in a chain reaction. The second is a highly developed sensibility toward movement, rhythm, content, and organization (which varies with the talented individual) and, thus, integration of thinking, feeling, and perceiving is experienced to a high degree by the talented person. The third is intuitive quality of imagination through which imagery important to the creative act is possessed to a high degree by the talented individual. The fourth, directness of expression, relates to the self-confidence expressed by the gifted individual in the act of artistic creation. The fifth is a high degree of self-identification with the depicted experience that is exhibited by the gifted individual.

Highly specialized knowledge and skill specific to each art form must be acquired by individuals before they can express themselves in that medium. Because it takes time to acquire this knowledge and skill, it is not unusual to find that screening of young children for talent in the arts in terms of potential is difficult. However, this may be more a function of psychometrics than a real problem. Capurso (1961), citing two studies on the subject of emergence of musical giftedness, suggests that the talents of musically gifted children generally reveal themselves during early childhood, "... with the exception of a few masters such as Berlioz, Tschaikowsky and Wagner, most of the great musicians revealed their artistic gifts before their teen years'' (p. 318).

However, the Sward (1933) study of musicians who have performed in the New York Philharmonic and in the Boston, Chicago, and Philadelphia symphony orchestras received tuition under a master-teacher or in a conservatory between ages of 3 and 16. A few examples of this are Arthur Rubenstein (age 3), Jascha Heifetz (age 5), Harold Samuel and Gregor Piatigorsky (age 15), and Ossip Gabrilowitsch, Walter Gieseking, and Mischa Mischakoff (age 16). This suggests that although musical talent may manifest itself early in a child's life, it does not mean that talent will not also manifest itself through the whole range of the school years. Maturational, environmental, and other related variables do play important roles in the emergence of musical talent, as they do in other forms of talent as well.

PSYCHOMOTOR ABILITY

Psychomotor abilities involve the combined function of body and mind: the practical intelligence of Thorndike; the kinesthetic-motor ($k{:}m$) abilities of Vernon's hierarchical model of intelligence that involve such factors as practical, spatial, mechanical, and physical; or the figural dimension of Guilford's structure of intellect. Abilities such as these are found in people who are good all-round repair persons, mechanics, engineers, draftspersons, clerks, truck drivers, airplane pilots, football players and other athletes, and the like.

Theoretically, if one uses Vernon's model of intelligence, then, g enters into all of psychomotor performance. If the structure of intellect is used, then, the figural dimension processed by mental operations as they deal with the informational input and output of the product dimension is involved. However, Guilford gives little information on psychomotor ability as it relates to the structure of intellect, although he makes some reference to the cognition of visual-figural systems and to psychomotor skills as being information related (Guilford, 1967). In an earlier discussion drawing on the work of Fleishman and Hempe (1955), Guilford (1958) identifies seven kinds of psychomotor abilities (strength, impulsion, speed, static precision, dynamic precision, coordination, and flexibility) involving the body as a whole or its various parts (trunk, limbs, hands, and fingers) and to which may be added the parts of speech. Interpreting the information relative to the whole body, Guilford indicates that there is evidence that only two of the abilities are general in nature, namely, general strength and general reaction time, which is obtained from positive intercorrelations of tests applied to various body parts.

Guilford's paper offers valuable suggestions on the measurement of each of the seven abilities as they relate to the whole body or parts of it. For instance on the measurement of trunk strength, he suggests the following:

Abdominal pivot—examinee pushes body around with hands on floor, with back arched.

Push-ups—lying prone, examinee pushes body off floor repeatedly with arms.

Leg raising—examinee raises leg to height of head when in sitting position.

To measure articulation speed, Guilford suggests the following:

Maximal rate of oral reading.
Normal rate of oral reading.
Speed of articulation (repeating a consonant).
Spelling (in a dictation test).

Apart from speculation of a few other psychomotor abilities, like McCloy and Young's (1958) muscular endurance, circulatory and respiratory endurance, agility, and power as well as the possible innate nature of general factors (involving the whole body) as compared to experience-related regional factors (associated with parts of the body—the pianist who develops strong fingers or the cyclist who develops strong legs) little else is said.

Another discussion on the subject (Saphier, 1973) identifies psychomotor abilities as kinesthetic awareness, visual perception, and auditory perception (also referred to as sensorimotor performance, psychomotor competence, motor coordination and planning). These psychomotor abilities involve the ability to coordinate, control, and direct movement as well as position the voluntary muscles, whose measurable components are (Saphier, 1973, p. 58):

1. **Laterality**—*knowing that there are two separate sides to the body (the left and the right) and being able to identify them and move them.*
2. **Directionality**—*being able to relate movement from a fixed position (perhaps one's own body) to away, under, over, into, out of.*
3. **Ocular pursuit**—*ability to follow a moving object with one's eyes (and later using one's eyes as guide for one's body).*
4. **Balance.**
5. **Body image**—*knowing what and where various parts of the body are (ignoring for the moment the affective component of this factor).*

Saphier gives no direct description of measurable components of visual perception although he relates it to both perceptual speed in reading and visual motor skills tested by the *Bender-Gestalt Visual-Motor Coordination Test* as they relate to reading achievement. He suggests that auditory perception may be thought of in terms of the ability to discriminate among different sounds, auditory memory, and auditory figure/ground discrimination (or auditory closure to distraction).

The main thrust of Saphier's (1973) paper appears to lie in the identification of these psychomotor abilities for diagnoses and remediation of learning disabilities. One of Saphier's concluding remarks considers the state of the art in the domain of psychomotor abilities as rather primitive, where distinct factors or elements in the P-M spectrum have not yet validly isolated separate and irreducible factors.

CONCLUSIONS

The first of the USOE categories of giftedness, general intellectual ability, suggests a single mental ability akin to Binet's conception of general intelligence and, to a lesser extent (although as relevant) to Wechsler's conception of global capacity and to Spearman, Burt, and Vernon's g factor. This category of giftedness can be traced to the strong influence of IQ and its extensive and dominant position over the years as the major criterion for the identification of the intellectually gifted. Although, in itself, general intellectual ability does not include the changing conceptions of the construct intelligence or the measures that have developed with it, there are five categories of giftedness that do bear relationship to the construct, although not clearly delineated as mental ability. Creative or productive thinking, for instance, can be identified in the structure of intellect model mainly as divergent thinking abilities. In terms of the overwhelming evidence that pure intelligence is not measureable; that it can be found reflected in the intellectual activity required of a person by test tasks; that many different abilities are available, with one or more retrieved for handling an intellectual assignment on different occasions; and that intelligence does depend on learning; it would be more appropriate to modify the term general mental ability to read intellectual abilities, the measurement of which may include a general intelligence index and indices of intellectual excellence similar to those of the Guilford model.

Academic aptitude, or the capacity to do well in school subjects, can best be approached by determining the level of achievement of learning in various school subject areas through standardized achievement tests. Although teacher-made tests can be used to measure the level of school learning at a particular point of time, their highly local and specific nature will not adequately serve the purpose. Besides, even standardized achievement tests, whose design and intent are not generally leveled at superior students, may not have sufficient ceiling to give it the power of discriminating the really top students from the rest.

Much is known about leadership and the qualities that are involved in it, but, as yet, initiative appears to be lacking to design procedures for the identification of leadership talent. This is largely due to the complexity of this facet of ability, especially because it not only involves the possession of intellectual and creative thinking abilities as well as personality traits peculiar to the individual but also the dynamics of the individual and group as they interact relative to task and situational variables. Hence, any attempt to identify leadership talent must pivot on a multimodal approach.

Another category of giftedness lies in the visual and performing arts area, where at the highest levels of functioning intelligence, creativity, and feeling play important roles apart from the language system that is unique to the art form used for communication. It has generally been found that the more musically talented child tends to show this in the earlier rather than the later school years. However, to speak in the language of music with fluency, originality, and maturity requires some mastery of the fundamentals of the language of music. This is more noticeable in the middle and later school years through early adulthood although exceptions to this may be found in the precocity of music child prodigies.

No less easy to identify are abilities in the psychomotor domain, where one of the chief problems lies in seeing relationships between mind and body functioning. Measures that can give us adequate readings of psychomotor abilities with the power to identify exceptional talent in this area are yet to be designed.

3

APPROACHES
TO
IDENTIFICATION

OVERVIEW

This chapter discusses approaches to identify gifted individuals in the six areas of giftedness recognized by the U.S. Office of Education (USOE), and it points out that because appropriate measures for all kinds of giftedness are not available, less formal approaches at identification may have to be used. Group measures of general mental ability are considered as the most suitable for initial screening, these are, then, followed by individual measures. Three group tests of general mental ability are briefly described and attention is called to ceiling effects and test levels that may be used relative to gifted individuals. Standardized achievement tests to screen for academic aptitude relative to the gifted are also briefly examined. In addition, the measurement of divergent-production and creative thinking abilities, originality and creative imagery, and creative perceptions are given some attention. Both formal and informal approaches at identification for leadership, visual and performing arts, and psychomotor abilities are also described.

CHAPTER OUTLINE

Introduction
Identification of General Intellectual Ability
   California Test of Mental Maturity (Short Form)
   Otis-Lennon Mental Ability Test
   Scholastic Aptitude Test
Identification of Academic Achievement

INTRODUCTION

One of the chief concerns of educators over recent years has been the proper identification of the gifted child. This has found expression in the writing and research of many scholars, in numerous conferences on the gifted, and in the federal government's recognition of six categories of giftedness. Chapters 1 and 2 reflect the thought that people may be gifted in a number of different ways and that to regard a person with a high IQ as gifted to the exclusion of other classes of giftedness is to ignore the greater gifted population. It is now necessary to include among the gifted creative and productive thinkers, high achievers in school subjects, those with exceptional abilities for leadership, those high in psychomotor abilities, and those talented in the visual and performing arts.

Identification of these different kinds of giftedness may take the form of more formal to less formal approaches. Although measures are available for some components of giftedness, they are not applicable to all categories and sub-categories of giftedness. Where measures are available, we may arrange to use them—they should provide the objective evidence needed for the purpose of appropriate identification. Where measures are not available, identification procedures have to be less formal and direct observation according to certain criteria relative to a category of giftedness is used.

Philosophical and procedural differences as they relate to one or another category of giftedness present some difficulty. When one deals with intangibles, like intellectual potential, one can expect that views about it are bound to be different. The issues on the nature of human intelligence are far from settled: more is known about it today than in the time of Alfred Binet and Lewis M. Terman, but still more will be learned about it in years to come. There is the tendency today to accept J. P. Guilford's model of the structure of intellect as the apex of thought on intellectual functioning, and, apart from some scholarly disagreements concerning his conceptual framework, this appears to be so based on the logical evidence. Yet, with the continued refinement of available tools and procedures—to which may be added the invention of others—we may see changes in thought on the subject in the near future that would surprise us now.

To identify the gifted child, the identification process should have the versatility to pick out qualities of mental functioning that can indicate the potential to extend as well as to conserve the boundaries of human existence. Although one of the six USOE categories of giftedness is creative and productive thinking abilities, the potential to be creative or productive may enter into any one of the following three categories of gifted functioning: leadership, visual and performing arts, and psychomotor abilities. If one were to attempt to simplify these six categories of giftedness, one could regard general intellectual ability as the capacity to function at a high level of mental effectiveness relative to all kinds of verbal and nonverbal performance. The term echoes the theoretical models of Charles Spearman, Sir Cyril Burt, and P. E. Vernon relative to the g factor; Alfred Binet's theoretical concept of general intelligence; or David Wechsler's global capacity of intellectual functioning. In terms of its measurement correlates, general intellectual ability implies identification by IQ tests. Creative or productive thinking does not belong to this model but relates to Guilford's structure of intellect model with divergent production, redefinition, and transformation abilities as integral components of it.

Academic aptitude, the potential to achieve at high levels of success in school subjects, relates closely to general intellectual ability and IQ tests modeled to predict its potential. Guilford's analysis and comments of test items on IQ tests indicate that no place is given to divergent production, little, to evaluative thinking abilities. Aptitude to perform well in academic subjects necessitates the use of cognition, memory, convergent production, and evaluative thinking abilities. The extent to which academic aptitude can contain creative components is worthy of some thought.

On the matter of visual performing arts and psychomotor abilities, high levels of performance should necessitate at least above average to bright levels of general ability as well as above average to high levels of creative functioning. If the special skills and knowledge involved in these two areas of exceptional talent relate to performing what is known well with little use for innovation, then, high

APPROACHES TO IDENTIFICATION

levels of creative functioning do not have to be identified as well. However, exceptional talent in these two areas of giftedness should reflect ability to go beyond the known.

High level of leadership potential almost requires the possession of high intellectual abilities and creative thinking abilities together with an understanding of, and sensitivity to, others. Again, we are faced with the problem of differentiating the administrator who maintains the status quo, perceiving and using the rules slavishly, from the manager of human relations who functions in a dynamic and innovative way, depending on changing circumstances and events.

In a recent reply to some editorial musings in the *Gifted Child Quarterly,* Torrance (1978b) suggests (1) that, although identification of the gifted relative to the six USOE categories of giftedness is useful, instruments for identifying all of these types of gifted and talented are not available and (2) that, although attempts to develop them are healthy, it is uncertain that people in gifted and talented education are willing to put out the considerable work involved in developing such instruments. These are important observations and suggest that there are many limitations to appropriate and adequate identification of the varieties of giftedness. If attempts were to be made to provide comprehensive and complete facilities for this identification, it would take years to reach the gifted beneficiaries. For the time being, the best approach to take is to work with what resources we have and apply them in the best way we can.

This problem of identification can be alleviated considerably by flexibility, so that formal procedures are used if they are available, informal procedures if they are not. Some treatment of the variables associated with each of the six USOE categories of giftedness was given in Chapter 2 (pp. 38–62). Here, formal and informal approaches at identification of giftedness, especially as they relate to teacher accessibility and use will receive attention.

IDENTIFICATION OF GENERAL INTELLECTUAL ABILITY

To identify the general intellectual ability of a child, it is common practice to determine the child's IQ. It is well known that individual tests of intelligence, like the *Stanford-Binet* and the Wechsler scales, are the most likely to provide the best evidence of this kind of giftedness. However, because these tests are time consuming, relatively expensive to administer, as well as inaccessible to teachers (training and certification is needed to use these psychological instruments), group tests that claim to do the same job have been widely used, among which are the *California Test of Mental Maturity,* the *Lorge-Thorndike Intelligence Test,* the *Henmon-Nelson Tests of Mental Ability,* the *Otis-Lennon Mental Ability Test,* the *Pinter General Ability Tests,* the *Primary Mental Abilities Test,* the *California Test of Mental Maturity (Short Form),* the *College Qualification Test,* the *Kuhlmann-Anderson Test,* and *Raven's Progressive Matrices.*

Terman (1919) recognizes the problem of using the *Stanford-Binet* in a school setting and advocates the use of the group test as an initial screening device, qualifying this by saying that scores in group tests should not be a substitute for information derived from an individual test. On group measures, Martinson (1974) suggests that they ought to be used for screening rather than for final identification. Put in another way, gifted children may be best identified by group tests in an initial screening with a later, more accurate identification by means of an individual measure of intelligence. Of course, this is a less expensive and time-consuming approach because fewer children will be involved in the final identification process. Support for this approach comes from several studies (e.g., Martinson, 1961; Pegnato, 1955) that found group measures of intelligence misidentify children, usually showing children as scoring lower IQs on group measures of intelligence than on individual measures, like the *Stanford-Binet*, with differences as much as 30 IQ points. This is attributed to a number of factors especially relative to the composition of the test and its ceiling effects. It must be realized that most tests of intellectual potential have not been especially designed with the gifted in mind, but rather for the general population—unlike the *Concept Mastery Test* Terman developed to identify gifted children in his famous longitudinal study. In content, these tests are limited and, hence, do not provide a suitable challenge to those children of exceptional intellectual capacity. Further, because of a limited number of test-items on such measures, overall indices of intellectual capacity are depressed and inaccurate readings follow.

Of the many group measures available (see O. K. Buros's *The Seventh Mental Measurement Yearbook,* 1972), three measures are selected for discussion here as examples of instruments that teachers with some background in psychometrics may use if appropriate interpretation is to be made of scores derived from them. The measures are the *California Test of Mental Maturity (Short Form),* the *Otis-Lennon Intelligence Tests,* and the *Scholastic Aptitude Test.*

CALIFORNIA TEST OF MENTAL MATURITY (SHORT FORM)

The *California Test of Mental Maturity* is a measure of intelligence intended to parallel the *Stanford-Binet* and provides information about the functional capacities that are basic to learning, problem solving, and responding to new situations (Sullivan, Clark, & Tiegs, 1963). The 1963 revision of the Short Form of the measure consists of seven subtests, each of which is expected to measure a different component of general mental ability: Opposites (Test 1), Similarities (Test 2), Analogies (Test 3), Numerical Values (Test 4), Numerical Problems (Test 5), Verbal Comprehension (Test 6), and Delayed Recall (Test 7).

The items on each of these subtests are both verbal and nonverbal, multiple choice in nature, and have been grouped according to four factors: Factor I— Logical Reasoning (Test 1: Opposites; Test 2: Similarities; Test 3: Analogies); Factor II—Numerical Reasoning (Test 4: Numerical Values; Test 5: Numerical

Problems); Factor III—Verbal Concepts (Test 6: Verbal Comprehension); and Factor IV—Memory (Test 7: Delayed Recall). The Short Form of the measure has eight articulated test levels that cover the grade and age range from preschool to adult levels.

Directions are read verbatim to the testee and time limits for each of the subtests are prescribed, with total actual testing time varying from 39 to 43 minutes, depending on the level used. The Short Form of the measure may be hand or machine scored and provides Mental Ages (MAs) and IQs for verbal, nonverbal, and the combined components of the test.

Details concerning the construction, reliability, validity, and relevant data may be found in an examiner's manual and several other supplementary publications (Sullivan, et al. 1963). See also the accompanying notes. Generally, estimates of internal consistency of the measure range from $r = .59$ to $r = .95$, and test-retest reliability coefficients range from $r = .48$ to $.93$, depending on the level of the test, its language or nonlanguage sections, and a composite of these sections. Validity of the measure is determined by correlating verbal, nonverbal, and composite IQs from the *California Test of Mental Maturity* with IQs from the *Stanford-Binet* and several group tests. Content validity, using the *Stanford-Binet* as the criterion, ranges from $r = .60$ to $r = .77$ (verbal), $r = .56$ to $r = .65$ (nonverbal), and $r = .66$ to $r = .78$ (composite), with indices in the .70s to .80s when group measures are used as the criteria. About 200 subjects at each test level were used to obtain these data. Higher reliability and validity coefficients are reported for the higher rather than the lower levels of the test. Normative data reported in the examiner's manual is highly representative of the student population in the United States.

Besides deviation IQ, MA, standard score, and percentile norms are provided for the verbal and nonverbal sections as well as the composite score—to this may be added the provision of standard scores and percentile norms for factor scores.

An assessment of the relative merits of the *California Test of Mental Maturity (Short Form)* shows the need for some improvement of the examiner's manual, especially to make clear what the norms represent in the section describing the scaling procedures. Information on concurrent and predictive validity of the four factors also helps in the interpretation of factor scores. Because there is a lack of such information, it would be best to use the total test IQ for identification and the language and nonlanguage IQs for differentiating the mode of intellectual strength. All in all, however, the value of the test relates to its identification of both a verbal and nonverbal IQ as well as a composite IQ.

OTIS-LENNON MENTAL ABILITY TEST

The *Otis-Lennon Mental Ability Test* (Otis & Lennon, 1967) is a revision of the earlier Otis tests (*Otis Self-Administering Tests of Mental Ability* and *Otis Quick-Scoring Mental Ability Test*). Consistent with the earlier versions, the

NOTES ON RELIABILITY AND VALIDITY

Validity

The extent to which a test measures what it intends to measure is the extent to which it is valid. There are three major kinds of validity relating to a test (*American Psychological Association Standards for Educational and Psychological Tests and Manuals,* 1966), namely, content validity, criterion-related validity, and construct validity:

1. Content validity relates to the degree to which items drawn from a situation, process, or area of knowledge are representative so that we can judge proficiency on the basis of responses to them.
2. Criterion-related validity is information that tells us how closely scores on a test relate to other, more direct measures of the quality, trait, or behavior tested. If the criterion selected is another test administered at the same time so that relationship between the two can be established, we are attempting to determine concurrent validity. If we are interested to know how well information on a test will forecast future performance or achievement, we relate this test information to expected accomplishment as a criterion to establish the predictive validity of the test.
3. Construct validity refers to the theory, or rationale, on which a test is based. The extent to which the test bears out the theoretical referent of the test is the extent to which the test has construct validity.

Reliability

Reliability of a test refers to the degree of its accuracy or consistency and stability. We are interested in two kinds of reliability. One relates to the internal composition of the measure, which we may determine, for instance, by comparing the odd items with the even items of the test. Another relates to the relative consistency of one form of a test with an equivalent form of the test or the same form of a test used again after a lapse of time. This is called test-retest reliability. We are also concerned about the reliability of scoring a test because more than one user will be involved. Information about the consistency of scoring is referred to as interscorer reliability.

For more detailed information on the concepts of validity, reliability, and other statistical terms as well as the computation involved, the reader may want to refer to a book on measurement or statistics, for instance, Anastasi (1976) or Philips (1973).

---

present Otis-Lennon test comprises a variety of items aimed at measuring general mental ability. The measure is designed for use from kindergarten (K) to grade 12. There are two primary levels of the test, each containing 55 items and all of which are pictorial. Its purpose is to measure mental processes of classification, quantitative reasoning, following directions, and comprehension of verbal concepts. There are three elementary levels and one advanced level of the measure. The first of the elementary levels has 80 items. It measures reasoning by analogy in addition to the mental process of the elementary levels. The other levels also contain 80 verbal and nonverbal items (synonyms, opposites, verbal and figural analogies, and number series), each is structured in a spiral omnibus fashion that measures a number of mental processes, with emphasis on abstract reasoning.

Testing time varies from 30 to 50 minutes, depending on the level of the test, and a single score is obtained that presumes to measure the verbal-educational (*v:ed*) component of *g* relative to Vernon's hierarchical structure of intellect. The measure provides deviation IQs, percentile ranks, and stanine norms. There is also a technical manual for the test that reports respectable reliability and validity data with standardization on a population of about 150,000 students (about 6,000 at K level and 12,000 for each of grade 1 to 12) selected from 117 school systems from all 50 states to provide representative and sound norm data. In addition, the manual provides guidelines for appropriate interpretation of the measure that can be used by a teacher who has preparation in basic psychometrics. The technical information in the manual is stated with clarity.

SCHOLASTIC APTITUDE TEST

The Scholastic Aptitude Test of the College Entrance Examination Board is one of several tests developed for use in selecting students for admission to college. It is generally taken in the senior year of high school. Students who need to take such an examination in their junior year are administered the *Preliminary Scholastic Aptitude Test,* a shorter but comparable form. However, the *Scholastic Aptitude Test* is most suitable for the identification of intellectually gifted students and may even be administered to them in their first year of secondary school.

The test consists of a verbal and a mathematical section, and scores are provided for each of the two sections. The items of the measure are constructed in a best-answer multiple-choice format, with 3 hours allowed for taking the test. The mathematics section attempts to measure ability for dealing with concepts rather than mathematical achievement although some knowledge of elementary mathematics is necessary for its application in the solution of problems. The same goes for the verbal section, where a wide reading background that has developed vocabulary and reading skill over a period of years and that allows for facility in reading comprehension, perception of analogical relationships, and the like, is a decided advantage. The measure has been most carefully developed and the extensive research and ongoing refinements of the instrument have produced a technically sound instrument. Achievement on the *Scholastic Aptitude Test* for the verbal and mathematical sections is reported in standard score units. Additional technical information on the measure may be found in Angoff, 1971.

The three group measures briefly described are examples of instruments that can be used to identify gifted children and youth for general mental ability. The first two are generally more appropriate to screen the gifted in elementary and junior high school years because test-ceiling effects can become noticeable with highly precocious youth. In selecting test levels for screening, the ones recommended by the test publisher may be followed. However, if there is reason to believe in advance that the subjects to be tested are highly able, it might be more appropriate to administer the test at a higher level than recommended. This approach was used successfully by Khatena (1975b) in Project Talented and Gifted with the *California Test of Mental Maturity (Short Form)* to identify students nominated as gifted by their schools for possible selection in the project. The *Scholastic Aptitude Test* has a ceiling high enough to discriminate among able students and is best suited for identification of highly gifted students in their junior and high school years. Stanley (1977b) and his associates have been using the mathematics section of the *Scholastic Aptitude Test* for the identification of mathematically precocious youth to participate in the Educational Acceleration Program at The Johns Hopkins University. Students as young as 10 and 13 years have been identified in this way.

IDENTIFICATION OF ACADEMIC ACHIEVEMENT

Another way to identify the intellectually gifted is by way of their academic achievement and, often, such identification has gone hand in hand with measures of IQ. It has been long established that those who do well on IQ tests have been found to do well on achievement tests. Where IQ measures attempt to measure capacity to achieve well in school, academic achievement tests attempt to measure what learning has occurred in terms of knowledge of facts and principles, to which may be added the ability to apply them in complex and frequently lifelike situations.

Attainment in learning may be measured relative to performance on school subjects in a specific class, in which case it is often teacher-made tests that are administered, or it may be measured relative to the learning expected of pupils of certain grade levels in schools located all over the country, in which case a standardized test is administered. In the latter case, a pupil's academic achievement in one place may be compared with the performance of others of the general population taking the test. Relative to gifted pupils, it is the standardized test that best serves the purpose of identifying gifted pupils in academic subjects.

In selecting an instrument, consideration must be given to the effectiveness of the measure as an identifier of academically gifted pupils. The same problem of ceiling effects also exists for measures of academic achievement because most measures have not been specifically constructed with the gifted in mind. There is no single instrument that is available to measure effectively the academic achievement of pupils at all grade levels because specialization in different school subjects increases with advancement of grade level. In the lower grades, a measure evaluating the achievement in many school subjects seems appropriate, whereas, in junior and senior high school, achievement tests in each subject area appear to be more appropriate for identifying the academically gifted pupil. Sometimes a combination of both kinds of measures serve individual needs best.

Another issue relates to the lack of appropriate reliability and validity data, even though other considerations, like item analyses, content selection, and largeness of the norm population, are handled with care. This adds to the difficulty of picking just the right measure for the purpose of identifying gifted students. It must be assumed, because the gifted student is several grades above grade-placement level, that it would be more appropriate to begin administering a form of the measure, say, two or even three grades above the usual one recommended. This is especially the case when tests that measure a number of different subject areas have been constructed relative to recommended grade levels. It is especially useful for the teacher involved in identifying academic achievement to make some educated guesses about the level of attainment of the children about to be screened according to past experiences with their educational achievement.

For an account of available measures, test users should consult O. K. Buros's *The Seventh Mental Measurement Yearbook* (1972). Among the many achievement tests available are the *California Achievement Test,* the *Iowa Tests of Basic Skills,* the *Metropolitan Achievement Test,* the *Stanford Achievement Test,* the *High School Arts and Humanities Test,* and the *American College Test.*

STANFORD ACHIEVEMENT TEST

The *Stanford Achievement Test* was designed to measure the knowledge, skills, and understanding that are considered important and desirable outcomes of the major branches of the elementary curricula (Kelley, Madden, Gardner, Gardner, & Rudman, 1965). The present edition of this measure is organized in five batteries for use at various grade levels from grades 1 to 9 (Elementary Levels: Primary Batteries I and II, Intermediate Batteries I and II, and the Advanced Battery). Each test battery comes in four forms (W, X, Y, and Z) matched for content and difficulty with slight overlapping of content between adjacent batteries.

Nine subtests of the Intermediate Battery Level II measure the content areas of word meaning, paragraph meaning, spelling, language, arithmetic computation, arithmetic concepts, arithmetic applications, social studies, and science; eight subtests of the Advanced Battery measure the same content areas except for word meaning. The tests are fundamentally power, not speed tests, although all subtests are timed for ease of administration because time limits are calculated to give nearly all students sufficient time to attempt all questions that they are capable of answering correctly.

HIGH SCHOOL ARTS AND HUMANITIES TEST

There is also a test for students in grades 9 to 12 that is called the *High School Arts and Humanities Test*. The publisher describes this test as measuring knowledge and understanding in the areas of classical and contemporary literature, music, art, dramatics, and philosophy. The test consists of 65 multiple-choice items and comes in Forms W and X. It takes 40 minutes to complete.

Responses to test items can be hand or machine scored. Information on construction, reliability, validity, and other related data may be found in the administration directions and the technical report of the measure. Some incompleteness of certain aspects of reliability and validity data of this test is indicated, for instance, by Merenda (1965). But he comments that the *Stanford Achievement Test* batteries remain in the forefront of those available to school personnel for use below the senior high school level, and he recommends its continued adoption and use.

AMERICAN COLLEGE TEST

The *American College Test* like the *Scholastic Aptitude Test* is one of the most widely used measures for college entrance purposes and is administered five times a year to high school seniors. The battery consists of four tests: English usage, mathematics usage, social studies reading, and natural sciences reading. In addition, a biographical inventory of nonacademic achievements, aspirations, special campus needs, and perceptions of college is also included in its test booklet.

The English-usage test consists of 75 items that relate to fairly long reading passages and has a time limit of 40 minutes. The mathematics-usage test is made up of 40 items in arithmetic, algebra, and plane geometry; it has a 50-minute time limit. The social studies reading test contains 52 items and has a time limit of 35 minutes. It calls for information based on four reading passages and miscellaneous facts from the social studies area. The natural sciences reading test contains 52 items based on four reading passages of scientific and general science content; it has a 35-minute time limit.

The items in these tests are all multiple choice in form; scores in each of the four subject areas as well as a composite score are provided. These are presented in scaled scores from 1 to 36. Item analyses show that construction and selection of item content need improvement. Data on reliability of the measure need to be better. Validation of the test is extensive, and it consistently achieves good results. Although the measure is not free from criticism, its chief strength lies in its predictive validities vis-à-vis criteria of college success. Various guides, such as a supervisor's manual, a counselor's handbook, and an interpretive booklet for students, are available. There is also a technical report produced in 1965. The

APPROACHES TO IDENTIFICATION

American College Test is a measure that can be used to advantage to identify academically gifted high school students.

The standardized achievement tests described can be used for the screening of the academically gifted student. The *Stanford Achievement Test* batteries are appropriate for students in the elementary school and junior high school grades, whereas the *American College Test* is appropriate for senior high school screening purposes. Where ceiling effects are anticipated for the *Stanford Achievement Test,* it may be necessary to screen at a level or two above that recommended by the test publisher, an approach successfully used in Project Talented and Gifted, Huntington, West Virginia, by Khatena (1975b) using the *Stanford Achievement Test.* However, standardized tests, although helpful in the identification of academically gifted students, do not tell us everything about the individual screened. Turnbull (1978), the president of Educational Testing Service, has pointed out that we are prone to have fallacious assumptions of three kinds about standardized tests: the micrometer fallacy—investing test scores with a precision they never possessed; the whole-person fallacy—the tendency to read into achievement test scores much more than they really tell (the scores are simply the amount a student has learned in a given subject); and the preparation fallacy—the expectation that the test will compensate somehow for the differences in the academic development of children whose learning opportunities have differed dramatically.

IDENTIFICATION OF CREATIVE TALENT

Creativity is a complex construct that is the source of apprehension and misgivings, especially in terms of its measurement correlates. There is considerable lack of agreement over the definition of the term because the word creativity has, through usage, become associated with many aspects of creative behavior and mental functioning, ranging along a cognitive and emotive continuum. Hence, any attempt to construct measures to identify creative talent must begin with a precise definition of the term.

Among the foremost psychologists in the field of creativity measurement are J. P. Guilford and E. P. Torrance. Generally, their measures give major roles to abilities known as *fluency, flexibility, originality,* and *elaboration;* however, their approaches to measurement differ. Whereas Torrance (1966, 1974b) attempts to measure these abilities through the presentation of several complex tasks designed to trigger the expression of several abilities at one and the same time, Guilford (1967) attempts to measure divergent thinking by using a test format that generally requires the subject to respond to many stimuli, each of which measures a specific component of the structure of intellect.

As to the associative conception of creativity, there are the following measures: (1) those constructed by Wallach and Kogan (1965); these attempt to arrange associative conditions for the production of many and unique associates and are scored for both number and uniqueness of response, which are not very different from the concepts of fluency and originality; (2) the one constructed by Mednick and Mednick (1967) that attempts to arrange three associative stimuli for the production of a single remote or original associate; (3) those contributed by Torrance, Khatena, and Cunnington (1973) that attempt to provide conditions of free association for the production of original or statistically infrequent associations; (4) the free-association comparison relative to the production of originality that was developed by Schaefer (1975); and (5) the free-association measure of originality developed by Starkweather (1971) for preschool children.

In addition to these, there are instruments that identify the creative individual (1) by means of biographical or creative perception instruments: the *Alpha Biographical Inventory* (IBRIC, 1968), the *Biographical Inventory: Creativity* (Schaefer, 1970), the *Group Inventory for Finding Creative Talent* (Rimm & Davis, 1976, 1980), and the *Khatena-Torrance Creative Perception Inventory* (Khatena & Torrance, 1976b); (2) by motivational-attitudinal-type instruments: the *How Do You Think?* inventory (Davis, 1975), the *Personal-Social Motivational Inventory* (Torrance, 1958); (3) by a creative self-concept measure: *How Do You Really Feel About Yourself?* (F. E. Williams, 1971b); (4) by measures of conformity, nonconformity, and willingness to try the difficult: respectively the *Form Board Test* and the *Social Conformity Test* on the one hand and the *Target Game* on the other hand (Starkweather, 1971); (5) by a measure of creative transactualization called the *Creative Behavior Disposition Scale* (I. A. Taylor, 1972); (6) by a measure of thinking style that involves right and left cerebral hemispheric functioning, namely, *Your Style of Learning and Thinking* (Torrance, Reynolds, Ball, & Riegel, 1978); and (7) by *Thinking Creatively in Action and Movement* (Torrance & Gibbs, 1979).

A variety of personality inventories have been used rather successfully in studying creative personalities although not primarily measures of creativity. Among the best of them are the *Allport-Vernon-Lindzey Study of Values* (1951), the *California Psychological Inventory* (Gough, 1956), the *Omnibus Personality Inventory* (Hiest & Yonge, 1968), the *Myers-Briggs Type Indicator* (Myers, 1962), the *Runner Studies of Attitude Patterns* (Runner, 1973; Runner & Runner, 1965), and the *Gough Adjective Check List* (Gough, 1960).

Several effective approaches for identifying the characteristics of creative individuals have emerged from the Institute of Personality Assessment and Research of the University of California at Berkeley. These include life history interviews, personality-trait ratings, adjective checklists, the Q-sort method, multiple regression analyses to predict the level of creativeness, and the capacity for metaphor, mosaic construction, and puzzles to test insight (Barron, 1958, 1969; Crutchfield, 1951; MacKinnon, 1978). To this list must be added Walkup's (1971) informal interview processes as a method of identifying creative individuals.

Few instruments are available on the assessment of creative achievement. A variety of techniques have been used by researchers to assess creative achievement, for instance, checklists and indicators of real-life creative achievements. There has been little, if any, sustained effort to develop measures for the purpose of assessing creative achievement relative to school subjects (Torrance, 1977a) or to objectives of courses in teacher education and certification (Torrance & Hall, 1980). Anastasi (1976) has indicated that more than divergent thinking is involved in the assessment of creative achievement because the critical evaluation phase follows the uninhibited divergent-production phase for genuine creative achievement to occur. The brainstorming approaches of A. F. Osborn and S. J. Parnes appear to be related to this perception—where delayed judgment and free wheeling, followed by evaluation against some set criteria of value and usefulness, are steps in the process. The closest approach to the measurement of creative problem solving, although it does not undertake to measure creative achievement in areas of school subject matter, is the *Purdue Elementary Problem-Solving Inventory* (Feldhusen, Houtz, & Ringenbach, 1972); there is also a measure of future problem-solving performance by Torrance and Horng (1978). The measurement of creative achievement, whether in science, engineering, art, music, or other fields of human endeavor, requires a complex pattern of aptitudes and personality traits peculiar, appropriate, and specific to these special areas of knowledge (Anastasi, 1976).

Identification of creative talent has been approached in a number of ways that include the measurement of creative thinking abilities, originality and creative imagery, and creative self-perceptions.

CREATIVE THINKING ABILITIES

Divergent-Production Abilities

The geometric representation of mental functioning conceived by Guilford as the structure of intellect comprises three dimensions of abilities: five kinds of mental operation, four kinds of content, and six kinds of informational form or product (Figure 4, p. 49).

Divergent production is one of the five mental operations of the structure of intellect that processes the four kinds of information (content) organized in six ways (product). It requries testees to produce their own answers to test items and not choose from alternatives given to them. Divergent production calls for the use of several creative thinking abilities that include fluency, flexibility, originality, and elaboration.

The various measures of creative thinking produced by Guilford and his associates relate to the divergent-production abilities of the structure of intellect and, in the main, have been used with adult and adolescent populations, although some of their work has involved younger children (Guilford, 1967, 1973). However, Guilford (1975) discusses the creativity measures for children described in his 1973 work that are aimed at grades 4 to 6 (although also usable with adults) and says that, in the main, he has revised the adult test forms (especially in rewriting the instructions that were appropriate for children) based on a series of factor analyses. His tests of creativity for children are made up of 10 tasks, each measuring 1 of 10 of the 24 divergent-production abilities: Names for Stories, What to Do with It?, Similar Meanings, Writing Sentences, Kinds of People, Making Something Out of It, Different Groups, Making Objects, Hidden Letters, and Adding Decorations. The first five tasks are verbal, the rest are nonverbal. Details about these tasks can be found in the test manual. Measures relevant to 18 of the 24 divergent-production abilities (as they relate to adults) are described in *The Nature of Human Intelligence* (Guilford, 1967), but they do not include divergent-figural relations (DFR) nor divergent symbolic transformations (DST); measures of the four behavioral components of divergent-production abilities are described in Guilford, Hendricks, and Hoepfner (1976).

Guilford's (1967, 1973) measures of divergent thinking are timed tests. This is based on the rationale that timing is critical to accurate testing. Scoring of responses to each task is not difficult and, with some practice, gives consistent results. Guilford recommends that scoring by an inexperienced scorer be checked by another person, and, where disagreement occurs, an expert should act as moderator. Interscorer reliability is provided in the manual for *Creativity Tests for Children* (Guilford, 1973) relative to each of the 10 tasks for different school populations, and, on the average, correlation coefficients derived range from .64 to .92. Similar evidence from investigators using the test—not available in the manual for measures of adult and adolescent performance—has been reported to be in the .90s. Split-half reliability coefficients range from .60 to .80; but Guilford (1967) observed that tests of divergent thinking are not noted for high reliability because of fluctuations in motivation, in set, and the dependence on a number of irrelevant determining circumstances. Guilford has also indicated that factorial validity is the best evidence for construct validity and that the extensive research prior to the publication of the measures that identify each test as a component of the structure of intellect bears this out. However, evidence of criterion-related validity is generally lacking although some is available in a few scattered independent studies. As this relates to the *Creativity Tests for Children* (1973), the manual reports some evidence of predictive validity as derived from correlations of test scores with teacher judgments although Guilford cautions that the validities of teacher judgments can be questioned. Further, concurrent validity evidence that Guilford attempted to generate by using total scores of the verbal and figural batteries of the *Torrance Tests of Creative Thinking* (1974b) that were available did not turn out as expected, with significant correlation indices found for three of the test tasks—one with the figural and two with the

APPROACHES TO IDENTIFICATION

verbal Torrance measures. Tentative norms are given in C scores and centile equivalents that relate to groups of adults and ninth-graders for most of the tests and to fourth-, fifth-, and sixth-graders for all the children's tests.

Torrance and Creative Thinking Abilities

Guilford (1967) measures creative thinking abilities largely by way of divergent production so that a person is required to respond to many stimuli, each of which sets out to measure a specific ability, whereas Torrance measures creative thinking abilities by presenting several complex tasks designed to trigger simultaneous expression of several creative mental operations that give major roles to fluency, flexibility, originality, and elaboration (Torrance, 1974b). A recently developed, streamlined scoring and interpretative manual for his figural tests (Torrance & Ball, 1980) expands the scoring dimensions of these measures, details of which can be found on p. 53.

Torrance defines creativity as a "process of becoming sensitive to problems, deficiencies, gaps in knowledge, missing elements, disharmonies, and so on; identifying the difficult; searching for solutions, making guesses or formulating hypotheses about the deficiencies; testing and retesting these hypotheses and possibly modifying and retesting them; and finally communicating the results" (Torrance, 1974b, p. 8). This construct is central to the *Torrance Tests of Creative Thinking* (1966, 1974b).

The *Torrance Tests of Creative Thinking* consist of alternate forms of verbal and figural measures, both of which present activities in the visual modality that relate to the creative process and involve different kinds of thinking. The measures were carefully constructed to make the activities interesting and challenging for individuals at all educational levels, from kindergarten through graduate school. The *Torrance Tests of Creative Thinking* can be either individually or group administered. The verbal forms consist of seven subtests: Asking Questions, Guessing Causes, Guessing Consequences, Product Improvement, Unusual Uses, Unusual Questions, and Just Suppose Activities; the figural forms consist of three subtests: the Shape Test, Incomplete Figures, and Parallel Lines or Circles. The verbal measures are scored for fluency, flexibility, and originality, whereas the figural measures are scored for these abilities as well as elaboration. Scores for these abilities are obtained for each subtest and then combined to give total creative indices in fluency, flexibility, originality, and (for the figural measures) elaboration. No composite single creative index is recommended.

The *Torrance Tests of Creative Thinking* are timed tests built on the premise that a certain degree of press is required to provoke creative mental functioning within a framework of encouragement aimed at making legitimate divergent thinking. Awarding credit for creative productions has never been an easy matter; any attempt to do so brings with it a certain element of subjectivity. With the *Torrance Tests of Creative Thinking,* a good measure of success has been attained toward objectivity by quantification of responses so that by counting the number of relevant responses; the number of different categories of response; the infrequent, but relevant, responses; and the number of new ideas or details added to the basic idea produced by individuals (their fluency, flexibility, originality, and elaboration scores respectively) can be determined. Interscorer and intrascorer reliability coefficients range from .86 to .99 and average .95 between trained scorers and the author. The most difficult trait to score is originality (figural or verbal), and, hence, lower interscorer reliability coefficients can be expected although Torrance will not accept anything less than coefficients of .90. He indicates that lower interscorer reliabilities for originality result most often from "failure to scan adequately the listed originality weights" and that those for elaboration result most often from "failure to give credit for subtle forms of elaboration such as shading, unusual uses of a line, and symbols that express feeling or emotional tone" (1974a, p. 18). Few studies of test-retest reliability, where the complete batteries of the alternate forms of the Torrance measures were administered to the same individuals, have been done. Reliability coefficients obtained from these few studies range from the .70s to the .90s, with indices for the verbal tests being higher than for the figural tests.

Torrance has paid attention to content, construct, concurrent, and predictive validity relative to creativity as a process. Such an approach relates the kinds of abilities necessary "for successful operation of the process in various situations or for the production of various kinds of products [or] of personality characteristics, group dynamic variables, and other environmental characteristics that facilitate or impede the kind of functioning described by the process definition" (1974b, p. 21). Hence, Torrance uses this general approach for the validation of his measures of creative thinking abilities. For content validity, the tasks' instruction and scoring procedures are based on the best theory and research available: selection of task items was made on the basis of information drawn from the lives, performance, and research of eminent creative people as well as from the theory and research on the functioning of the human mind. Great care was taken to exclude technical or subject-matter content from the tasks. Several studies involve the comparison of personality characteristics of high and low scorers on the Torrance tests, others involve simple correlations between test scores and other measures, and still others—conducted mainly with high school children and adults—assess growth in creative thinking relative to experiments and provide evidence on the construct validity of the measures (Torrance, 1974b), although no clear picture appears to have emerged as yet (Anastasi, 1976). The concurrent validity evidence that is presented and the fine points of these relations that is discussed relate to peer and teacher nominations, sales productivity, and educational achievement. Attention to predictive validity is also given by Torrance, the test author. This relates to evidence obtained from short-range and

80

long-range predictive-validity studies that set out to determine whether scores obtained on the *Torrance Tests of Creative Thinking* at different stages of education predict socially relevant creative behavior in adult life. Positive results were reported. Norms are given in T scores for fluency, flexibility, originality, elaboration and these relate to the alternate forms of the verbal batteries. The norm population consists of those at every educational level, from kindergarten to graduate and professional school. It is multiracial and multiethnic in composition, and it is intended to be representative of the middle range of most school populations. Means and standard deviations for students from kindergarten through the college graduate levels are also provided so that norm tables can be constructed as well for special uses by individual test users.

THINKING CREATIVELY WITH SOUNDS AND WORDS

Another measure of creative talent as it relates to originality and imagination, imagery, and analogy is *Thinking Creatively with Sounds and Words* (Torrance, Khatena, & Cunnington, 1973). It is made up of two measures of verbal originality entitled, *Onomatopoeia and Images* and *Sounds and Images*. Both components come in alternate forms for adults (Forms 2A and 2B) and for children (Forms 1A and 1B). The logic of both measures hinges on the operation of the creative imagination to effect a break away from the perceptual set of audio or verbal stimuli to bring about the production of original responses (Khatena & Torrance, 1973).

Onomatopoeia and Images presents auditory-visual stimuli in the form of onomatopoeic words. These words have semantic and sound elements that are tied to associative bonds of referential and inferential meanings established through usage. When presented to the listener, these words act as sets from which the listener must break away by using what Coleridge refers to as the more conscious and less elemental secondary imagination (1817/1956) to produce new combinations of meaning. The sound component of these words subtly strikes the listener and stirs the emotional base of intellect, providing a tendency toward the irrational response. It is in the intellectual emotive interaction that the mechanisms of the creative process function most effectively to produce the original. *Sounds and Images* presents auditory stimuli in the form of sounds that range from the simple to the complex. Built on the same rationale as *Onomatopoeia and Images,* these sounds also act as sets when presented to the listener who must break away from them to produce original verbal images. Like onomatopoeic words, these sounds require that the intellect interact with emotion to evoke an imaginative response.

Both measures have certain built-in conditions that help listeners use their creative imagination: they allow for progessive warm-up, stress the legitimacy of divergent thinking, provide freedom from threat and evaluation, and invite listeners to regress for the purpose of breaking away from inhibiting meaning and sound sets and, thus, produce original verbal images. The administration of the tests is standardized by presenting all instructions on long-playing records. A narrator prepares the subjects for the test by explaining its nature and purpose and calls for the use of the imagination to create original verbal images. In *Sounds and Images,* four sounds (simple to complex) are presented three times, with a 30-second interval between one sound and the next; in *Onomatopoeia and Images,* onomatopoeic stimuli (5 for the children's version and 10 for the adult version) are presented four times with a 30-second (children's version) or 15-second (adult version) interval between one word stimulus and the next. Verbal images are scored for originality, much like the *Torrance Tests of Creative Thinking,* based on the principle of statistical infrequency and relevance so that credits from 0 to 4 may be awarded to a response. A manual (Torrance et al., 1973) that accompanies the measures provides detailed scoring information with many examples. A norms-technical manual (Khatena & Torrance, 1973) provides interscorer and other reliability information as well as validity and normative data. Interscorer reliability and odd-even reliability coefficients reported are in the .90s; test-retest with varying time intervals reported reliability coefficients that range from the .70s to the .90s. Construct, content, and criterion-related validity coefficients derived from studies of personality, attitudes, biographical information, experimental manipulation, and the like, provide the necessary support. Norms are given in standard scores with a mean of .50 and a standard deviation of .10; the norm population is representative of all age-grade levels measured by the tests. Means and standard deviations for students from grade 3 to the college graduate level are also provided for comparison so that test users may construct local norms where these are needed.

Research on creative imagination imagery with these instruments (Khatena, 1978b) has led to the development of a scoring procedure that identifies the production of creative analogies (Khatena, 1977b). Studies on analogy production show that direct analogies are most frequently produced, that self-involvement in analogy production is less frequent so that fewer personal analogies are produced, that fantasy analogy production is even more infrequent, and that there is very little occurrence of symbolic analogy. Preference for the production of analogies with simple image structure rather than complex image structure is also evident (e.g., "John sings like a crow" rather than "John sings like a featherless crow on a winter's day."). Highest credit is given to the less frequently produced kind of analogy and image with scores ranging from 0 to 3 for the kind of analogy produced, 0 or 1 for the image structure given, and a combined score that ranges from 0 to 4 points. As yet, the scoring guide for creative analogies is in unpublished form.

82

Considerable evidence has accumulated to support the use of the autobiographical instrument as a screening device for giftedness and creativity. Instruments to measure an individuals's perception of himself or herself in the form of checklists, questionnaires, and inventories have been found to be an efficient way of identifying creative talent (e.g. Roe, 1963; C. W. Taylor, 1958). One such inventory that serves this purpose effectively is the *Khatena-Torrance Creative Perception Inventory* (Khatena & Torrance, 1976a, 1976b), which consists of two measures: *What Kind of Person Are You?* and *Something About Myself.* The measure is primarily designed to identify creatively gifted adolescents and adults, but it has been used with children aged 10 and 11 years (e.g., Khatena, 1975b).

The first measure, *What Kind of Person Are You?,* is based on the rationale that the individual has a psychological self whose structures have incorporated creative and noncreative ways of behaving. The purpose of this measure is to present verbal stimuli to trigger those subselves that would yield an index of the individual's disposition or motivation to function in creative ways. It contains 50 items of paired characteristics randomly arranged in a forced-choice format so that an item may call for a choice between a socially desirable and a socially undesirable characteristic or between a creative and a noncreative characteristic. The subject is asked to choose one of each pair and mark this on an answer sheet. The test is easily administered and intepreted and yields a creative index obtained by counting the number of correct responses out of 50. In addition to a creative perception index, *What Kind of Person Are You?* yields five factors (Bledsoe & Khatena, 1974). Acceptance of Authority relates to being obedient, courteous, conforming, and to accepting the judgments of authorities. Self-confidence relates to being socially well adjusted, self-confident, energetic, curious, thorough, and having good memory. Inquisitiveness relates to always asking questions, being self-assertive, feeling strong emotions, and being talkative and obedient. Awareness of Others relates to being courteous, socially well adjusted, popular or well liked, considerate of others, and preferring to work in a group. Disciplined Imagination relates to being energetic, persistent, thorough, industrious, imaginative, adventurous, never bored, attempting difficult tasks, and preferring complex tasks.

The second measure, *Something About Myself,* is based on the rationale that creativity is relfected in the personality characteristics of individuals, in the kind of thinking strategies they employ, and in the products that emerge as a result of their creative strivings. The purpose of the measure is to obtain an index of a person's creativity by the number of positive choices made relative to the items in the three categories of creative functioning. *Something About Myself* consists of

50 statements. The subject is asked to indicate on the answer sheet whether or not the statement is applicable. The test is easily administered and interpreted and yields a creative index obtained by counting the number of positive responses out of 50.

Something About Myself, in addition to a creative perception index, yields six factors (Bledsoe & Khatena, 1973). Environmental Sensitivity involves openness to ideas of others; relating ideas to what can be seen, touched, or heard; interest in the beautiful and humorous aspects of experiences; and sensitivity to meaningful relations. Initiative relates to directing, producing, or playing leads in dramatic and musical productions; producing new formulas or new products; and bringing about changes in procedures or organization. Self-strength relates to self-confidence in matching talents against others, resourcefulness, versatility, willingness to take risks, the desire to excel, and organizational ability. Intellectuality relates to intellectual curiosity, enjoyment of challenging tasks, imagination, preference for adventure over routine, a liking for the reconstruction of things and ideas to form something different, and a dislike for doing things in a prescribed routine. Individuality relates to preference for working by oneself rather than in a group, seeing oneself as a self-starter and as somewhat of an eccentric, being critical of others' work, thinking for oneself, and working for long periods without getting tired. Artistry relates to production of objects, models, paintings, and carvings; musical compositions; receiving awards, prizes, or having exhibits; and production of stories, plays, poems, and other literary pieces.

Both components of the *Khatena-Torrance Creative Perception Inventory* are not timed tests. Designed for quick and easy administration, the measures can be administered either individually or in group settings, and each generally requires from 5 to 15 minutes to complete. Scoring is simple and rapid: a credit of 1 point is awarded for each positive response on *Something About Myself,* whereas 1 point is awarded to responses on *What Kind of Person Are You?* according to a scoring key. In either case, scores range from 0 to 50. Scoring keys are provided for factor orientations. The test manual also provides information on odd-even reliability coefficients, which range in the .90s, and the test-retest reliability indices are in the .90s as well. Interscorer reliability coefficients from .97 to .99 are reported. Careful attention is given to content validity and item-selection procedures; and construct validity is derived from factor analyses and studies of attitudinal relationships. Criterion-related validity coefficients are derived from studies of personality variables, biographical information, creative ratings, and experimental manipulation. The norm population is representative of college adults and adolescents from grades 7 to 12. Norms are given for the total scale and for factor scores in standard score units with a mean of 5 and a standard deviation of 2. In addition, profile charts are provided for each test component.

IDENTIFICATION OF LEADERSHIP ABILITY

The ability to lead comprises not only intellectual ability but also other personality variables that, in themselves, do not sketch a reasonably good picture of leadership but that derive relevance from interactive effects with groups of followers, varying situations, and related variables. A considerable body of theory and research has accumulated over the years and has been reviewed and summarized by a number of scholars (e.g., Fleishman, 1973; Stogdhill, 1974). In general, the factors found to be most highly associated with leadership can be classified as follows (Stogdill, 1974:

1. Capacity
2. Achievement
3. Responsibility
4. Participation
5. Status
6. Situation

This list should point to the complexity of the task of identifying leadership. For one thing, there is no single psychological measure that can perform this task. The published measures that are available, like *The Leadership Ability Evaluation* (Cassel & Stancik, 1961) and *Leadership Evaluation and Development Scale* (Mowry, 1964/1965), are either inappropriate or inadequate as relating to rationale, item analysis, reliability, validity, and scaling. Cecil A. Gibb's observation that, ''Psychological research has never been able to identify or assess leadership ability'' (Gibb, 1972, p. 1148) is to the point.

The recognition by the USOE that leadership ability is another area of talent that needs identification in the selection process for programs of the gifted presents a real problem. There is no single adequate means for identifying such talent, unlike intellectual academic achievement or creative thinking abilities. Attempts to do this at best must be considered exploratory. However, there is a real need for development of adequate procedures to identify leadership ability and, in the absence of appropriately constructed instruments, some interpolation from the general findings of leadership research may offer fruitful direction.

The six categories of characteristics associated with leadership presented by Stogdill (1974) appear to offer comprehensive clues for the development of identification procedures that may be used in schools. Let us take each category in turn and examine the possibilities of using not only the psychometric approach but also the other resources we have. Or, let us create new approaches where there is the need to shape procedures for the identification of leadership ability in the classroom.

CAPACITY

Capacity relates to intelligence, alertness, verbal facility, originality, and judgment. A measure of general or multifactor intelligence may be used to derive information regarding all these characteristics except originality. For this, we shall have to use a measure of originality or creative thinking abilities that will give information on abilities, such as fluency, flexibility, elaboration and originality. Group and individual tests of intelligence and creative or divergent thinking abilities (see pp. 67–68) may be used. It should not be difficult to find and use this information, which is generally already avaliable in student records. Where these are not available, arrangements need to be made to select and administer measures appropriate to the information needed. With respect to the level of intelligence, the search should be among those who might be classified as bright normal and above, depending on the group that is to be led. Hollingworth (1942) observes that, among children with a mean IQ of 100 the IQ of the leader is likely to fall between 115 and 130 IQ, which means that the leader is likely to be more intelligent but *not too much more* intelligent than the average of the group led. This is a situation of relevance for the identification of the ability level of a leader in the regular classroom.

ACHIEVEMENT

Achievement relates to scholarship, knowledge, and athletic accomplishments. In this dimension, some consideration needs to be given to the kind of leadership intended for identification. As leadership relates to task performance of an academic nature, scholarship and knowledge go together; good achievement tests and student performance in class assignments should provide the necessary information. Like intelligence, achievement level may not need to be extremely high, but for the leader, certainly higher than the achievement level of the followers. As leadership relates to groups organized for games and athletics, information about physical prowess, knowledge, skills, and experience are the key factors of identification; the best information of this kind can be obtained from direct observation of the individual possessing these qualities and the way he or she uses them in the relevant group activity. Once again, the psychomotor approach is not the answer in this area of leadership.

RESPONSIBILITY

Responsibility relates to dependability, initiative, persistence, agressiveness, self-confidence, and the desire to excel. For this dimension of leadership, both direct observation (either by teacher or peer) and a personality inventory may be used to advantage. Of particular relevance is the *Khatena-Torrance Creative*

Perception Inventory, whose components *What Kind of Person Are You?* and *Something About Myself,* not only provide information on creative perceptions of individuals but also the qualities of initiative, persistence, self-confidence, the desire to excel, as well as many other traits not mentioned that also contribute to leadership. Direct observation of qualities exhibited by students in their everyday classroom and playground activities will provide valuable information. Where spontaneous situations do not provide sufficient data, then, situations that do evoke the manifestation of those qualities not easily observed may be arranged. Projects that invite group work, involve monitorial duties, or require special study or construction tasks can be arranged for this purpose with little difficulty. Relative to direct observation, some written record of observed data is most helpful.

PARTICIPATION

Participation refers to activity, sociability, cooperation, adaptability, and humor. Just as in the dimension of responsibility, direct observation and an inventory may be used in the ways suggested. Qualities in more than one of these dimensions may be found in a single inventory. For example, humor, cooperation, adaptability, sociability, as well as activity (in the sense of energetic) are characteristics that are found in *What Kind of Person Are You?*—where self-perceptions may range from the creative to the socially desirable. Adaptability can be associated with flexibility, which is a quality found in *Something About Myself* and which is also identified as one of the creative thinking abilities on the Torrance or Guilford measures.

STATUS

Status relates to socioeconomic position and popularity. On socioeconomic status, leaders as compared to nonleaders tend to come from a background superior (although not in the extreme) to that of the average of their followers. This information can easily be found in school records or by knowing the student well. Popularity can best be identified by direct observation.

SITUATION

Situation relates to mental level, status, skills, needs and interests of followers, objectives to be achieved, and so on. One of the best ways to identify these characteristics is to create a situation in the class where a task needs to be performed. Thus, achievement objectives of the group can be listed and the skills and interests of the various members relative to various aspects of the task can be identified. Then, discussion among members of the group can follow. All this may preface a sociometric analysis of relations in this group as it relates to the task at hand. Analysis of the data should give clues to both the leader (or leaders of the group) as this relates to the task (or subtasks) at hand as well as to the other variables mentioned. The tester may stop here or follow it up with the organization and activitation of the group or subgroups to work on the specific task and, thus, make direct observations. This will, in all probability, provide the information on personality-situation interaction and other variables as they relate to leadership.

Relative to mental level as it involves social aspects of intelligence, the best source of information is Guilford's measures of the behavioral component of the structure of intellect, where behavioral content relates essentially to nonverbal information involving attitudes, needs, desires, moods, intentions, thoughts, and the like, that occur in human interactions. These functions, especially in relation to the divergent thinking operations and the product dimensions of the structure of intellect, provide reasonably good clues to one dimension of leadership, for instance, as behavioral content relates to divergent thinking situations there may be found:

Behavioral units. For example, Expressing Mixed Emotions, which requires a listing of as many different things that individuals might say if they were both disappointed and jealous; or Alternate Picture Meanings, which presents a line drawing of a face that has a somewhat ambiguous expression and individuals are asked to list alternate interpretations of the psychological meanings of the expression.

Behavioral classes. For example, Multiple Behavior Grouping, which presents either a list of statements that need to be classified in different ways or line drawings of faces, hands, or other body parts from which one selects small groups of drawings, each possessing common attributes of the psychological disposition indicated.

Behavioral relations. For example, Creating Social Relations, which contains pictures of people—usually two—with some possible connection between the members in each picture.

Behavioral systems. For example, Creating Social Situations which calls for several story plots, when given three characters: (a) fearful woman, (b) angry man, and (c) unhappy child. A sample response may be: (c) brings home a poor report card; (b), the father, is angry with (c); and (a), the mother, is afraid that (b) will hurt (c).

Behavioral transformation. For example, Multiple Expression Changes, which presents a number of faces, all of the same sex, each with a different expression and with three related events given, like: "A man trips a lady who is walking; the man apologizes to the lady; the lady becomes angry." The task lies in the selection, in turn, of sets of three faces for the man to go with each step in the series of events; further, each set selected after the first requires a revision or transformation of the man's sequence and attitudes.

Behavioral implications. For example, Suggested Feelings and Actions, which is a test that presents a situation, like: "Late at night when A and her family are in their mountain cabin, she hears over the radio that a forest fire is raging a few miles away." The task requires the thinking of different emotions and corresponding actions arising from the situation.

If some assessment procedure for leadership ability can arise out of the preceding discussion, perhaps it might be organized as shown on the accompanying form.

LEADERSHIP ASSESSMENT RECORD

1. Socioeconomic position: _____Superior _____Above average _____Average

2. Intelligence: Verbal IQ _____ Nonverbal IQ _____

              Total IQ _____ Source _____

3. Creative thinking abilities: Verbal originality _____ Source _____

                        Figural originality _____ Source _____

4. Achievement: _____ Source _____

           _____   _____

           _____   _____

           _____   _____

5. *Inventory of personality traits:*

    _____ Intelligence (bright normal or above average)

    _____ Alertness and keen awareness of environment

    _____ Verbal facility (fluency of speech)

    _____ Originality (novel, clever, remote ideas)

    _____ Judgment

    _____ Scholarship (better than average grades)

    _____ Dependability (knows how to get things done)

    _____ Knowledge (specialized knowledge)

    _____ Initiative

_____ Persistence

_____ Aggressiveness

_____ Self-confidence

_____ Desire to excel

_____ Activity (energetic)

_____ Sociability (participates in more group activities)

_____ Cooperation

_____ Adaptability

_____ Humor

_____ Popularity (and prestige)

Note: Information for this inventory may be generated by the teacher, by the pupil reporting about himself or herself or about someone else the pupil knows, and by the parent.

6. *Sociometric data:*

7. *Case history data:*

8. *Information from other sources:*

Source: J. Khatena, *Music, Art, Leadership and Psychomotor Abilities Assessment Records,* p. 2. Copyright © 1981 by J. Khatena and published by Allan Associates. Reprinted by permission.

IDENTIFICATION OF VISUAL AND PERFORMING ARTS ABILITY

Identification of talent in the visual and performing arts areas is not an easy matter. Not only do we have to face the many categories of talent present but also the lack of good instruments to measure them. This is further complicated by (1) the differential manifestation or presence of observable talent at different age and grade levels and (2) specialized knowledge and skills relative to each talent may have been acquired and may be mistaken for real talent. Theory and research suggest that generally talented individuals in the visual and performing arts are bright, that creativity is a significant energizing factor in talent, and that specific to the art form there exist highly specialized abilities that require the language and skills peculiar to that art form for their expression. Hence, any approach at identification of talent in the areas of visual and performing arts must recognize and handle these variables.

The procedures for the identification of two areas of talent, music and art, will be discussed here. Several components are involved in each of these areas of talent; two of these, intelligence and creativity, can be considered to be common to all areas of talent. In any case, a general screening for these abilities may one day provide information for all students in school; reference to student records will give the needed data. However, talent does not involve mental abilities alone and, depending on the area of talent, its identification will hinge on what specialized abilities, personality traits, and productivity are sought. Screening books on measurement informs us that there are a few measures unique to the area of music abilities although, with the exception of probably two or three, the measures are generally poor indicators of musical talent; that there are even fewer measures for art-talent potential and that none are really appropriate for spotting out talented students in the elementary and secondary schools and that no measures of talent for drama exist.

Consequently, if psychometrically appropriate and sound instruments are not available, identification of the gifted in these areas of the visual and performing arts will have to depend on observational approaches. In practice, identification of musical and art talent is done by audition, an observational form that requires an individual to demonstrate by performing before, or presenting a portfolio of products to, an expert who subjectively determines the extent of talent possessed, which, then, acts as the predictor of future talent growth. Such experts should be alerted to seek out not only superior ability to reproduce but also the ability to be innovative, with the tendency to break away from the more conventional nature of the art form.

MUSIC ABILITIES

To identify the gifted child in music, we must recognize that we are looking for someone in possession of musical aptitude rather than for the acquisition of musical knowledge and skill, although some of this will enter into the screening operations. Definitions of music talent are many: the ability to retain, recognize, and reproduce a short musical phrase; to have absolute pitch; the ability to recognize intervals; to have a feeling for tonality; to love music; or to have general intelligence. But clearly no simple definition of musical talent exists (Lehman, 1968). Then, there is the theoretical orientation that regards musicality as made up of a hierarchy of talents, many of which are independent of one another (Seashore, 1938), or that regards music talent as comprising a number of elements subsumed under a general factor of musicality (Mursell, 1932). Lehman (1968) differentiates between those tests that are designed to measure innate capacity for musical learning, even though no such learning may have taken place (aptitude tests), and tests that are designed to measure how much has been learned or accomplished at a particular time (achievement tests). He also points out that musical ability includes both aptitude and achievement, whereas neither of the two include one or the other. Hence, musical aptitude tests must be so constructed that the musical training an individual may or may not have had will not affect the result in any way.

Among the many tests of music talent available is the *Seashore Measures of Musical Talents* (Seashore, 1919; Seashore, Lewis, & Saetviet 1960), which is the oldest. Others are *Kwalwasser-Dykema Music Tests* (Kwalwasser & Dykema, 1930), *Standardized Tests of Musical Intelligence* (Wing, 1939, 1961), *Drake Musical Aptitude Tests* (Drake, 1954), *Musical Aptitude Profile* (E. Gordon, 1965), and *Measures of Musical Ability* (Bentley, 1966).

Common to most measured elements in music are tonal rhythm, pitch, time, and intensity. Other elements measured by one or another music test relate to quality, consonance, melodic taste, timbre, and harmony. Nearly all these published measures are deficient and few report technically sound information. The best among them are probably the Wing, E. Gordon, and Bentley measures. The author has a preference for Gordon's *Musical Aptitude Profile* because it gives relatively more complete information on musical aptitude.

The *Musical Aptitude Profile* (E. Gordon, 1965) is an objective measure of basic musical aptitude designed for use with students from grades 4 to 12 and does not concern itself with historical or technical facts about music. The basic factors measured by the test are Tonal Imagery (Part I: Melody; Part II: Harmony), Rhythm Imagery (Part I: Tempo; Part II: Meter), and Musical Sensitivity (Part I: Pharasing; Part II: Balance; Part III: Style). The complete battery of seven tests includes practice songs and directions on recorded tape. The tests are made up of original short selections composed for violin and cello by E. Gordon and performed by professional artists. Subjects are asked to compare a selection with a musical answer to decide if the two are alike or different, exactly the same or different, or which is a more musical performance. Total testing time is 1 hour and 50 minutes. Each of the three main divisions of the battery may be administered during the time limits of a regular class period.

To measure originality and other creative thinking abilities, the measures developed by J. P. Guilford, E. P. Torrance, and J. Khatena described earlier in the chapter may be used, especially *Creativity Tests for Children* (Guilford, 1973) and *Thinking Creatively with Sounds and Words* (Torrance, Khatena, & Cunnington, 1973). Creative personality characteristics can be identified by using the *Khatena-Torrance Creative Perception Inventory* (Khatena & Torrance, 1976a, 1976b). It is of value to refer to the less widely known, but nonetheless important, attempt of Vaughan (1971) to develop a measure of creative music talent because her approach may give clues to the design of badly needed identification measures in music.

Other behaviors that pertain to musical performance and production may be best identified by observation. The accompanying checklist offers one possible approach.

MUSICAL BEHAVIOR ASSESSMENT RECORD

_____Able to hum or sing in tune

_____Know how to make a tune loud or soft for effects

_____Shows awareness of difference between production of good from bad sounding notes

_____Has a sense of rhythm

_____Can keep time to a tune

_____Can beat different time with rhythm changes in a tune

_____Knows when to accent different beats for effect

_____Able to vary loudness and softness of beat for effect

_____Can hum or sing in harmony with another person without the aid of musical notes

_____Remembers tunes easily

_____Remembers rhythm easily

_____Quick to learn a new tune

_____Quick to learn a new rhythm

_____Can sing another tune that resembles a known but not an identical tune

_____Can dance to a tune

_____Can dance to tunes with different rhythms

_____Sings, dances, or plays an instrument everyday

_____Given an incomplete melody can add tune to complete it

_____Makes own tunes

_____Plays an instrument by ear

_____Plays more than one instrument by ear

_____Can read simple music

_____Can write a simple tune

_____Has a good voice

_____Enjoys listening to music

_____Likes producing music with others

Source: J. Khatena, _Music, Art, Leadership and Psychomotor Abilities Assessment Records_, p. 3. Copyright © 1981 by J. Khatena and published by Allan Associates. Reprinted by permission.

ART ABILITIES

Identification of able students in art is also difficult. There is no completely satisfactory tests of aptitude in art, especially during the school years of individuals. Guilford (1968) has described some figural abilities that are important to artistic talent—ideational and expressional fluency, spontaneous and adaptive flexibility, and elaboration—in the divergent-production area of the structure of intellect and that are measurable as follows (Guilford, 1967):

Figural units. For example, Sketches, which present a simple basic figure to which is to be added just enough detail to make a recognizable object; Monograms, which require arrangement of such letters as A, V, and C to make many different monograms as if they were initials of a name.

Figural classes. For example, Alternate Letter Groups, which present a set of capital letters, like AHVTC, for the formation of subgroups, each of which makes a class that has all straight lines according to the figural properties of AHVT.

Figural systems. Emphasis is on organization of visual elements into wholes, for example, Making Objects Test, which requires the use of two or more of several given simple geometric forms to construct a named object.

Figural transformations. These are concerned with adaptive flexibility and are in line with the emphasis on shift, for example, Planning Air Maneuvers, which involves the planning of sky writing two capital letters in succession as efficiently as possible with an airplane pilot given instructions as to start, finish, and turns of the airplane.

Figural implications. For example, Decorations, which outline drawings of common objects, like pieces of furniture and articles of clothing, are each repeated two times with instructions for filling them in with decorative additions.

These figural abilities have been included and modified in Guilford's *Creativity Tests for Children* (1973). Guilford's measure includes a verbal and nonverbal section with five items in each. By administering the whole test to students from grades 4 and up, not only will information about an individual's aptitude for talent in art be obtained (figural tasks: 6 to 10, namely, Making Something Out of It, Different Groups, Making Objects, Hidden Letters, and Adding Decorations) but also information about his or her creative thinking abilities (using the whole test of 10 tasks).

Another very useful measure for this purpose is the figural forms of the *Torrance Tests of Creative Thinking* (Torrance, 1966, 1974b), from which information about the figural fluency, flexibility, originality, and elaboration of a student can be derived—all abilities that are important to art talent. This measure comprises three subtests that require students to use their imagination to respond

94

to various shapes and lines that are given to produce pictures of which no one else would have thought. Scoring the test by the published scoring guide gives fluency, flexibility, originality, and elaboration scores in the figural dimension that should tell us about an individual's potential to be creative. However, if the drawings are looked over with care, some indications of art talent may also be observed, although subjects are not asked to produce any pictures that can be considered as meeting any artistic standards as such. So at one and the same time, important elements of both creativity and art talent may be identified.

Specific art ability measures are not many. Among them that require production of drawings for the purpose of assessing art potential are the *Horn Art Aptitude Inventory* and the *Knauber Art Ability Test*. The *Advanced Placement Program in Studio Art* offers identification of art potential for college placement. The *Meier Art Judgment Test* and the *Meier Aesthetic Perception Test*—of little concern to us here—measure the ability to judge art but require no drawing ability.

In brief, the *Horn Art Aptitude Inventory,* suitable for high school seniors, does not concern itself with advanced skills in art, but rather with predicting future success in artistic activities. It requires subjects to draw simple pictures after which they are to compose more elaborate pictures according to a few given lines as clues. The scoring is subjective but uses various works of quality as criteria. The *Knauber Art Ability Test,* a much older test constructed in 1930, requires subjects' actual drawings and rearrangement of pictorial compositions. Responses are scored for quality according to a key that is provided.

Early attempts to assess artistic aptitudes were based on measurement of art judgments or preferences between "good" and "bad" compositions of well-known works of art (e.g., the *Meier Art Judgment Test).* Unlike these attempts, the *Advanced Placement Program in Studio Art* (Dorn, 1976) is designed to appraise the quality of studio art performance by recognizing all the highly subjective elements used in the creation of an art work. A portfolio—comprised of four original art works of a specific size and several 2-×-2 slides that document other works—is submitted with the help of the subject's school to Educational Testing Service. The examination consists of three sections. In Section A, the student's four original compositions of a given dimension are evaluated for quality; in Section B, the student's group of slides or film that show work over an extended period in his or her area of concentration is evaluated; in Section C, two slides submitted by the student, each showing proficiency in four broad areas—spatial illusion, drawing, color, and organization of three-dimensional materials—are also evaluated. The judging is done by a number of experts in the field who rate the components of the portfolio, giving place to uncommon responses in art. All this is done with great care; reliability of evaluations is ensured by the training of the judges before and during their reading of all three sections of the evaluation. This evaluation of the gifted in studio art performance, although not yet perfect, is considered a step in the right direction for measuring the ability of high school students to benefit from a college education in art.

To identify a gifted student in art, some consideration needs to be given to intelligence (because students who are highly talented in art are generally quite bright); to creative thinking abilities, especially as manifested in the visual figural dimension; and to talent specific to art, which is identified not only through psychometric tests but also through actual productions. One of the surest ways to spot gifted children in art is in their productivity frequency and level. Talented children are often seen communicating their ideas and feelings nonverbally in their drawings, paintings, and related art forms. Visual narrative, quality that is considered a catalyst, or a basic and primary element that activates other aspects of artistic giftedness, is observable in the works of young children (Wilson & Wilson, 1976). The Wilsons cite Alan Garner, Julian Green, and C. S. Lewis as examples of writers who used "visual narrative as children until they were able to use words with sufficient facility to convey the subtlety and complexity of the worlds they were busily creating" (p. 432–433). It is also visual narrative that leads gifted children to produce a vast number of drawings: "For gifted young people [visual] narrative is the train engine which pulls with it the freight cars of tension and relief, emotions and feelings, repressions and sublimations, symbolizations and expanding aspects of reality" (p. 435).

The teacher who is involved in the difficult job of identifying the gifted child in art needs to become familiar with both the personality characteristics and some important observable behaviors of such creative children. To derive information concerning traits of the creative personality, the teacher could use the *Khatena-Torrance Creative Perception Inventory*. As for observable behaviors relevant to art talent those shown in the accompanying form are suggested.

ART TALENT BEHAVIOR RECORD

_____Scribbles earlier than most other children in the class
_____Produces many ideas in drawings or paintings
_____Initiates drawings
_____If given a situation, takes it to develop new ones
_____Unusual and interesting visual imagery in drawings
_____Drawings show imagery expanding in chain reaction
_____Sensitive use of art materials
_____Sensitive handling of techniques
_____Highly developed sense of movement in drawings
_____Highly developed sense of rhythm in drawings
_____Great feel for color
_____Sensitive to order and organization in work

_____Varies organization of elements to suit different situations
_____Interest content
_____Tells a story
_____Expresses feelings
_____Shows confidence when undertaking a drawing
_____Intense personal identification with experience depicted
_____Produces many drawings
_____Enjoys expressing self in art
_____Likes adding details to basic idea
_____Flexible in use of art materials
_____Innovative in selection and use of art materials
_____Tends to want to draw unusual situations
_____Has unusual ideas for pictures

Source: J. Khatena, _Music, Art, Leadership and Psychomotor Abilities Assessment Records,_ p. 5.
Copyright © 1981 by J. Khatena and published by Allan Associates. Reprinted by permission.

IDENTIFICATION OF PSYCHOMOTOR ABILITY

There are a number of measures available on identification of psychomotor abilities as they relate to the diagnosis of (1) learning disabilities and their remediation through careful curriculum planning and (2) dysfunctions of one kind or another (Bialer, Doll, & Winsberg, 1974; DeGuire, 1971; Frostig, 1967). Tests favored to provide base line information regarding language and perceptual measurements are the _Illinois Test of Psycholinguistic Abilities,_ the _Weschsler Intelligence Scale for Children (WISC),_ or the _Stanford-Binet._

If weakness in the visual or visual motor domain are suspected, measures like the _Development Test of Visual Perception_ or the _Bender-Gestalt Visual-Motor Coordination Test_ have been used. Other tests are available for the dimensions of auditory-perceptual weaknesses and motoric or coordination disorders. There are no instruments aimed at measuring strengths that indicate talent potential in the psychomotor abilities area. Hence, there is a need for caution in selecting procedures for the identification of exceptional abilities in the psychomotor domain.

Psychomotor abilities are involved in many human activities and can be observed when a person learns to read, write, or speak; when a person performs one skill or another as this is related to games or athletics; when a person is engaged in manipulating various tools, machines, and equipment; or, again, when a person is engaged in musical, art, oratorical, or dramatic performance. The degree to which psychomotor related variables are present in each of these activities varies. Obviously, other conditions must prevail, like the presence of intellectual ability, and specific talent as well as affect and motivation.

In attempting to identify levels of psychomotor abilities, it would seem appropriate to screen for level of intellectual ability, ability specific to the talent area, creative thinking abilities if the psychomotor ability calls for innovation (e.g., carpenters who design new kinds of furniture, musicians who improvise on their instruments), level of development of the total body or its parts relative to the ability sought (e.g., strength, impulsion, speed, static precision, dynamic precision, coordination, or flexibility). If the Wechsler scales are used, for instance, the subtests in the performance area (Digit Span, Picture Completion, Picture Arrangement, Block Design, Object Assembly, Digit Symbol, Coding, and Mazes) should give some valuable information about the subject's performance IQ as well as information on visual motor coordination (Block Design, Object Assembly, Digit Symbol on the *Wechsler Adult Intelligence Scale (WAIS);* Coding on the WISC; and Mazes), visual organization (Block Design and Object Assembly), and perceptual organization (Picture Completion and Block Design.

Two measures that may be found useful at the secondary school level are the *Differential Aptitude Tests* (grades 8 to 12) and the *Multiple Aptitude Tests* (grades 7 to 13). The purpose of the *Differential Aptitude Tests* is to provide information on the multiple abilities of boys and girls for educational and vocational guidance. Of the eight subtests, Clerical Speed and Accuracy (measures speed to respond in simple perceptual tasks), Mechanical Reasoning (measures ability to reason in the mechanical field as well as understand mechanical and physical principles in familiar situations), and Space Relations (measures the ability to deal with concrete materials through visualization) are most pertinent to psychomotor abilities. The other five subtests are Verbal Reasoning, Numerical Ability, Abstract Reasoning, and Language Usage (Spelling) and Language Usage (Grammar). The authors of this measure are Bennett, Seashore and Wesman (1963).

The *Multiple Aptitude Tests* (Segal & Raskin, 1959) is aimed at providing comprehensive differential aptitude data to help individuals taking the test both to understand their potentialities and to make wise academic and vocational decisions. Of the nine subtests (four factors), four subtests are relevant to psychomotor ability:

Perceptual Speed (Factor II) comprises two tests: Language Usuage (a measure of a subject's ability to spot grammatical, spelling, punctuation, and capitalization errors) and *Routine Clerical Facility* (a measure of a subject's rate and accuracy for checking sameness and differences in names and numbers).

Spatial Visualization (Factor V) comprises three tests: Spatial Relations (two dimensions) Spatial Relations (three dimensions), and Applied Science and Mechanics (measures understanding and application of principles that explain the actions of fluids and machines).

Common to both the *Differential Aptitude Tests* and *Multiple Aptitude Tests* are the identification of psychomotor abilities of clerical speed, accuracy, and facility, mechanical reasoning, and spatial relations.

Guilford (1958) tells us that three tests are generally used in the analysis of psychomotor abilities: (1) tests of physical fitness, (2) apparatus tests, and (3) printed tests:

Tests of Physical Fitness require little, if any, equipment; are often administered in a physical-educational and athletic setting; and involve the whole body or large portions of it.

Apparatus tests involve movement, from finger reactions to gross bodily movement. Often (although not as often as desirable), when administered with the first types of test, they show overlap, especially if the same muscle groups and similar movements are involved.

Printed tests are paper-and-pencil tests given in group settings that involve movement that is fairly well restricted to fingers and hands.

For a complete description of how to measure the activity of the total body and each of the body parts (trunk, limbs, hands, and fingers) as they relate to the factors of strength, impulsion, speed, static precision, dynamic precision, coordination, and flexibility, the reader is referred to Guilford's "A System of the Psychomotor Abilities" (1958).

A good test of physical fitness with national norms is the *Youth Fitness Test* published by the American Alliance for Health, Physical Education, and Recreation (Hunsicker & Reiff, 1976). Other approaches to the identification of outstanding psychomotor abilities arising out of observation of expressed talent include nominations by parents, teachers, and peers.

The degree to which psychomotor is psychological will determine the extent to which, and what kind of, psychological measures may be used. Where perceptual and kinesthetic motor abilities are involved, they may be identified by tests if any are available. Otherwise, situations may have to be created—if no measures are naturally available—that will make for observable expressed talent in the psychomotor domain.

There are numerous difficulties in the identification of psychomotor abilities. These include not only the lack or nonexistence of suitable measures but also the age level at which outstanding psychomotor-abilities potential manifest themselves. Sometimes the difficulty presents itself by stretching the concept of talent to include ability to weld, to operate a chain saw, to plow, to type, or to adjust a spark plug—and all these activities are in the psychomotor domain. It is one thing to identify talent that relates to, say, a gifted budding figure ice skater, all-round athlete, or footballer; it is another to identify potential psychomotor skill that could benefit from learning and to call this gifted. Giftedness in the psychomotor area must be more than potential or realized skill; it must include more generalizable attributes to function at an exceptional level in the nonverbal area of mind and body and have the additional capacity to extend the boundaries of the known.

The identification problem of abilities in the psychomotor domain is great and cloudy, and the present state of knowledge on the subject is relatively primitive. The Office of the Gifted, USOE, showed an awareness of this problem in its decision to omit psychomotor abilities as a category of giftedness when it called for proposals for funding for the fiscal year 1978-1979.

However, for those who would care to attempt to identify talent in the domain of psychomotor abilities, the author has included a form that directs attention to the derivation of useful data for that purpose and that may be used to fit individual needs and dictates of the situation. Four categories of information are included: the name of the talent area, test data, nominations, and other relevant information. Any survey of psychomotor abilities potential should have some frame of reference; this will be largely determined by the area of talent in which the search is initiated. Generally, mental ability and academic-achievement levels can range from average to bright and above. If creative potential appears to be related to the talent area, information about creative thinking abilities may be obtained. Reference was made (p. 76) on the availability of *Thinking Creatively in Action and Movement* developed by Torrance and Gibbs (1979) for use with children between 3 and 8 years old. Specific psychomotor abilities, like high levels of mechanical reasoning and spatial-relations abilities, give the specific focus needed. Observations of a subject's behavior and activity that may lead to nominations by parent, peer, and teacher, and sometimes even by the individual concerned, will provide valuable information as well. Other information, like products and performances, provide added dimensions to the identification process.

PSYCHOMOTOR ABILITIES ASSESSMENT RECORD

1. Name of talent area: _____

2. Test data: General intelligence _____

              Academic achievement _____

              Creative thinking abilities (if applicable) _____

              _____

              _____

              _____

              _____

Abilities specific to talent: _____

_____

_____

_____

_____

3. Nominations: Self _____

Peer _____

Parent _____

Teacher _____

4. Other relevant information: _____

_____

_____

_____

_____

_____

_____

Source: J. Khatena, *Music, Art, Leadership and Psychomotor Abilities Assessment Records,* p. 6. Copyright © 1981 by J. Khatena and published by Allan Associates. Reprinted by permission.

CONCLUSIONS

The widespread recognition that there are many kinds of giftedness has found expression in the six USOE categories of giftedness. Identification approaches have fluctuated between the formal and less formal, depending on the availability of psychometric resources and appropriate instrumentation. On the matter of intellectual functioning, Guilford's model of the structure of intellect has provided the best logic and direction for thought and instrumentation design for more than one category of giftedness.

Although the position is far from clear, it is generally thought that intelligence plays an important role in most of the other categories of giftedness. Academic aptitude or achievement is well known for its very high positive relationship with general intelligence as measured by IQ. A moderate level of intelligence appears to be required for creativity to function well. In the area of leadership, the intelligence level of the leader is expected to be higher than the average intelligence of the followers. It has been observed that high levels of performance in the visual and performing arts may require above average to very bright levels of general intelligence and, depending on the level of creativity involved in the activity, creative thinking abilities of above average to high levels are needed. High levels of creativity are most pervasive, for instance, in musical composition and art, and, wherever the art form requires a breaking away from tradition or the production of a new form, creativity is present. For high-level functioning of psychomotor abilities, the general intelligence level of a person can be expected to be average to bright normal, with greater emphasis on nonverbal components of the intellect.

The energizing functions of creativity may enter into most categories of giftedness. Where mental operations and behavioral correlates of each of the talent areas call for innovation or the production of the new, creativity becomes a prerequisite.

On the matter of qualifying as gifted in the several categories of giftedness, only a small percentage of individuals (2.5% or less) can be said to have very superior ability. However, the levels of giftedness as they relate to IQ may be lower in one state than another to meet differing needs of people in different situations. Judgments as to what IQ level determines giftedness, are not often well informed and largely political in origin.

Where psychometric measures are used, a good rule of thumb in statistical terms is two SDs above the mean relative to the ability measured. If a mean standard score is 100 and the SD is 15, then, a person who is highly gifted on the measured ability must have $100 + 15 + 15$ (i.e., two standard deviations above the mean), or a standard score of 130. This means that anyone obtaining a score of two SDs or more above the mean on an ability may be considered gifted relative to the ability measured. Of course, if the selection requirements are to be more stringent and only about 0.5% of the people screened are to be regarded gifted, then, only those whose standard scores are three SDs above the mean on the ability measured need be taken. It is not advisable to screen for superior abilities below two SDs above the mean. This procedure allows one to pick superior children on one or more ability or abilities relative to the test scores derived and relative to the group from which one intends to select them. National norms are usually given in the norms-technical manual of the test, but, by using the method described, you will be able to derive local and often highly relevant norms because your group of children may not be a part of the group used by the test constructor to derive norms.

In attempting to identify a gifted child, a fruitful and less expensive approach would be to obtain initial information from those who are close to the child, like parents, teachers, coaches, and peers, about one or more of the child's gifts. This may be followed up with screening that can include observations of the child by trained personnel and, when available, by tests. What measures are selected will depend on the circumstances, resources, personnel, and set criteria. Where teachers are asked to do the screening because they are qualified, they should do the screening themselves and not delegate it. Certain measures may only be administered by trained professionals; if this is the case, then, their services must be sought.

A useful approach to screen students for superior abilities in general would be to obtain information regarding the student's level of (1) general ability (preferably verbal and nonverbal as well), (2) creative thinking abilities, (3) achievement in school subjects, and (4) specialized information relative to a talent area in which the student is expected to show excellence, and where no measures are available for this, a checklist may be used as a guide for gathering observational data.

4

CREATIVE
IMAGINATION
IMAGERY

Creative imagination and its imagery correlates have importance for productive learning of children generally and for the gifted specifically. The relevance of incubation, right-brain activity, and imagination to creative problem solving and imagery are discussed. Other subjects considered are the physiological correlates of imagination and the research on imagination imagery, which shows a lack of study of imagery as it relates to creativity. The problem of measuring imagery is examined and two measures are identified as useful to the study of creative imagination imagery and analogy. Studies of these measures include procedures for stimulating imaginative thinking, effects of time press on the production of analogy and originality, developmental patterns in original verbal images and analogies, sense modalities as they relate to originality, and autonomy of original image production.

CHAPTER OUTLINE

INTRODUCTION

For the most part, research on creativity has focused on problems of instrumentation; nurture of creativity; creativity and groups of exceptional children, including the gifted; and creativity as it is affected by ethnic and cross-cultural variables. Although much has been learned about creativity over the years, little has been done to explore the relationship it bears to the creative imagination and its imagery and analogy correlates. In recent years, however, some substantial research has been done on creative imagination and imagery, and the findings have considerable relevance to more productive learning for children in general and for the gifted in particular (Gowan, 1978b, 1978c; Khatena, 1978b, 1978c, 1978e).

The magic and mystery of the imagination set in motion by creative energy have given articulation to the world, transforming reality to dreams and dreams to reality. Poets regard imagination as some force outside of themselves that is responsible for creative experiences and works. This force, which sets in motion their creative acts, has often been referred to as the Muses. William Blake describes imagination as "spiritual energy" in whose exercise we experience in some way the activity of God. It has also been called "an ability of prime importance" by Samuel Taylor Coleridge because human beings in their creative activity simulate the creative act of God. Coleridge considers imagination as seminal rather than equivalent to perception, and he differentiates it as primary imagination and secondary imagination:

The primary imagination I hold to be the living power and prime agent of all human perception, and as a repetition in the finite mind of the infinite mind of the eternal act of creation in the infinite I AM. The secondary I consider as an echo of the former, co-existing with the conscious will, yet still as identical with the primary in the kind of its agency, and differing only in degree, and in the mode of its operation. It dissolves, diffuses, dissipates, in order to re-create; or where this process is rendered impossible, yet still, at all events, it struggles to idealize and to unify. It is essentially vital, even as all objects (as objects) are essentially fixed and dead. (Coleridge, 1817/1956, p. 167)

William Wordsworth refers to imagination as another name for "absolute power," identifying it with "clearest insight," "amplitude of mind," and "Reason in her most exalted mood."

Imagination as an action of mind to produce new ideas and insights, to generate new hypotheses, and to be involved in the act of problem solving has been explained to us, for instance, by Gerard (cited in Ghiselin, 1955) or Bowra (1969):

When we use our imagination we are first stirred by some alluring puzzle which calls for a solution, and then by our own creations in the mind, we are able to see much that was before dark or unintelligible. (Bowra, 1969, p. 7)

Eccles (1958/1972) sees creative imagination as brain activity. For a brain to exhibit creative imagination, it must have a sufficient number of neurons with a wealth of synaptic connections that have the sensitivity to increase their function with usage so that they may form and maintain a wealth of memory patterns (engrams). For the creative to occur, such a brain must also have a unique capacity for unresting activity that continually combines and recombines these patterns in novel ways.

Research on the creative imagination by Khatena (1973c, 1975a) has led him to define the function of the imagination as the chemistry of mental processing in which interactive intellectual and emotive forces participate in stimulating, energizing, and propagating the creative act. Other research over the past few years (de Bono, 1971; Olson, 1977; Samples, 1975; Sperry, 1974) has attempted to explain different modes of mental functioning in terms of the left and right hemispheres of the brain: "Although each hemisphere shares the potential for many functions, and both sides participate in most activities, in a normal person the two hemispheres tend to specialize" (Ornstein, 1972, p. 51). The left brain specializes in the handling of incoming perceptual information and processes it by means of language into a logical-analytical thought and decision in a continual stream of internal discourse that accompanies consciousness. By removal of left-hemisphere functions through relaxation, meditation, hypnosis, fantasy, daydreaming, sensory deprivation, or similar states, right-hemisphere imagery can occur. The right brain specializes in the handling of divergent thinking operations, intuition, insight, invention, metaphor, analogy, and the production of creative imagination imagery. Jaynes (1976) locates creative imagination imagery in the Wernicke area of the right cerebral hemisphere. It goes on there all the time although overlaid most frequently with left-brain or dominant-hemisphere cognitive activity, which Gowan (1978b, 1978c) has likened to the static of a radio receiver. When this activity of the left hemisphere abates, some type of resonance phenomena is set up, of which the first evidence is "vibrations" followed by the occurrence of imagery.

Johannes Brahms attributed the source of "vibrations" prior to musical composition to an "awe-inspiring experience" with his Maker. When he felt the urge to compose, he said:

I begin by appealing directly to my Maker . . . I immediately feel vibrations which thrill my whole being. . . . In this exalted state I see clearly what is obscure in my ordinary moods; then I feel capable of drawing inspiration from above as Beethoven did (Brahms cited in Abell, 1964, pp. 19–21)

Brahms, then, describes that while he is in a semitrance-like state, these "vibrations" take the shape of distinct mental images that precipitate the flow of ideas that give birth to musical composition:

Those vibrations assume the form of distinct mental images. . . . Straightaway the ideas flow in upon me, directly from God, and not only do I see distinct themes in the mind's eye, but they are clothed in the right forms, harmonies, and orchestration. Measure by measure the finished product is revealed to me when I am in those rare, inspired moods (Brahms cited in Abell, 1964, pp. 19–21)

In an analysis of the process of high creativity in musical composers, Gowan (1977) identifies three phases:

1. The prelude ritual, which may be conscious or unconscious, that often ends with an invocation.
2. The altered state of consciousness (creative spell) during which the creative idea is born. It starts with vibrations, is followed by mental images, and, then, by the flow of ideas that are finally clothed in form. This syndrome often proceeds with extreme and uncanny rapidity in what is always referred to as a trance, dream, revery, somnambulistic state, or similar altered condition.
3. The postlude, in which positive emotions about the experience suffuse the participant.

INCUBATION, RIGHT-BRAIN ACTIVITY, AND IMAGINATION

Incubation is an important activity of the brain in the creative process; it is that stage in creative thinking and problem solving when mental events, earlier set in motion by deliberate and intensive preparation, are energized to become autonomous for the occurrence of fruitful insights that lead to good solutions to problems. The time taken may vary from a moment to days to months and is beyond the awareness of the creator. The potentiality, when in use, taps the preconscious—Harry Stack Sullivan's "not-me" or the Aladdin cave according to Gowan (1978b). For instance, Coleridge before the composition of "Kubla Khan" had been working with various technical devices and reading Samuel Purchas's *Pilgrimage*. On falling asleep from the effects of an anodyne (a derivative of opium), taken to relieve him from "a slight indisposition," he experienced a vision in a dream that found poetic expression:

In consequence of a slight indisposition, an anodyne had been prescribed, from the effects of which he fell asleep in his chair at the moment that he was reading the following sentence, or words of the same substance, in "Purchas's Pilgrimage": "Here the Khan Kubla commanded a palace to be built, and a stately garden thereunto. And thus ten miles of fertile ground were inclosed with a wall." The Author continued for about three hours in a profound sleep, at least of the external senses, during which time he has the most vivid confidence, that he could not have composed less than from two or three hundred lines; if that indeed can be called composition in which all the images rose up before him as things, *with a parallel production of the correspondent expressions without any sensation or consciousness of effort. On awaking he appeared to himself to have a distinct recollection of the whole, and taking his pen, ink, and paper, instantly and eagerly wrote down the lines that are here preserved. (Coleridge, 1817/1956, p. 181)*

Gowan (1978b) says:

Incubation is the mental analogy of physical gestation in which an ovum is developed into a baby. Incubation is the process of metamorphosis and right hemisphere imagery is the vehicle through which incubation produces creativity. (p. 30)

This concept is given focus and relevance in a number of studies on creative imagination imagery, especially as these relate to stimulating the use of creative imagery and autonomy of imagery in which incubation plays an important role in the production of original verbal images. Of particular interest are two measures of originality: *Onomatopoeia and Images* and *Sounds and Images* that are combined under the title, *Thinking Creatively with Sounds and Words: Norms-technical Manual* (Khatena & Torrance, 1973). These instruments (discussed in Chapter 3) are used in most studies of creative imagery and have their roots in the incubation process as it relates to imagination imagery and analogy (Khatena, 1976b, 1978b, 1978e).

All in all, the main characteristics of incubation can be summarized as follows: (1) it depends much on intensive and careful preparation; (2) it requires no conscious or voluntary thinking of the problem in hand; (3) it functions (under optimum conditions) either through relaxation or rest with no interference from conscious thought about the problem or, when attention is given to solving other problems, through a series of incubations; and (4) it facilitates right-hemisphere or creative imagination imagery for creative solutions to occur.

The French mathematician Henri Poincaré (cited in Ghiselin, 1955) informs us that incubation (or the work of the unconscious mind) was present when he was involved in analyzing difficult problems. Hermann von Helmholtz spoke of the solution to problems coming to him early in the morning, especially while he walked in wooded hills on a sunny day. Wallas (1926), identifies the involvement of four distinct steps—preparation, incubation, illumination, and verification—in his famous paradigm of the creative problem-solving process, with incubation as the stage when a person is not deliberately involved in thinking about a problem.

There have not been many studies on incubation. Several studies (Patrick, 1955) found that creative people experience, and even deliberately use, the process of incubation prior to poetic composition. Mednick, Mednick, and Mednick (1964), define incubation of creative performance as "a stage of the process during which no active attempts at solution are being made but which nevertheless results in improvement of performance" (p. 84). They also studied the effectiveness of specific associative priming of relevant associative elements on the incubation of creative performance as measured by the *Remote Associates Test* (Mednick, 1959) in two experiments, and they found such priming effective.

Vargiu (1977), theorizing on the subject, suggests that the function of imagination may be thought of in terms of the activity of creative energy fields that are both mental and emotive. Drawing on the analogies from the world of physics, he tentatively defines the creative process as, "a large number of simple 'mental elements' within the boundary of a 'creative energy field' which have such properties that (1) each mental element will respond to the influence of the creative field, and (2) all mental elements can interact with one another" (p. 23). To illustrate this, he describes the well-known behavior of a thin layer of iron filings in the presence of a magnet:

> At first, the field is too weak to set the iron particles in motion. They are held in position by friction. As the intensity of the magnetic field increases, some of the iron particles overcome friction and begin to move, interacting with the nearby granules in a way that increases the overall magnetization. This in turn sets other particles in motion, accelerating the process and starting an "avalanche effect" or "chain reaction" which causes the pattern to suddenly form itself, independently of any further approach of the magnet. (1977, p. 23)

He suggests by analogy that mental events pass through the stages of preparation, frustration, incubation, illumination, and elaboration; and the suddenness of illumination he explains as "avalanche effect":

> *Thus the illumination comes to our consciousness as something new, something unexpected. It is produced by the creative field, of which we are not aware, and when it occurs it is beyond our conscious control. So it generates in us the unique and paradoxical impression of an unknown source that leads to deeper knowing, of a blinding flash that leads to clearer vision, of a loss of control that leads to greater order. (1977, p. 24)*

Before illumination, there is the state of incubation. Vargiu suggests that this state is not a statistically random ordering of mental elements. Rather, it is the dynamism involved by the creative energy field that, in the initial part of the creative process, passes through the stages of preparation, confusion, and frustration that lay the groundwork for incubation and illumination:

> *The initial part of the creative process—from preparatory activity to confusion and frustration—can thus be seen as having a three-fold purpose: supplying material on which the creative field can play; overcoming friction by setting this material into motion, thereby making it more responsive to the influence of the creative field; and providing conceptual "seeds" through which the creative insight relates to the problem. It is common knowledge among creative people that the intensity of the preparatory stage often determines how closely the insight will fit the problem. The stages of confusion and frustration have only a subsidiary function, but are psychological means we may need to justify saying what amounts to "the hell with it," and turning our attention elsewhere. We then move on to the incubation stage, the crucial and delicate period during which the often very weak creative field can act on the mental elements without the disturbance of our conscious manipulation, and therefore in the cumulative, coherent fashion that leads to illumination. (1977, p. 27)*

Vargiu, then, expands this model to include the emotional field that runs intact with the mental elements, tending to organize these mental elements into configurations that correspond to their own energy patterns. It is this interaction between the mental elements and the emotional field that constitutes the very essence of imagination so that images are formed in the mind and energized by feelings.

The function of creative imagination involves intellectual abilities as well as energy fields that operate in various ways to lead to incubation, creative imagery, and illumination in the creative process. Drawing from the Guilfordian conception of intellectual abilities and Wallas's and Vargiu's thoughts on creativity and problem-solving processes, it is possible to perceive abilities energized by magnetic fields of forces—both mental and emotive—as central to creative functioning. Activity set in motion by imagination causes these forces to act and interact with each other and with intellectual abilities. This activity may be deliberate or ongoing without our full awareness; however, if a problem is presented for processing this activity, incubation is induced and often produces imagery that leads to illumination and problem solution. This is illustrated in Figure 5 (Khatena, 1979c).

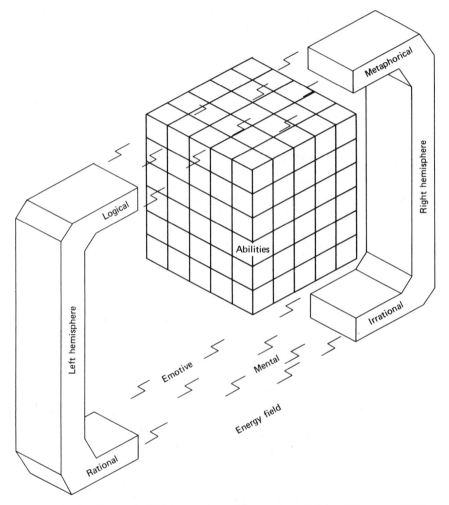

Figure 5   Intellectual abilities activated by energy fields. (Khatena, 1979c. Copyright © 1979 by J. Khatena, published by Allan Associates. Reprinted by permission of J. Khatena.)

Not so long ago, Eccles (1958–1972) presented his speculations on the function of imagination and creativity based (as he said), on secure evidence concerning the way information is conveyed to the cortex with a specificity that makes subsequent interpretation possible. In attempting to explain the characteristics of a brain exhibiting creative imagination, he speculates that:

The creative brain must first of all possess an adequate number of neurons, having a wealth of synaptic connection between them. It must have, as it were, the structured basis for an immense range of patterns of activity. The synapses of the brain should also have a sensitive tendency to increase their function with usage, so that they may readily form and maintain memory patterns. Such a brain will accumulate an immense wealth of engrams of highly specific character. In addition this brain possesses a peculiar potency for unresting activity, weaving the spatio-temporal patterns of its engrams in continually novel and interacting forms, the stage is set for the deliverance of a "brain child" that is sired, as we say, by creative imagination. (p. 40)

IMAGINATION IMAGERY

Some of the most beautiful things we say derive their energy and effectiveness from the creative imagination and the images they produce. It is creative imagery that often provides the artist or poet with the central idea for a picture or poem (Richardson, 1969). For instance, Wordsworth's lamentation for someone for whom he dearly cared is expressed in the lines of one of his Lucy poems:

A violet by a mossy stone
Half hidden from the eye!
—Fair as a star when only one
Is shining in the sky.

The image of a violet against the background of a mossy stone is naturally beautiful in color, texture, and vitality: it represents the girl (implied in the four lines) as alive and within reach although she may pass unnoticed (i.e., "half hidden from the eye"); and, just like the flower, she is delicate, fragile, and transient. The second image of the girl as a star shining alone in the sky reiterates her beauty but this time as gem-like, something beyond compare and remote although permanent. The imagery of these lines, congruent with the central notion of someone beautiful, once alive but now dead, transforms fact into poetry (Khatena, 1978f).

Much of the brain activity relative to creative imagination has to do with imagery or the reexperiencing of images and their language correlates. Eccles (1958/1972) goes on to suggest that, by association, the image is evocative of other images and that, when these images of beauty and subtlety blend in harmony and are expressed in some language—verbal, musical, or pictorial—they evoke transcendent experiences in others and, thus, we have artistic creation of a simple or lyrical kind. To this kind of imagery, Eccles would add an entirely different order of image making, one that provides the illumination that gives new insight or understanding and that, relative to science, may take the form of a new hypothesis that embraces and transcends an older hypothesis.

For example, Charles Darwin's theory of evolution or Friedrich Kekulé von Stradonitz's experience of imagery just prior to, and contingent on, the illumination that led to the structure of the carbon ring, which became the foundation of organic chemistry. A description of his experience follows:

I turned my chair to the fire and dozed. Again the atoms were gamboling before my eyes. The smaller groups kept modestly in the background. My mental eye, rendered more acute by visions of this kind, could now distinguish larger structures, of manifold conformations, long rows sometimes more closely fitted together, all twining and twisting in snake-like motion. But look! What was that? One of the snakes had seized hold of its tail and the form whirled mockingly before my eyes. As if by a flash of lighting I awoke. (Kekulé von Stradonitz cited in Koestler, 1964, p. 118)

Albert Einstein tells us that images not words or language served him as elements of thought. The principle of the rotating magnetic field appeared to Nikola Tesla in images that were as sharp, clear, and solid as metal or stone: this illumination revolutionized electrical science (Ghiselin, 1955).

Imagination imagery may be said to be the province of Land's (1973) mutualistic stage and Gowan's (1974) creativity-psychedelic, stages that relate to higher levels of psychological functioning (these and related stages are discussed on pp. 148–162). It is at these stages that high-level combinations and connections are made by analogy and metaphor and at which time the preconscious is tapped. Transformation occurs when movement taking place from a lower level or order moves to a higher level or order by means of the process of destructuring and reintegration (Khatena, 1979a).

FUNCTION OF IMAGERY

In psychology, an image is defined as a perception in the absence of an external stimulus irrespective of the sense modality in which it occurs. R. Gordon (1972) tells us that when she speaks of an image she speaks of:

The perception of forms, or colors, or sounds, or smells, or movements, or tastes in the absence of an actual external stimulus which could have caused such perception. This does not mean that such external stimuli did not present themselves in the past nor that the image is independent of such past experi-

ences. But it does mean that at the time of the perception of the image no such stimulus is present. (p. 63)

Individuals perceive the external world through their senses and record messages about the world in their brain as images that are later retrieved from storage in the absence of the original stimulus event. These images can be photographic likenesses without the mediation of emotive-motivational processes unique to each individual, but this is unlikely. Images can be expected to differ from one person to the next although the original stimulus events were the same. The image has the importance of giving coherence to a multitude of sensory input data about the world: it orders events, experiences, and relationships; it links the past and present and projects the future; it is the repository of experiences, needs, and frustrations; it projects the uniqueness of individual personality; it provides information about the inner life (private world) of the individual; and it is the key to man's creativity (Khatena, 1979b).

R. Gordon (1972) examines at length this privacy and exclusiveness of the image world unique to each individual, which musicians, artists, and filmmakers assume with "arrogant certainty" to be similar. That our image worlds are so different from one another is natural because a great many variables affect them, among which are dimensions of content, sense modality, flexibility-rigidity, divergency-convergency, autonomy-control, and active-passive. These dimensions are further affected by whether a person's imagery is predominantly reconstructive or constructive and inventive. R. Gordon suggests that, perhaps, these are the distinguishing features of the artist or the creative versus the nonartist or the critic. To these different dimensions of imagery she includes the world of the synaesthetic, where "visual images evoked sounds and tastes, and tones mixed up with colors and touch sensations" (p. 66). Edgar Allan Poe in one of his poems "hears" the approach of darkness; in another, Poe describes sensations that accompany death (Wilson, 1931):

Night arrived; and with its shadows a heavy discomfort. It oppressed my limbs with the oppression of some dull weight, not unlike the distant reverberation of surf, but more continuous, which beginning with the first twilight, had grown in strength with the darkness. Suddenly lights were brought into the room . . . and issuing from the flame of each lamp there flowed unbrokenly into my ears a strain of melodious monotone. (Edgar Allan Poe cited in Wilson, 1931, p. 13)

Different artists need different kinds and combinations of imagery (e.g., the playwright, film-maker and theater director need imagery that includes both visual and auditory images, whereas the artist needs imagery that is primarily visual and the musician needs imagery that is primarily auditory). These differences in imagery also vary for artists in different cultures (e.g., a Chinese artist's sketches of London that look more like China than England) or for artists living in different times (e.g., Shakespearian costumes marked Elizabethan England rather than the times the story assigned to the play. R. Gordon concludes that although the image world of an individual is personal and private it is open to influence and change. Arieti (1976) writing on the subject of art, the individual, and society perceives the magic synthesis that leads to invention, discovery, and eminence in the individual's dynamic relationship and creative exchange with society.

PERCEPTION IMAGERY AND ART

By visual arts, we mean drawing, painting, sculpturing, designing, and related productions of art forms that appeal to the eye; by performing arts, we mean music, dance, oratory, drama, and all other related forms of art that require performance. Persons engaged in the production of such works of art have to possess certain talents that allow them to perceive the ordinary world with an uncommon eye, one that stores as images sensory impressions that go beyond the visual, auditory, and kinesthetic—where sensory boundaries are crossed so that, for instance, what is heard is seen, what is touched is visualized. To this may be added a sensitivity to rhythm and a depth for feeling that, when energized by the creative imagination, brings about a magic synthesis of the elements that result in an image that is precursor to a work of art (Khatena, 1979b).

Arieti (1976) says that individuals may paint what they see (e.g., a tree, human being, an animal), in which case they rely on perception; or they may paint by remembering, not by looking at what they saw. In the latter case they resort to imagery (e.g., the earliest expressions of art in caves were made by artists who relied on their own images because the animals they portrayed were not in the caves). Artists who rely on imagery have first to perceive the object before they can evoke it through imagery. They may always check what they are doing through imagery by seeing the object before they evoke it through imagery. Or they can always check what they are doing through imagery by seeing the object in reality, thereby reexperiencing the original perception (something that the cave dwellers probably did in the course of their paintings).

Perception of an object, of course, is affected by thoughts, feelings, and past experiences so that the inner representation of the outer object is not an exact replica. Paul Cezanne, for example, did not wish to reproduce nature in mirror-like fashion, as was conventionally done, but to represent it. After a long period of realism, his art opened the door to subjectivity. Following him, the subjective element in art grew in importance, leaning more toward the primary than the secondary process. That is, there was greater reliance on imagery and imagination than on perception and memory, thereby allowing a fuller and more profound expression of the human spirit. No longer are artists bound by the dictates of the retina: they can soar in the realms of fantasy propelled by the emotions, and they can symbolize rather than describe or narrate. In a more general sense, humans have found that through art forms they can break the seal that locks them fast to their inner world, and they can communicate, with least distortion, the essential nature of the original message (R. Gordon, 1972).

Gowan (1975) sees art as the final product in the parataxic (i.e., experiences the numinous received as images) totemization of the traumatic aspects of the numinous element: by art the individual finds external form for fears, fantasies, and psychic tensions constructively and, in doing so, achieves catharsis and simultaneously produces objects of social value, beauty, and delight. The production of a masterpiece is explained by Gowan as:

> The long journey from the collective unconscious (archetypes) to the personal unconscious (icons) through creativity to the personal preconscious, and finally to external collective display (art). (p. 227)

On the subject of art as image-magic, Gowan draws our attention to the parataxic mode, which, he says, is characterized by the production of images that first served as the objective of magic elements (symbols)—which is the origin of visual art—then as signs (icons), and finally as pictures (modern art). In creating images that find expression in some form of art, humans gain autonomy, purpose, and security. This therapeutic magic finds expression in Pablo Picasso's reaction on seeing the first exhibition of African art in Paris:

> Men had made those masks and other objects for a sacred purpose, a magic purpose, as a kind of mediation between themselves and the unknown hostile forces that surround them, in order to overcome their fear and horror by giving it a form and an image. At this moment I realized that this was what painting was all about. Painting isn't an aesthetic operation; it's a form of magic designed as a mediator between this strange, hostile world and us, a way of seizing power by giving form to our terrors as well as our desires. When I came to that realization, I knew I had found my way. (Picasso cited in Collier, 1972, p. 174)

IMAGINATION IMAGERY AND RESEARCH

Relatively little research has been done on imagery, especially as it relates to the creative imagination. In fact, Durio (1975) points out that there is an almost complete absence of experimentally based research into the relationship between imagery and creativity. One of the major causes for this can be traced to the rejection of imagery by John B. Watson and the ascendency of behaviorism in the 1920s. In a journal editorial, Sheikh (1977) points out:

116

Watson regarded mental images to be nothing more than mere ghosts of sensations and of no functional significance whatever. His judgment led to the relegation of mental imagery to the background, and subsequently a preoccupation with the verbal processes increasingly dominated the psychological scene. (p. 1)

The readmission of imagery as an appropriate subject of study in psychology after 30 years of ostracism followed renewed interest by American psychologists in cognitive processes in the early 1950s (R. R. Holt, 1964; Richardson, 1969). The renewal of interest in imagery may be due to the view that images are indirect reactivations of earlier sensory or perceptual activity rather than mental mechanisms (Bugelski, 1970). However, this resurgence of interest in imagery by psychologists of various persuasions—whose writings have established the significance of imagery as important to scientific inquiry in the field beyond any doubt (Sheikh, 1977)—has tended to confine itself to the study of after imagery, eidetic imagery, and memory imagery (Paivio, 1971; Richardson, 1969).

In attempting to integrate studies on imagery that have such titles as hypnagogic imagery, perceptual isolation imagery, hallucinogenic drug imagery, photic stimulation imagery, pulse current imagery, sleep deprivation imagery, meditation imagery, and the like, Richardson (1969) suggests the term imagination imagery. He makes a distinction between memory imagery and imagination imagery as used in the traditional sense:

The memory-image *of a hammer that I now have in my mind's eye is of an old bookcase at the back of my garage. The visual image of hammer of no particular weight or type and with no other personal reference marks would be a* generic image. *But the mental picture of a hammer with a solid gold head and a smooth ivory handle would be an* imagination-image *because I had never seen such a hammer until a moment ago when I constructed an image of it. (pp. 93–94)*

Studies on imagination imagery have covered the following types of imagery.

Hypnagogic imagery. Imagery that comes in the semidream state between sleep and wakefulness.

Perceptual isolation imagery. Imagery that occurs when external stimuli are radically reduced under controlled conditions.

Hallucinogenic drug imagery. Imagery chemically induced from such drugs as LSD, peyote, and mescaline.

Photic stimulation imagery. Imagery evoked by any relatively slow, rhythmic visual stimulation that induces a trance-like state or drowsiness.

Pulse current imagery. Imagery induced by electrical impulses that are externally applied to the temples to stimulate the appearance of imagery.

Nondrug-induced hallucination imagery. Imagery like that experienced by schizophrenics, mystics, and shamans.

A common finding in all these studies is that there is a reduction of the external stimuli that operate on individuals to a level that frees them to attend to an inner world of stimulus events and allows them to experience imagination imagery (Richardson, 1969). However, the need to study types of creative imagination imagery, hitherto neglected, has been stressed by both Paivio (1971) and Richardson (1969).

Richardson only cites two studies on the creative correlates of imagination imagery: the first, on perceptual isolation, found that the number, clarity, and complexity of visual images experienced during a 2½-hour perceptual isolation period correlated with scores on J. P. Guilford's creativity measures administered before the experience (Kubzanski, 1961); the second was on the facilitative effects of LSD on 11 different conditions believed to be important to the creative problem-solving process (Harman, McKim, Mogar, Fadiman, & Stolaroff, 1966). Since then, several other studies on imagination imagery as it relates to creativity have been done.

Krippner, Dreistadt, and Hubbard (1972) summarized and discussed a group of studies that attempted to relate the right (nondominant), hemisphere of the brain to the creative person's experience of nonordinary reality through hypnosis, visual imaging processes, psychedelic drugs, dreams, extrasensory perception, and self-actualization.

On the subject of hypnosis, creativity, and the imagination, there are two comprehensive reviews that document the area: one by Bowers and Bowers (1970), the other by Sheehan (1972).

A study by Hanard (1972) on right-hemisphere function, imagery, and creativity hypothesized that the direction in which a subject looks when given a problem indicates that it is the opposite side of the brain that is active. He found that, when subjects were presented problems of a reflective nature, they tended to move their eyes to the left, which meant that the right brain was active. These subjects also produced more visual imagery and scored higher on a test of creativity.

Green and Green (1977) studied the relationships of creativity, hypnagogic imagery, and relaxation and found that "a kind of reverie or near-dream state [was induced] in which intuitive ideas and solutions came to consciousness in the form of hypnagogic images" (p. 124).

Leonard and Lindauer (1973) explored the relationship between participation in aesthetic activities (English, art, music and theater) and imagery arousal as measured by self-rating scales. They found that participation in aesthetic activities and imagery arousal were significantly correlated and that imagery scores differentiated aesthetic participation with little evidence of sex difference. No causal link between the two variables was found, and the authors suggest that both may be related to a third variable, namely, creativity.

Torrance (1972c) studied the tendency of adolescents and young adults to produce images of unusual visual perspective on the Repeated-Figures Activity section of the Torrance tests, which is used as a predictor of creative achievement. He found that the number of objects presented in unusual perspective on the Circles part of the test was moderately and significantly related to the criteria of adult creativity for Quality of Creative Achievement, Quality of Peak Achievements, and Creativeness of Aspirations. Objects presented in usual or common perspective are unrelated to these criteria.

In addition, a few other papers have attempted to find relationships between creative talents in music and the ability to produce original verbal images (Torrance & Khatena, 1969) and the relationships of personality characteristics, activities and attitudinal patterns, and the production of original verbal images (Khatena & Torrance, 1971, 1973).

Two papers that have added to the growing interest in the area of the creative imagination relate to source material on discovery by analogy (W. W. J. Gordon, 1974) and on metaphorical thinking and the production of similes (Schaefer, 1975). Studies have also dealt with the creative imagination and imagery-analogy correlates (Khatena, 1975a) and the production of original verbal images of deaf and hearing children (Johnson & Khatena, 1975).

MEASUREMENT OF CREATIVE IMAGINATION IMAGERY

One of the major problems of studying the function of imagination imagery has been the lack of objective measures. The early work of Richardson (1969) and a more recent paper by White, Sheehan, & Ashton (1977) bring to notice that self-report measures are among the most widely used for imagery assessment. White et al. suggest, in their conclusion, that *Betts Questionnaire upon Mental Imagery* is the most influential of the scales available. Several other measures whose development and construction can be traced to this earlier instrument have promoted a substantial body of research as well.

Betts QMI Vividness of Imagery Scale (Sheehan, 1967) developed by Sheehan, is a shortened form of the earlier instrument. A number of studies using this scale have shown that individual differences in imagery vividness are related to such variables as intentional and incidental recall, personality characteristics, spelling ability, creative self-perceptions, improvement of swimming skills, and discriminative reaction time. The *Gordon Test of Visual Imagery Control* (R. Gordon, 1949) differentiates autonomous from controlled visual imagery. Scores on this measure relate positively with stereotyped imagery, reversal rates of the Necker cube, mental disorder, mental practice, paired associate learning, extrasensory perceptions, creative self-perceptions, and the like. The *Vividness of*

Visual Imagery Questionnaire (Marks, 1973), the *Imaginal Processes Inventory* (Singer & Antrobus, 1966, 1970), the *Questionnaire on Imagery Control* (Lane, 1974), the *Individual Differences Questionnaire* (Ernest & Pavio, 1971), and the *Imagery Survey Schedule* (Cautela & Tondo, 1971) are several other measures that have been used in the study of imagery.

The need for appropriate instruments to study imagination imagery and its correlates in creativity has not ceased and has been, in part, relieved by the construction and development of instruments that attempt to measure creative abilities (e.g., Guilford, 1967; Torrance, 1966, 1974b). Although Guilford and Torrance did not directly attempt to measure creative imagination in terms of its imagery correlates as such, the measures they produced do suggest that the study of imagination imagery may begin with the study of creative abilities. At least there now exist measures of creative components of intellectual functioning, and these have prepared the way for the study of creative imagination imagery.

Of particular value to the study of creative imagination imagery and analogy have been two measures of verbal originality: *Onomatopoeia and Images* and *Sounds and Images,* which are the components of a test battery called *Thinking Creatively with Sounds and Words* (Khatena & Torrance, 1973; Torrance, Khatena, & Cunnington, 1973). *Onomatopoeia and Images* and *Sounds and Images* come in alternate forms for adults (Form 2A and Form 2B) and for children (Form 1A and Form 1B). Both these measures have been fully described on pp. 81–82.

STUDIES OF CREATIVE IMAGINATION IMAGERY AND ANALOGIES

The function of creative imagination and its imagery-analogy correlates are explored in several studies. They can be grouped as those relating to stimulating the creative imagination and its originality correlates and those relating to the effects of time press on the production of original verbal images as well as studies on the developmental patterns in the production of original verbal images, the production of original verbal images by deaf and blind children, the physiological correlates of original images, and the autonomy of imagery and originality (Khatena, 1978b).

STIMULATING THE CREATIVE IMAGINATION AND ORIGINALITY

A facet of the creative potential that has intrigued many a scholar in past years is the positive responsiveness of this potential to the effects of nurture. This responsiveness is based on the assumption that creative thinking is the heritage of all human beings whose mental functioning is not obstructed or impaired by nature or environmental forces (Maslow, 1959; Osborn, 1963; Rossman, 1931; Royce,

120

1898). Developmental acceleration of creative mental functioning through planned environmental enrichment has been claimed, and it is generally substantiated by the compendia of creative imagination research of Parnes (1958, 1960) and the works of Osborn (1963), Parnes, Noller, and Biondi (1977a, 1977b), Torrance (1972a), Youtz (1962), and others. On the whole, reported improvements in creative performance by means of tests of creative thinking reinforce the view that much can be done to help individuals realize their creative potential.

A variety of training procedures have been used to improve creative behavior and mental functioning as measured by tests of creativity, generally with great success. These have included principles of creative problem solving, idea-generating techniques, free association, and incubation (Feldhusen, Treffinger, & Bahlke, 1970; Maltzman, Bogartz & Breger, 1958; Mednick, 1962; Osborn, 1963; Parnes & Meadows, 1959; Torrance, 1965b). There seems to have been very little direct attempt to stir the imagination to produce original verbal images as such by using creative thinking strategies. However, experiments that tried this approach used one to five of these thinking strategies: breaking away from the obvious and commonplace, transposition, restructuring, synthesis, and analogy (Khatena, 1969a, 1969b, 1970ab, 1971cd), 1975a, 1977a).

Breaking Away from the Obvious and Commonplace

Breaking away from the obvious and commonplace is a strategy that requires a person deliberately to think in a way that is not habitual or customary, with an openness for the clever, unusual, and novel. For the purpose of illustrating the operation of this thinking strategy, subjects are given an example of a square and asked what could be done to produce an object using the square so that the object would be original. The instructions point out that one way of doing this is to break away from the square set. The examples of a clock and a pipe for better smoking are given. The square, then, serves as a figural stimulus. As a verbal stimulus, the word "roar" can be given. Examples are then set up for comparison and a response in terms of definition is considered commonplace—*to talk noisily* or (the more obvious) *the sound a lion makes*. A response that is imaginative rather than definitive is regarded as having creative strength, like *blood gushing out of a wound*.

Transposition

Transposition is taught in terms of the transference of an existing structural or functional relationship of a phenomenon from one mode of expression to another. As a figural stimulus, two circles are presented, one being larger than the other, and simple instances of transposition are made in terms of space, music, algebra, and linguistics. The verbal stimulus of "thunderstorm," representing the disequilibria of natural elements, is the expression of a heard relationship. The point being made is that, in transposing this heard relationship of disequilibria to disequilibria in other sense modalities (sight, taste, touch, smell), the subject shows imaginative strength. One example of such a transposition that expresses itself in the sense modality of taste is *a grape-drenched palate*.

Restructuring

In restructuring, we are supposed to reorganize something that appears to us to be organized in a certain way in such a manner that it may only slightly resemble the original. The exercise requires a perception of the parts that comprise the object presented, a breaking down of these parts either by physical or mental manipulation, and a conception of how these components can be put together in a new way so that a new phenomenon emerges. Take, for example, a human figure constructed with three triangles, four rectangles, and four semicircles presented to a child on a flannel board. To illustrate the operation of this strategy, the geometrical shapes are pulled apart and reassembled as an automobile. The child is, then, instructed to pull the same pieces apart and put them together to make a picture no one else would think of creating. Restructuring that involves words can also be given. For instance, a picture of the *Three Wise Men of Gotham* is shown to a child. As warm-up activities, the child is encouraged to ask questions that cannot be answered by merely looking at the picture as well as guess at both why events in the scene are taking place and what the consequences of these events are. This is, then, followed by getting the child to restructure three elements of the picture, namely, the three wise men, the bowl, and the sea, into an unusual and interesting story.

Synthesis

Synthesis is a strategy that requires, with the aid of the creative imagination, the organization of bits of information and various objects into something unique. Unlike restructuring, the act of synthesis allows more freedom for manipulation and expression. Similar methods may be used to produce creative combinations. Students do not have to be given all the materials needed to construct a creative product; sometimes they are required to use their initiative to acquire what they need to supplement what is given to them. If a child is presented with 30 geometric shapes in a plastic bag, he or she may use all of them in various combinations to make a picture or scene. As an illustration of the operation of this thinking strategy, the child may be shown on the flannel board a picture of two girls on a see-saw so that only 18 geometrical shapes are used from the bag. The picture, then, can be pulled apart to combine with as many of the remaining 12 pieces as desired to make a different picture or scene—one that is original. Synthesis may also involve the use of words. For example, a child can be shown a picture of *Wee Willie Winkie* and encouraged to ask questions and guess causes and consequences (in much the same way that was described for restructuring)—all of which require the use of the imagination. Next, a second picture, *The Schoolmaster and His Student,* can be shown and followed by similar warm-up activities. The child, then, can be asked to tell a story using a combination of the characters and situations in both pictures and be encouraged to use his or her imagination to make the story unusual and interesting.

Analogy

Analogy involves comparison of similarities between two unlike objects in the context of familiar experiences to facilitate understanding. Analogies have been talked of in different ways, but, quite recently, they have been described in creative problem-solving terms by the synectics group (W. J. J. Gordon, 1961). To communicate thoughts, feelings, or experiences that do not easily lend themselve to expression, a search for some familiar situation to which the thought-feeling complex can be related ensues—a process of making the strange familiar or the familiar strange and thereby allowing insights into hitherto concealed relationships. These mechanisms (i.e., making the strange familiar or the familiar strange) are operations involved in the making of creative analogies and have been presented in synectics as personal analogy, direct analogy, symbolic analogy, and fantasy analogy.

In personal analogy, a relationship is found between the person making the comparison and some other phenomenon with which this person and others are familiar. Suppose a person wants others to know how thin he is without having to give a lengthy description, he may say, "I'm as thin as a stick." Or, suppose a person wants to tell someone that she is very happy, she may say, "I'm as happy as a lark."

Just as with personal analogy, direct analogy finds a relationship between two unlike phenomena but without self-involvement. To produce a direct analogy, the I of the comparison above may become *she* or Jean and read, "Jean is as thin as a stick." Another direct analogy relative to being fat is, "John is as fat as a pig." And, if the activity is focused on eating habits, the analogy becomes, "John eats like a pig."

In symbolic analogy a sign (symbol) is found for a phenomenon to be described that has as many similar characteristics as the phenomenon itself. For instance, if there is need to describe someone as dependable, strong, stable, consistent, and so on, without using too many words, then, selection of some phenomenon (animate or inanimate) that approximates these qualities may be made. For example, the Rock of Gibraltar has been traditionally known to have such qualities: the Rock, then, can serve as a sign (symbol) of the qualities possessed by the person in mind. Using symbolic analogy, she may then be referred to as, "The Gibraltar of my life" or "Jean is as firm as the Rock."

In fantasy analogy, at least the comparison object or subject must be imaginary. Myths, legends, allegories, fairy tales, and the like, are all rich sources of imaginary materials for comparison: the Devil, Medusa, Pandora's box, Ariel, the rainbow, the dragon, the Garden of Eden, paradise, Sugar Candy Mountain, Jekyll and Hyde, and so on. Suppose the information to be conveyed is that someone is very wicked, evil, and murderous: such a person may be compared to Hyde, "John is Hyde himself" or "Leonora's whispers stirred the Hyde in John."

Imagery can be described as mental pictures (images) that have organized themselves into some kind of pattern. One thing this does is to make some sense of the world for the persons making images. They are very much like artists in the act of creating the world the way they see it: in the canvas of their mind, there appear images as they react to the world they see and, like artists in the act of painting a picture, they give organization and meaning to these images. How they depict their world, what details they include, the choices they make of colors, the style they choose, and the extent to which they allow their emotions to become involved are all dependent on their emotional-intellectual make-up and the creative energizing forces at work at the time.

Here, then, analogy was used to explain imagery that is compared to a painting: the mind is the canvas on which perceptions of the world are patterned. Imagery could have been compared to a painting with no attempt at elaboration. Instead, further details are added to the basic image—the individual is compared to an artist whose mind is a canvas. Thus, by extending or elaborating the comparison, the images are combined to make a more complex image pattern. To put it in another way, "Imagery is a painting on the canvas of one's mind." This is a complex image pattern. Simple and complex image patterns can be used in the act of comparison. The more highly imaginative a person is, the greater the tendency to use more complex images. Whether personal, direct, symbolic, or fantasy analogies are created, imagery is used. More often than not, analogies with complex patterns tend to be more interesting and provocative than simple image patterns, for instance, "Mary sings like a crow" when compared to "Mary sings like a featherless crow on a winter's day."

Figures of Speech

In making analogies, several well-known figures of speech based on agreement, similarity, or resemblance—simile, metaphor, personification, and allusion—may be used.

Simile

A simile is a form of comparison between two things that are different except in a single characteristic to which one wants to call attention: "John is as *fat* as a pig," where John and pig are different in kind and yet possess one characteristic in common, namely, being *fat*. By focusing attention on John's corpulence in this way, John is effectively described as *fat* without lengthy description.

Metaphor

A metaphor is a condensed or implied simile. A comparison using this form attempts to relate two things differing in kind as if they were both similar or even identical: "John is a pig." Here John is identified with the pig and with the implication that he does not only resemble the pig by being *fat* but also by possessing other piggish qualities. Thus, by calling John a pig, one is suggesting that John is not only fat but also greedy, filthy, stinking, and so on.

Personification

Personification is a form of comparison that attempts to give lifeless objects or abstract things attributes of life and feeling. One well-known example is "time marches on," in which "time" is given attributes of a human being moving forward on foot to indicate the steady passing of time.

Allusion

Allusion is yet another form of comparison that makes use of familiar phenomena in literature, mythology, legend, present-day happenings, and so on. To explain or describe something without having to say much, this something can often be related to something else that is well known, for instance, by biblical allusion: "She proved to be a good Samaritan" or by literary allusion "David is the Falstaff of our company."

Figures of Speech in Analogies

Each of the four figures of speech described can be used as comparison forms in the four kinds of analogies. The simile, "John is as fat as a pig," or the metaphor, "John is a pig," are both direct and analogies. If a simile or metaphor is to be used in the form of personal analogy, for instance, personal involvement in the comparison is necessary: "I'm fat as a pig" or "I'm a pig."

Personification can be used in personal analogy and direct analogy as in the éxample, "I walked with death in Vietnam" or "Death took her for his bride."

Allusion may also be used in personal analogy form: "I turned him to stone with my glassy stare" or "The bad news struck him down with the force of Jove's thunderbolt." These are examples of allusion in the direct analogy form. The first allusion refers to the head of Medusa, the second to the destructive energy of the chief Greek god. Symbolic analogy was earlier illustrated as a comparison in the form of simile and metaphor. The Rock of Gibralter was used as the symbol of dependability, strength, stability, and consistency in the simile, "Jean is as firm as the Rock," or the metaphor, "She is the Gibraltar of my life." If the allusion to "cornerstone" (with St. Peter in mind) is to be used as the comparison figure, then, by saying "John is the cornerstone of our diplomacy in the Far East," there is the implication that John has not only the qualities of dependability, strength, stability, and consistency but also is the most important single building block upon which the superstructure of our diplomacy is to be maintained.

The same figures can be used to great effect in fantasy analogy. For instance, jealousy has been described in Shakespeare's *Othello* as "the green-eyed monster." In simile form, the comparison may read: "His jealousy, like the green-eyed monster, will devour him"; in metaphor form: "Beware of jealousy, the green-eyed monster that destroys everything in its path."

Two studies with college adults as subjects (Khatena, 1970b, 1971d) show that, in general, exercise in the use of the five creative thinking strategies (see pp. 121–126) increased the probability of original verbal image production as measured by both *Onomatopoeia and Images* and *Sounds and Images*. A third study with music majors in college (Khatena & Barbour, 1972) used three of the five thinking strategies as training procedures, namely, breaking away from the obvious and commonplace, restructuring, and synthesis as well as Osborn's (1963) idea-spurring questions (Barbour, 1971), which encourage group ideation of rhythmic and melodic elements. The results favored the use of creative thinking strategies in the context of brainstorming to encourage the imaginative manipulation of rhythmic and melodic elements and, thus, increase the production of original verbal images. Another study (Khatena & Parnes, 1974) explored the effects of exposing college adults to a creative problem-solving program (Parnes, 1967a, 1967b) over one semester and found that experimentals produced more original verbal images than controls.

The question of whether the creative level of subjects has any influence on the results of training was also explored (Khatena, 1973b). It was found that creative level had no significant effect on training adults to think imaginatively with onomatopoeic words, that is, both creative and less creative people benefited from training to think in creative ways.

The findings of two studies as they relate to developmental patterns described later, pp. 130–132) suggest an experiment designed to find out if college men and women, identified as high and low creatives by the use of *Something About Myself* (Khatena & Torrance, 1976a, 1976b), could be taught to use personal, symbolic, and fantasy analogies with complex image structure more frequently than direct analogy with simple image structure (Khatena, 1973a, 1977b). In two earlier experiments with college adults (Khatena, 1970b, 1971c), analogy was used as one of five components of a creative training program (Khatena, 1969a, 1969b) and a significant increase in the subjects' originality scores was reported. However, the analogy training in these two studies did not differentiate the four analogy categories and the image structure, whereas Khatena's (1977c) training program on analogy attempted not only to differentiate the analogy categories and image structure but also to show that analogy can be structured in terms of some well-known figures of speech. The subjects—college juniors (24 men and

76 women), randomly assigned to two treatment groups—were taught the use of analogy in the following sequence:

1. They were first introduced to a description of analogy and imagery.
2. Then, exercises on the use of personal, direct, symbolic, and fantasy analogy followed, at first with a simple image pattern, next with a complex image pattern.
3. They were, then, introduced to four well-known figures of speech based on agreement, similarity, or resemblance (i.e., simile, metaphor, personification, and allusion) and shown how each of these could be used to structure each of the four kinds of analogies. This was followed by some practice in their use.
4. Further practice exercises using the four figures of speech were given with instructions and clues relative to the composition of analogies.
5. A final set of exercises with all clues withdrawn, except for (1) a set of instructions that reminded subjects to use what they knew about analogies, images, and figures of speech and (2) single-word stimuli that subjects were to use for analogy making.

The subjects of the experimental group were exposed to the training program for 200 minutes (50 minutes multiplied by four sessions) over a period of 10 days; following the fourth session, the subjects were administered *Onomatopoeia and Images* as a posttest. Their responses were scored for originality, based on the principle of statistical infrequency by using the published scoring guide. In addition, their responses were analyzed by a frequency count for the use they had made of the four kinds of analogy and the two kinds of image structure.

Generally, high creatives and low creatives who were taught obtained significantly higher originality scores than high and low creatives of the control group. This is consistent with the findings of another study (Khatena, 1973b) that showed both high and low creative college adults benefit from exposure to the creative training program described. In addition, all experimentals and controls were found to use the direct analogy simple image pattern to the other analogy-image types. Again, this is consistent with the adult study on analogy (Khatena, 1972c) discussed later.

In the main, it was found that all subjects producing direct analogies preferred the simple to the complex image structure; high and low creatives of both groups produced more complex images than low creatives of both groups. In addition, only one symbolic analogy and a few fantasy analogies were produced by both groups; experimentals produced more fantasy analogies than controls.

Although the training program significantly increased the originality means of the experimental group, it did not serve to increase the use of personal, symbolic, and fantasy analogy strategies significantly nor was it noticeable that use of any figure of speech strategy was made in the subjects' production of analogies.

EFFECTS OF TIME PRESS ON ORIGINALITY AND ANALOGY PRODUCTION

It was suggested by Rhodes (1961) that creative people could be identified through their person (personality characteristics), process (thinking operations), products, and press (the way they responded to stress situations)—abbreviated as the four P's. Much has been done in the areas of person, process, and product (e.g., Barchillon, 1961; Barron, 1969; Guilford, 1967; Khatena & Torrance, 1973, 1976a, 1976b; MacKinnon, 1971; Mednick, 1962; Roe, 1963; Schaefer & Anastasi, 1968; Taylor, 1958; Taylor & Ellison, 1967; Torrance, 1962a, 1965c, 1966), but relatively little has been done with press.

Maltzman et al. (1958) showed that associative processes at work can be urged to produce uncommon responses by mere repetition in the presence of verbal stimuli. Mednick et al. (1964) studied the effects of associative priming in the context of incubation, the stage at which associative processes are set to work to produce original verbal responses. Cunnington and Torrance (1965) explored the effects of progressive warm-up on the production of original verbal responses. Khatena explored the effects of press in terms of the repetition of stimuli (onomatopoeic words) to fixed and variable time-interval schedules with adults, adolescents, and children (1970a, 1971b, 1972b, 1973f, 1973g).

The adult version of *Onomatopoeia and Images* (Khatena & Torrance, 1973) presents 10 onomatopoeic word stimuli four times over fixed intervals of 15 seconds between the presentation of one word and the next, whereas the children's version presents 5 onomatopoeic word stimuli in the same multiple-presentation format with fixed intervals of 30 seconds between the presentation of each onomatopoeic word. The repeated presentation of onomatopoeic verbal stimuli to fixed time intervals with recorded encouragement from a narrator to be imaginative and produce original verbal images served as the experimental variable of press. The measures were administered to groups of college adults, adolescents, and children respectively.

The results of the study with adult subjects showed that the quality of original verbal images improved with each repetition and appeared to be best on the third and fourth presentations of onomatopoeic word stimuli (Khatena, 1970a). In the same study, another group of college adults were administered the adult versions of both *Sounds and Images* and *Onomatopoeia and Images* (Khatena & Torrance, 1973). The former is a measure of verbal originality that presents four sound stimuli three times at fixed intervals of 15 seconds between each sound stimuli presented and the next; the latter presents onomatopoeic word stimuli four times at fixed time intervals of 15 seconds between each onomatopoeic word and the next. The subjects were identified by their past achievements and by the results of several measures of creativity, like the *Torrance Tests of Creative Thinking* (Torrance, 1966, 1974b) and the *Remote Associates Test* (Mednick &

128

Mednick, 1967). The results of the study also showed the same progressive gains on both measures; the best performance was on the third presentation.

Both adolescents (12 subjects to 15 years old) and children (subjects 8 to 11 years old) showed similar progressive gains for the four presentations of onomatopoeic word stimuli at fixed intervals of 30 seconds; the greatest gains were in imaginative performance occurring between the first and second presentations (Khatena, 1973g).

In the next three studies (Khatena, 1971a, 1972b, 1973f), recorded texts of *Onomatopoeia and Images* were modified in the adult version to include variable time intervals of 5, 10, and 15 seconds for each of the four presentations with unlimited time; in the children's version, there were time intervals of 10, 20, and 30 seconds with unlimited time. These measures were presented to several groups of adults, children, and adolescents who were identified as high, moderate, and low creatives through their self-perceptions—for adults the measure used was *Something About Myself* (Khatena & Torrance, 1976a, 1976b); for children the measure used was *Sounds and Images* (Khatena & Torrance, 1973).

The results of the study with adults (Khatena, 1973f) showed that highly creative subjects when given 15 seconds time press in the third presentation produced superior original verbal images as compared to the moderate and low creatives. However, given unlimited time in the fourth presentation, only high creative men maintain their superiority over moderate and low creative men and women although still doing better than low creative women.

The study with adolescents (Khatena, 1971a) showed high creatives as producing better original verbal images when given as much time as they needed in the fourth presentation. In addition, they produced just as well if not better than their moderate and low creative peers when restricted by the time deadlines (10, 20, and 30 seconds) in the first three presentations.

A third study with children (Khatena, 1972b) showed high creatives as producing superior original verbal images as compared to moderate and low creatives when the time deadline was not so acute as in the 30-second interval of the third presentation or when the time interval was removed in the fourth presentation. Further, it was found that high creative boys and girls and low creative girls did better when given as much time as they needed than when the time interval was 10 seconds, whereas, moderate creative boys and low creative boys and girls did just as poorly when greatly pressed for time as when they were relieved of it. When time press was stringent, all groups were badly affected; some time press was necessary for high creative boys and girls, but less time press was necessary for the rest.

In summary, the results of the five studies indicate that (1) when the time interval is fixed, the imagination of adult subjects functions effectively to produce original verbal images given sufficient warm-up and (2) the imagination of children and adolescents is more rapidly sensitized to produce original verbal images. Further, when the time interval is varied and subjects are identified as high, moderate, and low creatives, the imagination of high-creative adults and children operates best in producing original verbal images when given moderate time deadlines, whereas the imagination of high-creative adolescents functions best when given as much time as needed.

With college students as subjects, Khatena (1978d) explored the effects of fixed time press versus freedom from time press on the production of analogies as well as the production of original verbal images as it relates to time/no time press in four presentations. Khatena (1977c) developed a scoring guide for creative analogies and images that was used in this study so that responses to onomatopoeic word stimuli were scored for production of personal, direct, symbolic, and fantasy analogies as well as for simple and complex image patterns on a scale of credits ranging from 0 to 160 points for the adult version of the measure. Responses were also scored by the standard procedure for scoring original verbal images according to the principle of statistical infrequency (Khatena & Torrance, 1973). The findings of this study showed that (1) more original verbal images were produced by college adults in untimed conditions; (2) originality increased and peaked in the third presentation, with a small decrease in the fourth presentation; and (3) although the untimed condition had significant influence on the complexity of creative image production, it did not have significant influence on the production of creative analogies.

DEVELOPMENTAL PATTERNS IN ORIGINAL VERBAL IMAGES AND ANALOGIES

Development of creative thinking abilities as related to originality and production of verbal images was studied by using *Onomatopoeia and Images* and *Sounds and Images* with both the general population and special groups of children that included the deaf, blind, and gifted.

Briefly, two cross-sectional studies explored the production of original verbal images by children 8 to 19 years old (Khatena, 1971b) and 9 to 19 years old (Khatena, 1972a) and showed that children at age 9 and 10 produced less original verbal images with some recovery at age 11. This found support in a longitudinal study (Khatena & Fisher, 1974) of a group of 8-year-olds over a four-year period.

Several studies were also done with deaf and blind children as subjects. One study on the production of original verbal images by deaf and hearing children between the ages of 10 and 19 (Johnson & Khatena, 1975) found that hearing children produced significantly more original verbal images than deaf children and that, although hearing children did not show any clear improvement as they grew older, deaf children showed significant improvement with age. Another study (R. A. Johnson, 1975) attempted to assess the differential effects of training deaf subjects the denotative meaning of the onomatopoeic words of the test because it was hypothesized that familiarity with onomatopoeic words was a function of age, which would account, in part, for the significantly higher originality scores of older deaf children. The results of the study showed that subjects who were taught the onomatopoeic words obtained significantly higher originality scores than those who had not been so taught.

A third study explored whether blind adolescents are more creative relative to the production of original verbal images than sighted adolescents when critical variables, such as intelligence scores, are taken into account (R. A. Johnson, 1977). Both *Sounds and Images* and *Onomatopoeia and Images* were individually administered to about an equal number of low-ability blind and sighted adolescents who were unable to record or spell their own responses. It was found that blind adolescents produced more original verbal images. It was also found that adolescents of high intelligence produced more original verbal images than their counterparts of moderate and low intelligence.

In addition to these studies on the production of original verbal images, several studies (Khatena, 1972c, 1973d, 1977a) explored the production of personal analogy, direct analogy, symbolic analogy, and fantasy analogy with simple and complex image structure by children, adolescents, and adults. The measure used was *Onomatopoeia and Images;* the responses were scored for analogies and image structure.

Khatena (1972c) engaged in a descriptive study of a group of 141 high-original men and women selected from a population of 1000 subjects who were attending colleges or universities in many parts of the country. The subjects' verbal responses were analyzed in terms of the four analogy categories (personal, direct, symbolic, and fantasy), which were further differentiated as simple or complex images. The results showed that high original men and women significantly preferred to use the direct analogy form and simple rather than complex image structure.

A second descriptive study (Khatena, 1973d) explored the production of analogies and images by 122 high-original boys and 126 high-original girls selected from a group of 598 boys and 963 girls between the ages of 8 and 19 who attended schools in West Virginia, Georgia, and Ohio. Their responses were also categorized in terms of the four analogy categories and differentiated by image structure. Analysis of their responses showed that most of the analogies produced were in the direct analogy form; no symbolic analogies were produced. It was also found that both boys and girls at all age levels between 8 and 19 years produced the direct simple image analogy most frequently, with boys producing somewhat more complex images than girls. The evidence also suggested that as children grow older they tend to produce less simple and more complex direct analogies, with 12-year-old boys and 13-year-old girls producing the complex image most frequently and with a corresponding reduction in the production of the simple image. Further, it was found that the production of both the simple and complex image was least and most frequent for boys at the ages of 9 and 12 respectively; for the girls at the ages of 8 and 13 respectively.

The evidence of these two studies suggest that high-original children, like high-original adults, show a significant preference for the direct analogy as the main creative thinking operation; that the absence of symbolic analogies in children's analogy-image production finds support in Jean Piaget's cognitive development theory structure; that the infrequent use of fantasy analogy by both adults and children may be the result of insufficient exercise and inadequate reinforcement of these kinds of thinking operations; and that there is an overemphasis on objectively dealing with the world around us and, what is more, an undeveloped disposition for what Coleridge has required of his readers, "a willing suspension of disbelief."

Here are examples of the creative analogies produced by these original adults and children in response to the onomatopoeic words (shown in parentheses) that illustrate the function of the imagination: the adult group produced such analogies as: "staccato movement in Mozart" (ouch), "essence of soul" (murmur), "a mesh of fishhooks" (jingle), "eyelids of a unicorn" (whisp), "my life on a humid sweltering day" (flop), "an anvil falling from a balloon" (zoom), "Peter at the third cock's crow" (stutter), "splashing hot water on cold feet" (fizzy); the children's group produced such analogies as: "a bird landing heavily on her nest" (buzz), "a tree growing out of its bark" (moan), "a handful of fingernails scratching on a blackboard" (groan), "violin on a dog's nerves" (ouch), "eraser tearing paper by mistake" (groan), "barber cutting a man's hair fast" (jingle), "a frightened lizard" (zoom), "a witch melting" (fizzy).

PHYSIOLOGICAL CORRELATES OF ORIGINAL VERBAL IMAGES

Bugelski (1970) has explained that a resurgence of interest in imagery by American psychology may be traced to the view that images are indirect reactivations of earlier sensory or perceptual activity rather than the outcome of mental mechanisms at work. Holt (1964) has indicated that an obvious feature of imagery lies in its sensory referents and, drawing from definitions given by dictionaries of psychology, Drever (1963) describes imagery as a revived sense experience in the absence of sensory stimulation.

Lindauer's (1972) survey on sensory correlates of imagery and their evoking stimuli suggests that, although sensory aspects of imagery are an essential phenomenological feature of imaging, studies of the individual differences of sensory imagery are insufficiently understood and that, relative to the role of sensory imagery in learning, they are little considered. This discussion also focuses attention on several major conclusions: that current studies indicate an

132   CREATIVE IMAGINATION IMAGERY

overall reliance on the visual and auditory sense modalities when it is the gustatory, tactile, and olfactory sense modalities (especially in recall) that should receive greater emphasis; that better recall is not necessarily dependent on any one particular sensory mode; that there are qualitative differences among the senses in arousal and recall of imagery that go beyond mere quantification of their general nature and functioning; that different degrees of imagery for sensory materials may be functionally equivalent; and that other important variables—like type of learning paradigm used, organizational factors, the concrete-abstract attribute of meaning, and sex differences, with emphasis on individual differences in the study of learning and imagery—should receive attention in future research.

A viable direction for research relates to creativity, imagery, and various modalities. Schmeidler (1965), using a quantifiable version of Francis Galton's original breakfast-table questionnaire (1880), found low positive correlation between imagery scores and a measure of creativity; Leonard and Lindauer (1973) found a significant correlation between participation in aesthetic activities (relative to English, art, music, and theater) and imagery arousal (as measured by self-rating scales) to ease and vividness of imagery produced in response to 45 sensory words equally distributed in five sense modalities (i.e., vision, sound, touch, taste, and smell). In addition, imagery scores differentiated aesthetic participation scores.

However, little has been done to investigate creative self-perceptions, originality, and imagery production as they relate to the functions of the several sense modalities. Of particular note are two studies, one that explored the relationship between vividness of imagery production and creative self-perceptions (Khatena, 1975d) and a second that explored the use that college adults—identified as high, moderate, and low originals—make of the visual, auditory, cutaneous, gustatory, olfactory, and organic sense modalities in their production of original verbal images (Khatena, 1976d).

In Khatena's 1975d study, 107 college adults were administered three measures concurrently: (1) *Betts QMI Vividness of Imagery Scale* (Sheehan, 1967; White et al., 1977), (2) *Something About Myself,* and (3) *What Kind of Person Are You?* The last two are the components of the *Khatena-Torrance Creative Perception Inventory* (Khatena & Torrance, 1976a, 1976b).

The 7-point scale of the *Betts Questionnaire upon Mental Imagery* was modified into a 5-point rating scale, the *Betts QMI Vividness of Imagery Scale,* by omitting two intermediate categories for ease of recording responses directly on IBM computer cards, scoring, and analyzing the data. It was felt that little or no loss in discriminatory power would follow. Subjects were asked to rate the vividness of the image produced to each of 35 items, 5 in each of the sense modalities by reference to the following scale: perfectly clear and as vivid as the actual experience (1); moderately clear and vivid (2); not clear or vivid, but recognizable (3); so vague and dim as to be hardly discernible (4); and no image present at all, you only know that you are thinking of the object (5).

An example of 1 item in each of the 7 image categories is as follows: the exact contour of face, head, shoulders, and body (visual); the whistle of a locomotive (auditory); sand (cutaneous); running upstairs (kinesthetic); salt (gustatory); new leather (olfactory); and a sore throat (organic). The ratings of each set of 5 items were added and averaged to give 7 mean-score ratings relative to the 7 sense modalities, and ratings of all 35 items were added and averaged to give a mean vividness-of-imagery index.

Scores on the two perception measures, *Something About Myself* and *What Kind of Person Are You?* (Khatena & Torrance, 1976a, 1976b) were correlated with scores on the seven subscales and total scores of the *Betts QMI Vividness of Imagery Scale*. Significant *rs* were found between the visual and cutaneous sense modalities and creative self-perceptions on both measures and between the auditory dimension and creative self-perceptions on *Something About Myself*. Further, the vividness-of-imagery index and the creative self-perception index as derived from the total scores of the *Betts QMI Vividness of Imagery Scale* and *Something About Myself* measures were also significantly correlated.

A second analysis of the data divided subjects according to their total scores on the *Betts QMI Vividness of Imagery Scale* into three groups: vivid imagers, moderate imagers, and weak imagers. Means and SDs of their creative self-perception scores on both measures were obtained. It was found that mean creative self-perception scores on the *What Kind of Person Are You?* of vivid imagers were somewhat higher than those of the moderate and weak imagers, with the greatest and least variance in creative self-perception mean scores for the vivid and moderate imagers. Creative self-perception mean scores on *Something About Myself* showed a similar pattern for vivid, moderate, and weak imagers. The same pattern in the variance was also found. However, this information was not found to be significant even though tentative clues were offered by it.

Khatena's 1976a study explores experimentally the use that college men and women identified as high moderate and low originals make of visual, auditory, cutaneous, kinesthetic, gustatory, olfactory, and organic sense modalities in their production of original verbal images. The study also attempts to find out if by exposing these subjects to various sound stimuli with instructions to produce imagination imagery mental sets would be created that would cause the subjects to make greater use of the auditory sense modality in their production of original verbal images. In addition, the warm-up effects of such exposure on originality scores were examined.

In this experiment, 77 college adults (33 men and 44 women) were randomly assigned to two treatment groups. Controls were given a 40-minute break; experimentals remained in the room and were given a set of instructions and some practice in rating the vividness of auditory images they produced. As an example, they were given the statement, "an airplane zooming above," and were asked to image with their mind's ear and rate the vividness of the image on a 5-point scale. This was followed by 10 items with similar instructions and exercises: "crashing of waves against rocks," "a bomb explosion," "hammering on metal," "bowling," "dripping water," "howling of the wind," "beat of the drum," "sawing wood," "cork popping," and "chime of a clock."

Sounds and Images, a measure of verbal originality described earlier, was administered to the subjects. The three repetitions of a group of four recorded audio effects interspersed with narrated instructions that forced the listener to reject commonplace associations for free-wheeling and imaginative ideas served as the independent variable. Subjects were instructed to apply the prior practice in rating the vividness of their auditory images to produce original verbal images by using the auditory sense modality. The exercise on *Sounds and Images* took 20 minutes. All subjects of the two treatment groups were assembled and administered Form 2A of *Onomatopoeia and Images* (see p. 81). Verbal images produced were scored according to the published scoring guide for originality as well as for the seven sense modality categories of the *Betts QMI Vividness of Imagery Scale* (Sheehan, 1967); however, in analyzing this data, it was found necessary to place the images produced into categories of visual, auditory, organic, visual-auditory, and two or three sense modalities combined as well as to categorize those images that fell into the symbolic dimension.

Verbal images produced on *Onomatopoeia and Images* were scored for originality, and use of various sense modalities. The results for originality showed no significant differences in mean originality scores owing to training, sex, or training × sex. The results for the various sense modalities showed that there were no significant differences in scores owing to training, originality level, training × originality level, and training × originality level × sense modality. However, significant differences in means were found for the use of the several sense modalities (visual, auditory, visual-auditory, combined two modalities, more than two modalities combined, and those in the symbolic dimension) and for interaction effects of level × sense modality.

Here are a few examples of the images produced with reference to onomatopoeic stimulus and sense modality:

Visual—wrinkled (meander), melting butter (ooze).
Auditory—thunder (rumble), soft echoing vibrations (moan).
Visual-auditory—raindrop to an ant (moan), swarm of bugs (crackle).
Organic—indigestion (rumble), excitement (buzz).
Kinesthetic-cutaneous—squeezing jello in your palm (ooze).
Visual-organic—lazy enjoyment (meander).
Visual-auditory-organic—angry throat (moan).
Visual-auditory-kinesthetic—clash of horns when two bulls fight (rumble).

Generally it was found that the visual, auditory, visual-auditory, two modalities combined, and two or three sense modalities combined were used in the production of verbal images.

AUTONOMY OF IMAGERY AND ORIGINALITY

Following the studies of Jaensch (1930) on eidetic imagery, autonomy of imagery was differentiated by R. Gordon (1962). She distinguished between autonomous and controlled imagery: autonomous imagery tends to take its own course and is independent of other mental functions, controlled imagery is integrated into the total personality. In a study on factors associated with the formation of national stereotypes, R. Gordon (1949) used a test she developed, the *Gordon Test of Visual Imagery Control*. This measure called for a yes, no, or unsure response to 12 questions, 4 of which, are (R. Gordon cited in Richardson, 1969, pp. 155–156):

1. Can you see a car standing in the road in front of a house?
2. Can you see it in color?
3. Can you now see the same car lying upside down?
4. Can you see it get out of control and crash through a house?

A positive response fetched 1 point, whereas a negative response received 0 credit. R. Gordon categorized subjects who scored 12 points as controlled imagers and those who scored 11 points or less as autonomous imagers. The findings of this study showed that subjects whose imagery was autonomous produced conventional stereotyped images in response to national stimulus words, like Englishman or Chinese, owing to their experiences earlier in life than the less stereotyped images of subjects whose imagery was controlled. She also found (Gordon, 1950) no significant mean differences in the reaction scores of neurotics with autonomous imagery versus neurotics with controlled imagery as to the reversal rate (normal, fast, or slow) of a Necker cube although significant differences were found when individual scores were analyzed. Another study (Costello 1957) showed that dysthymics and hysterics when compared with normals were relatively just as autonomous in imagery, with dysthymics having vivid, hysterics having weak, and normals having either vivid or weak autonomous imagery.

In McKellar's discussion of imagination imagery (1957) and autonomy, imagery, and dissociation (1977), autonomy of imagery is stated as fundamental and central to hypnagogic imagery, where images appear to follow their own course independent of the person experiencing them. However, such imagery will often surprise the experiencer by their highly creative or unreproductive character. This is much like Coleridge's experience of imagination imagery immediately before and during the composition of "Kubla Khan." Another instance is the cinematographic imagery of Enid Blyton relative to the occurrence of her ideas for the Noddy stories:

I shut my eyes for a few minutes with my portable typewriter on my knee. I make my mind a blank and wait–and then, as clearly as I would see real children, my characters stand before me in my mind's eye. . . . The story enacted almost as if I had a private cinema screen there. . . . I don't know what is going to happen. I am in the happy position of being able to write a story and read it for the first time at one and the same moment. . . . Sometimes a character makes a joke, a really funny one that makes me laugh as I type it on my paper and I think "Well, I couldn't have thought of that myself in a hundred years!" and then I think: "Well who did think of it?" (Stone, 1974, p. 209)

However, until Khatena's studies (1975c, 1976a, 1978o) there had been no scientific study of autonomy of imagery as it related to variables of creativity. This became the occasion of Khatena's studies on the subject, one of which also related to the use of sense modalities.

The first study (Khatena, 1975c) explored the relationship between autonomous imagery and creative self-perceptions of college adults who were given the *Gordon Test of Visual Imagery Control* and *Something About Myself.* For this study the scoring procedure of the Gordon scale was modified so that imagery was classified as less autonomous (high controlled: 12 to 9 points), moderately autonomous (controlled: 8 to 5 points), and more autonomous (low controlled: 4 to 1 point). The creative self-perception measure was scored as described earlier: 1 point was awarded to each positive response, with scores ranging from 0 to 50. The results showed that more autonomous imagers obtained higher mean creative perception scores than moderately and less autonomous imagers, and moderately autonomous imagers obtained higher scores on creative perception than less autonomous imagers.

The second study (Khatena, 1976a) explored the relationship of autonomy of imagery and production of original verbal images. In this study, the Gordon scale and *Onomatopoeia and Images* were the two measures used. Details of the scoring of both these measures have already been described. Here, there was one modification made in the Gordon scale because two thirds of the 90 college adults of this study fell into the less autonomous or high controlled imagery category, they were further divided into two subgroups within this category, namely, High Controlled Group 1 (12 and 11 points) and High Control Group 2 (10 and 9 points), and the remaining one third fell into the moderately autonomous or controlled category (8 to 5 points)—no subjects scored 4 or below for inclusion in the more autonomous imagery category. The results of Khatena's studies showed that moderately autonomous imagers produced significantly more original verbal images than imagers of the two high controlled groups.

Khatena's 1976d study found that college adults most frequently tend to use visual, auditory, or the visual and auditory senses combined in producing original verbal images, and they show a preference for multiple sense modalities (i.e., the combining of two or more senses). This suggested a third study to Khatena (1978a) that explored the use of single sense modality versus multiple sense modalities in the production of original verbal images as related to image autonomy level. In this study, 72 college adults were administered *Onomatopoeia and Images* and the Gordon scale. Scores on the Gordon scale range from 0 to 12; because none of the subjects scored below 5, they were divided into moderately autonomous or controlled (8 to 5 points) and less autonomous or high controlled (12 to 9 points) as in the Khatena, 1975c study. Verbal images produced in response to onomatopoeic words were analyzed for seven sense modalities (i.e., visual, auditory, cutaneous, kinesthetic, gustatory, olfactory, and organic). However, most images produced were of the visual, auditory, or the combined visual and auditory modalities. For example, in response to "meander," the verbal image "stream" was produced. This shows the use of a single sense modality (visual) as distinct from "a dog sniffing around in the morning" (visual-olfactory) or "walking on clouds" (visual-kinesthetic) where use is made of multiple sense modalities. Analysis of the data showed that the two groups of imagers produced original verbal images using multiple sense modalities more frequently than a single sense modality. However, autonomy of imagery does not appear to influence the use of single or multiple sense modalities in the production of original verbal images, and the findings concerning the frequent use of the visual, auditory, and the visual-auditory sense modalities combined are consistent with those of the 1975c study.

CONCLUSIONS

This chapter attempts to capture some of the essence of the nature and function of the creative imagination. For the most part, studies on imagination imagery as activated by creative energy are relatively few. One reason for this can be traced to the difficulty of measuring imagination imagery and its creative correlates. This has tended to move measures away from self-report instruments to those that require the production of images that are closely allied to projective techniques. The instruments found to be valuable in the study of creative imagination imagery comprise the two components of *Thinking Creatively with Sounds and Words*. These two measures have been used in the study of stimulating creative imagination, the effects of time press, developmental patterns (including those with adolescents and deaf and blind children), physiological correlates of imagery, and autonomy of imagery.

By using several creative thinking approaches to stimulate the creative imagination, important implications for productive learning were discovered. The function of stress in productive work affects people differently at different age levels and should be taken into account in the learning situation. The decrease in children's productivity of creative imagination imagery and analogy at about the ages of 9 and 11 is consistent with Torrance's findings of the fourth-grade slump in creative thinking abilities; a similar drop appears to occur in children's eidetic imagery (Richardson, 1969). These factors led Gowan (1978a) to raise the following question: "Can this be due to a transfer from the right hemisphere processing of images to the left hemisphere?" This ought to alert us to prepare to nurture creative imagination imagery more intensely during this and prior school-age periods of a child's life.

The studies of deaf and blind children gave some clues about their production of original verbal images as compared to other children with their senses intact. Some interesting speculation about the superiority of blind over sighted adolescents in the production of original verbal images are offered by R. A. Johnson (1977):

> The use of imagination and of creative thinking are critical for the blind. Objects and events that must be imagined are more original and unique than what one does not have to imagine. Too, the sighted adolescent, who is already familiar with many of the stimulus objects in the verbal originality tasks, may search the environment for common cues which trigger common responses probably more statistically infrequent.
>
> A second possible explanation for the apparent superiority of the blind adolescent concerns the conformity issue. In order to be creative, one must risk being labelled different. Perhaps, the blind adolescent has received more encouragement for participation in self-initiated learning activities, and in general is more independent. (p. 10)

The findings about the use of the senses of hearing, sight, hearing and sight, and two or more of the other senses combined in the production of creative imagination imagery by high originals offer clues to the use of these sense modalities for more effective learning communication and provide interesting implications for the study of special groups and their unique input-output sensory patterns. Autonomy of imagery offers an unusual correlate for identification of the creative imaginative thinker and possibly a different approach to measurement of the creative personality.

Of major concern should be the application of some of these findings to encourage gifted students to become more creative. The thinking strategies suggested apply both to cognitive and affective frames of reference in whose interplay the original emerges. Gifted children must also learn about incubation because it allows ferment and has an autonomy—operating at speeds and levels beyond measurement—to generate insightful images that lend themselves to the fruitful solutions of problems. Autonomy of imagery, where the creative process operates to produce images that have a life of their own, must also become a part of the mental equipment of gifted students. An acute awareness of the world through as many senses as possible can only lead to greater dimensions of creative thinking and imaging. A gifted child who can achieve this is at a decided advantage. Details of the application of these principles to encourage gifted students to be creative are to be found in two publications by the author: *Teaching Gifted Children To Use Creative Imagination Imagery* (Khatena, 1979c) and *Creative Imagination Imagery Actionbook* (Khatena, 1980).

5

DEVELOPMENT
OF
INTELLECT
AND
CREATIVITY

OVERVIEW

We now turn to approaches to the study of the intellect as it is affected by age. These have centered on the psychometric, developmental stage, and systems approaches. Development is considered as continuous and discontinuous. The concept of continuity in growth is derived from the mental testing movement and pivots largely on the study of intelligence and, more recently on the study of creativity. Development as discontinuous is discussed in terms of both the Erikson-Piaget-Gowan developmental stage theory and Land's transformation theory. Attention is also paid to thought on sociocultural effects on the creative development of geniuses in their formative years and some of the educational implications of these effects. The chapter concludes with some comment on the relationships of the approaches discussed.

CHAPTER OUTLINE

141

INTRODUCTION

Although much has been written about the development of the intellect, it has mainly referred to the general population. Relatively little has been done to generate information regarding developmental patterns of the gifted intellect. The works of Lewis M. Terman and his associates on the gifted provide the single best source of information on the subject. Much of the information on the developmental aspects of intellectual functioning relates to general intelligence and its factor components, which are mainly derived from the *Stanford-Binet,* Wechsler scales, and like measures of intelligence. Although Guilford (1967) discusses intellectual development relative to the abilities identified through the factor analysis of L. L. Thurstone and T. Kelley (i.e., the relevance of their findings to the abilities of his structure of intellect model, even though the model's developmental correlates, in themselves, have not been systematically investigated), nearly nothing has been done to study the developmental patterns of the complex intellectual abilities of the gifted.

Approaches to the study of intellectual development in the general population and the gifed are categorized as quantitative (having roots in measurement) and qualitative (having roots in developmental stage theory). The quantitative approach can be traced to the construction and use of the *Stanford-Binet* in the 1920s, and, as it relates to the gifted, to the application of the measure in Terman's *Genetic Studies of Genius.* To this may be added those tests that used other measures of intellectual functions, especially the Wechsler scales. Interest in finding information about the developmental patterns of creative thinking abilities can be traced to the measures developed by E. P. Torrance, J. Khatena, and their associates. The qualitative approach to the nature of the intellect as it relates to age has its roots in Jean Piaget's developmental stages and, more recently, in Gowan's model and Land's model with reference to creativity. On the one hand, development of the intellect is conceived as continuous; on the other hand, it is conceived as discontinuous. The picture that emerges from all these contributions is relatively sketchy and to some extent confusing and even incomplete. This can, in part, be attributed to the expanded concept of intellect and a number of other variables, for instance, whether intelligence is predetermined or subject to change, the effects of a changing environment, the appropriateness of test items in a measure for all age levels, sampling and related psychometric problems, and, in some ways, to the lack of empirical study and the generally speculative nature of developmental stage theory.

Development is the product of maturation and nurture. Maturation is the unfolding of a design that is essentially innate, and there is nothing external that has the power to influence it; nurture is the intervention of the environment (physical, educational, social, etc.) as it interacts with innate patterns to facilitate its fullest expression. The term growth is used to describe the measurement of development and is concerned with increment and decrement, whereas maturity indicates the attainment or completion of a particular stage of development and a readiness for the next stage (Olson, 1959).

These terms not only refer to the quantitative changes that are expected to take place with the increase in chronological age, where growth (the measured consequences of these changes) is regarded as continuous, but also to qualitative changes that are expected to take place in an individual as growth, seen as discontinous, is the attainment of higher levels of maturity as the individual passes or makes the leap from one sequence of development to the next and higher level so that the sequence recurs. Although the view of intellectual development as continuous derives its logic and force from psychometrics, the view of development as discontinuous derives its rationale and energy from observation, the clinic, and philosophical speculation.

DEVELOPMENT AS CONTINUOUS

As a starting point for regarding development as continuous, we need to go to the work of Terman and his associates with the *Stanford-Binet,* the *Concept Mastery Test* (a measure of intelligence constructed by Terman for use with high school students), and his studies of gifted children. The measures were used to identify precocious children from grades 3 to 8 and to study their intellectual growth, behavior, and personality characteristics as they increased in chronological age to midlife. A portrait of the Terman gifted group is given in chapter 1. When compared to the general population, Terman's gifted group continued to maintain their intellectual superiority and, with few exceptions, the superior child becomes the superior adult (Oden, 1968). In the 12-year internal between the two administrations of the *Concept Mastery Test* to 768 of his gifted subjects (422 men and 346 women), Terman found that they actually increased their scores in adulthood, contrary to the notion of "early ripe, early rot" (Bayley & Oden, 1955).

Mental growth takes place gradually and continuously from birth to maturity, but at what age this growth ceases is debatable. For instance, the slowing down in rate of growth that takes place during the early teens for most mental functions reaches its peak in the middle twenties (Bayley, 1949; Wechsler, 1958). But evidence from the Harvard Growth Studies show intellectual gains up to nearly 30 years of age, 2% of which are found to take place after the age of 21 or 22. As this relates to the 768 gifted whose mental growth was measured longitudinally by the *Concept Mastery Test* (a measure that calls for a knowledge of symbols and abstractions and the ability to use these relations to each other), Bayley and Oden (1955) see in the gains made on the test implications that this kind of knowledge and ability improves in superior adults, at least through 50 years of age. Owen's longitudinal study (1953) provides corroborating evidence.

The conflicting evidence about the amount of decrement and the time when this sets in has been attributed to the nature of the measures used (Bayley & Oden, 1955) and the instrument's lack of power to differentiate changing abilities at the upper levels of intelligence (Shock, 1951). The relationship between age and scores on a measure of general intelligence appears to be one of gradual but accelerating decline (Jones & Conrad, 1933). Age exerts a differential effect on various mental functions, for instance, vocabulary scores are found to be higher at age 60 than at 20, but nonverbal reasoning scores appear to decline substantially by age 50 (Foulds & Raven, 1948). Not all intellectual functions decline with age, and the abilities for knowing, vocabulary and information show continuous increase into later adult years. All of this is supported in several studies (Berkowitz, 1953; Corsini & Fassett, 1953; Owens, 1953). Wechsler (1950) discusses the growth of children's intelligence and indicates that various levels of mental maturity are reached by children at different periods of their lives, for instance, the attainment of the mental maturity of 15-year-olds can vary between 5 years 6 months to 15 years 6 months. Mental growth relating to digit span, for example, shows rapid increase to age 11 and little thereafter, whereas memory ability improves rapidly to age 14 and vocabulary shows a more gradual and steady development. Generally, growth curves for most intellectual abilities resemble the vocabulary growth curve, characterized by a rapid rise in test scores during the first few years and gradually slowing down as age 15 is reached— apart from a brief spurt occurring between the ages of 10 and 12. An exception to this is the age curve for memory span of digits where the line connecting mean scores at successive age levels consists of a series of risers connected by plateaus of varying breadths, which suggest that growth is discontinuous for some mental abilities (Wechsler, 1950). The problem of changes in intelligence with age is summed up by Wechsler (1958):

> *General intelligence as evaluated by pragmatic criteria appears to maintain itself unimpaired over a much greater portion of adult life and to decline at a much slower rate than do the mental abilities by which it is inevitably measured. Our general answers have been that sheer ability enters as only one of several factors of intelligence, that factors like drive, interest and motivation also operate in varying degrees as determinants and that learned responses, stored information and general experience may substitute for or better serve the individual than original aptitude. To these may be added the fact that at different ages different skills or abilities contribute varying amounts of whatever is needed for effective performance. (p. 142)*

Guilford (1967) observes that the age at which an individual reaches the maximum score on a measure of intelligence varies from test to test and that, because we cannot be sure if the ceiling of a test is high enough to measure higher levels of ability or abilities, we really do not know if the test actually measures the maximum of an average person. Further, just because the average reaches a maximum level, it does not mean that all members of the population cease to grow at that age. In fact, the growth curve of each individual is unique because within the context of upward development there may occur periods of little or rapid change relative to different rates of development in different intellectual abilities. These findings have important implications for the gifted, whose mental growth curve can be expected to show far more idiosyncratic features than those of the general population.

Hunt (1964) cites W. Johannsen, the Danish geneticist, as making a distinction between the genotype (inherited) intelligence of an individual which cannot be measured, and the phenotype (innate) intelligence, which interacts with various circumstances and experiences that can be directly observed and measured. Hebb (1949) makes a similar observation in terms of two kinds of intelligence: *Intelligence A* or the capacity for development and *Intelligence B* or the product of *Intelligence A* interacting with the environment, which is measured, however imperfectly, by tests. Both recognize the great importance of experience in the development of innate potential.

For a model of intelligence that incorporates the interactive elements of innate ability and environment, we may have to go to the structure of intellect (Guilford, 1967). The five mental operations (cognitive, memory, convergent production, divergent production, and evaluation) are predetermined and designed to act on an information dimension whose roots lie in the child's environment and comprise contents-times-products interaction. The development of intelligence occurs as a result of interactions between these categories and the five hereditary determined operations.

In his development, the child learns how to bring together the three aspects as represented by the three parameters of the structure of intellect in the various combinations, each combination being unique. How well any particular combination develops depends upon how much and how effectively he exercises that combination, and these circumstances depend upon what his environment offers to him and the needs he has for coping with these offerings. Individuals differ with respect to how much they have exercised each kind of combination, by necessity or by incidental involvement. (Guilford, 1967, p. 417)

Guilford rejects the Garret hypothesis (1946) that abilities found by factor analysis are differentiated from a single general intellectual ability prevailing in infancy and early childhood in favor of many abilities relative to the structure of intellect. Of course, he is uncertain as to how extensively this model does apply at early age levels because it is difficult to produce tests appropriate to structure of intellect factors for those age levels and to determine if the factors are morphologically the same as those found for adolescents and adults.

All in all, there are no direct studies of either the general population or the gifted on the rate of growth of abilities related to the structure of intellect. However, Guilford (1967) cites the Stott and Ball study (1963) that identifies 31 intellectual and 5 psychomotor factors (but no g factor) by analyzing items from a number of test batteries for infant and preschool children, and he cautiously attempts to relate these factors to structure of intellect categories. The 31 factors, he says, represent the five operation categories—four content categories and five of the six product categories (the category of classes is missing).

One dimension of the structure of intellect, divergent production, has stirred up considerable interest and has led to a number of studies on the creative development of American children as measured by the *Torrance Tests of Creative Thinking* (Torrance, 1966, 1974b). What has emerged from cross-sectional studies is a generalized developmental curve that shows decrements in creative thinking just before entry into grade 1 and in about grades 4, 7, and 12, with growth peaks occurring between grades 3 and 4 and again in about grade 11 (Andrews, 1930; Torrance, 1962a, 1963, 1965c, 1967b). Of the several drops in creativity, the worst seems to occur at about the fourth grade or at age 9; this is often termed the fourth-grade slump in creative thinking abilities. It has been observed that it is at this time that children experience the greatest amount of personality disturbances, behavior problems, learning difficulties, and the like. Torrance (1968) checked this by doing a longitudinal study with 100 children over a period of four years. What he found was corroborating evidence: on the average, slumps in fluency, flexibility, originality, and elaboration occur at the fourth-grade level. However, Torrance also found that, although 45% to 61% of the children showed decline, a few children did show increase in creative thinking abilities. In general, children were found to improve their scores in the fifth grade although the scores obtained were relatively lower than those in the third grade. These findings led him to explore this slump in creative thinking abilities in several other cultures to determine if a similar pattern existed (Torrance, 1967b). The evidence of this extensive study led him to conclude that, although development in some cultures is relatively continuous and in others there is little noticeable growth during the elementary school years, most cultures do show discontinuity in the development of creative thinking abilities. Generally, discontinuities in growth occur at the end of the third grade or at the beginning of the fourth grade although with some groups such discontinuities did not appear until the sixth grade. Torrance attributes the fall in creative thinking abilities to stress and the demands made on the children:

> *There are a number of indications that these discontinuities occur within a culture whenever children in that culture are confronted with new stresses and demands. When Christian missions and similar groups establish schools in underdeveloped areas, they apparently bring both a stimulating and disrupt-*

ing influence on development, producing discontinuities in creative development. (1976b, p. 301)

Several longitudinal studies on creative behavior dealing with short-range prediction (Torrance, 1963; Weisberg & Springer, 1961) and long-range prediction (Torrance, 1972b; Witt, 1971)—described in Chapter 1—attempted to determine the extent to which children identified as creative in their early years by the *Torrance Tests of Creative Thinking* would continue to show themselves as creatives 6 to 12 years later through their talented achievements or accomplishments. The information provided by the studies cited appear to have as their intent the validation of the Torrance measures rather than an exploration of the developmental aspects of creative potential. Therefore, they do not directly contribute to the discussion on the continuity of development. However, in Torrance's 12-year predictive study, reference is made to the fact that although originality on the *Torrance Tests of Creative Thinking* was a good predictor of creative achievement and aspiration for students in grades 9 through 12, it was not for those in grades 7 and 8. This was attributed, in part, to an expected slump in the students' creative thinking abilities. The information available on the rises and falls in creative thinking abilities—derived largely from cross-sectional studies and supplemented somewhat by longitudinal findings relating to children in the elementary school years—presents an incomplete picture of the developmental characteristics of creative potential. There still appears to be a need to study developmental patterns in creative thinking abilities longitudinally from childhood through adulthood.

In an attempt to find out if the same conditions applied to the production of original images, the children's versions (Form 1A and Form 1B) of *Onomatopoeia and Images* (Khatena & Torrance, 1973) were administered to 1365 children (680 boys and 685 girls) between the ages of 8 and 19. These children attended schools in Georgia, Ohio, and West Virginia. It was found that these children experienced two slump periods in their ability to produce original verbal images. This decrement manifested itself around the fourth- and fifth-grade levels or at the age of 9 or 10. The recovery that followed this drop was soon overtaken by another slump at the tenth-grade level or at age 15. Small sex and age fluctuations do not alter the basic pattern, and these findings are congruent with earlier research on the subject (Khatena, 1971b).

The earlier manual of *Sounds and Images* (Cunnington & Torrance, 1965) also includes some data on the fourth-grade slump as determined by Form 1 of the measure (now Form 1A), but a number of the Minnesota subjects at the third-grade level are not differentiated by sex. For the sake of comparison data, fourth-grade data for boys and girls were combined. The mean difference between the third and fourth grades was found to be highly significant. Consequently, a study designed to find out if the same developmental pattern occurs in the production of original verbal images was carried out (Khatena, 1972a). In this study, Form 1A and Form 1B of *Sounds and Images* (Khatena & Torrance, 1973) were administered to 665 children (352 boys and 313 girls) selected from several schools in West Virginia. It was found that girls experience a slump in ability to produce original verbal images in response to sound stimuli at 11 although this was not found to be statistically significant. At age 9, girls show lower means than at age 10. Boys seem to do better at age 9 but with increasing age the differences even out. Both boys and girls experience a spurt in their productivity at age 12 with a leveling off at the age levels that follow and reach their peak at ages 14 to 19.

These two studies of children's production of original verbal images generally indicate drops in children's originality especially in the upper elementary grades (grades 4 to 6) or between the ages of 9 to 11. When this was checked by a longitudinal study (Khatena & Fisher, 1974) using *Onomatopoeia and Images* to measure the production or original verbal images with a group of 8-year-olds over a 4-year period, it was found that loss in originality occurred in children between the ages of 9 and 10 or at about the fourth-grade level. There was some gain at the age of 11. These findings lend further support to Torrance's observations concerning the fourth-grade slump in creative thinking abilities.

DEVELOPMENT AS DISCONTINUOUS

Wechsler observed (1950) that the growth curve for the memory span of digits, unlike other growth curves (e.g., vocabulary and information), consists of a series of risers connected by plateaus of varying breadths. This may, in part, be due to units of measurement that are too large or insufficiently discrete or owing to certain mental abilities that are, contrary to current views, discontinuous functions so that increase or decrease can only occur by certain amounts or quanta. This discontinuity is in keeping with thought on the subject of growth in terms of developmental stages.

The seven ages of man perceived by Shakespeare about 400 years ago prefaces any discussion of developmental stages. Sigmund Freud talked about the five developmental periods of sexual libido nearly a century ago, and Maslow (1954), Piaget (1950), and Sullivan (1953) have all stated that there are qualitatively different developmental stages, each with different specific emphases. Piaget (1950) identified cognitive developmental stages; Erikson (1950) identified affective developmental stages; Kohlberg, Kohlberg & Mayer (1972) identified moral growth stages; and J. Simpson (1966) identified psychomotor stages. That the concept of developmental stages holds great importance for education today has been well expressed by Bailey (1971):

It seems to me that the most liberating and viable educational reforms of the next several years will come through the building of curricular and other educative activities around some of the developmental insights of men like Piaget, Bruner, Erikson, Bloom and Maslow. Although much separates these scholars in terms of analytic style and specific fields of concentration, they all seem to hold to the idea that human beings go through fairly discrete stages of development and that each stage calls for rather special educational treatment. And all of these men seem to be united in their belief that the maximization of human potential within the constraints of each life stage is the best way of preparing for succeeding stages. (p. 14)

Gowan (1972, 1974) attempts to combine Erik Erikson's affective stages and Jean Piaget's cognitive stages with his own on creativity, psychedelia, and illumination (extending the five stages of Piaget to eight), resulting in the Erikson-Piaget-Gowan periodic developmental stage chart (Table 2). Further, Gowan focuses attention on a periodicity of three that results in similarities between stages 1, 4, and 7, stages 2, 5, and 8, and stages 3, 6, and 9; reinforces

Table 2   The Erikson-Piaget-Gowan Periodic Developmental Stage Chart

Attentional Modes → Developmental Levels ↓		Latency 3 it, they The World	Identity 1 I, me The Ego	Creativity 2 thou The Other
Infant	ERIKSON (affective)	Trust vs. mistrust ①	Autonomy vs. shame and doubt ②	Initiative vs. guilt ③
	PIAGET (cognitive)	Sensorimotor vs. chaos	Preoperational vs. autism	Intuitive vs. immobilization
Youth	ERIKSON (affective)	Industry vs. inferiority ④	Identity vs. role diffusion ⑤	Intimacy vs. isolation ⑥
	PIAGET-GOWAN (cognitive)	Concrete operations vs. nonconservation	Formal operations vs. schizophrenia	Creativity vs. authoritarianism
Adult	ERICKSON (affective)	Generativitiy vs. stagnation ⑦	Ego-integrity vs. despair ⑧	(Agape-Love) ⑨
	GOWAN (cognitive)	Psychedelia vs. conventionalism	Illumination vs. senile depression	

Source: J. C. Gowan, *The Development of the Psychedelic Individual,* p. 51. Copyright © 1974 by J. C. Gowan. Reprinted by permission.

the concepts of discontinuity, succession, emergence, differentiation, and integration as components of escalation; deals with the significance of dysplasia, or malformation, in development as the splitting of cognitive and affective stage levels in malfunctioning individuals; and emphasizes self-actualization as escalation into higher developmental stages.

An individual goes through three stages of development, namely, latency, identity, and creativity, at each of the three levels of growth, namely, infant, youth, and adult. Herewith, is a paraphrase of Gowan's description (1972) of these developmental stages (Khatena, 1978c, p. 98–100):

1. The Latency Period *(Stages 1, 4, and 7)*

For the infant (0–1), this is the period when he gets to know the things around him, to experience the thing character of the world. As a youth (7–12) he begins to know things for their size, shape, form, and color and what one makes out of them. As an adult (16–40) he is concerned with others who are important to him such as children, their productions, art creations, and other "mental children."

Common to the infant, youth, and adult is his immersion in the world of senses. Things get done, changes occur, no self-consciousness is felt, very little time is left to assess feelings or to be concerned with the questions of "Who am I?". Accomplishments strengthen and prepare the person to search for his identity.

2. Identity *(Stages 2, 5, and 8)*

The infant, youth, and adult are concerned here with questions like "Who am I? Why do I exist? How am I in relation to others? What happens to me when I die? Will I be saved?" During these times the person searches within himself for answers, withdraws rather than returns, defies authority rather than obeys it, and "marches to the music of a different drum." At each stage, he tries to come to terms with himself: as an infant he searches for his identity, as a youth he redefines it in terms of the meaning of his life and death in the cosmos.

Others find it difficult to live with an individual passing through these stages—the infant with his negativism, and adolescent with his idealism, demand for independence and rebellion against authority both by his attitudes and actions. During this time of turning into himself and away from the world it is easy for him to believe that no one understands him, often spending too much time in self-examination, forgetting the real world outside himself leading to moodiness resulting from the discrepancy between what he wants to be and what he finds he can be and do.

3. Creativity *(Stages 3, 6, and 9)*

During stages 3 and 6, which deal with love, the person passes from love of self through love of parent of the opposite sex to generalized love of people of both sexes and to love of one person of the opposite sex. Stage 9 may very well exist where love is for all mankind given in the way of Buddah and Christ (Agape-Love).

Gowan sees love as required for creation both physically and mentally. That is why stages 3 and 6 are important: creativity first develops during stage 3 when a person gains control of his environment through affectional relations with the parent of the opposite sex such that "boys" who are affectionately close to their mothers and "girls" who are unusually close to their fathers, during 4 to 7 years, tend to become more creative than others of similar ability. It is during this period that warm affection given by the opposite-sex parent freely enlarges the bridge between the fantasy life and real world of the child.

Again in stage 6, adolescent creativity is normally enhanced through the inspiration of loving and being loved by a person of the opposite sex; however, in some cases of adolescent love, consummation involving physical relations tend to reduce the high energy potential aroused but when delayed or partly prevented from being used, great art, music and literature result.

Love in our lives is seen as central to creativity so that if we want to be creative we should put more love into our lives. Although the developmental process of stages 3 and 6 naturally emphasize creativity, it is not completely absent at the other stages of development. Love and creativity may enter into our lives environmentally at any time and the degree to which love is abundant is the degree to which creativity is likely to be present. However, a good start in stage 3 is expected to give the best assurance that creativity will occur again in stage 6.

Within each of the three stages, development occurs through cycles of escalation whose objective is emergent creativity in the personal unfoldment of the individual. Escalation, or the raising of the level of action by discrete jumps, much like moving up an escalator or a flight of stairs, is described as an aspect of developmental process that involves increasing complexity and embraces five different, but interrelated, attributes of development; namely, succession, discontinuity, emergence, differentiation, and integration (see Table 3). Succession implies a fixed order within a hierarchy of developmental stages, with the rate of succession from one stage to the next (the extent of development) at any one stage relatively flexible and dependent on the nature of the organism and its environment. This is called *hierarchicization* by Piaget and leads to *decalage*

Table 3   The Components of Escalation

Component	Description	Piaget's Nearest Term	Relevant Material
Succession	A fixed order of hierarchical stages	Hierarchicization	Dysplasias (cultural and personal lags)
Discontinuity	A discrete succession of discontinuous equilibration	Equilibration	Each stage has characteristic properties and tasks
Emergence	The budding and making of the implicit, explicit	Consolidation	Budding
Differentiation	Fixation and shift in emphasis	Integration	Fixed metamorphosis
Integration	A gestalt of structures d'ensemble	Structuring	Summation structrues d'ensemble (parts which assemble to make a whole)

(developmental spread), depending on personal and cultural idiosyncracies. Discontinuity involves an ordered and discrete sequence of equilibria, like a series of stairs—what Piaget has termed equilibration—so that any attempt to escalate from one level to the next requires additional input of energy. Emergence involves budding and the making of the implicit, explicit in the flowering of characteristics unseen before: it is the debut of new powers—what Piaget calls consolidation—at which time a given stage is simultaneously a summation of the accomplishments of previous stages and a preparation for the tasks of the next stage. Differentiation refers to the attribute that clarifies, fixates, and metamorphoses the emphasis in successive developments (e.g., the teenager who seems to have outgrown the family and regards himself or herself as a prisoner with only the telephone as a lifeline to age mates. Piaget has no word which exactly fits this definition, the nearest word Gowan (1974) considers to be Piaget's definition of integration (restructuring and coordination). Integration sums the other attributes into a higher synthesis with greater complexity and unites them into a gestalt Piaget called structures d'ensemble—it is very much like driving a car on an open road in overdrive with feelings of freedom and elation that come from the sense of using the automobile to the utmost for which it was designed. Accordingly, Gowan (1974) considers the Piagetian term: structuring as fitting his definition better since Piaget's concept of integration means reemphasis. As a result of this process, the environment may have maximum or minimum effect on the individual, depending on the individual's position in the cycle. Continual environment stimulation, however, is required for escalation into the higher (self-actualizing) levels (Gowan, 1972).

Gowan (1974) describes dysplasia as a lag, arrest, or slowdown of some part of an individual's development relative to the time it should occur. When one aspect of the psyche (e.g., affective) continues to escalate although another aspect (e.g., cognitive) becomes arrested, he calls this relative dysplasia to differentiate it from the disparity between the stage of development the individual, relative to age, ought to be and the different stage where he or she actually is, or absolute dysplasia. Where relative dysplasia occurs between the affective and cognitive stages, it is the cognitive that tends to lag behind in most cases. Exceptions to this may occur for instance when (1) a 10-year-old girl with an IQ of 150 is in stage 4 (industry) affectively but is in the cognitive stage of formal operations and, hence, reasoning in syllogisms; or (2) a brilliant youth, aged 14, although still in stage 5 (identity), already has escalated into cognitive stage 6 (creativity) and is producing original works of music, poetry, or mathematics; or (3) a bright and idealistic young adult of 23 has escalated into cognitive stage 7 (psychedelia) although affectively is only in stage 6 (intimacy).

There are three higher cognitive stages than those named by Piaget (Flavell, 1963). They go with the intimacy, generativity, and ego-integrity periods respectively and are called creativity, psychedelia, and illumination. These stages involve increasing mind expansion beyond formal operations (convergent thinking) and, hence, are increasingly rare, even in intelligent, healthy adults. Facilitation of escalation into these stages by various kinds of educational, therapeutic, sensitivity training, meditational, and allied techniques is in the process of becoming a major movement for superior adults.

The answer to questions like "Why should there be developmental stages at all?" or "Why cannot development, like growth, be one smooth accretion?" lies in the critical aspect of energy transformations in the individual. The transformation and focusing of energy is the essence of both the developmental and the creative process. Because the amount of energy available for use is not enough to be expended on the three areas of the world (it, they), the ego (I, me) and the other (thou) simultaneously, energy must be focused through attention and expended on first one and then another of these three aspects; this process is what leads to the three-phase periodicity of the developmental stages.

One of the unnoticed consequences of the periodic nature of the developmental stages is that the first barriers to accomplishment of the tasks of a given developmental stage are the negative polarities of the previous stage in the same column (the stage three back from a specific developmental stage). Thus, for children in stage 4 (industry), mistrust is the barrier to concrete operations; in stage 5 (identity), shame and doubt plague young adolescents in their identity crises; in stage 6 (intimacy), it is guilt and immobilization that keeps individuals from happiness in sex or joy in creative performance; in stage 7 (generativity), it is inferiority that makes individuals feel inadequate for the grandeur of generativity and psychedelia; and in stage 9 (ego integrity), it is role confusion that prevents ego-integrity; and so on.

Developmental stage theory can be regarded as carrying over the discontinuity principle of the quantum theory to behavioral science. Escalation is the jump from one riser to the next on the developmental staircase; energy from the organism is required for such jumps, but certain freedoms are gained thereby. If we ask, "What is escalating?", one answer appears to be ego strength that helps control and develop the creative imagination, which may be seen in a comparison between the horrors and dread of night terrors in the child or the beauty and simplicity of a musical or a mathematical product in the adult. Developmental process centers around stabilizing and controlling the creative imagination and harnessing it to constructive, not destructive use. We shall see later that this activity is related to the preconscious.

Studies by Arlin (1975) and Weinstein and Altschuler (n.d.) corroborate earlier views of such psychologists as Jean Piaget (cognitive stages) Erik Erikson (affective stages), and Robert J. Havighurst (adolescent developmental tasks). Arlin (1975) predicts a developmental cognitive stage following Piaget's formal operations stage, calling it problem solving (Gowan's creativity stage), which Epstein (1977) considers a prediction of a hitherto unknown stage. That Piaget did not formulate this and other stages beyond formal operations can perhaps be attributed to the unwillingness of Piaget's children to continue to submit themselves to the daily drudgery of observation (Gowan, 1979d).

An interesting resemblance to Gowan's stages 4, 5, 6, and 7 can be found in four of Weinstein and Altschuler's (n.d.) levels of self-knowledge. Their analysis of student stories led to the identification of the following four stages with relevant descriptive information (Gowan, 1979d, p. 52–53):

Concrete Operations *(Stage 4): Stream of consciousness reporting of separate images with no causality, nothing but separate feelings, and no overall start and finish.*

Formal Operations *(Stage 5): Report of feelings with start and finish of story, and a moral, causal outcome; however, no pattern across situations.*

Creativity *(Stage 6): Strong personal feelings in report of personality characteristics and personal style of which the story is an example, but outcome is fatalistic, working out the same across different situations.*

Psychedelic *(Stage 7): Choice, responsibility and autonomy enter reports, with the individual able to change his response pattern.*

Although some differences exist between Gowan's and Weinstein and Altschuler's informational categories, the developmental trend of these stages clearly follows periodic developmental stage theory.

Koplowitz (1978) proposed that two higher stages beyond the usual Piagetian cognitive ones exist: (1) a systems stage, where the individual understands complementarity, homeostasis, and interdependence (resembling Gowan's creativity or stage 6 and (2) a unitary operational thought stage, where the individual understands that the manner in which the universe is perceived is only one of several possible constructs (resembles Gowan's psychedelic or stage 7). This is consistent with the current view expressed by others that there may exist higher cognitive stages beyond Piaget's formal operations stage (e.g., Arlin, 1975; Epstein, 1977; Gruber, 1973; Vygotsky, 1974).

ACCELERATION VERSUS ESCALATION

The importance of acceleration in escalating individuals to higher levels of mental functioning is little known. Such questions as "Can acceleration of gifted children in any developmental stage produce escalation?" or "Do gifted children automatically escalate into higher developmental stages at an accelerated pace or do they need educational intervention to bring it about?" are to the point. Although evidence as to the positive effects of acceleration in learning is available (Gowan & Demos, 1964; Stanley, Keating, & Fox, 1974), no clear-cut research evidence exists as to whether acceleration in fact produces escalation (Epstein, 1977). Except, note the observations that (1) brighter individuals have the advantage of moving more quickly through successive stages, (2) although precocity across stages is clearly present it may not be as pronounced within stages (Keating, 1978), and (3) advance organizers were facilitative of children's acceleration from the preoperations level to the concrete level (Ausubel, 1978; Lawton, 1976; Lawton & Wanska, 1976).

THE PRECONSCIOUS IN DEVELOPMENTAL STAGE THEORY

Khatena (1978c) has described the preconscious in developmental stage theory, drawing from Gowan's recent works (1974, 1975). The term preconscious originated with Freud who divided the mental life of the psyche of a person into unconscious, preconscious, and conscious. This is very simply explained by Sullivan (1953) as the bad-me, not-me, and good-me. Bad-me (the unconscious), refers to that part of our mental life that stores ideas and drives that cause too much pain, anxiety, or guilt to us if we are conscious or aware of them; we store these ideas and drives in the unconscious to defend the self (ego) by pushing the ideas aside (repression) and in other ways. Of course, these ideas and drives remain active in our unconscious and without our awareness are the cause of some of our behaviors. Sometimes we notice them when our defenses are relaxed (as in dreams), in slips of the tongue, or when we are under the influence of alcohol or drugs. Good-me is that part of our mental life of which we are aware and which can be called the conscious positive self-concept. Not-me is the part of our mental life where frightening and uncanny experiences occur, like those we meet in dreams and nightmares.

> *The personification of the not-me is most conspicuously encountered by most of us in an occasional dream while we are asleep; but it is very emphatically encountered by people who are having a severe schizophrenic episode, in aspects that are to them most spectacularly real. As a matter of fact, it is always manifest . . . in certain peculiar absences of phenomena when there should be phenomena; and in a good many people . . . it is very striking in its indirect manifestation (dissociated behavior) in which people do and say things of which they do not and could not have had knowledge, things which may be quite meaningful to other people, but are unknown to them. . . . This is a very gradually evolving personification of an always relatively primitive character—that is organized in usually simple signs in the parataxic mode of experience, and made up of poorly grasped aspects of living, which will presently be regarded as "dreadful," and which still later will be differentiated into incidents which will be attended by awe, horror, loathing, or dread. (Sullivan, 1953; pp. 162–163)*

It is the preconscious not-me area of our mental life that is the source of much of our creativity (Gowan, 1974), and, in a series of analogies, Gowan explains that the preconscious can be considered:

> *as an ever refilling well wherein all creative men have learned to dip their bucket, or as a great computer, containing in its data banks all knowledge, and creativity is but the process of operating the terminal console. Or it can be considered as a great collator, chewing up the events and ideas of the day, and rearranging them into other forms and patterns, or like an enlarged fluid container, with a permeable membrane through which (by osmosis) creative ideas are leaked into consciousness. (1975, p. 301)*

Gowan has illustrated this last analogy by comparing the preconscious to an enlarged fluid container through whose permeable membrane creative ideas leak into the consciousness (1974, p. 83):

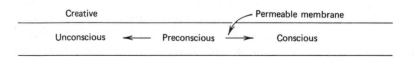

DEVELOPMENT OF INTELLECT AND CREATIVITY

Gowan also tells us that the preconscious is the source of man's creativity, especially if it is strengthened, protected, and enlarged through regular use and through increased mental health. At first creative persons make intuitive use of their preconscious—when leaks occur through the permeable membrane, as it were by osmosis—which manifests itself in works of art of one kind or another. At a higher level of creativity (psychedelia or state-of-mind expansion that takes place naturally without the help of drugs), the barriers that separate the unconscious and conscious are thought of as doors that swing open to let in, as it were, the resources of the preconscious for cognitive processing and production (Gowan, 1974, p. 83):

If the preconscious becomes open to persons in this way, then they become creative. Gowan (1975) explains this in terms of the printing of a new edition of old newspapers. He compares the preconscious to an editor who obtains the material needed for the new edition from the archives of the unconscious, which contain all the editor's past experiences in chewed-up and digested form—a vast assortment of biological impulses, tabooed acts, rejected compromises, affected pains and pleasures, remembered facts, personal feelings, horrifying nightmares, and a host of other material. What the new edition is to be will depend on the extent to which the editor finds the unconscious accessible.

Stage 6 in the periodic-table stresses creative forces at work. This is an intuitive kind of creativity that prepares a person for the psychedelic creativity of stage 7 when the resources of the preconscious become available, not so much by chance but almost at will.

The preconscious, like fire, makes a good servant but a bad master. The developing relationship between the individual and the preconscious starts as a scary and traumatic encounter, but become more humanistic through the parataxic procedures of creativity. It is like the developing relationship between a young child and a young colt. At first the child is afraid of the horse, and cannot ride him; the horse is skittish, unbroken and unpredictable. Eventually through many intermediary stages, the child learns to ride the horse and the horse is taught to accept the rider, until finally the man is complete master of the animal, now fully amenable to his commands. (Gowan, 1978c, p. 219)

Gowan asks us to observe an important happening in nature and in human life that he relates to a transformation of energy that takes place from one stage of development to the next higher stage of development. This, he calls periodicity, which "occurs when the same pattern of events is seen to run through higher development as has been contained in a corresponding pattern from a lower sequence" (1974, p. 49)—something that seems to have escaped the notion of human development theorists.

GENERAL SYSTEMS AND DEVELOPMENTAL STAGES

That intelligence consists of many abilities that are possibly defined by the structure of intellect is not enough. We need to recognize that ability is one dimension of the multimodal construct, to which needs to be added energy (derived from emotive-motivational fields of forces)—ability needs to be energized before it can become active and operable. Further, note that the conceptual model of developmental stages as it relates to the periods of an individual's life when verbal and nonverbal creativity can be most effectively activated holds significant implications for the gifted. In addition, any attempt at educational facilitation has to bear in mind the abilities potential the individual has attained. Attempts made over the past 25 years to realize these and related issues, especially as they impinge on the gifted, include the designing of theoretical constructs, models, or plans. Examples of such structures or systems can be seen in Guilford's structure of intellect model and the Erikson-Piaget-Gowan periodic developmental stage chart (Table 2).

Recently, the search for models and plans has been intensified, and attempts have been made to discover constructs that would allow for conceptions of greater order and generalizability. Seeing principles in patterns for the derivation of even higher levels of order has attracted no small attention and has given rise to some extremely valuable contributions to thought. Theoretical speculation rooted to, and deriving insights from, such disciplines as biology, physics, chemistry, mathematics, and psychology has produced a way of thought that has been called General Systems. Langham (1974), originator of the Genesa model prefaced his version of General Systems with the following questions:

If you had a magic key that would fit all makes of truth would you use it? If it revealed principles and made them available to you, would you use them? If it unveiled answers to your problems, would you be happy? (P. 177)

In the past few years, drawing from the advances in scientific and mathematical thought, Stuart Dodd, Derald Langham, George Land, John Gowan, and several others have each attempted to find general principles to explain existence and behavior. Interacting with one another by mail, visits, and meetings (such as those in 1974 and 1975 that were held at the Creative Problem-Solving Institutes in Buffalo, New York), they attempted not only to convince one another of the significance of their systems but also to find a system of systems. As Gowan and

DEVELOPMENT OF INTELLECT AND CREATIVITY

Dodd (1977) observe, "because General Systems theory is about generalities and not specifics it is difficult to explain" (p. 47). However, Land tells us that the idea of General Systems is not complicated but just the opposite—simple (i.e., to discover the fundamental laws of nature that apply in theory and practice to everything). Relevant to the concepts of growth and development are Gowan's developmental stage theory (see p. 148) and Land's transformation theory (Land, 1973; Land & Kenneally, 1977).

LAND'S TRANSFORMATION THEORY AS A SYSTEM

Land prefaces a discussion of his model with several highly relevant observations about systems (Land & Kenneally, 1977 pp. 12-17) which is paraphrased as follows:

1. In a system, it is important to differentiate the parts of the system from the whole system and to see their relationship to each other as well.
2. Things move from states of disorder to states of order and from these states of order to disorder before attaining higher states of order.
3. The scientific method encourages partialistic thinking through analysis to a solution—solving always creates new problems because the part effects the whole.
4. Systems may be seen as subsystems of larger systems.
5. A whole system may be identified by its organization, by its boundary that sets it apart from its environment (where it takes in things from and puts things out into its environment), and by its synergetic character (because a mature system is more than the sum of its parts).
6. The self-regulation of a system must have more than negative or positive feedback. It must have feedforward, or shared regulation, so that new information derived from the environment continuously provides for proper connection and adaptation to the system's changing environment.

Then comes the key concept of his theoretical model—growth. He defines growth as, "the process by which things become connected with each other and operate at higher levels of organization and complexity" (Land & Kenneally, 1977, p. 19) and as that which guides all systems and subsystems (Figure 6).

Land summarizes and extends these basic concepts to include his transformation model (Land & Kenneally, 1977, pp. 19-20):

A general system starts with a very high degree of polarity—that is, on the one hand great disorder, and on the other hand, great order.

At this initial stage connections are made between order and disorder by dominance and absorption—control. Initial order grows at the expense of the disorder. If successful, a pattern of order—an identity—is discovered and the

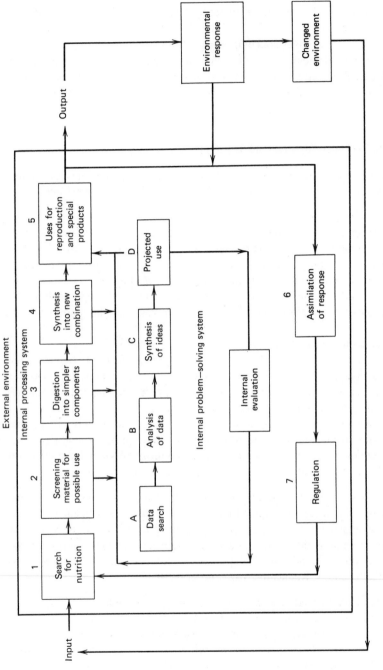

Figure 6 Transformation problem-solving model. (Land, 1973. Copyright © 1973 Random House, Inc. Reprinted by permission of Random House, Inc.)

160

system passes into its second stage, that is, the pattern is copied with few changes and either produces or connects to likenesses. The relationships in this stage, rather than those of control or being controlled, now change to those of influence and being influenced. *Rapid growth is possible since there is a pattern to follow. Inevitably the second stage of growth will use up its environment, i.e., run out of materials that fit easily into the initial and modified patterns. When this happens, the third stage of growth is reached in which the growing thing is forced to accommodate differences in the environment to continue growing. It is at this point that it becomes very sensitive and responsive to its environment and its* relationships shift from the influence type to those of mutual sharing, *simply because that is what works.*

Once a system has absorbed all the differences it can within its environment, and because they are shared, the differences become new sameness and the organism finds a new identity. It must begin to relate to a new and broader environment—a new disorder—and the process starts all over again at a higher level.

Here we have in essence Land's three distinctly different forms of growth. The first three stages he labels accretive, replicative, and mutualistic; the fourth, which represents a transition to a new and higher level of development, he names transformation.

On the relationship of General Systems and the creative process, Land suggests four different kinds of creativity and techniques that related directly to his four stages of growth:

1. The most primitive level of creativity simply produces enlargement of an idea or concept (accretive stage)—a change in scale creating a "supermarket from a grocery store." This has been identified by J. P. Guilford and E. P. Torrance as the ability to elaborate.
2. The next level of creativity makes modifications in the form of the pattern but not in its basic function (replicative stage)—modification that could lead to the improvement of something, making it lighter, stronger, more efficient, and so on. This is similar to A. F. Osborn's use of categories to induce shifts in creative thinking, which E. P. Torrance, for instance, has called flexibility.
3. The next higher level of creativity relates to the making of high-level combinations, analogies, and metaphors (mutualistic stage).
4. The fourth level relates to transformation, where invention—or the recombination of the old concept at a higher level of relationship to the environment— occurs and involves destructuring and reintegration.

These four stages of creativity are most clearly illustrated in the following example:

If we look at the process of a child putting together a Tinker Toy, first we see exploration to discover a pattern—a simple box for example. Level two follows by adding other boxes, modified to accomodate different shapes and sizes. At the third stage all the pieces that can be easily made into boxes have been exhausted and the child begins to make rearrangement in order that the odd pieces that didn't fit well at first can now become a part of the whole. This mutual stage of combining differences not only produces a new looking whole, but uses up the Tinker Toy.

This is where we run into the level-four problem—and opportunity. If this whole structure is now to join with other things in the room where the child is playing—the child must take an entirely new viewpoint toward *his creation. In a sense the beauty and perfection of the whole he created must be dismembered to accomodate its joining with other things in his environment. (Land & Kenneally, 1977, p. 23)*

GOWAN'S DEVELOPMENTAL STAGE THEORY AS A SYSTEM

Gowan's (1972, 1974, 1975) contribution to General Systems comes from his developmental stage theory. Like Land, he perceives growth as an essential phenomenon of his system but prefers to regard it as development; making a distinction between the two, he says that "development is to growth as quality is to quantity—the apple enlarges but it also ripens."

Gowan observes that, although Land's evolutionary process approach and his individual development process approach are diverse, they obey the same laws of nature (Land & Kenneally, 1977). Interaction between Gowan and Land in 1976 at the Creative Problem-Solving Institute in Buffalo, New York, in an attempt to find common ground for their two systems, led to some creative insights for bonding their models, the implications of which are yet to be worked out. However, it led Gowan to reiterate that "the developmental cycle is discontinuous and not continuous as previously believed."

Gowan's system pivots on the development of the creative individual and so concerns itself with those stages of development optimal to creative interactions of the inner and outer worlds of the individual, which is Land's third (mutalistic) stage in his interpretation of the creative process. Transformation in Land's model is little different from Gowan's periodicity: both preface the entry into the next higher level of growth or development. In both the models, the highest level of the creative process that prepares for transformation involves the functioning of analogical and metaphorical brain activity and the tapping of the preconscious. At present, some would refer to this as right-brain functioning or the functioning of the creative imagination and its imagery correlates (see p. 107).

Briefly, then, imagination imagery may be said to be the province of Land's mutalistic stage and Gowan's creativity and psychedelic stages, which relate to

DEVELOPMENT OF INTELLECT AND CREATIVITY

high levels of psychological functioning. It is at these stages that high-level combination and connections are made by analogy and metaphor and at which time the preconscious is tapped. Transformations occur when movement taking place from a lower level of order moves to a higher level of order through the process of destructuring and reintegration.

CULTURE, CREATIVE DEVELOPMENT, AND EMINENCE

So far development has been viwed as an individual phenomenon, and as it relates to the intellect and creativity, it has been discussed as continuous or discrete. That individual development cannot be treated as isolated from its sociocultural origins has been emphasized by both Arieti (1976) and Simonton (1978). Both ask the crucial question of why creative geniuses appear at a certain time and place in history and not at another, and both would attribute this to certain sociocultural events that significantly affect creative development of individuals. Like others before them, they recognize that the appearance of men of eminence takes place irregularly and in clusters.

Simonton (1978) focuses attention on conditions that facilitate or hinder the emergence of creative giants. In addressing himself to historical circumstances responsible for the emergence of such geniuses as Shakespeare, Michelangelo, Beethoven, and Aristotle, Simonton makes a critical distinction between two phases of a creator's life, namely, (1) the sociocultural events that may have influence on the period of a creator's productivity (e.g., warfare and its aversive impact on a person's output at a certain career point) and (2) the sociocultural events that may have influence on the creator's developmental period. The latter phase is far more important to the emergence of eminence:

> Perhaps a special set of political, cultural, and social conditions is most conducive to the development of creative potential in a youthful genius. In adulthood, that creative potential then becomes fully actualized in the form of prolific and significant creative productivity. Thus, it is quite conceivable that the creative genius is either made or broken during childhood, adolescence, and early adulthood. So complete knowledge of the historical forces behind a creative genius requires that productive and developmental period influences be carefully segregated (Simonton, 1978, pp. 181–188)

Simonton indicates that developmental periods of childhood and adolescence through adulthood tend to be more significantly affected by external events than do specific periods of productivity that enjoy immunity to external events, with the exception of physical illness and war. He identifies seven variables that have influence on the creative development of individuals: formal education, role-model availability, zeitgeist, political fragmentation, warfare, civil disturbances, and political instability.

1. Formal education is an important influence on the individual's creativity while growing up, but, beyond a certain point, it can inhibit creative development by enforcing an overcommitment to traditional perspectives. This finds support in some research that suggests the relationship between IQ and eminence is spurious and that an IQ beyond 120 bears little relationship to creativity.

2. Availability of eminent creators as role models for emulation is of great importance to the emergence of other eminent creators, so that the more role models there are for emulation during the developmental period of a genius, the greater the increase in creative potential. Generally, it is to be expected that emulation occurs in the same discipline, for instance, precocious musicians will be influenced by an eminent musician rather than by someone in the scientific or literary fields who has preceded them. If such influence crosses disciplines, the impact may not always be beneficial as seen in the negative effects of religious activity on creativity in philosophy. To this may be added the adverse effects of role-model availability on creative development when the presence of an excess of role models may lead a potential genius to make a premature commitment to a particular school of thought that makes a disciple of him rather than a leader.

3. On the matter of zeitgeist, Simonton's research shows that major minds in the history of ideas are neither ahead nor representative of their time, rather they tend to be behind their times. He explains that, unlike lesser thinkers, eminent thinkers are most influenced by the zeitgeist dominating the intellectual scene during their developmental period, which leads them to be preoccupied with elaborating the ideas to which they were most exposed and to act as synthesizers, that is, making prior accomplishments into a single unified philosophical system.

4. Political fragmentation, or the existence of many independent states within a civilization, engenders cultural diversity that significantly affects creative development more than it does creative productivity because it shapes the content of the creator's intellectual base toward an openness to experiences, change, individualism, and material welfare.

5. Constant warfare, however, in the lifetime of the youthful creative genius has the opposite effect on his or her creative development by discouraging those intellectual qualities that are shaped by political fragmentation.

6. Civil disturbances (i.e., popular revolts, rebellion, and revolution) have a potent influence on creative development although, at times, such exposure can have a negative impact.

7. Of all these influences, political instability is the one that is detrimental to creative development because to be creative an individual must find the world somewhat predictable and controllable and personal efforts must have some prospect of eventual fruition.

Simonton's conclusions about the significance of sociocultural conditions on creative development not only explain the rarity of eminence in our times but also direct our attention to those shaping influences in our society that are responsible for facilitating or hindering the development of creativity during the formative years of our young and growing gifted. It may be that of greatest relevance today is the overemphasis on the formal aspects of formal education and the insufficient emphasis on the need for emulating eminent men and women. This may, in part, be responsible for young geniuses of our day being conservationist rather than men and women of the frontier. However, we can expect the blunting edge of formal education to some extent by the inclusion and integration in the curriculum of creative ways of learning (Khatena, 1978c; Renzulli, 1973; Torrance & Myers, 1970; Williams, 1971b) and of arrangements for the education of a variety of abilities (Guilford, 1977; Meeker, 1969), as well as for the use of creative imagination, imagery, and right-brain processes (Gowan, 1978b, 1978c, 1980; Khatena, 1979c; Torrance, Reynolds, Ball & Riegel, 1978).

Turning to Arieti (1976), we find that he comments on Kroeber's (1944) cataloging of the occurrence of geniuses in the various disciplines of science, mathematics, music, literature, and so on, with no explanation offered for this clustering. Gray (1961, 1966), continuing in Kroeber's wake, compiled a curve of creativity for Western civilization that agreed with Kroeber's main findings on the emergence of genius in clusters so that blossomings occur several times during a civilization, that such peaks are rare and do not characterize most of civilization's course, and that these peaks are of unequal duration. In attempting to explain this, Gray advanced an epicyclic theory that views history as a series of concurrent cycles—economic, social, and political—with each cycle passing at different rates through four different stages: formative, developed, florescent, and degenerate. It is at the coincidence of the florescent and developed stages of the three cycles that clusters of creativity occur. Gray's analysis of history in terms of his epicyclic theory indicates that favorable economic, social, and political factors promoted creativity.

Concerning the shaping of genius by culture or culture by genius, Arieti (1976) points out that there exist a number of differing views. On the one hand, there are those who would give nearly all the credit to culture, regarding highly creative individuals not as rich personalities but as measures of cultural expression (Kroeber, 1944), or as indices of the growth of their culture (Gray, 1966), or as passive representatives who express their times (L. R. White, 1949). On the other hand, there are those who would attribute to these geniuses either the making of culture (Galton, 1870) or the remaking of culture by them before they are made by it (James, 1880).

Two significant conclusions reached by L. A. White (1949) were that invention or discovery would occur only if culture makes available materials and ideas necessary for the synthesis and that, if this were the case, invention or discovery would become inevitable under normal conditions of cultural interaction. However, Arieti (1976) suggests that the capacity of the individual who makes the significant synthesis must not be overlooked, which L. A. White (1949) does because *the significant synthesis is the creative process* itself, whose significance and unpredictability appear magical.

Analysis of the work of Kroeber (1944) and others convinced Arieti (1976) to conclude that individual possibility for genius is much more frequent than the occurrence of genius, that potentiality for creativity exists, that it can be activated, and that some cultures promote creativity (such cultures he calls creativogenic). Arieti regards the potentially creative person and the creativogenic culture as two essential components of creativity. Individuals, he suggests, make roughly two contacts with culture: the one relates to individuals' use of certain of their biological equipment to understand their environment and satisfy their needs; the other relates to individuals' acquisition of things already present in the culture that are mediated by interpersonal relationships. Both the individual and culture are perceived as open systems so that the individual gives to culture and takes from it. When a culture is creativogenic, it makes available to an individual creative elements that are perceived or accepted as such if similar characteristics exist within the individual. This then, prepares the way for a magic synthesis that will produce innovation, which, in turn, is offered to, and becomes a part of, culture. A creativogenic society offers the individual the possibility of becoming great, but it does not make the occurrence of greatness automatic. Arieti discusses nine conditions present in a creativogenic society that will facilitate greatness:

1. Availability of cultural means (an elite to preserve these cultural means; accessibility to equipment, materials, etc.).
2. Openness to cultural stimuli (cultural stimuli are present, requested, desired, and made easily available).
3. Stress on becoming, not just being.
4. Free access to cultural media for all citizens without discrimination.
5. Freedom—or even retention of moderate discrimination—after severe oppression or absolute exclusion is an incentive to creativity.
6. Exposure to different and even contrasting cultural stimuli.
7. Tolerance for, and interest in, diverging views.
8. Interaction of significant persons.
9. Promotion of incentives and rewards.

Simonton (1978) and Arieti (1976) both recognize that geniuses have the potential to become eminent and that actualization can occur through creativity. Whereas Simonton, who makes a distinction between creative productivity at certain times in a person's life, sees creativity as a part of development in an individual's formative years, and identifies those cultural conditions that may facilitate or hinder creative development, Arieti looks at creativity as a dynamic exchange of two open systems, the individual and creativogenic culture, with certain conditions that facilitate the emergence of eminence. Arieti emphasizes the conditions in a culture that can be expected to foster creativity; Simonton examines cultural conditions that affect creative development. The combination of both these views can only enhance our understanding of creative development still further.

CONCLUSIONS

The psychometric approach to describe developmental characteristics of intellect emphasizes continuity of growth and age, with the rate of growth decelerating until it peaks at anywhere from age 16 to 28. Everyone does not agree with this nor with the time at which decline sets in. As measures of creativity developed, a similar emphasis concerning creative growth as continuous emerged. And, a noticeable decline in creative thinking abilities was found to occur during several periods of a child's life. These declines were seen to be especially severe during the middle elementary school years, but there was some recovery at age 11 (or in grade 5). Wechsler (1950) makes the interesting observation that, after a rapid growth of the first few years, there is a gradual slowing down of development in intellectual abilities as age 15 is reached, except for a brief spurt between the ages of 10 and 12 because, at about that time, the decline and catch-up in creative thinking abilities appear. Is it possible that there is some relationship between the quickened growth of certain intellectual abilities at the expense of others? Could it be that continued emphasis in the first few years of schooling on left-brain activity (e.g., reasoning, logical thinking, knowing, and remembering) has an effect on the development of certain intellectual abilities at the expense of creative thinking abilities?

Developmental stage theory and transformation theory subscribe to and emphasize discontinuity in growth and development. Rather than consider growth as occurring at a rising, but decelerating rate, with age, both these thereotical models speak of rising from one level of development to the next higher level of development. Where Gowan (1972) describes growth in terms of escalation from one age period to the next in the repeated triad cycle of infancy, youth, and adulthood, Land describes growth in terms of rises to higher levels of functioning in triads that are not necessarily contained by chronology. Both models imply the attainment of peaks in functioning within any one stage of development in preparation for the entry into the next higher level of development. Instead of decline in growth, Gowan (1972) speaks of dysplasia relative to a model of growth that has united the cognitive and affective in its design and of healthy development, which necessitates the growth of both cognitive and affective components at each stage and level. If the growth of one component (cognitive or affective) takes place without the other, dysplasia occurs. Growth for Land relates to survival so that, when the mutualistic stage is reached, a transformation must take place to a next higher level for the recurrence of a similar pattern of growth that prepares for the next transformation to occur at an even higher level than the one before—otherwise death follows. Grow or die is central to his model. Creativity is essential to growth in both models: Gowan sees its energy in love and its source of productivity in the preconcious with the "gentling of the preconscious" (Gowan, 1978c) serving the individual as the key to intellectual development and productivity; Land sees creativity as entering into mental functioning from the lowest level of accretive growth to the highest level of mutualistic growth, where order grows from its lowest to highest forms—at that time destructuring of the order is necessitated before a reintegration or transformation into a higher order can take place. It is at the mutualistic stage that creativity makes use of high-level combinations, analogies, and metaphor, whose province (as we observed) lies with the preconscious and right-brain functioning.

Whereas quantitatively determined growth is specifically related to the intellect, qualitatively determined growth is related to the interactive effects of intellect and affect (Gowan, 1972) and is characteristic of growth of nearly all kinds of life (Land, 1973). Finally, whereas the psychometric approach derives data for growth curves empircally (note that these relate to average scores obtained with considerable variation from individual to individual), the developmental stage approach derives data from observation, speculation, and scientific findings.

The sociocultural origins of creativity and its development in individuals adds another dimension to creative development. Simonton (1978) identifies six of seven sociocultural conditions during the lifetime of youthful geniuses that may facilitate their creative development toward actualization in adulthood and eminence (two of which have immediate and strong educational implications); he also suggests the reduction of an overcommitment to formal aspects of education beyond a certain point and the increased emphasis on making available role models of eminence for emulation. Arieti's (1976) conception of genius acquiring eminence by creative transactions with a creativogenic society and the conditions that determine such a society not only provides an explanation for the occurrence of a renaissance but he also suggests the possibility of precipitating such an outcome by arranging conditions appropriate to it. The nine conditions he suggests may very well find application in schooling and help develop a more effective and fruitful educational climate that will maximize creative development of young gifted children toward eminence in adulthood.

To place these views in the perspective of the chapter as a whole, we find, for instance, that the theorizing of Gowan and Land and the empirical research of Torrance and Khatena on the development of the creative person gives focus to the individual, whereas Simonton would attribute the important effects of cultural conditions as shaping the creative development of an individual. It is Arieti who sees in the dynamic relationship and creative exchange of the individual and his society a magic synthesis that leads to invention, discovery, and eminence.

Most of the studies and discussions about intellectual development have centered in general on children as they grow up. There is a substantial gap in our knowledge about the intellectual development of gifted children. Although it is not difficult to interpolate how findings concerning children in the general population apply to gifted children—and some of these may be of high relevance—studies peculiar to the gifted are needed. The many hypotheses about development, especially from the approaches of developmental stage theory and General Systems, are yet to be explored and validated. In these, lie some potent future directions to the study of the intellectual development of gifted children. In addition, work needs to be done to find specific applications of the sociocultural origins of creative development in educational settings so that our gifted will be transformed by magic synthesis to men and women of eminence.

6

GUIDANCE

OVERVIEW

Here we attempt to deal with guidance of the gifted from several fresh perspectives. Unlike psychotherapy, whose province is the treatment of abnormal problems of adults, guidance deals with developmental problems of normal children as they strive toward self-actualization and higher states of mental health. It should be preventative and leveled at good mental health rather than crisis oriented and remedial. Guidance of creative development, which is seen as essential, is discussed in terms of developmental stages, growth and transformation, creativogenic sociocultural conditions in contemporary and historical perspectives, and suggestions for facilitating creative functioning. Stress is identified as a common source of problems. The purpose of guidance is conceived as preparing an individual to master stress by developing interpersonal skills and using intellectual abilities to cope with it constructively. Attention is also given to academic and career guidance; two examples of career guidance models are described: (1) the Guidance Institute for Talented Students (GIFTS) career development model, based on a developmental-motivational rationale and (2) the sociodramatic model, based on the dynamics of group creative problem solving and role playing in dramatic situations. Concluding remarks recommend that guidance of the gifted be perceived in terms of a multiplicity-of-resources approach that derives life from development and motivation toward self-actualization, coping with stress, and group creative problem solving in dramatic situations.

170

CHAPTER OUTLINE

INTRODUCTION

A recognition of individual differences falls, as we have seen, within the developments of humanistic psychology. This brings to mind the efforts of Lewis M. Terman and others, beginning in the 1920s, to know more about highly intelligent individuals, how to identify them, and what qualities and behaviors they possess as they grow up to midlife. Research on Terman's superior students (1925) as they grew to midlife was reported in four follow-up studies (Burks,

Jensen, & Terman, 1930; Oden, 1968; Terman & Oden, 1947, 1959). The geniuses studied in this research grew to be gifted adults who maintained their intellectual ability, had lower mortality rates, enjoyed good physical and mental health, manifested minimal crime, ranked high in education and vocational achievements, were active in community affairs, and held moderate political and social views—two thirds of them felt that they had realized their potential.

Another study (Cox, 1926) concludes that geniuses are characterized in childhood not only by superior IQ but also by traits of interest, energy, will, and character that foreshadow later performance. However, Oden (1968), in attempting to assess correlates of vocational achievement and genius, compared 100 most successful and least successful men geniuses and found that the most successful men came from families of higher socioeconomic status who gave their children encouragement to succeed; ranked higher as adolescents in volitional, intellectual, moral, and social traits; and had more self-confidence, perseverance, and integration toward goals. In addition, although scholastic achievement had been similar in grade school, half of the least successful men had graduated from college.

The fact that not all the subjects were successful suggests that gifted individuals are not entirely free from problems in spite of their general health and well-being; the Terman (1925) and Oden (1908) studies indicate that some gifted individuals are prone to emotional and social difficulties. For instance, L. A. Hollingworth (1926) and Terman (1925) have both pointed out that students with IQs of 170 and above experience difficulty in making adequate social adjustment. Kenmare (1972) concludes that geniuses are also characterized as being typically schizophrenic because of the difficulty they have in synthesizing their personal life and their existence as an impersonal creative process. Burnside (1942) believes that social maladjustment begins in the preschool years and may be prevented by appropriate adult supervision and wise guidance:

> The brilliant child is yet too immature to learn the lesson of "suffer fools gladly." Here begins the emotional maladjustment of isolationism. They [sic] are friendly and need companions of their own age who can understand and reciprocate their efforts at social contacts. Failure to achieve this may lead to a life of phantasy or disillusionment and bitterness of chicanery. (p. 224)

Barbe (1954) notes that, although gifted individuals are ahead of their age mates in mental capacity, this in no way makes them misfits. The problem arises when they are rejected because other children do not understand them. It is only then that they may become stereotype bespectacled introverts. Torrance (1962a, 1965a) pays considerable attention to the problems that gifted children face as a result of their conflicting interaction with society and the cultural environment. The creative energizing force that dominates the lives of highly gifted children sets them up in a position of independence and nonconformity in relation to the

172

group of which they are members. This often leads to confrontations of one kind or another, confrontations that require gifted children either to learn to cope with arising tensions or to repress their creative needs. Therefore, the one reaction leads to productive behavior and mental health, whereas the other leads to personality disturbances and breakdown. Torrance (1979c) reiterates the need to provide a refuge somewhere in the system for creative children and adults who are often under a great deal of stress:

> Society is still harsh in its treatment of creative persons, especially children. Almost inescapably, the creative child will come into conflict with the "authorities" in the system or establishment. He will experience frustration and must have a source of encouragement and support. He must have a right to fail without being ostracized or ruined. (p. 367)

PERSPECTIVES IN GUIDANCE FOR THE GIFTED

Much that is written on the subject of guidance tends to focus attention on providing guidance in the areas of educational and vocational guidance with some recognition given to problems that children face and to approaches to guidance that involve school counselors, teachers, and parents (e.g., Durr, 1964; Gold, 1965; Hildreth, 1952, 1966). Children need guidance. This has been emphasized again and again, but the problem of arranging for effective guidance hinges on the absence of a curriculum for guidance. A curriculum for guidance is found in developmental stage theory, especially in its cognitive and affective relational aspects (Gowan, 1979a). Gowan (1979c) charges that present-day practice of guidance (1) confuses psychotherapy with guidance—it sees the former as concerned with the treatment of abnormal problems of adults that involves association with them on a private and long-term basis, and it sees the latter as concerned with developmental problems of normal children that involves association on a short-term basis; (2) tends to consider the panacea concept of positive self-regard as not only necessary but also sufficient, whereas, in some aspects of developmental counseling (e.g., vocational counseling), individual diagnosis and prescription is absolutely essential because what is needed, for example, is specific job-opportunity information more than support; and (3) is similar to a pathology medical model (as seen in psychotherapy) where attention is crisis oriented; this has been outmoded by Maslovian concepts and, therefore, school guidance should be preventative and leveled at positive development toward the maintenance of good mental health.

Gowan (1979a) prescribes fresh perspectives for guidance so that emphasis is on counseling students with normal developmental problems as these relate to performing tasks that will ensure cognitive and affective development appropriate to developmental stage theory. Further, he requires that counseling go beyond establishing a positive self-concept in the counselee and go into areas of specific vocational, educational, interest, and motivational needs that provide the right kind of information for better decision making. In addition, guidance needs to take a preventative rather than remedial stance, providing those opportunities and conditions that will facilitate students to higher levels of creative development toward self-actualization and mental health.

In a substantive work on the subject, Gowan and Demos (1964) point to the relative recency of the guidance movement, beginning with the inception of vocational guidance in schools (Smith-Hughes Act of 1917); the extension of guidance concepts beyond the vocational to include all aspects of childhood and developmental tasks; proliferation of the counselor's tools, especially testing; and to the more global and clinical aspects of people and their problems. Other developments that came more slowly were the growing recognition (1) that guidance of the gifted was important because the gifted, too, face problems, among which are choices to be made from many attractive alternatives; (2) that there was too early tracking into a specialized occupational structure before related interests were developed; that there were problems attendant on upward mobility as well as problems of socialization and peer relations; and that there was a lack of appropriate and genuine adult-role models.

Conant (1958) observes that "guidance in the broadest and deepest sense of the term is essential for adequate development of the academically talented student . . . guidance must be comprehensive, continually available and realistic in terms of desirable educational objectives" (pp. 74–75). The importance of having a guidance program for the gifted was reiterated by Gowan (1979a) who perceives guidance for the gifted as the carrying over of the principles of guidance and their modification to provide differential guidance in the context of developmental acceleration.

The observation made a number of years ago by Gowan and Demos that no comprehensive statement about guidance for the gifted had been written (except for their book, *The Education and Guidance of the Ablest* [1964], and *Guiding Creative Talent* by Torrance [1962a]) applies today. For the most forward theoretical view of guidance for the gifted, we must rely on Gowan (1972; 1979a). Although many have addressed themselves to the problem (Barbe, 1954; Hildreth, 1952; Martinson, 1961; Passow, 1957; Strang, 1958), they have not much advanced thought on the subject. In the main, their writings advocate the need and importance for guidance of the gifted as this relates to educational, vocational, and personal guidance that would involve the counselor as well as the teacher, parent, and community.

For more recent views on the subject of guidance for the gifted, we have to turn to a special issue of the *Gifted Child Quarterly* devoted to guidance (1977) and to the second edition of *Educating the Ablest* (Gowan, Khatena, & Torrance, 1979) in which several papers are reported that reflect the thought of the Re-

174

search and Guidance Laboratory at the University of Wisconsin (Madison) along with pertinent editorial comments that reflect perspectives that are forward looking and germane to the development of counseling concepts and practice for the gifted. An article by Zaffrann and Colangelo (1977) views differentiated guidance for the gifted from a developmental perspective, drawing from Gowan's theoretical model and giving particular focus to (1) social and educational concerns, (2) career and vocational concerns, (3) gifted women, (3) developmental arrests, dysplasias, and malfunctioning. Zaffrann and Colangelo advocate a counseling program for gifted children that would take these concerns into account to facilitate mental health and creativity through the affective domain. Perrone and Pulvino (1977) also subscribe to the developmental stage model but emphasize the development of creative functioning in terms of right-hemisphere functioning and the metaphorical mind (Samples, 1975). They contrast right-hemisphere functioning with left-hemisphere functioning and the rational mind (Jean Piaget), field-independence with field-dependence behaviors, and divergent thought with convergent thought. However, they support the need for both halves of the brain to be productive. They also see that creativeness is best produced by affective support and cognitive stimulation, with the implication that counseling needs to take this into account. Gowan's editorial comments praise this article as an excellent start in the right direction but suggest that several other components follow the development sequence they propose.

Gowan (1980) cites Fischer (1974) on the specialized functions of the right and left cerebral hemispheres and the need to know which one predominates (because some people are dominantly convergent and others dominantly divergent in thinking styles) before we can maximize the learning and mental functioning of an individual. Hence, education should emphasize the development and perfection of the talents of the gifted rather than attempt to develop more generally talents that are not present. That is why differential learning modes are essential to the nurturance of creativity and should be an important consideration of guidance. Further, Gowan calls attention to the primary importance of the developmental stages in the model, pointing out that convergent thinking is followed by divergent thinking in the structure of intellect model as formal operations is followed by creativity, the next higher cognitive stage. This suggests that a more fruitful approach to the educational guidance of the gifted would be a stricter adherence to the order of developmental stage theory. The most common form of dysplasia prevents cognitive escalation to creativity in young adults and Gowan (1972) considers that this should be the prime focus of guidance for the gifted so that escalation of all parts of the psyche of an individual beyond the fifth developmental stage of formal operations can move toward full creativity and self-actualization. Finally, he points to the importance of guidance in the synergestic development of the individual because, when all aspects of the psyche are functioning harmoniously, higher levels of creativity and self-actualization emerge and major creative works as well as continued personal development after sexual maturity follow.

GUIDANCE OF CREATIVE DEVELOPMENT

We have already discussed the creative development of an individual in terms of developmental stage theory and transformation theory. The extent to which developmental stage theory relates to the gifted and its guidance implications were examined in terms of the Gowan-Erikson-Piaget model of developmental stages (Gowan, 1972). As for Land's (1973) growth model and transformation theory, there is no discussion on the gifted and their need for guidance within his system. However, the importance of these topics needs to be emphasized and some relevant implications for guidance of the gifted will receive some attention later in our discussion. Moving to the conception of an individual's creativity and its relationship and interaction with society, we find some interesting and thought-provoking views advanced by Arieti (1976) in terms of two open systems in dynamic energy exchange relations: the extent to which society shapes the individual's creativity and the specific society's value for it. To this may be added Simonton's view (1978) that sociocultural conditions exercise significant influence on the creative development of youthful geniuses during their lifetime. The import these ideas have for the gifted and their guidance will also receive treatment.

DEVELOPMENTAL STAGE THEORY

Briefly, developmental stage theory is based on the rationale that development is discontinuous. Individuals as they grow up from infancy to adulthood and beyond are seen as passing through three dvelopmental stages three times, each time at a higher level. Developmental characteristics of individuals relate to concerns of: the nature and function of the world (latency), themselves as persons (identity), and creative functioning (creativity) during infancy, youth, and adulthood. Details of each of these stages is presented in a matrix that relates the affective stages of Erik Erikson and Sigmund Freud, the cognitive stages of Jean Piaget, and the creative stages of J. C. Gowan (see pp. 149–155). Here we are concerned with Gowan's (1972) escalation and dysplasia as they relate on the one hand to cognitive and affective development and on the other hand to creativity and self-actualization.

Development occurs through cycles of escalation whose five attributes are discontinuity, succession, emergence, differentiation, and integration. Continual environmental stimulation is required for escalation into higher levels of creative functioning as the individual moves toward self-actualization; the extent to which this stimulation has maximal or minimal effect depends on the individual's

176

position in the cycle of development. Gowan's model (1972) goes beyond Piaget's formal operations stage to include three additional ones that, in turn, go beyond Erikson's stages of intimacy, generativity, and ego-integrity (i.e., creativity [stage 6], psychedelia [stage 7], and illumination [stage 8]), stages that involve further mind expansion that is rare even among healthy and intelligent adults. The important thing is the need for escalation to bridge one developmental stage to the next to overcome developmental discontinuity; hence, facilitation of the process should be one of the major concerns of guidance. Facilitation of superior adults may be effected in several ways. These include various kinds of educational experiences, therapy, sensitivity training, meditation, and so on, all of which can be adapted for use with young gifted people.

When malformation occurs in development so that individuals are either behind the stage of development in which they should be or develop affectively but not cognitively (or vice versa), dysplasia is said to have occurred. The former is referred to as absolute dysplasia, the latter as relative dysplasia. Dysplasia may be single or double; it cannot be more than this because of the triplicity of the model. Dysplasia produces a block to development and commonly prevents cognitive escalation to creativity, causing some kind of neurotic dissonance. This is a problem that gifted children may face and is one of the prime reasons for their need of guidance. The main purpose of such guidance, then, is to assist the gifted to develop as completely as possible to bring about escalation of all parts of the psyche beyond stage 5 (formal operations) through stage 6 (creativity), stage 7 (psychedelia), and stage 8 (illumination) toward higher levels of creative functioning and self-actualization.

Khatena (1978c) observes that discontinuity in the development of creative thinking abilities takes place between the ages of 5, 9, 13, and 17 with an especially severe drop occurring at about age 9 or in the fourth grade. This coincides with stage 4 of the developmental stage model and occurs again in stage 5. The fourth-grade slump in creative thinking abilities was also explored with other cultures, and Torrance (1967b) found that cultural variables and stress had a lot to do with the discontinuity.

To achieve their creative potential, the gifted have guidance needs, which Gowan (1972) emphasizes occur in stages 6, 7, and 8. However, information on developmental discontinuity in creative thinking abilities indicates that an earlier handling of the problem is required. Escalation from the intuitive (stage 3) and the creative (stage 6) in Gowan's model needs to take place at about stage 4 (concrete operations) without loss in creative functioning. Having been alerted to the restricting, stressful, and inhibiting times in the child's life during the elementary to middle elementary school years that preface the fourth-grade slump, guidance for the gifted can focus on prevention of much of these cramping influences to remedy or remove those variables that cause discontinuity in the child's creative development. Khatena (1978c) suggests some counteracting measures:

We have been in search for ways and means to overcome the problem of decrements in creativity especially at a time when children seem to be very vulnerable, and Torrance and others have shown conclusively that by arranging proper stimulating conditions and opportunities for creative achievement that much can be done to prevent the fourth grade slump. Gowan has added the dimension of love which tends to prepare and predispose the person for creative thoughts and acts, and for appropriate links that may be established between the conscious and preconscious so that the ability to dip into the preconscious to bring back creative ideas at will is developed.

It would be very useful to help your child to be creative during the ages of 4 and 6 or stage 3, especially if you observe that he shows signs of being low in his ability to be creative. You might also give him many opportunities to be creative around the ages of 9 and 10 years which is within stage 4 of the Gowan developmental model (7–12 years). Of course you will have to be on the lookout for the times when he is exposed to much stress, and over long periods of time; so do what you can to take some of it away. Entry points into varous levels of schooling do expose your child to stress and you should be particularly watchful over the pressures brought to bear upon him by his new surroundings, teachers, friends and learning. With your understanding and help he may avoid this difficult period of his life, or overcome these pressures while continuing to maintain his creativity and be productive. (pp. 106–107)

GROWTH AND TRANSFORMATION THEORY

We discussed Land's growth model as it relates to creativity and identified stages in the growth process that are organic to his transformation theory. As the accretive stage relates to creativity, it involves enlargement of an idea or concept and is elaborative; the replicative stage involves modification of form or pattern while still retaining similar function and is called flexibility; the higher levels of creative functioning that occur in the mutualistic stage involve metaphor, analogy, imagery, and the tapping of the preconscious; and the fourth level involves destructuring of the existing and coexisting patterns so that reintegration (restructuring) takes place, which, at one and the same time, effects transformation to the next higher level of creative functioning and, thus, prepares to repeat the same cycle of increasing order.

It has been observed that these stages of ever-increasing order are not necessarily affected by chronology and may occur at any time in a person's life relative to a situation or mental event. As it relates to the gifted, one implication for guidance that emerges is the need to assist the individual through these cycles of growth at one level of creative functioning to similar cycles of growth at increasingly higher levels. Creative thinking has been found by many (e.g., Torrance, 1972a) to be malleable and responsive to intervention or training procedures.

178

Experiences can be arranged to encourage the individual to pass from elaborative and flexible thinking to creative thinking, which calls for the use of the creative imagination, imagery, and analogy and includes restructuring and synthesis (Khatena, 1978b, 1978e) energized by love and facilitated by the accesibility of the preconscious through its frequent use (Gowan, 1978b, 1978c).

Land (1973) considers the importance of a growth system that necessitates not only feedback (positive or negative) but also feedforward. Individuals interact with the environment and are in constant dynamic relation with it so that they receive input from it. This input is subjected to mediation processes that are involved in what Piaget has termed assimilation and accomodation and, in turn, gives output to the environment. In the numerous transactions that occur between individuals and their environment, growth takes place each time at succeedingly higher levels. Herein lies another occasion for guidance, and arrangements for appropriate environmental stimulation leveled at facilitating the development of creative functioning with proper positive reinforcements (feedback) can be provided for the creative development of the gifted child. This approach can be expected to pave the way toward escalation to higher stages of creative functioning within the growth cycle.

CREATIVE DEVELOPMENT AND SOCIETIAL INFLUENCES

Drawing from the most cogent observations of both Simonton (1978) and Arieti (1976) concerning the creative development of individuals and their relationship to society, we begin to see the importance of guidance when approached from yet another perspective.

Of the seven sociocultural conditions identified by Simonton (see p. 164) as affecting youthful geniuses during their lifetime, six were found to be facilitative of creative development toward self-actualization and eminence. Of these, two have guidance as well as educational implications, namely, formal education and role models for emulation. As important as formal education is to children's creativity as they grow up, there comes a point beyond which an overcommitment to tradition inhibits creative functioning. We have seen it as partly responsible for the drop in creative thinking abilities, particularly at about the fourth grade as well as several other times in the schooling of children (Torrance, 1967b). We are also well aware of the pressures exerted by education on children to conform to prearranged educational experiences, with consequent press and its ill effects on their mental health (Gowan & Bruch, 1971; Torrance, 1962a). These pressures can cause stunting of the creative development of gifted children and call for guidance so that, while the children acquire the knowledge and skills that are needed for living, they do not sacrifice their creativity. Guidance can be given to them to circumvent these restrictions so that they begin to learn in ways that will lead to productive and higher states of creative development. For this, we may find many helpful suggestions from Torrance and Myers (1970), Gowan and Bruch (1971), and Khatena (1978c) among others.

Eminent creators as role models for emulation appear to be very important to the emergence of other eminent creators, and the effects are maximized and more predictable if emulation occurs in the same discipline and especially during the developmental period of genius. This has particular significance for guidance because arrangements can be made not only to bring to notice historical and contemporary creative eminents to gifted children for emulation but also, where feasible, to make plans for mentoring by bringing eminent people together with gifted children for face-to-face interaction.

Arieti (1976) views the individual and society as two open systems in dynamic exchange. He calls creativogenic a society that offers the individual the possibility of becoming great and focuses our attention on nine conditions present in a creativoenic society that facilitate such an occurrence (see p. 166). For the gifted child, several of these conditions take on significance and guidance has an important role to play to assist in developing greatness. Drawing from Arieti's observations, the following guidance approaches are suggested:

Guidance can ensure that gifted individuals find accessible other talented and gifted people with whom they can work, learn, and interact as well as be stimulated by them toward productivity. Also, guidance can see that materials, supplies, equipment, and the like, for activities and experiences needed for creative functioning and advancement of their talent are made available to the gifted.

Guidance can make gifted children more aware of what their culture can offer. It can arrange for opportunities whereby gifted children receive what they desire or request of cultural stimulation and that they are exposed to different and even contrasting cultural stimulation.

Guidance can emphasize continued striving towards self-actualization.

Guidance can develop gifted children's tolerance for and interest in divergent views.

Guidance can assist gifted children attain high levels of creative functioning and achievement, arrange for systems of incentives and rewards that move from the extrinsic to the intrinsic, and endorse the shift toward intrinsic reward.

To make the gifted develop and realize their creative potential has paramount significance for guidance. We have attempted to perceive guidance implications by drawing from developmental stage theory, growth and transformation theory, and historical and sociocultural perspectives. Here we reiterate the suggestions offered for the guidance of gifted children:

1. One major concern of guidance should be to provide continual environmental stimulation to facilitate escalation toward higher levels of creative functioning and self-actualization. Several ways used to facilitate superior

180

adults can be adapted for use with gifted children and youth, these include the provision of various educational experiences, therapy, sensitivity training, and so on.

2. When dysplasia occurs, guidance is needed to assist the gifted to develop as completely as possible (i.e., cognitively and affectively) and to effect escalation of all parts of the psyche beyond Gowan's stage 5 and through stages 6, 7, and 8 into creativity and self-actualization.

3. Guidance of the gifted can take the form of counteracting measures to alleviate the discontinuity in creative mental functioning that include the arrangement of stimulating conditions and opportunities, the fostering of love that makes accessible the preconscious for creativity, the encouragement in the use of creative imagination, and the reduction of stress.

4. The gifted can be assisted through their creative growth cycles to move from lower to higher ones by providing them with experiences and activities aimed at developing their creative thinking abilities and using metaphor, imagery, and analogy.

5. Appropriate environmental stimulation to facilitate the creative development of gifted children should include effective positive reinforcements (feedback), information that allows for escalation to higher stages of creative functioning within the growth cycle.

6. To counteract the adverse influences of formal education that may stunt the creative development of the gifted, guidance can be given to them to acquire the necessary knowledge and skills for living without sacrificing their creativity. This should be done in such a manner that the gifted learn in ways that lead to productivity and higher states of creative development.

7. Guidance can be given to the gifted to emulate historical and contemporary eminent creators and arrangements can be made, where feasible, for face-to-face interaction with these models.

8. Eminent men and women of talent, materials, and equipment can be made accessible to the gifted for the advancement of their creative development and talent expression.

9. The gifted can be guided to an awareness of the diversity and richness of cultural offerings that will stimulate them to creative striving and self-actualization.

10. The gifted can be assisted to attain the highest levels of creative achievements so that they may obtain both extrinsic and intrinsic rewards with an appropriate preference for intrinsic rewards.

GUIDANCE TOWARD MASTERY OF STRESS

Another facet for guidance as it relates to gifted students is the nature and function of stress and the approaches to cope with stress, not in a remedial but in a preventative sense. This is consistent with earlier observation on the positive thrust of guidance as it concerns itself with the normal development of gifted individuals. Stress interferes with development toward mental health, creativity, and self-actualization. Individuals are constantly bombarded with all kinds of stress from one moment to the next in their lives, and they are repeatedly put in the position of having to make adjustments and adaptations to stress, otherwise disorientation and breakdown become inevitable. The Terman studies (Terman & Oden, 1959) on gifted children who grow up to midlife have reitereated that the gifted are generally mentally healthy individuals; however, not all of them have remained so throughout their lives and, for these, early promise has not been fulfilled. Although one may attempt to find an explanation in specific events in their lives, what appears to be a common factor is stress and their inability to deal successfully with it. One of the most significant conceptions of this problem that holds considerable implications for guidance of the gifted is the idea that mental health involves constructive rather than adjustive response to stress (Torrance, 1965a).

Assessing the various concepts of mental health, Torrance distinguishes between those related to the perceptions of society and those related to the perceptions of professional mental health workers. He draws on his research with the *Imaginative Story,* an instrument that calls on children to write original stories when given divergent titles, such as "The Monkey That Flies," "The Lion That Does Not Roar," "The Man Who Cries," "The Doctor Who Became a Carpenter," and "The Hen That Crows". A fuller treatment of this can be found in *Guiding Creative Talent* (Torrance, 1962a). Torrance calls to our attention that mental health, which is perceived by society as reflected in these stories, requires conformity to behavioral norms as the alternative to destruction, brings relentless pressure for the well-rounded personality, emphasizes convergency because divergency is equated with mental illness and delinquency, and overemphasizes sex roles so that any deviation from appropriate masculinity and femininity is also associated with mental illness and delinquency. From the findings of the stories, Torrance constructs a picture of what a mentally healthy person in our society is like:

First, he must conform to the behavioral norms of his society. He must be well rounded and must work hard to correct any irregularities in development. If some aspect of development has lagged, he must neglect all else and achieve the expected standard. If some function or skill has been developed to an unusually high level, he must deliberately neglect further development along this line or suppress it. Individuals whose behavior is "different" are usually labeled as mentally ill (crazy, wild, etc.) or delinquent (naughty, bad, etc.). Regardless of natural inclinations and talents, the mentally healthy person according to this dominant position must conform to his society's concepts of masulinity or femininity. (1965a, p. 9)

Of the many professional attempts to define mental health—these have varied from simplistic single-sentence definitions to comprehensive and multiple-criteria listings of the well-adjusted person—Jahoda's (1958) approach appears to be the most pertinent. She suggests that appropriate adjustment toward mental health involves (1) attitudes of an individual toward his or her own self (accessibility to consciousness, correctness, feeling about the self, and sense of identity); (2) growth, development, or self-actualization (self-concept, motivational processes, and investment in living); (3) integration (a balance of psychic forces in the individual, a unifying view of life, emphasis on the cognitive aspects of integration, and resistance to stress); (4) autonomy regulation of behavior from within and independent behavior); (5) perception of reality (perception of need distortion and empathy [social sensitivity]); and (6) environmental mastery (ability to love; adequacy in love, work, and play; adequacy in interpersonal relations; efficiency in meeting situational requirements; capacity for adaptation and adjustment; and efficiency in problem solving).

It is not so much a lack of agreement as to what consitutes mental health as it is the attempt to express in words a multivariate and complex phenomenon—some words identifying units of the construct, other words classifying and systematizing these units into larger categories, and yet other words omitting detail for a global construct. Torrance (1965a) defines mental health as, "the healthy, complete functioning of the mind" whose proper operation may suffer interference from many forces within individuals as well as from the external environment. He labels this interference stress. It is in the use of individual's potentialities as resources to cope constructively with stress that offers guidance significant direction.

BEHAVIOR UNDER STRESS

Drawing information from survival research, Torrance (1965a) identified both the stressful physical conditions that can lead to death (e.g., water or food deprivation, extreme heat or cold, sleep deprivation) and the stressful psychological aspects of these conditions (e.g., shock, mental confusion, inefficiency, apathy, suicide) as they affect healthy mental functioning. He adds other conditions that bear no threat to life (e.g., interpersonal irritations, failure to achieve ambitions). When these conditions are not severe, he observes that such behaviors as overcompensation, heroism, increased speed, efficiency, planning, the use of higher levels of intellectual functioning to approach full potential, and the like, are called for so that death or breakdown can be prevented. Consequently, it is the function of professionals of mental health to prevent the occurrence of such breakdowns and help individuals in their living, study and career aspirations.

Stress can be regarded as an interference to the normal and full functioning of

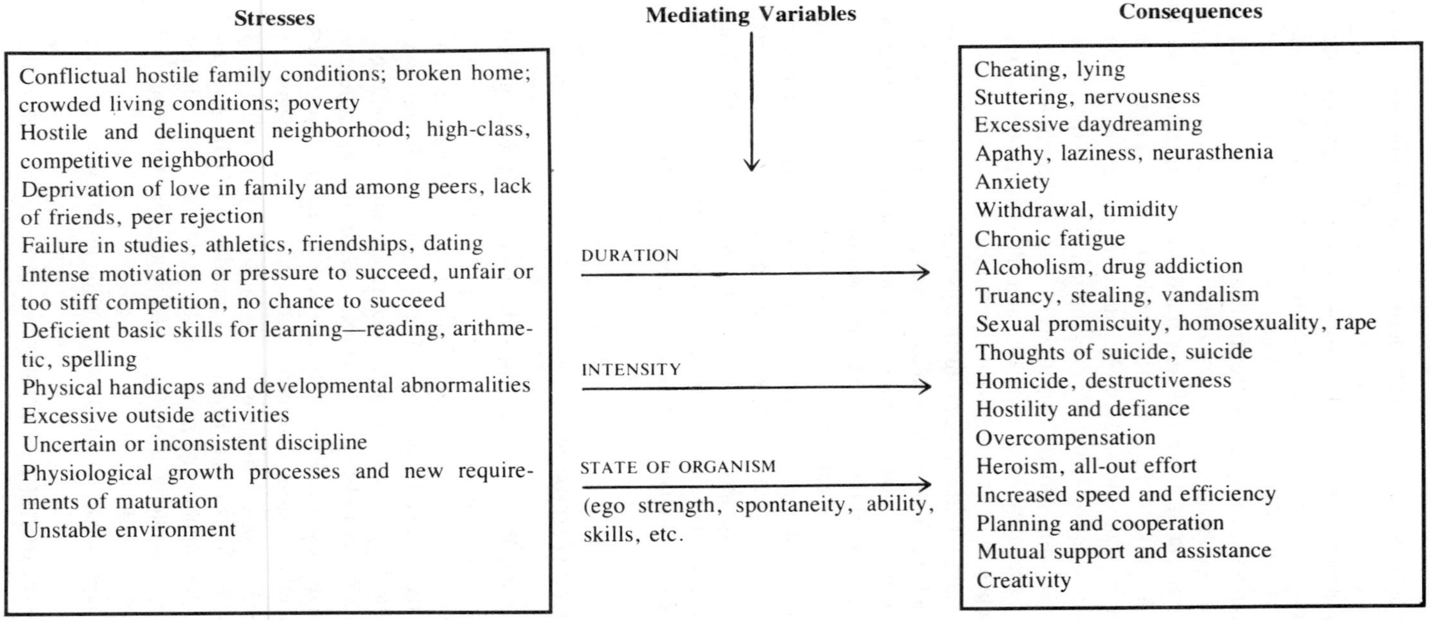

Stresses

Conflictual hostile family conditions; broken home; crowded living conditions; poverty

Hostile and delinquent neighborhood; high-class, competitive neighborhood

Deprivation of love in family and among peers, lack of friends, peer rejection

Failure in studies, athletics, friendships, dating

Intense motivation or pressure to succeed, unfair or too stiff competition, no chance to succeed

Deficient basic skills for learning—reading, arithmetic, spelling

Physical handicaps and developmental abnormalities

Excessive outside activities

Uncertain or inconsistent discipline

Physiological growth processes and new requirements of maturation

Unstable environment

Mediating Variables

DURATION

INTENSITY

STATE OF ORGANISM
(ego strength, spontaneity, ability, skills, etc.)

Consequences

Cheating, lying

Stuttering, nervousness

Excessive daydreaming

Apathy, laziness, neurasthenia

Anxiety

Withdrawal, timidity

Chronic fatigue

Alcoholism, drug addiction

Truancy, stealing, vandalism

Sexual promiscuity, homosexuality, rape

Thoughts of suicide, suicide

Homicide, destructiveness

Hostility and defiance

Overcompensation

Heroism, all-out effort

Increased speed and efficiency

Planning and cooperation

Mutual support and assistance

Creativity

Figure 7 Typical stresses encountered and the mediation of their effects. (Torrance, 1965a. Copyright © 1965 by Wadsworth Publishing Company, Inc., Belmont, Calif. Reprinted by permission.)

mental abilities that otherwise assist individuals to cope with their problems. Torrance conceives of behavior under stress as a process through which specific stresses, mediated by duration and intensity as well as the state of the organism, fetch a variety of possible responses (Figure 7). Specific stresses stem from situations that involve person, family, learning, and environment generally, and they may take the form of conflict, hostility, love, deprivation, disability, failure, and developmental changes which may cause a variety of negative or positive behaviors.

STRESS DURATION AND INTENSITY AFFECTING BEHAVIOR

When stress occurs and lasts for a short period of time, mastery of it is more likely to take place than if the duration is prolonged, which often leads to ineffective coping and eventual collapse. This is regardless of the ability level of the emotional condition of the individual. If stress is mild, improved performance, increased activity, learning, and so on, result; however, if stress is extremely intense, deterioration of performance and eventual breakdown can be expected. Further, mild but prolonged stress is even more damaging, and more breakdowns stem from prolonged stress than from brief intense stress. It is important to know the process of adaptation to the duration of stress so that breakdowns can be prevented. This process relates to normal functioning that suffers interference from stress. The onset of stress causes shock, which temporarily adversely affects both intellectual performance and emotional control. This arrest is followed by rapid overcompensation and maximum effort, which restores proper intellectual performance and emotional control and, in turn, is followed by a recovery toward continued normal functioning. Should stress continue over a prolonged period, fatigue with decreasing mental efficiency and emotional control sets in. This ultimately leads to collapse or breakdown (Figure 8).

STATE OF PERSON AFFECTING BEHAVIOR

Another mediating variable between stress and its behavioral consequences is the state of a person and the great variability that exists among individuals relative to this. The extent to which an individual achieves mastery over a stressful situation depends on a great number of variables, among which are the presence or absence of coping skills, specific relevant ability, physical disabilities, and prior experience or training for dealing with the stress. The mediation of ego-strength has much to do with the slowing down, speeding up, or prevention of the stress adaptation process described above.

When failure to cope with a stressful situation occurs, it means that the stress is more than the individual can handle. Generally, when an individual is unable to adapt to the experienced stress, it is to some degree because there is a loss of

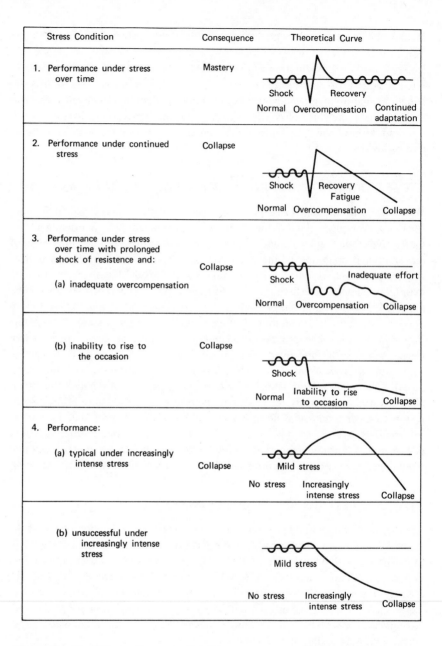

Figure 8   Conditions of stress and their consequences. (Torrance, 1965a. Copyright © 1965 by Wadsworth Publishing Company, Inc., Belmont, Calif. Reprinted by permission.)

anchor in reality (i.e., contact with the environment) or a lack of structure has occurred. The disorganization that ensures, in turn, causes stress and leads to a problem of successful adaptation to stress. Included among a variety of factors that bring about the disorganization and disorientation of an individual can be the strangeness or instability of the situation, with demands for handling it in ways unfamiliar and nonhabitual to the individual; threats to the individual's central value system; changes that occur too rapidly for efficient processing; or inadequate skills for coping with overwhelming requirements. For mastery of the stressful situation, the individual needs help to reorganize and a structure that can lead to appropriate anchors in reality.

PROBLEMS STRESSFUL TO GIFTED STUDENTS

Torrance (1967a) illustrates stress as affecting the gifted student as well as the process of adapting to it:

Let us consider the gifted student who suddenly encounters academic failure. When the stress (failure in a school subject) is suddenly encountered, there is first shock and lack of adaptation. Perhaps there is resistance to accepting the reality or seriousness of the failure. The student may wonder if some mistake has been made, blame the teacher or some other external source, or reason that he "just slipped up" or that "the test was no good." In successful adaptation, there will be rapid overcompensation, improved methods of study, increased energy in studying, longer study hours, etc. With recovery there will be a levelling off of performance and the restoration of emotional control; but if the teacher persistently refuses to recognize the improved performance and holds on to his original assessment of [the] student's ability and achievements, we can envision the consequences. The frequency of breakdowns among gifted students under such conditions is well known to anyone who has worked very long with gifted students.

Let us say that our mythical gifted student, after the first shock and acceptance of the seriousness of his failure, puts forth a maximum effort. At first he succeeds, but the course and the standards of the instructor become increasingly more difficult. He is pushed to use more expensive coping devices. He may increase his speed of reading and writing, obtain expert help, work with another student, or exercise greater ingenuity and creativity. If these expensive energies continue to be required by his academic program and there is no let up in the demands, some kind of breakdown will occur eventually. The result may be withdrawal from school, delinquency, thoughts of suicide or even suicide. He may react by cheating and deceit, excessive daydreaming, apathy, hostility and defiance, etc.

In another case, our gifted student may be unaccustomed to challenges that require "all out" performance. His attempt to rise to the occasion may be weak and inadequate and his collapse may come rapidly. Some gifted students consistently fail becuase they never find anything they consider worth their best efforts. Others keep thinking that they can "get by" with less than their best.

In still another case, our gifted student may fail altogether to recognize the seriousness of his failure. He makes no effort to overcompensate or "go all out" and immediate collapse follows. He simply waits until it is too late. In another situation, he may be so surprised, shocked or hurt by the failure that he will panic, become apathetic, and is unable to take any constructive action. Such behavior may be seen in withdrawals from school, serious mis-behavior, and the like. (pp. 4–5)

We have just seen how a gifted student who experiences the stress of academic failure may respond to it in a number of different ways, which could result under varying conditions in mastery of stress or collapse or breakdown. Other stressful conditions that lead to a variety of problems for the gifted relate to: (1) the numerous educational and occupation opportunities available to them and the wise choices they have to make, sometimes even before they are ready to make them; (2) the unusual need for them to develop specialized interests that go with certain professional occupations, even if their true interests lie elsewhere; (3) the gifted appraising and conceptualizing themselves at higher levels than age merits; (4) the early awareness of developmental tasks before physical readiness; and (5) the unusual pressures exerted on them by parents, teachers, and peers (Gowan & Demos, 1964; Rothney & Koopman, 1958).

To these problem-causing situations Gowan and Demos (1964) add: (1) gifted students' confusion over the dual norm group that leads to their instability to discriminate between situations that are applicable to all persons equally regard-less of ability and situations that are more in line with gifted norms, for which different expectations may be held; (2) a lack of challenge, especially in the elementary school curriculum; (3) a failure to find friends of the same age; (4) a lack of occupational information; (5) a lack of motivation; (6) an impatience with routine learning and the dull classroom; (7) an independence in thinking and judgment; (8) a resistance to conformity; (9) hypersensitivity and vulnerability to criticism; (10) a desire to excel with perfectionist tendencies; (11) a passion for the truth and a desire for meanings beyond the obvious, which may lead to dissillusionment and rebellion against "irrelevant" society; (12) an uneven pat-tern of intellectual abilities; and (13) physical and emotional handicaps.

Torrance (1962a) observes that society applies coercive influences on di-vergency and even on outstanding performance; that individuals who use creative talent often alienate themselves from friends; that tremendous pressure is placed on individuals to be well rounded; that there exists a misplaced emphasis on sex

188

roles, and that efforts toward the establishment of sex norms during early childhood pervade the educational life of individuals; that the school may not permit and even may retard the performance of individuals to learn on their own; that there is a lack of awareness that creative individuals have the desire to attempt difficult and even dangerous tasks, seek to discover their potentialities, and achieve their self-concepts creatively, and that they may possess different values from the norm; that many misinterpret the motivations of high creatives, who cannot seem to stop working and who create difficulties for themselves by deliberately trying to be different in search for their uniqueness—even rejecting their society's demand for them to surrender their individuality; and that the gifted are often in psychological isolation and estrangement from parents, teachers, and peers.

All these situations bristle with stress-inducing conditions that call for effective adaptive and adjustive behaviors toward mastery of stress. As we have seen, maladaptive behavioral patterns can only lead to collapse and breakdown and are not only tied to the intensity and duration of stress but also to the mediating variable of individual differences and to coping reactions. The problems identified above arise from the creative needs of gifted persons and their transactions with society and the external world, which do not often lead to need satisfaction. Khatena (1973e, 1978c) discusses problems attendant on the repression of creative needs and points out that, if repression is prolonged and adjustment maladaptive, this could lead to neurosis and even psychosis.

Repression of his creative needs may lead the highly creative child to become outwardly conforming, obedient and dependent, with damaging consequences to his concept of self. It may also lead to serious learning disabilities and behavioral problems. In preferring to learn by authority he sacrifices his natural tendency to learn creatively by questioning, guessing, exploring and experimentation. As a result he loses interest in and is resistant to learning. Development of awe for masterpieces and a spread of feelings of inadequacy from deficiency in one area of learning to other areas of learning where no deficiency exists follow. Further, much of the agressive behaviors in the classroom that the highly gifted child exhibits can be traced to his inability to use creative and scientific thinking strategies to overcome his tensions. These tensions often arise from his reactions to a school curriculum that is unchallenging, repetitive, reproductive and boring, before they become problems that result in his misbehavior.

The more serious problem of prolonged enforced repression of the creative child's needs may lead to emotional problems and neurosis, and even psychosis (e.g. Gowan, 1955; Torrance, 1962a). Neurosis as you know is a condition generated by acute and prolonged anxiety states and can be very much the case of continued repression of creative needs especially in the context of conflict situations. Neurosis hinders rather than facilitates the functioning of the creative process contrary to popular opinion. Kubie (1958) writing about this subject suggests that many a creative man of the arts and sciences refuses therapy because he erroneously believes that his "creative zeal and spark" is dependent upon his neurosis; what is really essential is that the preconscious process functions freely to gather, assemble, compare and reshuffle ideas in the activity of creation.

Torrance (1962a) writes of psychosis relative to maladjustment of the creative individual in a special sense. In psychosis resulting from the blocking of creative energies, thinking is often paralyzed and the imagination functions in a way that cannot distinguish between reality and irreality. The creative individual who has his productivity blocked may develop behavior traits similar to those of psychotics whose reaction to reality may be very much like the behavior of the paranoid personality in some respects, or his behavior might become withdrawn or schizophrenic. (Khatena, 1978c, pp. 89-90)

GUIDING THE GIFTED TO MASTER STRESS

The thrust of guidance for the gifted in mastering stress should be toward prevention rather than cure. The many problems that gifted students face arise often from their uniqueness attempting to find expression and even asserting itself in a society that does not understand this, will not tolerate it, and will even attempt to stifle it. Individuals assuming the role of counselor must recognize this position if they are to begin rendering effective and productive service. They must begin by attempting to understand the nature and function of giftedness and the special characteristics and needs of the gifted individuals with whom they have dealings; to indentify the conditions that are likely to thwart, obstruct, or prevent healthy development and expression of uniqueness; and to provide appropriate conditions for counselor-counselee interaction to occur. Preventative guidance also requires that the counselor anticipate stress-inducing conditions to provide his gifted charges the opportunity to acquire those skills that can be used to cope with stress from its onset. Among the several approaches that can be taken to guide the gifted toward mastery of stress are the development of interpersonal skills and the use of intellectual abilities that include problem solving.

DEVELOPING INTERPERSONAL SKILLS

We have already pointed out that gifted individuals in trying to be themselves and to realize their talents come into conflict with parents, teachers, peers, and larger groups. Others feel threatened by the uniqueness of the gifted and, in one way or another, pressure the gifted to be like everyone else. In the counseling situation, the gifted need to understand their situation and that, so long as they have

190

interaction with others, they will have to cope with this pressure and learn how to continue to be individualistic and unique without antagonizing others and, thus, bring about difficult and hostile conditions leveled at preventing their healthy development and actualization. Therefore, guidance should help gifted children to recognize their outstanding talents, which may be threatening to others, and to learn that one way of gaining acceptance is by putting such talents to use to serve the larger group and so build up what Pepinsky (1960) has called a credit rating. Torrance (1962a) advises helping gifted children maintain the characteristics that are essential to creativity as well as teaching them skills for avoiding or reducing to a tolerable level social sanctions that will be leveled at them. As this relates to gifted elementary pupils, he advises the following behaviors to serve as a useful model in guiding gifted children to overcome the tendency to be obnoxious without sacrificing their creativity:

Help the gifted child maintain his assertiveness without being hostile and aggressive. He must be aware of his superiors, peers and subordinates as persons. He may work alone but he must not be isolated, withdrawn or uncommunicative. In the classroom he must be sociable but not intimate. He must "know his place" without being timid, submissive, or acquiescent and must speak "his mind" without being domineering. As he tries to gain a point, he can be subtle but not cunning or manipulative. In all relationships, he must be sincere, honest, purposeful, and diplomatic. In the intellectual area, he must learn to be broad without spreading himself too thin, deep without being "bookish" or "too scientific," and "sharp" without being overcritical. (Torrance, 1962a, p. 156)

Another important facet of this kind of guidance must relate to help prevent gifted children from experiencing isolation or estrangement from teachers and peers (or reducing this where it exists). Gifted children have an intense need to communicate with others and sometimes may not be in a position to do this. The counselor may help them learn to tolerate some separateness or assist them in finding someone with whom they can communicate—perhaps another gifted child who may have common interests.

Not enough emphasis is given in the counseling situation to gifted students' use of their many intellectual abilities, which grow more effective in their dealings with others as they grow older. With growing intellectual maturity, gifted individuals can more accurately perceive the attitudes, interests, and abilities of others and, thus, gain those interpersonal skills that will allow them to deal with others in more constructive ways. Just as a person with practice can become more skilled in debating, so, too, gifted children can become more skillful in their transactions with others with experience. The counseling situation may arrange for a variety of experiences that may help to clarify the gifted child's relations with others to develop greater competence. The sociodramatic technique—drawn by Torrance (1975b; Torrance & Myers 1970) from J. L. Moreno and applied to children so that they may learn in creative ways—can be of great value in the counseling situation. A problem that a gifted child faces may be presented, clarified, and handled toward finding a solution by means of role playing in a dramatic situation. The outcome may be the discovery of the true causes of the problem as well as alternative behaviors that can be adopted to prevent or avert the problem. In these ways, the causative factors of stress may be identified and become apparent to the gifted child, with the purpose of preparing him or her to anticipate antagonistic stress-inducing behaviors and circumscribe them with alternative behaviors that may produce more tolerant and nurturant reactions from others. As these interpersonal skills are acquired, gifted individuals are more likely to experience little or no stress; if stress occurs they will be in a more knowledgeable position to cope with, and master, it for normal and healthy mental functioning.

USING INTELLECTUAL ABILITIES TO COPE WITH STRESS

As children grow older and have increasing command of their intellectual abilities, they learn to substitute intellectual approaches for the more primitive strategies they had used to cope with emergency situations. Torrance (1965a) emphasizes the importance of using intellectual resources toward constructive behavior when dealing with stress, and he examines these in terms of the five thinking operations of the structure of intellect: cognition, memory, convergent thinking, divergent thinking, and evaluation. Of the five mental operations, the first three entail the least expenditure of energy, whereas divergent thinking and evaluation require the greatest. Hence, Torrance suggests that cognition, memory, and convergent thinking if first called into play usually allow for some reserve energy so that productive and evaluative thinking can handle stress when needed.

Cognition and Stress
Cognition can assist a person to recognize when a situation becomes serious enough to require some adaptive action to avert disaster before it is too late. Often, many of us experience stress in a situation because we are not familiar with it; knowing something about a situation before actually experiencing it helps reduce anxiety and allows for more efficient functioning. Related to this is the identification of the components of a problem or structuring it to know the situation as well as possible for what it is; thus, not only does the situation become familiar but also the course of action that is to be taken becomes apparent. Knowing the causes and anticipating the consequences of certain actions are more likely to lead to successful adaptation to situations. A certain amount of remembering of past experiences and evaluating the situation—its structure and plan of action—come into play as well. Cognition can also be used to ensure that

192

one thinks well of oneself and expects to succeed, and it further allows for the understanding of feedback information relative to performance under stress so that behavior can be rapidly modified toward successful adaptation. Knowing information provides the essential basis for problem-solving behaviors and appropriate decision making. As indicated, cognition calls for the use of less expensive energies. Therefore, understanding the situation and knowing what to do allows persons to handle a large number of stressful situations and conserve more energy to solve other problems by using productive and evaluative thinking, which assist persons to recover speedily from the shock of stress. Thus, they return to normal functioning and a fuller awareness of self and the environment with the excitement and joy that, in turn, increases their mental health.

Memory and Stress

Memory abilities are very important in relation to stress. By their use a person may recall experiences that were stressful and examine how stress was handled, the success or failure of the strategies used, the modifications made in the process of successful adaptation, and the mastery of the stress. Thus, memory provides a frame of reference for handling other stressful situations. Of course, when different experiences are appraised, evaluation may also have a part to play in the process so that decisions can be made in dealing with these new situations. Stress may also be related to lapses in memory, which may not only give rise to discomfort but also hinder effective coping in emergency situations. It is important, then, to arrange for conditions that will facilitate appropriate storage for effective retrieval. Memory of oneself, of one's liabilities and assets, of the use of personal resources to cope successfully with stressful situations, and so on, are important because these remind individuals that they are not without means in an emergency. Remembering one's acquired knowledge and skills and their availability for use can assist an individual when coping behaviors are required. How to interact with others is also important and remembering how this was done in previous encounters with others should not only help one cope with stress but also circumvent stress by appropriate interpersonal behaviors. To this may be added that memory provides an individual with a frame of reference to structure or prestructure situations as the need arises for successful adaptation.

Convergent Thinking and Stress

Convergent thinking is considered important in coping with life's stresses as well. In general, it requires the use of less expensive energies than other thinking operations, and it is usually the easiest and quickest way of coming up with answers. For persons who have limited abilities it is the most efficient method on which they can rely for their actions concerning the thoughts of others. Consequently, it reduces intolerance of disagreement. Convergent thinking, then, relates to coping with stress by individuals keeping in line with the thinking of the group and, thus, they are less likely to create stress. Sometimes, however, trying to arrive at the one best or common solution is not without difficulty and can lead to an accumulation of stress that may become overwhelming. It is well known that having the same answers as others brings with it social-approval status, satisfaction of certain needs and other rewards, and allows convergent thinkers a rapport with others and their environment that is certainly tension reducing both for convergent thinkers and the group to which they belong.

Divergent Thinking and Stress

The role of divergent thinking in coping with stress involves the ability to deal with the excessive rate of change in our world—reliance cannot be placed on the single solution to a problem, which may become obsolete as soon as it is identified, but must be placed on the capacity to produce many alternative solutions in keeping with changing conditions. If tried methods prove to be repeatedly unsuccessful, frustration can be avoided by using divergent thinking to produce fresh approaches and strategies to handle the problem. Fatigue, which sometimes sets in during a coping situation, can be removed by divergent thinking because some wild exciting idea with the promise of fresh possibilities can revitalize and energize a person to increase efforts toward successful adaptation. Besides, with a reserve of many ideas and possible solutions to a problem, the prospects of making better decisions increase, and this is accompanied by gains in confidence that one will successfully overcome the problem. In addition, the generation of many possible alternative solutions prepares persons to anticipate many possible outcomes that are less likely to be stressful; rather, they can be expected to increase one's hopes for successful coping. Divergent thinking frees individuals in terms of their own uniqueness and allows them to be more comfortable with themselves and be authentic persons with consequent benefits in their relations with others and the world.

Evaluative Thinking and Stress

Evaluative thinking requires the most use of expensive energy, and its role in coping with stress is an important one. It is essential for a person to recognize the seriousness of a situation, but this not only calls for the operation of cognition and memory but also for appraisal of the situation so that a decision can be made for adaptive action. Here evaluation entails maintaining contact with the environment and structuring the situation to anticipate the consequences of action and so prevent shock. In appraising a situation for the making of a decision, individuals learn to recognize and accept their limitations, thereby reducing the number and seriousness of errors in their plans for coping more effectively with stress. Biases of unconscious motivations that interfere with evaluation abilities in the making of decisions can also be corrected so that coping with stress can be more successful. By the process of evaluation, a mass of data can be given simple

194

structure and proper emphasis for easier use to cope with stress in a situation. Further, evaluation is important for the testing of the reality and efficacy of the divergent thinking used in producing solutions to problems.

STRATEGIES FOR COPING WITH STRESS

After discussing the nature and role of the above five thinking operations as they relate to stress, Torrance (1965a) offers several useful strategies that he has drawn from approaches to cope with life. These strategies may call for one or more abilities in the coping situation, namely, risking and avoiding, mastering and failing, overloading and unloading, denying need and making peace, and encouraging the continued fight. These strategies are expected to aid pupils to develop more effective ways of dealing with such common stresses relative to curricular and career choices; to realistic self-concept development; to coping with pressures of the peer group, school, and society; to changing patterns of nonachievement and delinquency, and so on.

Risking and Avoiding

All individuals at one time or another find themselves in the position of having to make decisions. In school, students have to make decisions about educational or vocational choices; if gifted, they have many more alternatives from which to choose. Decisions also have to be made that relate to student's developmental tasks as well as their relations with others. The more uncertain or unfamiliar the situation, the greater the hesitance to make decisions, and often an appeal for help is made to the counselor, teacher, or parent. Those in the counseling situation must resist the temptation to make the decision for the students. Instead, the cause of this hesitance needs to be found, the students need to be assisted in obtaining adequate information about the problem and become reasonably familiar with the situation to the extent that some willingness to attempt or risk a decision can take place. We do know that highly gifted individuals are often risk takers; yet, there may be times when a situation may so overwhelm these students that some reassurance needs to be given so that there is some reduction in the risk before a decision is made. The students may test a tentative decision before going on to make a final decision; that is, they may be allowed a second chance and, thus, be able to alter the course of action before it ends up in failure for them. The technique of limited commitment suggested by Cooper (1961) may be tried. An action can be divided in a way that commits limited resources to it until the student can make up his or her mind or the situation can be simulated on a small scale to try out a plan of action before fully implementing it. Gifted students should be encouraged to take educated risks to cope with problems that face them, even if, in some instances, this may lead to failure. Some prior preparation in risk taking should keep to a minimum the expense of wasted resources.

If avoidance of decision making in students is evident, corrective action lies in finding out the cause of insecurity, which, if deep rooted psychologically, may be beyond the help that a teacher or a parent can give. One approach that may be taken is to let students avoid decision making as to where they personally stand on an issue which may help them know the extent to which they could use their judgment. In addition, the students should be well informed about the decision they have to make and encouraged, even pressed, to make a preliminary or trial decision. The success of their decision may persuade them to move further on in the decision-making process. Guidance can assist gifted individuals to learn the strategies of risking and avoiding in decision making. In addition to the approaches suggested, counselors can show the connections between conduct and consequences; give dramatic examples; offer criticism and encouragement to help individuals define the limits of a situation or have the limits defined for them (Redl & Wattenberg, 1959); and cultivate the habit of thinking of as many causes and consequences of one's behavior as possible (Torrance, 1965a).

Mastering and Failing

Many individuals are unwilling to take risks or are reluctant to make changes in their lives because there is fear of the unknown. Learning and occupational choices may also be approached in this way, and, with highly gifted students, the wide array of choices can sometimes be overwhelming and indecisiveness results. The counseling situation can help in a number of ways to alleviate this problem. Students may be helped to understand the situation that face them, and, where possible, some actual preliminary experience can be planned for them. As this relates to a choice of occupations, arrangements may be made for some trial on-the-job experience in several locations. Such a learning experience should be prefaced by some preparation of the students as to what to expect in the situation. It should be followed up by an analysis of the experience before the students make a decision about a vocation. Role playing can be a very valuable technique to make the unknown familiar and can be used where actual experience is not available or as a complement to it. Structuring and restructuring an experience are extremely valuable methods in assisting students to obtain as much information as needed for a new or forthcoming experience. Through these methods, students can know what the requirements are and assess if their academic, personal, and special-talent resources can meet them; if not, they can assess what else needs to be done and, then, make plans for the attainment of the necessary resources so that expected mastery over the situation can be gained. If a situation is too big or difficult to handle some restructuring appears to be needed and students will require assistance in understanding the situation. Therefore, they turn to their groups for mutual support and encouragement so that appropriate decision making can follow. In the event of failure to cope with the situation, the counselor would do well to help students recognize what went wrong so they can correct the error where possible; if the students do not have the skills to do this, the counselor will need to help them develop these skills. It is important that students learn the virtue of admitting mistakes. Counseling can help them do this more easily because by such admissions students will find themselves in a learning set that will reduce the chances of further errors and prepare them for fresh solution finding and appropriate verification. Such an approach will prevent students from collapsing under the stress of failure, profit by their mistakes, and prepare them for renewed attempts at coping with greater probability of success and mastery.

Overloading and Unloading

Another strategy for coping with stress is the mechanism of overloading-unloading. Overloading is caused by an accumulation of stress that becomes burdensome to individuals. Release must be found for it before individuals can give their attention to learning and career goals or be able to recognize the seriousness of a situation. The process by which such release can occur has been described as unloading or relieving oneself of tensions. The counseling situation affords individuals the opportunity to unload their pent-up feelings—just the opportunity to gripe about things or talk things over will free individuals and help them clarify their position and see the stress for what it really is. Then, they can begin to make a more accurate appraisal of their needs and decide on an appropriate course of action that should lead to achievement of their goals.

Structuring and restructuring the situation applies here, too, because once unloading has taken place, individuals are better able to handle their situation intellectually and the counselor can give the necessary guidance toward structure that will facilitate effective decision making. Much of the problem of overloading is related to the availability of time and its economical use in terms of the way activities are organized. Relative to this, unloading can be achieved by taking a task that is perceived as much bigger than it really is in the context of the limited time for its accomplishment and break both the content of the task and the time available into smaller and more manageable units and, then, make a plan of how best to handle each unit in turn until the task is completed. The counselor can give valuable guidance in this respect, for example, to students who are overwhelmed by the magnitude of preparing for an important final examination. By reducing anxiety, the counselor will make it possible for students to attack the problem successfully. Some practice in the use of this and the other strategies discussed should provide students with useful operations to prevent the occurrence of future overloading.

Denying Need and Making Peace

Conflicts between the needs of individuals and the demands of situations (e.g., frustration, fatigue, hostility) interfere with the effective functioning of evaluative thinking abilities and result in bad judgments. Hence, the counseling situation should assist the gifted student to resolve these conflicts before encouraging better decisions. Torrance (1965a) suggests aids to resolve these conflicts that involve counteracting the threat in some way by the use of objective information, the passing of time that may change the odds, a willingness to endure and not surrender, the recognition that the problem may need more mental effort or expensive energies, and strategic withdrawal. Decisions that involve others must also be accepted by them; their acceptance can be facilitated if the decision is congruent with the interests, intentions, and goals of the group.

Encouraging the Continued Fight

A valuable approach in coping with a problem that begins to become too much for an individual is encouragement and support from the group of which the individual is a member to persevere and not give up the fight. The counselor's awareness of this powerful source of coping energies is important because arrangement can be made in the counseling situation for this climate. Occasionally, students need to be aroused or spurred to greater effort by being countershocked out of their apathetic, paralyzed, or surrendering state and learn with counselor assistance and support how best to make full and better use of their personal resources (e.g., religion, values, sense of humor, acceptance of support from others.) The use of expensive energies if demanded over a long period will lead to breakdown and must be recognized by the counselor. However, to continue the fight, the use of expensive energies may be necessary and, for a time, its value to help students overcome their predicament cannot be emphasized more. In addition to the use of expensive energies, students may be counseled to keep busy and plan activities for continued stimulation because in this lies their chance to continue the fight with every possibility of eventual success.

ACADEMIC AND CAREER GUIDANCE

We have approached guidance of the gifted from two theoretical positions as they relate to creative development and stress, and we have touched on personal, academic, and vocational counseling in coping with developmental changes and stress. This section will look at academic guidance of the gifted student more closely and indicate the implications this may have for career guidance of the adolescent student. Further, guidance has so far been thought of in terms of the counseling situation. Although we have referred to counselors as the ones giving guidance, teachers and parents should also be thought of as having important roles in the counseling situation. There are some areas of counseling that can best be handled by the teachers, not only the educational aspects of guidance but also, at times, other advice and the implementation of such advice. There are other areas of counseling that parents can handle best, such as the problems of very

198

young children and some aspects of personal problems. Ideally, a counselor should be available to children in both elementary and secondary schools and continuity in counseling should be the goal, but this does not happen in most educational situations. That is why it is so important that counselors, teachers, and parents work closely together to complement one another so that guidance works at an optimal level. Hence, it seems more appropriate to emphasize counseling as determined by situations rather than counseling as determined by designated counseling roles.

ACADEMIC GUIDANCE

Some years ago Strang (1960) differentiated the guidance of gifted children as it applied to three school-age levels: the preschool child, the elementary school child, and the adolescent. At the preschool level, it is the parent who is responsible for giving guidance. The areas of help needed by children relate to goals toward character and personality development and include recognition of, and respect for, the rights and feelings of others; the ability to make, carry out, and accept the consequences of decisions; satisfaction in success and the willingness to try again in the event of failure and disappointment. Guidance of elementary school children becomes the responsibility of teachers as well. In general, teachers take an active part in the development of the total child with special emphasis on intellect, whereas parents continue with the guidance that has shaped the children since birth, leaning more and more on teachers for the academic guidance of children.

Strang (1960) points out that in the elementary school guidance for the most part is indirect, being generally related to the children's on-going activities. In a nutshell, teachers guide as they teach, giving sensitive and continuous developmental guidance, with the goal of guidance leveled at fostering an "ever-increasing self-understanding on the part of the child—understanding of what he can do well, what he might learn to do, what his limitations are, and the kind of person he is becoming" (p. 144), thereby assuming more responsibility for what the child is, does, and becomes. In addition, teachers have the responsibility of stimulating and satisfying the intellectual curiosity of the gifted, promoting academic learning, and creating a favorable learning environment that will maximize the realization of their potential. Gold (1965) suggests that it is not only in the early years of children's schooling, but also throughout their school life that an interest in academic activities for their own sake should be fostered. And, at the same time, an appreciation for the demands of the world requiring advanced scholastic achievement for top-level jobs should be developed. The gifted elementary student, Gold says, should be given the opportunity:

to try his wings with more advanced mathematics, science, art media, musical performance and appreciation, literature, ceative writing, dramatics, social sciences and industrial arts. Laboratories, shops, and studios where the youngster can work under minimal supervision provide excellent settings for such exploration. Foreign language laboratories and programmed materials may also be employed by gifted students for independent self-discovery. (p. 368)

When there are guidance counselors in elementary schools, they should help teachers understand their pupils so that they may guide the students as they teach; assist in the modification of classroom procedures, where necessary, to meet the special needs of gifted students; advise both parents and teachers about the children's exceptionality and make them aware of special opportunities and programs available to enhance the children's development and talent; act as patron and supporter of the creatively gifted; and work with the principal, administration, and committees to make conditions in school more conducive to the development of gifted children (Durr, 1964; Strang, 1960; Torrance, 1962a).

At the secondary school level, guidance generally rests with the the counselor although the teacher can, and sometimes does, assist the adolescent; parents can also play an active role to complement the work of both the counselor and the teacher. Academic guidance for gifted students at this juncture of schooling pivots on adequate and appropriate preparation for advanced work that will facilitate college studies; a recognition of special leanings of talent for certain areas of knowledge and arranging for suitable dvelopment of these preferences to the accelerated levels that these gifted students are capable of achieving (e.g., mathematics, science, foreign languages, and art); the availability and accessibility of information about special programs and projects that are designed for gifted students (e.g., the Study of Mathematically Precocious Youth [SMPY], a project at The Johns Hopkins University that is under the directorship of Dr. Julian C. Stanley; the programs for the gifted at the Talcott Mountain Science Center in Avon, Connecticut, under the directorship of Dr. Donald P. Lasalle; or the Governor's Honors Programs in Georgia and North Carolina). The fact that gifted students have a variety of interests and strengths make choices of school curricula at this level quite difficult, and the counselor has the special task of helping gifted students achieve a focus so that selection of areas of study have a coherence and direction that will rapidly lead to distinctive development of the students' intellectual assets toward academic actualization.

The counselor ought to be able to communicate effectively with parents, teachers, and school administrators about their precocious students, who require special support, attention, and acceleration, and be persuasive enough to assist in fulfilling these needs. It may be possible for enterprising and dynamic counselors to initiate curricular changes that will provide the optimum intellectual stimulation and learning relevant to the gifted or, where this cannot be attained within the school, to arrange for similar relevant exposure by using the resources of a neighboring university or the larger community. It would be of immense value to

200

have qualified counselors who have flexibility in their dealings with gifted students because they should not be surprised to find that many gifted students do change their minds about what they want to do, which necessitates a review of goals and a replanning of students' directions. Counselors may also be faced with the need to guide gifted students to choose study areas that will prepare them for the many alternatives of higher education because such students have been known to change courses several times in college or to revise their study plans just at the point of college entry.

Gowan and Demos (1964) in their discussion of intellectual adjustment advise counselors to bear in mind that continuous guidance of youth is necessary at all stages and that they can foster an aura of expectancy about going to college (as if everyone needs it and each one will receive a scholarship). Citing Brandwein (1955), they point to the value of the subject teacher as having a predisposing relationship with the gifted student, a relationship in which a general willingness to spend time and show pains exists, motivation to succeed in the curriculum is planned through a system of rewards and reinforcements, failure can be faced, and authority questioned. To these, Gowan and Demos add the need to provide gifted youth with the opportunity to thresh out some basic questions in senior seminars, problems and fears that beset all, including themselves, so that gifted students may in a give-and-take situation experience intellectual adjustment that will bring with it reassurance of their fears, provision of a modicum of emotional experience, and the practice of verbal interchange on a subject while under some tension beyond that of the recitation of factual knowledge. Further, the plight of the high upward mobility of gifted youth from low socioeconomic backgrounds should receive the counselor's attention. Not only will it be helpful to listen and offer explanation to young persons undergoing this problem—who may be cynical about what they are approaching and ambivalent about what they are leaving—but also to expose them, in the presence of the group, to the activities toward which they are heading (e.g., cultural, social, or work activities) and even show them the possibilities of scholarships, other financial sources, or part-time jobs and assist them in acquiring such help. Where parental rejection exists, the counselor needs to find alternative adult models and, if it is not to be the counselor, then, it could be other professionals or men and women of breadth and culture. Gowan and Demos also emphasize the need for such a student to have a protégé, a parent-like person who gives without expectation of return, thereby blunting the "predatory force which he has needed to break through the social barrier" and finding in the patron or mentor an example of the ability to help and nurture others for emulation.

CAREER GUIDANCE

Career guidance until very recently went under the heading of vocational guidance and is, in the main, the concern of the secondary school although sometimes its relevance harks back to the elementary school years. Very closely associated with educational guidance, career (vocational) guidance emphasizes the creation of conditions in the school setting whereby gifted students can be assisted to know their abilities and potential and be guided to see possibilities for their use and realization. On the one hand, guidance may show the way to suitable occupations that often require special training; on the other hand, guidance may assist in the planning of a program of studies that lead to a college education. This may postpone definite career choices to the sophmore or junior years in college and this is to be expected of the intellectually gifted. Many academically gifted students are often not ready to select a career while in secondary school (Gold, 1965) because vocational choices for them are complicated by the many alternatives from which they must select. Indecisions must not be regarded as weakness. Gifted students must not be pressured to select a career just because others are doing so at that time; they may need counselor assurance that it is quite all right to delay making the choice. Intellectually able students may need to be made aware that such indecision should not preclude their selection of a college education; in fact, they should be guided and encouraged to consider advancing their education in college, where during the first two years they can select a curriculum that is a part of the general studies' requirements. Thus, there is little or no loss to their academic or professional training when more highly specialized areas of study are required in preparation for their chosen career. Further, the counselor can advise students on the selection of a college relative to talent, interest, availability of scholarships, and related opportunities as well as provide data on college admission times and the like.

Gowan and Demos (1964) suggest the value of summer jobs or experiences to help gifted students know what they do not want to do, which can be important in eventually shaping what they do want to do. The counselor can use this experience as a clue to the appropriate guidance to be given such students. There is something to be said for growing into career choice. Although this can be frustrating to all concerned, it is better that gifted youth know themselves and to what they would like to aspire than that they plunge into a career that may prove to be a dead end with little or no room for challenge to their full potential toward growth and actualization. The importance of proper matching of aptitudes and interests in guiding the highly able person to make a career choice have been repeatedly emphasized by both Gowan and Demos (Gowan, 1979a; Gowan & Demos, 1964). They suggest that:

Where aptitudes and interest are both high in an area, the counselor could point this out. Where interests are strong and aptitudes weak, he may warn against it; and this may be a useful form of elimination. Where aptitudes are strong and interest weak, he had better keep silent, for fear of prejudicing the client against it. Finally, where both aptitudes and interests are weak, he can

202

generally get the youth to agree that this area is out at once. (Gowan & Demos, 1964, p. 261)

A recent collection of papers on career education for gifted and talented students (Hoyt & Hebeler, 1974) that emerged as a product of a federal project is relevant to our discussion. Its purpose was to develop materials that could serve as curriculum guidelines in career education for the gifted and talented. Recognition is given to the multifaced nature of giftedness as it relates to the six U.S. Office of Education (USOE) categories of giftedness (now reduced to five with the exclusion of psychomotor ability). However, emphasis is placed more on the world of work (for which the individual should be primed) than on the needs of growing individuals in determining the kinds of careers they should choose and for which direction must be found. Although some attention is given to individual students (e.g., in the papers on identification and on the characteristics of gifted and talented students, and career development needs) the orientation of the work, in the main, can be summed up as follows (Hoyt, Evans, Mackin, & Mangum, 1974):

> *Career education is the total effort of public education and the community to help all individuals become familiar with the values of work-oriented society, to integrate those values into their personal value systems, and to implement those values into their lives in such a way that work becomes possible, meaningful, and satisfying to each individual. (p. 15)*

Concern for providing the best vocational counseling for gifted students produced a variety of career guidance models (e.g., Ginsberg, 1951; Walz, Smith, & Benjamin, 1974) and recently has found expression in several others, two of which will receive some attention. One, developed by Perrone, Karshner, and Male (1979) of the University of Wisconsin (Madison) Guidance Laboratory and called the Guidance Institute for Talented Students (GIFTS) career development model, approaches guidance from a developmental-motivational position; the second, developed by Torrance (1976b) of the University of Georgia and based on group dynamics, applies sociodramatic principles to career guidance and is called sociodrama in career education.

GIFTS Career Development Model

Perrone, Karshner, and Male's (1979) model attempts to provide a theoretical rationale for career development of talented students toward an understanding of their different career patterns. It draws upon Eriksonian developmental stage theory and Maslovian need-motivation theory and is presented as a two-dimensional model, with awareness of self and others, action orientation, and goal attainment as one dimension and safety, love, esteem, and self-actualization needs as the other dimension.

Selected concepts from Erikson's developmental stage theory and Maslow's need-motivation theory integrated with the GIFTS dimension of the model are considered as adding important energizing and dynamic qualities to help explain differential patterns in career development. Perrone and his associates (1979) suggest that the implied continuum of each cell of this two-dimensional model (Table 4) shows the dynamics structuring the individual's orientation to each of the domains that facilitate development toward a career.

The authors assume that (1) each column represents a world orientation based on the individual's interaction with the environment (2) each row represents change and growth that move from security to self-actualization (and in the case of regression that moves in reverse); and (3) people will operate from one or more developmental levels at different times of their lives owing to personal and environmental reasons. In brief, the concerns of career guidance that are found in case study examples of talented individuals include (1) the mistaken notion that the talented are capable of attaining anything to which they aspire; (2) the difficulty the talented experience in reconciling their value system with those of others; (3) a premature commitment to career choices based on school subjects in which the gifted attained distinction, with the hazard of their remaining per-

Table 4   Maslow/Erikson Theoretical Constructs

Gifts Career Development Model	Security/ Safety	Social Acceptance/ Love	Self-Esteem/ Achievement	Self-Actualized
Self-awareness & understanding	Trust of self to mistrust of self	Self-acceptance to rejection of self	Competent to incompetent	Integrated to compartmentalized
Social awareness & understanding	Trust of others to mistrust of others	Accepted by others to rejected by others	Competence seen by others to incompetence seen by others	Integrated to compartmentalized
Action orientation (organizing/ planning)	Risk to non-risking	Toward others acceptably to toward others unacceptably	Pro-active to reactive	Meaningful to irrelevant
Goal attainment (action/ evaluation)	Self-confidence to self-protection	Achieve membership to rejection of membership	Goal achievement to goal failure	Integrity/ generativity to despair/stagnation

Source: P. A. Perrone, W. W. Karshner, and W.W. Mole, *Career Development of Talented Persons*, p. 4. Copyright © 1979. Reprinted by permission.

petual students; (4) the search for a career as a principal means of support; (5) a conflict between achieving excellence and fitting in and being accepted; (6) the great need of the gifted for mastery and thoroughness may cause them to fixate on detail at the expense of obtaining a good gestalt; (7) the severe delay of certain psychosocial needs, which result from an expectation of an extended education; (8) the extension of the dependence-independence conflict, which results from an extended preparation for a career entry; (9) the significant changes that occur both in the individual and the nature of the work during the period of the student's extended preparation; (10) the perception of many gifted women that marriage and careers are exclusive, which leads them to make unnecessary compromises in career planning; (11) the ability to adapt and adjust to new peer referent groups as the gifted move from high school to college; and (12) the need to redefine themselves as gifted and talented in a new context (these being relative terms) and to adjust or adapt their behavior accordingly.

This model underscores the authors' conception of career guidance as an on-going process, beginning in early childhood and proceeding throughout the life of the child until he or she attains adulthood—and beyond. This differs from the more limited view of educational and vocational guidance as preparing children through appropriate education that eventually leads to a job or career. The model attempts to see career directions in the context of the whole life of children as they develop into adults, taking into account their needs, motivations, goals, and interactions of self with others at each phase of their lives. Viewing career guidance in this way gives dimension and greater significance to early thoughts on vocational guidance and makes it an advance worthy of notice.

Sociodrama in Career Guidance

Another approach to career guidance that is of great value is sociodrama, a technique that combines the strengths of role playing in dramatic situations and the group creative problem-solving process. Sociodrama was first developed in the 1940s by Moreno (1946) and later refined and elaborated by him (Moreno, 1952; Moreno & Moreno, 1969) and others (e.g., Haas, 1948; Klein, 1956). Torrance (1975c) and Torrance and Myers (1970) have shown that the problem-solving process in sociodrama can be as deliberate and disciplined as any other creative problem-solving approach (e.g., W.J.J. Gordon, 1961; Osborn, 1963; Parnes, 1967a), and Torrance (1975c) has described, for instance, how it may be used to study problems that may confront us in the future. In a monograph, Torrance (1976b) discusses how the principles and techniques of sociodrama may be applied to career education and formulates a methodology that combines role playing, creative problem solving, and career education objectives within the sociodramatic approach. Role playing, although popular as a method in career education and inherent in the relevant instructional and curricular materials developed for the purpose, does not help students know their abilities and interests as these relate to careers nor does it take into account career education objectives. In addition, it does not have well-defined procedures for facilitating the creative process toward creative problem-solving outcomes, whereas sociodrama applied to career education does.

Sociodrama is primarily based on an educational methodology whose focus is preventative rather than therapeutic. It is group or social-problem centered and can be used in almost any physical setting, including the classroom. The intent in sociodrama is to give guidance by education of the individual in the context of the group, and, as applied to career education, the prime focus is on a problem or conflict expected to arise in a career, especially as this relates to the application of knowledge or acquired skills. The problem or conflict may be handled by the creative problem-solving process in a sociodramatic situation. The steps, which are similar to the Osborn-Parnes method of creative problem solving, include:

1. Defining the problem.
2. Establishing a situation (conflict) in operational terms so that deferred judgment is used.
3. Casting characters (protagonists), keeping in mind that participation is voluntary and not prearranged.
4. Briefing and warming up actors and observers by the director for possible alternatives; some preparation of the acting situation and setting.
5. Acting out the situation by using a variety of production techniques to dig deeper into the problem in a psychologically safe atmosphere where freedom to experiment with new ideas, behavior, and problem-solving ways are provided.
6. Cutting the action whenever actors are no longer in character or are unable to continue, or the episode comes to a conclusion, or the director perceives the opportunity to stimulate higher levels of thinking by moving to a different episode.
7. Discussing and analyzing the situation, the behavior, and the ideas produced; according to some criteria, evaluating the alternatives generated toward selection of an effective solution.
8. Making plans for further testing or implementing ideas for new behavior that is similar to the selling, planning, and implementing stage in creative problem solving.

The fact that sociodrama calls for the use of both the rational and emotive in processing the problem dramatically makes it a viable approach to career education. To put this in terms of present-day terminology, both the right and left hemispheres of the brain are required to function so that linear thought (e.g., analytic, logical, verbal, and sequential thinking) and nonlinear thought (e.g., global, creative, nonverbal, and imaginative thinking) are combined and directed toward the solving of a problem sociodramatically.

206

A sociodramatic session involves a director; one or more actors, or protagonists; and a group as a participating audience. The subject of the drama is a problem or conflict situation that needs definition, examination, exploration, and clarification toward solution finding. The creative problem-solving steps by which this may be effected have already been described. There are several ways of approaching the creative handling of the situation and these are described as production techniques. Drawing from Moreno (1946) and his own works, Torrance suggests 14 sociodramatic production techniques that may be applied to career education, briefly these are the: (1) direct presentation technique, (2) soliloquy technique, (3) double technique, (4) multiple double technique, (5) identifying double and contrary double technique, (6) mirror technique, (7) role reversal technique, (8) future projection technique, (9) auxiliary world technique, (10) magic shop technique, (11) high chair and empty chair techniques, (12) therapeutic community technique, (13) magic net technique, and (14) reality level sociodrama.

These production techniques, used in sociodrama relative to career education, may involve one or more of the following: the application of subject-matter knowledge and skills, for instance, to career problems, conflicts, uncertainties, predictions, and so on; the encouragement of incubation toward the development of original ideas and fresh insights; the discovery of new problems in applying information to career problems; the exploration of role requirements in different careers as well as the personal qualities and learning necessary for them; effective decision making, accurate observation, and awareness of the feelings of others; the encouragement of deliberate predictions as well as planning future implementation of decisions and exploring ways of changing behaviors in preparation for them; experiencing different occupational roles and constructing lifestyles associated with various career choices and future conditions; predicting consequences of career decisions and new lifestyles; and elaborating alternative courses of action and evaluating decisions.

The audience also plays an important role in sociodrama and, as this involves the creative problem-solving process, the audience may play research and problem-solving roles not ordinarily found in sociodrama. Members of the audience may be asked by the director to identify with the protagonist and supporting actor (auxiliary ego), to act as observers, to offer alternative strategies for problem presentation or to think of alternative solutions, to serve as public opinion, to analyze the action at any stage of the creative problem-solving process as deemed relevant, to play a purely supportive role for the protagonist or auxiliary ego, or to act as consultant. Any one of these roles may be taken by the audience in career education as they relate to core objectives and specific career education needs of the group at the time.

Although Torrance does not mention the gifted in his discussion of sociodrama as applied to career education, the use of creative problem-solving sociodrama is as highly relevant to the gifted as it is to all students. The multipotentiality of gifted students make career choices extremely difficult, and sociodrama offers a viable approach to help gifted students discover vocational direction that will both match their abilities and interests and place attendant problems in appropriate context. The creative problem-solving process that gifted students use in a dramatic situation not only assist them to apply the knowledge and skills they have acquired about various careers but also to test their validity before a participating group that is expected to assist them to identify and clarify the problems they may face, to generate ideas and hypotheses that will need to stand the test of supportive scrutiny, and to arrive eventually at some sound decision making. It is more likely, at present, that gifted students will find themselves in a heterogenous class setting rather than in one constituted of other gifted students. In either setting, sociodrama can be expected to operate effectively, the one providing the context of a social group with whom the student is more likely to interact in the world of work and who may provide an atmosphere more congenial to career education, the other providing a stimulating social context of peers who are probably facing similar problems in need of resolution. In addition, gifted students have the opportunity of experiencing in sociodramatic circumstances career possibilities and attendant conflicts that range from those of the present world of work to those of the future.

CONCLUSIONS

This chapter offers some fresh perspectives on guidance of the gifted that focus on (1) counseling normal children to help them overcome problems of development toward self-actualization and good mental health, (2) the importance of facilating creative development of gifted children, (3) the interference of normal functioning by stress and the strategies to master it to prevent breakdown, and (4) counseling as preventative and situational. All these derive their strength from theoretical roots that can only envigorate approaches to guidance generally and to the guidance of the gifted in particular. A growth and development psychology that includes creativity as an essential component, the psychology of stress and its mastery through the use of the intellect and the development of interpersonal skills, and a social psychology that brings into sharp focus the dynamics of group creative problem solving and role playing in dramatic situation call into play a multiplicity of resources for guidance. These psychologies hold great significance and high relevance for personal, academic, and vocational guidance and can provide explanations for many of the problems connected with underachievement and the problems of special groups, which include gifted women and the culturally diverse (topics that will receive attention in chapter 7).

The literature has made it evident that there is a lack of good counseling and counselors, either because the education system is unable to support sufficient numbers of professional counselors in schools to make their work effective or because the school principal adulterates counseling functions by assigning counselors to other than counseling chores. Where there are professional counselors, their effectiveness becomes dissipated in the overwhelming press of student academic advisement and there is little time or energy left for real contact with individual students who themselves are reluctant to go to the counselor for help.

Any administrative arrangement or model guidance program for the gifted cannot neglect to take into account the essentials of creative development, the variety of stress factors impinging on the individual and affecting behavior, the preparatory work that must go into equipping the individual with coping skills, individual counseling circumstances, and the arrangement of situations whereby problems can be brought into the open for processing toward solutions through the use of sociodrama. Ideally, a counselor should have charge of a small number of students. They should get to know them intimately, not only for placement of course work (this is often done with only a superficial acquaintance of the pupil and background and is often restricted to the fact that the student is in a certain grade and about to prepare to study in the next higher grade) but also for their abilities; talents; interests; hobbies; motivations; interpersonal relations with schoolmates, teachers, family and others; the kind of problems they may be prone to experience, and so on. Certainly, the counselor needs to work in close cooperation with teachers and parents as well as with other counselors who may also know these students. The counselor's orientation should not be one that expects to treat symptoms in crisis situations, but one that expects to improve the mental health of students—prior and frequent association with students coupled with a thorough understanding of them will allow this to operate effectively. It is of the utmost importance that students must feel that the counselor is approachable and accepting, someone in whom they must have trust and with whom they can communicate freely, someone who is there when needed and who can be depended on to provide direction when necessary as well as stand aside and permit growth when this is about to take place.

7

___

PROBLEMS
OF
SPECIAL
GROUPS

OVERVIEW

In this chapter, underachievement is discussed as a relative and multivariate term. The clauses of underachievement are better understood than are its remedies, which are recognized as multiple and complex and as stemming from the individual, the home, the school, and other related areas—physical, sociocultural, economic, and psychological. Underachievement as it affects girls is discussed in terms of sex differences, careers of gifted women, and developmental stage theory. In addition, the effects of cultural diversity on underachievement receives attention, pivoting on the problems of definition, identification, and nurture.

CHAPTER OUTLINE

INTRODUCTION

In the early years of the gifted movement, one of the major concerns revolved around the problem of identification and its measurement correlates. The Lewis M. Terman studies (see pp. 12–17) focused on the highly intelligent individual who (generally) attended the city schools of California. Unlike the advantage we enjoy today in the availability of measuring instruments, Terman had to develop such instruments from scratch. In addition, he had little to guide him by way of previous contributions on the gifted and was himself the major initiator of this branch of knowledge. To most of us, he is known as the father of the gifted movement. Terman did not take into account socioeconomic factors in his research on the gifted, variables we now take for granted in our research and practice. Nor did he pay appropriate attention to the gifted population living in rural areas. But it is only because we have been made more acutely aware of the significance of these shaping influences by the contributions of others who followed and built on Terman's work that more and more of us take into account these factors when we become involved in identifying, educating, and guiding the ablest.

Today an expanded conception of giftedness strongly persuades us to look not only for the gifted with high IQs but also for those who are gifted in other dimensions as well. That is why we cannot rely alone on IQ tests to identify the gifted but must turn to other procedures to identify the creative individual, the leader, the talented musician, the nonverbally gifted, and so on. Much of this has to do with more than innate abilities. It has to do with the interactive influences of environment, which include the physical, social, and psychological forces that shape and direct the development of abilities so that they express themselves in numerous and different ways.

Consequently, any approach to identify, educate, and guide the gifted must take into account the effects of these mediating variables. It means, for instance, that we have to reassess the suitability of available measures to identify the gifted among those who have not had the same intellectual, social, and psychological advantages as those for whom certain measures were designed. We are referring to the culturally disadvantaged, different, or diverse gifted, those who are penalized by identification instruments whose content and idiom are not designed for use with their groups. Other groups affected by environmental-cultural shaping influences and related press factors are those who do not do as well in school as their high-potential allows or who discontinue schooling. This might, for example, be attributed on the one hand to interference and retardation because of emotional difficulties or physical handicaps or on the other hand to sex bias that could arrest, retard, or divert the development of potentially gifted girls toward actualization. The subject of special groups (the culturally different or diverse), their problems, and suggestions for dealing with them will be considered in terms of underachievement in this chapter.

GIFTED UNDERACHIEVERS

In the main, underachievement has been generally defined as a deficit condition in schooling and specifically defined as poor performance and low grades in school subjects. It would be preferable to regard it more broadly, that is, not only as achievement below expected performance in school subjects but also as achievement in terms of expressed talent potential and productivity. In another sense, underachievement can and should be regarded (in terms of developmental theory) as dysplasia, where both cognitive and emotive components of the psyche escalate to higher levels toward self-actualization. There is the tendency to regard underachievement in terms of a student doing badly in subject areas rather than to consider underachievement as arrest of normal development. In this respect, we need to consider the gifted girl who may never achieve full realization of potential as an adult (owing to arrest in cognitive development but not in affective development) or, if such actualization of potential occurs, it may happen much later in her life.

A certain looseness attends the term underachievement. Its meaning appears to

212

depend on whether we are comparing the achievement of an individual with that of a group or whether we are comparing an individual's actual performance with what his or her IQ says he or she is capable of doing. As we have seen, the predictive validity of IQ can be questioned (pp. 17–24). It is well known that IQ is generally a good predictor of success in schooling although not necessarily in all academic areas because it is dependent on certain abilities that are specific to subject areas as well as other related variables, such as interest, motivation, attitude, and the like. Therefore, the term underachievement can only be used in relative terms. In fact, it has been pointed out that lack of success in dealing with the concept of underachievement is not only related to the complex nature of its causes but also to the fact that precision is lacking in its definition (Gowan, Khatena, & Torrance, 1979).

Some years ago, Gowan (1955) was discussing the underachieving gifted child and defined underachievement in general as performance that places the individual 1 SD or more below his or her ability standing in the same group. Performance that, when applied to gifted children, identifies them as underachievers if they fall in the middle third in scholastic rank and as severe underachievers if they fall in the lowest third in scholastic rank. Gowan believes his definition needs wider acceptance. Another definition, by Shaw (1960), states that, ''the underachiever with superior ability is one whose performance, as judged either by grades or achievement test scores, is significantly below his high measured or demostrated aptitudes of potential for academic achievement'' (p. 15). Both definitions are highly relevant. Of the two, Gowan's reference to percentiles makes his more operational. However, such definitions reflect the more traditional view of underachievement as it relates to IQ and scholastic achievement. Apart from the fact that we are beginning to be more accepting of varieties of giftedness, we have also begun to recognize the importance of bringing to greater fruition the creativity in gifted individuals. McGuire, Hindsman, King, and Jennings (1961)—writing on the relationships of various personality variables, especially creativity and achievement—considers divergent thinking as an underlying dimension of intellectual functioning that acts as a catalyst to productivity and, hence, is significant to achievement. Gowan and Demos (1964) point out that the works of C. McGuire on achievement, J. P. Guilford on intellect, and E. P. Torrance on creativity (to which may be added J. W. Getzels and P. W. Jackson on creativity and intelligence) have given us a different perspective of achievement:

Formerly a discrepancy between narrow-spectrum measures of intelligence and achievement in school marks was laid to motivational aspects (the ''over'' and ''underachiever''). But if narrow-spectrum tests do not measure all of the intellect, and if creativity is an important part of what is missing in tests, then the research of Getzels and Jackson on the ability of creative

youngsters to achieve as well as narrow-spectrum tested gifted children makes
considerable sense. If we broaden our measurement of ability to wide-
spectrum testing which includes more of the Guilford factors, we may consid-
erably lessen the variance necessary to assign to motivational factors. The
intelligent underachiever may underachieve because he is not creative rather
than because he is not motivated. (pp. 298–299)

Any definition of underachievement must include the discrepancy between actual and expected levels of attainment. Levels that are not limited to scholastic achievement as predicted by IQ but that go beyond such achievement to other dimensions of talent and their realization. Therefore, the kind of question to ask is: Are persons identified as having extraordinary gifts in art or music expressing their talent at a level compatible with that identified, if not above it? or Are the individuals who show a superior capacity to lead others actually fulfilling their anticipated promise? If we are to conceive these achievement levels in statistical terms, we should be able to expect that in whatever area of talent a person has been identified as superior, (2 SDs above the mean in that area of giftedness—intellect, art, music, leadership, etc.), that person should express the talent in ways considered superior and, if measurable, at about 2 SDs above the mean. Of course, at present, this may not always be easy or even practical to do, but an expanded concept of underachievement must be cognizant of this so that efforts will continue to find ways and means to make such an approach possible. Note that underachievement for the gifted can, then, be recognized as performance below superior level. The same applies to levels of superiority between 1 and 2 SDs above the mean that are considered levels of excellence by those systems that identify a larger population of individuals as gifted, those who are not necessarily the cream of the crop yet are nonetheless talented. Underachievement, it must be emphasized, is a relative term, especially in the context of a multivariate concept of giftedness and its statistical implications.

CAUSES OF UNDERACHIEVEMENT

The causes of underachievement have been investigated with greater success than have the procedures used in efforts to correct or cure underachievement (Gowan, 1979a)—human nature and society (being what they are) will probably not allow the condition to be eliminated (Newland, 1976). A considerable number of studies on the subject have identified causes that are peculiar to the individual, that is, underachievement largely brought about by the individual's transactions and interactions with immediate family, school, society and the larger environment (e.g., Angelino, 1960; Gallagher, 1975; Strodtbeck, 1958; Whitmore, 1980). The reasons behind the causes have been classified in a number of different ways, one being McIntyre's (1964) physical, sociologic, economic, or

214   PROBLEMS OF SPECIAL GROUPS

psychologic reasons—or all these variables combined. It is well known that many physical illnesses have a detrimental effect on the studies of bright individuals although, on occasion, such conditions spur a student to high levels of attainment (Anastasi, 1958). Common problems of sight, hearing, infection, disease, malnutrition, and the like, may hold students back, limiting their enthusiasms, interests, and capabilities and, thus, lead to underachievement. The debilitating effects of adverse socioeconomic conditions (discussed in more detail on pp. 236–244) are significant factors in underachievement and turn on such circumstances as poverty, low level of aspiration and motivation, language deficits, ethnic difference, and differential cultural contexts (see Bonsall & Stellfre, 1955; Frierson, 1965). As they relate to psychological factors, the causes of underachievement include various kinds of mental ill health and emotional disturbance, which are often rooted in the climate of home and family and the stress of interactions with parents and others as the individual grows up (Gallagher, 1975; Gowan & Demos, 1964; McIntyre, 1964). Whitmore (1980) suggests that underachievement as it relates to gifted elementary underachieving students can be described in terms of three distinct behavioral syndromes: (1) the aggressive gifted child, (2) the withdrawn gifted child, and (3) the erratic, less predictable child who vacillates between aggression and withdrawal.

DYNAMICS OF THE HOME AND FAMILY

Achievement has much to do with a child's upbringing. It depends on the kind of relationships shared with father, mother, and siblings; it requires stability of parents' relations—a family life that is not torn by continual disagreements, fights, and other disruptions, which may lead to separation or divorce; it is facilitated by the educational level of parents and a stimulating home environment; it thrives on high levels of aspirations, affectional support, and reinforcement; and it needs appropriate models. When these do not exist, achievement congruent with potential is threatened and underachievement may be the expected consequence.

Studies have attempted to identify the extent to which underachievement can be attributed to the relationship of bright children with their father or mother. Strodtbeck (1958) suggests that, if the power of the father is great (the higher the socioeconomic status, the greater the power of the father), the son can be expected to be less achieving than the dominant father. Certainly, the level of aspiration on academic matters of father and son can be expected to be similar; when the aspiration level of the father is low, underachievement can be anticipated for the son (Shaw, 1960). Underachieving boys appear to identify not with their fathers but with other male figures, for instance, a teacher, an uncle, or a minister, probably because of negative feelings toward the father (Kimball, 1953), which are generated by the father's hostility to, and rejection of, the son

(Karnes, McCoy, Zehrbach, Wollersheim, Clarizio, Gostin, & Stanley, 1961). If parents are too autocratic or authoritarian, developmental arrest and consequent underachievement follows (Gallagher, 1975; Gowan, 1957) although, when the parent in question is the mother, there appears to be some difference in the way the son and the daughter are affected. That is, when father and mother are both highly authoritarian and low in acceptance, the son shows poor academic performance; when the mother is low authoritarian or laissez-faire, the daughter tends to show poor academic performance (Drews & Teahan, 1957; Pierce & Bowan, 1960).

This subject is further discussed by McIntyre (1964) in terms of passive-aggressive trait disturbance, which is the most common cause of underachievement, more so in boys than girls. Briefly, the characteristics of passive-aggressive children include dawdling, stubbornness, pouting, sullenness, procrastination, inefficiency, and daydreaming. Such children are sometimes cocky and obnoxious; they do not fight back directly and outwardly but rebel through a form of inaction; they want freedom but cling to dependency, caught between the desire to be nurtured and the refusal to be dominated; they have difficulty accepting or having to face reality; they appear calm and without anxiety outwardly, but they seethe with resentment; and they may appear disinterested, unmotivated, lazy, self-sufficient, unsociable, and lonely.

McIntyre (1964) points to the observation of Grunebaum, Hurwutz, Prentice, and Sperry (1962) that the parents of such children tend to confuse the aggressive activity that is involved in learning, achievement, and success with aggression, which involves hostile and hurting impulses. Consequently, they may not actually want their sons to achieve in school because to achieve is to hurt. When parents do not share executive functions in the home, one parent may be dominant and the other submissive. As for a boy in such a family, if the mother is dominant and the father submissive, the mother overprotects and infantalizes her son; if the father is dominant (strict and explosive) and the mother submissive (assuming a position of helplessness to deny her own hostility toward the father), the son tends to perceive that it is dangerous to become a man. In either case, the son is a pawn in the game and transfers the anger and resentment felt for the parents to the teacher. He mistakes the parents' disinclination that he learn in school for a demand for high performance; therefore, he may try to get even with his parents by underachieving in school. As for a girl in such a family, being generally passive, dependent, and nonassertive she is less likely to resent her parents' neurotic demands and her parents become upset only when she starts to fight back. Passive-aggressive girls appear lazy and uncaring and, unlike boys who often hide their feelings, are more willing to share their feelings with others and even anxious to discuss their upsetting experiences.

Underachievers appear to come from homes where parents are either overindulgent and overprotective or indifferent and rejecting. Homes where there is less

216

identification with, and more rejection of, parents and where an unstable climate exists because of parental disagreement on child-rearing practices. This prevents the establishment of standards of behavior and excellence for the child to follow (Gowan & Demos, 1964). Against such a familial background, it is not easy for a growing child to escalate from one stage of development into the next higher stage of the Gowan-Piaget-Erikson periodic developmental stage chart (Gowan, 1972), and developmental arrest or dysplasia can be expected, with consequent detrimental effects on the achievement level of the student.

Underachievement viewed as failure in some developmental tasks leads to an internalization of conflict that involves hostility, resentment, aggression, projection, regression, overdependence, fear, withdrawal, and escape tendencies (Gowan & Demos, 1964). For instance, children who experience developmental arrest do not learn the joy of real work and accomplishment to assist them to find status among their peers and authority figures but depend on satisfaction derived from earlier developmental stages. Further, boys, being slightly less mature than girls, sometimes find that their parents expect more of them than necessary, thus, causing a more problematic introduction to cultural demands (Gowan, 1957). Some of the major causes of underachievement viewed as failure in certain developmental tasks are (Gowan and Demos, 1964, pp. 306–307):

1. *The child's own difficulties with the task.*
2. *The lack of skill of the parents in handling early relationships, such as trust, toilet training, industry, independency training, etc.*
3. *Psychotic or neurotic involvements of the child.*
4. *Failure of the school properly to stimulate the child.*
5. *Lower parental socioeconomic status, which interferes with the intellectual component of developmental task attitudes, especially at higher levels.*
6. *Lack of parental education, which also inhibits the intellectual components of developmental tasks at their highest levels and operates to cut off professional occupational choices.*
7. *Environmental and sub-cultural attitudes which similarly impede intellectual development tasks at their highest level.*
8. *Parental, environmental and cultural attitudes, which (a) reinforce, clannishness and inhibit the breakaway of the child, and (b) promote authoritarianism and dependence on fate and super-natural authority and inhibit the "do-it-yourself," entrepreneur, risk-taking "reasonable-adventurer" type individual.*
9. *Parental attitudes of over-protection and over-indulgence, which prevent children from having early independence experience and do not put enough stress into the environmental background.*
10. *Parental, environmental and school attitudes of antiintellectualism, lack of respect for scholarship and hard work necessary to attain it.*

We need to focus on the underachiever in the school setting because, when we talk about underachievement, we usually refer to students who do not do as well in school subjects or obtain the kind of grades that their IQs tell us can be expected. Underachievement may be general or specific (Raph, Goldberg, & Passow, 1966). If it is general, it is more likely related to personal difficulties that are psychological in nature. If it is specific, its occurrence is precipitated by difficulties in the acquisition of knowledge and skills—in such subjects as reading or arithmetic at the elementary school levels and language or mathematics at the upper levels of schooling—and, often, underachievement may be a function of intellectual ability (differentiated from general to specific with increasing age) as much as it may be inadequate learning of the fundamentals that hinders the mastery of more advanced learning. However, psychological disturbances and specific learning difficulties are not independent of one another as related causes of underachievement. The problems of home and family are not left behind when the child comes to school: these problems preface all activities in school, hindering or facilitating the child's progress in academic and nonacademic areas. This is not to say that psychological disturbances do not occur in the child's life at school owing to the demands of others (e.g., teachers, peers) and the press of learning, but a child relatively free of serious home and family problems comes to school with a mentally healthy predisposition to benefit from educational experiences. It must also be remembered that the difficulties that a child encounters in learning a school subject may cause disturbances, but these are less likely to jeopardize the achievement of the child if they are symptomatic of specific learning content rather than personal problems.

In general, most studies on underachievement concentrate on nonschool-related variables, such as personality characteristics, adjustment, self-concept, peer attitudes, and parental background, rather than on classroom behaviors, study practices, and the school (Gallagher, 1975; Raph et al., 1966). Studies of underachievement and school-related variables find that college and high school underachievers dislike their professors and courses (Dowd, 1952; Wilson & Morrow, 1962) and spend fewer hours on their studies, do less homework, use poorer study techniques, and have lower grade aspirations than achievers (Dowd, 1952; Frankel, 1960; Wilson & Morrow, 1962); that they are poorly adjusted to school rules and procedures (Granzow, 1954); that, when the assignments appeared too long or difficult they become easily discouraged (Lum, 1960); that they are inclined toward school, to attend school, and to study science, and mathematics, but are less apt to plan college courses in the pure sciences and liberal arts (Frankel, 1960; Lum, 1960; Wilson & Morrow, 1962); that their most prominent characteristic is withdrawl from schoolwork, often engaging in nonverbal activity in another area than the one studied—this is especially noticeable

218   PROBLEMS OF SPECIAL GROUPS

with arithmetic (Perkins, 1965); and that their major problem rests not on the mechanics of study but on motivation and attitude (Westfall, 1958).

Other observations of school-related causes for underachievement (Bricklin & Bricklin, 1967; Goldberg & Passow 1959; Strang, 1960; Willard, 1976) include changes in schools; poor preparation owing to lack of basic instruction that results from frequent absences or irregular attendance; poor, laborious, and discouraging study habits; bad teaching, unsympathetic and insensitive teachers, drill classes, busy work, or a curriculum that fails to interest and challenge to high endeavor; educational pressures and unrealistic expectations at home that may lead to rebellion; a teacher who is satisfied with adequate rather than capacity performance, an attitude that can destroy the incentive to achieve; and the rigidity and narrowness of classroom activity that inhibits productive learning, which allows creativity to wither before it matures. Gowan (1957) comments on underachievement as the result of interference with creative learning and expression and the consequent lack of approval:

The gifted underachiever . . . appears to be a kind of intellectual delinquent who withdraws from goals, activities, and active social participation generally. As a child, his initial attempts at creative accomplishment may not have been seen by others as "worthwhile" but only as "queer" or "different." The blocking of this avenue of rewarding behavior by others, tending as it does to reinforce his often overcritical appraisal of the disparity between his goals and achievements, may blunt his work libido, stifle his creativity, and consign him to a routine of withdrawl and escape as the most tolerable method of insulating his ego from hurt in an alien and uninterested world. (p. 101)

In an interesting paper, Roth and Meyersburg (1963) lay the responsibility of underachievement on the student. They suggest that poor achievement does not arise from an incapacity to achieve but is an expression of student choice not to prepare for the kinds of academic performance that will be evaluated; that the possession of poor academic skills is an outgrowth of previous choices for poor achievement; that choice for poor achievement may be expressed as overall limited achievement or as achievement in deviant channels; and that the patterns of poor-achievement choice are enduring, do not undergo spontaneous change, and may be considered related to personality or character traits. However, Whitmore (1980) makes an interesting observation about the differing perceptions by teachers, parents, and pupils as to who is to blame for underachievement:

Teachers perceived the problem as the child's attitudes and behavior, often relating that to inadequacies of the home. Parents perceived the problem first of all as the school's lack of responsiveness to the educational needs of their child, and secondly as the child's stubbornness in wanting things his way and unwillingness to try hard enough to do better. The children blamed the school or, more often, themselves. All of them, to varying degrees, had integrated the feedback from teachers, parents, and peers to conclude that they were the problem—something was wrong with them since school was "okay" for everyone else. (pp. 86–87)

Underachievement and DeWitt Clinton High School

One of the most persuasive discussions on gifted underachievers stems from information obtained from the DeWitt Clinton High School, a boy's high school in New York City (Raph et al., 1966). As underachievement pertains to school dynamics, phenomenological factors were identified that related to self-concept, self-ideals, motivation, and adult models. The authors found that a positive self-concept consistently related to school mastery more than it did to intelligence. They see in White's (1959) competence-motivation construct a plausible explanation for their findings that young underachievers realistically appraised the discrepancy between their ability and their performance on school or task-related items regardless of geographical location or socioeconomic level. At the same time, the authors recognized the problem of finding a theoretical justification for a self-concept that was either the cause or the effect of scholastic attainment. This leads the authors to suggest that:

Applied to school achievement, White's [1959] focus would postulate that later academic skill and satisfaction in mastery might well be related to the pleasures derived from such competencies. Put more concisely, "I can do" becomes "I am," in that satisfaction in mastery becomes linked to the self-concept. (Raph et al., 1966, p. 182)

Raph and her associates also found from interviews with underachieving boys of the DeWitt Clinton High School that underachievers tended to minimize their ability, evaluating themselves as "pretty average," "about like others," and so on, to avoid both social ostracism from their peers and the more stringent demands of adults. This finds corroboration in the observations that the peer culture does not support outstanding school attainment (Coleman, 1961; Tannenbaum, 1960) and that the gifted child is, in the first place, a minority of one (Torrance, 1962a).

On the subject of self-ideals, Raph and her associates found that underachievers did not appear to see the discrepancy between poor class performance and future professional aspirations or desired status. Insofaras underachievers are able to see this gap, they perceive the narrowing of this discrepancy in terms of doing more than achievers; but, if they are unable to bridge the gap, they may experience greater stress, which may call for the use of defensive maneuvers to reduce the dissonance. Further, underachievers may meet this discrepancy by

220

withdrawing entirely from the demands of school to become truants and eventually school dropouts.

Raph and her associates also found that underachievers of DeWitt Clinton High School attributed their success or failure to particular teachers. The authors attempted to find an explanation for this excessive responsibility that was placed on the teacher by these adolescents in the dependency on extrinsic motivation (e.g., good grades, parental and teacher approbation). Therefore, when no reward was available, seeking reward shifted to projecting blame. These underachievers also blamed themselves for poor school performance in terms of not having studied enough, on laziness, and the like, and justified their lack of application to good intentions but an inability to fulfill them when the time came. The authors recognized the complexity of finding explanations for such irrational factors and perceived in this possible clues for understanding the disparity between ability and performance.

McClelland, Atkinson, Clark, & Lowell (1953) say that need-achievement may offer another plausible explanation for underachievement. They cite Atkinson's (1960) conceptualization of two dispositions being activated in a performance situation, namely, achievement-motive and motive to avoid failure:

[Atkinson] postulates that these two opposing tendencies, to approach and withdraw, are inherent in any activity when the behaving individual expects that his performance will be evaluated and that the outcome will be either a personal accomplishment or a sense of incompetence. He bases a number of predictions on this model, among them that individuals whose need for success is stronger than their fear of failure will try harder and perform better than individuals with the reverse pattern, i.e., those whose fear of failure is stronger than the need for success. (McClelland et al., 1953, p. 188)

The problems concerning adult models were also given attention. The DeWitt Clinton studies found that underachievers came from disrupted familites, that fathers of underachievers made frequent reference to their own college aspirations and not those of their children; that mothers seemed to be more concerned with their boy's school performance (Raph et al., 1966); that academic failure and hostility toward a family member demanding success were related (Kirk, 1952); and that for high need-achievement to develop, a boy needed more autonomy from his father and a high degree of involvement from his mother, including both reward and punishment (Rosen & D'Andrade, 1959).

The Cupertino (California) Experimental Program for Gifted Underachievers

Another interesting account of the gifted underachiever in the context of schooling grew out of Whitmore's (1980) concern for elementary school students who were problems. She thought those problem students might be gifted, but they were excluded from special classes provided by the Cupertino Extended Learning Program because they did not score high enough on the *Stanford-Binet* to be considered intellectually gifted. Whitmore arranged to work with several of these students whose mental giftedness was concealed by the natural tendency of teachers to focus on their problem behaviors and lack of achievement. She found that their most common handicap was learning disabilities directly related to perceptual-motor skills. The underachievers discovered in the Cupertino Experimental Program were identified as belonging to one of four etiological types: (1) the learning disabled, (2) the behaviorally disorded or emotionally disturbed, (3) the neurologically handicapped or minimally brain damaged, and (4) the paralyzed perfectionists. This classification, it was felt, would indicate the source of their learning or achievement problems and so help to determine appropriate individual treatment programs.

Whitmore's study (during 1968 to 1970) of 29 underachieving gifted (6 students participating for both years, 13 participating for just the first year, and 10 who entered the class the second year and continued for one or two years after 1970) not only gave her clues about the nature and possible sources of their problems but also several useful directions to be taken. These include (1) the need for early identification of the gifted so that the emphasis is placed on potential for superior performance rather than on actual achievement and (2) the importance of providing preventative intervention or early remediation before negative attitudes and counterproductive habits become firmly established and resistant to influence. She is emphatic on the point of gifted children being made underachievers by specific handicaps—by a dull, meager curriculum that destroys motivation to achieve in school; by inappropriate teaching strategies that are incompatible with their learning styles; and by a lack of adult assistance to the child in need of learning how to handle socioeconomic conflict to gain self-control and set realistic self-expectations. This is underscored by her underachievers' observations that the development of their negative feelings, problem behaviors, and underachievement can be traced to (1) a perceived lack of genuine respect for them as individuals; (2) a competitive social climate; (3) inflexibility and rigidity in expectations of student performance, curriculum choices, sequence of learning experiences, and lack of time and opportunity to pursue individual interests; (4) stress on external evaluation; (5) predominance of the failure syndrome and criticism, (6) adult-teacher control; and (7) an unrewarding curriculum.

Whitmore's educational philosophy sees no difference in the educational programs provided for the achieving or underachieving gifted, except in the amount of teacher time and effort directed toward such objectives as enhancing self-esteem, developing social skills, and remedying academic deficiencies. Consequently, the gifted educational program provided to underachievers at Cupertino is considered by her appropriate for gifted achievers, and, although designed for the elementary level, can (with certain changes) be adapted for use at the secondary level. Evaluation of this experimental program at the end of two years and in the 1972 and 1975 follow-up studies have indicated the tentative effectiveness of such an approach, and Whitmore expects this to be directional of efforts to provide educational alternatives for gifted underachievers.

The Dropout Problem

A major outcome of consistent underachievement is eventual withdrawl from school—the dropout problem, which is a serious waste of talent resource. Several studies have indicated that a fair number of dropouts are gifted or talented. For instance, Bridgeman (1960) estimates that 55% of the boys and 70% of the girls in the top 30% of high school graduates do not complete college. An Iowa study by Green in 1962 (cited in Gowan & Demos, 1964) found that out of 735 high school dropouts, 29 of them or 3.95% were of the talented population. French (1968) reported that there were 1800 high-ability dropouts during 1964–1965 in Pennsylvania, a state with one of the lowest dropout rates.

In general, the symptoms and causes of youngsters leaving school have been listed and categorized as primary factors and other related factors by Kowalski and Cangemi (1974), p. 2.

PRIMARY FACTORS	OTHER RELATED FACTORS
Low reading ability	Low scholastic aptitude
Low IQ	Dislike of school
Low socioeconomic status	Unhappy family situations
Parents formerly dropouts	Home pressures
Pregnancy	Performance below potential
Frequent absence and tardiness	Feels rejected by the school
Retention	Poor work habits
Broken homes	Perception of school as a hostile unhappy
Alienation	place
Avoiding participation in extracurricular	Lack of self-confidence
activities	Lack of self-knowledge
Pupil–teacher relationships	Lack of self-acceptance
Consistent failure to achieve in regular	Lack of self-control
schoolwork	Feelings of insecurity
Frequent changes of schools	Sex problems
Record of delinquency	Is resentful, defiant, and rude
Desire to find employment	Shows rebellious attitude toward authority
	Daydreaming; excessive fantasy behavior
	High needs for love, acceptance, and
	attention

PRIMARY FACTORS	OTHER RELATED FACTORS
	Disinterested in school
	Low self-esteem
	Poor social adjustment
	Fatalistic attitude
	Emotional maladjustment
	Immaturity

Strom (1967), discussing the general population of dropouts, points to factors relating to the culture of poverty' that predispose familial tendencies to foster drop-outs; to the incorrect emphasis on grades as indices of learning; to an antiquated, intellectual secondary school curriculum designed for the cultured few, with little recognition for differing needs of individuals; to the imposition of "nonsensical" experience that goes under the name of education; and to the problem that such students do not perceive that they are learning anything of value. On the matter of the high incidence of dropouts, Strom prefers to consider this to be more a symptom of the school's chronic disorder than of the individual's, and he persuasively questions us:

Do we not overwork the language or doctrine of individual differences and yet seldom employ this practice in teaching and evaluating children? Do we not insist that children remain in school because it is good for them when, in fact, for those whose history of failures is constant this is socially sadistic? Do we not tell the student he ought to choose what's right and yet limit his right of choice by giving him no alternative within the curriculum? Is tyranny a word for events on foreign soil or does it include the practices of some public schools? Until potential drops are individually helped to succeed, schools will collectively fail. (p. 31)

It takes little to recognize the relevance of these questions for the highly able dropout as well. There is no doubt that the whole area of underachievement and its culmination in dropping out of school is a very complex one indeed. The variables are many, interactive, and cumulative. Sometimes the bright student may drop out for financial reasons, but, more often, the reasons relate to personality patterns, personal adjustment problems, sex roles, cultural expectations, limited programs in schools (Gowan & Bruch, 1971) or, for girls, dropping out because of marriage or pregnancy (French, 1968). There is also the struggle for individuality as adolescents seek to find themselves and to assert their independence in an environment that demands strict adherence to rules; it is not that they reject learning, rather it is a protest against required conformity in a school setting (French, 1968; Gallagher, 1975). What dropouts appear to be concerned

224

about is that school does not prepare them for the real world and that their teachers tend to be unfeeling and insensitive to their needs (French, 1968; Strom, 1967). Moreover, as a group, highly able dropouts are mentally healthy (Gallagher, 1975).

DYNAMICS OF OTHER FACTORS

Other dimensions of underachievement relate to handicaps of one kind or another, for instance, physical disabilities or emotional disturbances. Handicapped students often pass unrecognized as potentially gifted—their disabilities conceal their possibilities. To educators and psychologists only recently made aware of this group of students as a talent pool, unfamiliarity and lack of experience have obstructed its visibility. Not only is there the problem of a wider acceptance of the concept of handicapped gifted and the selection of appropriate programs for them but also the selection and development of proper instruments for their identification. The greater the awareness and understanding of the hindrance and obstruction that disabilities pose to these gifted, the more will it be accepted that average or below average attainment in school is a function of the handicap and not of the ability. Generally, underachievement is said to have occurred when a student has performed below capacity as measured by IQ or achievement test scores. In the case of gifted students with handicaps, it could be that, because their capacity level is not known, underachievement by them may be mistaken for performance of less able students and so may pass unnoticed. Besides, the facts that other areas of talent are not identified by IQ or achievement scores and that talent in nonintellective areas, for example, may be overlooked is applicable to the handicapped gifted too. However, there is very little, if any, sustained research on the handicapped gifted. Gerken (1979) points to the need for better identification methods and guidance provision for the handicapped gifted and talented, but the literature is still too spotty to offer significant direction.

Emotional factors as they interfere with the proper mental functioning of gifted individuals have received attention both in the discussion of stress (see pp. 181–198) and in terms of home, family, and school dynamics. Emotional factors as they affect achievement in schooling will not be dealt with here. The subject of learning disability as it affects the achievement of gifted students has also received some attention in the discussion on factors of underachievement relative to findings at DeWitt Clinton High School, (see pp. 220–221), this is referred to as specificity of underachievement (Raph et al., 1966), where, if underachievement in a content area is severe enough, it may affect performance in other content areas. Raph and her associates also point out that different abilities are needed for the mastery of different content areas, and they anticipate Meeker's (1967, 1968, 1969) direction on learning disabilities as they relate to the structure of intellect components determined by the Stanford-Binet and Wechsler scales. Related observations that gifted children with learning disabilities not only show an extreme range of discrepancies among their several aptitudes but also are very sensitive about these discrepancies were made by Gowan and Bruch (1971). This further confirms Guilford's (1967) remark that we possess many different abilities, as illustrated by the structure of intellect, some of which are less developed than others; it is partly because of this that we do not do so well in all subject areas. On the physically handicapped gifted child (e.g., blind, hard of hearing, speech impaired, or those with other physically crippling handicaps), little has been done, especially, as it relates to educational programs. What training is given to teachers or to students with particular handicaps has been approached primarily from special educational opportunities for the handicapped, which do not help teachers or students to learn how to challenge the handicapped gifted (Gowan & Bruch, 1971).

Recognition that handicapped individuals may also be gifted, especially as the handicap relates to adverse socioeconomic conditions, has received considerable attention in the literature (e.g., Baldwin, Gear, & Lucito, 1978; Maker, 1976, 1977; Torrance, 1977a, 1977b), and approaches at identifying talent in the handicapped gifted (Karnes & Bertschi, 1978; Maker, 1976) and providing educational facilitation (Maker, 1977; Vantour, 1976) have also received some recent attention. However, one of the best sources of information on the subject is to be found in a work by Pringle (1970) that is based on case studies of gifted handicapped children in England. Of particular relevance, for instance, is one of Pringle's three case studies concerning the effect of physical handicaps on gifted children, a paraphrased version of which is presented here:

Toby aged 9 years 9 months with an IQ of 133 was born with a cleft palate, which necessitated seven operations before age 5 years. He had a bad speech defect, was weak verbally, severely retarded educationally, regarded as a slow learner by his principal, read 2½ years and spelled 3 years below his age respectively, but did arithmetic at about his age level. Timid, well behaved, and anxious, Toby seemed "miles away," had few friends and feared the teacher, disliked school and often feigned various ailments, slept badly during term time (i.e., the time when school was in session) and was most unhappy. Generally, his parents were very supportive and loving; however, there was a time when his mother, torn between letting him stay at home and making him go to school despite his pleas, taxed him with laziness and letting down the family when he brought home a bad report, concluding that "he could at least try harder." Toby broke down in tears protesting that he had tried and was willing if she were willing to teach him at home to study for longer hours, even forfeiting play altogether. The mother realized the full extent of his unhappiness and arranged with the principal to have her son at the bottom of the lowest stream so long as he would be happy. It was not until a young, newly qualified, discerning teacher took Toby over that he was found to have in addition to the cleft-palate problem, high-frequency deafness, and defective vision. Equipped with a hearing aid, glasses, and an understanding teacher, Toby's attitude changed, and, in two terms with her, Toby had grown less timid and worried, participated willingly in oral work, eagerly talked about his interests, and made some quality contributions that set the teacher thinking whether or not Toby was in fact quite intelligent despite his poor educational attainments and his previous more experienced teachers' opinions. Referal to a diagnostician for examination confirmed that Toby was really a gifted child who experienced problems because of his physical handicaps primarily. (pp. 56–60)

Pringle's observation of subsequent developments in Toby's life follows:

One factor everyone had underestimated was the effect of the boy's changed attitude to learning on his determination to succeed. He asked his teacher for homework and got up every morning at six o'clock to do it; he persuaded his parents and teacher to give him private coaching during the Easter and summer holidays (even offering to pay for it out of his pocket money!). Periodic re-examination showed excellent acceleration in his rate of learning. But as he had to make up such leeway, I [Pringle] tried to persuade him that time was too short for him to catch up sufficiently to succeed in the examination on which he had now set his heart; I did this in an endeavor to avoid too deep a disappointment but he would not accept what seemed sound educational sense. In the event he proved to be the wiser: he won a place to a technical school where he did very well indeed. Eventually he became articled to an accountant and continued to pass successfully all the necessary examinations, in each case "first go". At the early age of twenty-one, he passed his finals and was admitted as an Associate of the Institute of Chartered Accountants.

Throughout the years he kept in touch with me, sending me school reports, photos and a press cutting when he went to Buckingham Palace to receive a Duke of Edinburgh award. (p. 60)

The reader is also referred to the case study of Martin, aged 5 years 11 months with an IQ of 175, who suffered from intermittent deafness and bronchial trouble. He disliked school and was bored and disillusioned, which an inexperienced young teacher misinterpreted as lack of ability. Another study worthy of note is the one of Jack, aged 10 years 9 months with an IQ of 142, who became partially paralyzed following an accident that left him speechless and unconscious for a time. But, nurtured to some degree of health although never regaining his former agility and prowess, he channeled his love for sport into refereeing, held his own in grammar school*, wrote verse, and painted.

UNDERACHIEVEMENT AND GIFTED GIRLS

We have, so far, considered underachievement as performance in school subjects that is below the level apparently predicted by general intellectual ability or IQ. In considering the underachievement of girls as they grow up to be women, we have to look at the problem not only in terms of achievement in school subjects below ability expectation but also in terms of those influences (perceived in a more general sense) that arrest achievement from escalating to higher levels of development and that should ultimately lead toward fulfillment and eminence.

SEX DIFFERENCES

The problems of girls beyond the studies that tease out sex differences have not received the attention they deserve. Earlier sources of such information can be found in the work of Terman and his associates. For instance, Terman (1930) brings to our notice his group of gifted child writers. Seven of the most gifted were girls, yet all the eminent adult writers in his study were men. This lead him to conclude that other than inherited variables must have a part in determining eminence. A similar observation by Carroll (1940) appears to confirm this. Gowan and Demos (1964) also point out that studies of high school students show a smaller number of gifted girls than boys as underachievers when grades were used as the criterion. In college, grades as a criterion show no noticeable sex differences in achievement, but test scores show boys excelling girls.

Terman and Oden (1959) found that at age 44, 50% of their gifted women were housewives with no outside employment; that of the remaining half of the women, 42% held full-time jobs, whereas about 8% held part-time jobs; that 12.5% of the group were teachers or administrators in elementary or secondary schools (as compared to 4% of men in like jobs); that 20% were secretaries or held other office positions (as compared to 5% of men in similar jobs); and that only 11% held professional positions (as compared to 45% men professionals). The remaining 6.5% held jobs in a number of other fields. To paraphrase Wolleat (1979, pp. 331–332) a decline in the professional and educational status of gifted women as a result of various personal and sociopsychological factors as well as ignorance about career development is noticeable so that:

(1) Women account for about 65% of the increased labor force between 1950

---

*A grammar school in England is a high school that prepares students for entry into college.

and 1960, 26% of which related to technical and professional jobs; decline between 1950–1960 is especially noticeable in women's participation in the natural sciences—chemistry: from 10% to 8.6%, physics: 6.5% to 4.2%, and in mathematical careers: from 38% to 24% (Torsi, 1975)

(2) 45% of professional and technical jobs held by women in the 1940s declined by the 1970s to 40%; whereas the number of women obtaining the bachelor's degree remained fairly constant during the period of 1940 and 1960 (i.e., 40%) a decline from 40% to 35% took place in the acquisition of the master's degree, and from 15% to 12% in the acquisition of doctoral degrees. (Theodore, 1971)

In attempting to find an explanation for these differences, various views advanced focus attention on slower maturational, emotional, and social development of boys as compared to girls; sociocultural pressures and values that assign different roles to, and demands on, boys and girls so that girls at an early age are expected to accept the status quo, whereas boys have fewer requirements to which they must conform. Further, the behavior of girls is more strictly regulated than boys; girls are expected by our male-oriented culture to accept the traditional role of preparing to become housewives and mothers rather than to pursue an academic or professional life. Although achievement is perceived as essential for boys, it is not so perceived for girls (Gowan & Demos, 1964; Havighurst, 1961; Morse & Bruch, 1970; D. Rogers, 1969).

PROBLEMS AFFECTING CAREERS OF GIFTED WOMEN

Wolleat (1979) offers one of the best discussions on the problems that have implications for the career guidance of gifted women. She discusses such subjects as sex typing of social roles, creativity, achievement motivation, direct versus vicarious achievement, and contingency and discrepancy factors as important explanatory variables for underachievement in gifted women.

Sex Typing of Social Roles

Morse and Bruch (1970) consider the sex typing of social roles one of the major contributing causes of underachievement in gifted women. Sex typing brings to the fore the fact that achievement toward eminence by men in the professions is a cultural expectation and, hence, looked on favorably, whereas similar accomplishments by women are regarded as attained at the expense of sex-role expectations and, as such, meet with disapproval. Gifted women aspiring to careers conflict with the prevailing social image and often are dubbed "masculine," whereas their men counterparts who pursue artistic interests are labeled "feminine." This masculine-feminine bipolar sex-orientation is said to be responsible for many of the conflicts experienced by gifted women in the pursuit of careers.

Creativity

It is quite well known that femininity and masculinity are creative-related traits when possessed by members of the opposite sex. Creative people have been found to accept opposite-sex characteristics in themselves, for instance, assertiveness in women and aesthetic inclinations in men, and to allow into consciousness behavior that others would repress (Bruch & Morse, 1972; MacKinnon, 1968). When a person, either man or woman, is identified as having both masculine and feminine traits, that person is considered to be psychologically androgynous (Bem, 1976). This concept of androgyny is found in the discussions of Torrance (1962a, 1963) on creative individuals who, at the same time, possess both feminine and masculine traits (e.g., sensitivity versus autonomy and independence). This served as the rationale for Torrance's (1962a) development of such deliberately divergent titles as "A woman who swears like a sailor" or "A man who becomes a nurse," for example, in his *The Imaginative Story*. Wooleat (1979) suggests that research may show that more similarities in dominant characeristics exist between creative men and women than we realize and that the differences between them arise primarily from socialization practices that tend to reinforce men to achieve and women to be nurturant. To this may be added the conflict that a gifted woman experiences owing to the fact that society expects her to possess as an adult woman quite a different set of characteristics than she is expected to possess as a gifted person if she is to be regarded as a mentally healthy woman (Broverman, Broverman, Clarkson, Rosenkrantz, & Vogel, 1970).

Achievement Motivation

McClelland (McClelland et al., 1953) defines motivation in terms of strong affective association that relates goal anticipatory response with pain or pleasure. He states that, in terms of motivation for achievement, this could be traced to basic motivational patterns that were set early by child-rearing practices as well as by competition relative to a standard of excellence, unusual accomplishment, and involvement over a long period of time. However, his approach to identify high and low achievers was not found to discriminate between high- and low-achieving girls (Pierce & Bowman, 1960). This prompted Horner (1972a, 1972b) to find an explanation for this difference in a dimension that went beyond Atkinson's (1960) conceptualization of two opposing tendencies that approach or withdraw in a performance situation, namely achievement-motive and motive to avoid failure. Although these two dispositions are considered by Horner as appropriate to an achieving man, a third motive, which she calls motive to avoid

230

success, is also present in some women. This is especially so when women are in competition that involves both sexes and suppression of performance by the woman is perceived as necessary to get around the problem of being labeled a failure as a woman because of successful achievement. This is troubling to the gifted woman, who has to resolve the conflict of her dual tendencies to achieve and to act in a nurturant role.

Wolleat (1979) suggests that the psychological implications of the motive to avoid success in mixed sex competition can be found in attribution theory (Ickes & Layden, 1979), which attempts to explain the relationship between performance and one's perception of the causes of successful or unsuccessful performance. Causal attributes appear to fall into four categories: ability, effort, task difficulty, and luck. Generally men as a group tend to attribute success to ability (stable internal factor) and failure to effort or luck (unstable or external factors), whereas women view their success in terms of luck or ease of task and their failure to lack of ability, which makes persistence in a task unlikely and success expectation low. Of relevance is the observation that bright girls do not anticipate success as readily as boys (Walberg, 1969). What is more, teachers nearly always attribute girls' failure to intellectual inadequacies and boys' failure to lack of effort or motivation (Dweck, Davidson, Nelson, & Enna, 1978a, 1978b).

Direct Versus Vicarious Achievement

Another interesting perspective concerning the career development process relates to the extent one gains status and reward through self-achievement or through the achievement of others—what Lipman-Blumen and Leavitt (1976) have termed direct versus vicarious achievement. The traditional role of women places them in the position to obtain status and achievement vicariously through facilitating the efforts of their husbands and children who obtain their status and achievement directly. A personal communication of J. D. Pedro in 1978 (cited in Wolleat, 1979, p. 335) as bringing to Wolleat's notice the relationship of vicarious versus direct achievement as well as planning involvement or avoidance. He reported that girls who are high on direct achievement tend to be more advanced in their career planning than girls who intend to depend on vicarious achievement, whereas boys, except for some intrasex differences, are strongly direct-achievement oriented. Thus, the process of socialization, acting on these psychological attributes, makes it more difficult for gifted women than for gifted men to achieve eminence, even though their ability potential may be equal. Besides, as Morse and Bruch (1970) observe, achievement of gifted women toward eminence in a career may be obstructed by probable interruption of education during their child-bearing years, lack of mobility, or getting a late start. With a family, even goal-directed women may take many more years to achieve their career goals.

Contingency and Discrepancy Factors

The contingency factor is another relevant element in the resolution of the conflict of career and family goals as experienced by gifted women. Wolleat (1979) points out that the marriage patterns in the United States find men marrying women who are either below or at their own educational level, whereas women marry men whose education level is the same or exceeds their own. As a consequence, the pool of desirable husbands is greatly reduced for gifted women, who may then delay graduate- and professional-level education until a suitable husband is found. Such delay by married gifted women may be related to the anticipated difficulties of finding highly specialized jobs in the same locality for both themselves and their husbands. There is also the case of those women who slow down their educational advance so that they will not graduate ahead of their husbands because this may pose the problem of whose career comes first, with consequent painful decisions. Hence, we find such solutions as contingency planning, delaying education, or reducing the discrepancy between career and family goals. Instances of reduction of discrepancy include the choice of occupations that are compatible with the "female" or nurturant role (e.g., teaching or nursing) or participation in male-dominated professions on a part-time basis. These difficulties do not affect the career patterns of men and, hence, do not require the use of contingency planning or the reduction of discrepancy between career and family roles for men.

UNDERACHIEVEMENT RELATED TO DEVELOPMENTAL STAGE THEORY

More recent perspectives on the gifted girl as she grows into a woman approach the problem from a developmental point of view. Earlier, we discussed the development of an individual as occurring in stages, and J. C. Gowan's periodicity table represents a combination of the cognitive stages of Jean Piaget, the affective stages of Erik Erikson, and Gowan's creative stages. An individual passes through three stages—growing from infancy through youth to adulthood—so that, within each stage of development, the person passes through three phases and each time at a higher level toward creativity and self-actualization.

EXPANSION OF GOWAN'S MODEL

One of the most cogent attempts to grapple with the problem of the gifted woman in terms of developmental process is a paper by J. Simpson (1977) that expands Gowan's model without changing its form. She includes Perry's (1970) connotative mode and Kohlberg's moral mode (Kohlberg & Mayer, 1972) as well in the developmental stages of infant, youth, and adult. She points out that the divisions in the periodicity table are not as definite and clear cut as they appear to be and that some overlap and continuity from one stage to the next can be expected. Further, Gowan's terms of escalation and dysplasia (absolute and relative) are described. Dysplasia for Perry finds expression in the terms of temporizing (a prolonged pause in development, which may last for a year or more—as if forces are gathering for the next step forward); retreat (active denial of the potential of a particular stage because of anxiety, resentment, passive resistance, or rebellion reactions, thus, retreating to an earlier stage of reassurance and freedom before choosing to reengage in the ''new'' stage); and escape (denying or rejecting implications for growth, being encapsulated or limited to a particular stage). Kohlberg (Kohlberg & Mayer, 1972) uses the term horizontal decalage (spread across the range of basic physical and social actions, concepts, and objects to which the stage potentially applies). Like Gowan's escalation, horizontal decalage is more important than acceleration if healthy development to the next stage is to occur. J. Simpson (1977) reminds us that developmental tasks in the affective domain are not completed in the same stage in which they are begun. Rather, there is a continuous process that is begun in one stage, more fully developed and integrated in the next two succeeding stages, and finally completed in the fourth stage so that regression under stress may occur.

WOMEN AND DEVELOPMENTAL STAGES

What has all this to do with women? J. Simpson (1977) suggests that for many women more time will be spent in certain stages of development and there will be an uneven progression through these stages. For instance, she says that women will have to spend more time in the affective domain fulfilling affiliation needs (stage 4) and parental needs (stage 7); more time in the cognitive domain at the conventional level of moral commitment (stage 5); more time with formal operations; and more time in connotative development (stage 6):

These are the areas that I see the typical, traditional woman as spending most of her adult life in. I am not unbiased as to the ''traditional woman's role'' having spent most of my adult life as primarily wife, homemaker and mother; but I am coming to realize, more and more, that this role is not for all women for all time, and that, as needs are filled in one stage, a woman or any individual, can be freed and stimulated to move on to the next—that a woman who is reaching toward self-actualization, or ego-integrity, can fill different roles at different times of her life, perhaps more so than a man. (J. Simpson, 1977, p. 378)

To find a theoretical explanation, J. Simpson refers us to Erikson's (1973) thesis concerning a productive inner body space located in the center of a woman that is superior to the missing penis. The woman who can reflect on this inner space without apology is one who can direct her own unique talents and viewpoints toward leadership in the affairs of man, moving as it were into stages of creativity, self-actualization, ego integrity, postconventional morality, and commitment. At this juncture, it appears appropriate to focus attention on Bruch's (1972) insightful perspective of the creative-productive woman in terms of Bruch's comments on the affective aspects of Gowan's model:

> The questions raised by Gowan (1972) as to the affective relationships of girls with their fathers in the initiative stage and to the affective developments in the intimacy period and thereafter in his later elaborations of creativity development, will need careful validation as to their applicability to women. Again, the Eriksonian bases for these periodic stages may be biased towards development in men. Women in our more emancipated age have more choices open to them for choosing whether to marry or not to marry, whether to be totally, partially, or not-at-all involved in child-bearing and child-rearing, etc. Although Torrance (1971) found some women to experience creative gratifications in child-rearing, he also cited that the number of children was negatively correlated with the criteria of creative achievement and aspiration.
>
> The Eriksonian sequence of adult development is also representative of the cultural norms, but creative persons generally do not fit these norms. Even professional women who marry and have families somewhere along their adult developmental stages may observe several patterns of time-out for child-bearing and rearing, short or long periods, earlier or later in adult ages, with larger or smaller numbers of children so that during the generativity stage there may be no peaceful time available for access to the proposed psychedelic level of inner awareness. It is therefore anticipated that several patterns of development of various adult levels of creativity will be found in creative women, from the intimacy period onward.
>
> For example, intimacy for the woman who does not marry may mean simply learning to care deeply for another human being so that the warmth estimated as a creative-productive characteristic may emerge. It may not lead at all to actual generativity, although this could be experienced vicariously through the contacts possible in working with the children of others. The professional woman who is married may have other patterns dependent upon the necessity for study time enroute to an advanced degree, the postponement of family, or the care of children by others. The realities of financial struggles while the wife (and the husband) progress to advanced levels of study, and the wife's lowered likelihood of receiving scholarship aid, set varying sequences upon women's creative development. (p. 8)

SELF-ESTEEM AND IDENTIFICATION

Another theoretical position on sex-linked differences in the developmental process relates to self-esteem and identification. In 1971, Judith Bardwick wrote that, in the main, boys' self-esteem is achievement based and girls' self-esteem is acceptance based. It may be that girls, being dependent on others and reinforced by significant others for esteem, do not find esteem within themselves because such esteem can evolve only when an individual sets goals and frequently achieves them. Bardwick perceives identification as a process involving both parents. The girl identifies with the personal qualities and maternal role of the mother while simultaneously identifying with her father whom she loves and by whom she is loved. Should rejection of maternal-role-model-related variables occur, a girl may identify more strongly with her father's role activity and perceive herself as more capable of achieving success and self-esteem in male-oriented activities. This ties in with the observation that children who relate more with opposite-sex parents are more likely to facilitate the development of their creativity so that the development of a sense of self-esteem and achievement in stages 4 and 5, which are more difficult for girls, allows an individual to move into the creativity of stage 6 (J. Simpson, 1977).

AFFILIATION AND ACHIEVEMENT

Most adult women see affiliation in the nuclear family as critical to their achievement of self-esteem. Atlhough the motives to achieve in other areas are considered important, they can be only secondary to the need for affiliation. Generally, it is only after women feel secure in the family and have esteem as females that a reemergence of achievement motivation may occur. At that time, mature women may assume multiple roles—taking for granted their family affiliation, they may go to college and extend themselves in various directions toward higher developmental stages. That women tend to remain in this stage of development longer than men may be attributed to their feelings of security and happiness because they can be dependent and protected while fulfilling the vital role of mother. Achievement motivation can and often recurs when women have no longer the need to take care of dependent children and can turn their attention to maintain self-esteem by moving on to new stages of development. Those women who cannot move to the next higher stages of development experience a form of escape (Perry, 1970) or dysplasia (Gowan, 1972). This may result because their affiliative, love, productive, and care roles (affective areas of stages 6 and 7) are the most culturally acceptable.

UNDERACHIEVEMENT AND THE CULTURALLY DIVERSE

An important contribution to our understanding of human beings and their behavior comes from the works of social anthropologists like Ruth Benedict, Otto Kleinberg, Clyde Kluckhohn, Margaret Mead, and others. In attempting to find answers to questions concerning some of the problems faced by individuals growing up in an American environment, these social scientists chose to study the institutions and behavior patterns of less complex social groups both in this country and elsewhere in the world. Almost without exception, these scholars concluded that many of the problems experienced by our youth arise from cultural shaping and conditioning.

CULTURAL DIVERSITY IN THE UNITED STATES

The diversity observable even among the different peoples living in this country can be attributed to cultural variance. Although language differences contribute to the complexity of cultural variability in other lands more than in the United States, the fact remains that the English used in this country among its subcultural groups is not altogether the same. Variation not only exists in the spoken tongue but also in the denotation and connotation of word meaning as well as word usage. To complicate matters, fresh waves of Spanish- and Asian-speaking immigrants keep entering the country to add further dimensions to cultural diversity.

For some time, this country has been well known as a melting pot of people from many parts of the world. Although many of the differences among these peoples have dissolved into a common American culture, some differences still remain to characterize American culture as comprising a number of subgroups as well as several nondominant, generally low socioeconomic subgroups, which include native Indians, black Americans, Mexicans, Puerto Ricans, Chinese, Vietnamese and other Asian subgroups, and the like. They all share a common American education and culture although still maintaining some aspects of their own cultural heritage, which makes for cultural diversity in this country.

IQ AND THE CULTURALLY DIVERSE

American schooling generally levels itself at the average student. It is a repository of the middle-class culture and value system, which operate as major educational influences that shape the lives of students. The educational design for years has included learning and testing as important elements. The growing recognition of individual differences in ability and needs has manifested itself in the rise of the testing movement and in the provision of a differential curriculum. Students have been tested for achievement over many years, mainly to evaluate learning outcomes but sometimes IQ information is also used for educational placement. As advocates for special education were being heard and federal or state legislation was passed to provide opportunities for exceptional children (one might include the gifted as a category of exceptionality although the term seems generally to be applied to those students with handicaps or disturbances), identification of general intellectual ability, as measured by IQ tests, was the common practice. Children would, then, be categorized for purposes of education along a continuum, from educable mentally retarded through average to highly intelligent and genius levels. Using a frame of reference that is uniquely white middle class both in terms of test items and norm groups, traditional IQ measures would compare the performance of students from culturally diverse groups with the performance of students for whom the tests were really designed—only for the results to show deficits for the culturally diverse, who are called culturally deprived, disadvantaged, or different.

Goddard (1908, 1911) first used an American translation of the Binet measure in institutional settings, but cultural bias showed this approach to be unsuitable. Terman's design of an American version of the Binet measure proved to be more productive. It is ironic that, whereas the *Stanford-Binet* recognized the need to construct a measure of intelligence that would reflect the cultural difference and uniqueness in this country, it limited itself to the dominant white middle-class population of Americans and their culture. In addition, the underlying assumption that the *Stanford-Binet* is an instrument relevant for use with all Americans without regard to cultural diversity and socioeconomic factors is faulty. Comparison of different groups of people to norms that do not include their groups violate good measurement rules and, without question, introduce extraneous variables that contaminate the results. It is to be expected, then, that readings on the measures for people who are different from the norm group and for whom the items of the test were not designed, both by way of language idiosyncracies and content, would not be correct and more than likely would show deficits. Clearly, such people rather than being called disadvantaged should be regarded as being *at a disadvantage*. Much of the controversy over mental capacity of blacks as compared to whites as measured by IQ scales (e.g., Gage, 1972; Jensen, 1969; Shockley, 1972) could have been avoided had the thrust of the arguments been directed toward cultural diversity of the population rather than deficits among blacks with a biased frame of reference as the criterion.

Underachievement of the culturally diverse is an interesting dimension. It relates to problems of semantics; it calls into question the suitability and validity of instruments currently in use; and it points to educational programs that generally do not take into account the needs and interests of students from different cultural groups. Underachievement used more commonly to measure learning of school subjects below the level predicted by capacity must be thought of afresh because the discrepancy that exists in instrumentation to identify mental capacity may lead to inaccurate predictions of school learning and attainment.

THE PROBLEM OF DEFINITION

Of the many problems that confront us when we are trying to make up our minds about special groups, the problem of definition obtrudes. In selecting a word to name a group relative to certain attributes, we are sometimes not fully aware of the connotations of the word that are assigned so that, although in some respects the denotative meaning of the word communicates those attributes that fit it, in other respects emotive implications and overtones may be inherent in the usage of the word. It is of value, then, to take a second look at such words as deprived, disadvantaged, different, and diverse—words used commonly to describe minority groups as it pertains to their culture. The first two words have negative connotations: deprived suggests deliberate withholding, whereas disadvantaged suggests lack. Both words indicate deficit conditions that attend a present state of being and imply comparison to a frame of reference expected to apply to the whole referent population.

It is of importance to remember that, when we refer to the culturally different and diverse, we mean to include ethnically different groups, about whom the word disadvantaged especially loses its meaning. For, as Gowan (1969) points out, the scion of a Jewish or oriental immigrant family, even though poor, may not be culturally disadvantaged. Rather, the alien cultural tradition may actually give advantage in terms of a rich cultural background, which may account for the rapid rise of many descendents of immigrants to managerial and professional positions. Gowan also asks us to note how Cuban emigrés with similar handicaps as Mexican-American families, who are customarily regarded as culturally disadvantaged, have made rapid adjustment to American life, whereas the Anglo-Saxon Kentucky hillbillies have failed to adjust in three centuries. Further, he considers that the word disadvantaged is ostensibly related to poverty and low socioeconomic status in the family and goes on to define disadvantaged not so much in ethnic terms but as being reared by poor, lower class, native parents who are out of the cultural mainstream.

The selection of one or another of the four terms to denote a minority group will vary depending on whether the user's perspective relates to differences among a variety of cultural groups or to differences between a group and some standard relative to a trait or behavior pattern. This problem has led Baldwin (1978), Fraiser (1979), Fuchigami (1978), Torrance (1977b), and others to question the validity of the deficit terms deprived and disadvantaged and to suggest the use of such terms as different, diverse, or minority as more appropriate words.

We have already discussed the concept of giftedness, and its multifaceted

238   PROBLEMS OF SPECIAL GROUPS

nature is just as highly relevant when we refer to the gifted minority (Fuchigami, 1978) or to the gifted culturally diverse (Baldwin, 1978; Fraiser, 1979) or different (Torrance, 1977b). Cultural and socioeconomic factors tend to veil the talent potential of these gifted groups, consequently hindering true readings and proper identification. Baldwin's (1978) diagrammatic representation of innate capacity interacting with environmental influences and functioning-performance levels brings into sharp focus the complexity of identification and educational programming for gifted culturally diverse individuals (Figure 9).

The importance of this conceptualization should be underscored because emphasis moves from individual variables that affect minority-group children to their interactive effects, which are illustrated by Baldwin's examples of Carmen, José, Tommy, Lon, and Elain:

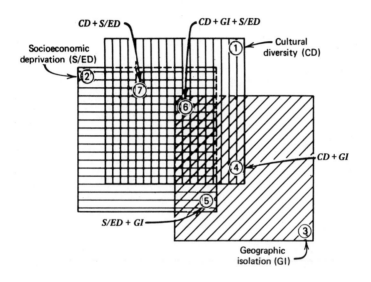

Figure 9 Interrelations among the three variables used to define the gifted child with unique needs. Area 1 represents cultural diversity. Area 2 represents socioeconomic deprivation. Area 3 represents geographic isolation. Area 4 represents culturally diverse children affected by geographic isolation. Area 5 represents the interactive effects of socioeconomic deprivation on children in geographic isolation. Area 6 represents the effects on culturally diverse children of socioeconomic deprivation and geographic isolation. Area 7 represents cultural diversity affected by socioeconomic deprivation. (Baldwin, 1978. Reprinted by permission.)

Carmen, a Puerto Rican student, who is culturally diverse is also socio-economically deprived, so his problems are different from José who has a language difference along with his cultural diversity but whose parents are not economically destitute. Tommy lives on a farm, is poor, and is from a different culture. Plans for identifying and planning for individuals in his situation should include consideration of all three of the variables. Lon is an Asian student who has just come to this country to escape the political problems of his native land; he cannot speak English but his family is able to live moderately well. Therefore, he falls in the category of cultural diversity. Elain is a Black student whose parents have just moved back to America after serving the government in Europe and Africa. She is culturally diverse but other support systems have diminished the effects of this variable on her functioning level. She would not be the primary concern of this programming [sic]. (p. 4)

THE PROBLEM OF IDENTIFICATION

The selection of students for participation in gifted programs or projects in and out of school brings into sharp focus the problem of identification. The general narrowness of identification approaches according to IQ and achievement has already received attention. The growing recognition that there exist varieties of talent that must be taken into account in the identification-selection process leads to some embarrassment when it is found that appropriate procedures are not available for some areas of talent. This appears to be further complicated by cultural-diversity factors so that not only is there the problem of designing instruments or procedures for the identification of a multiplicity of gifts but also the problem of making these approaches relevant and meaningful for the many cultural groups that constitute American society.

Of the many well-known discussions on the important issues of identification and nurturance of the culturally different gifted (e.g., Clark, 1965; Fantani & Weinstein, 1968; Gallagher & Kinney, 1974; Riessman, 1962), there are three that merit special notice. One, by Samuda (1975), focuses attention on issues pertaining to the measurement of abilities of minority groups; the other, by Bruch (1975), examines issues that involve the assessment of creativity in the culturally different. To these must be added Torrance's (1977b) discussion, which deals not only with major issues and trends in the discovery and nurturance of giftedness in the culturally different but also provides the unique conceptualization of using creative positives both for purposes of identification and education.

Samuda's (1975) comprehensive treatment of the subject points to six tendencies that focus attention on expansion and elaboration rather than on discontinuance in the use of psychometric approaches as they relate to the measurement of ability of minorities. The six tendencies are:

1. Present testing practices are unfair to the culturally different.
2. The need for better trained test administrators who are sensitized to the special problems of cultural diversity as related to traditional measures, which may result in misreadings and possible misinterpretations.
3. The use of measures of the environment to bolster and supplement scores on IQ tests.
4. The relevance of a pluralistic sociocultural model for testing minorities so that IQ measures take into account the characteristics of individuals in the context of their family and sociocultural group.
5. The need to develop new measures that incorporate language features unique to individuals who are part of minority groups.
6. A focus on the use of instruments for description and diagnosis rather than for selection and prediction.

Bruch (1975) identifies four areas of concern on measurement generally and on measurement fallacies in IQ and achievement testing specifically as these relate to cultural differences:

The first issue points to the use of IQ measures based upon middle-class mainstream culture and values that overlook or underestimate the abilities of minorities. The need then is to turn away from the "deficit" model to the "difference" model (whose measurement focus is on the characteristics fostered by a particular culture), and the "bicultural model" (whose measurement focus is on the inclusion of a combination of relevant cultural and mainstream characteristics).

The second issue has to do with the neglect of known subcultural values, abilities, and specific knowledge in current instruments and procedures, and the need for modification of standardized instruments that will take into account word usage in various culturally different groups that may dictate culturally right but mainstream-wrong answers, and testing that will utilize the personal style qualities of culturally different children.

The third issue pivots on motivational negatives related to educators, test administrators, and test administrations combined: bias in favor of the traditional IQ, lack of acceptance of cultural pluralism and its measures, and mainstream bias that interferes with the acceptance of other cultural values thus preventing the recognition of the [fact that] cognitive or behavioral strength of the culturally different are factors delimiting the perspectives of educators; and the negative expectancies of test administrators, the emotional resentment for a mainstream culture test by the culturally different child with consequent display of low motivation are testing related problems that suggest the need for good rapport especially in individual testing and appropriateness of the social setting.

The fourth issue is concerned with fallacies of measurement among cultur-

ally different groups, namely, the attitude that giftedness can only be iden-
tified by means of the objective test, the assumption that IQ measures are
reliable and valid for culturally different children, the belief that IQ tests
measure innate ability without the influence of experience, and the assump-
tion that IQ tests measure unitary ability (contrary to Binet's conceptualiza-
tion of the abilities called into play in his measure of intelligence) rather than
a multi-intellectual approach. (pp. 166–169)

Common to both Samuda's (1975) and Bruch's (1975) observations are the
inadequacies inherent in the conceptualization that test measures constructed for
use with members of the majority culture are just as appropriate for use with
members of diverse subcultures. There are also questions on the relevance of
item content, reliability, validity, and related psychometric procedures as well as
on their administration and interpretation for cultural minorities. Another common issue is the need for measures to take into account the influence of experience and differences of language usage in the context of cultural diversity. Both
Samuda and Bruch see the need for training testers and developing test administration procedures that reflect an orientation toward a difference model and that
point away from a deficit model. Samuda's observations concern the need for the
development of new measures for diagnosis and prescription that incorporate
special language characteristics of minority groups and serve as open-ended
probes that include atypical patterns and varieties of learning. A departure from
traditional testing and deficit models, Samuda's (1975) concepts have neglected
to emphasize both a multitalent approach and a search for the abilities that are
especially encouraged by culturally different groups (Torrance, 1977b). Bruch
(1975) offers a more future-oriented and balanced summary of the issues (Torrance, 1977b). However, she includes the need for assessment procedures (1) that
go beyond IQ so that multiple talents and creativity can be identified and (2) that
recognize the value of identifying such talents by more informal observational
procedures that take into account environment, experience, and cultural diversity. Her conceptualization of the problem is in line with Torrance's (1977b)
emphasis on the need for a nonpsychometric approach whose rationale is to
identify the talents of the culturally different by means of creative positives.

About the best, most comprehensive, and forward-looking discussion on the
discovery and nurturance of giftedness in the culturally different is Torrance's
(1977b) monograph whose purpose, in the main, is to provide a resource book of
alternatives. The problem is perceived as complex and pivots mainly on issues of
the identification and development of giftedness. Torrance points to the inadequacies of traditional tests that, for instance, deny culturally different students
special educational opportunities, prevent access to higher education, incorrectly
place minority children in programs for mentally retarded students (Astin, 1975;
Goolsby, 1975), and, by means of the issues and consequences associated with

242

test usage, thwart the discovery of giftedness among the culturally different (Bruch, 1975; Kamin, 1974; Miller, 1974; Samuda, 1975). Further, the ineffectiveness of educational programs for culturally different children and the need for different alternative education relevant to them are pointed out by many (Coleman, 1973; Edmonds, Billingsley, Comer, Dyer, Hall, Hill, McGehee, Reddick, Taylor & Wright, 1973; Jencks, 1973; Torrance, 1977b).

On the matter of identification, there have been attempts to correct the inadequacies of the traditional measures, these have included translations (e.g., Spanish and English versions of the *Wechsler Adult Intelligence Scale,* [*WAIS*] the *Wechsler Intelligence Scale for Children,* [WISC] and the *Inter-American Series: Test of General Ability*) as well as scoring refinements that tend to highlight the specific strengths of culturally different and disadvantages groups (e.g., Bruch's work with the *Stanford-Binet,* 1971; Mercer's *System of Multicultural Pluralistic Assessment* [*SOMPA*] [Mercer & Lewis, 1978]). To these may be added measures with no verbal content, minimal instructions, and no time limits (for some measures) that can be adapted for use with culturally different children (e.g., *Arthur-Point Scale* [Arthur, 1947]; *Chicago Non-Verbal Examination* [Brown, 1963]; *IPAT Culture-Fair Intelligence Test: Scales I, II,* and *III* [Cattel & Cattel, 1963];* *Test of General Ability* [Flanagan, 1960]; *Raven's Progressive Matrices Test* [Raven, 1947]).

Torrance considers that most of the instruments described, regardless of various adaptations, appear to have racial and sociocultural biases. He suggests that only two instruments that are useful in the identification of giftedness lack cultural bias—the *Torrance Tests of Creative Thinking* (Torrance, 1966, 1971, 1974b) and the *Manual for Alpha Biographical Inventory* (Taylor & Ellison, 1966), which can be used to discover talent in minority groups but is not yet commercially available.

Other possibly unbiased approaches to the identification of culturally different children exist but are either not easily available (e.g., the *SOI Learning Abilities Test* [Meeker, 1979b]†) or not as yet ready or developed for use (e.g., the *Creative Binet* [Bruch, 1968] and the *Multiple Talent Evaluation* [C. W. Taylor, 1969]).

An approach that turns away from the traditional culture-free test to culture-specific procedures to assess ability is the *Black Intelligence Test of Cultural Homogeneity (BITCH)* (R. L. Williams, 1972b, 1972c) a measure that consists of 100 multiple-choice questions to be answered as black people would answer them. Two other measures are the *Black Awareness Sentence Completion Test* (R. L. Williams 1972a) and *Themes Concerning Blacks* (R. L. Williams 1972d). R. L. Williams's basic idea is now used in several developmental projects and

*IPAT = Institute for Personality and Ability Testing.
†SOI = structure of intellect.

may eventually give rise to the construction of measures for identifying gifted-ness in other minority groups (Torrance, 1977b).

First, review our discussion (pp. 79–82) of the *Torrance Tests of Creative Thinking* (Torrance, 1974b) and *Thinking Creativity with Sounds and Words* (Khatena & Torrance, 1973; Torrance, Khatena, & Cunnington, 1973). To that discussion must be added Torrance's observation of the relevance of these mea-sures in the identification of the creative potential of minority children. The open-ended nature of the measures permits students to respond in terms of their own experiences regardless of what these may have been, and the testees can use whatever language or dialect they find most comfortable. The *Torrance Tests of Creative Thinking* were designed to be used with children, youths, and adults from the kindergarten through graduate and professional school levels. Thus far, it has been translated and used in at least 25 different languages. The many studies that Torrance cites support the relevance of his measures for identification of talent in minority groups. In particular, those studies should be noted that have found that the *Torrance Tests of Creative Thinking* appear to assess abilities that are little influenced by heredity (Pezzulo, Thorsen, & Madus, 1972; Richmond, 1968) but are most susceptible to the influence of experience (Davenport, 1967). However, it is interesting to note A. R. Jensen's remarks on black-white dif-ferences (with strong hereditary leanings) to Emily Harris of "Report on Educa-tion Research" (May 2, 1979) in an interview at the American Educational Research Association Convention in San Francisco: (1) he attributes racial dif-ferences mainly to Spearman's *g* loading on IQ measures owing more to com-plexity than to content per se and (2) he sees the differences as developmental and not confined to the verbal areas so that black children perform nearly like white children who are a year or two younger on Eisner's developmental free drawing scale.

Continued refinements of the *Torrance Tests of Creative Thinking* by Torrance and his associates have resulted in the construction of a streamlined scoring procedure for the figural components of the battery. Not only can the measure provide a creative index that is a better indicator of giftedness than can standard scoring but it also gives additional information of strengths that can be used in the planning of learning activities that are consistent with the concept of emphasizing creative positives. Other facilitating conditions for effective testing of minority groups relate to appropriate warm-up; the use of language or dialect in which students are most comfortable; and the quality of the test settings.

The expanded conception of giftedness has not only made us aware of the multidimensional nature of giftedness but also has brought into sharp notice the deficiencies of psychometric procedures, if not their inappropriateness for the discovery of varieties of talent. Torrance says this prompted him to consider nontest ways of identifying the creatively gifted (1962b), which he saw as more urgently needed for talent identification and development among economically

244   PROBLEMS OF SPECIAL GROUPS

disadvantaged and culturally different students (Torrance, 1973, 1974a). This found expression in a more comprehensive system for both discovery and nurturance of talent. Torrance (1976a, 1976b, 1977b) discusses how each creative positive may be discovered in turn; its importance; its evidence among the culturally different; its use in the curriculum; and its use in developing careers. Based on the rationale of creative positives, he lists the following characteristics as indicative of talent among the culturally different (1976b, p. 14; 1977b, p. 26):

List of Creative Positives

1. *Ability to express feelings and emotions.*
2. *Ability to improvise with commonplace materials and objects.*
3. *Articulateness in role playing, sociodrama, and story telling.*
4. *Enjoyment of and ability in visual arts, such as drawing, painting, and sculpture.*
5. *Enjoyment of and ability in creative movement, dance, dramatics, and so forth.*
6. *Enjoyment of and ability in music rhythm, and so forth.*
7. *Use of expressive speech.*
8. *Fluency and flexibility in figural media.*
9. *Enjoyment of and skills in group activities, problem solving, and so forth.*
10. *Responsiveness to the concrete.*
11. *Responsiveness to the kinesthetic.*
12. *Expressiveness of gestures, body language, and so forth, and ability to interpret body language.*
13. *Humor.*
14. *Richness of imagery in informal language.*
15. *Originality of ideas in problem solving.*
16. *Problem centeredness or persistence in problem solving.*
17. *Emotional responsiveness.*
18. *Quickness of warm-up.*

THE PROBLEM OF NURTURE

Although the problem of nurture is one that affects all children generally and the gifted specifically, it has particular features when considered in terms of minority groups. The most productive thrust appears to be in the direction of the identification-diagnosis facilitation model discussed earlier (pp. 83–84) relative to the *Khatena-Torrance Creative Perception Inventory* (Khatena, 1977b; Khatena & Torrance, 1976a, 1976b). This measure includes creative positives and strengths of individuals in the context of cultural diversity (Torrance, 1976a, 1976b, 1977b). Another significant thrust can be traced to the use of process models relative to the structure of intellect (e.g., Meeker, 1977) and teaching strategy models (e.g., Joyce & Weil, 1972; Renzulli, 1977a; Sisk, 1976; F. E. Williams, 1970) that take into account cultural diversity factors.

Baldwin's (1978) discussion on curriculum and methods in terms of four components, namely, decisions relating to the planning for (1) strengths and weaknesses, (2) curriculum objectives, (3) evaluation procedures, and (4) an instructional system, may apply to most students in regular classrooms although specifically directed at providing some rationale for designing quality programs for gifted children. Although she does not speak much to the issue of programming for minority children in this paper, both her attempt to link curriculum and methods to the three dimensions of cultural diversity (Figure 9) and her table of descriptors aimed at providing clues for identification as well as planning give interesting perspectives and meaning to what she has to say for minority groups (Table 5).

Baldwin on Curriculum and Methods

Baldwin's conceptualization of curriculum and strategies is appraised by Fuchigami (1978) as similar to those of other test-oriented researchers. Although he compliments Baldwin for including references to all major contributors to curriculum design for the gifted, he finds it disconcerting that she does not attempt to show relationships among proposed approaches by followers of B. S. Bloom, J. P. Guilford, F. E. Williams, J. S. Renzulli, and others. He suggests that there is a great need for the various theoretical positions to be linked into a comprehensive whole to provide an overall framework for education of the minority gifted. The fact that we do not now have one confuses and frustrates both planners and practioners. Fuchigami's answer to the problem is a curriculum model for minority gifted children, spanning kindergarten through grade 12, to develop those skills and personality traits necessary for leadership. However, like Baldwin, he did not intend to include detail in the compass of this paper.

Fuchigami on Program Activities

In addition to the leadership curriculum concept, Fuchigami offers 12 program-activity ideas, which he considers might capture the imagination of some public- or private-funding source. They have relevance for all gifted students within the larger concept of cultural diversity (Fuchigami, 1978, pp. 74–75):

(a) *Regional schools or programs that enable gifted to transcend traditional school district boundaries. This idea could involve a variety of possibilities within and between districts, cities, counties, states, regions, and even nations.*

246

Table 5 The Most Common Descriptors for Children Affected by Cultural Diversity, Socioeconomic Deprivation, and Geographical Location

Descriptors	External and Internal Deficit	Possible Environmental Causality	Exceptional Characteristics to Look for	Intellectual Processing Ability Indicators	Horizontal/ Vertical Program Adaptation
1. Outer locus of control rather than inner locus of control.	**1.** Inability to attend to task without supervision.	**1.** Discipline does not encourage inner locus of control. Child is directed to follow directions. Tradition dictates strict adherence to directions.	**1.** Academic—retentive memory.	**1.** Convergent production of semantic units.	**1.** Contract activities—directed level development—counseling for trust—skill development.
2. Loyalty to peer group.	**2.** Inability to externalize behavioral cues.	**2.** A need to belong. Empathy for those in similar situation.	**2.** Psychosocial sense of humor; intuitive grasp of situations; understanding of compromise.	**2.** Affective behavior—possible indication of convergent production of behavioral units or classification.	**2.** Group activity debating counseling seminars—philosophy, logic—process and skill development.
3. Physical resiliency to hardships	**3.** Inability to trust or consider	**3.** Environment dictates need to sur-	**3.** Creative—tolerance for ambigui-	**3.** Divergent production.	**3.** Creative activities—counseling-

continued

Table 5 (continued)

Descriptors	External and Internal Deficit	Possible Environmental Causality	Exceptional Characteristics to Look for	Intellectual Processing Ability Indicators	Horizontal/Vertical Program Adaptation
encountered in the environment.	''beauty'' in life.	vive. Anger and frustration increase animalistic desire to survive. Alternatives, solutions are forced.	ties; insight; inventiveness; revolutionary ideas.		mentor relationship—process/skill development.
4. Language rich in imagery and humor rich with symbolism; persuasive language.	4. Perhaps only avenue of communication—standard language skills not used.	4. A need to use subterfuge in environment to get message across—a lack of dominant language skills—a need to fantasize through language—acute awareness of environment due to its effect on individual.	4. Creative fluency, flexibility, ability to elaborate, originality. Academic-retentive memory, ability to think systematically.	4. Divergent production of semantic classifications, systems relations, and transformations; fluency of thought evaluation of behavioral implications.	4. Writing and speaking emphases—debating—rhetoric analysis. Contemporary and historical literary comparisons. Literary product development.
5. Logical reasoning; planning ability and pragmatic problem solving ability.	5. Opinions disallowed in school situation.	5. Early responsibility related to survival.	5. Thinks in logical systems, uncluttered thinking, insightfulness, un-	5. System analysis; decision making skills.	5. Exposure to systematically developed strategies for solving problems;

logic.

...derstanding cause and effect.

6. Creative ability.	**6.** Lack of directed development of ability.	**6.** Need to use items of environment as substitute, e.g., dolls, balls out of tin cans; wagons, sleds out of packing boxes; dolls out of "corn husks."	**6.** Flexibility of thinking, fluency, special aptitudes in music, drama creative writing.	**6.** Divergent production of symbolic transformation; flexibility of thought.	**6.** Special classes in creative aptitudes, independent study, mentor, process, and content skills development.
7. Social intelligence and feeling of responsibility for the community; rebellious regarding inequities.	**7.** No opportunity to exercise behavior in community without censorship.	**7.** Social reforms needed to help community; high regard for moral obligation to fellow man; religious influence; tradition; survival dictates awareness of social elements related to survival.	**7.** Intuitive grasp of situations, sensitiveness to right and wrong.	**7.** Affective domain; Kohlberg's upper levels of moral development.	**7.** Leadership Seminars Community Service Participation—counseling, historical antecedents. Process and content skills.
8. Sensitivity and alertness to movement.	**8.** Lack of training and development.	**8.** Need to excel, toughness of environment, family, emphasis on physical prowess to substitute for lack of educational input.	**8.** Hand-eye coordination, physical stamina, skilled body movements.	**8.** Divergent production; convergent production of behavioral implication.	**8.** Special development classes, olympic participation, physical cultural classes.

Source: A.Y. Baldwin, G.H. Gear, L.J. Lucito, *Educational Planning for the Gifted.* p. 47. Reprinted by permission.

(b) *Year round educational programs involving special sessions at different locations.*

(c) *Special educational travel-study programs to locations like the Smithsonian Institute, National Aeronautics and Space Administration facilities, marine laboratories and so forth, operated by both public and private organizations, agencies, and industries.*

(d) *Special talent and leadership camps. Depending on location some could be operated on a year round basis and others on a seasonal basis. Gifted pupils would attend for varying lengths of time.*

(e) *Short term student exchange programs within the state, region and nation. The exchanges could mean opportunities to move from urban to suburban or rural settings and vice versa.*

(f) *Criss-cross national "walkabout" type programs whereby students could drop off for varying lengths of time to stay at hostel type homes and sample unique educational experiences in specialized centers of learning.*

(g) *Short term and part-time work-study internships with private industrial and business firms, public agencies, and foundation supported programs.*

(h) *Special cultural heritage programs for minority gifted so they can learn about their roots through a variety of activities and opportunities.*

(i) *Establishment of regional or national universities or educational learning institutes especially planned and staffed for genius or extremely high level gifted. These rare children are potential human treasures unique to humanity and should receive very special development opportunities for their talents and abilities. Such centers might also become available for children from other countries if provisions for their families could also be included.*

(j) *Special family programs and options that include all members of the family. The minority gifted from economically poor environments need special consideration by program planners to minimize concerns related to potential conflict and alienation in family relationships. Alternatives for family programs should range from simple inclusion of specially trained family caseworker/counselors to something as radical as family relocation options involving public or private employment for all working members of the family.*

(k) *Special schools. At a time when busing children is widely practiced, the gifted could be easily transported to special schools without the usual problems accompanying such practices.*

(l) *Short term boarding schools whereby students return home on weekends and holidays.*

Torrance on Nurture as Related to Talent Discovery

Torrance's (1977b) future-oriented focus on nurture as interrelated to the discovery of talent among minority groups commands our attention for its innovative, germane, and productive perspective. He suggests three alternatives designed to allow for harmony in selection and programming that would avoid selecting students on one measure of giftedness and, then, placing them in a program aimed at developing some other type of giftedness (pp. 65–66):

(a) Talent Development Center

For this alternative, students with some exceptional talent would be recruited. This talent might be in writing, one of the visual arts, drama, music, dance, science, politics, mathematics–even unconventional talents needed by society. All kinds of evidence would be accepted for evaluation, such as art products, musical compositions, photographs, videotaped performances, research reports, and samples of creative writing. The nature of the evidence would depend in part on the ingenuity and creativeness of the applicant. This alternative program would be designed to develop the student's particular giftedness and help the student create the kind of career he or she desires. The student would take courses in whatever departments would facilitate the development of the proposed career, including independent study under professors and specialists in the community or region. The director of this program would be a person expert in the field of career development.

(b) Future Studies Center

For this alternative, students gifted in future problem solving would be recruited and selected. The special alternative admissions criteria might be performance on the future problem solving tests developed by Torrance, Bruch, and Goolsby or some similar battery yet to be developed. The alternative program would develop abilities in future problem solving, futures research, and the like. The director of this program would be a qualified futures scholar. Students in the program would enroll in courses in whatever departments offer opportunities for developing the competencies needed in future studies or careers.

(c) Creative Studies Center

For this alternative, students gifted in creative problem solving would be recruited and selected. As admissions criteria, it is proposed that the Torrance Tests of Creative Thinking and the creativity score of the Alpha Biographical Inventory be used. Both instruments are relatively free of racial and socioeconomic bias. The program would be similar to the Creative Studies Program of New York State University College at Buffalo developed by Parnes and Noller and described in their book Toward Supersanity: Channeled Freedom (1973). In addition to the integrating core of creative studies, students might take some conventional major, or they might simply take courses throughout the college or university to enhance their skills as crea-

*tive problem solvers. The director of this program would have special exper-
tise in creative problem solving and in developing creative problem solving
skills in others.*

Other general approaches for articulating discovery and the nurturance of giftedness that are expected to cater to the varying local needs of the culturally different include:

1. The use of cultural positives (strengths) to discover giftedness in the culturally different and direct their development toward competencies that are required for success in the mainstream culture (e.g., the program developed in 1965 by Witt [1971] in New Haven, Connecticut).
2. The partial use of traditional criteria to select the minority gifted for exposure to an intermediate intervention program. The program would prepare them to move on to high-level opportunities in which their cultural strengths would be used as the basis for developing the intervention program (e.g., the program in the medical science area known as the High School Education Program at the University of Pennsylvania [HEP-UP] by Shepherd, [1972]).
3. Discovery of giftedness and programming based on creative positives (Torrance, 1977b) that was achieved through curriculum reform in all schools and by the development of special schools in the performing and creative arts (e.g., schools in Houston, New Haven and New Orleans are now partially testing this approach). The approach was tried on a short-term basis (Amram & Giese, 1968; Bushnell, 1970). However, the time involved was insufficient for helping the culturally gifted students attain their potential.
4. The selection of students who demonstrate giftedness in the cultural positives and who perform moderately well on traditional criteria to provide them with special support programs that will help them attain higher levels on the traditional criteria (e.g., Whimbey & Whimbey [1975] developed a type of cognitive therapy approach by which students are made aware of their strengths and weaknesses in thinking strategies and provided with directed, specific help to improve their thinking behavior).
5. The discovery and nurture of giftedness among the culturally different through programs of competition in those areas in which culturally different students frequently excel. Programs that are apart from the already existing successful athletics programs (e.g., creative writing, art, music, dance, and drama).

Additional guidelines include a difference rather than deficit model; the criteria of creativeness; a multidimensional model of giftedness; creative instructional methods and learning environment; careful avoidance of unreasonable financial demands and, where possible, opportunities for earning money to purchase educational materials; help for the culturally different gifted that moves them from feelings of alienation to feelings of pride in their special strengths with

252

opportunities to share the fruits of their strengths with others by means of planned learning activities, administrative procedures, and classroom-management procedures; a heavy reliance on such programs in learning, working in teams or small groups; and arrangement for these gifted to have sponsors, persons who can encourage and protect their rights when they are frustrated, discouraged, or abused and who can give them a chance to make it (Torrance, 1977b).

CONCLUSIONS

The special problems of the gifted are perceived in our discussion as facets of underachievement. These include the more conventional viewpoint of underachievement as arising from the discrepancy between predicted attainment through the IQ index and actual performance on school subjects that is below expected level; an expanded frame of talent reference that is multivariate and far more complex than hitherto considered to ascertain underachievement; the variability of sex generally and those factors that hinder gifted girls from achieving eminence; the omission from consideration of disability factors that can affect gifted students when making decisions regarding underachievement of potential; and the misinterpretation of IQ indices as predictors of achievement in schooling within the context of cultural diversity.

The complexity of underachievement has been generally recognized more in terms of causes that interfere with IQ-predicted school performance. This dimension is far better understood than are attempts to find a remedy although attempts to do so are not lacking. The real problem regarding the finding of an appropriate remedy is in the identification of specific causes. Often, the interactive nature of a multiciplicity of causes defies an adequate prescription on how to approach the correction of underachievement. What makes the problem even more complicated is that even a specific difficulty may not only have a multiple number of root causes but that the problem itself may be multidimensional. The complexity of the situation is further aggravated because underachievement may be conceived both as performance below par in school learning as well as poor performance toward higher levels of fulfillment and self-actualization. Cultural diversity calls into question the validity of underachievement narrowly conceptualized by traditional predictive procedures. This challenge almost demands a reorientation that will give cognizance to the multidimensional nature of talent, the use of a variety of test procedures and nonpsychometric approaches, the identification of specific talent strengths so that situations that are relevant to the development of such talent can be handled properly, the diagnostic value of identification for planning educational activities and experiences, and the design of programs that are innovative, flexible, forward looking, and significantly relevant to the complex dimensions of underachievement—programs that include strong guidance components to ensure high levels of achievement, mental health, and self-actualization.

8

NURTURE
OF
THE
GIFTED

OVERVIEW

The subject of nurture is discussed in terms of acceleration so that enrichment and escalation are included. To illustrate this, the approaches used in the study of mathematically precocious youth (SMPY) project and the enrichment triad are examined. Process education by way of teaching to structure of intellect abilities, divergent thinking, and affect—as these find practical application in curriculum materials—also receive attention. To these are added several creative problem-solving approaches, which include the Osborn-Parnes and synectics models, lateral thinking, sociodrama, and those generic problem-solving systems that relate to the structure of intellect and transformation theory. Further, motivation is discussed as are the principles of competence-effectance, incongruity-dissonance, and growth needs that relate to esteem, self-actualization, knowing and understanding, aesthetic needs, creative ways of learning, and future imaging. Comments concerning these several aspects of nurture bring the discussion to a close.

CHAPTER OUTLINE

INTRODUCTION

Many changes have taken place in our understanding of the gifted. These include recognition of the variety of talent potential that exists; the importance of creativity in the lives of the gifted; the nature of their intellectual and creative development, which is essential to the achievement of eminence; some of the problems they face; and the guidance they need. Yet, above all, professional educators want to know what to do with the gifted in the school setting. The subject of differential education for gifted children has received considerable attention over the years (e.g., Fliegler, 1961) and many approaches have been tried with varying success. These have included innovations with curriculum content and methodology, administrative arrangements within the school setting, and special projects. In addition, professional educators have also used services, facilities, and personnel outside the school setting.

For many years, process learning has been emphasized in education generally (e.g., Bruner, 1960). It has acquired renewed vigor and specific direction in an operational-informational theory of intelligence that is based on the structure of intellect and that brings into play both act and content in a comprehensive way (Guilford, 1972), with significant implications for school-learning events. Divergent thinking, creativity, imagination, and related dimensions of brain functioning have become important foci in the arrangement of educational experiences and have led educators of the gifted to suggest approaches to learning that are expected to maximize the intellectual development of gifted students so that they may move toward the frontiers and become not just conservers of knowledge but producers of it.

Not much has been written on the subject of motivation as it pertains to the gifted. Its significance, however, in producing commitment and goal direction toward achievement at the highest levels is just as relevant for gifted people as it is for people in general. Systems of motivation that appear to hold particular relevance for the gifted are those related to achievement through competence, incongruity-dissonance, growth motivation toward higher levels of self-fulfillment, and motivation inherent in creative learning.

This chapter, then, will concern itself with the treatment of approaches that are directed at facilitating the educational development of gifted children. These may be categorized, in the main, as acceleration (including curriculum and environmental enrichment, grade skipping, improved methodology, and administrative arrangements), process and skills approaches, and motivation.

ACCELERATION

Much has been written about acceleration and its related facets (e.g., Dehaan & Havighurst, 1965; Gallagher, 1975; George, Cohn, & Stanley, 1979; Gowan & Demos, 1964)—whether the subject directly concerns itself with the highly gifted or with the objective of arranging circumstances to allow students, in general, to achieve at a rate compatible with their capacity. In either case, there is recognition that the school does not, by and large, provide for the individual development of intellect in its attempt to make learning accessible to everyone. Educators find themselves frustrated in the day-to-day learning situation by the obvious unevenness of student intellectual growth. Various ways have been tried in the classroom by the practicing teacher to get around this problem so that students can be accelerated to express their potential more fully and with a better measure of success. Conceptualizing acceleration in the broader terms of the enrichment of content and methodology, educators have given some direction to:

Innovations with diverse grouping procedures that arrange and rearrange, relative to project assignments, the larger classroom group into more manageable subgroups to facilitate learning of the basics generally and of other school subjects specifically.

Learning materials and texts, making them more orderly, interesting, and attractive as well as providing related materials directed toward making a more appealing classroom environment, which is intended to enhance learning.

The larger methodology of various plans (e.g., the Dalton and Winnetka plans) and methods (e.g., project, center of interest, and playway methods)—frequently experientially based—that are intended to provide for individual and group development and that hark back to the attempts of the progressive movement of the 1930s.

The emphases on individualizing educational experiences that are either behavioristically oriented (e.g., operant conditioning and its application in programmed instruction) or cognitively-affectively based (e.g., taxonomy of educational objectives, structure of intellect, or self-directed learning).

ACCELERATION AS ENRICHMENT

Acceleration can be thought of in terms of horizontal and vertical enrichment although, more frequently, it is considered as resulting from enrichment. Horizontal enrichment provides more same-level educational experiences; vertical enrichment offers educational experiences of increasing levels of complexity. Such kinds of acceleration are the province of individual classrooms, which can, then, generalize to other similar individual school units. Recent application of this approach for gifted students, for example, has led to the establishment of a center, located in one school, to serve several schools in a district as well as state-supported or federally supported special projects. Although some variation in the practice exists at different levels of schooling (elementary, middle, junior, and senior high schools), the thrust is generally the same because the plan operates within the lockstep of grade levels. Problems faced in such acceleration are knowing how to ensure that such a practice is not decorative but functional as well as not limited (by the restriction of providing an advance in learning that is expected to take place in a grade or two above the one in which it actually occurs), but rather facilitative of intellectual development toward levels beyond the confine of grades.

ACCELERATION AS GRADE SKIPPING

Grade skipping, another form of acceleration that is little practiced (Bowman, 1955; Gowan & Demos, 1964; Stanley, 1977a), is fraught with the danger of causing gaps in the acquisition of learning and may bring in its wake psychosocial developmental problems, however, very highly gifted students are less affected by this. If grade skipping is the accelerative procedure used, then, the times chosen for its occurrence should be minimally discrepant. That is, students at certain grade levels will feel less shocked by the change educationally and psychosocially than at other grade levels. Proper timing in grade skipping as it relates to students of exceptional excellence can be recommended. Anticipated gaps in learning can be overcome by special preparatory educational experiences. However, a more fruitful approach appears to be accelerative learning without gaps, that is, a student's learning, for example, in certain subject areas, is continuous toward increasingly higher levels in nongraded schooling—the emphasis is on learning accomplishments, not on grade chronology. What remains important is that, as rapidly as their capacity will permit, students advance in their acquisition of knowledge and skill to the highest levels of achievement.

Acceleration thought of in this way can lead to the most productive results; but the constraints of administrative arrangements are definite problems and much needs to be done to find ways to overcome them.

Stanley (1977b) of SMPY at The Johns Hopkins University reminds us of a number of different ways that are available for gifted student acceleration:

Early entrance into school, preferably at the kindergarten level.

Early exit from school by skipping the senior year to attend the first year of college as a substitute.

Skipping grades, preferably the last one prior to moving from one school level to the next (i.e., skip grade 6 and go to grade 7 or skip grade 9 and go to grade 10).

Taking courses required in the senior year in grade 10 and grade 11 (and for some even earlier).

Completing two or more years of study in a subject in one year.

Using special mentors to pace, stimulate, and tutor brilliant students through various courses.

Obtaining credit through college board examinations or college departmental examination on entry into college to validate previously acquired learning.

Taking correspondence courses at high school or college levels from a major university.

Using self-paced (including programmed) instruction (an approach not recommended by SMPY).

Attending private and elementary school with distinct social or athletic advantages over public schools (also not recommended for students of IQ 140 and above by SMPY).

STUDY OF MATHEMATICALLY PRECOCIOUS YOUTH (SMPY) PROJECT

Although research has generally supported acceleration (e.g., Elwood, 1958; Gallagher, 1966; Klausmeier, 1963; Pressey, 1949; Ripple, 1961; Terman & Oden, 1947), it is not widely practiced. Education appears to favor enrichment over acceleration, with many parents not only hesitant to accept it for their children (Newland, 1976) but also wholeheartedly conspiring with educators to restrain able children from moving ahead at accelerated paces natural for them (Stanley, 1977a). On the subject of enrichment, Stanley is critical. Four main kinds of educational enrichment are identified:

Busy work that keeps the brightest students occupied with a great deal more of the subject they already know so well.

Irrelevant academic enrichment that provides brilliant students with a special academic course, such as high-level social studies, that is not congruent with the direction of their academic bent, or provides them with essentially new academic work, such as games or creative training that is divorced from subject matter.

Cultural enrichment that provides certain "civilized" experiences (e.g., music appreciation, performing arts, and foreign languages) beyond the usual school curriculum, which, although this may prevent boredom, it does not meet the students' specialized academic needs.

Relevant academic enrichment that is not sustained throughout the school years so that seven or eight years of special academic experience are followed by participation in the usual type of academic experiences, to the utter boredom and frustration of the able learner; even though such enrichment is sustained by a 13-year program (e.g., mathematics), it must be backed up by the provision of college credit.

Stanley (1977a) concludes that any kind of enrichment (with the exception of the cultural) without acceleration will tend to harm the brilliant student. The SMPY approach to acceleration emphasizes three phases:

1. The discovery of young students of high mathematical-reasoning ability (Stanley, 1977a; Stanley, Keating, & Fox, 1974). Youths selected by SMPY are generally between the ages of 12 and 13. The principal measure used is the *Scholastic Aptitude Test*—the mathematics component was found to be excellent for identifying high-level mathematical reasoners among seventh and eighth graders. The verbal (verbal reasoning) component of the *Scholastic Aptitude Test,* when administered to the high scorers on the mathematical component of the measure, was found to be of great value for predicting those students who would be able to accelerate their mathematical education radically. This measure is also used with other assessment procedures like the *Sequential Tests of Educational Progress,* an achievement battery.

2. During the description phase, the most talented are tested and studied further.

3. This leads to the developmental phase (the prime reason for SMPY), during which these youths are continually helped, and encouraged so that each is offered a smorgasbord of educational opportunity from which to choose whatever combinations (or nothing) are suitable to each individual. They are both encouraged and provided with the educational opportunity to study mathematics beginning with a course titled Algebra I. Or, skipping, they can go on to advanced courses in calculus, linear algebra, and differential equations (Stanley, 1979).

A special feature of the SMPY program is its diagnostic testing and the ensuing specific teaching of just those points not known to the student:

For example, many seventh- or eighth-grade youths who reason extremely well mathematically can score high on a standardized test of knowledge of first-year high school algebra even though they have not yet studied a school subject entitled "Algebra I." If, for example, such a student can answer correctly thirty out of forty items on Form A of Educational Testing Service's Cooperative Mathematics Algebra I Test in the forty-minute time limit, he has scored better than 89 percent of a random national sample of ninth graders did after studying Algebra I for a whole school year. Then the youth is handed back the test booklet, told which ten items he missed, and asked to try them again. If he still misses, say, six items, they are examined carefully and he is helped by a tutor to learn quickly those points that he did not know. After suitable instruction on just those points and on any points in the test about which he was unsure (e.g., items guessed right), he takes Form B of the test under standard conditions and his success is studied. In this way an able youth can often go on to Algebra II within a few hours, rather than wasting nearly all of a long, tedious 180-period school year on Algebra I. He already knows most of the material of the first course or can learn almost any not-yet known point almost instantaneously. This type of diagnostic testing and teaching of superior mathematical reasoners makes so much sense that we cannot understand why it is tried so seldom. SMPY has formalized the procedure into a day-long "algebra tutorial clinic." (Stanley, 1977a, p. 6.)

In addition, SMPY has developed a team of mathematically talented youths as expert tutors of other talented youths not much older than themselves. These youths work in a one-to-one relationship that resembles the tutorial system of Oxford and Cambridge universities. This approach is proving to be the fastest and best way to swiftly accelerate highly able youths in the study of mathematics. Mathematically gifted students are also offered much educational and vocational counseling and guidance along with memoranda and individual letters as well as a newsletter, *Intellectually Talented Youth Bulletin*. Since the inception of SMPY in 1971, communication has been directly with the youths themselves.

A more recent development is the program for verbally gifted youth. Just begun at the Johns Hopkins University with William George as its director, it is similar in pattern to SMPY. In the next few years, we can expect some interesting evidence from this program about the relevance and significance of this approach.

THE ENRICHMENT TRIAD MODEL

In another currently viable view on enrichment, Renzulli (1979a) calls into question the seeming appropriateness of many intrinsically valuable activities that are essentially indefensible as the mainstay of programs serving gifted and talented students. He offers instead an enrichment model aimed at both guiding the development of the qualitatively different and creating defensible programs for able students. Two program objectives are offered:

I. For the majority of time spent in the gifted programs, students will have complete freedom to pursue topics of their own choosing to whatever depth and extent they so desire; and they will be allowed to pursue these topics in a manner that is consistent with their own preferred style of learning. (p. 112)

II. The primary role of each teacher in the program for gifted and talented students will be to provide each student with assistance in (1) identifying and structuring realistic solvable problems that are consistent with the student's interests, and (2) acquiring the necessary methodological resources and investigative skills that are necessary for solving these particular problems. (p. 114)

These two objectives form the basic tenets of the enrichment triad model. This model comprises three different types of enrichment: (1) general exploratory activities, (2) group training activities, and (3) individual investigation of real problems. The first two are appropriate for all learners and the third—the major focus of the model—is for gifted students. Type I and Type II enrichment deal with strategies for expanding student interests and for developing the thinking and feeling processes. Thus, they represent logical input and support systems for Type III enrichment. It is the interrelationship of the first two types of enrichment with the third that is emphasized in this model. The underlying assumptions of enrichment in the model relate to (1) experiences or activities that are above and beyond the so-called regular curriculum, (2) activities (with the possible exception of some Type II activities) that must show respect for the learner's interest and learning styles and require the learner's sincere desire to pursue a topic or activity of his or her own choosing, and (3) the location of the enrichment—in and out of school and time, as needs dictate.

Briefly, Type I enrichment consists of exploratory activities and experiences designed to assist students become familiar with topics or areas of study expected to generate genuine interest that, in turn, will give clues both to the identification of a bona fide Type III enrichment activity and to the planning of Type II enrichment activities that will facilitate this. Three guidelines are suggested for Type I enrichment activities:

1. Students' exploratory activities must be purposeful and lead to alternative suggestions for further study.
2. Students should be exposed to a wide variety of topics or areas of study from which they can select problems for in-depth investigations (e.g., (1) by developing interest centers—in social sciences, physical and life sciences, mathematics and logic, music, the visual and performing arts, writing, phi-

losophy, ethics, social issues—that are stocked with appropriate books, old newspapers, documents, maps, and related materials; (2) by field trips; or (3) by inviting resource persons—local historians, poets, dancers, architects—who are actively engaged in contribution to the advancement of knowledge to make presentations to gifted students).

3. Teachers should find direction from these kinds of enrichment for planning Type II enrichment activities.

The main thrust of Type II enrichment activities pivots on training exercises leveled at developing thinking and feeling operations or processes that can enable the learner to deal more effectively with content. Various general terms, like critical thinking, problem solving, reflective thinking, inquiry training, divergent or creative thinking, sensitivity training, and awareness development, have been used to describe these processes—to which may be added such specific terms as brainstorming, analysis, synthesis, flexibility, originality, value clarification, and commitment. Renzulli (1979a) suggests B. S. Bloom and D. R. Krathwol's taxonomies of educational objectives and J. P. Guilford's structure of intellect as models that incoporate these thinking and feeling processes. He also indicates several sources of new curriculum materials that emphasize process rather than content objectives and that can be used for Type II enrichment. He notes that process may not always have content relevancy and that such activities can be appropriate without content focus. However, Type II enrichment must lead to Type III enrichment so that practicing process leads to actual use of these activities in real inquiry situations. It must be remembered that Type II enrichment activities should be purposefully selected to represent a logical growth of student interests and concerns that can bind Type I and III enrichment components of the model to provide a defensible rationale for its use.

Then, Type III enrichment activities follow and require the student to become an investigator of real problems. In this component of the model, the teacher has the important responsibility of ensuring that the student (1) identifies and focuses on solvable problems, (2) acquires needed methodological resources and investigative skills, and, of special importance, (3) finds appropriate outlets for products.

ACCELERATION-ENRICHMENT AND ESCALATION

Both J. C. Stanley and J. S. Renzulli have expressed apprehension about the looseness of enrichment. Stanley would have little to do with general enrichment approaches and moves toward a more precise focus of acceleration by narrowing the concept to the accelerative-enrichment of mathematical talent; Renzulli, on the other hand, recommends tightening enrichment into a three-component system that is leveled at a broader talent base with accelerative features in purposeful

262

enrichment that would make of the learner a competent investigator. The thrust of Stanley's program lies in the acceleration of highly specialized ability toward highest achievement in mathematics and its related areas; the thrust of Renzulli's model is toward preparation and fuller development of the gifted individual's cognitive and affective resources for more open-ended but well-organized learning situations. It may be that acceleration as perceived by Stanley is the effective route for the rapid actualization of mathematical talent of gifted junior high school students; the evidence is overwhelming in support of it, but the multidimensional nature of talent, as discussed earlier (pp. 34–63), may require different approaches for different talents as well.

Acceleration is important, but it is not the same as escalation (Gowan, 1979d); Renzulli, 1979a). The rate at which intellectual development is facilitated by acceleration does not ensure transformation to higher levels of intellectual functioning. (See the Erikson-Piaget-Gowan periodic developmental stage chart (p. 149). The reaching a certain stage of development prepares one for the welling up of those energies that are needed for the leap to the next higher level of functioning. Escalation to higher levels of intellectual functioning is really the key to the advancement sought for the fulfillment of potential and promise in the gifted. Where acceleration is the movement toward such an end, escalation effects transformations to higher levels of intellectual operations. The question to ask is not so much what we are accelerating the student into but will acceleration produce escalation into the next higher stage of intellectual development.

PROCESS APPROACH

Consistent with Renzulli's proposed model as it relates to Type II enrichment is the process approach to learning. This approach has been stressed over the years by many cognitivists (e.g., Bloom, 1956; Bruner, 1960; Cole, 1972; C. R. Rogers, 1967) and, more recently, by advocates of creative learning (e.g., Feldhusen & Treffinger, 1977; Meeker, 1969; Torrance, 1965c; F. E. Williams, 1972) because learning pertains to most children attending regular schooling. With the growth of the gifted movement (especially over the past 20 years) and the search for better ways to facilitate the intellectual growth and advancement of gifted students, recent advocates of process learning have turned their attention to the relevance of some of these approaches for the gifted student. The rationale of the process approach sees learning in the control of each individual and related to intellectual abilities and their emotive or affective correlates; finds expression (1) in techniques that familiarize individuals with their own capabilities and (2) in strategies that call for the use of these capabilities in learning that can effectively adapt to the needs of changing circumstances; implies the growth of abilities—in the conducive and facilitative climate of what C. R. Rogers (1967) has called psychological safety and freedom—to higher levels of mental functioning with the expectation of greater productivity. Renzulli's comments about process learning as training exercises (1979a) call to notice only one dimension of the intellect. Although it is true to say that at one level the learner is taught certain ways of thinking that are expected to enhance overall learning potential, the intent appears to be leveled at exciting the motivational emotive roots of mental functioning to bring about an involvement and commitment in the individual to escalate to higher stages of intellectual development. Although it may be true to say that most students in the act of gaining process tools through training exercises may go through the motions as a first step to intellectual development, there are some who make the connections and feel the vibrations that can project them beyond the beaten paths. What are some of these process tools that are used by gifted people more than any other group and that can, in fact, lead not only to fuller development but also to the much needed breakthroughs of our civilization?

Many approaches at training people to think in creative ways have been tried. Just a few years ago, Torrance (1972a), in reviewing the effects of training procedures and related variables on creative thinking as measured by the *Torrance Tests of Creative Thinking,* categorized these approaches in terms of problem solving, creative arts, media and reading programs, curricular and administrative arrangements, teacher influence and classroom climate, and motivational mechanisms. Another good source of information is the appraisal by Mansfield, Busse, & Krepelka (1978) on the effectiveness of creativity training. Their appraised, in the main, deals with:

1. The productive training program (e.g., Covington, Crutchfield, Davies, & Olten, 1974), a self-instructional program for fifth- and sixth-grade students aimed at developing creative problem-solving abilities and favorable attitudes toward problem solving.
2. The Purdue creative thinking program (e.g., Feldhusen, Speedie, & Treffinger, 1971) for students at about the fourth-grade level, which is designed to foster divergent thinking abilities of verbal and figural fluency, flexibility, originality, and elaboration.
3. The Parnes program (1967a, 1967b) for adults, which uses many techniques derived from Osborn's (1963) suggestions and particularly focuses on brainstorming—a three-step process (fact-finding, idea-finding, and solution-finding) that has two important underlying principles, namely, that the production of many ideas increases the chances of more good ideas and that deferred judgment does not permit criticism until all ideas have been produced (Osborn, 1963).
4. The Myers-Torrance workbooks (1964, 1965a, 1965b, 1966a, 1966b, 1968), which are designed to foster creativity in elementary school children through practice in activities requiring perceptual and cognitive abilities that are presumed to underlie creativity.

264

5. The Khatena training method (Khatena, 1970b, 1971c, 1971e; Khatena & Dickerson, 1973) that provides instruction and practice in five creative thinking strategies, namely, breaking away from the obvious and commonplace, transposition, analogy, restructuring, and synthesis. The method is designed for use with both children and adults.

6. A variety of other little-researched training programs that include the use of divergent production abilities; games; experiences from the visual and auditory senses; principles of general semantics; self-instruction to modify what persons say to themselves during problem-solving; focusing—to attend to, and reformulate, feelings; and synectics, which uses a variety of techniques to facilitate making the strange familiar, the familiar strange.

The major question posed by this appraisal is whether the creativity gains made by means of exposure to any of these programs would actually affect real-life creativity. The answer about the effects of such training on developing creative adult professionals is uncertain because their creativity may depend on the joint occurrence of a number of cognitive, motivational, and personality characteristics as well as on situational factors. Yet, it is recognized that, at nonprofessional levels, the training when integrated with instruction in a particular subject area is more likely to lead to productivity, for instance, in the writing of original stories or the conduct of original science projects. This should remind us of what Renzulli (1979a) has said regarding Type II enrichment activities that find application in Type III enrichment activities. The appraisal makes mention of the value and enjoyability of the training to students although its effects on attitudes are uncertain.

One thing to notice about all these programs is that, by and large, they are leveled at people in general with only an occasional study aimed at the gifted. On the whole, the picture is quite well sketched by the review although it is not altogether complete in terms of the availability of different training programs or materials (e.g., Feldhusen & Treffinger, 1977, 1980; Karnes & Collins, 1980) nor in terms of its supporting research, some of which needs updating. But these are not of concern here. What we need to examine are the generic roots of these and related approaches, which can be identified, in the main, through (1) the structure of intellect; (2) creative problem solving, future problem solving, and sociodrama; and (3) recent developments in creative imagination imagery.

THE STRUCTURE OF INTELLECT

One viable approach to the use of process in education is the structure of intellect model (Guilford, 1967) described in Chapter 2 (pp. 48–49). Another is Bloom's model (1956). But, where Bloom's taxonomy of educational objectives (knowledge, comprehension, application, analysis, synthesis, and evaluation) is linear and hierarchical, Guilford's is three dimensional and interactive (operations, contents, and products). In terms of the intellectual functioning of the learner, Bloom's taxonomy has its most direct parallels with the operations aspect of the structure of intellect. The little (or no) emphasis on contents and products of information make his taxonomy quite incomplete, and because there is no empirical validation by factor analysis, the philosophical basis of the categories have the status of untested hypotheses (Guilford, 1972). However, we shall see shortly how Bloom's taxonomy is an integral part of F. E. Williams's model (1972).

The structure of intellect is an informational theory of intelligence that depends on the environment for materials. Materials that may take any one of four forms (figural, symbolic, semantic, or behavioral), that may be organized in any one of six ways (units, classes, relations, systems, transformations, and implications), and that are acted upon by five different kinds of mental operations (cognition, memory, convergent production, divergent production, and evaluation). It has provided the rationale and procedures for the development of several training models that are now in use in schools and special projects all over the country.

To foster intellectual development, Guilford (1972) suggests that we have two goals, the first relates to the development of skills and the second relates to the stockpiling of specific items of information, thereby emphasizing possession of information (cognition) and its use (production). Two additional objectives should be involved in the evaluation and the retention of information. These goals are dependent on achievement relative to the other mental operations (Guilford, 1967).

The structure of intellect operationalizes abilities. Thus, theory informs practice in a way that not only permits the arrangement of exercises that use these abilities, thereby facilitating their continued development, but also gives direction to the planning of curricula that make the abilities functional. In addition, knowledge of the structure of intellect assists in the design of eaching methodology that requires the use of structure of intellect abilities as well as the construction of various assessment procedures that call these abilities into action. Guilford (1977) considers it important to ggve exercise to these abilities so that intellectual development can be maximmied; he points to the fact that first-rate musical performers or golf players, for instance, do not reach peak form and award-winning performance wiitout engaging in hours of special exercises. Practice appropriate to each intellectual ability is expected to promote increase in that ability, and this practice can be facilitated once children know the kinds of intellectual resources they possess. However, training of intellectual skills does not have to be restricted to the formal exercises specifically designed for that purpose but, with the proper emphasis, such training can be cultivated in regular course work. Teaching can be redirected to emphasize not just the formation of concepts weighted toward the cognition of semantic units but, more especially, to emphasize the exercise of other products (i.e., classes, relations, systems,

266

transformations, and implications) in whose involvement units of information acquire significance, meaning, and usefulness. Further, in the selection of a curriculum, provision should be made for both the development of general skills as well as for their immediate and special uses. The more courses that give exercise to structure of intellect abilities, the more transfer benefits can be expected to occur among them (Guilford, 1967, 1977).

The structure of intellect has provided the rationale for the development of many training procedures, especially as they relate to exercises in creative thinking (e.g., Davis, 1970; Renzulli, 1973; Schaefer, 1971). Insofar as the development of models is concerned, two are of particular interest to us. The first is a direct application and extension of the structure to education process (Meeker, 1969); the second augments the structure of intellect model with concepts borrowed from Bloom (1956), Krathwohl, Bloom, and Masia (1964), and Piaget (1967) in the context of classroom instruction (F. E. Williams, 1972). Both attempts were conceived for students in general, and their application in instructional settings is broadly based. This does not mean that the models have no relevance for gifted students. Both have much to offer to the intellectual development of gifted students by putting in their hands, as it were, tools that will allow them to cope with the detail of an ever-expanding curriculum. Sensitive to developing educational thrusts aimed at meeting the needs of gifted students, both M. N. Meeker and F. E. Williams have attempted to focus their models on the gifted. Meeker (1979a) shows the relevance of the structure approach in individualized education programs but does not say much more than she had previously on the potentiality of the model; F. E. Williams (1979b) finds commonality between the strategies in his model and those of Renzulli's enrichment triad but does not distinctly get away from the model's original intent to reach the student in general.

Meeker and the Structure of Intellect (SOI) Workbooks

Guilford (1977) recognizes that Meeker more than anyone else has done most of the work to find applications of the structure of intellect concepts to remedial education and to educational problems generally. Consistent with Guilford's thoughts on the development of intellectual abilities through educational experiences, Meeker (1969) observes that teaching a person how to use ability is as important as the mastery of prescribing content. That is why there is the need to go beyond measuring IQ to identify which abilities are more developed than others and to diagnose strengths and deficits so that educational experiences can be planned according to the learner's intellectual needs. Meeker believes that emphasis should shift, on the one hand, from strengthening and enriching curriculum and on the other hand, from refinements of acceleration approaches and teaching techniques, to the learning process itself. The structure of intellect is seen by her as a way to circumvent the philosophical problem of keeping pace with the continuous expansion of knowledge because, by its relative stability, it provides a frame of reference for the fashioning of learning experiences beyond curriculum content. It is also regarded as the basis of a cognitive therapy that levels itself by assisting students to overcome failure that can be attributed to the fact that they have not developed requisite abilities for success. A differentiated measure of abilities is the key to the identification of deficiencies and the structure of intellect can provide this. In this way, many intellectual failures can be corrected through direct exercise of prerequisite intellectual skills.

Meeker's (1969) practical thrust of Guilford's (1967) theoretical model brings to the practitioner an instrument that, if understood and properly used, can give greater meaning to the learning situation and the learner. Theory is operationalized into small learning components that recognize the interactive nature of ability, information, and the way it is organized. This permits the structuring of learning experiences that, at one and the same time, can identify and facilitate. One major outcome of this early work—which not only familiarized readers with the structure of intellect but also provided interpretation and uses for curriculum planning—was the development of the SOI *Abilities Workbooks* (Meeker, Sexton, & Richardson, 1970), which are leveled at training children to use structure of intellect abilities.

The *SOI Abilities Workbooks,* a takeoff from the theory-based curriculum suggestions of Meeker's earlier work (1969), are organized into five components (based on the five thinking operations) and each contains exercises that call into play the known interactive content and product dimensions in the context of curriculum materials. This approach is prescriptive and individualizes instruction based on a diagnosis of intellectual responses on an IQ measure, like the *Stanford-Binet* or the *Wechsler Intelligence Scale for Children (WISC)* (e.g., Meeker, 1969). The IQ can be translated into structure of intellect profiles by use of prepared templates with the assistance of a psychologist or psychometrist, who, then, prescribes tasks for the needed development of certain abilities. For the teacher who does not have the assistance of a structure of intellect profile from the psychologist, Meeker and her associates suggest that the workbook material be used so that teaching an ability begins with the units level (if a deficit exists or if a weak ability needs to be tied to a strong one), goes on to the classification level (the beginning of concept formation), then, to the relations and systems levels (may be taught together), and finally reaches transformations and implications (high-level abstract abilities associated with creative experiences). Further, this approach has both general and specific objectives that are clearly stated, its materials and instructions are outlined separately to assist teachers to find the individualized materials as they relate to the objectives, and procedures are given for evaluation and reinforcement.

The tasks are set up in a small-step-structure approach so that each one fits a defined structure of intellect factor and may serve as an example for the instruc-

268

tion to be used in the shaping of other similar tasks. The importance of approaching learning in this way is emphasized by the authors of the workbooks, and Meeker, in her introductory remarks, says:

> *Education, if based on the premise that it is necessary to teach children how to learn rather than [to teach them] content, or if based on the premise that we need to develop thinking abilities rather than subject matter, may manage to survive during this century. The clamor to train children in affective abilities [may] be best heard when we show that we can develop cognitive abilities demonstrated that somehow, magically, thinking does relate to affective growth. (Meeker et al., 1970, p. viii)*

Guilford has time and again pointed to the great need for the development of two very much neglected mental operations of the structure of intellect in schooling, namely, divergent production and evaluation thinking abilities. Students are required to use cognition, memory, and convergent thinking operations by their teachers' instructional materials as well as on the tests designed to measure intellectual potential or related educational outcomes. It is not surprising, then, that many educators have constructed and recommended various training procedures to give exercise in the use of the two neglected abilities, therefore, placing more emphasis on divergent and creative thinking. The intellectually gifted student generally uses creative thinking abilities less frequently. If we were to seek for the relevance of the *SOI Abilities Workbooks* to the superior student, it would appear that we could be selective in their use, especially choosing the *Divergent Production Workbook* and selecting tasks from the other workbooks that allow for the development of abilities in the transformations and implications dimensions. To illustrate this, two examples have been excerpted from the *Divergent Production Workbook* (Figures 10 and 11). However, to be consistent with Meeker's prescriptive approach, a structure of intellect profile may be obtained to give information on what abilities need to be developed. Such diagnosis, then, can lead to a prescription of needed exercise for certain intellectual abilities that can be effectively followed up in the series of tasks organized in these workbooks.

This diagnostic-prescriptive approach applies to reading and arithmetic. Meeker's later work (1979) needs to be consulted and will be treated in Chapter 9 (pp. 314–318).

Williams's Cognitive-Affective Interaction Model

Another adaptation of Guilford's theoretical model can be found in F. E. Williams's cognitive-affective interaction model (F. E. Williams, 1969, 1972). Similar to Guilford's, this model is three dimensional but modified to substitute contents, operations, and product dimensions for meaningful content to the teacher, strategies teachers use across content, and pupil behaviors produced as

CHILD'S NAME _____   CELL _____
                                SUBJECT _____
                                GRADE _____

OBJECTIVE:
To develop the ability to produce varied implications from given symbolic information.

RECOMMENDATION TO TEACHER	
MATERIALS:	**INSTRUCTIONS** **GENERAL:**
Pencil Duplicated exercise	

<table>
<tr><td colspan="2">

Math

Name _____ Date _____

Write new equations using these letters.
The new equations must be based upon the
equations.

Example:
Given: A + B = C

New Equations:
C − B = A
B + A = C

1. Given: D + F = E

New Equations:

_____

_____

2. Given A − B = C

New Equations:

_____

_____

</td><td>

SPECIFIC:
Follow the directions on the exercise.

EVALUATION OF PROGRESS:

</td></tr>
</table>

REINFORCEMENT TECHNIQUES:	*Task: Equations*

*Figure 10   Divergent production of symbolic implications. (Meeker, Sexton, &
Richardson, 1970. Copyright © 1970 Mary Meeker, SOI Institutes, Richmond,
El Segundo, Calif. Reprinted by permission of Mary Meeker.)*

CHILD'S NAME _____ CELL _____
                                    SUBJECT _____
                                    GRADE _____

OBJECTIVE:
To develop the ability to produce unusual, remote or clever responses involving reinterpretations or new emphasis on some aspect of an object or situation.

RECOMMENDATION TO TEACHER	
MATERIALS: Short story—verbally or visually presented Sample story: (lower grade) Three men built houses. One man built his house on the sand and no foundation under it. Everyone thought he was very foolish. Another man built his house on the dirt with no foundation. The third man built his house on a great flat rock. The house built on sand lasted only a week, for the winds blew it down. The house built on the dirt lasted six months and the house built on the rock is now 200 years old!	**INSTRUCTIONS** **GENERAL:** Present the story to the student. Explain proverbs—give examples. Make the stories more sophisticated for junior and senior high students. **SPECIFIC:** After reading and/or hearing the short story students are assigned the task of making up their own proverbs as homework. **EVALUATION OF PROGRESS:** The proverbs will be read in class. Students will guess the interpretation.
REINFORCEMENT TECHNIQUES:	*Task: Proverbs*

Figure 11   Divergent production of semantic transformations. (Meeker, Sexton, & Richardson, 1970. Copyright © 1970 Mary Meeker, SOI Institutes, Richmond, El Segundo, Calif. Reprinted by permission of Mary Meeker.)

an outcome of an interaction between what teachers do and content. However, different from Guilford's model, the dimensions of Williams's model are neither altogether parallel nor interchangeable with the structure of intellect model, nor are they probably meant to be. Williams's model concentrates on divergent production operations without using specific structure of-intellect-cube terminology (e.g., divergent symbolic transformations [DST]; divergent figural implications [DFI]) but rather by using broader factor categories, like fluency, flexibility, originality, and elaboration, much in the way that Torrance (1974b) has used his creativity measures. The Williams model uses cognitive to mean the four creative thinking abilities and designates three personality traits as well as imagination as the affective component. The same model, gives focus to curriculum strategies and to teaching strategies—both of these were not in the original intent of the structure of intellect although they seem to have been perceived by Guilford as important educational implications of his model (Guilford, 1967). Meeker (1969) translated them into classroom practice.

One face of the structure (D1) deals with curriculum (subject-matter content) as it relates to art, music, science, social studies, arithmetic, and language; a second face (D2) deals with teacher behavior (strategies/modes of teaching) as it relates to paradoxes, attributes, analogies, discrepancies, provocative questions, examples of change, examples of habit, organized random search, skills of search, tolerance for ambiguity, intuitive expression, adjustment to development, study of creative people and process, evaluative situations, creative reading skill, creative listening skill, creative writing skill, visualization skill; and a third face (D3) deals with pupil behaviors (cognitive [intellective] and affective [feeling]).

One of F. E. Williams's (1969) first remarks on the subject of finding a suitable model for encouraging creativity in the classroom identifies the inadequacy of taxonomical models, such as Bloom's taxonomy of educational objectives in the cognitive domain (1956), Piaget's stage theory of intellectual development (Flavell, 1963), and Krathwohl's taxonomy of objectives in the affective domain (Krathwohl et al., 1964). F. E. Williams states that taxonomies are deficient (1) because their components are conceived in hierarchical order; (2) because they hold that the creative process (defined by many as synonymous with such mental processes as hypothesizing, synthesizing, inventing, associating, transforming) is only found within the higher stages or levels of the taxonomies; and (3) because of the erroneous assumption that children are incapable of higher level thinking before the earlier levels are mastered and until the children reach the adolescent and adult stages of development. F. E. Williams maintains that there is also a need to include the affective dimension of cognitive functioning in process models, citing both Krathwohl and his associates and Piaget: "Nearly all cognitive behaviors have an affective component" (Krathwohl et al., 1964); "[There is a] close parallel between the development of affectivity and that of intellectual functions, since these are two indissociable aspects of every action'' (Piaget, 1967).

F. E.Williams tells us that what is needed is a morphological rather than a taxonomical model to take into account both the cognitive and affective behavioral dimensions. Guilford's structure model describes an interrelated classification of intellectual abilities within only the cognitive domain (F. E. Williams 1972). Although an affective-taxonomical model is available, it is unidimensional. Therefore, morphological interaction model that takes cognizance of cognitive and affective dimensions of behavior as these function with curriculum and teaching strategies was perceived to be badly needed. This gave F. E. Williams the rationale for his cognitive-affective interaction model.

The model found expression in a *Total Creativity Program* (F. E. Williams, 1972), which comprises five books, two poster sets, two audiotapes, a teaching strategies packet, and an instructor's manual. It is designed so that it gives practical assistance to teachers in almost any classroom; requires no large-scale innovative or drastic changes and needs no expensive materials or equipment to supplement methodology that is in current use; provides a spontaneity in learning that encourages pupils to desire involvement in creative learning experiences; and can be used for teacher training in both regular and in-service programs. The program received a very favorable review by Cole and Parsons (1974), who presented it "not only as simply another elementary school curriculum innovation—although it is indeed an excellent one—but as an elaborate and well designed instructional system from which much can be learned not only by other educators, but also by researchers and curriculum developers as well' (p. 206).

Currently F. E. Williams (1979) is attempting to find a relationship between Renzulli's enrichment triad model, which is leveled at differentiated education for gifted students, and his own cognitive-affective interaction model, which is designed to promote better education for most students. He states that these two models complement one another well so that the enrichment triad serves as a guide to what should be done and the cognitive-affective interaction model offers a multistrategy approach on how to get it done, thus, yielding results. Neither model is taxonomic or hierarchical, rather, each one is morphologic and interactive. F. E. Williams illustrates how the two models fit each other:

TYPE I ACTIVITIES USING EXPLORATION STRATEGIES

Paradoxes	Self-contradictory statement or observation
Attributes	Inherent properties, traits, or characteristics
Analogies	Similarities or situations of likeness
Discrepancies	Unknown elements or missing links
Provocative questions	Inquiries bringing forth exploration or discovery

| Examples of change | Exploring the dynamics of things by alterations, modifications or substitutions |
| Examples of habit | Sensing rigidity and habit-bound thinking |

TYPE II ACTIVITIES USING TRAINING STRATEGIES

Organized random search	Organized structure randomly leading to a production
Skills of search	Skills of historical, descriptive or experimental search
Study creative people and process	Analyze traits and study process of eminent people
Evaluate situations	Setting criteria, deciding, critical thinking
Creative reading skill	Idea generation through reading
Creative listening skill	Idea generation through listening
Creative writing skill	Self-expression through writing
Visualization skill	Expressing ideas in visual form

TYPE III ACTIVITIES USING PRODUCTION STRATEGIES

Tolerance for ambiguity	Tolerating open-ended situations without forcing closure
Intuitive expression	Sensing inward hunches and expressing emotional feelings
Adjustment to development	Developing from rather than adjusting to experiences or situations
Evaluate situations	Deciding upon solutions and productions by consequences and implications
Creative writing skill	Self-expression through written production
Visualization skill	Expressing ideas in visual form

One of the two examples given by F. E. Williams (1979) to show how the two models are complementary in operation relates to an ungraded lesson idea in mathematics for a whole class that begins with Type II enrichment activities (pp. 5–6):

A teacher should randomly select five objects in the classroom for measurement. Length of room, height of ceiling, area of table, volume of box, and circumference of opening in wastebasket are some suggestions. Divide the class into smaller work groups, three to four students, asking each group to choose a recorder. This person records the group's measurements. Students should be told there will be two tasks for them to become involved in both requiring group activity.

The first task is for each group to estimate or predict measurements of the five selected items in the room without use of any specific measuring instru-

274   NURTURE OF THE GIFTED

ments. No rulers are allowed at this time. Only improvisations are accepted, and groups are told they are to create clever ways to predict measurement of the five things. Watch groups and observe what happens (divergent productions). If at this moment students do not know how to obtain area, volume, or circumference measurements, now is the perfect time for a teacher to step in and present such facts.

After all groups have guessed by improvisation some ways for predicting the five measurements and have them recorded, now pass out a yard or meter stick to each group. The second task is to arrive at actual measurement of the five things in some definite units of measure (convergent productions). Two sets of recordings have now been obtained, the first by improvised predictions, the second by actual measure. This gives each group two types of data to work on further.

The task at hand now is for each group to design some kind of graphic system representing a comparison between improvised guesses and absolute measures. Suggestions might be use of bar graphs, line or pie charts, or combinations thereof. If the class has had no training in graphing techniques, now is the time to present such information. Sophistication of unit conversion and graphic representation of the two sets of comparative data will depend on prior knowledge, experience and grade level of the groups (Renzulli Type II training activities using two Williams strategies organized random search and evaluate situations cuing for both divergent and convergent productive thinking).

Students motivated by such training activity could be challenged to move on into Type III production activities. Some may become intrigued with ideas for designing an original graphic system by comparing subjectively predicted data arrived at under improvised conditions against objectively accurate data arrived at under measured conditions. A few most inquisitive might wonder how to arrive at area or volume of an irregularly shaped object such as the trapezoidal form of a wastebasket. At this time they should be introduced to the principles of calculus and, if they so desire, allowed to pursue work in higher mathematics as an individual or with a small accelerated group. (Renzulli Type III activity applying Williams strategy adjustment to development).

We have seen so far that both Meeker and F. E. Williams have adapted the structure of intellect for use in the classroom situation, the one arranging for learning across the five mental operations and the other including the dimension of divergent thinking. Both approaches are three dimensional and interactive, with Meeker's directly related to the structure cells of Guilford's model and F. E. Williams's drawing more broadly from the factorial components of divergent thinking but including feeling categories that take cues from Krathwohl's affective educational objectives and draw on the creative personality research of D. W. MacKinnon, F. Barron, E. P. Torrance, and others. Although recognizing the importance of affective roots of intellectual abilities and their functioning, F. E. Williams separates them in his model. Meeker's approach, however, omits affect altogether, unless one reads affective characteristics into behavioral-content categories. Both advocate the development of teacher competencies and a way of facilitating effective use of their approaches with children. Direction for the use of both these models with gifted students arise from direction for their use with most children. If the development of creative mental function in gifted children is the primary goal, then, either model can serve this purpose well.

CREATIVE PROBLEM-SOLVING APPROACHES

Another significant process approach that can be effectively applied to the education of gifted children is creative problem solving. Evidence about the complexity of problem solving can be found in the literature of general psychology, where experimental studies that have used a variety of problem-solving tasks, such as Maier's string-and-hatrack problems, Luchins's water jars problems, syllogisms, mechanical puzzles, and concept attainment, are reported. Other evidence has come from the research of animal psychology, where a variety of problem situations in the form of mazes, puzzle boxes, discrimination tasks, detour situations, and field and configuration problems have been used to understand problem solving. Yet, another important source of information on problem solving can be traced to factor analysis and its finding that problem solving is factorially complex—sufficient evidence exists for the problem-solving aspects in episodes to allow for a generic picture, from which is derived problem-solving models (Guilford, 1967). In addition, another problem-solving model has emerged from a biopsychological process approach to understand the universe, which is called transformation theory (Land, 1973).

One can view problem solving as a process by means of sequential steps, such as those proposed by Dewey (1910), Johnson (1955), Rossman (1931), Vargiu (1977), Wallas (1926), and others. Then, too, there are its adaptations to research methodology, where creative problem-solving procedures have found expression in the activities of the Creative Education Foundation (e.g., Osborn, 1963; Parnes, 1967a, 1967b) and those who have been directly influenced by the sequential-steps process (e.g., Covington et al., 1974; Feldhusen, Treffinger, & Bahlke, 1970) as well as those influenced by the related procedures of synectics (W. J. J. Gordon, 1961; Prince, 1968) or lateral thinking (de Bono, 1974, 1976)—nearly all these procedures call for the use of facilitative strategies that include attribute listing, questioning, brainstorming, and morphological analysis. The unique application of the principles of creative problem solving to sociodrama provides yet another approach, one that uses the metaphor of the stage in which participants serve the function of both audience and protagonist for resolution of conflict (Torrance, 1975a). Or, one can view problem solving as a process rooted to larger conceptual systems with particular reference to the structure of intellect problem-solving model (Guilford, 1967, 1977) and the biopsychological process and transformation theory problem-solving model (Land, 1973).

Problem Solving as Sequential Steps

John Dewey's problem-solving steps are (1) sensing a difficulty, (2) locating and defining it, (3) suggesting possible solutions, (4) considering consequences, and (5) accepting a solution. Others who followed him made minor modifications to these steps or elaborated on them; of particular interest are those steps suggested by Rossman, following his study of 700 inventors (1931). To Dewey's steps, he added the surveying of available information and the formulation of new ideas. The steps proposed by Wallas (1926) omit Dewey's first two and begin with preparation (information gathering) and incubation (unconscious workings of the mind), going on to two others, which are similar to Dewey's fourth and fifth steps but called by Wallas illumination (emergent solutions) and verification (the testing and elaborating of solutions). Wallas omits the final step of solution acceptance. Theorizing on the problem-solving aspects of creativity has led Vargiu (1977) to propose problem-solving steps similar to Wallas's, except that Vargiu added frustration as the step following preparation and changed verification to elaboration, which, in any case, is included as part of the process of solution testing. These four approaches are shown in Table 6, and, as we shall see, are taken into account by the structure of intellect and the biopsychological process and transformation models.

These problem-solving steps form the basic principles of creative problem-solving approaches, two of which we shall now discuss.

Osborn-Parnes Creative Problem-Solving Approach

The principles of creative problem solving are discussed in *Applied Imagination* (Osborn, 1963) in several different ways. The well-known procedure for group-think, better known as brainstorming, has four basic ground rules, which are said to lead to effective creative problem solving. Osborn advocates that criticism be ruled out, freewheeling be welcomed, quantity of ideas be desired, and combination and improvement of them be sought.

In describing the principles and techniques of deliberate idea finding, Osborn offers two significant approaches to creative problem solving used as a training procedure, namely, deferment of judgment and quantity breeds quality. To this he adds yet another significant contribution to the principles of brainstorming: the application of a three-step process in creative problem solving (1962, p. 20):

Table 6 Several Sequential-step Approaches to Creative Problem Solving

John Dewey	Joseph Rossman	Graham Wallas	James Vargiu
Difficulty felt	Need or difficulty observed		
Difficulty located and defined	Problem formulated		
	Available information surveyed	Preparation or information collected	Preparation
			Frustration
		Incubation or on-going unconscious activity	Incubation
Possible solutions suggested	Solutions formulated	Illumination or emergent solutions	Illumination or solutions avalanche
Consequences considered	Solutions critically examined	Verification or testing and elaborating solutions	Elaboration
Solution accepted	New ideas formulated		
	New ideas tested and accepted		

I. *Fact-finding*

Problem definition: picking out and pointing to the problem.

Preparation: gathering and analyzing the pertinent data.

II. *Idea-finding*

Idea-production: thinking up tentative ideas as possible leads

Idea-development: selecting from resultant ideas, adding others, and reprocessing by means of modification, combination, rearrangement, substitution, and so on.

III. *Solution-finding*

Evaluation: verifying the tentative solutions by tests and otherwise.

Adoption: deciding on and implementing the final solution.

In this way, Osborn incorporates the alternation between creative and evaluative thinking (elsewhere described as green-light and red-light activity) and the principle of deferment of judgment (Osborn, 1962).

Parnes and his associates applied and extended these principles in several publications (Parnes, 1967a, 1967); Parnes, Noller, & Biondi, 1977a, 1977b), in courses at the State University of New York College at Buffalo, and in the annual and regional Creative Problem Solving Institutes. His illustration (Figure 12) of the creative problem-solving process (Parnes, 1967a) indicates that a problem situation appears to the experiencer as unclear (a fuzzy mess) so that problem definition at this point cannot relate to the real problem at hand. As a result of careful exploration to uncover the facts contingent on the problem, or what S. J. Parnes calls problem finding, sufficient clarity may result and recognition of the real problem may occur. This, then, should lead to idea finding or brainstorming (often encouraged as a group process), which can be expected to produce many alternative solutions. To facilitate the generation of ideas, criticism must be deferred and freewheeling welcomed for wild or silly or impractical ideas may spark ideas in others that will lead to a breakthrough idea toward a practical solution. At this time, the production of many ideas is to be encouraged because this may lead to the production of quality ideas. This prepares the way for the improvement of ideas and a number of procedures that may be used to facilitate such improvement, including hitchhiking on the ideas of others, idea-spurring questions (e.g., Put to other uses? Adapt? Modify? Magnify? Minify? Substitute? Rearrange? Reverse? Combine?), free association, analogies, forcing relations, using various sense modalities, and so on. Once several solutions are identified, they may be subjected to evaluation—according to some agreed on relevant criteria (e.g., cost, time required, usefulness, social acceptance)—and followed by an acceptance of the most appropriate solution so that it may be used as a lead to a successful plan of action.

Other emphases that relate to the creative problem-solving process (Parnes et al., 1977a, 1977b) are:

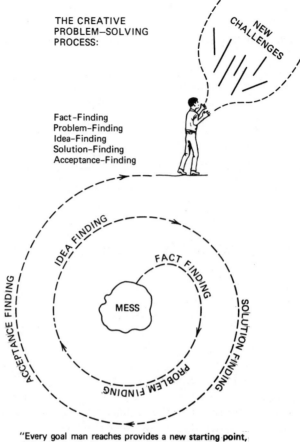

THE CREATIVE
PROBLEM—SOLVING
PROCESS:

Fact-Finding
Problem-Finding
Idea-Finding
Solution-Finding
Acceptance-Finding

NEW CHALLENGES

IDEA FINDING

ACCEPTANCE FINDING

FACT FINDING

MESS

SOLUTION FINDING

PROBLEM FINDING

"Every goal man reaches provides a new starting point,
and the sum of all man's days is just a beginning."
Lewis Mumford

*Figure 12   Typical flow of the creative problem-solving
process. (Parnes, 1967a. Copyright © 1967 by Charles
Scribner's Sons. Reprinted by permission of the publisher.)*

1. The dynamic/delicate balance between judgment and imagination; between
   the open awareness of the environment through all the senses and the deep
   self-searching into layer-upon-layer of data stored in the memory; between
   logic and the emotion; between the processes of making it happen and those
   of letting it happen; between the insights and the action.
2. The presence of sensitivity, synergy, and serendipity illuminates the creative
   process that requires divergent thinking: *sensitivity* implies great awareness

through all the senses; *synergy* occurs when two or more elements, on becoming associated, bring about an emergent element that transcends its parts; *serendipity* results from an awareness of relevancy in accidental happenings.

3. The practice in coping behavior that programs nurturing creativity give.
4. The productive consequences of stimulating the brain with such processes as deferred judgment and various idea-stimulating techniques.
5. The challenge of keeping creativity alive through creative calisthenics to prevent the atrophy of talents and to develop the creative muscles through exercise; the excitement of self-discovery through creative education that provides its own reason for being and its own self-stimulation so that a person's entire life can be built around the intense desire to learn.

Parnes in 1975 brought to our notice some fresh thoughts on his conception of creative problem solving. The variety and diversity of the Creative Problem-Solving Institute's experience, teaching, and research have led Parnes to reformulate some of his thoughts on the creative problem-solving process and procedures expressed by the activities of the Creative Education Foundation. Atlhough reaffirming the basic tenets of the Osborn-Parnes system, Parnes underscores the basic philosophy of the Creative Problem-Solving Institute as always "growing" and "becoming" (Land, 1973) rather than as "become." The Institute's eclectic program not only includes its five-step process of fact, problem, idea, solution, and acceptance finding but also has interlaced processes that come from synetics, sensitivity training, art, fantasy, meditation, body awareness, and so on, hence, subscribing to the concept of balanced growth. Parnes (1975) comments on the problem-solving process as follows:

> *Thus the problem solving process becomes one of opening up the self to the fullest possible awareness of the storehouse of energy and resources within oneself—in one's vast mental library of life experience—as well as in the vast data of the external world. Problem solving becomes the task of finding the greatest number of interconnections and interrelationships among these vast resources, including the layer upon layer of primary information stored in our brain cells from birth and even from embryonic states. One searches for the kinds of synergistic connections that one can make toward the solution of one's problems, one's goals, one's wishes, one's aspirations, one's hopes, one's dreams—for oneself, one's family, one's group, one's society, one's world, one's universe. (pp. 26–27)*

A shift in emphasis by Parnes and his associates on the use of the imagination and judgment in problem solving has taken place—from its sequential occurrence to its more generalized occurrence through all the creative problem steps. Thus, there is unleasing of the imagination, which is to be gradual while the judicial abilities are concurrently strengthened; stretching of the imagination to all creative problem-solving stages rather than restricting it to the idea-generation stage; and, in the problem-definition stage, there is to be more effort in the acquisition of a multiplicity of viewpoints of the problem. This is what Parnes and Biondi (1979) term the delicate balance. This brings to mind two pertinent questions: "How loose a person can stay before falling apart?" and "How tight can one remain before freezing up?" The authors, then, say that if judgment is no longer to overwhelm the imagination in decision making, we shall have to maintain the *deferjudiced* stance that will allow us to oscillate comfortably between *nojudice* and *prejudice, looseness* and *tightness,* with full awareness that nothing is final.

Synectics Approach to Creative Problem Solving

Another viable approach to creative problem solving is synectics, which has its origins in the works of W. J. J. Gordon (1961) and Prince (1968). In the main, they have operated as Synectics Incorporated, serving the needs of business and industry. Synectics is a term borrowed from the Greeks to mean the joining together of different and apparently irrelevant elements. W. J. J. Gordon (1961) tells us that synectics attempts to integrate individuals who come from different backgrounds (e.g., physics, mechanics, biology, geology, marketing, or chemistry) into a problem-stating-and-solving group and calls for the conscious use of the preconscious to increase the probability of success in problem-stating and problem-solving activity. Part of the time, a group (there are about six) attacks invention problems to find out their origins; part of the time, a group devotes itself to the implementation of concepts that have been developed as solutions (i.e., building working models, conducting experiments, investigating market potentials), an activity considered most important in a synectics project. The several functions of the group include keeping in touch with ongoing projects, learning how others overcome specific problems to understand more about the invention process, and teaching select candidates from client companies to use the synectics method.

The theory of synectics is based on the assumption that people can increase their creative efficiency if they understand the psychological processes that set it to work and that the emotional or irrational is more important than the intellectual or rational, the understanding of which can increase the probability of success in a problem-solving situation. The creative process is defined by synectics as the mental activity in problem stating and solving that results in artistic or technical inventions. Several psychological states considered for successful inventive effort include the ability to tolerate and use attitudes, information, and observation that do not appear to be relevant to the problem in hand. A companion state is the ability to play or to sustain a childlike willingness to suspend adult disbelief, this includes:

1. Play with words, meanings, and definitions (this involves transposing a specific invention problem into a general word or statement).

282

2. Play in pushing a fundamental law or a basic scientific concept out of phase.

3. Play with metaphor.

Two very important processes of synectics are (1) making the strange familiar and (2) making the familiar strange. The first relates to the need to understand the problem, whereas the second requires a new way of looking at the known world. Four mechanisms, each metaphorical in character, that are identified with making the familiar strange are, personal analogy, direct analogy, symbolic analogy, and fantasy analogy. These are essential to successful problem solving because through them we are consciously able to tap the preconscious.

Personal analogy results from the personal identification with elements of a
   problem, which releases the individual from viewing the problem in terms
   of its previously analyzed elements (e.g., Friedrick Kekulé von Stradonitz
   identifying himself with a snake swallowing its tail developed an insight
   into the benzene molecule in terms of a ring instead of a chain of carbon
   atoms).

Direct analogy is a mechanism that describes the comparison of parallel facts,
   knowledge, or technology, and it has been found that a biological perception of physical phenomena produces generative viewpoints (e.g., Alexan-
   der Graham Bell's perception of the human ear led to the invention of the
   telephone).

Symbolic analogy uses objective and impersonal images to describe the problem.
   It is a compressed description of the function or elements of the problem
   (qualitative rather than quantitative), and it is immediate and complete in a
   blurt out of association (e.g., selecting a key word that has some connection
   with the problem, empathize with it to produce a title representing the
   problem as in a book title).

Fantasy analogy involves wish fulfillment, where imaging can lead to all kinds
   of magical solutions that prepare the way for their translation into practical
   terms (e.g., the problem of inventing a vaporproof closure for spacesuits
   was solved by imaging a skinny demon as a wire pulling together imbedded
   springs in rubber, that is, stitching with steel).

Other details of these mechanisms and their correlates in figures of speech and imagery can be found in Chapter 4 (pp. 121–127).

Application of these principles in a synectics problem-solving session is dis-cussed by Prince (1968)—W. J. J. Gordon's colleague—as a series of steps that flow into one another in an excursion that leads to a point of view about a potential solution to a problem, which, if not satisfactory, yet prepares the way for other excursions through the same process. A modified version of Prince's (1968) flowchart with attending explanations is shown in Figure 13.

Some fresh insights from synectics research had led Prince (1975) to present a theory of thinking and problem solving called mindspring. It is a theory that is

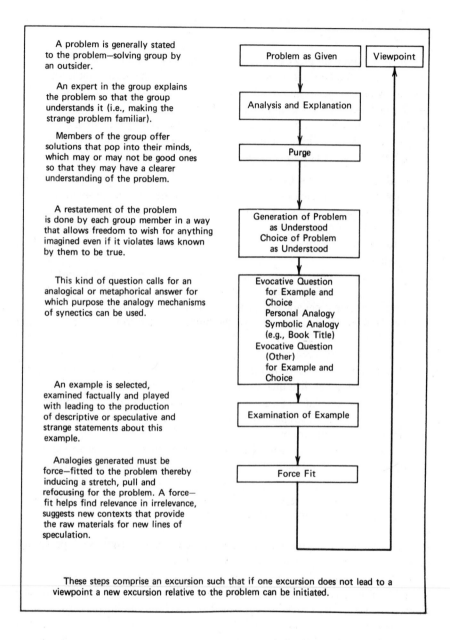

A problem is generally stated to the problem-solving group by an outsider.

An expert in the group explains the problem so that the group understands it (i.e., making the strange problem familiar).

Members of the group offer solutions that pop into their minds, which may or may not be good ones so that they may have a clearer understanding of the problem.

A restatement of the problem is done by each group member in a way that allows freedom to wish for anything imagined even if it violates laws known by them to be true.

This kind of question calls for an analogical or metaphorical answer for which purpose the analogy mechanisms of synectics can be used.

An example is selected, examined factually and played with leading to the production of descriptive or speculative and strange statements about this example.

Analogies generated must be force-fitted to the problem thereby inducing a stretch, pull and refocusing for the problem. A force-fit helps find relevance in irrelevance, suggests new contexts that provide the raw materials for new lines of speculation.

Problem as Given   Viewpoint

Analysis and Explanation

Purge

Generation of Problem as Understood Choice of Problem as Understood

Evocative Question for Example and Choice Personal Analogy Symbolic Analogy (e.g., Book Title) Evocative Question (Other) for Example and Choice

Examination of Example

Force Fit

These steps comprise an excursion such that if one excursion does not lead to a viewpoint a new excursion relative to the problem can be initiated.

Figure 13   Synectics problem-solving flowchart. (Prince 1968. Reprinted by permission from the "Journal of Creative Behavior," 1968. Volume 2. No. 1. published by the Creative Education Foundation, Buffalo, N.Y.)

not only cognitive but also emotive, drawing strength from playfulness, ambiguity, analogical relationships, imagination, and related variables. Overemphasis on precise, accurate thinking over the years has severely restricted and repressed approximate thinking essential to learning. Consequently, Prince suggests the need for balance between precision and approximation. A person should be able to oscillate between a tolerance for approximation and a wish for perfection as well as swing from the logical and rational to the nonlogical and irrational (much like the delicate balance of imagination and judgment expressed by Parnes & Biondi [1975]), what Prince calls thinking attitudes.

Mindspring theory comprises five elements with operations that are cyclic (i.e., wish, retrieve, compare, transform, and store), with imaging an important relative to each as shown in Figure 14.

1. Wish. Wishing is useful and is another form of exploratory thinking. Because it is not concerned with reality, it can open a person's eyes to new possibilities. Wishing gives temporary freedom from reality and can be a powerful benefit in problem solving when it can be used as a thinking tool. Many definitions of a problem can be formed by wishing. As every problem is loaded with implications and facets, a series of wishes that deal with them can enrich thinking and evoke fruitful images in preparation for unexpected retrieval opportunities.

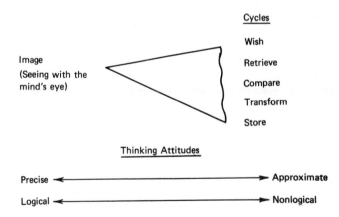

THE MINDSPRING THEORY

Image
(Seeing with the
mind's eye)

Cycles

Wish

Retrieve

Compare

Transform

Store

Thinking Attitudes

Precise ◄————————————► Approximate

Logical ◄————————————► Nonlogical

Figure 14   The Mindspring Theory. (Prince 1975. Reprinted by permission from the "Journal of Creative Behavior," 1975, Volume 9, No. 3, published by the Creative Education Foundation, Buffalo, N.Y.)

2. Retrieve. Retrieving brings to notice the astonishing inner resources possessed by individuals, the memory or experience bank with billions of bits of information that cover or are relevant to nearly every human activity or problem. The difficulties in gaining access to some of this data relate to the expectation that our retrieval services is poor, to our intolerance of approximations, and to the belief that we should steer clear of problems where we lack precise knowledge. Some strategies that can assist us over the retrieval problem are: idea getting, use of analogy and paradox, picture making, and cloud watching.

3. Compare. Comparing presupposes standards and the learned response of applying everything to them. Ideas are aborted if they do not appear perfect, and because wishing, imaging, and transforming are so repressed, their work is invisible to us. Actually, we are in command of the Muse to push ideas around at will. Comparing does not have to be a negative activity, rather, it can assume the stance of looking out for the positive or the pro qualities in an idea. An idea is not a simple monolithic proposition but a spectrum of implications, which, when sorted, range from the acceptable to the unacceptable.

4. Transform. Good transforming features an intense awareness of one's freedom to retrieve, image, and mutate *anything* in *any way* one wishes. An idea in its final form may bear no discernible relation to its initial retrieval and through successive approximations gain direction toward a solution.

5. Store. Storing involves taking possession of the new by connecting it to approximations we already have, for example, relating the new experience of the needles of a pine tree to the stored experience of hair to call forth a response from a child like, "That tree is hairy." This leads to the bold guessing habit (approximate retrieving) that will make better learners of us.

Lateral Thinking

Edward de Bono (1967, 1970) offers lateral thinking as another approach to thinking and problem solving. He observes that there are two fundamentally different sorts of thinking, vertical and lateral thinking. Vertical thinking is like digging the same hole, going deep and proceeding rigidly along the path of highest probability; lateral thinking proceeds imaginatively along a variety of low-probability paths in the hope of generating new and better approaches to the problem. There is the need in lateral thinking (1) to let go of the obvious and the danger of being trapped by it and (2) to avoid proceeding carefully from stage to stage to allow the emergence of a more imaginative step at some point.

The mind, de Bono (1970) says, does not behave in the ideal logical way—in the act of solving a problem, the very efficiency of logic may lead a person in the wrong direction, thus, he suggests that there is a need to shift attention from the problems themselves to the way the mind tackles them. In addition, de Bono emphasizes the importance of the approach to a problem rather than the efficiency with which that approach is followed up. He points out that the approach selected has much to do with habit, attitude of mind, or even emotion.

Repeatedly, de Bono (1975) emphasizes that thinking is a skill and, like any skill, it can be developed and improved. It accounts for his great insistence on the necessity for practice of creative thinking skills. Unlike the attempts of F. E. Williams (1972) or Meeker (1969) to incorporate the curriculum of school subjects in the teaching of thinking skills, de Bono is of the opinion that practice in thinking can be provided most effectively outside regular subject-matter courses and content specific to one or another area of human interaction or occupation.

In his training programs, de Bono (1974, 1976) provides practice to develop skills of elaboration. The problem solver lists the requirements for a product or solution in order of importance and uses the list as a guide to work out a solution. This procedure de Bono consideres important because an idea that does not fulfill the requirements of a situation can have little value. In his *Thinking Course for Juniors,* de Bono (1974) would have adults talk with a child about the child's creative problem solving, using the following sequential steps: praise, clarification, criticism, and amplication. The first two steps are expected to reinforce children to open up to themselves and the problem and prepare them to evaluate their work critically relative to the requirements set when first encountering the problem or during the clarification process. Moving on to the amplification step allows children further opportunity to open up to modifications, additions, elaborations, future plans, and so on. If we compare these steps with those offered in Table 6, we can see that de Bono's first step (praise) is unique because, unlike the other problem-solving steps, attention is given to the problem of getting started, a kind of warming up that is encouraged and receives positive acknowledgement at the start. This opening up of problem solvers increases their chances of resistance to premature closure and, thereby, allows for the creative process to work more effectively.

Other aspects of de Bono's (1970, 1971, 1975, 1976) training procedures relate to the use of such devices as chance, humor, models, synthesis, diversion, and fantasy to avoid the easy acceptance of alternatives immediately on occurence and to foster the careful consideration of both sides of issues as well as to search for new and unusual perspectives, which are central to lateral thinking. Attention is given by de Bono to the training of the problem solver in the use of different ways to conclude (bring about closure) and to differentiate whether a conclusion is tentative, changeable, or definite. De Bono also considers emotions as most important to lateral thinking. Emotions, he says, come before thinking; however, if thinking occurred first, then emotions would give it power. Because emotions may be either facilitative or inhibitory, it is important for problem solvers to know if emotions are affecting their thinking at the time of the problem-solving activity. Further, de Bono favors drawing as a medium for training children in problem-solving, and, almost exclusively, uses this as a method of instruction in his problem-solving course.

SOCIODRAMA AS AN APPROACH TO CREATIVE PROBLEM SOLVING

Another group approach to creative problem solving that is effective in attempts to solve not only present-day problems but also those that can be anticipated in the future is sociodrama. In Chapter 6 (pp. 205–208), sociodrama as it applied to career guidance (e.g., Torrance, 1975c, 1976b; Torrance & Myers, 1970) received some attention. Sociodrama places the principles of creative problem solving in a deliberately contrived, living, dramatic context, in that a group or social problem is examined with the assistance of various production techniques. In a sense, it combines the principles of creative problem solving and synectics—the metaphor is the stage and the play is the drama of life.

Sociodrama viewed as a creative problem-solving technique can be used to bring about a unity of opposites, and, in this respect, it echoes Moreno's (1946) theory of the unity of mankind which is reflected in his works on psychodrama and sociodrama. Citing the research findings of Barron (1969) and MacKinnon (1978), Torrance (1979b) tells us that highly creative individuals incorporate many sets of opposites in their personality so that, at one and the same time, they tend to be more masculine and more feminine; more independent in their thinking and, yet, more open to suggestions and information from others; more conforming and more nonconforming; more playful and more serious and more hardworking, and more humorous and graver than their less creative counterparts. Creativity that emerges from a collision of these opposites appears to highlight the essence of the problem, in whose resolution unity of these opposites is attained. One deliberate training procedure that can do this is sociodrama.

The basic conflict is brought to the surface when the problem is defined in a sociodramatic setting. This, then, leads to the decisions that have to be made for the selection of the roles that should best illustrate the conflict (e.g., Parent versus parent? Parent versus child? Child versus teacher? Patient versus physician? Employee versus employer?), with the experiences of the sociodrama group giving clues for these decisions. Group consensus on the selection of conflicting roles that should bring out the greatest number of aspects of the conflict is followed by the casting of characters and the establishing and enacting of the conflict situation. In this way, highlighting of each conflicting role is effected, even to the point of exaggeration at times, to increase the chances of obtaining a creative solution to the problem.

Torrance (1975c) tells us that it is not often that initial confrontation in a sociodrama results in a solution that will bring about a unity of opposites; it may be necessary to use some special production techniques to effect a resolution.

Such a resolution may occur through the soliloquy technique. For example, following a very heated confrontation between two protagonists of a sociodrama, each of the actors may be asked to soliloquize about their feelings and emotions regarding the confrontation. As the two actors verbalize their silent,

288   NURTURE OF THE GIFTED

unspoken feelings and thoughts, the unity of opposites may occur and a solution may be instantaneous. After the actors have verbalized their feelings, they may also be asked to brainstorm alternative solutions to the conflict and this may also result in a solution that represents a unity of the opposites and is more satisfactory to both protagonists than either of the initial solutions that engendered the conflict. (Torrance, 1979b, p. 56)

The usefulness of double and multiple double production techniques that are effective in bringing about a unity of opposites, promoting interdisciplinary thinking, and bringing a variety of viewpoints to the problem is emphasized:

Double Technique: *In this production technique, one of the actors in a conflict situation is supplied with a double who is placed side by side with the actor and interacts with the actor as "himself." The double tries to develop an identity with the actor in conflict. By bringing out the actor's "other self," the double helps the actor achieve a new and higher level of creative functioning. The Actor-Double situation is usually set up following the use of a Direct Presentation after the actor has withdrawn from the conflict. He imagines himself alone in the woods, walking along the street or in a park, or sitting at home. This production technique may also be used following the Soliloquy technique to speed up or facilitate the production of alternative solutions.*

Multiple Double Technique: *This is a variation of the "standard" double technique and is especially useful for bringing different points of view to bear on a conflict situation and provides a good vehicle for group brainstorming. The actor in the conflict situation is on stage with two or more doubles of himself. Each portrays another part of the actor (different moods, different psychological perspectives, etc.). (Torrance, 1975c, pp. 189–190).*

One production technique that Torrance used successfully with young and disadvantaged children is the magic net game. Pieces of nylon net in various colors (36 × 72 inches) serve as the magic net. Torrance and Myers describe the magic net game as follows:

In the "Magic Net" game, about ten children were given pieces of net and invited to choose whatever role they desired. They were then asked to "feel" themselves into these roles in various ways. Next, the entire group would be invited to make up a story, using the roles chosen by the actors wearing the "Magic Net." The story is enacted as it is told by the audience. Usually, one story teller begins a story and others continue it. In some cases, it has been found helpful to give the story teller a "Magic Net" to overcome his self-consciousness and to identify him clearly. (1970, p. 89).

The authors point out that an interesting feature among younger and older disadvantaged children is the tendency to choose similar roles chosen by their peers, indicating a strong need of support by peers for coexperiencing roles. Where a child would dare to choose a unique role, reinforcement by way of other children taking a similar role sometimes was observed to be necessary. For instance, Pamela, a 6-year-old, extremely timid girl chose to be a bear in a princess story. But she did not act the role, despite the magic of the net and the director's encouragement, until three agressive boys were selected by the director to play supporting bear roles. Then, she became a bear with zest.

A graduate student who was working with Pamela commented as follows concerning her behavior on that day:

"Pamela had been so quiet and had not been a part of the creative drama, dance, song, or play until today. Then she was given a magic net and decided to be a bear. She was too timid and withdrawn to be a good bear even with encouragement. Dr. Torrance, realizing this, reinforced her with some more bear children. She became an excellent bear. She overcame some of her shyness and began to interact with the group, not just in play acting. Her success seemed to change her whole self-image. Pamela in her quiet voice entered into the group problem-finding game and gave some very intelligent problems. She was anxious to participate and contribute to the group ... I saw a sense of achievement in her approach.

Earlier I could not get her to concentrate and study the picture when she did the Picture Interpretation Test. *She would answer questions without studying the picture. But, today, she would look at pictures and study them. She was able to make up an entire story of "Smokey Bear" from the pictures. I was amazed that she knew so much.*

Her self-image is very poor, maybe because of her sense of failure in the first grade. But the one feeling of success at being a bear and Dr. Torrance's congratulations changed her self-opinion. She found today that she is far more intelligent than I had dreamed. She lacks confidence and being unsure and inhibited can be taken for signs of a low I.Q. But when the inhibition is broken, you can see that she is not dull but too afraid to exert and show her abilities." (Torrance & Myers, 1970, pp. 89–90).

For a detailed account of other production techniques the reader is encouraged to refer to Torrance, 1975b; Torrance 1976b; and Torrance and Myers, 1970.

Sociodrama can not only be used as a procedure for creatively solving present problems but also as an approach to project oneself into the future and, by assuming a variety of roles in numerous situations, perceive relevant problems arise and, then, brainstorm ways of dealing with them. Futurists have developed disciplined ways for studying the future (e.g., Hencley & Yates, 1974) so that anticipation of probable events will minimize surprise and choices now made may influence the shaping of the future. In keeping with this thinking, Torrance (1975c, 1979b) advocates (among other techniques) the use of the audience techniques of sociodrama to give glimpses of infinity and to help people attain a future orientation to a given problem. He suggests using the future projection technique, a production technique requires actors to show how they expect a conflict will shape up in the future. Intense warm-up and communication of known particulars of the situation are regarded as essential, and, generally, involves dyadic brainstorming between director and protagonist. Sometimes the audience may also participate in constructing the future situation, drawing from the acquired information about the future. This production technique may tap various states of consciousness to include daydreaming, expanded awareness, internal scanning, and stored memories (Torrance, 1975c). In *The Search for Satori and Creativity,* Torrance (1979b) presents an interesting practice exercise that calls for the writing of one's own future scenario:

> *Try writing your own future scenario. . . . You had probably thought a great deal about what you want to accomplish in life and you perhaps have some new ideas now. You have doubtless thought about what you want to accomplish through your occupation. You have thought about the kinds of knowledge you want to acquire and what you want to achieve in regard to your family, your community, and society.*
>
> *Imagine that it is now 25 years hence. Write a scenario of a day or a week in your life as it might occur 25 years from now. A scenario is simply a description of a sequence of events that might possibly happen in the future. A scenario is usually developed by studying the facts of a situation and selecting a development or set of developments that might occur, and imagine what might follow. Use predictions about the future, and try to describe a specific day or week in your future career.*
>
> *In writing your scenario, use primarily the present and past tenses. In other words, imagine that your future is here—now! Your scenario should reflect what you have achieved, the kind of life you are living, and what is happening in the world. It should reflect the changes that have occurred in yourself and in the world. It should also communicate your hopes and aspirations. (pp. 203–204)*

CREATIVE IMAGINATION IMAGERY

The nature of creative imagination imagery and the procedure for stimulating its occurrence toward productivity as it relates to creative thinking strategies (breaking away from the usual and commonplace, restructuring, synthesis, analogy), incubation, autonomy of imagery, and sense modalities and imagery were dealt with in Chapter 4. Read this chapter on creative imagination and note that it provides yet another viable process approach to encourage creative mental functioning as a precursor to invention and discovery. Teaching the gifted to use creative imagination imagery as a training tool for learning in the various areas of knowledge is to prepare for the deliberate use of near inaccessible mental resources in the service of both verbal and nonverbal creativity.

One powerful facilitator of such creative functioning is *Thinking Creatively with Sounds and Words: Norms-Technical Manual* (Khatena & Torrance, 1973), an instrument of verbal originality and imagery, whose *Sounds and Images* (Cunnington & Torrance, 1965) component was once used to stimulate imaginative story and verse writing as take-off activities from responses to the test. This procedure is being revived and is expected to extend to the *Onomatopoeia and Images* (Khatena, 1969b) component as well. The nature of these tests, in the context of right- and left-brain activity, invite some interesting speculation about processing of input auditory-visual-verbal stimuli for output as verbal images. *Sounds and Images* presents auditory stimuli alone, whereas *Onomatopoeia and Images* presents stimuli that are at once auditory, visual, and verbal (see Chapter 3 for more specific information on the tests). The listener receives information with instructions to be imaginative and produce original verbal images. When, for example, *Onomatopoeia and Images* is administered both right- and left-brain activity is induced because of the multidimensional stimuli. As input data, the auditory-visual components of onomatopoeic words stimulate the production of right-brain images while their verbal aspects set in motion decoding processes of the left brain to act with right-brain productivity almost simultaneously. Image activity, the province of the right brain, follows. It includes the use of the imagination in the destructuring, reintegration, and transformation processes, which leads to the emergence of new imagery for transference to the left brain for encoding in language that is ready to be recorded in verbal written form on the response sheet. Because it requires the symbiotic relationship of both halves of the brain in creative endeavor, such activity is of great value. It calls for the exercise of verbal and image functions that are rooted in the springs of creativity. The instrument that is able to involve this activity is a powerful tool that can be directed for use with gifted students to make them verbally and nonverbally creative. Experiences for the gifted can be planned in directed imagery, incubation, image autonomy, and the like, not only for exercising creative imagination and image processing but also for preparing imagery activity as an integral part of learning in the areas of language and literary composition as well as in the areas of visual and performing arts, which include drama, music, dance, and art (see pp. 120–140).

The fourth-grade drop in the development of creative-thinking abilities and visual imagery received some attention in Chapter 5 (pp. 147–148). Techniques that attempt to alleviate this problem have been the concern of many investigations, for example, in the writings of Torrance, 1965c, 1972a. The main reasons emphasized to account for this drop are, by and large, the effects of socialization and acculturalization and their educational implications. Gowan (1979d, 1980) in his discussion of this drop in creativity at the fourth-grade level calls our attention to the extinction of right-hemisphere imagery that results from overteaching the left-hemisphere functions of reading, writing, and arithmetic and the lack of stimulation of right-hemisphere functions that is caused by the lessening or the absence of music and art in the curriculum with a related lack in the use of right-hemisphere stimulation procedures. Elicitation of right-hemisphere imagery, he suggests may be accomplished either indirectly by stilling the overiding left-hemisphere functions (receiving incoming perceptor information and internal discourse) or directly by stimulating the right hemisphere while the left is operant. In qualitatively better elementary science teaching, where care is given to manipulation and discovery in the laboratory, Gowan sees a way of preserving the functions of the right-hemisphere with its incubative imagery that leads to creative production. Thus, not only is a change from Piagetian formal operations to creativity accelerated but also a more complete formal operations stage in which both sides of the brain engate in symbiotic operations, rather than the left side alone, is achieved. Further, Gowan points to the fact that gifted students, unlike average students, need to be taught not for consumer science knowledge but for creative scientific production in preparation for creativity in later life. That cognitive stimulation of the right brain and education of imagery can be effected in science as well as in art and music if spatial empirical methods are adopted is a new discovery and must be used more fully. We have already cited Albert Einstein that, even in science, imagery and not logic produces creative discovery.

SYSTEMS AND CREATIVE PROBLEM SOLVING

A systems approach to creative problem solving offers a larger conceptual model of organized information on the subject. It takes into account many related variables, positioning them in sequential processes that, on the one hand, are both interrelated and interactive and, on the other hand, forward moving to a point where the completion of a problem-solving activity is looped to the inception of another. Two such approaches come to mind, the one arising from the structure of intellect (Guilford, 1967), the other from the study of biopsychological processes (Land, 1973). Both are designed to show the relationship of a person to his or her environment in the act of processing information to solve problems, with the one approach giving conceptual focus to biopsychological connectedness of the internal processing and problem-solving systems (transformation problem-solving model and the other to intellectual functioning (structure of intellect problem-solving model). In addition, both models are self-regulatory and dependent for their success on positive and negative feedback as well as (to use Land's term) feedforward (shared regulation) because newly generated data would feed the system continuously for adaptation and adjustment to an ever-changing environment.

Transformation Problem-Solving Model

The model proposed by Land (1973) has already been discussed (pp. 159–162). To this needs to be added Land's observation that the function of biological processes and system, as they occur within human thinking and problem-solving processes, is represented by the same steps that living organisms follow (see Figure 6 p. 160) (Land, 1973, p. 103):

I. Searching *for available knowledge and information.*
II. Analyzing, *breaking down, and* digesting *the data.*
III. *Manipulating the information through imagination into new* synthesis, *into a hypothesis or idea.*
IV. *Internally projecting the* use *of the idea.*
V. *Evaluating the solutions for their "fitness," that is, their potential effect and value and the probable* feedback *that will be received.*

The satisfactory completion of the internal processing of a problem finds transfer into the primary growth system and its tryout in the external world. Land suggests that the brains of humans may be, in fact, miniature evolutionary laboratories where, through experience, each one of us can observe the evolution, mutation, and selection processes as they proceed in our minds at any one time.

Structure of Intellect Problem-Solving Model

Guilford (1977) considers that the best place to see the components of the structure of intellect working together is in problem solving and creative thinking. A problem is encountered when it becomes necessary to go beyond the items of information that we have already structured, then, a need arises for new intellectual activity that goes beyond comprehension or understanding to include productive thinking. Guilford sees the necessity for a general problem-solving model that not only serves creative production but also takes into account the traditional models of problem solving, the structure of intellect categories, and related conditions. Thus, he presents the structure of intellect problem-solving model (Figure 15).

The model in Figure 15 is a communication system (also called an informational-processing model) showing events of a problem-solving episode that are spread out in time, from start to finish, with input from the environment (E) and input from the soma (S). The latter (S) is concerned with body parts and includes the feeling and motivational states of an individual. The arrows in the

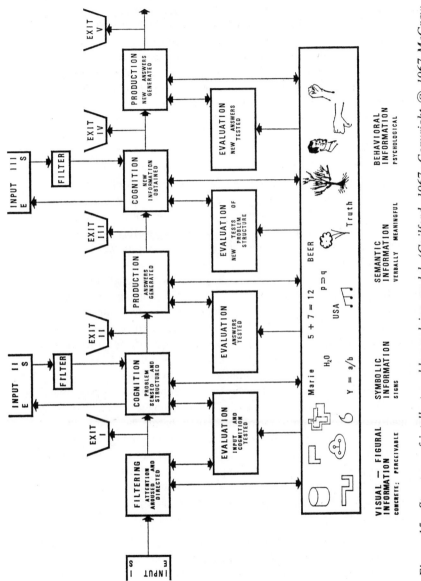

Figure 15 Structure of intellect problem-solving model. (Guilford, 1967. Copyright © 1967 McGraw-Hill. Reprinted by permission of McGraw-Hill Book Company.)

diagram show that information flows at times in a one-way and at other times in a two-way connection. All structure of intellect operations, with the exception of memory, are involved, as indicated in the rectangles of the problem-solving model. Memory storage and retrieval underlies and contributes everything that goes on. Examples of different kinds of structure of intellect contents organized as units, systems with some relations, and implications can be found in memory storage at the base of the model. Information transmitted from memory storage to cognition and production operations may at times pass through the filtering function of evaluation, but at other times it may be transmitted directly to the mental operations for processing, as in the case of suspended judgment. Evaluation is ongoing at every step of the problem-solving process. The other input sources (Input II and III) relate to an individual's active search for further information in the environment, shown by the upgoing arrows from cognition to input stations and with relevant filtering by evaluation to and from memory storage also indicated. The several exit stations indicate cessation of problem-solving activity (e.g., a complete ignoring or rejection of the problem [Exit I]; the recognition that the problem is not important, impossible to solve, or active postponent of problem solving for the time being, possibly with intention to renew the activity following incubation [Exit II]; or a satisfactory solution is reached [Exit III]).

An important feature of the model is the generous allowance for looping that involves feedback information (e.g., for each cognitive and memory phase there is the loop from cognition [production], which can be repeated many times). It is this looping that allows some flexibility with respect to order of events, for instance, the need for backtracking to earlier stages of the problem-solving process or even going back to the environment for additional fact finding when we discover our failure to solve a problem is due to wrong cognizance of the problem. This leads to a restructuring of the problem and a new round of problem-solving operations, thus, focusing attention on the fact that there may be more than two cycles of problem-solving activity before the goal is attained.

Creative activity in the structure of intellect problem-solving model is said to occur whenever divergent production takes place; it not only happens in the generation of possible solutions but also plays a part in structuring the problem. Besides, transformation is also a creative activity in the model and may occur not only as a function of divergent production but also in any of the operations that include convergent production.

In a certain organization, dissatisfaction developed with the financial information that was provided. The first thought was that the accounting system was in need of revision. But further investigation revealed that it was a personnel problem; a problem of lack of communication among certain key individuals. It was a behavioral problem rather than a semantic or symbolic one. This transformation came at the cognition stage in the SIPS [structure of intellect problem-solving] model.

More obviously, transformations play roles at the production stage. We are frequently faced with the need of finding an object that will serve some unusual purpose; a redefinition is required. For example, we need to start a fire and no match or cigarette lighter is at hand. The sun is shining, so it occurs to us to use a pocket magnifying glass as a condensing lens to focus the sun's rays to start a fire. A reading glass is transformed into a fire starter. (Guilford, 1977, pp. 164–165)

The production stations in the model (Figure 15) represent both divergent- and convergent-production operations because, in recalled information, some element of transfer is involved in both operations when differentiation of the use of divergent or convergent production must be specified in the required response, for instance, the many names that can be given when asked to name American writers of the first half of the 20th century (divergent production) versus the one name given when asked to name the American writer who wrote the story of a certain archbishop (convergent production).

Guilford reiterates that his model is generic and may not fit any particular episode of problem solving, therefore other special flow charts of models that are specific to the needs of certain types of problem solving may have to be developed. Further, he brings to our notice helping and hindering variables in creative thinking and problem solving. Paraphrased here, they include:

(a) *Environmental influences of family home and society.*
(b) *Motivation whose primary source is intrinsic and associated with achievement, competence, and cognitive congruence; and whose secondary source of satisfaction lies in the approval of others, the desire to be different and avoid the trite and banal, the preference for complexity; in addition, are those dimensions of interests in different kinds of thinking (e.g., reflective thinking, logical thinking, autistic versus realistic thinking, convergent thinking, divergent thinking, and tolerance for ambiguity).*
(c) *Informational-memory store that assists in the generation of ideas is not a sufficient but necessary condition for creative production.*
(d) *Flexibility (a ready shifting from class to class, transformations in divergent production activities, and redefinition or transformations in convergent production) versus rigidity or the blocking of these processes.*
(e) *Group thinking or brainstorming, mainly at the structure of intellect problem-solving step of production but also at other places.*
(f) *The ruling out of criticism during the idea-generation session to avoid reduction in creative output.*
(g) *Attitudes and emotions that tend to suppress the flow of ideas (e.g., sex roles*

taken too seriously, too much attention or pressure to norms; emotional states, like prejudice, fear, anxiety, envy, negativism, apathy, and complacence; respect for authority figures, attempts to please others to "get ahead", and lack of self-confidence). (Guilford, 1977, pp. 165–169)

To Guilford's list must be added those strategies and tactics designed to promote increased effectiveness in problem solving that include broadening the problem, breaking the problem into subproblems, asking questions, suspending judgment, extending effort to generate ideas, listing of attributes, forced relationships, brainstorming, morphological analysis, incubation, altered states of consciousness (e.g., visual thinking, relaxation, mediation), inducing transformations (e.g., adapt, modify, substitute, magnify, minify, rearrange, reverse, and combine), and criteria for evaluation.

MOTIVATION

Relatively little has been said about motivation as it pertains to the gifted beyond a discussion of achievement as it finds focus in academic underachievement and related factors, such as sex, socioeconomic and ethnic differences, school environment, and familial and societal influences and models (e.g., Alpert, 1965; Dehaan & Havinghurst, 1965; Gold, 1965; Raph, Goldberg, & Passow, 1966). Some attention has also been given to personality and perception variables (e.g., Fleigler, 1965; Gold, 1965) and to the ability to generalize quickly in the content of internal and external motivational events (Newland, 1976). In the main, motivation as it relates to the gifted is conceived as intrinsic so that external shaping and confirming influences internalized become essential components of the inner controls of behavior.

Generally, there still exist differences of opinion as to what motivation is (Littman, 1958). Part of the problem lies in the fact that motivation is a logical scientific construct with no immediate sensory referent (Underwood, 1949). The term seems to have derived its meaning from animal and human studies that would attribute the forces that impel organisms to activity to external or internal sources. At least two important appraisals of motivation see the need for reinterpretation (Hunt, 1960; White, 1959). They see weaknesses in a dominant theory that claims that all behavior is motivated toward reduction or elimination of stimulation or excitation of the nervous system. Sources of such excitation or drive may be traced to internal stimuli that arise either from homeostatic imbalances and needs or as a result of intense and painful external stimulation. The concept of homeostatic imbalances and needs is implicit in both the traumatic notion of anxiety in psychoanalysis and in the conditioned or learned drive in behavior theory, without which, in either case, activation of the organism is not expected to occur. Related to this is the notion of habit or the recurrences of certain behaviors and not others. This idea is derived from concepts of fixation or conditioning, both of which are governed by the principle of effect—where gratifying or frustrating experiences on the one hand and positive or negative reinforcement on the other hand fetch behavior repetition that is drive reducing. Although both homeostasis and conditioned drive and fear are sound in their basic assumptions, they contradict fact and call for reinterpretation.

Research indicates that primary drive theory does not explain exploratory behavior, manipulation, and general activity (White, 1959). White consideres that a more satisfactory explanation lies in the organisms' effective interaction with the environment, which in terms competence. Competence is significant to growth and life itself because it imples the acquisition of tremendous power to bring the environment into the service of the organism. The motivational aspect of competence White calls effectance, which he assumes to be neurogenic in origin, that is, its energies are simply those of the living cells that comprise the nervous system. In effectance motivation, the organism carries on a continuing transaction with the environment by which its relations to the environment are gradually changed and satisfaction (or better, a feeling of efficacy) is achieved in a trend of behavior rather than in a goal gained becuase no consummatory climax is involved. Effectance motivation is aroused by stimulus conditions that offer variety and novelty of response so that interest is sustained when the action affects the stimulus to produce difference-in-sameness and wanes when the action no longer presents new possibilities.

Hunt (1960), too, does not find primary drive theory adequate and prefers to conceive living things as open systems of energy exchange that exhibit activity intrinsically and upon which stimuli have a modulating rather than initiating effect. He notes that this view implies that not all activity is leveled at reducing or avoiding stimulation and, in fact, that, under conditions of low and unchanging stimulation for a time, increases of stimulation become reinforcing and certain types of stimulation although intense and exciting are positively reinforcing. In addition, he suggests that motivational correlates of fear and anxiety are not the province of conditioning alone but are also the result of maturation and cognitive dissonace (i.e., disturbances arising from the mismatch or incongruity between acquired central patterns of past experiences and present ones). Drawing from various systematic theories that incorporate, the incongruity dissonance principle in one form or another, Hunt notes its value in making motivation and reinforcement, instrinsic to the organism's relations with its environment. That is, intrinsic (as it were) to the organism's information-processing, in which a built-in feedback system indicates discrepancy between present receptor inputs and residues of past experiences or stored information as the basis for anticipating the future. In this way, motivation and reinforcement are not extrinsic to the information processing and, hence, need not be the responsibility of others (viz., teachers, parents, and those in authority).

Although both White and Hunt indicate that the dominant view of motivation does not say everything about the subject and although they suggest alternatives in their reinterpretation by way of competence or incongruity-dissonance, they do not deny the relevance of drive, habit, reinforcement, and the like. However, they have questioned their underlying assumptions, which appear to be couched in all-or-nothing terms. A theoretical position that must be of interest to us is based on the preportency of needs, that is, Maslow's (1970) well-known theory of human motivation. Maslow recognizes the fundamental priorities of needs so that the ones most basic to life and survival (physiological and safety needs) take precedence over intermediate needs (those that relate to living and doing things with others—loving and belonging needs, esteem needs) and higher needs (those that occur when the more basic ones have been satisfied—self-actualization, desire to know and understand, aesthetic needs). Of course, the attainment of higher needs does not preclude the recurrence of the more basic ones. For most "normal" people, needs are only partially satisfied, which is probably realistically described by Maslow (1970) as decreasing percentages of satisfaction as we go up the hierarchy of prepotency. Also, as implied by the model, the hierarchy of needs is not a fixed order and some reversal is not uncommon, for instance, the need for self-esteem seems more important to some than love or the need for self-actualization by creative people seems more important despite other need deficits. Another essential aspect of Maslow's (1968) theory is that it is a growth model so that when *deficiency* needs (the lower four in the hierarchy) are satisfied, a striving for the satisfaction of the *higher being* needs follows. This, Maslow observes, is characteristic of healthy children who *enjoy* growing and moving forward, gaining new skills, capacities and powers. Maslow also makes a distinction between *good choosers* and *bad choosers*. He points out that many people allowed freedom of choice appear consistently to make good choices but that most tend to make choices that are self-destructive. The good choices tend to be made by people who are given the opportunity when higher needs emerge. Maslow perceives growth as occurring in the context of a never-ending series of situations that provides free choice between the attractions and dangers of safety and growth. To facilitate this, he suggests that those concerned with children's growth can assist in the gratification of their basic needs so that they can feel unthreatened and autonomous and make the growth choice more attractive and delight producing. Figure 16 is a simple diagram that illustrates a choice situation:

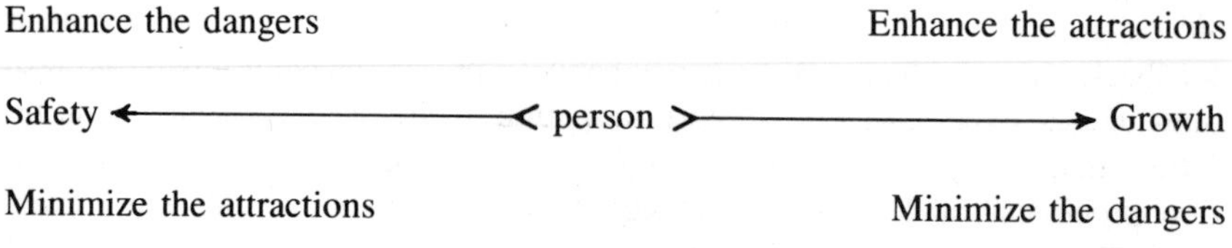

Enhance the dangers   Enhance the attractions

Safety ◄───────────────◄ person ►───────────────► Growth

Minimize the attractions   Minimize the dangers

Figure 16   Choices between safety and growth. (Maslow, 1968. Copyright © 1968 by Litton Publishing. Reprinted by permission of D. Van Nostrand Co.)

NURTURE OF THE GIFTED

These several theoretical positions have all people in mind. Hence, any discussion of their relevance for the gifted must be by way of extrapolation. Certain extrinsic factors can and do have positive and facilitative effects on gifted children, for instance, various forms of praise, recognition, and reward (which, in any case, are internalized) or the physical arrangements in the classroom and the more general learning situation. However, the major emphasis of these effects appears to lie with intrinsic factors that relate to cognitive-affective processes (including parents, peers, teachers, significant others, and schooling and reward systems) whose influences are internalized and to interaction with the internal environment (including abilities, informational-processing mechanisms, affective conditions, needs, and desires). Generally, the gifted depend more on internal than external control: they are autonomous, self-directed, and growth oriented; they possess superior mental abilities and talents that can be expected to aid them gain command of their environment; and they have extraordinary potential to move toward productivity and self-fulfillment. However, various interferences can obstruct this expected pattern and may call for some temporary external intervention and control as in the problems of underachievement in its larger sense (see pp. 211–253).

Motivational controls of special relevance to the gifted may be found in J. McV. Hunt's incongruity-dissonance principle, W. W. White's competence principle, and A. H. Maslow's need hierarchy. The incongruity-dissonance and competence principles operate, for instance, in both Land's (1973) transformation problem-solving model and Guilford's (1967, 1977) structure of intellect problem-solving model discussed earlier. Both these problem-solving systems are informational-processing models that in the problem-solving process engage in transactions with the external environment. As self-regulated systems, they provide feedback to the processing operations for the production of appropriate solutions to problems, which are, then, internalized as stored information to provide the basis for handling other problems. The more efficient or competent persons become in the handling of these operations and the greater the success they experience in arriving at solutions with attendant achievement satisfactions or feelings of efficacy, the more are they likely to want to repeat such activities. Inventors, for instance, have spoken of feelings of exhiliration, mastery, and superiority on successfully overcoming problems connected with a new invention and of the desire to seek new problems, overcome them, and discover solutions to reexperience similar feelings and satisfactions (Rossman, 1931). It appears that experiencing and participating in problem solving is in itself rewarding; that so many get involved in research, even without initial support or recognition, bears out this observation. Problem-solving activity is inherent in research methodology and has been often advocated for gifted students (Renzulli, 1979a; Torrance, 1965c).

Maslow's growth motivation model has also relevance for the gifted, especially as it relates to esteem needs, self-actualization, knowing and understanding, and aesthetic needs. Just as there is an intrinsic reward associated with problem solving that leads to a creative solution, product, or invention, so, too, then is self-satisfaction for individuals in the act of discovery, which boosts their self-esteem. To enhance this esteem of self, their products and solutions must be appreciated by others as well so that, in winning the acceptance and approbation of others, they not only achieve the others's esteem but also add to their own self-esteem. The importance of rewarding creative performance has been stressed by Torrance (1965c) and, in a somewhat related focus by Renzulli's (1979c) advice to arrange for outlets and exhibition of the gifted child's products. Esteem of self and esteem of others are very closely intertwined and, in fact, may be considered as two faces of the same factor. This being the case, esteem can be accepted as a strong energizing force that may determine the quality and direction of performance. Self-actualization, encompasses the notion of fulfillment of potential in its broader sense, but, in a narrower sense, it must include the successful accomplishment of atomistic expressions of potential, the cumulative effect of which must lead to self-realization. This view allows for an operational definition of self-actualization that can find implementation in the many success-ful outcomes of creative endeavor of the gifted, in their creations of various art forms, and in their scientific discoveries and inventions no matter how miniscule these may be. Knowing and understanding in both cognitive and affective dimen-sions are needs more apparent in the gifted than in others. These are pervasive to their intellectual and affective states and energize them to get to know the world around them rapidly as well as to make appropriate preparation for breaking new ground, stepping to the frontiers and beyond, and making new discoveries. Aesthetic needs are yet other forces that activate the gifted to be producers or consumers of the beautiful and true. These needs are essential to potential talent and its productive expression, especially in the literary, visual, and performing arts. Although arrangement of events and appropriate support can facilitate the realization of these needs (and they must be emphasized), the real needs come from within and must be recognized as the prime movers to the actualization of self.

The creative act has its own rewards, which, then, motivates the generation of other similar acts. Torrance (1965b) in his discussion on motivating gifted chil-dren with school-learning problems, advocates giving them a chance to use what they learn as tools in their thinking and problem solving, providing them with a chance to communicate what they learn, showing an interest in what they have learned rather than in their grades, giving them learning tasks of appropriate difficulty, according them a chance to use their best abilities, offering them the chance to learn in their own preferred ways, recognizing and acknowledging many different kinds of excellence, and providing genuine purpose and meaning to learning experiences. In later discussions of the subject (Torrance & Myers, 1970; Torrance, 1975b), it is shown that creative ways of teaching have built-in motivations for achievement. Some of the most essential characteristics of educa-

302

tional methods for facilitating creative ways of learning, are identified as incompleteness (or openness in motivating achievement; the production of something and, then the do of something with it; and having pupils ask questions. An even more powerful motivational force is a person's vision or image of himself or herself in the future—expectations of what persons will become relative to what they are in the present are considered powerful determinants of behavior (Torrance, 1979b; Torrance & Hall, 1980). Futurists, like Polak (1973), Singer (1974), and Toffler (1974), are strong advocates of such imaging by individuals. They believe that persons' images of themselves in the future can only lead them to strive for its actualization. There is much to be said for this, and educators must be alert to the task of preparing gifted students to use this significant motivational mechanism.

CONCLUSIONS

The subject of nurture has been, and will continue to be, the prime concern of formal education. In simplistic terms, although educators may want to know how gifted students are to be identified, they want to hurry on to the business of teaching them. What must be realized is (1) that identification and its measurement correlates are no longer regarded by many as ends in themselves but rather as the means to prescriptive education, where strengths and weaknesses in abilities provide the clues for designing instructional materials and procedures, and (2) that emphasis on teaching in the traditional sense has declined, to be replaced by the notion of arranging conditions that will take into account student abilities, interests, and intentions to facilitate learning toward productive development of potential that is unique to the individual. In other words, individualization of nurturing practices, a subject that will be further dealt with in Chapter 9, is fast becoming the key to superior educational opportunities for the gifted. We have seen it take shape in a fresh conceptualization of acceleration. This includes enrichment when a special aptitude for the language of mathematics is determined early and appropriate direction is provided for its fullest development; similar implications exist for special aptitudes for the language of words, which may go on to include the language of other symbolic and visual systems that enter into the fields of the sciences and arts. We have also seen this concept directed toward a tightening of enrichment that moves away from the decorative toward the functional, that conceives of enrichment as accelerative and productive, and that requires provisions to maximize individual growth potential. Individualizing learning experiences for ability development with special emphasis on divergent thinking and affect can be seen in the construction of program packages for that purpose—the arrangement of learning specific to need is a viable thrust in the right direction. There is also the important distinction that must be made between acceleration as cumulative and acceleration as transformative, the one (cumulative) provides the circumstance for optimum development within a certain area of learning, the other (transformative) allows acceleration to become the catalyst for growth (from a lower level of mental functioning to higher levels of mental functioning, which is expressed in the concept of escalation.

Much has been said about the value and development of creative thinking abilities, especially over these past 20 years, and various procedures have been designed—some concentrating on the mechanisms of the creative process, others finding application of these processes in curriculum materials. Almost any system of process education, if it is to be viable, will have elements of the productive, either by way of thinking operations or their application in problem-solving modes. These have particular relevance to the gifted. Not only should our concern be to assist the gifted to become independent planners of their own acquisition of knowledge and skills but also to assure they do so in ways that capture knowledge and skills for storage. Storage in forms that lend themselves to the generation of alternatives in acts of retrieval by their informational-processing systems so that the gifted become less prone to be regurgitators of the old rather than producers of the new. Various creative problem-solving approaches are available to prime the gifted for processing information toward increasing orders of creative functioning and productivity. More use of these approaches can be made by educators, and it is highly recommended to do so.

Although of high significance, motivation is the most nebulous aspect of learning. We have witnessed its power in shaping behavior and maintaining behavior at strength through manipulative arrangements when it is applied in terms of rewards and reinforcement. This has merit for certain kinds of learning and for people at certain intellectual levels, but it is not the answer to the question of how best to energize gifted people in particular to learn. We were reminded of the inadequacy of external manipulation as the prime and only mover in the learning context and the place of homeostatic imbalance, anxiety, and related drive-inducing states were questioned. The gifted, by nature of their potential, possess urging energies that characterize them as initiators of learning events. Motivation for them is generally intrinsic. It is when these energies are prevented their normal functions by various obstructing influences (e.g., family, peers, society, school, and the like) that gifted students become low achievers and the causes for concern. If these influences and controls can be internalized so that interaction with higher needs, abilities, informational-processing systems, and future imaging can occur, motivational controls can assume a power for the gifted that can impel them toward the highest levels of accomplishments and self-realization. Although much discussion about motivation research continues in the annual Nebraska symposia and the issues are far from settled, the several motivational controls discussed in this chapter have particular relevance for the gifted. They include competence-effectance, incongruity-dissonance, growth motivation related to esteem by self and others, self-actualization, knowing and understanding and aesthetic needs, creative ways of learning, and future imaging.

9

DIFFERENTIAL
EDUCATIONAL
MODELS

OVERVIEW

This chapter discusses several approaches at individualizing instruction for the student in general as well as some unique features of approaches that are specially conceived for the gifted student. Attention is also given to self-directed learning and mentoring and to the curriculum and the qualitative differences that distinguish the curriculum designed for gifted education. In addition, special programs and projects are looked at. Several representative special programs are selected for attention and comment is made as these relate to identification, instructional mode, learning environment, and the delivery system, which include the private school contribution as well as a variety of approaches reflected in the innovative projects that are in operation nationally. The chapter closes with a consideration of procedures for appropriately evaluating programs and projects.

CHAPTER OUTLINE

Introduction
Individualizing Education
   Individually Guided Education (IGE)
   Individualized Education Program (IEP)
   Individualized Education Program (IEP) Model for the Gifted and Talented
   The Structure of Intellect IEP Model
   Self-Directed Learning and Mentor Facilitation
   Curriculum
   Programs

INTRODUCTION

Nurturance of the gifted is a very complex phenomenon if potentiality is to be realized to its fullest. It involves so many contributory factors and interactive variables, including knowing and understanding (1) the gifted individually in terms of abilities, talents, needs, interests, motivations, developmental patterns, other areas of human functioning, and the like; (2) parents, teachers, the school, and the community, as well as the role each plays in preparing and implementing approaches for the cultivation of healthy behavior and growth; (3) educational processes and procedures, which create the conditions for due acceleration and escalation; (4) the effects of innovative educational arrangements by way of special programs, projects, and the methodologies for their effective implementation; and (5) the delicate balance that exists between curriculum content and process that calls for higher orders of mental functioning. Other relevant factors are those associated with the more formal support systems that deal with the preparation of teachers; legislation; funding; federal, state, and local plans to implement the law and spend the money allocated for the purpose in the most effective way; and the less formal support systems of local, state, or national parent and educator groups.

In particular, this chapter will concern itself with a discussion of recent thrusts at providing individualized educational programs, special projects and programs with their special approaches to nurture, and public and private school efforts. The supporting roles played by federal, state, and local agencies; parent and teacher groups; and teacher preparation programs will be dealt with in Chapter 10.

INDIVIDUALIZING EDUCATION

Thoughtful educators have repeatedly questioned traditional education for its ineffectiveness; emotional harmfulness; undemocratic nature; and unfairness, inflexibility and unresponsiveness to human needs (e.g., Conant, 1977; Glasser, 1966; Holt, J., 1964; Silberman, 1970); and for its unwillingness to meet the challenges of a changing world rapidly enough to produce educated people who are resiliant, adaptive, and forward looking enough to survive change and turn adverse conditions to advantage. The thrust has been too strongly in the direction of leveling instruction (which is confused with education) at a body of students rather than at the individual. The possibility for education to be personalized gave way (owing to such factors as small student populations, irregular school terms, poor pupil attendance, lack of commercial teaching materials, little communication among educators) to the emergence of the graded-school structure in the middle of the 19th century, which was one of the greatest inhibitors to individualizing instruction (Bahner, 1979). What followed in the wake of the graded school and its increased student body was a variety of graded curricular and standardized textbooks that helped to freeze the subject content for each grade. Reactions to the rigidity and stereotyping of schooling in favor of flexibility, which would allow greater attention to the needs of the individual student, included the Dalton, Winnetka, and Gary plans (Bahner, 1979; Ingas, 1979). None of these plans survived in the contest with traditional education (Ingas, 1979). To these plans must be added the less formalized approaches of playway and the project and center-of-interest-activity methods. Other similar reactions found expression in the teaching machine, programmed instruction, team teaching, and nongraded school approaches.

Attempts to respond to the call for schooling geared to the individual were expressed in a variety of approaches at grouping, ranging along the dimensions of time and homogeneity (Gowan & Demos, 1964), wherein segregation of individuals varied from temporary part-of-the-day work groups engaged in a certain specified task to more permanent arrangements that would keep the same individuals together for a whole year's education program. Grouping students of diverse mental abilities and achievement levels (especially as this related to basics, multiple interests, a variety of handicaps, and the like) was aimed at reducing heterogeneity among students on one or more variables to make individual differences and needs more discernable and achieve more effective instructional management. However, the evidence generated by various studies on the effectiveness of homogeneous grouping (grouping according to ability) has proved inconclusive (Gold, 1965; Gowan & Demos, 1964). What seemed to count was not so much grouping, but the rationale and accuracy of grouping purposed to differentiate content, method, and rate of learning (Eash, 1961; Ekstrom, 1961). Further, the observation made on the incompatibility of ability grouping and individualization by writers of the *National Society for the Study of Education (NSSE) 1962 Yearbook on Individualizing Instruction* compels us to look to other pertinent efforts at individualizing learning, among which are the procedures developed for Individually Guided Education (IGE), leveled at all children (Bahner, 1979), procedures developed for Individualized Education Programs (IEPs) leveled at the gifted (Meeker, 1979a; Renzulli & Smith, 1979b); and self-directed learning (Treffinger, 1975) with its facilitation by mentors (Gold, 1979; Runions, 1980).

INDIVIDUALLY GUIDED EDUCATION (IGE)

Bahner (1979), the chief designer of IGE, describes it as a comprehensive and systematic approach at managing the learning environment in a school or related setting. It is applicable to all types of curriculum from the basics to a humanistic approach. The IGE system emphasizes teacher behavior and the involvement of students and support persons (parents, school board members, and administrators). The IGE approach was developed in the 1960s by the joint efforts of the Institute for Development of Educational Activities (an affiliate of the Charles F. Kettering Foundation) under the leadership of John M. Bahner and by the Wisconsin Research and Development Center for Cognitive Learning led by Herbert J. Klausmeier. However, the alliance broke up and each organization went its own way to develop separate IGE programs. To follow Bahner's efforts, we find that the theory on which the IGE is based consists of two major dimensions: (1) learning and its logical relationship to the teaching act and (2) the role of the teacher and teaching.

Several theoretical concepts of learning applicable to all learners are built directly into IGE as follows (Bahner, 1979, pp. 66–70):

- Learning is increased when learners are clear about what is to be learned.
- Learning is increased when learners are involved in keeping to defined objectives and activities to achieve those objectives.
- Learning is increased when elements of the learning environment are matched to the learner's learning style and not to his or her age.
- Learning is increased when the learner is in a supportive environment with at least one instructor particularly concerned with enhancing the learner's self-concept and with sharing accountibility for the learner's learning program.
- Learning is increased when feedback regarding learning is almost immediate, is constructive, and involves the learner in the assessment analysis.
- Learning is increased when application accompanies or immediately follows initial knowledge and understanding; learning is further enhanced when the application is critiqued and a new cycle of planning, doing, and assessing further applications is commenced as soon as possible.

Teaching in IGE extends beyond the classroom to include (1) planning and evaluation that takes place before, during, and after the teaching act; (2) the relationships of all teachers in the building; and (3) the support and assistance the teacher receives from outside the school. In IGE the teacher has to deal with the change process in which (Bahner, 1979, pp. 70–74):

- The individual school is the strategic unit of educational change.
- Each school needs a process by which it can deal effectively with its own problems if it is to maintain continuous improvement.
- Basic changes in the effects of school (e.g., reading achievement, attitudes toward school) are lasting only when such changes include support of the administrative hierarchy and school board, when organizational structures are revised in response to the needs of the changes, when new modes of operation are assumed by the teachers involved, and when students modify their behavior appropriately.
- Most individual schools are not strong enough to overcome the inertia against change built into the school district and, therefore, require a supportive peer reference group.
- Teachers learn new roles best when the principles of learning discussed above are followed.

In application, this form of IGE has 35 outcomes that are identical for all levels of schooling, with differences occurring in the application and emphasis of outcomes from school to school. Based on the theoretical concepts listed above, IGE concerns itself with academic and nonacademic curricula, student evaluation, counseling, discipline, and the roles of administration, teachers, students, and parents.

INDIVIDUALIZED EDUCATION PROGRAM (IEP)

The IEP, as Treffinger (1979) has pointed out, represents a systematic approach to instruction of long standing. It is now receiving considerable attention because it is a condition of Public Law 94–142 relating to education of the handicapped. It has derived direction from earlier established thought on individualization and established procedures that are inherent, for instance, in the IGE program (Bahner, 1979), in Individually Prescribed Instruction (IPI) (Weisgerber, 1971a, 1971b), or in the texts on modular instruction (Russell, 1974). The rationale and procedures on which these individualized program packages are based are sound and are just as relevant for gifted students as they have been found to be for average and handicapped students. Some fundamental principles of the IEP as a useful tool for planning education for any student are proposed by Treffinger (1979, pp. 52–54):

(i) *There must be adequate time for thoughtful planning and training in instructional design so that the planning will not be busywork.*

(ii) *Effective planning requires accurate assessment data that will be relevant to the instructional decisions to be made.*

(iii) *An individualized program does not mean the student learns only in isolation.*

(iv) *An effective IEP may lead to the implementation of different learning outcomes for various students.*

(v) *An effective IEP provides for the utilization of many different instructional activities.*

(vi) *IEP development should involve a cooperative planning model utilizing input from many different sources.*

(vii) *There must be sufficient opportunity for effective implementing of many alternatives devised in the IEP.*

As these apply to gifted, talented, and creative students, Butterfield (1979) and Treffinger (1979) caution us to be sure that the IEP *truly* differentiates instruction *qualitatively* rather than quantitatively and by rate of learning alone. This observation was made earlier on the subjects of guidance and nurture and is equally significant in the design of IEPs for the gifted. To this we must add (1) that there is need to refine the focus of those individualized programs for gifted students that do not emphasize instruction, but rather stress learning according to the individual's bent and goals; (2) that there is need to move away from teacher-directed to student-directed learning whenever this is feasible; (3) that flexibility and change mechanisms are essential built-in devices for evolution to occur within what appears to be preset conditions of learning; and (4) that there must be no mistake that the program component in an IEP does not mean conditioning, but rather suggests some tentative directions for gifted students to follow. It is of some concern to this author that those who will engage in IEPs may mistake the fundamental precept of individualization of learning experiences for excessive structure and put the gifted in a straitjacket, as it were.

In his discussion on IEPs for the gifted, Treffinger (1979) indicates that the basic principle of planning an IEP is not detailed prescription of each activity, but rather *a flexible contract of services* to the student. This gives rise to specific recommendations for educators who plan to make IEPs effective tools in the management of instructional programs for gifted, talented, and creative students (pp. 54–58):

(i) *Attention should be given to the unique talents and characteristics of the student (emphasis on strengths and unique qualities are to be noted).*

(ii) *The IEP should also take into account student interests, motivation, and learning styles or preferences.*

DIFFERENTIAL EDUCATIONAL MODELS

(iii) *There must be attention in the general goals to each of the basic compo-nents of an effective instructional program for the gifted and talented (i.e., individualized basics, appropriate enrichment, effective acceleration, in-dependence and self-direction of learning, and issues of values and per-sonal development).*

(iv) *The IEP for gifted, talented, and creative students should be as much concerned with the unknown as with the known, and as much concerned with the future as with the past or present.*

(v) *The IEP should be concerned with methods for finding and solving prob-lems, making inquires, and doing research as well as with curriculum context.*

(vi) *Participation of the student is highly desirable in planning the IEP.*

(vii) *The IEP should provide a basis for effective coordination of learning resources at school, at home, and in the community (as this concerns* people *assistance,* places *where productive learning can occur,* processes *to be nurtured, and* products *that will result).*

(viii) *The IEP provides a foundation for effective coordination of regular educa-tional programming and special educational services.*

(ix) *The details of the IEP should be open to continuous monitoring and to revisions as appropriate (i.e., the IEP is to be a flexible document, with provision for careful monitoring of its contents and procedures, and the mechanism for revision and change).*

(x) *Record keeping should be explicit and objective, and should involve the student directly in the process.*

(xi) *The flexibility of the IEP for gifted, talented, and creative students does not remove the responsibility for systematic evaluation (i.e., evaluation should include explicit criteria to be specified in advance, and should incorporate documentation of student progress).*

At present, there are not many published accounts of IEPs specially developed for the gifted student; among the ones that have been designed on the basis of sound conceptual models (see p. 311–318) is that of Renzulli and Smith (1979b) and that of Meeker (1979a)—the IEP model for gifted and talented and the structure of intellect IEP model respectively.

INDIVIDUALIZED EDUCATION PROGRAM (IEP) MODEL FOR THE GIFTED AND TALENTED

As Renzulli and Smith (1979a) describe it, their IEP model has two major goals: (1) to provide teachers and administrators with a practical approach to indi-vidualization that includes both material and procedural steps for its implementa-tion and (2) to provide a valid rationale in support of such programming. This

IEP involves (1) three supporting models derived from research and theory of learning and instruction ([a] a characteristics model of gifted and talented students, [b] a learning process model that matches students to learning environments, and [c] an enrichment model that attempts to integrate regular curriculum experiences with those more appropriate to the gifted); (2) practical considerations (identification of strengths from various sources; buying time for recommended higher level experiences; cognitive-affective development; integration with the regular program; total faculty in-service training; and the development and organization of learning experiences that represent *true* differentiation; and (3) management (a system of organizing and implementing the theoretical and practical aspects of the model). These and the ways the several components interrelate are shown in Figure 17.

The assumptions underlying this model relate to the capability of the gifted to master the regular curriculum at a much faster rate and at higher levels of proficiency than their nongifted peers, the provision of special opportunities for the gifted to identify and pursue advanced-level areas of study of particular attraction to them through procedures described in the enrichment triad (see pp. 260–262), and the focus on individual strengths (both general and specific as these relate to higher levels of thinking, creativity, task commitments) with provision for their development in learning situations that are relatively unstructured.

The authors of the model call our attention to instruments that have been developed to identify and facilitate the enhancement of the strengths of the gifted, namely, the *Strength-A-Lyzer,* the *Interest-A-Lyzer,* the *Learning Style Inventory,* and the *Compactor.*

1. The *Strength-A-Lyzer* (Renzulli & Smith, 1978c) is used to record information about the gifted—their abilities derived from various test sources (intelligence, aptitude, and creativity); their interests and learning styles; teacher ratings and end-of-the-year grades in the various subject-matter areas. The end result should lead to recommended action to guide in the design of an individual program.

2. The *Interest-A-Lyzer* (Renzulli, 1977b) is used to find out students' individual present and potential interests so that educational experiences can be built around them. The four steps recommended for interpretation of student responses are (a) the sharing of responses in small-group discussions to discover each student's pattern of interest, (b) the grouping of students according to common interests that may lead to group or class projects, (c) the follow-up studies and discussions on the feasibility of activities to be carried out in terms of cost, time availability of resource persons and materials, and the like, thereby ensuring realistic parameters for the activity, and (d) problem focusing (probably the most important and complex of the four steps), an in-depth

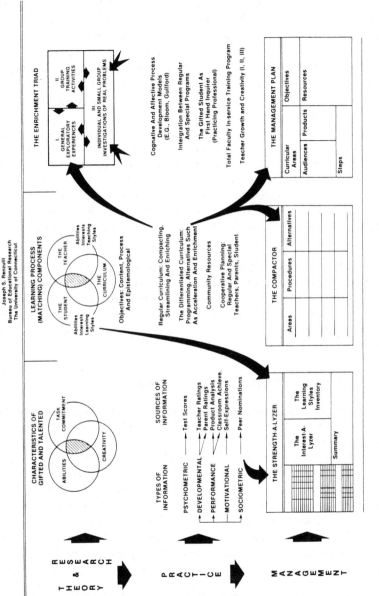

Figure 17 Individualized educational programming model—gifted/talented. (Renzulli & Smith, 1979b. Reprinted by permission of the publisher, N/S LTI on the Gifted and Talented, Los Angeles, Calif.)

treatment of which can be found in *The Enrichment Triad Model* (Renzulli, 1979a). The information thus obtained is recorded in the interest section of the *Strength-A-Lyzer*.

3. The *Learning Style Inventory* (Renzulli & Smith, 1978b) and its accompanying teacher version are used to find out both the strategies a student prefers when interacting with particular bodies of curricular materials (projects, drill and recitation, peer teaching, discussion, teaching games, independent study, programmed instruction, lecture, simulation) and the instructional strategies most frequently preferred by the teacher to facilitate a closer match between learning and teaching styles. Information thus derived is recorded in the appropriate section of the *Strength-A-Lyzer*.

4. The *Compactor* (Renzulli & Smith, 1978a) is a systematic plan for compacting and streamlining the regular curriculum so that (a) the competencies for later achievement are assured and the boredom of doing unchallenging work in the basic skills areas is relieved, and (b) the time saved can be used by students to pursue acceleration and enrichment activity. Information from the *Strength-A-Lyzer* gives direction to the compacting of certain curricular areas and to basic materials for acceleration and enrichment activities that are recorded respectively in the three columns shown in Figure 17.

The description of developing management plans for individual and small-group investigations attempts to provide the guidance necessary to implement the third component of Renzulli's enrichment triad, which requires inquiry and problem solving of real problems aimed ideally at adding to present knowledge or at creating a relatively new artistic product, including consideration of possible audiences and outlets.

THE STRUCTURE OF INTELLECT IEP MODEL

To Meeker (1979a) goes the credit for designing the structure of intellect IEP model whose major purpose is to tailor curriculum to fit an individual pattern of intellectual abilities based on a theory of individual intelligence. This model is closely linked to theory and has arisen directly from Meeker's earlier work on teaching to the structure of intellect abilities (see pp. 267–269). Meeker points out (1) that a knowledge of the structure of intellect model and training in its use and interpretation assists one to perceive students as individuals with multivaried intellectual aptitudes and faculties, (2) that this perception helps to identify individuals and group strengths and weaknesses precisely, and (3) that, consequently, a prescriptive structure of intellect program can be developed to strengthen areas of relative weaknesses and enhance areas of identified strengths. In this way, students in such special programs should experience a curriculum that is pertinent to both their abilities and to their basic educational needs.

314

For the implementation of this model, Meeker has developed the *Structure of Intellect Learning Abilities Test* (1979b), which comprises 24 of 120 predicted structure of intellect abilities so that cluster A diagnoses reading readiness, cluster B reading accomplishment, cluster C arithmetic readiness, and clusters D, E, and F creative potential in the figural, symbolic, and semantic areas respectively. The relationship between these structure of intellect factors and subject matter is presented in Figure 18.

An IEP using the structure of intellect model begins with an analysis of the raw scores of the 24 subtests, which can be hand or machine scored, to produce profiles of relative strengths and weaknesses. The test manual that describes the administration and scoring procedures uses two strategies for prescribing, the first is based on individual patterns of learning abilities with targets specifically keyed to individual abilities and the second is a more general grouping of

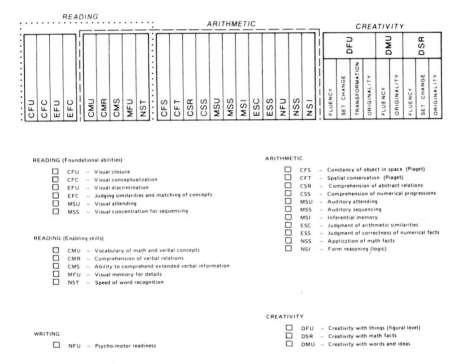

Figure 18 Relationship between structure of intellect factors and subject matter. (Meeker, 1979a. Reprinted by permission of the publisher, N/S LTI on the Gifted and Talented, Los Angeles, Calif.)

strengths and weaknesses. Once diagnosis takes place, prescriptions of an IEP for a gifted student follows and is based on the materials produced by Meeker, Sexton, and Richardson (1970), which were discussed on pages 267–269. A recent discussion (Hedbring & Rubenzer, 1979) on the subject of a structure of intellect based IEP is highly complimentary on the effectiveness of this approach. Meeker (1979b) also puts the assessments of the *Structure of Intellect Learning Abilities Test* in the broader context of total human functioning in the paradigm shown in Figure 19.

Meeker's interpretation of the paradigm relates the three areas with different kinds of giftedness, and her pertinent comments about each follow (1979b, pp. 15–16):

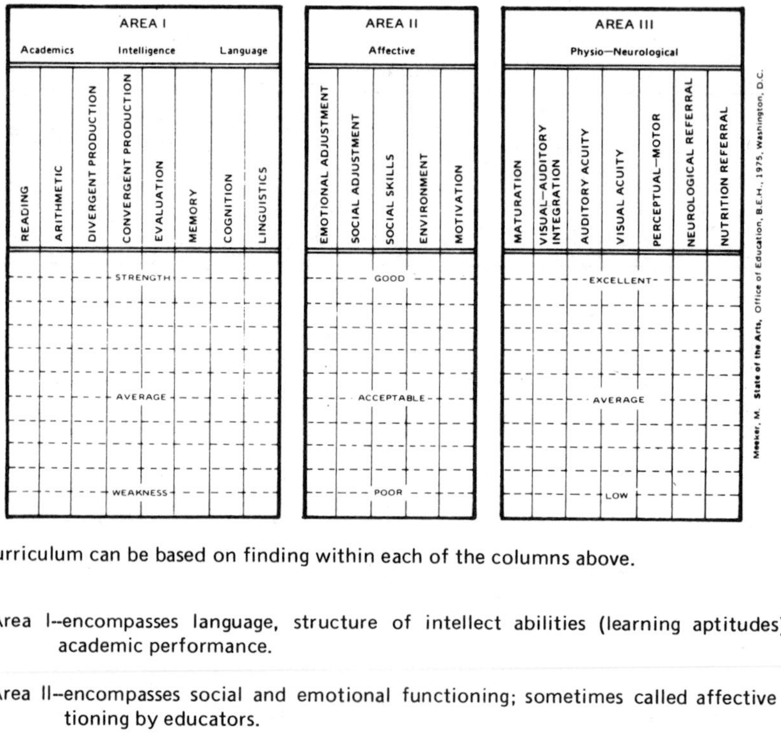

Curriculum can be based on finding within each of the columns above.

·Area I--encompasses language, structure of intellect abilities (learning aptitudes) and academic performance.

·Area II--encompasses social and emotional functioning; sometimes called affective functioning by educators.

·Area III--encompasses physiological and neurological functioning.

Figure 19   Paradigm of structure of intellect-learning abilities test assessments. (Meeker, 1979b. Copyright © 1979 Mary Meeker, SOI Institute, Richmond, El Segunda, Calif. Reprinted by permission of Mary Meeker.)

The academically gifted are, of course, performing at a gifted level in Area I. Typically they are excellent convergent producers with gifted memory abilities that bring them to the attention of their teachers. Individual Educational Plans (IEPs) can be made for all students in each one of the Area I columns using the SOI Sourcebooks, Task Cards, *and standard curriculum.*

We tend to equate giftedness with academic giftedness but there are gifts and talents in the other two areas as well. Area II giftedness can be assessed as well as Area I. An Area II giftedness is usually reflected in school leadership, social leadership, and interpersonal relations. Many Area I gifted need support and guidance in Area II.

In some ways Area III is the most neglected and yet any serious problem here will affect performance in Areas I and II. The best kind of education we can provide today would begin with excellent diagnosis in Area III. The earlier the diagnosis here, the better the chances for avoiding special education placement and long-term failure in average classrooms for students who enter school with Area III deficiencies. Many Area I potentially gifted are severely hampered by Area III problems which often go undetected. Area III giftedness is best described as talent and is shown in athletic, musical dancing, artistic, and skill-craft talent. In other words, the Area III talents depend upon motor functioning which is at gifted level—how the artist sees, how the musician hears, how the athelete coordinates body with eyes and ears. For example, the talented vocalist shows Area III giftedness; if the vocalist also creates the music, then that is a demonstration of Area I Divergent Symbolic giftedness, Semantic Divergent Production; the actor is gifted in Convergent Production and Memory in Area I, as well as in Area III where body movements communicate to the audience exactly what is expected to be interpreted from the action. The quarterback on a football team has Area III giftedness, but his decisions and changes in plays on the spot demonstrate Area I (Figural and Evaluation) giftedness. Area II giftedness is the motor skill underlying the Cognition overlay. In other words, giftedness, talents, leadership are human functions which are extremely outstanding performances in any one or more of the three areas. At the same time, any gifted person can be non-gifted in any of the other column functions in the paradigm.

Our search for giftedness will be more humane with the understanding that giftedness is certainly differential and may, for any individual, be confined to one area of special aptitude—that the identification of giftedness in one area should not carry with it the expectation that the person will be gifted in all areas. This is especially meaningful for the gifted whose greatest needs are in Area II, the social-emotional area. Since the gifted have a tendency toward acute sensitivity, feelings of being different, and loneliness (except for the Area II gifted), their motivation is easily diminished or extinguished when they are locked into an environment at home or school and that environment is neither supportive nor accepting. Equally damaging to the gifted are parents and teachers whose expectations approach perfection during childhood. And just as damaging is the forced competitiveness for "A's" in all subjects. Occasionally this perfectionism does stem from the student, and in these cases, support and teaching tolerance for failure becomes most important. Many of our potential gifted students fail to perform in Area I when their Area II needs are not met.

The paradigm reminds us that human functioning is multifaceted and while we may emphasize one aspect or another in nurturing development, we should not lose sight of the total human profile. The diagnosis of SOI abilities as they relate to the learning of school subject matter should be made on every student entering school. We talk about basic education—we forget that basic intelligence training is just as fundamental a part of education as is basic skills training.

SELF-DIRECTED LEARNING AND MENTOR FACILITATION

Another important methodological dimension of individualizing education is self-directed learning and its close relative, the mentor. The discussion up to this point has indicated that the emphasis in individualizing education for the gifted and talented has not been placed so much on learner control but on educator control of learning. This is not to say that IGEs, IEPs, and related arrangements do not take into account abilities, interests, styles of learning, and even, to some extent, active participation of the individual student in the planning of the programs. From all accounts, we must note that the major construct of individualized educational arrangements levels itself at providing for the individual student, even to the extent of encouraging independence in the choice of learning alternatives. Yet, what emerges from the methodology of the IGE and IEP is both educator dominance and design of student learning. The extent to which the student gains control of learning according to felt needs, motivations, interests, and aspirations—where the full compass of his or her abilities and talents can operate and be energized by personal commitment—is the extent to which individualized education becomes self-directional.

Those of us who are convinced that self-directed learning is the most suitable educational approach for gifted students also realize that we are confronted with the very practical problem of dealing with students who have been consistently programmed by general public schooling to develop responsive rather than initiatory learning habits. Placed in a gifted program where self-directed learning is an all-at-once requirement can be threatening and, even, anxiety producing. Students who during nearly all their educational life have had their learning mapped out for them are unlikely to know how to cope with a sudden change that puts them in total charge. Treffinger (1975) is correct in perceiving the need for gradual, even step-wise, transfer of such powers. His proposed plan of self-directed learning is worthy of some serious thought. It brings to our attention that self-directed learning is organized; is supportively structured (according to students' abilities, interests, needs, etc.); is individualistic, yet cognizant of social outcomes; is unselfish in addressing itself to learning goals and objectives; is involved with a variety of cognitive and affective processes and outcomes; necessitates good evaluation procedures that take into account evidence that goes beyond passing judgments on student efforts to include every conceivable evidence of the learner's progress or success; and involves the acquisition of skills through planned instructional experiences and the student's active participation in every phase of the learning process. The model of self-directed learning proposed by Treffinger (1975) involves (1) goal and objective setting, (2) assessing entry behavior, (3) planning and implementing instruction, and (4) assessment of performance.

Self-directed learning is important for inclusion in almost any educational experience or program for gifted students. It requires careful thought on the part of the planner and should iinlude adequate preparation for effective implementation—the background of the learner and the total learning situation must be carefully considered, the planning relationship of the educator and learner must be interactive and ongoing, and, possibly, one major outcome may be a brief written plan of action or proposal that specifies the problem, expected outcomes, and the methodology needed for the planned learning experience. Some flexibility and open endedness is desirable and should be included in the planning so that certain kinds of changes become allowable in the course of the learning without destroying its original integrity.

This brings us to another significant consideration that can be expected to attend effectively on self-directed learning, namely, the expert counselor, guide, or mentor—someone with high level expertise and competence in at least one area of knowledge, for instance, in science (e.g., astronomy, particle physics), mathematics (e.g., exponential functions, statistics, computer language), communication (e.g., eastern or western languages, comparative philology), aesthetics (e.g., music, art, drama), social and behavioral science, and the like.

The definition of such a function found meaning in Mentor, the faithful friend of Ulysses. Ulysses entrusted Mentor with the education of his son, Telemachus, during his absence in the Trojan Wars (Websters, 1962). Boston (1976) offers some fine insights about the mentor who combines the role of counselor, advisor, and companion. His analysis of the relationship between the mentor and student includes (1) mentor expectations of students (involvement in a total learning experience that gives equal place to doing and thinking, willingness to explore and experiment, feedback provision for more effective learning experience, demonstration of the acquisition of new skills, and growth orientation); (2)

mentor responsibilities to students (aware of being a personal and cultural role model, aware of teachable moments, ability to organize and give direction according to student needs, teaching by indirection, giving realistic appraisal of progress and dealing with conflicts, and creatively guiding the student through creative problem-solving steps); and (3) conditions for effective mentoring (arranging for the program to be experientially based, matching with care the student and mentor, making learning more open ended, and ensuring that both learning and its evaluation are competency based).

Lack of attention to mentorship in gifted education has been observed by several educators (e.g., Boston, 1976; Gold, 1979), and its infrequent use in education is attributed, in the main, to the inconvenience of implementing it administratively (Gallagher, 1975). However, among the several attempts to initiate mentor programs, the 10-year old Executive High School Internship Program (Hirsch, 1976) is considered by Gold (1979) as the major organized mentor effort to be found in the United States. He briefly describes it:

> The program aids local school systems in developing plans in which high-school students are given released time from their formal studies and are put in contact with volunteer community learders in business, industry, and the professions. Although this plan is not for the exclusive use of gifted or talented children, its value to them is of some magnitude. The period of released time is usually a semester, but may vary according to local conditions. In one school system a student might be released for a day per week during the second semester might be released for a day per week during the second semester of the senior year, while a student in another system might be released for an entire six-week period or longer, and still another system might opt for two afternoons per week for the entire year. (pp. 275–276)

Another such program is the Mentor Academy Program, which Runions (1980) describes as an alternative high school enrichment credit program for high-achievement students motivated to explore and expand their interests with mutually interested members of local shools, universities, professional agencies, and community services. Runions suggests that the Mentor Academy Program is different from other mentor-type programs:

> [It] totally integrates the mentor-training process by encouraging personal development of academic, career, and avocational knowledge and skills, while developing leadership/services skills through mentoring a high-achievement elementary school student, and the initiation of a life-learning process by the student that is self-supporting, self-directed, and self-transcending. (p. 156)

The Mentor Academy Program does not confine its attention to arranging for the matching of the self-directed learner with a suitable mentor. In fact, it is a formalized system of mentoring that consists of three interactive phases:

The first phase, the Basics Workshops, is a series of workshops designed to facilitate learning basic thinking skills, creative problem-solving skills, self-directed learning skills, academic research skills, aesthetics, leadership/service skills, mentorship contract skills, futuristics, and entrepreneur skills. During this month-long focus, the student also contacts academic, career, and avocational mentors to negotiate mutually agreeable conditions for sharing interests, identifies and begins to mentor an elementary school student, and designs a mentorship contract for an area of study.

The second phase, the Synergistic Seminars, is a practicum lasting approximately three months. Weekly seminars are held which are open to the whole school, and serve to introduce the students to a holistic approach in an area of study, update information about an area of study, and explore new developments in learning. The student also applies skills from the Basic Workshops in managing and monitoring a mentorship contract, and meets with a program facilitator in a regular basis.

The third and final phase, The Mentor Exchange, lasts approximately one month and is the time when students and mentors come together to share their learnings from the mentorship with interested members of the local communities and schools, organized and directed by the student mentor.

Over the five-month period, the student mentor integrates learning with six different mentors—a professor at the local university or community college, a career person, a senior citizen, an elementary school teacher, a high school teacher in the area of study, and the program facilitator who assists and supports the student in individualizing the program, linking up self-support systems, and anticipating post-program development. (Runions, 1980, p. 156)

Mentoring appears to be highly suited to the gifted student in the act of self-directed learning. By definition it provides for the individual needs of the self-directed learner; it shifts emphasis of teaching to guidance, which is more inclined to be nondirective; it sets the stage for a one-to-one relationship of two people with common interests and goals, generally over a reasonable period of time for the learning experience to lead to productive consequences; it requires the presence of competence on the one hand and a commitment to growth on the other hand; it paves the way not only toward intellectual stimulation and the acquisition of competence and achievement in the learning process but also allows for affective interactiviiy, which may result in the development of a research stance—a perpetual state of ferment that sees in the conclusion of a learning experience the beginning of yet others at even higher levels; and the predisposition to enter into meaningful relationships with other minds tuned to the best in human thinking and leveled at present and future extensions of the frontiers of knowledge and productivity.

CURRICULUM

Earlier discussion of educational provision for gifted students emphasized the importance of differential nurturance for them. Although it is true that there is commonality among all children, there are also differences unique to the individual, which are not difficult to recognize and accept. However, we are tempted, when discussing gifted students, to conceal these differences to some extent. In matters of curriculum, there is no lack of emphasis on teaching the basics. It is not the content that is questioned, but rather the unbending manner in which we approach the teaching of basics. It is good to know that thinkers like M. N. Meeker and J. S. Renzulli, for instance, offer alternative ways of teaching the basics within their models. To this must alss be added the observation that schooling should not direct itself to teach gifted students what it predetermines is essential for them to know, but rather schooling should add ferment to education that will lead students (even long after they have left the school confines) to be critical and creative thinkers of knowledge, independent in acquiring it, and generative in their expression of the new, unique, and valuable. Hence, the delicate balance between depth and breadth, specificity and generality, routine and variety, and conservation and creativity should be among the hallmarks of curriculum development for the gifted.

In pointing out the need for qualitative differences in the curriculum of gifted children (Gowan, Khatena, & Torrance, 1979), we have stressed the importance of including (1) deeper study than an average class could handle (e.g., in language arts, the study of phonetics, elementary philology, etymology, and the like, or in elementary mathematics, the study of higher arithmetic, numerical permutation and combination, trigonometry and logs, statistics, and so on); (2) a change in the teachers' function from directors of learning to facilitators so that teachers do not set themselves up as knowing everything there is to know but as leaders who show the way (when needed) to the storehouse of knowledge—in the use of libraries and in the development and acquisition of skills and information by means of the laboratory as well as through active participation in attempting to solve real problems by way of available outlets for resultant products; (3) individualized instruction, possibly with the assistance of computer terminals on shared time or with other programmed learning devices (the IGE, IPI, or IEP), to get around the accelerative consumption of curriculum materials by gifted students; (4) greater processing opportunities to curriculum material that would, for

322

instance, go beyond structure of intellect operations of cognition, memory, and convergent thinking on curriculum materials and extend to divergent thinking and evaluation that would require decision making from alternatives—to be accomplished by curriculum games, simulations, or a creative production (such as a poem, painting, or some other art form); and (5) the intentional use of curriculum materials to develop creative thinking.

It is not within the compass of this book to go into the curriculum of each subject area. Source information for this can be found in writings by experts in subject-teaching fields. Among the many curriculum aids that the reader will find useful are the National Education Association publications in the several subject fields of mathematics, social studies science, foreign languages, English, music and art; the periodic curriculum issues of the *Review of Educational Research* (Gowan & Demos, 1964); some valuable curriculum-planning approaches for educating the gifted child that include the areas of social studies, arithmetic, mathematics, science, creative writing, reading, foreign languages, art, music, and drama in a book of readings by Fliegler (1961); Gold (1965), and Gowan and Demos (1964) have also treated similar curriculum areas with more recent suggestions by Gallagher (1975) on modification of curriculum offerings in the content areas of mathematics, science, social studies, and language arts; and various articles in the *Gifted Child Quarterly*.

Screening the readings on planning curriculum for the gifted in the Fliegler (1961) book for proposed teaching strategies, the strategy that calls for the use of critical and creative thinking recurs most of all, especially for learning in social studies, creative mathematics, creative writing, and the creative arts. The use of the library for the location of information is next frequent in occurrence and is stressed for social studies, arithmetic, and creative writing. Other strategies vary from learning processes and teaching methods to administrative arrangements by means of grouping, acceleration, and enrichment, depending on the content area.

Gallagher (1975) makes some important observations about several content areas: (1) mathematics is not a static subject area where everything is known and the task is merely to master it, but rather it is a dynamic ever-expanding field dependent for its continued growth on the creative and innovative ideas of gifted students, scientists, and mathematicians; (2) gifted students need to understand that the true nature of science lies in the search for truth and the acquisition of the skills and methodology to permit it; (3) social studies curricula should pivot on the proper study of Man—to accomplish this, gifted students must be helped to understand the basic concepts of economics, sociology, and psychology, be introduced to controversial ideas, and be taught to use the tools needed for analysis as well as for the acquisition and evalution of additional information so that they can arrive at unbiased viewpoints. The emphasis in language arts is also on giving gifted students the opportunity to understand ideas of greater complexity and the systems of knowledge in that content field, to go beyond grammar and syntax and use literature as a means to appreciate past cultures, and to study values as the basis for making intelligent judgments about conflicting ideas.

Such a view about the development of more complex units and materials based on advanced conceptualization of curriculum is forward looking, germane, and consistent with contemporary thought on the subject. Gallagher (1979a) reiterates the importance of actual content as the heart of any differentiated program regardless of the particular learning environment in which it is delivered; he suggests the value of developing curriculum units around central seminal ideas, much like J. Bronowski's technique used in the television series, "The Ascent of Man." His reference to the importance of integrating content with learning process calls to mind those models developed, for instance, by Meeker, Renzulli, and F. E. Williams (see pps. 260-276). Although Gallagher (1979a) expects teachers to have a rough time providing direct services to gifted students because of the paucity of organized curriculum resources to draw on, it should be emphasized that, if the training of these teachers had included the proper learning of these various processes so that they really understood them and could put them to work, then—relative to their command of different subject areas—they could choose the delivery system of content to accommodate process. Ideally, curriculum resources that have incorporated these and other larger conceptual frameworks (if available) would simplify the task of many teachers of the gifted during the uneasy time of transition from teaching in the context of average education to education for excellence. But teachers of the gifted need to be resourceful and work with others in teams to shape new dimensions in content.

We must not overlook some valuable observations made about curriculum for the gifted by both Ward (1961) and Newland (1976). In a more traditional sense, Ward writes about curriculum in terms of experiences designed to promote civic, social, and personal adequacy; of emphasis in intellectual activity and creativity; of inclusion of the foundations of civilization, the study of the classics, and instruction of ideal moral behavior and personal and social adjustments. Newland defines curriculum in a broader sense to include content of subject matter extending beyond the school to all life's experiences, many of which can be tapped by educators to facilitate learning; he expects the gifted, because of their superior capacity for learning, to use verbal symbols and function conceptually as well as to have their life and learning space not limited to the present—or primarily committed to learning about the immediate social context—but that are part of what has been in the past and what will become in the future.

PROGRAMS

On the matter of programs and projects we come face to face with the many attempts over the years to provide special ways to help gifted students grow

324

educationally in the widest sense. The approaches have been numerous and have been centered within the school, generally regardless of administrative level (secondary or elementary), as integral components of the regular classroom or as satellites to it in specially assigned centers within a school that may cater to students of the school alone or act as a host center for students from several neighboring schools. Focus was found in a variety of programs in the form of innovative projects that were pheripheral rather than central to regular schooling, supplemental rather than basic. Occasionally these approaches were expressed in terms of special schools that, by and large, have been and may continue to remain private. If it was difficult to give a complete account of the programs and projects existing in the United States 15 to 20 years ago (Gowan & Demos, 1964), it would be impractical to attempt to do so now because of the proliferation of programming all over the country, envigorated by the relative availability of money direct from federal or direct and indirect from state, local, and private sources—although with the cuts in education by the Reagan administration financial support conditions may not remain the same. What stands out, however, is the fact that, with a few exceptions, not much that is being done (by way of programs) today is much different from that which was done in prior years. It is true that approaches have been given rather catchy titles and that the combination of elements that make up these programs have, to some extent, a certain freshness, but, in the main, practices have not veered much from what may be regarded as traditional innovations. However, they are three major exceptions: first, the programming, as it relates to an alternative reconceptualization of enrichment, is differential in level, purposeful, and directional so that the end of the exploratory and preparatory activities in the development of thinking skills and in the acquisition of scientific methodology leads to individual investigation, production, and communication outlets; second, the development of many intellectual abilities and processes and the acquisition of creative problem-solving and affective skills; and third, the diagnostic-prescriptive approach that attends learning events relative to curriculum and the individualization of this approach to meet the needs of the gifted student adequately.

Fox's (1979) overview of programs for the gifted and the talented is a good summary of the various ways that have been or are still being tried with variable measures of success, approaches that have received attention and documentation by many earlier sources (e.g., Dehaan & Havighurst, 1965; Gold, 1965; Gowan & Demos, 1964; Passow, 1958). Gallagher (1975, 1979a) has pointed out that modification of existing programs to meet the needs of gifted children specifically, as was done for exceptional children generally, could be brought about in three major areas:

1. By way of *content* (viz., changes within established subject areas, like mathematics or history, or in the inclusion of new content areas hitherto unavail-

able, like ethnics and value systems; more complex curriculum units and materials based on advanced conceptualization of a subject and developed around central seminal ideas; integrating content with attention to process; and individual and small group investigations of real problems).

2. By way of *special skills* (viz., developing problem solving and divergent and creative thinking skills; using the discovery method of learning as it relates to the work of J. P. Guilford, M. N. Meeker, E. P. Torrance, J. S. Bruner, and B. S. Bloom; and using creativity as it relates to something.

3. By way of *learning environment* (viz., creating a facilitative environment that may range from having a special meeting with the gifted a few hours a week to establishing a special school for the gifted and giving special attention to the needs of underachievement and cultural difference. However, it is more in keeping with current American special-education philosophy of least restrictive environment that one would move a child out of the regular program only as absolutely necessary and with return to the regular program as soon as the special needs are met; special schools or classes for the gifted are not looked on with favor, especially if it is felt that the same results can be achieved through a part-time special class or with the addition of a resource teacher in a regular classroom.)

Fox (1979) has added a fourth dimension, namely, *rate* of *instruction*. In commenting on content versus rate, she brings to notice the need to consider *mode of instruction,* where acceleration (defined as the adjustment of learning time to meet individual abilities of students) and enrichment (defined as the provision of learning experiences that develop higher processes of creativity in a subject area) should complement one another because both are necessary to meet the learning needs of gifted individuals. Further, on the subject of mode of instruction, she emphasizes that diagnostic-prescriptive teaching and its relevance for self-direction (self-paced learning) is the most useful strategy for fostering acceleration of learning rate. She expands learning environment to include appropriate equipment and facilities—essentials like computer terminals, science-of-language laboratories, and video-taping; internship experiences as they relate to community and government agencies for older students; homogeneous grouping; and well-trained teachers. To these she adds the development of an atmosphere of mutual trust, respect, and commitment to self-improvement. Her discussion on delivery systems includes special schools, with the compromise of satellite schooling or the school-within-a-school; learning centers or laboratories; early admission to school and to college—or admission with advanced standing, grade skipping, telescoped programs, subject-matter acceleration, accelerated and enriched classes, nonaccelerative enriched classes, individualized study, tutors, mentors and internship, within-class individualization, or mainstreaming. She concludes that no single concept can effectively

326   DIFFERENTIAL EDUCATIONAL MODELS

meet the needs of all gifted students. We can see in currently operating projects or those put into operation during the last half of the 1970s subscription to one or several of these delivery systems, which must include differential emphases within the instructional mode.

SPECIAL PROJECTS

The best single source of published information on current special projects for gifted students can be found in a special issue on the subject in the *Gifted Child Quarterly* (1979a). The 72 special projects covered may be regarded as representative of efforts around the country to provide educational opportunites that are not expected in regular school learning. They have features that, at one and the same time, may be linked to recent thought and to state guidelines (where these exist). Many projects, of course, include recent thought on identification, nurture, and delivery in an additive rather conceptual way. That is, they are projects that are not totally based on some broad conceptual model. Nonetheless, a few are so based. An example of such a project is one that would use the diagnostic-prescriptive structure of intellect model advocated by Meeker (1969, 1979a) that would include testing and instruction that quite precisely relate to the model. However, this is in contrast to most projects, which use a variety of enrichment procedures with no central frame of reference to give them coherence.

Information on the location, title, and administrative agency of these 72 projects tells us something about the vigor of participation in innovative approaches on the one hand and the absence of participation of some on the other hand. This is more likely due to lack of information than nonactivity. On the basis of this data, we see that 15 participating states have from 2 to 10 projects each that are at various stages of development. It is pertinent to indicate the shift that has occurred in programming—from an approach that was dominantly cognitive to one that is massively diversified. This shift is in keeping with the expanded concept of giftedness, which no longer focuses entirely on the intellectually gifted but has come to include the other five U.S. Office of Education (USOE) categories of giftedness (Jackson, 1979). Of the 72 projects, 15 are selected for discussion as they relate to identification, instructional mode of learning, delivery system, and evaluation (Table 7)—all reflect the shift to the expanded concept of giftedness.

IDENTIFICATION

The procedures used to identify gifted students for a project generally follow state guidelines, with most projects using individual or group IQ measures (more often than not) as a major criterion. Of the 15 projects listed on Table 7, IQ measures are used (e.g., Advanced Instruction Module (AIM), a project in San Diego, California, or Developing Divergent Modes of Thinking in Mentally

Table 7   Identification, Instructional Mode of Learning, Delivery System, and

Locale	Title of Project	Administrative Agency	Grade Levels	IQ	Cognitive Abilities	Creativity (CPS)[1]	Academic Achievement	Nominations	SOI[2]/SOILA[3]	Other	Time
Alaska (Anchorage)	Program for Academically and Creatively Talented (PACT)	Achorage School District	K–8		x	x	x	x			3 hours per week
California (San Diego)	Advanced Instruction Module (AIM)	Mt. Diablo Unified School District	K–6	x						x	6 hours per week
(San Diego)	SOI Demonstration Center	San Diego Unified School District	2–6						x		—
(Whittier)	Developing Divergent Modes of Thinking in Mentally Gifted Minors (MGM) Children	ESEA[5] Title III Project	1–8	x						x	Once a week
Connecticut (Avon)	Learning Lodge	Talcott Mountain Science Center ESEA[5] Title III & ESEA[5] Title IV–C Project	4–12	x		x	x	x			Week days, Saturdays, Summer
Idaho (Boise)	Four-School Enrichment Program	Boise School District	K–6	x		x	x	x			6 weeks interschool workshop
Iowa (Ankeny)	Ankeny Gifted and Talented Education (AGATE)	Ankeny School Board	K–8	x			x	x		x	3 hours per week
Kansas (Lawrence)	Primary Gifted Education	ESEA[5] Title IV–C Project	K–2	x			x				2½ days per week
Maryland (Baltimore)	Accelerated Mathematics for Gifted and Talented	Howard County Public Schools & Ellicott City Schools	7–8			x	x				Saturday (32 two-hour sessions)
New York (North Merrick)	Widening Interest Through New Experiences for Gifted Students (WINGS)	North Merrick School	4–6	x	x					x	1½ days per week
Oklahoma (Guthrie)	Exemplary Program	Guthrie School District	K–12	x				x			School year
Pennsylvania (Bethlehem)	Quest for Advanced Intellectual Development (QUAID)	Hannover School	4–6	x				x	x		School year
Texas (Alice)	Talented and Gifted Students	Alice Independent School District	8–12				x	x			5 days per week
Utah (Heber City)	Gifted and Talented Program	Wasatch School District	6–11			x	x			x	School year
(Sandy)	Identifying and Developing Gifted and Talented Students	Jordan School District	2–6								School year

[1]CPS = creative problem solving.
[2]SOI = structure of intellect.
[3]SOILA = structures of intellect learning abilities.
[4]IEP = individualized education program.
[5]ESEA = Elementary and Secondary Act.

Evaluation of 15 National Special Projects

Column groups: **Instructional Mode of Learning** — Content (Curricula Regular, Curricula Special, Other); Special Skills (Critical Thinking, Creative Thinking/CPS[1], SOI Abilities (Meeker)[2], F.E. Williams's Strategies, Enrichment Triad (Renzulli), Other (Bloom, Parnes, C.W. Taylor)); Environment (Peers Homogeneous, Class Heterogeneous). **Delivery System**. **Evaluation** — Tests (Cognitive Abilities, IQ, Torrance; Guilford, Achievement, SOI[2]/SOILA[3]); Observation (Product, Renzulli, Parent/Teacher/Peer, Informal Records).

Curricula (Regular)	Curricula (Special)	Other	Critical Thinking	Creative Thinking/CPS[1]	SOI Abilities (Meeker)[2]	F.E. Williams's Strategies	Enrichment Triad (Renzulli)	Other (Bloom, Parnes, C.W. Taylor)	Peers (Homogeneous)	Class (Heterogeneous)	Self-contained Class	Special School	Learning Center/Lab	Grouping (Cluster, Homogeneous)	Grade Skipping	Enrichment (General)	Acceleration	Individual Study	IEP[4]	Tutor/Mentor	Mainstreaming	Teacher Oriented	Other (Pull-out)	Cognitive Abilities	IQ	Torrance; Guilford	Achievement	SOI[2]/SOILA[3]	Product	Renzulli	Parent/Teacher/Peer	Informal Records
x						x										x	x	x					x	x	x							
x			x	x		x		x					x	x		x	x						x				x	x				
					x						x							x														
																		x	x													
				x			x				x			x				x					x									
				x	x	x					x			x				x									x		x		x	
x	x				x	x		x		x			x										x									
x																x	x	x					x								x	
x																		x									x					
	x						x				x		x	x		x		x											x		x	x
x	x		x	x						x										x							x					
x					x					x											x						x					
		x	x	x		x		x		x								x		x							x				x	x
x								x		x		x				x							x								x	
x				x						x												x										

329

Gifted Minors, a project in Whithes, California). However, it is the practice now to use multiple criteria in the selection process to include achievement and creativity tests (e.g., Identifying and Developing Gifted and Talented Students, a project in Sandy, Utah), as well as less formal observational-inventory-nomination types of indices so that psychologist, teacher, parent, and peer may all be involved at times. For example, the Program for Academically and Creatively Talented (PACT) (Anchorage, Alaska), the Learning Lodge of the Talcott Mountain Science Center (Avon, Connecticut), the Four-School Enrichment Program (Boise, Idaho), and the Primary Gifted Education (Lawrence, Kansas) projects all use multiple-assessment procedures. Of particular interest is the SOI Demonstration Center Project (San Diego, California), which uses structure of intellect measures (by means of the Meeker *SOI Abilities Workbooks* [1970] for identification in preparation for the development of those abilities. Generally, test information provides the main selection criteria although most projects depend on nominations and observational data as well.

INSTRUCTIONAL MODE OF LEARNING

At times, the instructional mode of learning may directly arise from a theoretical model, like the structure of intellect as M. N. Meeker has interpreted it or as F. E. Williams has applied it; at other times, the instructional mode of learning may include creative problem-solving processes by using the Osborn-Parnes approach and its related derivatives or, less frequently, the synectics approach, although in these 15 projects, there is no overt mention of the synectics approach being used. Often, projects will combine a number of process models, which include not only the ones mentioned but also B. S. Bloom's taxonomy, Piagetian concepts, and C. W. Taylor's multiple talent approach, to integrate them with the curriculum. It is not unusual for a project to concentrate its central efforts on process, particularly as process relates to creative or divergent thinking and problem solving, as well as on activities that are not necessarily curriculum based (it is more frequent to see the application of such thinking operations to curriculum correlates however). The most popular methodological approach is J. S. Renzulli's enrichment triad model. It has a distinct theoretical rationale and gives appropriate focus to the concept of enrichment that is deliberate and accelerative and that unites process and content toward production with suitable outlets for them. The uniqueness of the enrichment triad model lies not so much in its conceptual grasp as in its basic content. As a model of how to accomplish enrichment in the classroom, it is easily the best available. In terms of cognitive and affective creativity and their curriculum correlates, F. E. Williams's *Total Creativity Program for Elementary School Teachers* (1972) is another model that has won a great measure of acceptance. The more loosely conceived concept of general enrichment that still pervades many of the projects must be less effective

330

than its more precise relative, the enrichment triad. Acceleration, another feature of several projects, has found more precise focus in the Study of Mathematically Precocious Youth (SMPY) Project at Johns Hopkins; unlike the general accelerative features of the enrichment triad, it encompasses acceleration to higher levels of accomplishment in a subject area related to special abilities. Thus, SMPY possesses an unquestionable power of its own. There is no doubt that the need for different instructional modes of learning exists, not only according to abilities and special aptitudes but also according to age levels and developmental advances of gifted students. Hence, the definite need for IEPs that range from teaching individual abilities and talents by means of accelerative procedures in various content areas to interest-determined projects. On reviewing the projects, one finds few projects that are deliberate attempts to provide IEPs. Some exceptions are the Individualized Progress Program in the Madrona Elementary School, Seattle, Washington; the IGE program of Stevens Point, Wisconsin; the SOI Demonstration Center project of San Diego, California; and the Quest for Advanced Intellectual Development (QUAID) project of Bethlehem, Pennsylvania, which uses Meeker's structure of intellect diagnostic-prescriptive approach. However, it must be noted that 9 of the 15 projects listed do include individual study in their programs (e.g., the Talented and Gifted Students project in Alice, Texas).

Other interesting facets to this group of projects include the sound ecletic theoretical approach of Project Reaching Educators and Actualizing Children (REACH) in St. Paul, Minnesota, which has designed the development of creative thinking skills and their curriculum correlates within a teacher-training program. REACH operates within a five-level continuum model (basic thinking skills, higher level thinking skills, creative problem solving, self-initiated investigations, and creative living) in the expectation of finding gifted students functioning at the higher levels once they have received training in the first three levels within the regular classroom (Juntune, 1979). Significant effects of teacher understanding and competence in educating the gifted is also recognized and provided for in the "Teachers Are Gifted Too!" project in Vernal, Utah. This is a somewhat different conceptualization of teacher-in-service components (which many projects have included) because, in this project, preparation of teachers for the project is the independent variable that is expected to bring about positive changes to the pupils. Another effort, which relates to Project REACH in that it provides gifted education to all children in the regular classroom, is the mainstream approach to gifted and talented education provided by the Wesatch School District of Heber City, Utah. This project emphasizes C. W. Taylor's multiple-talent approach. It uses the *Biographical Inventory Form* developed by Taylor and his associates at the Institute of Behavioral Research in Creativity at Salt Lake City and is designed to train teachers as well to provide for the needs of gifted students. Another project implemented by The Child Development Research Group Program levels itself at highly precocious academically and intellectually gifted students whose performance on standardized tests is 4 SDs above the mean or better and whose academic program emphasizes enrichment, acceleration, and the creative use of abilities in a way that attempts to meet the individual needs of students. The Yakima School District of Washington State has the Futuristic Learners Program, a project that stresses both futures and leadership elements in its instructional model. Of special interest is the confluent model, a project that attempts to provide gifted students with moral education through cognitive and affective processes toward the acquisition of moral autonomy so that the individual becomes self-reliant and inner directed. This is a project of the Vestavia Hills School District of Alabama.

Looking over these projects, we find that most of them work with content of the regular school curriculum but that several give emphasis to specialized areas of knowledge that do not come within the province of general schooling (e.g., archaeology, values clarification, futurism, comparative cultures, astronomy, magic, ornithology). Further, most of the projects aim at developing abilities and special-thinking skills, with varying emphases depending on the project, relative to the works of B. S. Bloom, Jean Piaget, J. P. Guilford, E. P. Torrance, J. S. Renzulli, C. W. Taylor, F. E. Williams, and others. All in all there is a marked attempt by many of the projects to integrate curriculum with special skills, strongly focusing on meeting the individual needs of gifted students and, to some extent, developing suitable individual educational programs. What distinguishes these projects from earlier ones is the inclusion of a theoretical rationale, deliberate instruction to multiple abilities, and enrichment that is more precisely conceptualized and strongly accelerative.

Learning Environment
Closely allied to instructional mode is learning environment. Learning provides structure and rationale for educational provisions. Environment concerns itself with the content of the surroundings: location, the teacher, teaching style, teacher-student relationship, and the like; materials, equipment, and other essential facilities, like audio and videotape facilities, teaching machines, language or science laboratories, calculators, computer terminals; events and activities in the teaching-learning situation; community resources, including experts in the field made available on the school site; internships, which are essential for career education and provide on-the-job experiences that give preliminary know-how and perspectives to aspiring youth; and the classroom climate and interpersonal relationships. Both Gallagher (1979) and Fox (1979) remind us about these essentials, most of which are taken into account in good school practice in any case. The projects that we have discussed so far give proper attention to learning environment, emphasizing different aspects described according to project rationale, available resources, delivery system used, and the like. Most projects

DIFFERENTIAL EDUCATIONAL MODELS

recognize the need and importance of providing in-service training for their teachers, and, if the project is well designed, this will be consistent with its rationale. A carefully planned example of this in Project REACH. Most projects level themselves at providing enriched environme.. in nearly all areas of the school curriculum; some focus on those areas that enhance specific abilities of particular gifted students. The chief thrusts have been directed at providing general or accelerative enrichment to the intellectually or academically gifted student. There has been much less of an effort made to enhance the talented, especially in dance, music, drama, visual arts, and creative writing. The Alabama School of Fine Arts in Birmingham is an example of an institution that addresses itself to such needs, providing intensive training in these talent areas.

DELIVERY SYSTEM

Another factor of relevance is the method by which delivery of the program is effected. This can be accomplished in a number of different ways, including programs offered by both the regular and special school, administrative arrangements, learning centers and laboratories, tutors, mentors, and internships. The several delivery systems will be discussed in terms of school programs and other arrangements.

School Programs

The most common method of program delivery for many years has been the school. The delivery of special educational opportunities in the classroom may be through individualized instruction aimed at catering to the intellectual talent and interest needs of the gifted student or by grouping together highly able students in a single school for special learning events although, at the higher levels of ability, only a few are likely to qualify. The same procedures may be practiced with several classes that are at either the same or different grade levels, and a special room should be set aside by the school for activities that the gifted can share together. The procedures may vary in the secondary school when the nature and organization of the learning events lend themselves to individualization of education. However, by and large the same procedures can be implemented in the secondary school with careful thought and planning.

It is generally expedient to combine several schools and locate a home base in the most accessible of the schools or in a building that can be considered common to all participating schools, like a learning center. Or each school can take turns. A good example of this is the Four-School Enrichment Program operating in Boise, Idaho, for gifted students in grades K to 6 with a meeting place or open house located in each of the four schools on a rotating basis. Examples of secondary programs for mathematically precocious youth are those developed in

Maryland by the Howard County Public Schools, and Ellicott City Schools for seventh- and eighth-graders following The Johns Hopkins University model.

Another variation particularly suitable for secondary school students is the school-within-a-school arrangement (in principle much the same as the honors school) wherein, according to their abilities, gifted youth may receive instruction in academic subject areas from teachers assigned to this special task. At other times, these teachers participate with the rest of the student body in social events in learning nonacademic subjects. The same gifted students may operate as a homogeneous group and together undertake projects that may be public-service oriented or that may serve as the vehicle for these gifted students to interact with one another (Bristo, 1956; Fox, 1979). Furthermore, several schools might participate in a program, much like the multitalent enrichment program in Boise, Idaho, which caters to the specialized interests of gifted students in high schools with each of the four schools designated as a center of specialization in such areas as mathematics, the sciences, modern languages, and the visual and performing arts. In this way, students with special abilities can benefit from the specialized training they can obtain in these schools.

This brings us to what may be theoretically considered the ideal delivery system—the school specially designed for the gifted student, where all the special opportunities can be found in one place; where the best materials, resources, and teachers are available; where highly able students learn and interact with other highly able students in a wealth of experiential situations. Schools of this kind are incompatible with the philosophy of American public education and, hence, have little or no support from it. The best public efforts in this direction were expressed in the special schools of Baltimore, Philadelphia, New York City, and in a few other large metropolitan areas. Generally, however, it is the specialized high schools in the country that cater to the needs of the gifted. The often cited Hunter College Elementary Laboratory School or the Speyer School, both in New York City, were earlier manifestations of schools for the near-gifted that were provided by public education. In general, however, the best public efforts were made with the Governor's School in such states as Georgia, North Carolina, and Pennsylvania, which function in the summer rather than all year round. Other such schools are necessarily privately owned and privately managed, among them are, The Roeper School for the Gifted, The Mirman School for the Gifted, The Calasanctius School for the Gifted, and The Interlochen Arts Academy.

Some schools that offer summer programs can to some extent be considered as schools for the gifted for the duration of their programs if they enroll various categories of superior students for educational enrichment and acceleration, students who are identified and brought to a particular location where materials, equipment, and related resources generally excel those that are available in regular schooling, where the teachers are better prepared and selected for their

334   DIFFERENTIAL EDUCATIONAL MODELS special academic strengths or talents in the areas of the visual and performing arts, where instruction is decidedly superior, and where innovation can thrive. Perceptive educators have advocated approaching provision of special opportunities in the public school by means of summer programs in which it is much easier to bring together high-ability students in an atmosphere where various innovations can thrive, with the possibility of these innovations being incorporated into the regular year, and where the scope for elective programs can be considerably broadened to meet individual needs and inclination (e.g., Conant, 1958; Gowan & Demos, 1964; Merry, 1935).

In fact, summer schools have become an important vehicle for the delivery of programs for the gifted all over the country and may be offered jointly or seperately by a college and a school system. Often, we find school districts or centers of learning including "summer" programs in activities for the gifted during the rest of the year, on schooldays, or on Saturdays. However, it is in the Governor's School in the various states that we find sustained efforts to provide the gifted in a summer's duration what private schools attempt to achieve for their gifted students during the school year. The San Fernando Valley State University College and the San Bernadino City Schools summer offerings are well-known provisions for gifted students; others are the Learning Lodge for gifted science students at the Talcott Mountain Science Center in Avon, Connecticut, and the flagship summer programs offered by the Guthrie Public Schools in Oklahoma, which began in 1973.

One of the earliest attempts that has proved to be successful and enduring is the Governor's School of North Carolina initiated in 1963 under the sponsorship of Governor Terry Sanford with the assistance of the Carnegie Corporation of New York and local business foundation interests. The Governor's School is now an important extension of public education in North Carolina, operating under a special Board of Governors and administered by the North Carolina State Department. In a thoughful discussion of this school, Ward (1979) briefly describes student selection, instruction, and related information:

> Some 400 senior high-school students, selected by competition in academic areas, and by auditions in the fine and performing arts, are brought each summer to the school site at [Winston-] Salem [State] College in the Old Salem community of Winston-Salem for a seven-week period. There they pursue a program of study supplementing but not supplanting their studies in their home communities, in a curricular pattern geared as closely as possible to their respective aptitudes and interests. Tuition is free. There are no grades in the usual sense. The faculties for the various areas are meticulously selected for competence and distinction within the respective curricular fields, and they come from secondary schools and colleges in North Carolina and in other states.

The Governor's School is a prototype in differential education for the gifted, the first of such institutions among several that were to follow with similar concepts of purpose and program. Initially, it provided occasion for some exciting and adventurous thought on the part of its progenitors. And while a succession of able faculties and administrative personnel have made notable contributions in the operation of the program and in the substance of curricular activities over the intervening years, the character of the school has remained remarkably true to the original concepts as to the organization of the program and the structure of the curriculum (pp. 209–210).

An expansion of the Governor's School at Winston-Salem in the last few years has led to a replication of this model at the beautiful campus of St. Andrews Presbyterian College in Laurinburg so that each summer the Governor's School now operates on two campuses.

An interesting development that has taken place is the emergence of an experimental school for the gifted, privately funded but following the guidelines of the North Carolina Department of Education under the directorship of Dr. Rose Mary Lavicka. The write-up in *St. Andrews Newsletter* of November, 1979, on St. Andrews College for Kids (SACK) describes it as patterned after the British open classroom (i.e., a multiage grouping within a community of scholars). The school has only one full-time teacher (helped by a student intern as necessary), who aids professors with follow-up activities and assignments for the full academic year. Compared with the subject offerings in grades 5 to 9 of the public schools, SACK offers 13 to 16 different subjects. The instructional mode differs as well, in that students are encouraged to learn as much as they want through individual study. Small-group activities are included to give students the skills they will require for in-depth study, and self-learning is emphasized. It is expected that two years' exposure to this program will accelerate students to early college enrollment. Generally, SACK has as its rationale Renzulli's enrichment triad and is considered unique, in that it is primarily research oriented, involving the direct participation of college faculty in the instructional process.

We now move away from schools that operate for the most part during the summer or are experimental in nature—and, consequently, are dependent for their continuance on support funds from federal, state, or private agencies—and move on to consider several of the few private schools for the gifted that function on a regular basis and provide enhanced programs. Among these are The Mirman School for the Gifted in Santa Monica, California, The Calasanctions School for the Gifted in Buffalo, New York, The Roeper School for the Gifted in Detroit, Michigan, and The Interlochen Arts Academy in Interlochen, Michigan.

The Mirman School for the Gifted
Briefly, The Mirman School for the Gifted was designed to cater to the needs of the academically gifted of IQ 130 and above. Beginning in the home of Norman

and Beverley Mirman in 1965, the school moved to a new location in the Santa Monica Mountains in 1970 and in 1979 had an enrollment of 185. The school is most selective in its choice of teachers to work with their gifted students in programs from K to 8. The teachers at present number 14 (9 full-time and 5 part-time). A variety of enrichment procedures are used to enhance the educational development of the students; these include an accelerative and varied curriculum with appropriate support equipment and other facilities. Both individual and group work are encouraged and attention is given to building good self-esteem and to providing creative activities and expression in the arts and sciences. The school produces a newsletter and has strong parent support.

In 1970 the school had 80 students and 12 part-time faculty members, most of them experienced, accredited teachers. The teachers would shift subjects according to the mood of the class. Art, history, French, science, and music would give way to Greek mythology, new math, literature, English, and cursive writing (for tots who would be sternly restricted to printing in public school). Sudden spurts of tangential interest in midlesson would redirect the discussion toward political problems, Jackson Pollock, electronics, science fiction, and creative writing. The Mirmans told *McCall's* (Finder, 1970):

We don't consider the lesson plan a straitjacket. In the middle of Dante's Inferno, *for instance, one class wanted to create the circles of hell as an art project. So they did. During the study of Greek mythology, the children decided to study the Greek language. (p. 88)*

There is, however, nothing undisciplined, nothing fuzzy, or nothing abstract about this approach:

We try to teach our children how to think, to analyze, to evaluate. They're so glib verbally, it's very important that somebody pin them down. (p. 88)

The school appeals to its teachers, parents, and children for different reasons. Teachers delight in the small class size, their creative role in curriculum development, the satisfaction of working with bright kids who give good feedback. The parents are attracted because, in the Mirmans' (1970) view:

They're sometimes in awe of their child, and often desparate that he get a quality education. (p. 88)

As far as the children are concerned, their reasons for glee are apparent: their voracious appetites for learning are unchecked by anyone but themselves.

The Roeper School for the Gifted

The Roeper School for the Gifted in Bloomfield Hills near Detroit was founded by George and Annmarie Roeper in 1956. It admits highly motivated children with IQs of 120 and above after careful screening of the child and the motives of the parents for bringing the child to the school, their attitudes to special education, and the home environment. The school consists of two organizational units, a lower school with an enrollment of approximately 300 students in a nongraded, multiage, open-classroom environment and an upper school with an enrollment of approximately 200 students in grades 7 through 12 with each unit having a head person. A Board of Trustees is the governing body and establishes policy for the entire school. It is a nondenominational school with a scholarship program, which, in part, supports many of its students, thus, children of different socioeconomic backgrounds are included. Vital to the school's continuance are its guiding principles that focus on the dignity of all people and their right to enjoy free and honest expression, to share in our cultural heritage, and to participate fully in the family of Man. Like the Mirman School, its programs are conceptualized in terms of enrichment by means of the arts and science curricula, which are expected to accelerate the intellectual development of the students in a variety of settings that are common to all good schooling. It derives its strength from competent and innovative full-time instructors, from university professors, enthusiastic parental support, and superior facilities and equipment. The Roeper School has a fine newsletter, *Parent Communication,* as well as a journal, *The Roeper Review,* which not only reflect the school's activities but also contribute to thought on gifted education.

The Calasanctius School for the Gifted

The Calasanctius School, as described by its founder, Father Gerencser (1979), began as an experiment in the education of gifted and talented children from grade 5 to the college level in 1957 and expanded to include children from age 5 and up. Located in Buffalo, New York, the school serves the needs of people of all socioeconomic levels. Students are admitted mainly on the basis of high IQ (130 and above) and interest in the programs. Father Gerencser tells us that the curriculum of the school was not designed as a copy of other curricula, nor were so-called enrichment and acceleration methods to be used; rather, the program was to be a unified one built around the psychological and sociological needs of gifted children. Important features of the school's program include: planning for a six-year sequence of basic curriculum, usually after the fouth- or fifth-grade level, in preparation for the rigors of college-level study; exposure early in schooling to a variety of learning experiences in clearly circumscribed fields so that during the first three years all courses are required, except for the choice of foreign languages and in some areas of the creative arts; college-like scheduling of a variety of courses, that is, 10 to 15 subjects per week rather than the usual 5 per day—a challenge that gifted students seem to prefer; and the notion that creativity is a natural consequence of a broadened range of experiences in memory storage. Uniqueness of the program lies in its integrating qualities expressed, for instance, in three kinds of activities: (1) the Seminar Program, an independent research/study program under the guidance of a proctor to culminate after three consecutive years of work in the presentation of a serious paper or creative art work; (2) the Field Study Trip, which lasts from two to three weeks or less for younger children and the school year for the others; its objectives are to coordinate and integrate school learning experiences with real life situations, to open the minds of students to the variety of natural beauties around them and to the best of American achievement, and to nurture an understanding of the American experience; and (3) the Phenomenon-of-Man Program, which consists of a cluster of courses—taken in the fourth, fifth, and sixth levels of study over one to four semesters—that are aimed at introducing students to the richness of the history of ideas underlying human culture. Finally, students are evaluated not for the time spent in a course, but rather on actual knowledge acquired in an area. The program for students between 5 and 9 years of age is built on a combination of Jean Piaget's developmental stages, Carl Jung's archtypical approach regarding content, and a respect for the riches of children's eidetic imagery. Another feature of the program for the young was the teaching of foreign languages, including Japanese. The complicated nature of the program requires the assistance of a large number of highly informed teachers—the cream of the academic community—who complement the full-time highly competent faculty. Continuous in-service training and visits to other schools help the faculty to keep up to date and, therefore, to be highly effective in their role as teachers of the gifted. The school supports itself by tuition and fees, donations, and contributed services. Its important service to the gifted was recognized in 1976 when, in honor of its 20th anniversary, Calasanctius Day was proclaimed in Buffalo and in Erie County.

The Interlochen Arts Academy

The Interlochen Arts Academy, located in Interlochen, Michigan, began in 1962 as the country's first high school to emphasize the arts and academic subjects equally. It is the natural outcome of the early efforts of Dr. Joseph Maddy, who pioneered the idea that music education should receive full credit in the nation's schools, as well as National Music Camp, founded in 1928, and its expanded offerings in dance, drama, and art in the years that followed. The Academy is a special high school (grades 9 to 12) that provides talented students with comprehensive training in music, dance, theater, and the literary and visual arts as well as the other subjects to a high school curriculum leveled at preparation for college. The structure of the program allows as much latitude as possible to students, within sound educational standards for college-admission requirements, to arrange their own academic study. It offers small classes with highly qualified teachers, individualized instruction, tutorial assistance, opportunities for the exploration of topics of interest on an individual or group basis, promotion whenever the student is ready for it, and faculty who work together to integrate the academic curriculum with that of the arts. The school depends on tuition fees and contributions for support. It has a scholarship and financial aid program that make it possible for highly talented but needy students to attend the academy. The school operates as a day as well as a residential school and caters to an important need in Michigan.

Other Arrangements

Among the most common ways for the delivery of programs in schools are enrichment and acceleration (both of which have already received our attention). To what has been said about enrichment, let us add the organizational elements of centers in the classroom, school, or district. This is well reflected in several of the projects reported in the *Gifted Child Quarterly* (1979), among which are the SOI Demonstration Center or the Creative Problem-Solving Center in San Diego, California; the resource room or resource center of many projects, including Ankeny Gifted and Talented Education (AGATE) of Ankeny, Iowa, and Widening Interest Through New Experiences for Gifted Students (WINGS) of North Merrick, New York; or the Program for Academically Gifted Students of Mobile County Schools in Alabama. Students spend full time at these centers of learning or attend part of the time to participate in seminars, independent study or project work, creative problem-solving activities, tutorials, and the like, on a daily or weekly basis and are supervised or taught by a facilitator or coordinator of the gifted program. Acceleration may be incorporated in the activities of the centers to include advanced study of various subject areas. Acceleration is certainly an integral part of the individualized instruction by tutors and in the programmed materials as well as in the individualized programs (self-directed or teacher directed) as interpreted in diagnostic-prescriptive teaching methodology. Acceleration may also be thought of in terms of shortening the time students spend in school by grade skipping or by telescoping programs so that (1) at the junior high school level gifted students are placed in homogeneously grouped classes that cover three years of work in two years or (2) at the senior high school level gifted students eliminate or reduce the number of their electives, take courses in the summer, or earn credit by examination and, thus, graduate a year earlier (completing the curriculum in three rather than four years). Early admission to kindergarten or grade 1, or by reducing the number of years spent in the junior or senior high school (in the ways described), or by taking college courses while in high school to be able to enter college with advanced standing are all related facets of accelerative procedures that are frequently used. Emphasis on the function of the teacher—whether involved in individualizing in the regular classroom, serving as a tutor with expertise organized for direct instruction on a one-to-one basis, or as mentor with a less formalized instructional approach—is another dimension of program delivery that schools and innovative projects tap in their attempts to provide special educational opportunities to gifted students. To these must also be added the extension of the mentor relationship for secondary school gifted students who, by being given the opportunity to work with experts of the community in on-the-job situations, gain training and experience in their fields of interest. Such a relationship will give many gifted students the much-needed direction and preparation for the career choices they have to make and help to eliminate some of the problems that naive gifted students face on entering college because the diversity of their talents is not informed by practical experience.

EVALUATION OF PROGRAMS AND PROJECTS

There is no doubt that evaluation is an essential component of any program or project and that it can and often does turn out to be one of the most troublesome problems. Often, those who initiate educational activities as innovative practice do not give careful attention to evaluation in the planning stage of the program and, then, find out as the program is reaching its final stages that there is a real need to be able to say if the innovative approach has, in fact, proved effective. This is important because many who become involved in providing unique educational opportunities do look about initially, at least, for guidance. The findings generated by a project, whether positive or negative, can be of great value in determining the direction that should be taken. It is not uncommon to find project directors frantically searching for someone or some agency to effect a rescue at a time when the evaluation component has usually become a make-shift operation; more often than not, the evaluator is unable to control for alternative explanations of change other than those that may have occured because of the project experience. For any appraisal to be effective, those involved should be present at the planning stage of the project. In this way, control of extraneous variables, evaluative dimensions and stages, appropriate instrumentation, correct statistical analyses, and the like, can be woven into the total project.

There is also the distinction that has to be made between a project that has been found to be significant for the education of students and has become part of an educational program and a project that is in its try-out phase. In the first case, it is necessary to give careful forethought to the conceptual framework of the project so that an adequate grasp of the consequences that are expected become evident and that the events, circumstances, and related conditions that may give rise to the consequences, rather than the variables of the project itself, are also apparent. In the second case, it is necessary to ascertain if the results found to occur on the evaluation of the project during its trial run do in fact recur when it is in use. To test the effectiveness of a project that is supposed to bring about changes in participants, it is necessary to adhere to principles of best design relative to the project's goals. The design that will control for many interferences determines the kind of computation that is to be used. The project that has been accepted as effective and incorporated into an educational program does not need such an approach. Rather, the procedure is leveled at selection of appropriate ways to assess growth, achievement, and increased competence resulting from exposure to the program.

Another consideration for innovative projects is ongoing evaluation of the effects of the program components. Evaluation of this kind only provides information about student strengths and deficiencies; it also gives important feedback data for program refinement and further evolvement. Such evidence is invaluable in the final evaluation of the project as well. One of the most productive ways of appraising the effectiveness of a project is to plan it within a study design that provides information at the outset about (1) the students' intellectual and educational levels and personality, (2) other pertinent factors that may be expected to react or interact with the program offered, (3) performance changes that are expected to occur. The design should include feedback so that program changes and improvement can be made at various times in the life of the project (usually at the end of each project year—this may be limited to two appraisals) and there should be a final evaluation of the total project that involves students, the curriculum, and such other project components as in-service training programs; the effectiveness of contributions to the development of the project made by experts, parents, and community-related resources; and the overall management of the project. All the above were incorporated in the evaluation procedures of Project Talented and Gifted, an Elementary and Secondary School Act (ESEA) Title III Region II West Virginia project, during the period 1973-9176 (Khatena, 1975b, 1976e).

Renzulli (1975) and Renzulli and Smith (1979), in thoughtful discussions of the subject, cite some pertinent evaluation research that distinguishes between formative and summative evaluation (e.g., Scriven, 1967) and describe the kind of evaluation design used so that, on the one hand, one appraises ongoing outcomes of a project for feedback information that can be used for program refinement and evolvement, and, on the other hand, appraise the consequences of the project as a whole. It is the combined use of the two evaluation procedures that is preferred. Further, the role of evaluation determines the types of data to be generated, that is, for producet, process, and presage, each of which deserves attention. Renzulli notes that both evaluation designs and the kinds of data-generating factors have a distinct relationship, and, as we shall see later, he combines the two into a very useful evaluation matrix.

PRODUCT EVALUATION

Product evaluation can be regarded as the assessment of observable and measurable student outcomes arising from exposure to program elements in a project. The derivation of such information serves to document the changes that were expected to have taken place in the student. Procedures to measure this kind of

342   DIFFERENTIAL EDUCATIONAL MODELS

outcome present problems, especially as they relate to identifying changes of higher level process (as in creative problem-solving abilities). That human judgment of some kind is needed must be recognized, but, for this to be effective, some criteria need to be established. Criterion-referenced tests that truly assess the type of learning appropriate to gifted students should be used. Information on products may be obtained by expert ratings of student products and by frequency counts through the use of school logs, checklists, or analysis of school records as these relate to the accomplishment of important program objectives.

PROCESS EVALUATION

Process evaluation is concerned with assessing what goes on in the learning situation involving student and teacher behaviors rather than learning outcomes. Assessment of the actual dynamics of the learning circumstance may prove valuable, in that strengths and weaknesses of certain teaching strategies can be identified in the formative stage to give direction to appropriate emphases or refinements, and these may be used with caution in summative evaluation reports. The *Flanders Interaction Analysis System* (e.g., Amidon & Flanders, 1971) is offered as one of several assessment approaches. Another procedure suggested is the *Class Activities Questionnaire* based in part on B. S. Bloom's *Taxonomy of Education Objectives* and developed by Steele (1969), which attempts to measure the cognitive-affective dimensions of the instructional climate. To this may be added the *Barclay Classroom Climate Inventory* (Barclay, 1978), which attempts to measure expectations in the affective and social domains of learning.

PRESAGE EVALUATION

Presage evaluation is yet another source of data. It focuses on factors assumed to have significant impact on outcomes or products, factors that relate directly to the materials of a program. This approach is particularly useful for the evaluation of nonproduct dimensions of a program. An instrument developed by Renzulli and Ward (1969), entitled the *Diagnostic and Evaluation Scale for Differential Education for the Gifted* (DESDEG), can be used to differentiate clearly different components of a program for more careful analyses of each in an evaluation. The example given in the DESDEG for the identification component allows for examination of the comprehensiveness of screening and placement procedures, the variety of criteria used in identification, and the proportion of students selected at each grade level, thus, forcing a breakdown of information for the evaluator to see the identification system more clearly so that more meaningful questions may be asked and better judgments made.

On the subject of special problems encountered in evaluating a program,

OVERVIEW OF THE KEY FEATURES EVALUATION SYSTEM

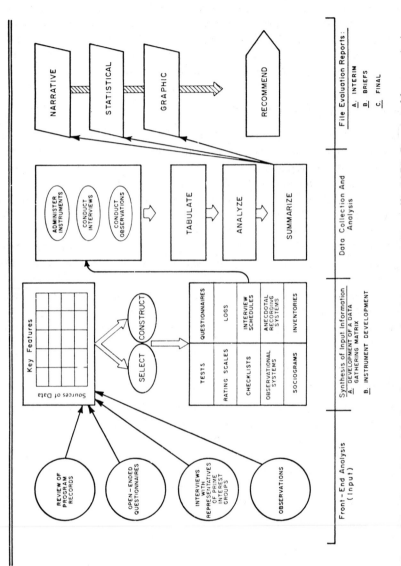

Figure 20 Overview of the key features evaluation system. (Renzulli, 1975. Reprinted by permission of the publisher, N/S LTI on the Gifted and Talented, Los Angeles, Calif.)

Matrix of Key Features and Sources of Data

Key Features

Sources of Data	Student Growth	Levels of Thinking and Classroom Conditions	Attitudes Toward Program	Identification Procedures	Etc.
Students	Pre- and Post-Tests of Creativity, Critical Thinking, etc.	*Class Activities* *Questionnaire* Interviews	Questionnaires Interviews (Random Sample)		
Program Teachers	Evaluation of Student Growth Forms (A Structured Anecdotal Report)*	*Class Activities* *Questionnaire* Logs	Interviews	Time and Effort Reports Follow-up Questionnaire	
Parents			Questionnaires Interviews (Random Sample)	Follow-up Questionnaire	
Student Selection Committee (Including Records)				Time and Effort Reports Rating Scale (on Usefulness of Information) Interviews Analysis of Records	
Non-Program Teachers	Rating Scale		Questionnaires Interviews (Random Sample)	Time and Effort Reports Follow-up Questionnaire	
Consultants	Student Product Rating Form				
Building Principals and Coordinators		Questionnaires	Interviews "Problems" Log	Time and Effort Reports "Problems" Log	
Secretaries				Time and Effort Reports	

Figure 21   Matrix of key features and sources of data. (Renzulli, 1975. Reprinted by permission of the publisher, N/S LTI on the Gifted and Talented, Los Angeles, Calif.)

Renzulli and Smith (1979b) point to (1) the difficulty of measuring the effects of the program on the development of higher powers of mind and advanced levels of awareness, interest, and other affective behaviors; and (2) the highly individualized objectives peculiar to each gifted student. Further, because gifted students are at the upper levels of standardized tests, the problem of statistical regression toward means and the low ceiling of tests can be expected to give inaccurate readings of their growth. These problems are attenuated by the cost factor of an evaluation, the need for trained personnel who should be involved at the very beginning of the project, and the attitude of project personnel toward the evaluator because an evaluation can constitute a threat to the continuity or dissolution of the project.

This leads Renzulli (1975) to suggest his Key Features System, found by him to be a particularly effective model for the evaluation of gifted and talented programs. The model consists of four sequential steps, namely, front-end analysis, synthesis of input information, data colection and analysis, and file-evaluation reports (Figure 20). He also suggests that, once identified, these key features can be organized in a matrix that has as one dimension key features and as a second dimension sources for the collection of data (Figure 21). The blank squares in the matrix can be completed according to the needs of the individual programs that are to be evaluated. Further details on this model can be found in Renzulli 1975 and 1979a.

Appropriate attention needs to be paid to the factors that relate to an effective evaluation system of projects at the proposal stage. It would be advantageous to seek the services of knowledgeable professionals to assist in the planning and writing of the proposal so that whatever goes into the proposal belongs to the conceptual framework of the project. The discering reader will recognize the meaning and quality of such an approach and will be more inclined to favor the project for funding. As competition for funding continues to increase, it will become more and more necessary to attend to the relevance of this dimension of a project.

CONCLUSIONS

Any view of educational opportunities for gifted and talented children must distinguish between educational provisions for all students and those specially designed for the able. The need for such differential education has been the concern of professional education particularly since the post-sputnik period of the 1960s. Using the familiar methodology of acceleration, enrichment, and various administrative arrangements, on the one hand, and the recognition of the wide varieties of giftedness (each of which speaks strongly for the existence of highly individual needs), on the other hand, educators have developed numerous approaches. These approaches have included individualization of education, at first formalized broadly for the general student in IGE and related programs. More recently, programs have been developed for the gifted, with particular emphasis on involving the students in determining learning content and rate as well as recognition of unique talents of individuals and how best to address their development—with tie-ins to educate abilities and to accelerative-enrichment conceptual frames of reference. Attempts at providing for individual differences and needs more precisely have found expression in the diagnostic-prescriptive approach that is leveled at identifying strengths and enhancing them as well as at alleviating weaknesses. Whereas Meeker's individualized approach uses specific curriculum content to educate singular components of the structure of intellect, Renzulli's more general approach hinges on the principles of his enrichment triad, leading to inquiry, problem solving, productions, and outlets. Further, the importance of self-directed learning and mentorship program models must not be viewed as separate individualized approaches to learning for the gifted, but rather as closely interactive components, which should result in productive learning and ferment.

These ways of catering to individual needs that bring into play process and curriculum content are one major departure in handling curriculum for the gifted. This approach is not doing more of the same thing nor is it only providing study of curriculum at higher levels to the able student, but it is deliberately arranging for the development of intellectual operations that may be organized as a creative problem system by which gifted students can attain greater command of their environment in preparation for interdependent relations with others. It is an invitation to creativity, to innovation, to adaptation, and to germination. Emphasis on process is not restricted to its application in curriculum but is broadened to extend and transcend learning boundaries to escalate to higher levels of mental growth and development. Another feature of a differential curriculum for gifted students relates to viewing the curricula not as completely known areas of study to be mastered but as ever-expanding areas as new knowledge is generated by the creative and scientific minds of our times—dyanmic rather than static. Further, curriculum should be thought of more as exposure to, and experience with, ideas (rather than as facts to be acquired and stored) and as the occasion for ferment that prefaces strides to the frontiers (rather than as the acquisition of information that delineates only the known). Movement away from the traditional curricula offerings to a multitude of fascinating areas of study is yet another dimension that must become increasingly noticeable and significant. These conceptualizations are not informing the development of special programs for the gifted and talented and are reflected in the numerous projects receiving support for being innovative (in one form or another) and that operate all over the country. We can also expect these projects to be integrated in various delivery systems by way of both public and private schooling. Good beginnings have been made and must continue to expand if we are to have a really differentiated curriculum for gifted students.

CONCLUSIONS

10

NATIONAL, STATE, EDUCATIONAL, AND OTHER SUPPORT AGENTS

OVERVIEW

This chapter discusses the thrusts the federal government has made in education of the gifted and the efforts to implement these programs by its agents, including the Office of the Gifted and Talented, the National/State Leadership Training Institute (N/S LTI), and the computerized services of the Council for Exceptional Children/The Association for the Gifted/Educational Resource Information Center (CEC/TAG/ERIC). Increase in state efforts to provide special educational opportunities for gifted students over the years receive attention as do parental involvement and initiative, both as individuals and as members of local or national organizations. In addition, teacher preparation is discussed in terms of individual suitability and training approaches, which include preservice and inservice teacher education programs.

CHAPTER OUTLINE

Introduction
Federal Efforts
   Office of the Gifted and Talented
   Council for Exceptional Children/The Association for the Gifted/Educational Resources and Information Center (CEC/TAG/ERIC)
   National/State Leadership Training Institute (N/S LTI)
State Efforts
Parent and Organized Efforts
Preparation of Teachers for Gifted Children

348

INTRODUCTION

Although our knowledge of the gifted and talented and what could be done for them has increased over the years, it has not been without considerable frustration owing to the obstructionism of a public education system that is essentially geared to a philosophy of egalitarianism. It was the achievement of a foreign power and its threatening implications in the form of sputnik that shook Americans out of their apathy and skepticism concerning the gifted. There was a definite turn of thought that separated pre- from post-Sputnik. Americans, at first, blamed the education system for curricular and instructional weaknesses in mathematics and science and reforms were sought. At about the same time, the National Defense and Education Act (NDEA) was passed. Bish (1975), speaking of the American reaction to sputnik, describes early national efforts of the National Education Association (NEA). With the assistance of grants from the Carnegie Corporation, the association designed and supported a project whose major function was to inform the American public about the urgent need to attend to the education of the gifted and talented. During its lifetime of 11 years (1958–1969), the project acted as a clearinghouse and center for the dissemination of information by way of various publications, organized conferences all over the country, and provided consultant services as well. As Bish (1975) observes, "It bridged a gap between the apathy of the post-war Fifties and the demands of the Seventies" (p. 288).

Serious initatory and supportive efforts of federal and state legislation and funding became noticeable in the 1970s; but now, in 1981, the proposed budget cuts in education by the Reagan administration introduces an ominous note in what otherwise might be considered an unprecedented period of growth in gifted education. The establishment of the Office of the Gifted and Talented in 1972 gave focus to the major thrusts for better educational opportunities for the gifted. The computer services of the CEC/TAG/ERIC in Reston, Virginia, served to bring information on the gifted to those who needed it. Dissemination of information and provision of in-service leadership activities by the N/S LTI envigorated the move for better opportunities for the gifted all over the country. To these must be added the significant efforts of parent and other organized groups and the contributions of the universities and colleges in preparing teachers by means of preservice and in-service training to assume the role and responsibility of facilitators of gifted and talented education. This chapter will concern itself with federal and state efforts, parents and organized group efforts, the preparation of teachers for gifted children, and considerations related to teacher preparation programs as well as preservice and in-service approaches to meet the needs for teachers prepared for the task of facilitating the education of the gifted.

FEDERAL EFFORTS

The challenge of the 1950s and the response to it described by Bish (1975) prepared the way for a truly significant step to counteract the problem (Khatena, 1976e). This took the form of an act of the U.S. Congress, which included in its amendments to the Education Act of 1969 (Section 806) provisions for gifted and talented children. The set was signed into law on April 13, 1970 (Marland, 1972a). The law required the Commissioner of Education (1) to determine the extent to which special educational assistance programs were necessary or useful to meet the needs of gifted and talented children, (2) to evaluate how existing federal educational assistance programs could be more effectively used to meet these needs, and (3) to recommend new programs (if any) needed to meet these needs. Further, the Commissioner was to report his or her findings, together with recommendations not later than 1 year after the enactment of the act (Section 806c of Public Law 91–230).

This led Commissioner Marland (1972a) to indicate the immediate steps the Office of Education could take to launch the federal program for the gifted and talented without new legislation and at the same time provide for long-range planning at the federal, state, and local levels by both the public and private sectors to alleviate systematically the problems identified by the study. These provisions would take the form of (1) a planning report on the federal role in education of gifted and talented children; (2) an assignment of program responsibility and establishment of a Gifted and Talented Program Group; this group would have a nucleus staff augmented by working relations with staff from programs throughout the Department of Education and would have significant potential to benefit gifted and talented children; (3) a nationwide inventory and assessment of current programs for the gifted and talented; (4) strengthening of state educational agencies toward more effective provision of educational programs for the gifted and talented through Title V of the Elementary and Secondary Education Act; (5) leadership development and training of representatives from the states at institutes whose programs would aim at the development of a strategic plan for the education of the gifted and talented; (6) career education models in line with the existing ones developed by the National Center for Educational Research and Development; (7) experimental schools devoted to the individualization of programs to benefit gifted and talented students (as a comprehensive design to effect education reform); (8) supplementary plans and centers relative to encouragement of Title III Elementary and Secondary Education Act (ESEA) in cooperation with the Office of Education Gifted and Talented Program Group to support still further the agencies within the states to provide special programs for the gifted and talented; (9) 10 regional offices with a part-time staff member to be identified as responsible for gifted and talented education and who would act as liaison with the national office of the Office of Education, provide developmental assistance to state agencies, effect continuous dissemination of information, and give management assistance to specialized regional activities as they arise; and (10) higher educational opportunities for the gifted and talented, which would be determined and implemented by the Office of Education Gifted and Talented Program Group.

Three years after their formulation, these objectives found realization in the establishment of the Office of Education for the Gifted and Talented, Office of Education Regional Part-time Directors, the ERIC Clearinghouse on the Gifted and Talented; the N/S LTI; internships in the Office of the Gifted and Talented; cooperative interstate projects supported by Title V (Section 505) funds; a gifted students symposium; and many state projects on the gifted and talented.

OFFICE OF THE GIFTED AND TALENTED

Discussions of federal responsibilities and efforts (e.g., Jackson, 1979; Lyon, 1976; Marland, 1972b) point out that the Office of the Gifted and Talented had its origins in the staff that prepared the Marland report and, at first, had no funds with which to operate. Under the leadership of Harold C. Lyon, Jr., assisted by Jane Case Williams, this office set itself up in an advocacy role to champion the cause of the gifted and talented, using the needs-assessment-survey information included in the Marland report (1972a) as a guideline, namely, that federal, state, and local funds for differential educational provisions had low priority for gifted and talented students; that fewer than 4% of gifted children were receiving services commensurate with their needs; that 57% of the school administrators said they had no gifted or talented students in their classrooms; that minority and culturally diverse gifted were hardly reached; that, although legislative or regulatory provisions existed for these students in 21 states, they were more by way of intent than actual provisions, with only 10 states having full-time personnel assigned to gifted-child education; that such children needed special opportunities and were not, in fact, doing well on their own; that the belief that gifted children came exclusively from upper middle class and wealthy families was a prevailing myth; that identification procedures were poor, funds were lacking, and, frequently, teachers and administrators were apathetic and even hostile to the needs of the gifted; that only 12 American universities were training teachers at the graduate level for gifted and talented students; and that the expected federal role in the delivery services to gifted and talented students was practically nonexistent.

Because the Office of the Gifted and Talented was faced with an enormous task and had meager resources, it took the following directions: (1) it adopted the strategy of sustained advocacy; (2) it used the leadership-training approach (with funds from the Education Professions Development Act) to further support professionals already interested in the gifted and talented; to reach key educators, opinion shapers, and legislators; to begin developing potential parent constituency; and to provide concrete skills in planning and program building at the state level; (3) it called on private foundation, business, industry, and community groups to assist in the endeavor of providing special benefits to gifted and talented students, using the national news media, extensive travel to speak to various groups, and writings in popular and professional publications; (4) it found a great deal of publicity for the gifted and talented through such programs as exploration scholarships (funds for which came from the Explorers Club and Expeditions International), scholarships provided by the Bureau of Indian Affairs, and a national symposium for gifted high school students (jointly sponsored by the American Association for Gifted Children and the Presidential Scholar's Program initiated by President Lyndon B. Johnson in 1964); (5) it alerted local and state education agencies to use creative grantsmanship techniques in their attempts to obtain funds for programs from various ESEA title categories; (6) it also sought support from the National Endowment for the Arts and Humanities, the National Science Foundation (NSF), the Robert Clark-Sterling Foundation, and other similar funding agencies.

Harold C. Lyon, Jr., wrote a letter on February 19, 1975, to friends of the gifted and talented noting that the Special Project's Act (Public Law 93-380, Section 404) gave his office the statutory authority to administer programs for this group and for the first time would shortly make funds amounting to $2.56 million available. He indicated that a call for proposals would shortly be forthcoming with the expectation that funds could be awarded for state comprehensive programs, for a consortium of academic institutions and internships carrying graduate credit and degree status to potential leaders, for a technical assistant project, for exemplary projects relative to special groups of gifted and talented youth, and for an analysis of requirements for the gifted and talented and their dissemination to practitioners. Although these funds did not amount to much when we consider their being spread over 50 states for an many as 1 million potentially gifted students, it must be noted that for the first time in the history of the United States a definite commitment to implement legislation for the gifted and talented was made. This must be recognized as the significant precursor to escalating support. Using the successful strategy adopted by the N/S LTI, the Office of the Gifted and Talented diverted half of its money to state educational agencies for professional staff development and to local projects and model programs with replication potential in their design—seeing in these ventures the great possibility of contagion and rapid spread.

The initial allocation of $2.56 million in 1976 for gifted programs was increased in 1979 to $3.78 million, and Public Law 95–561 as projected for fiscal year 1980, has an escalated amount of funds available of from $6.3 million to $25 million over a five-year period (Sisk, 1979). Of course, with the Reagan administration proposed cuts in education, such funds may not materialize. However, this new legislation, if allowed to become operational, will direct 75% of the federal appropriation to the states, 90% of which is expected to flow through competition to the local district of each state—with the requirement that 50% of the money must serve culturally disadvantaged gifted children (Lyon, 1979; Sisk, 1979). In addition, 25% of the Commissioner's discretionary funds will be distributed according to the Commissioner's priorities, namely, graduate-level training; statewide planning; and contracts for research, information products, and model products (Lyon, 1979). To these must be added Lyon's second communication (1979) that up to 100 monetary awards were being made available to young people for study in the humanities under the Gifts for Youth Projects Program and the National Endownment for the Arts and Humanities.

Apart from describing the new legislation that continued to give decided advantage to special provisions for the gifted and talented, Sisk (1979) reviewed the events during her term of office (1976–1979) and made the following observations and comments:

1. The increases in federal funds resulted from a greater awareness of gifted children's needs brought about through the efforts of state and local agencies and a variety of news media coverage.
2. The strengthening and funded support of nearly all education agencies has found expression in a multitude of innovative programs.
3. There has been a tripling of the number of funded local projects since 1976 and their positive efforts in terms of the dissemination of materials and local replications.
4. A call for proposals has gone out (1979) for models addressing the minority or disadvantaged gifted and talented program with emphasis on mathematics and science and the visual and performing arts.
5. There has been funding of a university consortium graduate-training program in the gifted that has trained over 45 leaders, many of whom now (in 1979) occupy positions in various universities around the country.

6. There is a continued emphasis (in 1979) on building leadership in the minority areas to work with minority gifted and talented, which is reflected in awards to black colleges for training teachers.
7. Fund awards have also been made to a mentor/teacher-training program with emphasis on creative problem solving (a N/S LTI as well as a regional effort).
8. Relative to future trends and needs, it was perceived that greater emphasis had to be placed on teacher training and in-service training to serve the regular classroom teacher who teaches gifted and talented students; that gifted curriculum institutes were needed; and that continued development of measures to identify all kinds of gifted and talented had to have priority.

COUNCIL FOR EXCEPTIONAL CHILDREN/THE ASSOCIATION FOR THE GIFTED/EDUCATIONAL RESOURCES AND INFORMATION CENTER (CEC/TAG/ERIC)

An important component of the national effort, which far exceeds the potential of the NEA's effort in the 1960s to disseminate information on the gifted, is the CEC's tie-in (officially since 1972) with, and operation of, the computer services of ERIC. Although supported by federal dollars, it was not perceived at the time as directly related to the federal approach of initiating and maintaining changes in education that would give special opportunities to American gifted children. Its major functions include the gathering, abstracting, and dissemination of information on the many aspects of gifted children and their education; the production of monographs, manuals, reports, and various studies; the computer search of special topics on an individual basis; the sponsorship of information related to research on gifted children and the best practices available for dealing with them. Over the past 7 years, the CEC/TAG/ERIC has performed these functions most effectively and is recognized as a significant vehicle for the establishment and operation of a communication network that has the capability of reaching everyone in the country who is concerned with the gifted. In the Clearinghouse facility, we have a power which no country in the world has at this time, for the storing and sharing of information in all matters pertaining to the gifted with maximum economy and efficiency. The fact that researchers, educators, parents, and others interested and concerned about the gifted have extensively used the CEC/TAG/ERIC facilities of one kind or another is testimony to its much needed functions.

NATIONAL/STATE LEADERSHIP TRAINING INSTITUTE (N/S LTI)

The highest priority perceived in 1972 by the Office of the Gifted and Talented was the need to strengthen state leadership. For this purpose the N/S LTI was created and funded, primarily under the Education Professions Development Act for a period of 3 years and administered by the Superintendent of Ventura County, California. The N/S LTI had the mission to train teams of five leaders for every state so that they would have significant input in the making of education policy. Each team was to consist of one state-level leader, one local education representative, two teachers, or parent or academic community, and one noneducator. The director of this effort has been, and still is, Irving Sato, who is assisted by an able staff whose several goals give focus to developing sensitivity to the educational needs of the gifted, in training educators teaching techniques relevant to gifted education, and in helping to plan for the special educational needs of gifted children at the state and local levels. In the first 3 years of its operation, the NS/LTI trained 48 state teams who developed state plans. It also trained the teams to plan long-term programs for the gifted, which they would implement on their return to their states. The teams would also provide the leadership for relevant legislation, funding, community support, and media coverage in their respective states. In addition, the NS/LTI has set up a national network of persons and agencies committed to gifted education; keeps people informed nationally through a monthly bulletin, visits, conferences, consultation, on-site technical assistance, and the like; and offers many important publications on various topics of interest. To date, the continued activities of the NS/LTI have trained a large number of educators, administrators, parents, and others. The frequency of their meetings can be seen in the rather comprehensive agenda listed in their monthly bulletin as well as in the quality of the institute's leadership program. All this is testimony to the effectiveness of their offerings.

STATE EFFORTS

The many projects and differential programs for gifted and talented students that have been, or are still, in existence around the country—as reported in a special issue of the *Gifted Child Quarterly* (1979) and in related sources (Passow, 1979)—are indicative of the spread of interest in providing special opportunities for such students. Recently, stimulated by the efforts of federal legislation that has expressed itself not only in money for various innovative projects but also in leadership training, conferences, the issuance of relevant information, and so on, many states have enacted legislation and allocated state resources to formalize provisions of special educational opportunities for gifted students. As yet, not all states have legislation and funds for the implementation of special educational opportunities, but many of those that do not have this advantage have set up (or are setting up) the machinery necessary to attain this end. What we now have are state provisions for the gifted along a continuum from relatively informal to quite formal and support funds that vary from state to state. Of course, there is room for considerable improvement. Several states had their own financed programs even before federal facilitation. In fact, they have served as models to many states now beginning such programs, among these are California, Connecticut, Florida, Illinois, Kansas, Maryland, New York, North Carolina, Ohio, Oregon, and Pennsylvania (see Gallagher, 1975; Gowan & Demos, 1964; Laird, 1971; Laird & Kowalski, 1972). It is also of interest that program provisions have emerged not only from state conceptualizations but also from local school districts, the latter initiatives have helped, in many instances, to establish a framework for planning at the state level. Thus, there is on the one hand the state-mandated provisions for the gifted in California and on the other hand the emergent provisions that derive their force from local efforts in Illinois (Newland, 1976).

A survey of educational provisions for gifted children conducted by Laird (1971) cites Dortha Jensen's 1927 study of the educational concepts and practices 45 school systems. She revealed, at the time, that "no system has as yet been able to devise really adequate provisions" (cited in Laird, p. 206) although the control of public education rests with the state. As important as this observation is for students in general, it is even more important for gifted students. If efforts on their behalf are to serve and continue, it must be the responsibility of the state to mother and nurture them. Laird's survey of the provisions for the gifted in the 50 states fetched 83% returns. An analysis of the returns provides information of state efforts before the federal thrust to envigorate differential education for the gifted in 1972, Information presented in the papers of Jackson (1979) and Zettel (1979) and in surveys conducted by the author (with assistance from Tina Hanaford and Diane Wolfe) in 1979 attempt to update the data on state efforts. Taken together, these studies show a significant increase in legislation, funding, program development, teacher training, state personnel assigned to the gifted and talented, and organized teacher-parent groups. The picture is incomplete in some of its details because (as in all surveys) some respondents did not fully complete all details and there were some nonrespondents.

The remaining portion of this section discusses state provisions in the light of the above three sources of data, and some attempt is made to comment on the pre- and post-1972 aspects of the data. For convenience, the several sources of data are organized according to the 10-item questionnaire that the author sent to superintendents of education of all states, the District of Columbia, and the territories of Puerto Rico, Guam, and the Virgin Islands in 1979. The questionnaire called for information on legislative provisions and funding, length of programs if in action, special educational opportunities and arrangements, categories of giftedness attended to in the identification process and related procedures for selection, teacher qualification requirements, provision for in-service training, presence of coordinators of the gifted at state and county levels, and the presence of organized parent-teacher groups for the gifted as follows:

1. *Do you have provisions for educating the gifted/talented?* Laird (1971) found that 20 states had some legislative provisions with 3 of them having no

funds, whereas 20 states were without legislation and funds. Gallagher's 1972 survey (1975) indicated that 21 states had legislation with special resources or incentives for local school districts. Khatena's 1979 survey (44 returns) found 28 states with legislation, 5 of which had no funds, and 12 states without legislation, 7 of which had no funds. Jackson (1979) informs us that at least 38 states make provision for the gifted and talented in their legislation or in the regulations of state educational agencies (or in both). Legislation in some cases expresses intent only, without specific financial provision. Of these 38 states, 16 fund every local education agency in the state for program support; 8 of these states instituted this policy after 1971. Further, Jackson adds that, because it is the state and local education agencies that bear 92% of all educational costs, we need to look toward them and not the federal government for continued development of programming, despite its significant contribution to the states since 1972. As things stand, approximately one third of the states fund programs statewide; another one third show interest in, and support for, planning, in-service training, and special projects; the remaining one third have little or no significant involvement on behalf of gifted and talented students, except for a few outstanding local programs.

2. *How long has your state had such a program?* According to Laird's (1971) findings, operating programs have been in existence for from 3 to 40 years (Connecticut, 40 years; Oregon, 19 years; Florida, 16 years; North Carolina, 10 years; Kansas, 9 years; Maryland and Rhode Island, 8 years; Illinois, 7 years; Pennsylvania, 6 years; West Virginia, 3 years). In addition, 12% of the states are considering providing programs in the future (Georgia, Idaho, Mississippi, Oregon). Khatena's 1979 survey found that 42 of the 44 responding states had programs for the gifted that were in existence for from 1 to 9 years or more so that three programs were 1 year old, 21 from 2 to 5 years old, 7 from 6 to 8 years old, and 11 were 9 years old or more. The states with programs of 9 or more years were California, Connecticut, Florida, Georgia, Illinois, Kansas, New York, Oklahoma, Oregon, Rhode Island, and Texas. This suggests that the remaining 31 respondent states must have felt, in one way or another, the vigor of the federal thrust.

3. *How do you provide special education opportunities to gifted students?* In 1971 and before, gifted education was generally provided (in some states) through regular schooling with an occasional project operating under one of the Title funds. Zettel (1979) reports that since 1974 21 states operate under a state-approved plan with another 21 states preparing such state plans. Khatena's 1979 survey shows that 25 states provide special educational opportunities to gifted students through regular elementary school and 32 states provide this at the secondary level—26 states through special projects (with federal, state, or local funds) and 38 states through a combination of regular and special projects.

4. *What kind of special educational opportunities are available?* Laird (1971)

found that provision for special educational opportunity concentrated on acceleration and enrichment although, in reporting by state, it was not clear what form either approach took. Where there were provisions for gifted classes, they used special curricula. The use of special equipment was reported by 4 states, Connecticut, Maryland, Washington, and West Virginia. The tallies showed 4 states using acceleration, 8 states using special curriculum, 7 states using enrichment, and 1 state using a variation of these procedures according to needs. Khatena's 1979 survey showed that out of the 44 states responding, 25 states used various administrative arrangements, 32 acceleration, 36 special curriculum, 38 enrichment, and 10 other procedures. A total of 22 states used all of the first four procedures.

5. *Which categories of giftedness do you attend to in the identification process?* The 1971 Laird survey shows that giftedness tended to be limited to general intellectual ability and academic achievement. Following the definition of the U.S. Office of Education (USOE), which includes six categories of giftedness, many states have broadened their definition of giftedness to include most, if not all, six categories. Zettel (1979) reports that consideration is given to IQ in 38 states, creative or productive thinking in 32 states, specific academic aptitude in 34 states, leadership ability in 26 states, and psychomotor ability in 23 states. This information shows that marked strides have been made in the 8 years following federal legislation. Khatena's 1979 survey shows that, in addition to attending to general intellectual ability, 36 states gave consideration to creative or productive thinking, 40 to specific adademic aptitude, 27 to leadership ability, 31 to visual and performing arts ability, with 23 states including all six categories of giftedness as criteria for purposes of identifying the gifted.

Another interesting aspect is the several ways in which certain states have approached a definition of giftedness. Zettel (1979) points to four principal ways that this is done in the statutes of the states: 9 states define the gifted as those with high intellectual capacity and scholastic attainment and define the talented as those possessing superior ability in leadership, the visual and performing arts, and psychomotor areas (e.g., Delaware); 16 states define the intellectually gifted under the general rubric of exceptional children (e.g., Alabama); 7 states include gifted and talented (without mention of the words) in their definition of exceptionality (e.g., New Mexico); and 4 states describe their gifted and talented as handicapped (e.g., Tennessee). Zettel also points out that 14 states make no reference to gifted and talented in their state codes or statutory language.

6. *How are the children selected for participation in your gifted programs?* Methods for selecting gifted children may vary from state to state. The Laird (1971) study reported that 11 states used group or individual measures and that 12 states used achievement tests, school grades, teacher judgment, or psychological judgment. It should be noted that no use of creative thinking measures was made at the time. According to the Zettel (1979) study, the states that subscribed

to the USOE six categories of giftedness would use appropriate measures to screen the students and, where needed and relevant, nontest indicators, like teacher or peer judgment and observation. Khatena's 1979 survey found that 35 states used both test and nontest indicators to screen gifted students, with Delaware and Washington using IQ, achievement measures, and nontest indicators (like teacher and peer judgment); and Colorado and Mississippi using IQ and achievement measures—Mississippi using nontest indicators as well. The cutoff point for determing the level of giftedness varies from state to state; as this relates to IQ, it is not uncommon to find this varies from 1 to 2 SDs above the mean (IQ from about 115 to 130 and above) and as it relates to achievement tests this varies between the 95th and 98th percentile levels.

7. *What qualifications are required of the teacher of the gifted beyond the bachelor's degree and general teaching certificate?* Laird (1971) tells us that, for some states, no special qualifications are required of the teacher of the gifted. He cites Connecticut, Idaho, Illinois, Mississippi, North Carolina, Oregon, Pennsylvania, Rhode Island, Washington, and West Virginia. In Kansas, only 26 hours of special casework is required. Louisiana and Florida require competency in the gifted child area of study. Presently, many states require that teachers be trained in the areas of the gifted and talented as well as have a bachelor's degree and a general teaching certificate. Khatena's 1979 survey shows that 11 of the 44 respondent states require a master's degree as well as certification in the gifted and talented area; 12 states require certification; 9 states require the master's degree in addition to the basic teaching qualification; and 20 of the 44 states require qualifications that range from experience teaching gifted children to a PhD or EdD degree.

8. *What in-service training (if any) do you provide or support for the teachers of the gifted?* According to Zettel (1979), 33 state education agencies conduct in-service training for teachers, administrators, support personnel, and parents. Khatena 1979 found that 31 states do this through college or university courses and conduct workshops; 36 states arrange for their personnel to attend local, state, and national conferences; and 9 states have related kinds of activities according to needs. In-service training—as a form of preparing individuals connected with the gifted, but who have had no experience with gifted education, or of sharpening the skills of individuals who have had the experience—has become increasingly popular. When compared with the no-data report on this subject in Laird (1971) study, one cannot help but conclude that the effectiveness of in-service training has contributed to its own rapid growth.

9. *Do you have a state and/or county coordinator for the gifted and talented?* Jackson (1979) makes the observation that about one fifth of the states had coordinators for the gifted in 1971, whereas this figure had increased to one half the states in 1977. Some further information from Zettel (1979) informs us that over half the states employ a full-time coordinator at state level to help initiate

and coordinate educational programs and services for the gifted and talented, with 19 states using state and 7 states federal funds or a combination of both. State coordinators in 9 states have three-quarter or half-time professional responsibilities to the gifted; 11 states have less than half-time state coordinators; 3 have no state coordinators. Khatena's data shows that 43 of the 44 states have state coordinators, with Louisiana having 50 at the county or local levels, California having 3 state coordinators, Maryland having 3 state coordinators and 1 in each school district, and Michigan having several at the county level. The figures released by N/S LTI in 1980 show that every state has at least 1 coordinator for the gifted and talented—California and Louisiana have 2; North Carolina has 3. There is no doubt that, in general, the states have responded to the trends in gifted education these past 8 years, if employment of state or local coordinators is any indication of this. The change in the number of states having coordinators from one fifth in 1971 to all states by 1980 is significant.

10. *Do you have parent/teacher groups interested in the education of the gifted and talented?* Zettel (1979) reports the presence of various advocacy groups: 36 state and local parent-advocacy groups for the gifted and talented; 21 active parent groups at state level, with 10 of these states having 2 to 3 of these groups—3 states having 5 groups and 1 state (California) has at least 40 active parent groups. Khatena's 1979 data show that 34 of the 44 respondent states have parent/teacher groups that work on behalf of the gifted and talented; some states have several such groups.

From the combined sources of information we can draw the conclusion that, whereas very little was done in the United States for gifted and talented students before federal legislation and funding, what was done tended to be more by way of local and less formalized efforts (except for a few states, like California, Connecticut, Florida, Illinois, and Pennsylvania). Much has happened following federal legislation that has envigorated the states to work on legislation at their own level and to formalize their provisions for gifted education. There is considerable ferment in the country at present and the increasing allocation of federal monies (prior to the budget cuts in education proposed by the Reagan administration) made available either directly or through state agencies and complemented by state financial support have activated the several related thrusts to provide for the gifted and their education. The barriers that were perceived by Gallagher in 1972, namely, insufficient financial support, inadequately trained personnel, inadequate curriculum development, inadequate referral and diagnostic techniques, lack of public interest, inadequate legal base, physical space and other limitations (1975) still persist but not all are at the same level of severity today. Other priorities will continue to command our attention, but federal and state legislation is making its influence felt. The number of trained personnel has sharply increased over the past few years, facilitated by the many conferences, workshops, and related activities at the state and local levels; the contributions of the leadership-training institutes; state certification requirements; and the formalized offerings in colleges and universities that fulfill certification needs and provide the training that leads to advanced graduate degrees. The discussion in Chapters 7 and 8 and in the first part of this chapter have given strong indication that curriculum development has made and can continue to make significant strides. The greater awareness of many kinds of giftedness that is finding application in identification and screening procedures have taken off some of the edge of this problem although by no means removing it. In this area, there is so much more that needs to be done, including the construction of new instruments, the refinement of those that exist, and more competent and extensive referral services. There is certainly more public interest than there was before, and this has been facilitated by the news media, advocacy groups, parent/teacher associations, law suits, and the like. The problem of having an adequate legal base has been offset by the recent passage of Public Laws 94–142 and Section 806c of Public Law 91–230 as well as by the fact that at least 38 states today have legislation and the remaining states will have such legislation before long. As for physical space, various administrative arrangements that make available special classrooms, locations shared by several schools in a district, demonstration and resource centers, and project facilities have alleviated this problem considerably. Jackson (1979), in reviewing the activities for gifted and talented these past few years, identifies five major developments: (1) the presence of better trained and equipped personnel in gifted education, many of whom possess a master's or doctor's (PhD) degree in the field; (2) the occurrence of significant policy changes at state level as well as legislative advances and developments in state departments of education, with the gifted receiving appropriate focus as a component of exceptionality, and the combined pressures of federal initiatives and the organized voice of parent/teacher groups who are prepared to go to the courts to ensure the rights of the gifted and talented; (3) the movement from a dominant cognitively oriented program to a diversification of programs that subscribe to the needs of the six USOE categories of giftedness by way of the model projects of the Office of the Gifted and Talented (e.g., visual and performing arts, creativity, early childhood, disadvantaged gifted, rural and community-based mentor programs); (4) a variety of pedagogical styles that have emerged from the diversification of programs (e.g., resource rooms, acceleration, enrichment, intensive one-to-one relationships with mentors); and (5) the propensity to piggyback on to community and private sector resources.

PARENT AND ORGANIZED EFFORTS

There is very little written on the parent effort to mobilize forces for change in the education of gifted and talented children. Most of what has been published has been by way of assisting parents to know more about the subject and directing them to possible actions they might take to facilitate needed changes (e.g., Hildreth, 1952; Khatena, 1978c; Nathan, 1979; Strang, 1960). Information of what is going on in gifted education in the United States reaches parents through the news media and magazine and journal articles—usually simplified for common consumption and often cursory; by way of conferences and training sessions conducted by various associations; through the N/S LTI; and through local district efforts. There is no doubt that in recent years, parents have been far more sensitized to giftedness, more cognizant of approaches that are needed for many kinds of giftedness, more aware of the state's responsibility to establish adequate provisions, and more pointed in their demands for the realization of their children's potential.

Many parents have recognized that they can play a number of roles that can effectively bring about or speed up opportunities for their gifted children to grow and achieve excellence. First and foremost is their role as facilitators in the home and the related environment. Abundant information about gifted children and what parents can do to enhance talent is becoming increasingly accessible. In addition, pertinent material can be found in the various issues of the *Gifted Child Quarterly,* which includes an article for parents in each issue. Among several other sources are the *Roeper Review* and, in addition, a special newspaper for parents of gifted children attending the Roeper School as well as the *National/State Leadership Training Institute Gifted and Talented Bulletin, (N/S LTI-G/T Bulletin)*, which has a brief section for parents and brief informational sketches on what is happening nationally as well as notes on useful materials that are currently available. Undoubtedly, parents can do much for their gifted children by acquiring the know-how from these and related resources. In this way, parents can effectively complement formal schooling efforts and, where no facilities are available in school, they can, as an interim measure, create the kind of climate at home to nurture and envigorate talent growth.

The second major role parents can play directs their efforts away from home toward a cooperative partnership with the school and its professionals. As individuals, parents serve as an informational base for those who are involved in the education of their children; as an effective follow-up service of the school that gives continuity to the work done in the classroom; as resource agents in and out of school for gifted students, depending on the measure of their expertise; and as the driving force for funds and related advantages in kind. Organized in local parent groups (especially as affiliates of gifted and talented national or state groups), parents become one of the strongest forces in initiating legislation and in acting in an advisory capacity to the school board, state and local agencies, principals of schools, and other administrators to bring about changes in curricula consistent with the best in thought and practice on gifted education and in the selction of procedures that qualify their children for special opportunities.

Organized efforts can be parent-shaped and may take the form of local district and state groups. There are a growing number of such effective groups, one of particular current significance is the Louisiana State Association for the Gifted under the leadership of Kay Coffey. The formation of a national organization of parents on behalf of gifted and talented interests will take time, effort, money, commitment, and a more stable economy to allow for sufficient and consistent funding of gifted programs. A more powerful approach would be for parents, either individually or as local groups, to belong or affiliate themselves to existing national associations for the gifted, the most viable of which at present is the National Association for Gifted Children whose membership consists of parents and teachers—and at one time even included gifted children. Another important and active organization—a component of a larger parent organization, the Council for Exceptional Children—is The Association for the Gifted, which has a totally professional educator membership. The professionals of both associations may also be parents, but, by and large, they are members primarily because they are professionals. However, the National Association for Gifted Children has many members who belong to it as parents. The membership thrusts of The Association for the Gifted have led to the formation of professional chapters in nearly all the states; the membership thrusts of the National Association for the Gifted have been leveled less at the formation of chapters (the several that do exist comprise both parents and professionals) and more at individual recruitment nationally as well as at school, public, and professional libraries both nationally and internationally. One of the main reasons for the direction of the thrust toward the library is its journal the *Gifted Child Quarterly*. Now that The Association for the Gifted also produces a journal, *Gifted, Creative and Talented*, a strong library membership for this association can also be expected in time. The National Association for Gifted Children has also made preparations to work toward the formation of chapters around the country, whose membership would primarily have parent emphasis. In its conferences these past few years, this national association has been giving a greater place to parent participation and, although it is still dominated by professional educators today, its executive board comprises several members who are parents. In the next 5 years, one can expect to see an increase in parent leadership and general membership and, if a delicate balance can be maintained between professional educator and parent interest and participation, the organization can become one with power and clout. When this takes place, the parents will have a delivery system for presence, advice, and press that will be hard to match.

Finally, parents, in their role as taxpayers, have the right to see that the laws of the land pertaining to the gifted are properly implemented. As we know, both Public Law 94–142, which, in essence, established the right to a free appropriate public education for all the handicapped children in the nation, and Public Law 91–230 (Section 806c), which established the right to free public educational provision for the gifted and talented, give parents the legal bases for demanding the opportunities that are rightly due to their gifted children. Where legislation relative to provisions for gifted and talented exist in their states, parents have access to due process of law to obtain their rights. Several parents have brought suits against school systems that have proved negligent. For instance, on June 6, 1975, the parents of Christopher Fisher brought suit against the Franklin County School System in Tennessee for denying their gifted son a suitable education program and related services. They won the right to be present at a multiassessment conference that was to determine the appropriate educational program and placement for their son (Zettel, 1979).

PREPARATION OF TEACHERS FOR GIFTED CHILDREN

So long as gifted students were not a population designated for special opportunities and remained in the regular classroom, there appeared to be no felt need for teachers of the gifted. Teachers with the usual professional training were the ones who took care of the educational needs of gifted students as they did the rest of the students in the regular classroom. Only a few states had special programs for the gifted before the federal legislation of 1972 and, for the most part, they catered to the academically gifted student and the programs were generally staffed by teachers of established professional competence who were not necessarily exposed to direct training experiences in gifted education. Laird (1971) indicated that a number of states with some provisions for the gifted did not require special qualifications for teachers of the gifted, these included states like Illinois, Oregon, and Pennsylvania where programs had been in operation for many years. Wilson (1957) was critical about the fact that programs for the gifted were in operation without interest or facilities for appropriately trained teachers. Emphases on the importance of special preparation for the teacher of the gifted is a more recent trend. French (1959) was probably right in his observation that both a lack of knowledge about teaching gifted children and no demand by the schools for teachers with special qualifications were factors that hindered special education offerings on the gifted. The several reasons for this condition advanced by Gowan and Demos (1964) focus attention on an egalitarian philosphy that assumes all teachers are suited to teach all children who are to be given equal educational opportunity; a school system that offers no financial incentive to attract the able teacher in this direction; the demand for teachers, especially at the elementary school level, in excess of supply, which tended to pull into education weaker candidates, to weaken standards of teacher preparation, and to produce teachers ill trained in mathematics, science, and basic language and communication skills; the lack of articulation between education faculties and the academic divisions in training teachers; the conformity of public schools, which increased attrition on the stimulating nonconforming teacher-type; and the lack of knowledge of what constitutes a good teacher in general and an effective teacher of the gifted specifically.

It was not until 1972 that the real need for specially trained teachers to manage differential education for the gifted persuaded colleges and universities, which had offered courses on the gifted sporadically and intermittently, to take significant direction toward preparation for undergraduate and graduate degrees and for fulfilling state certification requirements. Alongside, grew the less formalized and sustained approaches of organized in-service training, whose main purpose was to complement and enrich already-trained professional educators and to create a cadre of leaders in the field. The challenge to prepare teachers adequately to staff the rapidly growing number and variety of educational opportunities for gifted students has begun to be met by institutions of higher learning around the country, and, although much is still to be desired, considerable progress has been made since the 1970s. Teacher education for the gifted has assumed unprecedented vigor, powered by national and state (where applicable) legislation; envirogated by federal and state funds that find their way into projects, program developments, and related educational innovations; and supported by the efforts of the N/S LTI and the CEC/TAG/ERIC computer services.

A number of surveys (e.g., Laird, 1971; Laird & Kowalski, 1972; Bruch, 1977) attempted to find out which institutions of higher learning were offering courses and degree programs in gifted education. In general, their findings indicate a consistent growth of preparation opportunities in the number of institutions participating in training and in course offerings. These vary from a single course or several courses that are intended to lead to certification to degree programs which lead, in the main, to the master's degree and, to lesser extent, specialist degrees or a doctorate. There are also occasional programs at the bachelor's level, for instance, the programs offered at East Montana College, Kent State University, and the University of South Alabama, (Gold, 1979; Maker, 1975; *N/S LTI-G/T Bulletin,* 1976).

The author with the assistance of Tina Hanaford and Diane Wolfe conducted two surveys in 1979—one to obtain information on the opportunities for the preparation of teachers of the gifted at various universities in the country; the other to identify which states provided their teachers with in-service training pertaining to gifted children. For the first survey, about 3000 questionnaires were sent to four-year colleges and universities with graduate programs in the United States and its territories; these were addressed to the deans. Of 335 returns, 127 institutions indicated that they offered courses on the education of the gifted; 208 did not (Table 8). From 1 to 11 courses on the gifted were offered by a variety of departments: Human Learning and Development; Consumer and Public Service Division; Instruction and Curriculum; Educational Psychology; Elementary and Secondary Education; Special Education; Continuing Education; Administration; Counselor Education; Educational Foundations; Psychology; Educational Arts and Systems; Learning and Development; Professional Services; and Behavioral Sciences.

Table 8   Survey of Gifted Programs in Colleges and Universities

---

1. Does your university/college presently offer courses on the gifted?

    (a) Yes: 127
    (b) No: 208

2. If the answer is yes, how many courses are offered?

    No. of courses offered: 1 to 11

3. How long have these courses been offered?

    (a) Length of time: 1 to 25 years
    (b) Times per year: 1 to 3 semesters
                               1 to 4 quarters

4. How many faculty members do you have on your staff who teach courses on the gifted?

    (a) Full time: 0 to 4
    (b) Part time: 0 to 6

5. Do you have summer workshops?

    (a) Teachers of the gifted: 62
    (b) Gifted children: 15
    (c) Combined: 33

6. At what levels are courses taught?

    (a) Undergraduate level: 45
    (b) Graduate level: 105
    (c) Both levels: 58

7. What qualification does your program on the gifted lead to?

    (a) Teaching Certificate: 40
    (b) Master's Degree: 49
    (c) Doctor's Degree: 12
    (d) Master's and Doctor's Degree: 11
    (e) All three combined: 15

8. Is there any indication that you will expand your present programs?

    (a) Yes: 77
    (b) No: 39
    (c) Not as yet known: 12

    The length of time these courses had been offered ranged from 1 to 25 years, with 11 colleges or universities having offered courses for 9 or more years. The number of times these courses were offered part of the year or year round varied according to the university. The number of full-time or part-time faculty who were available to teach gifted courses ranged from 0 to 4 or 0 to 6, respectively, so that some universities would depend altogether on either part-time faculty or

Table 9   University/Colleges Offering Courses on Gifted Education

University/College	Professor	Courses	Level	Qualification		
Alabama, University of Tuscaloosa, Alabama	Dr. Carol Schlicter	5	Undergrad/Grad	Certification	Master	Doctor
Alaska, University of Anchorage, Alaska		2	Grad	Certification	Master	—
Alderson-Broaddus College Philippi, West Virginia		2	Undergrad	Certification	—	—
Alverno College Milwaukee, Wisconsin		1	Undergrad/Grad	Certification	—	—
Appalachian State University Boone, North Carolina	Dr. Richard Stahl	4	Undergrad/Grad	Certification	Master	—
Arkansas Tech University Russellville, Arkansas		2	Grad	—	Master	—
Augusta College Augusta, Georgia	Dr. Geraldine W. Hargrove	2	Grad	Certification	Master	—
Austin Peay State University Clarksville, Tennessee		1	Undergrad/Grad	—	—	—
Bank Street College New York, New York		1	Grad	Certification	Master	—
Beaver College Glenside, Pennsylvania	Dr. Steven P. Gulkus	7	Grad	—	Master	—
Bloomsburg State College Bloomsburg, Pennsylvania		2	Undergrad/Grad	—	Master	—
Boston College Chestnut Hill, Massachusetts		2	Undergrad/Grad	—	Master	—

continued

Table 9 (continued)

University/College	Professor	Courses	Level	Qualification	
Boston State College Boston, Massachusetts		1	Undergrad/Grad	—	—
Cabrini College Radnor, Pennsylvania		2	Undergrad	—	—
Calvin College Grand Rapids, Michigan		1	Grad	Master	—
Central Missouri State University Warrensburg, Missouri		1	Undergrad/Grad	—	—
Central State University Edmond, Oklahoma		2	Undergrad/Grad	—	—
Central Washington University Ellensburg, Washington		1	Undergrad/Grad	Certification	Master
Charleston, College of Charleston, South Carolina		3	Grad	—	—
Clemson University Clemson, South Carolina		1	—	—	—
Concordia Teachers College Seward, Nebraska		1	Undergrad/Grad	—	—
Connecticut, University of Storrs, Connecticut	Dr. Joseph S. Renzulli	6	Grad	Master	Doctor
Converse College Spartanburg, South Carolina		2	Grad	Certification	—
C.W. Post Center of Long Island University Greenvale, New York					—
David Lipscomb College		1	Grad	—	—

Institution	Contact	Number	Level			
Nashville, Tennessee		1	Undergrad	Certification	—	—
Delaware, University of Newark, Delaware		2	Grad	—	—	—
Delta State University Cleveland, Mississippi		2	Grad	Certification	—	—
East Central State College Ada, Oklahoma		1	Undergrad/Grad	—	—	—
Eastern Kentucky University Richmond, Kentucky		2	Grad	—	Master	—
Eastern Washington University Cheney, Washington		1	Undergrad	—	Master	—
East Tennessee State University Johnson City, Tennessee		4	Undergrad/Grad	Certification	Master	—
El Centro College Dallas, Texas		1	Undergrad/Grad	—	Master	Doctor
Emmanuel College Boston, Massachusetts		1	Grad	—	—	—
Emporia State University Emporia, Kansas	Dr. Roberta Petelli	5	Grad	Certification	Master	—
Evansville, University of Evansville, Indiana		1	Undergrad/Grad	—	—	—
Fairfield University Fairfield, Connecticut		2	Grad	—	—	—
Fairmont State College Fairmont, West Virginia		1	Undergrad	—	—	—
Florida, University of Gainesville, Florida		1	Grad	—	—	—

continued

Table 9 (continued)

University/College	Professor	Courses	Level	Qualification		
Fordham University New York, New York		2	Grad	—	—	—
Framingham State College Framingham, Massachusetts		1	Undergrad/Grad	—	—	—
Georgia College Milledgeville, Georgia	Dr. Catherine B. Bruch	3	Grad	Certification	—	—
Georgia, University of Athens, Georgia	Dr. Mary M. Fraiser Dr. E. Paul Torrance	11	Undergrad/Grad	Certification	Master	Doctor
Grossmont College El Cajon, California		2	Undergrad	Certification	—	—
Heed University Hollywood, Florida		1	Grad	—	Master	Doctor
Idaho State University Pocatello, Idaho		1	Undergrad/Grad	—	—	—
Illinois, University of Urbana, Illinois		2	Grad	—	—	—
Indiana University of Pennsylvania Indiana, Pennsylvania		5	Grad	—	Master	—
Iowa State University Ames, Iowa		3	Grad	—	Master	—
Jackson State University Jackson, Mississippi		2	Undergrad/Grad	Certification	—	—
James Madison University Harrisonburg, Virginia	Dr. Ted Christiansen	4	Undergrad/Grad	—	Master	—

Institution	Contact		Undergrad/Grad	Certification	Master	Doctor
Johns Hopkins University, Baltimore, Maryland	Dr. Julian C. Stanley	7	Undergrad/Grad	—	Master	—
Kansas Newman College, Wichita, Kansas	Dr. Lynn H. Fox	5	Grad	Certification	—	—
Kansas, University of, Lawrence, Kansas		8	Grad	Certification	Master	Doctor
Kean College of New Jersey, Union, New Jersey	Dr. Phyllis F. Kavett	6	Grad	—	Master	—
Kent State University, Kent, Ohio	Dr. Wilber L. Simmons	9	Undergrad/Grad	—	Master	Doctor
Lake Erie College, Painesville, Ohio		1	Grad	—	Master	—
Lehigh University, Bethlehem, Pennsylvania		3	Grad	—	Master	—
Lewis and Clark College, Portland, Oregon		1	Grad	—	Master	—
Lewis-Clark State College, Lewiston, Idaho		1	Undergrad	Certification	—	—
Long Beach City College, Long Beach, California	Dr. Barbara Clark	2	Undergrad/Grad	Certification	Master	—
Manhattanville College, Purchase, New York		—	Grad	—	—	—
Mansfield State College, Mansfield, Pennsylvania		3	Undergrad/Grad	Certification	—	—
Marshall University, Huntington, West Virginia		4	Grad	Certification	Master	—
Mars Hill College, Mars Hill, North Carolina		5	Undergrad	Certification	—	—

continued

Table 9 (continued)

University/College	Professor	Courses	Level	Qualification		
Maryville College Maryville, Tennessee		1	Undergrad/Grad	—	—	—
Meredith College Raleigh, North Carolina		1	Undergrad	—	—	—
Michigan, University of Ann Arbor, Michigan	Dr. Eleanor Hall	3	Undergrad/Grad	—	Master	—
Middle Tennessee State University Murfreesboro, Tennessee		2	Undergrad/Grad	—	—	—
Minot State College Minot, North Dakota		1	Undergrad/Grad	Certification	—	—
Mississippi College Clinton, Mississippi		2	Undergrad/Grad	Certification	—	—
Mississippi State University Mississippi State, Mississippi	Dr. Joe Khatena	5	Grad	Certification	Master	Doctor
Mississippi University for Women Columbus, Mississippi		1	Undergrad/Grad	Certification	—	—
Mississippi, University of University, Mississippi		2	Undergrad/Grad	Certification	—	—
Missouri, University of Columbia, Missouri		1	Undergrad/Grad	—	—	—
Montana, University of Missoula, Montana		1	Undergrad/Grad	—	—	—
Montclair State College Upper Montclair, New Jersey		2	Grad	—	—	—
Moorhead State University Moorhead, Minnesota	Dr. Max Spriggs	2	Undergrad/Grad	Certification	Master	—

Institution	Contact		Level	Certification	Master	Doctor
Morehead State University, Morehead, Kentucky		1	Undergrad/Grad	—	—	—
Nebraska, University of, Lincoln, Nebraska	Dr. C. Tomlinson-Keasey	4	Undergrad/Grad	—	Master	Doctor
New Mexico, University of, Albuquerque, New Mexico	Dr. Gary Adamson	5	Grad	Certification	Master	Doctor
New Rochelle, College of, New Rochelle, New York		5	Grad	—	—	—
New York College at Oneonta, State University of Oneonta, New York		2	Undergrad/Grad	—	—	—
North Adams State College, North Adams, Massachusetts		3	Grad	—	Master	—
North Carolina State University at Raleigh, Raleigh, North Carolina		4	Undergrad/Grad	Certification	Master	—
Northeastern Illinois University, Chicago, Illinois	Dr. Steve Lapan	—	Grad	—	Master	—
Northern Illinois University, DeKalb, Illinois	Dr. Barbara G. Ford	3	Undergrad/Grad	—	Master	—
Northern Iowa, University of, Cedar Falls, Iowa	Dr. James O. Schnur	2	Grad	—	Master	—
Northern State College, Aberdeen, South Dakota		1	Undergrad/Grad	—	—	—
Northwestern State College of Louisiana, Natchitoches, Louisiana	Dr. C.R. Kinard	3	Undergrad/Grad	—	Master	—

continued

Table 9 (continued)

University/College	Professor	Courses	Level	Qualification		
Oakland University Rochester, Michigan		?	Grad	Certification	—	
George Peabody College for Teachers Nashville, Tennessee		1	Undergrad/Grad	—	—	
Pembroke State University Pembroke, North Carolina		1	Undergrad	—	—	
Pennsylvania University University Park, Pennsylvania	Dr. Joseph L. French	4	Undergrad/Grad	—	Master	
Pittsburg State University Pittsburg, Kansas		1	Grad	—	Master	
Puget Sound, University of Tacoma, Washington		1	Undergrad	Certification	—	
Purdue University Lafayette, Indiana	Dr. John F. Feldhusen	—	Undergrad/Grad	—	Master	Doctor
Redlands, University of Redlands, California		1	Undergrad/Grad	—	—	
Rio Grande College Rio Grande, Ohio		1	Undergrad	Certification	—	
Saint Cloud State University Saint Cloud, Minnesota		2	Undergrad/Grad	—	Master	
Saint Leo College Saint Leo, Florida		1	Undergrad	—	—	
San Diego State University San Diego, California						
South Florida, University of	Dr. Dorothy Sisk	4	Undergrad/Grad	Certification	Master	

Institution/Location	Contact	No.	Level	Certification	Master	Doctor
Tampa, Florida	Dr. Linda Addison	11	Undergrad/Grad	—	Master	Doctor
Southeast Missouri State University, Cape Girardeau, Missouri		3	Undergrad/Grad	—	Master	—
Southern Illinois University, Carbondale, Illinois		4	Undergrad/Grad	—	Master	—
Southern Mississippi, University of, Hattiesburg, Mississippi	Dr. Frances A. Karnes	7	Grad	Certification	Master	Doctor
Southwestern Louisiana, University of, Lafayette, Louisiana		2	Grad	—	—	'
Tennessee, University of, Knoxville, Tennessee		1	Undergrad/Grad	Certification	Master	—
Texas A&M University, College Station, Texas	Dr. William R. Nash	2	Grad	—	Master	Doctor
Texas Tech University, Lubbock, Texas		2	Undergrad/Grad	—	—	—
Trinity College, Hartford, Connecticut		1	Undergrad/Grad	—	—	—
Tulane University, New Orleans, Louisiana		2	Undergrad/Grad	—	—	—
Utah State University, Logan, Utah		2	Undergrad/Grad	—	—	—
Walla Walla College, College Place, Washington		1	Undergrad	—	—	—
West Chester State College, West Chester, Pennsylvania		5	Undergrad/Grad	—	—	—
Western Carolina University, Cullowhee, North Carolina	Dr. Roy Cox	4	Undergrad/Grad	Certification	Master	—

continued

Table 9 (continued)

University/College	Professor	Courses	Level	Qualification	
Western Kentucky University Bowling Green, Kentucky		1	Undergrad/Grad	Certification	Master
Western Michigan University Kalamazoo, Michigan	Dr. Joseph J. Eisenbach	3	Grad	—	Master
Western State College Gunnison, Colorado		1	Undergrad/Grad	—	—
West Virginia University Morgantown, West Virginia		3	Grad	—	—
William and Mary, College of Williamsburg, Virginia		2	Grad	Certification	Master
William Carey College Hattiesburg, Mississippi		1	Grad	Certification	—
Winona State University Winona, Minnesota		1	Undergrad/Grad	—	—
Wisconsin, University of Milwaukee, Wisconsin		3	Grad	—	—
Wisconsin State University Platteville, Wisconsin		2	Undergrad/Grad	—	—
Wright State University Dayton, Ohio		2	Grad	—	Master
Wyoming, University of Laramie, Wyoming		1	Grad	Certification	—
Xavier University Cincinnati, Ohio		1	Undergrad	—	—

on full-time faculty to make the offerings. Summer workshops seemed to be quite common, with nearly 62 universities having workshops for teachers, 15 for gifted children, and 33 offered workshops for both groups. Undergraduate offerings were being made at 45 colleges, graduate offerings at 105 colleges, and 58 offerings were made at both levels. On preparation for degree and certification requirements, 40 institutions prepared teachers for state certification to teach gifted children, 49 offered the master's degree, and 12 offered doctor's programs; 15 institutions offered preparation toward both advanced degrees and certification. When compared to the findings of earlier survey of master and PhD programs in gifted education (*N/S LTI-G/T Bulletin,* 1976), which showed less than 30 colleges offering master's degrees and about 10 offering the PhD or EdD, the 1979 survey indicates that further growth in teacher preparation programs has taken place.

Expansion of current offerings on the gifted were anticipated by 77 institutions with 12 uncertain as to what else they might want to do. Additional information specific to what each of these colleges or universities offer can be found in (Table 9). Other sources of information on programs for the gifted can be obtained from the CEC/TAG/ERIC Clearinghouse on the subject of *Professional Training Programs in Special Education,* and from the recent N/S LTI announcements of graduate programs for the gifted. The 1977 summer issue of the *Gifted Child Quarterly* was specially devoted to the subject of training and a useful listing of current degree programs in gifted education by state and university was included. Information on nonrespondent universities and colleges offering degree programs on the gifted derived from these N/S LTI announcements and the *Gifted Child Quarterly* can be found in Table 10.

In a second survey, 54 questionnaires were sent to consultants for gifted and talented in each state as well as in the District of Columbia, the Virgin Islands, Guam, and Puerto Rico and fetched 35 returns. The questionnaire requested information about in-service training supported or provided by the state and other governments. The responses showed that 74% supported college or university training, 89% provided in-service workshops, and 91% supported state, local, and national conferences as sources of in-service training for their teachers. In addition, 7 states reported that they provided in-service training to their teachers by means of projects, demonstration centers, and in-service packages (Table 11).

CONSIDERATIONS IN TEACHER-PREPARATION PROGRAMS FOR THE GIFTED

One of the major concerns of any educator about teacher preparation relates to the suitability of the person who is to be prepared to teach children. Hence, many discussions about the subject begin with teacher characteristics and roles, appli-

Table 10   *Nonrespondent Universities/Colleges Offering Courses on Gifted Education*

University/College	Professor	Courses	Level		Qualification	
Alabama, University of Birmingham, Alabama	Dr. Gayle H. Gear	—	Grad	Certification	Master	—
Arizona, University of Tucson, Arizona	Dr. George Leshin	—	Grad	—	Master	—
Arizona State University Tempe, Arizona	Dr. Willard Abraham	—	Grad	Certification	Master	—
California State University Fresno, California	Dr. Peter Fast	—	Grad	—	Master	—
Columbia University New York, New York	Dr. Abraham J. Tannenbaum Dr. Harry A. Passow	—	Grad	—	Master	Doctor
District of Columbia, University of Washington, D.C.	Dr. Herbert Alf	—	—	—	—	—
Eastern Montana College Billings, Montana	Dr. C. Rockney Copple	—	Grad	—	Master	—
Georgia State University Atlanta, Georgia	Dr. Leonard J. Lucito	—	Grad	Certification	Master	Doctor
Kansas State University Manhattan, Kansas	Dr. Myrliss Hershey	—	Grad	Certification	Master	—
Michigan, University of Ann Arbor, Michigan	Dr. W. A. Ketcham	—	Grad	—	Master	—
New York College at Albany, State University of Albany, New York	Dr. Alexinia Y. Baldwin	—	Grad	—	Master	Doctor
New York College at Buffalo, State University of Buffalo, New York	Dr. Donald J. Treffinger	—	Grad	—	Master	—

Institution	Contact					
Northeastern Louisiana University, Monroe, Louisiana	Dr. Oliver Hensley	—	Grad	—	Master	Doctor
Northern Colorado, University of, Greeley, Colorado	Dr. Kenneth R. Seeley	—	Grad	—	Master	—
Ohio State University, Columbus, Ohio	Dr. Raymond H. Swassing	—	Grad	—	Master	Doctor
Oregon, University of, Eugene, Oregon	Dr. Fay Haisley	—	Grad	—	Master	—
Pennsylvania, University of, Philadelphia, Pennsylvania	Dr. Albert Oliver	—	Grad	—	Master	—
Santa Clara, University of, Santa Clara, California	Dr. Joyce A. Gerard	—	Grad	Certification	Master	—
Shippensburg State College, Shippensburg, Pennsylvania	Dr. James Payne	—	Grad	—	Master	—
South Alabama, University of, Mobile, Alabama	Dr. Marvin J. Gold	—	Grad Undergrad	Bachelor	—	—
Southern Connecticut State College, New Haven, Connecticut	Dr. Rudolph G. Pohl	—	Grad	—	Master	Specialist
Tennessee at Chattanooga, University of, Chattanooga, Tennessee	Dr. Caryl Taylor	—	Grad	—	Master	—
Utah, University of, Salt Lake City, Utah	Dr. Reed Merrill Dr. Calvin W. Taylor Dr. Joan Wolf	—	Grad	—	Master	Doctor
Virginia, University of, Charlottesville, Virginia	Dr. Virgil Ward	—	Grad	—	Master	Doctor
Washington, University of, Seattle, Washington	Dr. Maurice Freehill Dr. Mildred Kersh	—	Grad	—	Master	Doctor
Wayne State University, Detroit, Michigan	Dr. Thomas M. Buescher	—	Grad	—	Master	Specialist

Table 11 Opportunities Provided/Supported by States and Nonstates (Only Those Responding Are Listed)

State/Nonstate	College/University Courses	Workshops	Conferences	Other
Alaska		x	x	
Arizona			x	
Colorado	x	x	x	
Connecticut	x	x	x	
Delaware	x	x	x	
District of Columbia		x	x	
Georgia			x	x[1]
Hawaii	x	x	x	
Idaho	x	x	x	x[2]
Indiana	x	x	x	
Kansas		x	x	
Kentucky	x	x		x[3]
Louisiana		x	x	
Maine	x	x	x	
Maryland	x	x	x	
Michigan	x	x	x	
Minnesota	x	x	x	x[3]
Mississippi	x	x	x	
Montana	x	x	x	x[4]
Nevada	x	x	x	
New Hampshire	x	x	x	
New Jersey	x	x	x	
New Mexico	x	x		
North Dakota	x	x	x	
Ohio	x	x	x	x[5]
Oklahoma	x	x	x	
Rhode Island	x	x	x	
South Carolina	x	x	x	
Texas	x	x	x	
Utah		x		
Vermont	x	x	x	
Virginia			x	
Washington			x	x[6]
Wisconsin	x	x	x	
Wyoming	x	x	x	

[1]Georgia provides staff development workshops in the area of in-service training.
[2]Idaho is developing in-service training packages to be tested in 1979.
[3]Kentucky and Minnesota did not specify additional state provisions for in-service training.
[4]Montana has federal demonstration sites as part of its in-service training.
[5]Ohio's state consultant provides technical assistance to schools, including in-service training.
[6]Washington's in-service training program is aided by federal funding.

cable not only to teachers in general but to teachers of the gifted in particular. Another important consideration is the variety of giftedness currently perceived, which must have significant implications for any teacher-preparation program. Furthermore, attention must be directed not only to the need of determining the nature and level of content to be acquired—first, by the teacher and, then, transmitted to the gifted student—but also the procedures and learning operations that are associated with the generation of new knowledge and skills, with which gifted students need to be equipped if they are to achieve excellence and eventual eminence. It would be a sad omission not to recognize the interaction of these several dimensions in the learning situation. The better prepared teachers are about events that arise from these dimensions, the better will they be able to monitor their behavior and that of their gifted charges toward productive results.

TEACHER QUALITIES

Most of the comments on the numerous listings of descriptive characteristics of teachers of the gifted are far from complimentary. For instance, Gowan and Demos (1964) point to the lack of scientific study that has given rise to such lists and say that, for the most part, they are rooted to armchair speculation and could apply equally well to a practical nurse, an airline stewardess, or a sympathetic curator in a zoo. The fact is that, in attempting to describe a teacher for the gifted, various authorities, pupils, and parents have tended to picture a paragon of paragons relative to pedagogical virtues (Gold, 1965). Gallagher (1975) refers to listings of attributes of the teacher of the gifted as one of the favorite passtime activities of educators that borders on nonsense rather than on evidence. Gold (1979) concurs with Gallagher's observation, noting that a search of the literature reveals very little meaningful research on the characteristics that are unique to the teacher of the gifted.

Professionals with the formal designation of teacher of the gifted are as new as the planned attempts to produce them. Like so many aspects of gifted education that have been affected by broadened concepts of giftedness, hypotheses relating to the effectiveness of new programs, developmental processes, and philosophical speculations about what qualities can be expected of teachers of the gifted await scientific investigation. It may be that the survey approach to obtain data about the teacher of the gifted can be complemented by studies that are carefully designed to test the functional effectiveness of observed or speculated characteristics.

Table 12 attempts to order the many lists of characteristics presented by numerous studies and cited by critics in a way that minimizes repetition. The characteristics are differentiated as personal and professional and the information source for each characteristic is given. Some of the characteristics listed are common virtues of all good teachers (e.g., alertness, common sense, understand-

Table 12 Characteristics Expected of Teachers of Gifted Students

Personal	Source	Professional	Source
Accomplishments (broad range of skills)	13	Ability to direct students to achieve full potential and to encourage students to want to learn	2,4
Achievement needs are high	11	Admired	1
Alertness	1	Behavior (consistent)	6
Common sense	1	Caring, sympathetic, sensitive to student problems	2,7,14
Considerate, friendly, kindly	1,6,7	Cooperative	6
Constructive	1	Democratic	6,11
Creative (flexible, original)	8,2,6	Disposition good	6
Curious	1	Enjoys teaching	5,14
Decisive	1,8	Enthusiastic	3
Emotional balance	8	Experienced	3,11
Good health (energetic, physically superior, vigorous)	8	Fair, impartial	5,6,10
Hobbies (interesting)	8	Firm but not strict	5,12
Honest	12	High standards of achievement	1
Humor (good sense of)	5,6,8	High standards of behavior	1
Imaginative	1	Individual development encouraged	2,3
Independent thinker	13	Inspiring	1
Intellectual superiority (stature, acumen, curiosity)	2,3,13,14		

382

Characteristic	Reference
Intellectual growth sought	11
Intuitive	1
Love for learning	13
Patient	6
Positive	1
Resourceful	1
Self-confident	i
Thoughtful	1
Tolerant of new and different ideas	1
Understanding	1,5
Versatile, wide variety of interests	1,6,10,14
Intellectual growth through teaching	11
Interests varied (literature, arts, culture)	11
Knowledge of theories of learning	10
Likes working with children even during free time	8
Mature	11
Parent surrogate	8
Philosophy of education clear and consistent	10
Plucky in the face of teacher frustrations	7
Published articles	8
Recognition and praise used	1
Respect for children's goals and dreams	7
Responsibility among students encouraged	5
Sensitive to creative efforts of others	2
Supportive of innovative programs	11
Teaching proficiency (course content is well known, interesting, well organized, stimulating)	4,10,11
Thinking encouraged	
Trusts students, trusted by them	12

1. Abraham (1958)
2. Passow (1955)
3. Conant (1958)
4. French (1959)
5. Davis (1954)
6. Witty (1950)
7. Goodrich and Knapp (1952)
8. Brandwein (1955)
9. Neivert (1955)
10. Gallagher (1975)
11. Bishop (1968)
12. Torrance (1975)
13. Gold (1965)
14. Maker (1975)

ing, admired, consistent behavior, knowledge of theories of learning, and the various categories of teaching proficiency). How, then, can we distinguish traits of the good teacher from the teacher of the gifted. This is not an easy task and may, in fact, prove impractical. Gowan and Demos (1964) have suggested teacher effectiveness as an important dimension although recognizing the difficulty of identifying valid criteria. Some approaches for measuring teacher performance show a shift from teacher characteristics to the study of teacher behavior (e.g., Flanagan's critical incident technique [1949]; Amidon & Flanders's system of interaction analysis [1971]; or by means of rating scales Gowan [1955]) in an attempt, on the one hand, to assess teaching performance through authority and peer figures and, on the other hand, through tests of ability, background knowledge of subject, personality, interests, emotional stability, and pupil gain. Although Gowan and Demos (1964) direct our attention to several qualities that a teacher of the gifted can be expected to have in more abundance than a teacher of the average student (see Table 12). Gowan and Demos (1964) make a particular point of emphasizing inspiration as the key to the gifted student's striving toward excellence and by means of which "the torch of education is passed individually from a great teacher to each child" (p. 391). To them, "the best teacher . . . is not he who knows the most or teaches the most or counsels the most, but he who inspires the most" (p. 391).

Terman and Oden's (1959) report of teacher ratings of their gifted subjects and Torrance's (Torrance & Myers, 1970) teacher ratings of the ideal-pupil checklist, aimed at identifying the creatively gifted, provide the following 29 characteristics that are common to those listed as characteristics of teachers of the gifted. In this way a list of the traits that both intellectually gifted and creative children and their teachers have in common (except for the one related to teaching proficiency, which is peculiar to the professional educator) is attained:

1. Accomplishments: broad range of skills; well read.
2. Achievement needs are high; desires to excel.
3. Common sense.
4. Considerate, friendly, kindly, warm.
5. Caring, sympathetic, tender, sensitive to problems.
6. Creative (flexible, original).
7. Disposition is good, cheerful; mild mannered; permanence of mood, emotional balance.
8. Enthusiastic, excited about learning, exuberant.
9. Fair, impartial.
10. Firm but not strict; does not stand for foolishness.
11. Health is good; physically attractive, physically superior; energetic, vigorous.
12. High standards of achievement; critical of mistakes; works hard.

13. Honest, truthful.
14. Humor (good sense of).
15. Imaginative; lively imagination.
16. Individual development encouraged; eager to help when needed; thinks each person is an important individual.
17. Intellectual superiority (stature, acumen, curiosity); general intelligence high, intellectually brilliant.
18. Love for learning; intellectual growth sought.
19. Patient.
20. Recognition and praise used, generous with praise.
21. Respect for ideas, goals, and dreams.
22. Self-confident.
23. Sensitive to creative efforts of others; takes pride in accomplishments.
24. Tolerant; accepts new and different ideas.
25. Teaching proficiency (course content well known; interesting, makes interesting assignments; well organized; can usually make points clear; stimulating).
26. Thinking encouraged.
27. Trust (teacher trusts students and is trusted by them).
28. Understanding; tries to understand others' behavior.
29. Versatile; wide variety of interests.

This list, however, also needs to include aesthetic, social, and psychomotor traits of excellence before it can be said to reflect a fairly representative list of observable traits of teachers of the gifted.

The question now arises about the extent to which one can and needs to use this information to select suitable candidates for professional training, bearing in mind that, for the most part, those who enter as trainees already have general teaching qualifications. Maker (1976) recommends several criteria for the selection of teachers of the gifted, distinguishing between those qualities that should be expected of candidates for training programs and those qualities that the candidates would have acquired or developed by the time of college graduation. Minimum entry criteria of such candidates require that they have (1) knowledge of the variety of giftedness (as defined by the six USOE categories), (2) the ability to relate to those they will teach, and (3) the disposition to be open to change. These traits appear essential if the candidate is to communicate effectively with students and to adapt the special teaching approaches suitable for the gifted to the shifting needs of students. As minimum exit criteria, Maker recommends that graduating teachers of the gifted should know about those traits peculiar to the talent possessed and should be able and willing to serve as guide rather than as dictator as well as to use techniques that individualize instruction and facilitate emotional and social needs of gifted students. As for subgroups of gifted students, Maker points out that we know much about the intellectually, academically, and creatively able but little about those who are able in the visual performing arts, leadership, and psychomotor areas. She, then, goes on to suggest entry and exit traits required of these three subgroups.

The intellectually and academically gifted
    Entry requirements of trainees
        At least above average intelligence
        Possession of self-confidence and emotional stability
    Exit requirements of trainees
        Ability to use teaching competence to develop high-thought processes in students
        Extensive knowledge of basic concepts in a subject field of specialization and in related fields
        Command of machine and materials, which can be effectively used in teaching area

Creatively gifted
    Entry requirements of trainees
        High regard for imaginative ideas
        Respect for individual potentiality
        Recognize responsibility of the teacher and the group to the child
        Enhance student's self-image
    Exit requirements of trainees
        Provide a warm, safe, and permissive atmosphere
        Learn to use teaching techniques that further the development of creative thinking abilities applied to curriculum
        Develop creative problem skills

Methods to assess if candidates satisfy these requirements are also suggested and include:

1. Observe a candidate in a real or simulated learning situation.
2. Administer various personality and attitudinal inventories as well as locally constructed checklists relevant to the situation for which information is needed.
3. Use value clarification techniques.
4. Arrange for interviews by gifted students, parents, and teachers.

Maker (1976) emphasizes the use of a variety of techniques to evaluate the prospective teacher and shows a strong preference for use of the first of the above methods. Although it is generally feasible to apply these various criteria in the selection of candidates for teaching positions following training, it is not practical for the purpose of selecting students for enrollment in college courses. That is, unless some special funds make scholarships available for the training of special kinds of teachers, for instance, the federally funded consortium at Columbia University in New York City, which provides doctoral training for highly able student-teachers, or the creative leadership project at the State University College at Buffalo, New York.

APPROACHES TO TEACHER PREPARATION

Considerable attention has been given to the characteristics of teachers of the gifted but not to specific preparation of them—an observation R. A. Martinson made several years ago (cited in Marland, 1972a). At the time, however, teacher preparation programs relative to the gifted were few and scattered (Laird, 1971). Today, many more institutions of higher learning are involved in offering not only individual courses but also courses in an academic sequence that lead to a degree (see pp. 367–379). French's (1959) early survey of special education courses offered at colleges and universities revealed that 2 out of 122 offered a sequence of courses on the gifted and that of the 76 colleges that offered one or more courses in special education—totaling about 800 courses—only 34 dealt with the gifted. The picture over 20 years later has altered considerably. Compatible with vigorous public interest, the course offerings on the gifted have become more numerous and varied, with many institutions now offering preparation toward both graduate and undergraduate degrees in the area of the gifted. Of the 3000 colleges and universities sent enquiries about what provisions they had for the training of teachers in the area of the gifted, 134 responded positively. An analysis of their course offerings revealed 35 of 287 courses, or 12.2% were at the undergraduate level, whereas there was a preponderance of graduate level courses—252 courses, or 87.8%. The frequency with which these courses are offered are shown in Table 13. The top six courses are titled: Teaching the Gifted and Talented, Psychology of the Gifted, Introduction to Education of the Gifted and Talented, Internship/Practicum/Student Teaching, Curriculum for the Gifted and Methods and Measurement for the Gifted. The current variety of offerings is another noticeable factor. Different emphases can also be seen in course offerings in creativity, imagination, underachievement, learning disabilities, and the disadvantaged gifted.

Although the number of courses offered are many more today, there are only six major areas covered, with some overlap. Maker (1976) has identified these major areas and their course content:

Nature and Needs of the Gifted: *The content consists of topics such as characteristics, problems, myths perpetuated about gifted and creative children, psychological considerations, and identification measures.*

Materials and Methods in the Education of the Gifted: *Content usually centers*

Table 13 *Frequency of Graduate and Undergraduate Courses Offered on the Gifted and Talented*

Course Titles	Undergraduate	Graduate	Combine
Teaching the Gifted and Talented	8	55	63
Psychology of the Gifted	11	29	40
Introduction to Education of the Gifted and Talented	11	27	38
Internship/Practicum/Student Teaching	—	33	33
Curriculum for the Gifted	1	23	24
Methods and Measurement for the Gifted	2	19	21
Creative Problem Solving	—	10	10
Workshops on the Gifted and Talented	—	10	10
Research on the Gifted	—	7	7
Creativity/Developing Creative Talent	1	6	7
Nature/Nurture of the Gifted	—	6	6
Creative Expression for the Gifted	—	4	4
Individual Study	1	3	4
Special Topics in Education of the Gifted and Talented	—	4	4
Guidance for the Gifted	—	4	4
Mainstreaming the Gifted	—	3	3
Critique of Literature on the Gifted	—	2	2
Symbolic Aesthetic Processes	—	2	2
Learning Difficulties	—	1	1
The Disadvantaged Gifted	—	1	1
Teaching Mathematics to the Gifted	—	1	1
The Bright Underachiever	—	1	1
Psychology of the Creative Imagination	—	1	1
Total	35	252	287

around the most appropriate instructional strategies and materials to be utilized with the gifted. In many cases, time is spent in designing materials and in developing appropriate curricula units. Emphasis, in many instances, is also placed on techniques for individualizing instruction for the gifted.

Education of the Gifted: *A course of this type is usually concerned with exploring various programs and administrative arrangements currently in use in schools as well as other related issues.*

Seminars in the Education of the Gifted: *Seminars usually involve a less structured approach through which students explore topics of interest to them as well as controversial issues in the field. Independent study and related techniques are often utilized.*

Practicum in the Education of the Gifted: *Practica usually involve either a variety of practical experiences with gifted children or one in-depth experience, depending on the interests and needs of the students. Examples of some of the experiences provided are: student teaching in a program for the gifted; internships with consultants, administrators, and programs for the gifted; visitations to several programs for the gifted, observation of gifted students, including the writing of case studies and internships in state and federal programs for the gifted. (p. 22)*

PRESERVICE TEACHER PREPARATION

By and large, formal course offerings at colleges and universities teach to some qualifications, which may take the form of a degree, certification, or a combination of the two (see pp. 367–379).

Programs of teacher preparation of the gifted are offered by a variety of college departments, especially by departments of special education and educational psychology. The emphases in such courses, even though the content is quite similar, may be different according to the orientation of the department that is offering the program. Generally, these programs are leveled at preparing teaching personnel. One such exception is the program now offered by the Department of Educational Psychology at Mississippi University, which not only prepares candidates to be teachers but also to be psychologists of the gifted. Thus, the master's level, a student develops competencies of a psychometrist; at the doctoral level, this extends to the development of additional background and skills in educational and school psychology. With a greater awareness of the many needs of the gifted—ranging from identification of multiple talent, planning learning, and facing problems to giving guidance—a candidate with dual preparation in teaching and psychology is in a better position to serve a combination of these needs. Although many departments of educational psychology use the same basic courses and may even add a few more courses in their training programs, they conceptualize the program as one that prepares teachers. One of the best and most comprehensive teacher programs directed by a department of educational psychology is at the University of Georgia under the direction of E. P. Torrance. The program prepares candidates for master's and doctor's degrees with specialization in the education of gifted children. It offers at least 10 different courses on the gifted that contain such content as characteristics, learning disabilities, identification and assessment, supervision, and guidance as well as seminars, internships, and practica. The program includes up to 100 graduate quarter hours of electives. The gifted program at the University of South Florida, housed in the Department of Special Education, aims to prepare teachers of gifted children by offering courses that include the development of skills in using tests and test data, group dynamics, guidance, creative thinking, practice in the use of cognitive and affective skills, and action research. See Table 13 for further information on the subject. A few of the colleges that offer such programs have professors who have published on the subject, among them are: Johns Hopkins (Julian C. Stanley), University of Connecticut (Joseph S. Renzulli), Purdue University (John F. Feldhusen), University of South Florida (Dorothy Sisk), State University College at Buffalo, New York (Donald J. Treffinger), Columbia University (A. Harry Passow and Abraham J. Tannenbaum), University of Georgia (E. P. Torrance, Catherine B. Bruch, and Mary M. Frasier), and Mississippi State University (Joe Khatena) (Gowan, Khatena, & Torrance, 1979).

It appears to be important to have some rationale for the planning of the curriculum for these programs. In the main, programs at most, if not all, universities have evolved from one or two course offerings that were in the category of electives to programs leveled at preparing teachers of the gifted and, to a lesser extent, to programs with strong emphasis on psychology and guidance that lead to certification or to a degree. Colleges and universities instituting new programs have a good chance to decide what thrust they want to make and can design their programs to meet demands in a global way, taking as examples the experiences of other institutions of higher learning. New directions that pertain to the gifted, especially those of the late 1960s and the years of the 1970s, should be used to inform the design of new programs or suggest refinements of older ones. The move should be away from course offerings to the conceptualization of an overall plan that will meet the needs of gifted education. The following elements should be taken into account: (1) an expanded concept of intellect and talent and, more generally, giftedness; (2) measurement approaches that go beyond the IQ and standardized achievement test to include other formal and informal procedures that will allow not only for the screening of multiple talent but also that will take into account cultural diversity; (3) a better understanding of intellectual development that takes into account both cognitive and nonintellective factors in the context of developmental state theory, which at present, in the main, sadly lacking in the curricular programs on the gifted; (4) an appropriate emphasis on creativity, creative imagination, creative problem solving, creativity as occurring at various developmental phases, creativity in the context of culture, and creativity as the key to the productivity of giftedness with provisions for its enhancement; (5) the proper emphasis on all five Guilfordian mental operations that will allow for the delicate mesh of process and content in education; (6) an expanded concept of underachievement that includes not only schooling variables but such factors as cultural diversity and sex as well; (7) problems peculiar to the gifted, the role of stress and methods to cope with it relating to guidance and counseling with due regard to differential and developmental guidance; (8) curriculum and methodology relevant to gifted education that needs to be placed in the context of process education whose roots lie in the systems of J. P. Guilford, B. S. Bloom, Jean Piaget, J. S. Bruner, S. J. Parnes, E. P. Torrance, and J. C. Gowan on the one hand and in learning theories on the other hand; (9) motivational theories and approaches that find application to the gifted; (10) the specialized knowledge necessary to arrange educational experiences for special groups of gifted students, including those in the visual and performing arts as well as in leadership and psychomotor areas of abilities, those of culturally diverse background, those with special difficulties or disabilities, and the like; (11) the large community resources and support personnel and systems; the variety of technical and educational resources together with the skills needed to use those that are available; (12) the availability of differential training program models; the development of skills to do both basic and applied research on various aspects of the gifted so that not only will there be an awareness of the most recent trends in the field but also the disposition and competence to generate new ones.

These and related considerations should provide the broad theoretical framework needed for planning courses for a program. To approach program designing in this way is to ensure effective offerings, which, when in need of refinements or additions, can be made relative to the preparation program as a whole.

IN-SERVICE TEACHER PREPARATION

Unlike the basic college preparation program of teachers of the gifted, the in-service program approach attempts to enhance initial preparation of professionals who have already learned the job of teaching gifted students; to provide brief training episodes for some special purpose, like updating training by bringing to participants recent developments in the field; to prepare professionals to write state plans and proposals for funding; to produce a cadre of leaders; to provide examples of some of the best innovations recently introduced; and to inform paraprofessionals about matters pertaining to gifted children as well as ways by which they can be supportive of both children and educators or act as agents of change in legislation and its implementation. The delivery systems of in-service education for teachers of the gifted include summer institutes, demonstration projects, service centers, technical assistance, and related support activities (Gallagher, 1974; Maker, 1976; Ward, 1979).

Summer Institutes

The summer institute is an effective in-service approach where various groups involved in gifted education, including gifted students, can be conveniently brought together. The purpose of an institute is to provide training that unites textbook materials with field experiences to serve a variety of needs, like priming a team of teachers about to begin a program for the gifted in a school setting for the first time, keeping teachers informed of latest developments, enhancing or refining teachers already involved in teaching gifted children, and providing the opportunity for interactive experiences among professionals, parents, and gifted students who come together at an institute.

Gowan's editorial comments in his introduction to the "Teachers and Teacher Training" section in *Educating the Ablest* (Gowan et al., 1979) arises from 10 years' experience directing the San Ferando Valley State College summer workshops where teachers received training while teaching gifted students. Drawing from this experience, he points to the significance of integrating textbook learning with field experience that calls for (1) productive interaction of teachers, teacher trainees, counselor trainees, aides, parents, and gifted children; (2) inclusion in lectures and new cognitive models—like J. P. Guilford's structure of intellect, B. S. Bloom's taxonomy of educational objectives in the cognitive domain along with D. R. Krathwohl's taxonomy in the affective domain, Jean Piaget's cognitive developmental stages, Erik Erikson's eight stages of man, J. C. Gowan's developmental stage theory, J. S. Bruner's views on process education, and the Osborn-Parnes creative problem-solving technique; (3) the affective growth and development of staff and trainees; (4) training in developmental guidance that stems from developmental stage theory; and (5) paraprofessional support.

Maker (1976) gives examples of summer institutes: (1) eight institutes conducted by E. P. Torrance that aim to develop an increased awareness in graduate trainees to the creative positives of socioeconomically disadvantaged students, the skills to make use of these positives, favorable and realistic attitudes toward this disadvantaged group, and an increase in the repertoire of teaching skills within the context of university-course credit; and (2) the Illinois gifted programs, sponsored institutes on creative problem solving after the Osborn-Parnes model and on developing leadership. The N/S LTI on the Gifted and Talented continues to conduct two-week intensive institutes that are not soley designed for teachers but are leveled at developing cadres of leaders and conducting activities that include components related to the acquisition of knowledge, demonstrations, activities, interaction with peers, decision making, familiarization with the processes of change, and the like (Ward, 1979). Summer institutes may last for a few days or may continue for a 6- to 8-week period. Institutes may be initiated by any of a number of agencies, including the college, the local district or state, federal or state funded projects, of which the N/S LTI is one. For other examples of summer institutes, the reader is referred to the 1979 issue of the *Gifted Child Quarterly* on special projects and programs.

Demonstration Projects as Centers

A demonstration center is a vehicle of training that generally relates to innovative projects or models that have been found successful or are currently being tried. It is a good source of information and acts as a resource center for visiting trainees. The extent to which demonstration centers are viable, inventive, and dynamic is the extent to which they can serve as good examples to trainees in search of fresh approaches to gifted education or to provide an operational model for schools to observe or adopt if found effective.

Demonstration centers are usually supported by state or federal funds and may last anywhere from 1 to 3 years (5 years if extensions of funding permit). These centers are located in many parts of the country and are particularly abundant in California and Illinois. Several examples of these centers are described by Maker (1976); others can be found in the 1979 issue of the *Gifted Child Quarterly* on special projects and programs. Ward (1979) regards the demonstration project more as a failure than a success as a vehicle for teacher preparation.

Service Centers

Unlike the demonstration project, which generally is a trial for some innovation, the service center is a vehicle for providing technical assistance for the training of teachers and has the capability of drawing resources rapidly and effectively. Its strength lies in the ability to deliver quality goods, which may well be an important contribution in accelerating the refinement of the training repetoire of teachers of the gifted. Like the demonstration project, service centers derive their support from state and federal funds. For further information see Maker's (1976) account and the descriptions of service efforts in the special projects issue of the *Gifted Child Quarterly* (1979).

Technical Assistance Development System

Gallagher (1974) has written about the relative ineffectiveness of consultation services offered in the traditional way. An expert is invited to act as consultant to a workshop, institute, or project for one day and is gone the next, giving his or her *all* (so to speak) to the client rather than addressing the specific problems and needs that prompted the invitation in the first place. A viable alternative can be found in the technical assistance development system although not originally developed with the gifted in mind but for other special education groups. The system operates to provide on request assistance to local programs relative to some local problem. The system is staffed not only with educators familiar with gifted education but also with those who have expertise in such areas as curriculum development, program evaluation, or stimulation of creative activities. A technical assistance plan comprises (1) a needs assessment, (2) a formal contract of agreement that relates to personnel time and the manner of the delivery of the services, and (3) a talent bank that stores all kinds of information about the personnel and resources that are available. Gallagher believes that this approach to the training of teachers of the gifted can be superior to the standard preservice training model, especially in lieu of the fact that large numbers of qualified teachers are needed as soon as possible. Although this approach has merit and in many ways may even prove to be a superior organizational approach to brief workshops, consultative services of a one-shot-deal nature can hardly be said to be the alternative to a college or university education that the preservice training approach can provide. Ward (1979). Although commending the technical assistance development system as a means of upgrading education for the gifted and and talented, does not see how it can have more impact than preservice agencies.

Related Activities

In addition to the four kinds of popular in-service approaches described, there are several other useful related techniques. These include workshops in which invited experts share their ideas and opinions about the gifted and talented, point to directions that may be taken to develop program alternatives, bring to the notice of participants what is going on elsewhere for purposes of envigoration and modeling, and make known advances in theory and practice that the most current research has revealed; administrators, supervisors, and other professionals with experience in gifted education can also be brought in to advise and give ideas to teachers on the approaches that can be taken to enhance teaching content and methodology; teaching and demonstrations by gifted teachers can bring to notice an effective instructional technique or make known the availability of facilitation materials and resources and their use; and conversations can occur with indiviual teachers or in groups as follow-up work. In-school training is yet another approach of value. College professionals are actively involved in ongoing projects and can be invited to schools to conduct on-site a few weekly seminars on selected topics or problems. Another viable arrangement is one where several schools may get together and jointly arrange and support anyone of the above activities. Both Maker (1976) and Ward (1979) have suggested such activities as the committee approach, monthly training sessions, the team-study approach, teacher institutes, classes and study groups, individual reading and informal conversations among teachers—all contributory to in-service training. Ward emphasizes the importance of the presentation of concepts, materials, biases, and related information over mode of presentation.

Renzulli (1977a) suggests the relevance of streamlining the organization of workshops through his instructional management system (IMS), a model for developing in-service training modules for use by college faculty, consultants, or classroom teachers assuming leadership roles in staff development. The use of IMS is expected to prevent those haphazard approaches, as in other workshops, that do not allow for continuous development of participants. Renzulli regards the IMS short-term workshop as one of the few viable alternatives that can be used to meet the needs of gifted students. The IMS is leveled at assisting trainers to design, develop, and disseminate information about teaching strategies and instructional materials.

The IMS has three major objectives: (1) to compress much highly relevant information into a relatively short training period; (2) to provide a structure of knowledge about the topic or teaching strategy presented; and (3) to provide a series of packaged workshops that can be easily used by other trainers. Renzulli discusses four general types of informational content of IMS: (1) its rationale; (2) its packaged workshop activities (theoretical information, demonstration activities, samples of exemplary teaching, lists of exemplary programs, catalogs and descriptions of available materials, and materials' evaluation forms); (3) its student materials (no-fail introductory activities, student information about the IMS, guidelines for productivity in IMS, and advanced training opportunities and resources); and (4) its program evaluation. Renzulli perceives that it is by using the IMS that we can go beyond workshops that are merely informative and entertaining to provide gifted students with the tools for continuous learning and involvement far ahead of the single lesson or activity.

CONCLUSIONS

The post-sputnik response and the national expression for the felt needs of special educational opportunities precipated into legislation in the past decade slow but increasing funding for gifted education in the United States. National and state efforts have envigorated various dimensions of gifted and talented education all over the country. The inclusion of professional educators and parents in interactive and support roles and state and federal expressions of achieving an American dream toward excellence has just begun and will continue to prepare the way for one of the richest harvests of talent in this century before long.

The agency that is providing both the thrust and momentum at the federal level is the Office of the Gifted and Talented. Through N/S LTI and the CEC/TAG/ERIC computer services, the agency is not only disseminating information rapidly and effectively to reach a widely interested American public but has also created (and will continue to create) cadres of leaders organized in a newwork that will undoubtedly order local opinion and effort and continue to inaugurate and sustain special opportunities for the gifted and talented. Experience has confirmed that if a program is to be successful and continuing, it must be the result of the combined commitment and press of both local initiative (including professionals, educators, and parents as well as local education agencies) and the state agency (voluntarily or, if necessary, compelled by legislation to enact financial appropriations) to support attempts to provide special opportunities for gifted children at the local levels.

We are well aware of the meager beginnings in terms of adequately trained teachers for the purpose of implementing educational opportunities for gifted children. However, reorientation and envigoration of the states and their universities and colleges to the pressing need to produce qualified personnel for the task at hand has led to a variety of teacher-preparation offerings, which come under the categories of preservice and in-service training programs. Preservice training is concerned with preparing teachers for degrees, from the bachelor's to the doctorate, that may or may not include certification; in-service training is concerned with the enhancement of the preparation of qualified and experienced teachers in various matters pertaining to gifted education. Programs for this purpose will continue to make viable the implementation of special provisions for the gifted, with increasing excellence both in the preparation phase and in the delivery phase following training.

11

EXPANDING
HORIZONS

OVERVIEW

This chapter focuses on the emergence of the recognition for multidimensional giftedness, an area in which measurement correlates are yet incomplete and whose implementation is not without problem. Creativity as an escalating and transforming force of giftedness is seen as significant. The potency of creative imagination imagery as a precursor to new insights and discoveries in the arts as well as the sciences is recognized. Intellectual and creative development are seen as both continuous and discrete, and guidance is regarded as preventative and developmental. Recognition is given to an expanded concept of underachievement and the unique problems associated with special groups; emphasis is on education that gives proper place to accelerative enrichment, to process-curricula integration and to individualization of curricula and study. Another concern is future-oriented thrusts to meet adaptation to unpredictable changes by means of envigorating educational arrangements that go beyond the present boundaries of ordered curricula and methodology. To this is added the need for harnessing intrinsic motivational forces relative to competence, incongruity-dissonnance, feedback for feedforward processing, and the need satisfaction gained from esteem to actualization that is inherent in creative ways of learning. Finally, we perceive the conversion of peripheral innovative projects and programs to the central curriculum of education and the expansion of a variety of benefits from national and local support agencies as other necessary developments.

CHAPTER OUTLINE

INTRODUCTION

Formal education for the gifted is a 20th century phenomenon that has found a focus in events of the past 25 years or so. True, there was some recognition of excellence at various times in the history of civilization, but this was idiosyncratic and occasional, more often occurring after than during the lifetime of eminence. For the most part, there was resistance to those who would be different or to those who would not follow the norm. Society saw the gifted as a threat to their accustomed way of life and, in defense, would react in ways that would squelch talent. The few who saw importance and value in sustaining talent acted as patrons or mentors, and, in so doing, supported, protected, and facilitated the emergence of numerous great works to the continued delight of the many generations that followed. There were those less fortunate, for lack of patronage or mentorship, who succeeded in the face of impossible odds by sheer brilliance and grit, but there were those, too, who, overcome by adverse conditions, never made their mark in this world.

There were all kinds of gifted people around, but few had anything to do with facilitating their talent growth during the formative years of their lives. The compelling urgency of their talents directed their energies to surface and gained them recognition. They often did not know the real reasons why they found more problems than their fellows; they were nagged by the spirit of genius to actualize, even in the face of almost insurmountable difficulties; they prepared themselves for the eminence that was to follow; and they left behind a true wealth that is now

398

ours. There were brilliant politicians and statespersons; eminent orators, thinkers, musicians, and artists; literary giants; engineers; inventors of excellence; and others who, by their achievements and performance, have made a difference in the lives of their fellows and in the world inhabited by them. They became known and recognized as gifted people, but little was known about the nature and function of giftedness, the variety of abilities related to it, or the extent to which the environment held influence over talent and its expression until the rise of mental testing and its theoretical origins.

CHANGING CONCEPTIONS OF GIFTEDNESS

We have seen conceptual changes about mental functioning during the past 50 years that have moved from the position of an unchanging intelligence to the position that intelligence is malleable to some extent by experience; from a unidimensional to a multidimensional theory of intelligence; from intelligence that is native to an informational theory of intelligence; from a global intelligence comprising verbal and nonverbal components involving cognition, memory, reasoning, and, to a negligible extent, judgment to a three-dimensional interactive intellect model that comprises operations, content, and products combined to reflect the presence of at least 120 intellectual abilities. The mental operations of the structure of intellect go beyond the ones mentioned and include divergent production and evaluative thinking abilities. In the content dimension, the behavioral component gives due place to an area of mental functioning that is lacking in mental testing although earlier recognized as social intelligence. J. P. Guilford (1967, 1977) points to the relatively small place that classes occupy in mental tests as well as to the near neglect or omission of transformation and implications of the product dimension. Unlike other theoretical models of intelligence that subscribe to a relatively unchanging mental function, the structure of intellect offers a potent frame of reference and a tool for educating intellectual abilities and for maximizing their development and output. The structure of intellect provides what Guilford has called a kind of grammar for all thinking. Although it operationalizes intellectual functioning in a way that allows for more systematic measurement, it does not directly provide a place for the emotive-motivational dimension that is so important to divergent production more narrowly and creative thinking more broadly. Moreover, visual and auditory senses that find place in the figural-content dimension may in time be extended to include other sensory dimensions—especially the tactile and motoric—which may enter as test items beyond just the visual. We have also seen the potency of the model as its components are organized in a generic creative-problem-solving model. Guilford's model, more than any other on intellectual functioning, has pushed back the boundaries of thought on the intellect, and its full significance may only be realized with the turn of the next century.

THE U.S. OFFICE OF EDUCATION (USOE) CATEGORIES OF GIFTEDNESS

It is quite well recognized that giftedness is not to be equated with intelligence or intellectual abilities in themselves although these may come into play to a greater or lesser degree according to the talent potential and the kind of operation it is required to perform. The deliberations of those involved with the gifted resulted in 1970 in the identification of six broad areas of giftedness, of which general intellectual ability or intelligence is only one. It was recognized that specific academic aptitude, creative or productive thinking , leadership ability, visual and performing arts ability, and psychomotor ability (now discontinued as a category of giftedness by USOE) were five areas of giftedness. It is important that the federal government has given recognition to these areas of giftedness because prior to 1970 giftedness tended to be equated with general intelligence alone. This expanded concept of giftedness will soon find its way into legislation in all states and be implemented both in identification-selection and provision of specialized educational opportunities.

GENERAL INTELLECTUAL ABILITY

To pause a moment for a fresh look at the six USOE categories of giftedness, we notice that, in spite of the fact that in 1970 20 years had passed since the structure of intellect was made public, the policy makers were still clinging to the concept of general intelligence as an index of intellectual giftedness. It would have seemed more appropriate to have offered intellectual abilities as an alternative index, to say the least. Of course, the judgment to have general intellectual ability as a category of giftedness is rooted in well-established tradition and practice as well as the highly trained personnel that implement the testing of it. There is need for some reeducation of psychometrists, whose preparation limits them to perceive giftedness in terms of intelligence only. The validity of this is now repeatedly questioned, even as the sole criteria of intellectual giftedness. And an understanding is developing of the significance of having an operational-informational theory of intelligence that can reveal multiple intellectual abilities.

SPECIFIC ACADEMIC APTITUDE

The concept of specific academic aptitude as a category of giftedness is rooted to the recognition Spearman (1927) gives to specific abilities, in his two-factor theory of intelligence which is subsumed in the verbal-educational component of Vernon's (1927) hierarchical structure of human abilities. Aptitude, unlike achievement, is potential and its identification should serve as a predictor of certain kinds of learning, generally in the school-subject areas; achievement refs to measured outcomes of acquired learning. If it is a predictor index that is wanted, then, we should use the information derived from some measure of intellect or its relevant component; if a performance index is needed, then, a standardized test in a subject area should be used. However, what appears to be needed is some kind of prediction index so that a gifted student with special academic ability may be identified for some special program participation by using previous achievement indices in a certain area of specialization over time; standardized test data, if available, may well serve the purpose. It is quite common to find that radical accelerates, especially in mathematics, are identified by the mathematics component of the *Scholastic Aptitude Test*. What this does is to identify aptitude directly through achievement, which may include the use of intellectual operations of cognition, memory, convergent production, and (to a lesser extent) evaluation; it does not include the use of divergent production. Although such a measure may give us information about those having special academic aptitude, it is information that will not give us the basis for predicting those who have the capacity to extend the boundaries of knowledge in their area of specialization. It is in this regard that measures of specific academic aptitude need refinement. A reconceptualization of what abilities are to be put to work on specific curricula to reflect superior aptitude for learning in a certain subject area seems wanting. In the design of instrumentation for such a purpose, due emphasis ought to be given to divergent production, and evaluation mental operations as well as to their handling of specific academic material whose content can be organized in the product categories of classes, transformation, and implications. If the measures of intellectual abilities constructed by Guilford and his associates (Guilford, 1967) relative to the structure of intellect are not considered enough for the purpose of predicting those who would have the aptitude to do well in a certain subject area, then, other measures using the rationale of the structure of intellect need to be constructed. The operational definition of abilities relative to content and product dimensions give more precise direction to the design of instruments that can predict more fully how well a person may be able to handle advanced curricula. Pursuit of this approach should lead to the extension of boundaries in the identification of specific academic aptitude. Such investigations are waiting to be done.

CREATIVE OR PRODUCTIVE THINKING

In the recognition of the fact that people do think in creative ways and that traditional measures of intelligence do not provide them with an opportunity to reflect this, creative or productive thinking was selected as yet another area of giftedness. In terms of the structure of intellect, divergent production (or creative-productive thinking) is one of the five operations of intellectual functioning. But, this is a missing dimension in IQ measures. About 10 years before this dimension of mental functioning was officially recognized as a category of giftedness, work on the measurement of creative-productive thinking blossomed into measures of creative thinking abilities, the most comprehensive and well known of which are the *Torrance Tests of Creative Thinking* (Torrance, 1966, 1974b) and *Thinking Creatively with Sounds and Words* (Khatena & Torrance (1973). In addition, this is seen to some extent in the measures of divergent thinking designed for adults by Guilford and his associates. Theoretical formulations and construction of measures took life, in the main, from Guilford's pronouncements in the 1950s about the structure of intellect. If we are looking for a major advance in thought about intellectual functioning, we have it in Guilford and Torrance's development of the rationale and measurement of creative thinking. There is no doubt that boundaries in the field of measurement were extended by investigations in creative and divergent thinking, and they will continue to expand as we understand more of the underlying nonintellective factors of these abilities. The relevance and significance of this dimension of mental functioning, once recognized, led to studies in the 1960s that differentiated between high IQ and high creative thinking abilities. The intent was directed more toward asserting the importance of including creative thinking in the identification process than to fractionizing intellect as creative and noncreative. But the findings that 70% of the top 20% obtaining high scores on measures of creativity would be missed on a measure of IQ served almost to force a two-way approach to the study of intellectual functioning. If we pause to consider what mental operations are involved in creative thinking, we find that cognition, memory, convergent thinking, and evaluation all play their part in the process and that, as creative thinking is extended into problem solving, these several mental operations are noticeably called into action. A reorientation that would pull together the separate tugs of intelligence and creativity under a model, such as the structure of intellect, must lead to productive consequences. It may be that the traditional test format of identifying potential and aptitude would not leave out creative thinking but would give it its due weight and so provide information predictors for as many of the intellectual abilities as possible. The measures constructed by Guilford and his associates have already established the basic architecture to this end. It is now left for others competent in the field of measurement to break way from traditionalism in the testing movement and move in the direction of completing missing test components of the model, extending the boundaries of the model, and generally giving body to test-item correlates of the model as a whole.

Creative behavior is not just the result of creative thinking operations, but it is very much influenced by emotive-motivational forces that are peculiar to the individual and very much related to sociocultural variables. Expectations of predictive indices to creative accomplishments must be moderated by this consideration. This is a significant problem in the measurement of creative behavior, one that must inform test constructors and their critics. Being more susceptible to

402

variability, creative thinking may not offer the same kind of predictive validity that can be expected of measures of other intellectual functions. Attention needs to be given to the arrangement of conditions that will allow brief control of the dynamic properties of creative mental functioning for as near accurate a sample of its processes as it will allow. Because quantification is an important variable in arriving at a predictor index, there is much that remains to be done (1) to refine scouring procedures that minimize subjectivity and (2) to seek for alternative ways to fetch, count, and explain responses to test stimuli.

LEADERSHIP, VISUAL AND PERFORMING ARTS, AND PSYCHOMOTOR ABILITY CATEGORIES

If the identification of the gifted relative to general intellectual ability, special academic aptitude, and creative or productive thinking is not free from problems—in spite of the advances that have been made in these three areas both in theory and instrumentation—identification of the gifted in the categories of leadership, the visual and performing arts, and psychomotor abilities have even greater problems. For one thing, leadership was not linked with giftedness until the USOE pronouncements. As a field of study it had not concerned itself with identification of potential leaders with the view to enhance their development, but rather with the view to use such subjects in leadership roles for specific tasks. Consequently, much of the study on leadership involved adults, and the research data that were generated concerned traits and qualities of individuals. A definite step forward was taken when research recognized the complexity of the subject and turned its attention to the study of those variables that relate, on the one hand, to the dynamic interaction of the individual and group and, on the other hand, to situations. Hence, leadership must be associated with person, group, situation, and resultant interactions. There is no single instrument that can be used to predict leadership potential. At best, we must rely on intellectual and creative ability, achievement, and personality-trait measures to give us both the information we need to identify the personal dimension of leadership and the sociometric measures to determine the individual's relationship to the group relative to certain tasks. And we must observe the individual in a situation (real or simulated) that requires leadership. We have come a long way in our under-standing of the dimensions of leadership and have had to derive much of this information obliquely, from individual and social psychology and group dynamics rather than from gifted education. However, our grasp of leadership as a category of giftedness is still incomplete and awaits rigorous investigation. We have to move away from regarding leadership as an ability, for to do so is to oversimplify; the acceptance of leadership as a multidimensional phenomenon is necessary. There is much work ahead to develop an appropriate rationale for the identification of leadership and to design effective measures toward this end.

Giftedness in the visual and performing arts is, by and large, not as closely related to the language of words as it is to the language system of the specific art form. When outstanding people in the visual and performing arts are administered an intelligence test that is verbally weighted to a high degree, it is not surprising to find that they show themselves to be average or bright normal. The reason is that they are called on by the test to show how well they think in a language system they use less frequently than their art-form language system. Besides, the mental operations that are called into action do not include creative thinking, which for most of these individuals is essential to their expression in one art form or another. We are inclinded to point out that much nonverbal activity occurs in the thinking and performance repetoire of artists. Although this is a way of differentiating the verbally gifted from the nonverbally gifted or talented, it does not communicate that artists use language unique to their art, that considerably more right-brain activity takes place in their mental functioning, and that much imagery occurs—especially in the visual, auditory, tactile, and kinesthetic-motor sense modalities—both as input information for processing and as output forms of art expression.

Attempts have been made over the years to design measures of music and (to a lesser extent) of art talent by using the essentials of either of their language systems. However, these are yet to be proved effective predictors of talent brilliance. As yet, psychometric measures of other art talent are almost nonexistent. The recent shift from an awareness and appreciation of talent on the basis of product or performance to a need to identify talent potential for the purpose of providing special developmental opportunities brings with it a host of problems. Psychometric approaches appropriate for identification of other forms of giftedness may not be as suitable for artistic talent, and measures for this purpose remain to be developed. Alternative approaches must be sought that will ensure at least some elementary command of the language of the art form, the opportunity to apply this language in practice situations before assessment, and the exercise of the giftedness to allow creativity to manifest itself. In general, nonpsychometric approaches at identification of talent may be the key. If this route is pursued, then, observational procedures that contain criteria with specific relevance to the art form are needed to guide experts in the identification process. This approach requires close attention and study and may lead to, or be suggestive of, other alternatives. The problem of effectively identifying potentially gifted students in the dimensions of the visual and performing arts is a pressing one and cannot be ignored if we are adequately to implement the intent of providing special opportunities to these areas of talent.

Of all the areas of giftedness, the one that should present the greatest difficulty for purposes of identification is psychomotor ability. This is mainly due to the fact that many human activities call for some use of both mind and body, including the acquisition and use of reading, writing, and speaking skills; performance in atheletics and games; manipulation of tools and equipment; and performance in music, art, oratory, and acting. Psychomotor ability is generally used here in a generic sense, when it should more appropriately refer to abilities that take meaning (for purposes of identification) only insofar as they relate to a specific area, like psychomotor abilities in musical performance, in athletics, and in the operation of machines. An operational definition of each specialized area needs to be made before any attempt to measure the presence and level of the abilities can be made. There are no instruments that can effectively measure psychomotor ability in a general sense; the few measures of intellectual functions that call for the use of kinesthetic motor dimensions that are available, are not adequate. This area requires much careful study and industry before adequate approaches for the identification of psychomotor ability as a category of giftedness can be found. It is one thing to identify the nature and function of psychomotor abilities, but it is another thing to determine what constitutes giftedness in the area and the extent to which this can have predictive power. The problem is not so much knowing that someone is gifted in some area of psychomotor abilities but discovering that someone has the potential to become superior if given the right kind of opportunities. Definition that includes psychomotor ability as a category of giftedness has only made us aware of our responsibility to develop appropriate machinery for its identification.

SOME IMPLEMENTATION PROBLEMS

Identification of these several categories of giftedness present many problems that hinge both on theoretical issues that are far from settled and on practical considerations that make full implementation very difficult, if not inhibitive. It should come as no surprise to know that although many states have accepted the USOE categories of giftedness, they have not included all areas in their screening operations. As we have seen, not all that needs to be known about these six areas of giftedness is known to allow for the development of suitable instruments for adequate identification. Of the six areas, there is relative ease in locating measures to identify intellectual abilities, creative or productive thinking, and specific academic aptitude although some disagreement persists about their precision. The remaining three areas do not have similar facilities and can be expected to present many practical restrictions, even though adaptation of satellite screening procedures may be possible by way of administration, time, and cost. That is why screening plans, by and large, focus on the use of IQ and achievement measures and, to a much smaller extent (confined to relatively few states) focus on creativity measures. However, test administration in all these areas presents relatively little difficulty although the problem of scoring creative thinking measures and the expense of using a scoring service are factors of some concern. With these factors in mind, we are in a better position to understand the reluctance of many states to throw themselves into the identification of all six categories of giftedness. This results not so much because there is an unwillingness to recognize these varieties of giftedness but because there is sufficient uncertainty and instability that can enter into screening operations to call judgments in selection of gifted students into question. Another factor of importance is the trained personnel who run the testing units for the state—by professional preparation, they veer toward IQ and achievement measures. Because we do have an acute need for well-trained personnel in the screening and advisement of students in several categories of giftedness, a reeducation of those in office and appropriate preparation of those now in training appear to be increasingly necessary. Hence, we must recognize these problems and prepare ourselves to deal with them. It is unlikely that the search for better and different identification procedures will slacken; in fact, there is every indication that the need will continue to grow over the years.

CREATIVE IMAGINATION IMAGERY

The study of creative imagination imagery is rather new, but it is promising and provocative in itself and in its implications for creative education for all children in general and for gifted children in particular. Hardly 10 years have elapsed since Richardson (1969) and Paivio (1971) observed that little (if any) serious work had been done in the study of creative imagination imagery. The most important happening in the 1970s relating to the study of imagery is the fact that behaviorism relinquished its 30-year hold on this field of enquiry because of the resurgence of interest in imagery by psychologists of various persuasions. Their writings established beyond doubt the significance of this field of study, which over the past few years especially has led not only to a proliferation of research on imagery but also in the formation of two national or international organizations, the publication of a journal, and the organization of several major conferences.

Findings from various studies on eidetic memory and imagination imagery have become increasingly of value to psychotherapy and are quite extensively used by clinical psychologists to assist their patients to regain mental health. Although the value of imagery to learning has been established by B. R. Bugelski, A. Paivio, and others, it has not found its way, in any significant sense, as a valuable learning tool in the classroom. There is much work ahead to translate the findings of research in these several imagery domains into teaching practice. For example, we have hardly begun to touch the surface of one of the most significant resources of the human brain, the facilitation of learning.

The study of imagery as it relates to the creative imagination has just begun and should receive strong impetus from the brain research now being conducted. We have discussed the relationship of imagery, preconscious activity, and creativity; we have seen the importance of imagery in problem solving in the incubation and illumination stages; and we have the testimony of eminent persons in the arts and sciences about felt vibrations and imagery as a precursor to creative ideation, invention, or composition. We now seek ways to understand imagery better so that we may have greater control of its resources to stimulate and enhance the creative development of students.

In instrumentation, we have moved from simple self-reports to more complex ones, from self-reports and rating scales to projective measures. These have assisted the study of imagery considerably. Of interest in the study of creative imagination imagery are the two components of *Thinking Creatively with Sounds and Words,* namely, *Onomatopoeia and Images* and *Sounds and Images.* Through these measures we have been able to understand variables that relate to stimulation of creative thinking, problem solving and incubation, autonomy of imagery, developmental patterns, and the physiological correlates of imagery. Some research has been done in these several areas but more awaits to be done.

Editorial comments in *Educating the Ablest* (Gowan, Khatena, & Torrance, 1979), which introduce several papers on imagery, point to the importance of incubation in problem solving as a sufficient condition for illumination and production of right-hemisphere imagery. Although a good repetoire of educational techniques of preparation for creativity, like those proposed by F. E. Williams and M. M. Meeker, are available, equally strong techniques for incubation are hard to find. A measure of verbal originality, *Thinking Creatively with Sounds and Words,* allows and encourages production of imagery and analogies. On the subject of analogies Upton (1961) emphasizes the shift in the development of thinking from categorizations to analogy and finally to isomorphics, or a study of the equivalences in analogies. Thinking by analogy and imagery can be facilitated by various incubation techniques that sever the dominance of the left-ceberal hemisphere to allow right-cerebral hemisphere activity. Synergistic cooperation between the right and left hemispheres permits the former to pick up the images and the latter to translate them into alpha numeric form (Gowan, 1979b, 1979d). The importance of incubation in the creative thinking process must not be underestimated although its study is elusive experimentally (Olton, 1979) and presents problems. It is difficult to control what subjects do during the period of incubation, other than their incubation activity, except for brief periods that last for minutes only (Guilford, 1979). Besides, subjects have the task of avoiding premature closure so that they may give due emphasis to the role of transformation. However, enough is known about incubation to justify attempts to teach problem solvers to use it successfully (Guilford, 1979). Torrance (1979a) suggests a three-stage instructional model for enhancing incubation, namely, an introductory phase that arouses anticipation and heightens expectations; a second phase that deepens involvement along with commitment that goes beyond the superficial; and a third phase that keeps the thought process active.

Other ways to encourage gifted students to use incubation for the production of imagery have been suggested in *Teaching Gifted Children to Use Creative Imagination Imagery* (Khatena, 1979c) and *Creative Imagination Imagery Actionbook* (Khatena, 1980). Interest on incubation led both the *Gifted Child Quarterly* and the *Journal of Creative Behavior* (1979) to devote recent spring issues to this subject.

Research on creative imagination imagery can be expected to continue vigorously with special attention given to developmental factors; sensory disability and adaptations; various subgroups, including the gifted and talented and culturally diverse students; the design of new instruments and scoring systems whereby creative potential and personality variations can be identified; and the deliberate nurturant procedures that enhance not only educational development but also high levels of productivity. We are at the brink of important explorations and discoveries in the field of human abilities as they relate to creative functioning. These can be expected to go far beyond the quantification of responses to given test stimuli. We hope these studies will tell us something about intellectual processing—which is more far reaching than mere retrieval of information for processing by various mental operations—and give us knowledge of what, in fact, is involved in the process of metamorphosis and catalystic thinking.

DEVELOPMENT OF INTELLECT AND CREATIVITY

Nearly no attention has been given to developmental features of the gifted and talented by those concerned with gifted education. Most of what we know about developmental patterns of intellect and creativity has come from studies of the general population through the intelligence and the factor components of the Wechsler scales. Relative to the structure of intellect, no systematic attempts have been made to study developmental patterns, except for Guilford's inferences about those based on the factor analytic work of L. L. Thurstone and T. L. Kelley. As for the study of complex intellectual abilities of gifted children as they grow older, nearly nothing exists. It is interesting to note Guilford's rejection (1967) of Garrett's (1946) hypothesis. Garrett states that multiple abilities develop from the unitary ability of infants and young children. Multiple abilities, like those of structure of intellect, appear more clearly with increasing age. However, Garrett recognizes that his morphological factor model may not be the same for young children. But, there are as yet no studies in the direct rate of growth of structure of intellect abilities, and this opens up many research possibilities.

The study of intellectual and creative development may be approached in several ways. As it pertains to individual development, it may be regarded as continuous or discontinuous, information about this may be obtained from psychometrics or developmental stage theory respectively; as it pertains to the

408

individual in the context of general principles available to explain behavior, one has to go to a general systems theory, such as J. C. Gowan's on periodicity or G. Land's on transformation; and, as it pertains to the interaction of the individual with society, one can derive information from a study of historical patterns relative to the emergence of eminence or to the dynamic exchange between two open systems in a creativogenic society.

What contributions have these various approaches to the study of intellectual and creative development made? The psychometric approach has shown that both intellectual and creative development can increase in adulthood although some differentiation may have to be made among the functions of various abilities; that, at the upper levels, tests do not discriminate very well, depending on test ceiling and the intellectually superior subject; that experience plays a much greater role in the development of intellect than was earlier recognized; that fresh conceptualization of the nature and function of human abilities must follow in the wake of the informational-operational theory of intelligence in the structure of intellect, shifting in emphasis from a heredity view of unitary intelligence to an interactive heredity-environment view of multidimensional abilities; and that creative abilities suffer drops at various grade or age levels, the severest of which appears around the fourth-grade level (or between the ages of 9 and 10) with recovery levels not exceeding the level attained in the third grade.

Gowan's (1972) theory of the development of the creative individual provides some corroboration for this drop in creativity: the model shows the period of the elementary school years (stage 4) as a time of low creative potential when one can expect a slump in creative thinking abilities to occur, whereas in the stage before (or the preschool years) creative potential is high. Khatena's (1971b, 1972a) findings of the drop in the production of original verbal imagery at about the same time as the fourth-grade slump and the earlier finding of Jaensch (1930) on the decrement of eidetic imagery of children as they grow older leads Gowan (1979d) to speculate if this may not be the result of transfer from right-hemisphere processing of images to left-hemisphere processing of verbal materials. Gowan's developmental stage model extends the five cognitive stages of Jean Piaget to eight and gives emphasis to creativity in stages 3, 6, and 9; it also gives new dimension to the Eriksonian adult stages of intimacy, generativity, and ego integrity in creativity as well as psychedelia and illumination (the phases of mind expansion) in stages 7, 8, and 9 of the model.

Other contributions to thought on creative development relate to periodicity (a term carried over from quantuum theory into behavioral science) to indicate the occurrence of energy transformation that raises functioning from a lower to a higher level; to self-actualization as escalation to higher developmental stages; to the occurrence of dysplasia or slowing down of some part of an individual's development relative to the time it should take place; and to an emphasis on love as central to creation.

DEVELOPMENT OF INTELLECT AND CREATIVITY   409

In terms of general systems as the source of some fresh insights relative to development, we turn to Land's transformation theory and Gowan's developmental stage theory. Both seek general principles to explain behavior; both see growth or development as moving from lower to higher levels of functioning; both perceive development in triadic stages, with the attainment of one as preparatory to a transformation to the next higher level of development—but whereas Gowan discusses this in terms of escalation and dysplasia, Land speaks of it as destructuring and reintegration; and both see the involvement of analogical or metaphorical brain activity and imagery in the highest level of the creative process that prepares for transformation.

We turn to D. K. Simonton and S. Arieti for some fresh insights on sociocultural factors relating to the creative development of individuals, the former attributes greater importance to creators' developmental periods than to the periods of their productivity, whereas the latter sees creative development as emerging from the creative transactions of individuals with their creativogenic society. Of the seven sociocultural influences that affect creative development toward actualization and adult eminence, formal education and role models have significant implications for education. With what we know today about the procedures for enhancing creativity and intellectual activity, there is a good chance for reducing, if not preventing, the restriction and narrowness of formal education. We have seen how this adversely affects the continuity in the development of creative thinking abilities as identified by psychometric procedures, and we have also learned that many approaches have been applied with considerable success to offset some of the grosser aspects of these hindrances. It may be that with careful planning for an enlightened and stimulating curriculum as well as the adoption of appropriate attitudes and educational stance formal education will level itself at escalation and transformation, moving gifted students to higher and higher levels of achievement and growth toward an eminence so lacking in the present-day world. Good role models are hard to find, but there is nothing to say that we may not use the renaissance men and women of history along with those we can find today as touchstones for our gifted as they strive for eminence. Further clues for facilitating gifted children toward adult eminence may lie in several conditions expected in a creativogenic society. The extent to which we can adapt, adopt, and even create these conditions for use in gifted education needs to be explored. Certainly, we should seek out contemporary and historical figures of brilliance who not only act as repositories of cultural excellence but also perform the functions of role models. So that this aspect becomes functional, we need to make accessible materials, equipment, and all else that the studies need. Another condition for which to strive is exposure to all facets of culture (made available to everyone who can be prepared to enter into the experiences with active receptivity), which can transform storage into productivity. Emphasis in education should be on self-actualization toward interaction with significant people in a climate that encourages and tolerates divergent views. The condition that presents difficulty to design for gifted education deliberately is the condition that sees in freedom or retention of moderate discrimination after severe oppression or absolute exclusion as incentive to creativity. Where adverse conditions are present and release can be implemented, then, release must be tried as a means to provoke creativity to function and express itself. One might see in the propositions of both Simonton (1978) and Arieti (1976) many possibilities for scientific study.

GUIDANCE

Congruent with the concept that the gifted are people who can make it on their own and, hence, do not need educational and related facilitative intervention, guidance was not at first perceived a necessity for them. When it was realized that they, too, could benefit from guidance, proponents concentrated their efforts on providing educational and vocational guidance, in the main, and only to a lesser extent was guidance for adjustment problems provided. Gowan (1979a) perceived an absence of a curriculum for guidance and charged that, for rationale and procedure, guidance tends to draw on the medical model of psychotherapy, whose concern is the treatment of abnormal problems of adults on a private and long-term basis and where attention is crisis oriented. He maintained that guidance should concern itself with the developmental problems of normal children that involve association on a short-term basis and with preventative measures that will facilitate the individual to attain high levels of self-actualization and mental health. The importance of developmental stage theory, its creativity dimensions, and its key features of escalation and dysplasia are emphasized as basic curricula for guidance of the gifted because they give direction to a preventative stance in guidance whose thrust is toward facilitating gifted students to higher levels of creativity, actualization, and mental health. The need for guidance by gifted people who are striving toward higher levels of creativity finds corroborative evidence in Land's (1973) transformation theory, where growth cycles in creative functioning of a lower order move on to cycles of growth of increasingly higher order. The concepts of destructuring and reintegration at the mutualistic stage of each cycle prior to transformation to the next higher level of functioning has significance for guidance for the gifted because it provides the framework for a fresh look at success whereby the components comprising it are reexamined. This is followed by a restructuring of the field to include hitherto unperceived material and alternatives for a transformation that begins a new but higher level cycle of growth. Because the gifted are on a course of accelerative direction, escalation or transformation will ensure that intellectual and creative development proceed not to single frontiers of attainment but to frontiers in multiple planes of increasing order. There is nothing written on the subject of transformation theory as it relates to guidance, but the application of its apparent power needs careful thought and investigation. Together, Land and Gowan offer startling new directions for guidance.

Moving from the gifted person as an individual to the gifted person in interaction with others, we recognize that there are factors in a social setting that either facilitate or hinder his or her development. From Simonton (1978) and Arieti's (1976) observations of conditions that foster growth of gifted individuals to eminence, we learn that guidance can make accessible the emulation of historical and contemporary eminent creators as models and, where feasible, arrangements can be made for some of these eminent people to act as gifted mentors; that guidance can make available materials, equipment, varieties of cultural exposure and stimulation; and that guidance can apply a system of rewards and incentives, moving from the extrinsic to the intrinsic, to endorse efforts toward high levels of self-actualization.

Another forward-looking approach in guidance would be an inclusion of strategies to assist gifted students to cope or master stress. Much of this stress arises from the adjustment problems gifted individuals face from day to day in their transactions and interactions with a society that, generally, does not understand or tolerate divergence, which is often a reflection of the individual striving to express uniqueness. Recognizing that much of the stress experienced by gifted individuals has this circumstance as its origin, the counselor can, then, plan a course of action that subscribes to preventative rather than curative guidance. Torrance's (1962a, 1965a, 1967a) discussion of the subject has great relevance for counselors involved in the guidance of gifted students; among the approaches he suggests are those that hinge on the development of interpersonal skills and the use that can be made of the structure of intellect abilities and creative problem solving. This leads him to suggest several important strategies for coping with stress.

In the case of academic guidance for the gifted, the movement has been from assisting students to plan programs of study as they relate to regular school offerings to planning accelerative learning in school subjects at advanced levels or in making available many more study alternatives in areas of knowledge that are less frequently examined but that are of interest to gifted students. Emphasis has shifted in orientation from school subjects to individual development so that fresh attitudes toward guidance and the continuous guidance of students at all stages of growing up is deemed necessary. New attitudes toward guiding lower socioeconomic groups also need to be adopted so that understanding of the differential needs of the culturally diverse receive appropriate attention.

Career guidance (not so long ago known as vocational guidance) for the gifted does not only attempt to make varieties of job information and experience available but also takes into account the individual's needs and those that arise from the individual's interaction with the environment. This, in fact, is a major shift in

412

focus because it recognizes that addressing itself to information about the work world is insufficient. Individual differences must be taken into account and so must the transactions among individuals, the world of work, and the congruence that may emerge from the relations the individual's have with this outside world. The model proposed by Perrone, Karshner, and Male (1979) takes these and related factors into account so that the dynamics structuring an individual's orientation in the areas of self, social awareness, and understanding as well as the organizing and planning relative to goal attainment and its evaluation facilitate development toward a career. Just as in other areas of guidance, career guidance is thought of as an ongoing process that begins in early childhood and goes on for many years after adulthood is reached. Career guidance for the gifted takes into account needs, motivations, goals, interactions of self with others, and the varieties of job opportunities that can be expected to serve them in more substantial and profitable ways.

A dynamic procedure to facilitate career guidance of the gifted lies in socio-drama. It goes beyond the benefits of role playing to assist students to know their abilities, interests, and feelings as these relate to careers. Leveled at clarification and solution finding, it allows the creative problems solving process to approach the examination of potential problems in careers and calls into service the power-ful dynamism of drama. Primarily sociodrama for educational use is preventative rather than therapeutic; it is group centered and highly suited to the classroom; it is a viable approach to assist in the matching of multiple talent, abilities, and interests of gifted students and choices that have to be made over a variety of possible careers; it is a method that allows for group exploration, value clarifica-tion, fresh insights, and consensual validation of careers and their attendent problems—all seen in microcosm as preparation for the real thing. Sociodrama, then, must be seen as a valuable additional tool for guidance of the gifted both specific to careers and to related areas of guidance in general. It may become more widely used and, thus, may be the occasion for research aimed at testing its effectiveness.

PROBLEMS OF SPECIAL GROUPS

One of the chief concerns in the early years of the gifted movement was the development of appropriate measuring instruments where none existed for the identification of gifted students. This gave rise to the *Stanford-Binet,* whose underlying rationale was to sample hereditary-based intellectual traits of indi-viduals with little cognizance of environmental influences. In the selection of gifted subjects by Lewis M. Terman for his (1925) study, no place was given to socioeconomic variables; even the title of the study, *Genetic Studies of Genius,* emphasized genetics although the content of the various reports was leveled at understanding the nature and function of intellectually superior students as manifested in their experiences and accomplishments in the world as they grew up to middle life and beyond. We have moved away from both these positions to recognize the presence of multidimensional abilities that find development and usage through interactions with the environment. The hereditary-rooted components of mental operations are illustrated in the structure of intellect, which depends for its functions on different kinds of input information organized in different ways for processing and expression. It gives point to the fact that not all abilities receive opportunities for development and use and that lack of exposure to varieties of experiences are largely contributory to this, which forces attention to the importance of having an interactive heredity-environment model.

Reconceptualization of abilities as multiple rather than singular and as interactive heredity and environment based rather than solely heredity based have important consequences in our thinking about underachievement, which traditionally has been conceived as a mismatch between IQ potential and school achievement. We have moved to a position whereby we can regard underachievement relative to multipotentiality and, with our broadened concept of giftedness, this puts underachievement relative to abilities potential in proper perspective. If underachievement is thought of in terms of developmental stage theory, then, we move into the area of developmental arrest, or dysplasia, where cognitive or emotive development do not occur together at each developmental stage; as dysplasia refers to gifted women students, we have begun to recognize some of the developmental variables that prevent or hinder their rise to higher levels of functioning toward self-actualization and the potentiality for adult eminence. Underachievement has also come to be regarded as unfulfilled creativity, that is, an intelligent person underachieves not because of motivational lack but because of not having the opportunities to be creative. It is more appropriate today to consider underachievement not in the restrictive sense of lower performance level in schooling but to extend it to include all areas of talent where performance is below superior level. We now recognize that the handicapped gifted student's deficit functions in school subjects is not attributable so much to lack of ability as it is to the disability possessed. Hence, more appropriate orientations toward the disabled as a potential pool for giftedness can be expected. Further, we also recognize that nonintellective talent must not be mistaken for underachievement but that achievement has to be screened relative to several dimensions and different ways than assessment through school subjects allow. Our better understanding of sources of cultural diversity factors in underachievement can be expected to lead to better approaches at identifying talent potential, planning experiences for growth that accentuate creative positives and creativity, and providing programs that are future oriented. As underachievement relates to developmental arrest of girls growing up, we can now begin to understand contributary factors, like role expectation, sex typing of social roles, creativity that tends to be determined by socialization, different patterns of

414

achievement motivation, achievement that oscilates between direct and vicarious rewards, and reliance on factors of contingency and discrepancy.

What we know today about the problems of such spcial groups as the under-achieving, the handicapped, and the culturally diverse gifted; underachieving girls as developmentally arrested; and underachieving as a function of assessed potential and performance is more than we knew a few years ago. But, this is only the beginning. Not only will we need to continue to research these problems but also there is need for a continual search for special groups of gifted not as yet known so that we can maximize educational growth. Research must especially focus on these problems as they relate to proper indentificatiqn of potential in many areas of giftedness, bearing in mind the problems of measurement pertinent to these special groups, choice of criteria as appropriate predictors of achievement, selection of rationale, and planning for educational experiences that will facilitate growth unique to these groups of individuals. Particular attention should also be paid to developmental variables as they affect esclation toward higher levels of actualization of talent and as they test the relevance of hypotheses generated by these considerations. It will be hard to exhaust the possibilities of research in this area of giftedness, and this bears special relevance to the increasing awareness and expected support for different kinds of gifted students.

NURTURE

Of all other aspects of giftedness, it must be nurture that is of greatest interest to educators. It is their business and province of expertise. The educator should have more to say about nurture than on anything else concerning the gifted. This is primarily what the demand for legislation and funds is all about, namely, the provision of special educational opportunities for gifted students. We are led to ask the improtant question: How different are such provisions for gifted students in formal education than provisions for their less able, but average, peers so that these special provisions for them can be justified? Have changes, in fact, taken place these last 30 or 40 years to show that we have moved forward to differentiated and defensible educational programs in schooling for the gifted? If so, what are these?

For one thing, we can see a broadened conceptualization of acceleration emerging that includes enrichment. Accelerative enrichment should be the key concept to this approach of different educational opportunity. We have seen acceleration of various forms over the years, but the deliberate preparation, both in terms of identification and study arrangements, for radical accelerates gives this sharper focus and has begun to win convinced support in many quarters of the country. First tried in the area of mathematics, its success has led to development of a similar accelerative program for the study of language at advanced levels and can be expected to spread to other areas of knowledge as well.

The approach of identification here relates to special academic aptitude screened by standardized tests of achievement in both these areas so that performance on such tests can be used as a predictor index of aptitude. The general enrichment approach practiced is steadily giving way to a more deliberate, closely focused one that makes a distinction between exploratory activities and group-training activities that are suitable for the many in preparation for individual investigation of real problems and with production and recognition as end results for the few. Both approaches are leveled at accelerative enrichment. One approach follows a narrow track of high levels of academic achievement by study of a content area at advanced levels; the other approach is aimed at preparation for the acquisition of knowledge of content and process that leads to investigative competence and resultant productivity. However, what distinguishes accelerative enrichment now from earlier approaches is that it is not cumulative but transformative so that it produces escalation to increasing levels of intellectual growth.

Process education advocated for the many now finds relevance for gifted students and is expected to provide individual expansion of abilities, facilitate intellectual-affective growth, turn over direction of learning to the student, and allow for adaptation of knowledge and skills acquired to changing circumstances. The early emphasis on the need for process education in the 1930s found expression in the 1960s and 1970s in the construction of various training procedures to develop thinking tools that emphasize creativity and problem solving. The growing recognition of the added benefits of integrating process with curriculum has led to the development of several good models. Of particular note are two that have as basic rationale the structure of intellect—one uses all five Guilfordian mental operations and the other confines itself to creativity, combining it with an affective component in one dimension and teacher behaviors in another dimension. The early sequential problem-solving steps have developed into more elaborate paradigms that give greater emphasis to creativity, both in its cognitive and emotive aspects; more recently this has found powerful expression in the dramatic situation of sociodrama.

Another development in creative problem solving can be found in the systems approach, which offers a conceptual model that not only takes into account numerous variables in sequential order but also shows them as interrelated, interactive, and looped so that the conclusion of one problem-solving activity is the inception of the next. Further, the systems approach offers a generic model from which other models can take life. Emphasis is on the individual's transactions and use of the environment with positive and negative feedback and feedforward as important mechanisms in the problem-solving process, which are leveled at adaptation and adjustment in an ever-changing environment.

Of the several recent forward-looking expositions on educational nurturance (e.g., Gallagher, 1979a, 1979b; Gowan, 1979b, 1980; Passow, 1979; Renzulli, 1980; Sisk, 1980; Torrance 1977c), few truly provide vision for the future.

Among those that do, however, are found in the work of Gowan and Torrance. In the main, each foresees advances in education from a different stance, Torrance (1977c) in the year 2002 and Gowan (1979b, 1980) in Utopia after the manner of Aldous Huxley. Schools in the future, according to Torrance will have interdisciplinary curricular activities; research methodology; futures research and special programs with futuristic aspects stressed; creative problem solving; synectics; sociodrama; the Delphi technique, (a procedure used to make future predictions for consensus attainment); metaphorical, mechanical, and mathematical analogs; simulation games; and there will be places where a combination of teaching and learning techniques are used without question as to their relative merits. Gowan's Utopian schools emphasize developmental stages and escalation toward self-actualization, move from formal operations (convergent thinking) to creativity (divergent thinking) in the secondary school years, and include the study of biographies of geniuses and creative persons so that their outstanding lives are analyzed in accordance with the critical stages, environmental pressures, and the advantages that occurred at the periods in which they lived. Curriculum will include minicourses that reflect a dynamic view of humankind seen in the process of change and becoming, as found in energetics (the use of life energies, including some we do not understand), ecology (with a better appreciation of Spaceship Earth and the conservation of its resources), utopias (from Plato to Huxley), futuristics (the study of and planning for, the future), species evolution, social policy, historics (history from a dynamic point of view, like that of Toynbee or Spengler), the glass bead game (emphasizing the development and expression of ingenuity and invention in music, language, mathematics, and so on), and the study of the creativogenic society (where social institutions maximize creative talent). Creativity will be a solid part of the curriculum and directly taught (e.g., synectics, brainstorming, and structure of intellect applications according to the model (F. E. Williams and M. N. Meeker).

In addition, somatics (a term that is nearest to, yet different from, our physical education) will be taught not as group skills leading to aggressive behavior and team rivalries but as individual bodily exercises to reduce stress and thereby contribute to good health. In the domain of the normal state of consciousness there will be minicourses in science (e.g., astrophysics, particle physics, and astronomy (taught so that they will be understood by nonscience majors), mathematics (e.g., emphasis will be on exponential functions, binary notations and logs, computer and artificial languages), new scientific method (e.g., synchrony, which is the study of coincidence in time, space, and magnitude, and has much to do with resonance on the same frequency), scientific ethics (there will be more emphasis on probability function attached to truth-value theories), and history (will be seen from the perspective of historical progression of ideas liberating humankind, which is regarded as more important than historical progression of laws liberating humankind—all of which will be important units of the curriculum of the future. Communication theory comprising verbal study (e.g., phonetics; comparative philology; and both foreign languages and artificial languages that are made up by students and in which emphasis is placed on extensional and intensional use of words) and nonverbal study (e.g., gesture, expression in body, dancing, empathy, intuition, archetypes, images, dream ritual, and art) will be taught instead of language arts as we know them. Use will be made of the intensive journal method for creative writing, and flexibility of thinking will be developed by the study of metasymbolic calculus in which symbols acquire several meanings and running prose conveys double or triple meanings. Another important curriculum innovation will involve the learning of techniques of relaxation, meditation, time distortion, and the like, so that incubation can be encouraged for imagery to take place. Finally, the curriculum will include the development of a repertoire of theories rather than beliefs, the study of general systems, the study of neotics, and the analysis of the mind and consciousness.

Another closely related aspect of nurture is motivation. As motivation pertains to the gifted the emphasis is on the establishment of inner controls rather than outer controls, instrinsic rather than extrinsic. The emphasis shifts from habit and conditioning control to growth toward higher states and levels of functioning. For the gifted student, effective motivational forces are to be found in competence, incongruity-dissonance, feedback, feedforward information processing, growth needs relative to esteem self-actualization, knowing and understanding, and aesthetics. To these must be added the power of motivation inherent in creative ways of learning and the perception individuals have of what they would want to become in the future (Torrance, 1979b).

DIFFERENTIAL EDUCATIONAL MODELS

Effective nurture of the gifted involves the interplay of many variables, which necessitates a delicate balance for the best results. We realize from experience that teaching the gifted to make use of their intellectual resources more fully requires helping them to understand the processes involved and giving them the practice to use these processes so that they become accessible when needed. Process, in itself, is insufficient because it must be an integral part of learning content. Just like the interactive dimensions of the structure of intellect, process must react to or act on various kinds of curricular information that is organized in a number of different ways. Further, especially related to gifted students, the presence of wide variations in talent potential gives greater focus to individual differences and provision has to be made for this. Therefore, today there is an increasing emphasis on individualizing education by way of various individualized instruction programs, which appear to attack the problem of such provision with greater precision than the earlier efforts that stemmed from the innovations of the progressive movement to speak toward individual growth. The

418

mechanized individualization of learning through the teaching machine, which is based on the principles of operant conditioning, is of great value for the average and below average student. But, it will not serve the gifted the more learning moves they attain away from basics and as they reach higher levels of intellectual functioning. This is not to say, however, that judicious use of the teaching machine and programmed instruction for self-instruction in certain areas of basic information—preparatory to more advanced knowledge acquisition and thinking—cannot be made and whose energy lies not in extrinsic but in intrinsic motivation as competence increases.

One word of caution concerning the suitability of specific individualized instruction programs for the gifted student and the extent to which qualitative differences exist. Instruction provided by the teaching machine and programmed learning emphasizes the importance of efficient acquisition of basic content regardless of the individual; the approaches of progressive education are freer and the basic tenets of individualizing learning hinges on active participation and experience of the general learner. Unlike these approaches, individualized education for the gifted has in its design built-in provisions for uniqueness of individual talent and learning style; suitable instructional procedures; built-in conditions of flexibility and change; concern for the unknown and future as well as for the known, past and present; student invovlement in planning; inquiry tools and research methodology that call for the use of intellectual processes leveled at creative learning and production; and careful planning, management, and evaluation procedures that relate to explicit criteria, determined in advance, to document student change and progress.

Conceptualization of curriculum for the gifted has moved from the position of imparting to students as much as we know about various areas of knowledge to making accessible repositories of knowledge and exciting initiative in the students to discover this; from the memorization of fact and detail for quick recall to the productive learning of ideas that are seminal to higher levels of intellectual growth; from the narrower use of intellectual resources that are directional to the known and correct to the broader use of these resources that are generative of the unknown and possible; from the strictures of the regular school curriculum to the freedoms of curricula that are at the frontiers of knowledge; from an unidisciplinary to a multidisciplinary approach in the study of curricula; and from curriculum as information acquisition to curriculum as a tool to be used to gain access to ever-expanding horizons of excellence.

Special provisions for the gifted are associated with organizing curriculum and methodology as programs that are expected to better meet the needs of the gifted. Innovative aspects of programs are to be seen in projects that are peripheral rather than central to regular school offerings. Programs central to regular schooling are less frequently found in public schools but, instead, have found expression in special schools for the gifted, which have mainly tended to be private. By and large, our schools appear to be continuing in the traditional enrichment and acceleration practice familiar to us; the projects, although catchy in title, are with a few exceptions not highly innovative in conceptualization or practice. Special schools have considerable refinements to make relative to the kind of gifted pupils admitted to their programs and to the inclusion of the most recent thoughts on use of intellectual resources and processes that should be well integrated with their curricula: the movement must be away from traditional enrichment and acceleration to accelerative enrichment, which is a precursor of escalation to higher levels of intellectual growth. Projects tend to be less stable and have more transitory provisions for the gifted. Projects are the tryout grounds for innovative ideas. Often, however, they have not veered away from traditional innovations in practice, except for those that have struck out in the directions of accelerative enrichment; deliberate development of intellectual abilities and processes; problem solving and affective skills; and the adoption of the diagnostic-prescriptive approach, which uses curriculum purposefully to educate abilities in the context of individualization so that the needs of gifted students may be more adequately met. Sadly lacking in numbers are projects planned to provide for the nurture and development of talent in the many different areas of the visual and performing arts. There can be expected improvement of this and in identification procedures that will not just meet the requirements for administering several instruments to subjects but that will have the intent of screening for different kinds of gifts and talents central to the design of the program provisions of the projects. As for the number of operative projects, the past 10 years have shown a substantial increase and there is every indication of the continuance of this trend. What is highly desirable is that more and more of these projects become integrated as a function of regular schooling rather than continue as satellite eruptions that are threatened with the surgery of noncontinuance of financial support. Finally, what distinguishes present-day evaluation approaches from those used before is the demand for more efficient evaluation procedures that not only assess the projected exit outcomes of a project relative to its design and objectives but that also provide information on an ongoing basis for program refinement at various stages so that feedback becomes feedforward information for continued growth. Certainly, this is a more informed evaluation approach that can be expected to be essential to any project designed for the gifted from here on.

THE GROWING INTEREST IN TALENT DEVELOPMENT

The early efforts of Terman launched the gifted movement in the 1920s and matured in the 1950s in partnership with the creative movement that found focus in Guilford's expanded concept of the intellect and were subsumed as dimensions of humanistic psychology. The prizing of individual worth and its potentiality for growth and becoming, the increasing awareness by society of the value of talent and the need to cultivate it for the common good, the related development of screening measures, the recognition of a variety of talents, the realization that creativity is an essential human dimension of power for health and productive ascent, the expanded understanding of the transcendental nature of development and growth that moves an individual from lower to higher orders of functioning, and the increasing acceptance of parapsychological factors as they lend themselves more to scientific investigation are all in the province of humanistic psychology and have important implications for the gifted. We have seen how research has contributed to our understanding of these and related areas in the 12 milestones identified by Gowan (1978a). Milestones that have influenced thought concerning the gifted as it relates to identification and construction of a variety of measures as well as it relates to individual development and its theoretical formulations, especially in developmental stage theory, guidance, socioeconomic and cultural diversity variables, the falibility of measures, the relationship between intelligence and creativity, the nurture of creativity, and the need for counteraction to underachievement problems.

A major impact of the gifted and creative movements can be seen in the passage of federal legislation in 1970—official recognition given for the first time in American history. It was the single most important event in public education for the gifted and talented. All prior activities and efforts were but preparatory to this main event. A decade of initiative by the National Education Association (NEA) with the support of the Carnegie Corporation performed the important function of sensitizing the American public to the need for special provisions for the gifted by means of dissemination of information through its publications, conferences, and consultative services. Thereby, it became one of the earliest and most significant advocacy groups that not only bridged the apathy of the early 1950s and the needs of the 1970s but also precipitated legislative activity in Congress in favor of the gifted. The years that followed saw the establishment of the Office of the Gifted and Talented; the computerized dissemination services of the CEC/TAG/ERIC, the organization of the Leadership Training Institute (LTI); the envigoration of state activity; the rise of organized parent groups, whose initiative was direct or through professional associations; and the designing and implementation of teacher-preparation programs. All of this was in the cause of the gifted. The most recent legislation of 1979 escalated funding from $2.5 million to $25 million over a period of five years. This is now threatened by the Reagan administration's budget cuts in education. However, where there was no strong federal leadership, the establishment of the Office of the Gifted and Talented provided it. The role of this office as an advocacy group since its inception in 1972 was necessitated by a lack of funds; with the planned increase of money, however, some significant revision in its role took place. During its term of sustained advocacy, the office used the leadership-training approach, which prepared appropriate press for legislative funding; it sensitized private foundations and business enterprise to the needs of gifted education, thereby supplementing the meager resources at its command by securing funding for nationally competitive scholarships and symposia for gifted students; and it alerted state and local agencies to obtain funds from various federal sources where no direct allocations of funds for the gifted existed. Consequently, a great many special projects, either funded directly from funds allocated to the Office of the Gifted and Talented or from several Elementary and Secondary Education Act (ESEA) Title sources, came into existence. Its contributions and commitments to teacher training, special provisions for the minority gifted, development of instrumentation for multitalent identification, and curriculum features should grow.

The N/S LTI is the right arm of the Office of the Gifted and Talented. Its mission has been to produce groups of five leaders in each state to champion the cause of the gifted, to establish a network of persons and agencies committed to gifted education, to keep people informed through its monthly bulletin and other publications of what is currently happening in the field, and to bring together gifted educators, administrators, and parents in conferences on specially selected themes in gifted education, all of which continue to produce leaders and maintain their efficacy.

The role of the CEC/TAG/ERIC computer services in gifted education is significant. It has made possible the mass storage of relevant data on the gifted and talented for easy and rapid retrieval at relatively low cost; it is a machine service that satisfies the need of information for general consumption and for research. Its low costs make many categories of data on the gifted accessible, ranging from informal papers, bibliographies, custom searches (on request), abstracts, full-length reports on specially selected topics, and the like. Such a service has great potential and we can expect that in the next few years it will provide significant support to the escalating development of the gifted movement.

The National Association for Gifted Children has played a significant role in advancing thought on, and interest in, the gifted, and it has evolved (for more than a quarter of a century) into the most viable independent association of the gifted in the country. The association is managed by a distinguished executive board comprising a national representation of scholars, teachers, and parents and also has administrators and libraries as members. It has been responsible for (1) stimulating and encouraging research on, and education of, gifted children; (2) making available and disseminating scientific information concerning gifted children; (3) encouraging study of the problems and practices in working with gifted children; (4) providing classroom teachers with opportunities to study improved methods of working with gifted children; and (5) publishing and reporting on scientific and experimental investigations that relate to gifted children and on improved practices for working with them, especially through its *Gifted Child*

422

Quarterly, the association's pulse of the gifted movement. To Ann Isaacs, the founder and first editor of the *Gifted Child Quarterly,* must go the credit of conceiving and producing that journal; to John C. Gowan must go the credit of refining, extending, and giving stature and scholarship to the journal; and to the Editorial Board and the Board of Directors go the credit of supporting and nurturing the transition and emergent functions of the journal, which keeps in touch with the national and international membership. Recent changes have resulted in the election of Don J. Treffinger as the Editor and the appointment of Joyce Juntune as the Executive Director, whose combined functions were held by Gowan for several years. The presidents since 1974 who were responsible for escalating the association to higher levels of achievement and service were John C. Gowan, Faye Shaffer, Joe Khatena, and Juliana Gensley. They will be followed by John F. Feldhusen and Catherine B. Bruch for the period 1981–1985.

At state level, the significant change is that of legislation to provide special opportunities for the gifted and talented as well as the money to implement them. Although a number of states had been financing special education programs for gifted students, they were not many; mandated provision is a phenomenon of the 1970s. Although some states have legislation for this purpose, many do not; however, the wheels have been set in motion for the purpose by federal legislation and the spirit and activity of the times. Despite the Reagan administration's budget cuts in education, we can expect all 50 states to have legislation and to provide some financial support for the education of the gifted where little or none existed. As this develops, the interests of many kinds of giftedness will receive the attention due them in time. Another outcome of these activities will be the appointment of state and local coordinators of the gifted to provide the necessary leadership for the implementation of special education opportunities—many have already been appointed and the appointments that remain should shortly be accomplished. In-service teacher preparation will continue to be stepped up as more and more trained teachers are needed.

Parents are no longer passive about the education provided for their gifted children. They have become a potent voice for changes in gifted education, one that will continue to be heard. And they know that the power is with them. The number of roles they play range from being a facilitator of their gifted child at home; interacting with the teacher in cooperative partnership to increase the effectiveness of their child's educational experiences; participating as members of organized advocacy groups who press for legislation, funding, and educational change and who resort to due process of law to see to the implementation of their children's rights.

We are far removed from the position of having no teachers specially prepared to be educators of gifted students; yet, in some ways, we have only just begun our efforts to provide sufficient numbers of adequately trained teachers to staff the increasing number of positions that are being created for them all over the country. Preparation is basically given in the preservice programs of colleges and universities, generally at the graduate level. Course offerings fluctuate from single to multiple and are designed to meet certification requirements (where these are necessary), degree requirements, or both. With the expanded concept of giftedness, it has become necessary to introduce a variety of course offerings so that any university or college offering a program of preparation, rather than single courses, usually includes four basic categories of course material, namely, psychological foundations, teaching strategies and materials, practicum, and research. Selection of teachers for these areas of preparation relative to special qualities although highly desirable, would not be found to be practical. Certainly, where control of trait factors is difficult, preparation can alert trainees about the special nature of their task and the need to develop those behaviors and competencies that will mark them for the role of educators of excellence. An important complement and immediate facility is the in-service approach of teacher preparation. This can be specially designed to reorient trained teachers for the new task at hand, keep them abreast of new knowledge in the field, and ensure the application of their acquired competence in the direction of nurturing excellence.

CONCLUSIONS

As we draw to a close, it is appropriate to appraise briefly the development of thought in the education of gifted students. A priority has been to make some sense of the term gifted. We have discovered that the semantics of the word includes multidimensional abilities and talent that are peculiar to the individual; that environment plays a much larger part in interacting with hereditary factors to facilitate the unfoldment of excellence than we realized; that the social value system determines what is or is not giftedness; that creativity is the single most powerful energizing factor in human functioning, which goes beyond abilities to include the interactive influences of intellective, emotive, and motivational forces; and that goal-directed behaviors and task commitment add operational dimension to its productivity. Although we possess many more assessment devices today, we have a long way to go before the several categories of giftedness can be appropriately identified. Successful construction of well-designed instruments is waiting for those who are willing to invest time and effort. We must not minimize the problem of implementation, which includes trained personnel whose understanding goes beyond IQ and academic achievement as indices of giftedness; nor must we minimize the problem of providing money to carry out the task. Of all the areas of giftedness, one of the least explored is that of development. Some data are available on intellectual and creative development, but little else is available that relates to other areas of talent. Information about the development of gifted students can provide important clues to what we may

424

do to maximize the growth of their potential. What we know about the severe drop in creative thinking abilities is helping us to offset this problem to some extent by stimulating creative processes, alleviating stress, and providing needed support at critical developmental phases. Certainly, developmental stage theory and its extension to include creativity have great import for educational practice and counseling. Periodicity to indicate the transformation of energy required for escalation to higher levels of functioning is pertinent to creative leaps, which are so necessary for gifted students in their move toward actualization and eminence. This alerts us to changes in mental growth that occur among the gifted and transend acceleration. The triadic model of the developmental stage theory is a systems approach to account for discontinuous growth in individuals. An interesting variation of this systems approach is transformation theory, which cuts across chronology to account for many kinds of growth, each occurring at different stages and levels in triadic sequence (accretive, replicative, and mutualistic). As the organized pattern approaches perfection, it begins to break down or destructure; reorganization (or reintegration of the elements) and inclusion of other elements follow, prepartory to the transformation that is to take place for the next triadic movement at a higher level. This has importance for the creative development of gifted students, especially in their aspirations for higher levels of intellectual growth as well as for guidance. On the issue of guidance, we are tending to move away from intervention that is crisis oriented and therapy rooted to guidance that concerns itself with the developmental problems of normal children and that is rooted in prevention rather than cure. An important feature of guidance today is creativity and the direction that is to be taken to facilitate its development in gifted students so that they may achieve high levels of intellectual functioning toward self-actualization and mental health. We have learned something about the nature of stress and its inhibitory and destructive characteristics, which guidance can reduce (if not prevent) by equipping gifted students with various coping strategies. Guidance today and in the future can be expected to integrate academic and career advisement and direction; it should shift to a continuous emphasis. We have also become aware of the importance of the benefits of a creativogenic society on the gifted individual; however, if we cannot have this in macrocosm, then we should attempt to achieve it in microcosm so that conditions can be created to foster creative growth maximally in a school setting. Any attempt to cater to gifted individuals today must bear in mind the interests of special groups. These interests may relate to an expanded concept of underachievement, minority and culturally diverse factors, disabilities and handicaps, and the special developmental problems of girls in a society that stereotypes sex-role behaviors. We can look forward to increasing support from various national, federal, state, and local agencies and organizations. As more people become increasingly knowledgeable about giftedness, we can expect legislation and funding in all the states that will mandate special opportunities for the gifted. We can also expect institutions of higher learning to become more responsive to the task of training the best teachers for the education of the gifted.

Land's (1979) address on the future of education in terms of his transformation model—which is consistent with other theoretical models of growth (e.g., those of E. Fromm, J. C. Gowan, A. H. Maslow)—anticipates change as inevitable if continued survival is to take place. Relevant to education in general, Land makes a number of observations, such as moving from high levels of disorder through order (normal success) to high levels of order (integrative complexity) or, concerning thinking and brain functions in particular, as moving from stimulus-response—involving brain stem activity of *perceiving* and *acting* (Phase I)—through copying and modifying—involving midbrain and limbic system functions of perceiving, *analyzing, evaluating,* and acting (Phase II)—to creating—involving cortex processing of perceiving, analyzing, synthesizing, evaluating, and acting (Phase III). Education emphasizes, in the main, learning for mastery. But Land sees learning as moving beyond mastery to creativity, where integration of differences to produce the new occurs to meet the challenges of change for the purpose of growth. Although other educators have pointed to the importance of cultivating creativity, it is Gowan who (like Land) reiterates its importance in individual development, perceiving in its nurture the escalation to higher levels of human functioning. The importance of creativity to the gifted student's development cannot be minimized for it has power to transform giftedness to eminence as it moves from the restrictions of the known to the frontiers of the unknown and beyond. We are also reminded by Land (1979) that if growth is to occur, the change sequence of conservation, collapse, and transformation must happen. The turning point from Phase II to Phase III brings about the problem of the bump that is, with success there is the tendency to overshoot and a kind of diminishing return sets in at the end of Phase II, at which time the system begins to break down. Education innovation in the 1960s designed to meet this problem did not work and lead to the back-to-basics movement—a little bump or reaction to unforseen change may result in reverting to the initial pattern. Perpetuating the past Land considers *educative catastrophe*. For growth to occur in education, it is important that change be facilitated without too many educative catastrophes. Understanding the transition that needs to be made between Phase II to Phase III and being able creatively to bridge or combine differences more rapidly would help the advancement of education and whose relevance extends to the numerous developments in gifted education today. The rich diversity of approaches that may appear separate in the nurturant process, procedures, and programs practiced need to be pulled together to become integral components of curricula and central to regular schooling. But not without controls for change and transformation to higher and more productive levels so that education creates open systems of energy exchange for dynamic growth.

REFERENCES

Abell, A. M. *Talks with great composers*. Garmisch-Partenkirchen, West Germany: G. E. Schroeder-Verlag, 1964.

Abraham, W. *Common sense about gifted children*. New York: Harper & Bros., 1958.

Allport, C. W., Vernon, P. E., & Lindzey, G. *Study of values: Manual of directions* (Rev. ed.). Boston: Houghton Mifflin, 1951.

Alpert, R. Motivation to achieve. In M. J. Aschner & C. E. Bish (Eds.), *Productive thinking in education*. Washington, D.C.: National Education Association, 1965.

Amidon, E. J., & Flanders, N. A. *The role of the teacher in the classroom: A manual for understanding and improving teacher classroom behavior*. Minneapolis, Minn.: Association for Productive Teaching, 1971.

Amram, F. M., & Giese, D. L. *Creativity training: A tool for motivating disadvantaged students*. Minneapolis: University of Minnesota Press, 1968.

Anastasi, A. Heredity, environment, and the question "how?" *Psychology Review,* 1958, *65*(4), 197–208.

————. *Psychological testing*. New York: John Wiley, 1976.

Anastasi, A., & Schaefer, C. E. Note on the concepts of creativity and intelligence. *Journal of Creative Behavior,* 1971, *5*(2), 113–116.

Andrews, E. G. The development of imagination in the pre-school child. *University of Iowa Studies in Character,* 1930, *3*(4).

Angelino, H. The low achiever: A closer look. *The Oklahoma Teacher,* 1960, October, p. 12.

Angoff, W. H. (Ed.). *The college board admissions testing program: A technical report on research and development activities relating to the scholastic aptitude test and achievement tests*. New York: College Entrance Examinations Board, 1971.

Arieti, S. *Creativity: The magic synthesis*. New York: Basic Books, 1976.

Arlin, P. Cognitive development in adulthood. *Developmental Psychology,* 1975, *11*(5), 602–606.

Arthur, G. *Arthur-point scale*. Chicago: Stoelting, 1947.

Astin, A. W. *The myth of equal success in public higher education*. Atlanta, Ga.: Southern Education Foundation, 1975.

Atkinson, J. W. Personality dynamics. *Annual Review of Psychology,* 1960, *11,* 255–290.

Ausubel, D. P. Defence of advance organizers. *Review of Educational Research,* 1978, *38*(2), 251–259.

Bahner, J. M. Individually guided education. In E. Ingas & R. J. Corsini (Eds.), *Alternative educational systems*. Itasca, Ill.: F. E. Peacock, 1979.

Bailey, S. K. Education and the pursuit of happiness. *UCLA Educator,* 1971, *14*(1), 14–18.

Baldwin, A. Y. Introduction, In A. Y. Baldwin, G. H. Gear, & L. J. Lucito (Eds.), *Educational planning for the gifted*. Reston, Va.: Council for Exceptional Children, 1978.

Baldwin, A. Y., Gear, G. H., Lucito, L. J. (Eds.). *Educational planning for the gifted*. Reston, Va.: Council for Exceptional Children, 1978.

Barbe, W. B. Differentiated guidance for the gifted. *Education,* 1954, *74,* 306–311.

Barchillon, J. Creativity and its inhibition in child prodigies. In *Personality dimensions of creativity*. New York: Lincoln Institute for Psychotherapy, 1961.

Barclay, J. R. *Appraising individual differences in the elementary classroom: A manual for the Barclay Classroom Climate Inventory*. Lexington, Ky.: Educational Skills Development, 1978.

Bardwick, J. *Psychology of women*. New York, Harper & Row, 1971.

Barron, F. The psychology of imagination. *Scientific American,* 1958, *199,* 155–166.

————. *Creativity and psychological health*. Princeton, N.J.: D. Van Nostrand, 1963.

————. *Creative person and creative process*. New York: Holt, Rinehart & Winston, 1969.

Bayley, N. Consistency and variability in the growth of intelligence from birth to eighteen years. *Journal of Genetic Psychology,* 1949, *75,* 165–196.

Bayley, N., & Oden, M. H. The maintenance of intellectual ability in gifted adults. *Journal of Gerontology,* 1955, *10,* 91–107.

Bem, S. L. Probing the promise of androgyny. In A. G. Kaplan & J. P. Bean (Eds.), *Beyond sex-role stereotypes: Readings toward a psychology of androgyny*. Boston, Mass. Little, Brown, 1976.

Benedict, R. *Patterns of culture*. London: Routledge & Kegan Paul, 1935.

Bennett, G. K. Seashore, H. G., & Wesman, A. G. *Differential aptitude tests*. New York: Psychological Corporation, 1963.

Bentley, A. *Measures of musical ability*. New York: October House, 1966.

Berkowitz, B. The Wechsler-Bellevue performance of white males past age 50. *Journal of Gerontology,* 1953, *8,* 78–80.

Bialer, I., Doll, L., & Winsberg, B. G. A modified Lincoln-Oseretsky motor development scale: Provisional standardization. *Perceptual and Motor Skills,* 1974, *38,*

Binet, A., & Simon, T. Méthodes nouvelles pour le diagnostic du niveau intellectuel des anormaux. *Année Psychologique,* 1905, *11,* 191–244.

Birch, J. W. Early school admission for mentally advanced children. *Exceptional Children,* 1954, *21,* 84–87.

Bish, C. E. The academically talented project: Gateway to the present. *Gifted Child Quarterly*, 1975, *19*(4), 282–289.

Bishop, W. Successful teachers of the gifted. *Exceptional Children*, 1968, *34*, 317–325.

Bledsoe, J. C., & Khatena, J. A factor analytic study of "Something about myself." *Psychological Reports*, 1973, *32*, 1176–1178.

———. Factor analytic study of "What kind of person are you?" test. *Perceptual and Motor Skills*, 1974, *39*, 143–146.

Bloom, B. S. (Ed.). *Taxonomy of educational objectives, handbook I: Cognitive domain.* New York: David McKay, 1956.

Bonsall, M., & Stefflre, B. The temperament of gifted children. *California Journal of Educational Research*, 1955, *6*, 162–165.

Boston, B. *The sorcerer's apprentice: A case study in the role of mentoring.* Reston, Va.: Council for Exceptional Children, 1976.

Bowers, K. S., & Bowers, P. G. *Hypnosis and creativity: A theoretical and empirical rapproachment* (Research Report No. 11). Unpublished manuscript, University of Waterloo, Canada, 1970.

Bowman, L. Educational opportunities for gifted children in California. *California Journal of Educational Research*, 1955, *6*, 195–200.

Bowra, C. M. *The romantic imagination.* New York: Oxford University Press, 1969.

Brandwein, P. *The gifted child as a future scientist.* New York: Harcourt Brace, 1955.

Bricklin, B., & Bricklin, P. *Bright child—poor grades: The psychology of under-achievement.* New York: Dell, 1967.

Bridgeman, D. S. Where the loss of talent occurs and why. In *College admissions: Vol. 7. The search for talent.* New York: College Entrance Examinations Board, 1960.

Bristo, W. *How New York City schools provide for gifted.* New York: New York City Schools, Bureau of Curriculum Research, 1956.

Brown, A. W. Chicago non-verbal examination. New York: Psychological Corporation, 1963.

Brown, E. K., & Johnson, P. G. *Education for the talented in mathematics and science.* Washington, D.C.: Department of Health, Education, and Welfare, 1952.

Broverman, I. K., Broverman, D., Clarkson, F. E., Rosenkrantz, P. S., & Vogel, S. Sex-role stereotypes and clinical judgments of mental health. *Journal of Consulting and Clinical Psychology*, 1970, *34*, 1–7.

Bruch, C. B. *The creative Binet.* Paper presented at the *Council for Exceptional Children Conference*, New York, April 1968.

———. Modification of procedures for identification of the disadvantaged gifted. *Gifted Child Quarterly*, 1971, *15*(4), 267–272.

———. *Sex role images influencing creative productivity and non-productivity in women.* Paper in the symposium presented at the Southeastern Psychological Association, Atlanta, Ga., April 1972.

———. Assessment of creativity in culturally different children. *Gifted Child Quarterly*, 1975, *19*(2), 164–174.

———. Current degree programs in gifted education. *Gifted Child Quarterly*, 1977, *21*(2), 141–153.

Bruch, C. B., & Morse, J. A. Initial study of creative productive women under the Bruch-Morse model. *Gifted Child Quarterly*, 1972, *16*(4), 282–289.

Bruner, J. S. *The process of education*. Cambridge: Harvard University Press, 1960.

———. The act of discovery. *Harvard Educational Review*, 1961, *31*(1), 21–32.

Bugelski, B. R. Words and things and images. *American Psychologist*, 1970, *25*, 1002–1012.

Burks, B. S., Jensen, D. W., & Terman, L. M. *The promise of youth: Genetic studies of genius* (Vol. 3). Stanford Calif.: Stanford University Press, 1930.

Burnside, L. Psychological guidance of gifted children. *Journal of Consulting Psychology*, 1942, *6*, 223–228.

Buros, O. K. (Ed.). *The seventh mental measurement yearbook*. Highland Park, N.J.: Gryphon Press, 1972.

———. (Ed.). *Tests in print* (Vol. 2). Highland Park, N.J.: Gryphon Press, 1974.

Burt, C. The structure of the mind: A review of the results of factor analysis. *British Journal of Educational Psychology*, 1949, *19*, 100–111; 176–199.

———. The psychology of creative ability. *British Journal of Psychology*, 1962, *32*, 292–293.

Bushnell, D. D. Black arts for black youth. *Saturday Review*, *53* (July 18, 1970), 43–46; 60.

Butterfield, S. M. Some legal implications. In *Developing IEPs for the gifted/talented*. Los Angeles, Calif.: National/State Leadership Training Institute on the Gifted and Talented, 1979.

Campbell, D. T., & Fiske, D. W. Convergent and discriminant validation by the multitrait-multimethod matrix. *Psychological Bulletin*, 1959, *56*, 81–105.

Capurso, A. Music. In L. A. Fliegler (Ed.), *Curriculum planning for the gifted*. Englewood Cliffs, N.J.: Prentice-Hall, 1961.

Carroll, H. A. Intellectually gifted children: Their characteristics and problems. *Teachers College Record*, 1940, *42*, 212–227.

Cassel, N., & Stancik, E. J. *The leadership ability evaluation*. Los Angeles, Calif.: Western Psychological Services, 1961.

Cattell, R. B., & Cattell, A. K. S. *IPAT culture fair intelligence test: Scales I, II, and III*. Champaign, Ill.: Institute for Personality and Ability Testing, 1963.

Cautela, J. R., & Tondo, T. R. *Imagery survey schedule*. Unpublished questionnaire, Boston College, 1971.

Chemers, M. M., & Rice, R. W. A theoretical and empirical examination of Fiedler's contingency model of leadership effectiveness. In J. G. Hunt and L. L. Larson (Eds.), *Contingency approaches to leadership*. Carbondale: Southern Illinois University Press, 1974.

Clark, K. B. *Dark ghetto*. New York: Harper & Row, 1965.

Cole, H. P. *Process education: The new direction for elementary secondary schools*. Englewood Cliffs, N.J.: Educational Technology Publications, 1972.

Cole, H. P., & Parsons, D. E. The Williams total creativity program. *Journal of Creative Behavior*, 1974, *8*(3), 187–207.

Coleman, J. S. *Social Climates*. Washington, D.C.: U.S. Government Printing Office, 1961.

———. Equality of opportunity and equality of results. *Harvard Educational Review*, 1973, *43*(1), 129–164.

Coleridge, S. T. [*Biographia litereria*]. New York: Dutton, 1956. (Originally published, 1817.)

Collier, G. *Art and the creative consciousness.* Englewood Cliffs, N.J.: Prentice-Hall, 1972.

Conant, J. B. *The identification and education of the academically talented in the American secondary schools* (NEA Conference Report). Washington, D.C.: National Education Association, 1958.

_____. *The citadel of learning.* Westport, Conn.: Greenwood Press, 1977.

Cooper, J. D. *The art of decision making.* Garden City, N.Y.: Doubleday, 1961.

Corsini, R. J., & Fassett, K. K. Intelligence and aging. *Journal of Genetic Psychology,* 1953, *83,* 249–264.

Costello, C. G. The control of visual imagery in mental disorder. *Journal of Mental Science,* 1957, *103,* 840–849.

Covington, M. V., Crutchfield, R. S., Davies, L., & Olton, R. M. *The productive thinking program: A course in learning to think.* Columbus, Ohio: Charles E. Merrill, 1974.

Cox, C. M. *The early traits of three hundred geniuses: Genetic studies of genius* (Vol. 2). Stanford, Calif.: Stanford University Press, 1926.

Crutchfield, R. S. Assessment of persons through a quasi group-interaction technique. *Journal of Abnormal and Social Psychology,* 1951, *46,* 577–588.

Cunnington, B. F., & Torrance, E. P. *Sounds and images: Teachers' guide and recorded text* (Adult and children's version). New York: Ginn, 1965.

Cutts, N. E., & Moseley, N. *Teaching the bright and gifted.* Englewood Cliffs, N.J.: Prentice-Hall, 1957.

Davenport, J. D. A study of the performance of monozygotic and dizygotic twins and siblings on measures of scholastic aptitude, creativity, achievement motivation, and academic achievement. (Doctoral dissertation, University of Maryland, 1967). *Dissertation Abstracts,* 1968, *28,* 3865B. (University of Microfilms No. 68–03350).

Davis, G. A. *Imagination express.* Buffalo, N.Y.: D.O.K., 1970.

_____. In pursuit of the creative person. *Journal of Creative Behavior,* 1975, *9*(2), 75–87.

Davis, N. Teachers for the gifted. *Journal of Teacher Education,* 1954, *5,* 221–224.

de Bono, E. *The five-day course in thinking.* New York: Basic Books, 1967.

_____. *Lateral thinking.* New York: Basic Books, 1970.

_____. *The dog-walking machine.* New York: Harper & Row, 1971.

_____. *Thinking course for juniors.* Dorset, UK.: Direct Education Services, 1974.

_____. *Think links.* Dorset, UK.: Direct Education Services, 1975.

_____. *Thinking action.* Dorset, UK.: Direct Education Services, 1976.

DeHaan, R. F., & Havighurst, R. J. *Educating gifted children.* Chicago: University of Chicago Press, 1965.

Dewey, J. *How we think.* Boston, Mass.: D. C. Heath, 1910.

Dorn, C. M. The advanced placement program in studio art. *Gifted Child Quarterly,* 1976, *20*(4), 450–458.

Dowd, R. J. Underachieving students of high capacity. *Journal of Higher Education,* 1952, *23,* 327–330.

Drake, R. M. *Drake musical aptitude tests*. Chicago: Science Research Associates, 1954.

Drever, J. *A dictionary of psychology*. Baltimore, Md.: Penguin, 1963.

Drews, E. E. M., & Teahan, J. E. Parental attitudes and academic achievers. *Journal of Clinical Psychology*, 1957, *13*, 328–332.

Durio, H. F. Mental imagery and creativity. *Journal of Creative Behavior*, 1975, *9*(4), 233–244.

Durr, W. K. *The gifted student*. New York: Oxford University Press, 1964.

Dweck, C. S., Davidson, W., Nelson, S., & Enna, B. Sex differences in learned helplessness: II. The contingencies of evaluative feedback in the classroom and III. An experimental analysis. *Developmental Psychology*, 1978, *14*(3), 268–276. (a)

Eash, M. J. Grouping: What have we learned? *Educational Leadership*, 1961, *18*, 429–434.

Eccles, J. C. The physiology of imagination. (Originally published 1958.) In *Readings from "Scientific American."* San Francisco: W. H. Freeman, 1972.

Edmonds, R., Billingsley, A., Corner, J., Dyer, J. M., Hall, W. H., Hill, R., McGehee, N., Reddick, L., Taylor, H. F., & Wright, S. A black response to Christopher Jencks' "Inequality and certain other issues." *Harvard Educational Review*, 1973, *43*(1), 76–91.

Edwards, A. J. *Individual mental testing: Part I—History and theories*. San Francisco: Intext Educational Publishers, 1971.

Ekstrom, R. Experimental studies of homogeneous grouping: A critical review. *School Review*, 1961, *69*, 217–226.

Ellison, R. L., James, L. R., Fox, D. G., & Taylor, C. W. *The identification and selection of creative artistic talent by means of biographical information* (Report submitted to the USOE/HEW, Grant No. OEG-8-9-540215-4004 (010), Project No. 9-0215). 1971.) Washington, D.C.: U.S. Government Printing Office, 1971.

Elwood, C. Acceleration of the gifted. *Gifted Child Quarterly*, 1958, *2*(1), 21–23.

Epstein, H. T. Growth spurts. In J. Chall & A. F. Mirsky (Eds.), *Education and the brain*. Chicago: University of Chicago Press, 1977. (77th Yearbook of the NSSE)

Erikson, E. H. *Childhood and society*. New York: W. W. Norton, 1950.

————. Inner and outer space: Reflections on womanhood. In S. Berg (Ed.), *About women*. Greenwich, Conn.: Fawcett, 1973.

Ernest, F. J., & Pavio, A. Imagery and verbal associative latencies as a function of imagery ability. *Canadian Journal of Psychology*, 1971, *25*, 83–90.

Evans, M. The effects of supervisory behavior on the path-goal relationship. *Organizational Behavior and Human Performance*, 1970, *5*, 277–298.

Fantini, M. D., & Weinstein, G. *The disadvantaged child: Challenge to education*. New York: Harper & Row, 1968.

Feldhusen, J. F., Houtz, J. C., & Ringenbach, S. The Purdue elementary problem-solving inventory. *Psychological Reports*, 1972, *31*, 891–901.

Feldhusen, J. F., Speedie, S. M., & Treffinger, D. J. The Purdue creative thinking program: Research and evaluation. *NSPI Journal*, 1971, *10*(3), 5–9.

Feldhusen, J. F., & Treffinger, D. J. *Teaching creative thinking and problem solving*. Dubuque, Iowa: Kendall/Hunt, 1977.

————. *Creative thinking and problem solving in gifted education* (2nd ed.) Dubuque, Iowa: Kendall/Hunt, 1980.

Feldhusen, J. F., Treffinger, D. J., & Bahlke, S. J. Developing creative thinking: The Purdue creativity program. *Journal of Creative Behavior,* 1970, *4*(2), 85-90.

Feldhusen, J. F., Treffinger, D. J., van Mondfrans, A. P., & Ferris, D. R. The relationship between academic grades and divergent thinking scores derived from four different methods of testing. *Journal of Experimental Education,* 1971, *40,* 35-40.

Fiedler, F. E. A contingency model of leadership effectiveness. In L. Berkowitz (Ed.), *Advances in experimental social psychology* (Vol. 1). New York: Academic Press, 1964.

———. *A theory of leadership effectiveness.* New York: McGraw-Hill, 1967.

Finder, J. Living with people: The Mirman School. *McCall's,* 97(11), 41; 74-75; 87-88.

Fischer, R. Hallucinations can reveal creative imagination. *Fields Within Fields,* 1974, *11,* 29-33.

Flanagan, J. C. Critical requirements: A new approach to employee evaluation. *Personal Psychology,* 1949, *2,* 419-426.

———. *Test of general ability.* Chicago: Science Research Associates, 1960.

Flavell, J. H. *The developmental psychology of Jean Piaget.* New York: D. Van Nostrand, 1963.

Fleishman, B. A. Twenty years of consideration and structure. In E. A. Fleishman & J. G. Hunt (Eds.), *Current developments in the study of leadership.* Carbondale: Southern Illinois University Press, 1973.

Fliegler, L. A. (Ed.). *Curriculum planning for the gifted.* Englewood Cliffs, N.J.: Prentice-Hall, 1961.

———. Commentary on "Motivation to achieve" by R. Alpert. In M. J. Aschner & C. L. Bish (Eds.), *Productive thinking in education.* Washington, D.C.: National Education Association, 1965.

Foulds, G. A., & Raven, J. C. Normal changes in the mental abilities of adults as age advances. *Journal of Mental Science,* 1948, *94,* 133-142.

Fox, L. H. Programs for the gifted and talented: An overview. In A. H. Passow (Ed.), *The gifted and the talented: Their education and development.* Chicago: University of Chicago Press, 1979. (78th Yearbook of the NSSE)

Fraiser, M. M. Counseling the culturally diverse gifted. In N. Colangelo & R. T. Zaffrann (Eds.), *New voices in counseling the gifted.* Dubuque, Iowa: Kendall/Hunt, 1979.

Frankel, E. A comparative study of achieving and underachieving high school boys of high intellectual ability. *Journal of Educational Research,* 1960, *53,* 172-180.

French, J. L. (Ed.), *Educating the gifted: A book of readings* (Rev. ed.). New York: Holt, Rinehart & Winston, 1959.

———. The highly intelligent dropout. *Accent on Talent,* 1968, *2*(3), 5-6.

Frierson, E. C. Upper and lower status gifted children: A study of differences. *Exceptional Children,* 1965, *32,* 83-90.

Frostig, M. Testing as a basis for educational therapy. *Journal of Special Education,* 1967, *2*(1), 15-34.

Fuchigami, R. Y. Summary analysis and future directions. In A. Y. Baldwin, G. H. Gear, & L. J. Lucito (Eds.), *Educational planning for the gifted.* Reston, Va: Council for Exceptional Children, 1978.

Gage, N. L. IQ heritability, race differences and educational research. *Phi Delta Kappan,* 1972, *53*(5), 308-312.

Gallagher, J. J. *Research summary on gifted child education*. Springfield, Ill.: Office of the Superintendent of Public Instruction, 1966.

———. Technical assistance: A new device for quality educational services for the gifted. *TAG Newsletter*, 1974, *16*, 5–8.

———. *Teaching the gifted child* (2nd ed.). Boston, Mass.: Allyn & Bacon, 1975.

———. Issues in education of the gifted. In A. H. Passow (Ed.), *The gifted and the talented: Their education and development*. Chicago: University of Chicago Press, 1979. (78th Yearbook of the NSSE)

———. Research needs for education of the gifted. In *Issues in gifted education*. Los Angeles, Calif.: National/State Leadership Training Institute on the Gifted and the Talented, 1979. (b)

Gallagher, J. J., & Kinney, L. (Eds.). *Talent delayed—talent denied: A conference report*. Reston, Va.: Foundation for Exceptional Children, 1974.

Galton, F. *Hereditary genius*. New York: Appleton, 1870.

———. Statistics of mental imagery. *Mind*, 1880, *5*, 300–318.

Garrett, H. E. A developmental theory of intelligence. *American Psychologist*, 1946, *1*, 372–378.

George, W. C., Cohn, S. J., & Stanley, J. C. (Eds.). *Educating the gifted: Acceleration and enrichment*. Baltimore, Md.: The John Hopkins University Press, 1979.

Gerencser, S. The Calasanctius experience. In A. H. Passow (Ed.), *The gifted and the talented: Their education and development*. Chicago: University of Chicago Press, 1979. (78th Yearbook of the NSSE)

Gerken, K. C. An unseen minority: Handicapped individuals who are gifted and talented. In N. Colangelo & R. T. Zaffrann (Eds.), *New voices in counseling the gifted*. Dubuque, Iowa: Kendall/Hunt, 1979.

Getzels, J. W., & Jackson, P. W. The meaning of "giftedness": An examination of an expanding concept. *Phi Delta Kappan*, 1958, *40*(2), 75–78.

———. Occupational choice and cognitive functioning: Career aspirations of highly intelligent and of highly creative adolescents. *Journal of Abnormal and Social Psychology*, 1960, *61*(1), 119–123.

———. Family environment and cognitive choice: A study of the sources of highly intelligent and of highly creative adolescents. *American Sociological Review*, 1961, *26*, 351–359.

———. *Creativity and intelligence: Explorations with gifted children*. New York: John Wiley, 1962.

Ghiselin, B. (Ed.). *The creative process*. Berkeley: University of California Press, 1955.

Gibb, C. A. The principles and traits of leadership. *Journal of Abnormal Psychology*, 1947, *42*, 267–284.

———. (Review of *Leadership evaluation and development scale*.) In O. K. Buros (Ed.), *Seventh mental measurement yearbook*. Highland Park, N.J.: Gryphon Press, 1972.

Gifted Child Quarterly. 1977, *20*(3). (Special issue on Guidance.)

———. 1979, *22*(3). (Special issue on Special Projects.) (a)

———. 1979, *23*(1). (Special issue on Incubation.) (b)

Ginsberg, E. *Occupational choice: An approach to a general theory*. New York: Columbia University Press, 1951.

434

Glasser, R. The design of instruction. In J. I. Goodlad (Ed.), *The changing American school*. Chicago: University of Chicago Press, 1966. (65th Yearbook of the NSSE)

Goddard, H. H. The Binet and Simon tests of intellectual capacity. *The Training School*, 1908, *5*, 3–9.

———. Ten thousand children measured by the Binet measuring scale of intelligence. *Pedagogical Seminary*, 1911, *18*, 232–259.

Gold, M. J. *Education of the intellectually gifted*. Columbus, Ohio: Charles E. Merrill, 1965.

———. Teachers and mentors. In A. H. Passon (Ed.), *The gifted and the talented: Their education and development*. Chicago: University of Chicago Press, 1979. (78th Yearbook of the NSSE)

Goldberg, M. J., & Passow, A. H. A study of underachieving gifted. *Educational Leadership*, 1959, *16*, 121–125.

Goodrich, H. B., & Knapp, R. H. *Origins of American Scientists*. Chicago: University of Chicago Press, 1952.

Goolsby, T. M. Alternative admissions criteria for college. In *Non-traditional approaches to assess the academic potential of black students*. Atlanta, Ga: Southern Regional Education Board, 1975.

Gordon, E. *Musical aptitude profile*. Boston, Mass.: Houghton Mifflin, 1965.

Gordon, R. An investigation into some of the factors that favor the formation of stereotyped images. *British Journal of Psychology*, 1949, *39*, 156–157.

———. An experiment correlating the nature of imagery with performance on a test of reversal of perspective. *British Journal of Psychology*, 1950, *41*, 63–67.

———. *Stereotypy of imagery and belief as an ego defense*. London: Cambridge University Press, 1962.

———. A very private world. In P. W. Sheehan (Ed.), *The function of imagery*. New York: Academic Press, 1972.

Gordon, W. J. J. *Synectics: The development of creative capacity*. New York: Harper & Row, 1961.

———. Some source materials in discovery-by-analogy. *Journal of Creative Behavior*, 1974, *8*(4), 239–257.

Gough, H. G. *California psychological inventory*. Los Angeles, Calif.: Consulting Psychologists Press, 1956.

———. The adjective check list as a personality assessment research technique. *Psychological Reports*, 1960, 6, 107–122. (Monograph supplement)

———. The underachieving gifted child: A problem for everyone. *Exceptional Children*, 1955, *21*, 247–250.

———. Dynamics of underachievement in gifted students. *Exceptional Children*, 1957, *24*, 98–101.

———. The education of disadvantaged gifted youth. In J. C. Gowan, J. Khatena, & E. P. Torrance (Eds.), *Educating the Ablest* (2nd ed.). Itasca, Ill.: F. E. Peacock, 1979.

———. The development of the creative individual. *Gifted Child Quarterly*, 1971, *15*(3), 156–174.

———. *The development of the creative individual*. San Diego, Calif.: Robert R. Knapp, 1972.

_____. *The development of the psychedelic individual.* Buffalo, N.Y.: Creative Education Foundation, 1974.

_____. *Trance, art and creativity.* Buffalo, N.Y.: Creative Education Foundation, 1975.

_____. Creative inspiration in composers. *Journal of Creative Behavior,* 1977, *11*(4), 249–255.

_____. Creativity and gifted child movement. *Journal of Creative Behavior,* 1978, *12*(1), 1–13. (a)

_____. Incubation, imagery and creativity. *Journal of Mental Imagery,* 1978, *2*(2), 23–32. (b)

_____. The role of imagination in the development of the creative individual. *Humanitas,* 1978, *24*(2), 197–208.

_____. Differentiated guidance for the gifted: A developmental view. In J. C. Gowan, J. Khatena, & E. P. Torrance (Eds.), *Educating the ablest* (2nd ed.). Itasca, Ill.: F. E. Peacock, 1979. (a)

_____. Education of the gifted in utopia. In J. C. Gowan, J. Khatena, & E. P. Torrance (Eds.), *Educating the ablest.* Itasca, Ill.: F. E. Peacock, 1979. (b)

_____. *New trends in counselling.* Address presented at the Expressive Therapies and Creative Education Gifted Programs Conference, University of Georgia, Athens, March 1979. (c)

_____. The use of developmental stage theory in helping gifted children become creative. In *Issues in gifted education.* Los Angeles, Calif.: National/State Leadership Training Institute on the Gifted and the Talented, 1979. (d)

_____. The use of developmental stage theory in helping gifted children become creative. *Gifted Child Quarterly,* 1980, *24*(1), 22–28.

Gowan, J. C., & Bruch, C. B. *The academically talented: Student and guidance.* Boston, Mass.: Houghton Mifflin, 1971.

Gowan, J. C., & Demos, G. D. *How to enhance effective leadership.* Unpublished manuscript. California State College at Long Beach, 1962.

_____. *The education and guidance of the ablest.* Springfield, Ill.: Charles C. Thomas, 1964.

Gowan, J. C., & Dodd, S. C. General systems: A creative search for synthesis. *Journal of Creative Behavior,* 1977, *11*(1), 47–52.

Gowan, J. C., Khatena, J., & Torrance, E. P. (Eds.). *Educating the ablest* (2nd ed.). Itasca, Ill.: F. E. Peacock, 1979.

Granzow, K. R. A comparative study of underachievers, normal achievers, and over-achievers in reading (Doctoral dissertation, University of Iowa, 1954). *Dissertation Abstracts,* 1954, *14,* 631–632. (University Microfilms No. 00-07, 563)

Gray, C. E. An epicyclical model for western civilization. *American Anthropologist,* 1961, *63,* 1014–1037.

_____. A measurement of creativity in western civilization. *American Anthropologist,* 1966, *68,* 1384–1417.

Gray, C. E., & Young, R. C. Utilizing the divergent production matrix of the structure of intellect in the development of teaching strategies. *Gifted Child Quarterly,* 1975, *19*(4), 290–300.

Green, E. E., & Green, S. Beyond biofeedback. New York: Delacorte, 1977.

Gruber, H. E. Courage and cognitive change in children and scientists. In M. Schwebel and J. Raph (Eds.), *Piaget in the classroom*. New York: Basic Books, 1973.

Grunebaum, M., Hurwutz, I., Prentice, N., & Sperry, B. Fathers of sons with primary neurotic learning inhibitions. *American Journal of Orthopsychiatry, 1962, 32,* 462.

Guilford, J. P. Creativity. *American Psychologist, 1950, 5,* 444-454.

———. A system of the psychomotor abilities. *American Journal of Psychology, 1958, 71*(1), 164-174.

———. *The nature of human intelligence*. New York: McGraw-Hill, 1967.

———. Creativity in the visual arts. In J. P. Guilford, *Intelligence, creativity, and their educational implications*. San Diego, Calif.: Robert R. Knapp, 1968.

———. Some misconceptions regarding measurement of creative talents. *Journal of Creative Behavior, 1971, 5*(2), 77-78.

———. Intellect and the gifted. *Gifted Child Quarterly, 1972, 16*(2), 175-184; 239-243.

———. *Creativity tests for children*. Orange, Calif.: Sheridan Psychological Services, 1973.

———. Varieties of creative giftedness: Their measurement and development. *Gifted Child Quarterly, 1975, 19*(2), 107-121.

———. *Way beyond the IQ*. Buffalo, N.Y.: Creative Education Foundation, 1977.

———. Some thoughts on incubation. *Journal of Creative Behavior, 1979, 13*(1), 1-8.

Guilford, J. P. Hendricks, M., & Hoepfner, R. Solving social problems creatively. In A. M. Biondi & S. J. Parnes (Eds.), *Assessing creative growth: The tests—book one*. Buffalo, N.Y.: Creative Education Foundation, 1976.

Guilford, J. P., & Hoepfner, R. Creative potential as related to measures of IQ and verbal comprehension, *Indian Journal of Psychology, 1966, 41,* 7-16.

Hanard, S. R. Creativity, lateral saccades and the non-dominant hemisphere. *Psychological Reports, 1972, 34,* 653-654.

Harman, W. W., McKim, R. H., Mogar, R. E., Fadiman, J., & Stolaroff, M. J. Psychedelic agents in creative problem solving: A pilot study. *Psychological Reports, 1966, 19,* 211-227.

Hass, R. B. The school sociatrist. *Sociatry, 1948, 2,* 283-321.

Hassan, P., & Butcher, H. J. Creativity and intelligence: A partial replication with Scottish children of Getzels' and Jackson's study. *British Journal of Psychology, 1966, 57,* 129-135.

Havighurst, R. J. Conditions productive of superior children. *Teachers College Record, 1961, 62* 524-531.

Hebb, D. O. *The organization of behavior*. New York: John Wiley, 1949.

Hedbring, C., & Rubenzer, R. Integrating IEP and SOI with educational programming for the gifted. *Gifted Child Quarterly, 1979, 23*(2), 338-345.

Hencley, S. P., & Yates, J. R. *Futurism in education: Methodologies*. Berkeley, Calif.: McCutchan, 1974.

Henry, N. B. (Ed.). *Education for the gifted*. The Chicago: University of Chicago Press, 1958. (57th Yearbook of the NSSE)

Hiest, P., & Yonge, G. *Omnibus personality inventory, form F: Manual*. New York: Psychological Corporation, 1968.

Hildreth, G. H. *Educating gifted children*. New York: Harper & Bros., 1952.

———. *Introduction to the gifted*. New York: McGraw-Hill, 1966.

Hirsch, S. P. Executive high school internships: A boon for the gifted and talented. *Teaching Exceptional Children*, 1976, *9*(1), 22–23.

Hollingworth, L. S. *Gifted children: Their nature and nurture*. New York: Macmillan, 1926.

———. *Children above 180 IQ Stanford-Binet*. New York: World, 1942.

Holt, J. *How children fail*. New York: Pitman, 1964.

Holt, R. R. Imagery: The return of the ostracized. *American Psychologist*, 1964, *19*, 254–264.

Horner, M. S. The motive to avoid success and changing aspirations in college women. In J. Bardwick (Ed.), *Readings on the psychology of women*. New York: Harper & Row, 1972. (a)

———. Toward an understanding of achievement—related conflicts in women. *Journal of Social Issues*, 1972, *28*, 157–175. (b)

House, R. J., & Dessler, A. The path-goal theory of leadership: Some post hoc and a priori tests. In J. G. Hunt & L. L. Larson (Eds.), *Contingency approaches to leadership*. Carbondale: Southern Illinois University Press, 1974.

Hoyt, K. B., Evans, R. N., MacKin, E. F., & Mangum, G. L. *Career education: What it is and how to do it* (2nd ed.). Salt Lake City: Olympus, 1974.

Hoyt, K. B., & Hebeler, J. R. (Eds.). *Career education for gifted and talented students*. Salt Lake City: Olympus, 1974.

Hunsicker, P., & Reiff, G. G. *Youth fitness test manual*. Washington, D.C.: American Alliance for Health, Physical Education, and Recreation, 1976.

Hunt, J. McV. Experience and the development of motivation. *Child Development*, 1960, *31*, 489–504.

———. The implications of changing ideas on how children develop intellectually. *Children*, 1964, *11*(3), 83–91.

Ingas, E. Introduction to alternative educational systems. In E. Ingas & R. J. Corsini (Eds.), *Alternative educational systems*. Itasca, Ill.: F. E. Peacock, 1979.

Institute for Behavioral Research in Creativity (IBRIC). *Development of the ALPHA biographical inventory*. Salt Lake City: Author, 1968.

Jackson, D. M. The emerging national and state concern. In A. H. Passow (Ed.), *The gifted and the talented: Their education and development*. Chicago: University of Chicago Press, 1979. (78th Yearbook of the NSSE)

Jaensch, E. R. *Eidetic imagery*. London: Routledge & Kegan Paul, 1930.

Jahoda, M. *Current concepts of positive mental health*. New York: Basic Books, 1958.

James, W. Great men, great thoughts and the environment. *Atlantic Monthly*, 1880, *46*, 441–459.

Jaynes, J. *The origin of consciousness in the breakdown of the bicameral mind*. Boston, Mass.: Houghton Mifflin, 1976.

Jackson, D. M. The emerging national and state concern. In A. H. Passow (Ed.), *The gifted and the talented: Their education and development*. Chicago: University of Chicago Press, 1979. (78th Yearbook of the NSSE)

Jaensch, E. R. *Eidetic imagery*. London: Routledge & Kegan Paul, 1930.

Jahoda, M. *Current concepts of positive mental health*. New York: Basic Books, 1958.

James, W. Great men, great thoughts and the environment. *Atlantic Monthly,* 1880, *46,* 441–459.

Jaynes, J. *The origin of consciousness in the breakdown of the bicameral mind.* Boston, Mass.: Houghton Mifflin, 1976.

Jencks, C. Inequality in retrospect. *Harvard Educational Review,* 1973, *43*(1), 138–164.

Jensen, A. R. How much can we boost IQ and scholastic achievement? *Harvard Educational Review,* 1969, *39*(3), 1–123.

Johnson, D. M. *The psychology of thought and judgment.* New York: Harper & Row, 1955.

Johnson, R. A. Word knowledge and production of original verbal responses in deaf children. *Perceptual and Motor Skills,* 1975, *41,* 125–126.

————. *Verbal originality in the absense of sight: Blind versus sighted adolescents.* Paper presented at the meeting of the 24th Annual Convention of the National Association for Gifted Children, San Diego, Calif., October 1977.

Johnson, R. A., & Khatena, J. Comparative study of verbal originality in deaf and hearing children. *Perceptual and Motor Skills,* 1975, *40,* 631–635.

Jones, H. E., & Conrad, H. S. The growth and decline of intelligence. *Genetic Psychology Monograph,* 1933, *13,* 223–298.

Journal of Creative Behavior. 1979, *13*(3). (Special issue on Incubation.)

Joyce, B., & Weil, M. *Models of teaching.* Englewood Cliffs, N.J.: Prentice-Hall, 1972.

Juntune, J. (Ed.). *Gifted Child Quarterly,* 1979, *23*(3). (Special issue on local projects)

Kamin, L. J. *The science and politics of IQ.* New York: John Wiley, 1974.

Karnes, F. A., & Collins, E. C. *Instructional resources for teaching the gifted.* Boston, Mass.: Allyn & Bacon, 1980.

Karnes, M. B., & Bertschi, J. D. Identifying and educating gifted/talented nonhandicapped and handicapped preschoolers. *Teaching Exceptional Children,* 1978, *10*(4), 114–119.

Karnes, M. B., McCoy, G. F., Zehrbach, R. R., Wollersheim, J., Clarizio, H. F., Gostin, L., & Stanley, L. Factors associated with underachievement and overachievement of intellectually gifted children. *Exceptional Children,* 1961, *27,* 167–175.

Keating, D. (Review of *The Gifted and the Creative: A Fifty-Year Perspective* edited by J. C. Stanley, W. C. George, & C. H. Solano.) *Gifted Child Quarterly,* 1978, *22*(2), 167–170.

Kelley, T. L., Madden, R., Gardner, E. F., & Rudman, H. C., *Stanford achievement test.* New York: Harcourt Brace Jovanovich, 1965.

Kenmare, D. *The nature of genius.* Westport, Conn.: Greenwood Press, 1972.

Khatena, J. *Exercises in thinking creatively: Teacher's guide (children's version).* Unpublished manuscript, East Carolina University, 1969. (a)

————. The training of creative thinking strategies and its effects on originality (Doctoral dissertation, University of Georgia, 1969). (University Microfilms No. 70-1172.) (b)

————. Repeated presentation of stimuli and production of original responses. *Perceptual and Motor Skills,* 1970, *30,* 91–94. (a)

————. Training college adults to think creatively with words. *Psychological Reports,* 1970, *27,* 279–281. (b)

REFERENCES

———. Adolescents and the meeting of time deadlines in the production of original verbal images. *Gifted Child Quarterly*, 1971, *15*(3), 201-204. (a)

———. Production of original verbal images by children between the ages of 8 and 19 as measured by the alternate forms of "Onomatopoeia and images." *Proceedings of the 79th Annual Convention of the American Psychological Association*, 1971, *6*(1), 187-188. (b)

———. A second study training college adults to think creatively with words. *Psychological Reports*, 1971, *23*, 385-386. (c)

———. Some problems in the measurement of creative behavior. *Journal of Research and Development in Education*, 1971, *4*(3), 74-82. (d)

———. Teaching disadvantaged preschool children to think creatively with pictures. *Journal of Educational Psychology*, 1971, *62*(5), 384-386. (e)

———. Development patterns in production by children aged 9 to 19 of original images as measured by "Sounds and images." *Psychological Reports*, 1972, *30*, 649-650. (a)

———. Original verbal images of children as a function of time. *Psychological Reports*, 1972, *31*, 565-566. (b)

———. The use of analogy in the production of original verbal images. *Journal of Creative Behavior*, 1972, *9*(3), 209-213. (c)

———. *Analogy and imagination: A study guide*. Unpublished manuscript, Marshall University, 1973. (a)

———. Creative level and its effects on training college adults to think creatively with words. *Psychological Reports*, 1973, *32*, 336. (b)

———. Imagination and production of original verbal images. *Art Psychotherapy*, 1973, *1*, 113-120. (c)

———. Imagination imagery by children and the production of analogy. *Gifted Child Quarterly*, 1973, *17*(2), 98-102. (d)

———. *Problems of the highly creative child and the school psychologist*. Paper presented to the meeting of the Southeastern Region of the National Association of School Psychologists, White Sulphur Springs, W.Va., November 1973. Unpublished manuscript, Marshall University, 1973. (e)

———. Production of original verbal images by college adults to variable time intervals. *Perceptual and Motor Skills*, 1973, *36*, 1285-1286. (f)

———. Repeated presentation of stimuli and production of original responses by children. *Perceptual and Motor Skills*, 1973, *36*, 173-174. (g)

———. Creative imagination imagery and analogy. *Gifted Child Quarterly*, 1975, *19*(2), 149-160. (a)

———. *Project talented and gifted second evaluation report*. (ESEA Title III, Region II W. Va.) (Prepared for the West Virginia State Department of Education.) Unpublished manuscript, Charleston, W. Va., 1975. (b)

———. Relationship of autonomous imagery and creative self-perceptions. *Perceptual and Motor Skills*, 1975, *40*, 357-358. (c)

———. Vividness of imagery and creative self-perceptions. *Gifted Child Quarterly*, 1975, *19*(1), 33-37. (d)

———. Autonomy of imagery and production of original verbal images. *Perceptual and Motor Skills*, 1976, *43*, 245-246. (a)

_____. Creative imagination imagery: Where is it going? *Journal of Creative Behavior,* 1976, *10*(3), 189–192. (b)

_____. Original verbal imagery and its sense modality correlates. *Gifted Child Quarterly,* 1976, *20*(2), 180–186. (d)

_____. Educating the gifted child: Challenge and response. *Gifted Child Quarterly,* 1976, *20*(1), 76–90. (c)

_____. *Project talented and gifted final evaluation.* (*ESEA Title III Region II* W. Va.) (Prepared for the West Virginia State Department of Education.) Unpublished manuscript, Charleston, W. Va., 1976. (e)

_____. Analogy strategies and production of original verbal images. *Journal of Creative Behavior,* 1977, *11*(3), 213. (a)

_____. The "Khatena-Torrance creative perception inventory" for identification, diagnosis facilitation and research. *Gifted Child Quarterly,* 1977, *21*(4), 517–525. (b)

_____. *"Onomatopoeia and images": A preliminary scoring guide for creative imagination imagery and analogies.* Unpublished manuscript, Marshall University, 1977. (c)

_____. Some thoughts on the gifted in the United States and abroad. *Gifted Child Quarterly,* 1977, *21*(3), 372–386. (d)

_____. Autonomy of image and use of single or multiple sense modalities in original verbal image production. *Perceptual and Motor Skills,* 1978, *46,* 953–954. (a)

_____. Creative imagination through imagery: Some recent research. *Humanitas,* 1978, *14*(1), 227–242. (b)

_____. *The creatively gifted child: Suggestions for parents and teachers.* New York: Vantage Press, 1978. (c)

_____. The effects of time press upon the production of creative analogies. *NCAGT Quarterly Journal,* 1978, *4*(1), 6–13. (d)

_____. Frontiers of creative imagination imagery. *Journal of Mental Imagery,* 1978, *2*(1), 33–46. (e)

_____. Identification and stimulation of creative imagination imagery. *Journal of Creative Behavior,* 1978, *12*(1), 30–38. (f)

_____. Some advances in thought on the gifted. *Gifted Child Quarterly,* 1978, *22*(1), 55–61. (g)

_____. *Teaching gifted children to use creative imagination imagery.* Starkville, Miss.: Allan Associates, 1979. (c)

_____. Creativity, general systems and the gifted. *Gifted Child Quarterly,* 1979, *23*(4), 698–715. (a)

_____. Nurture of imagery in the visual and performing arts. *Gifted Child Quarterly, 1979, 23(4), 735–747. (b)*

_____. *Music, art, leadership and psychomotor abilities assessment records.* Starkville, Miss.: Allan Associates, 1981.

Khatena, J., & Barbour, R. L. Training music majors in college to think creatively with sounds and words. *Psychological Reports,* 1972, *30,* 105–106.

Khatena, J., & Dickerson, E. C. Training sixth grade children to think creatively with words. *Psychological Reports,* 1973, *32,* 841–842.

Khatena, J., & Fisher, S. A four year study of children's responses to onomatopoeic stimuli. *Perceptual and Motor Skills,* 1974, *39,* 1062.

Khatena, J., & Parnes, S. J. Applied imagination and the production of original verbal images. *Perceptual and Motor Skills,* 1974, *38,* 130.

Khatena, J., & Torrance, E. P. Attitude patterns and the production of original verbal images: A study in construct validity. *Gifted Child Quarterly,* 1971, *15*(2), 117–122.

————. *Thinking creatively with sounds and words: Norms-technical manual* (Research ed.). Lexington, Mass.: Personnel Press, 1973.

————. *Khatena-Torrance creative perception inventory.* Chicago: Stoelting, 1976. (a)

————. *Manual for Khatena-Torrance creative perception inventory.* Chicago: Stoelting, 1976. (b)

Kimball, B. Case studies in educational failure during adolescence. *American Journal of Orthopsychiatry,* 1953, *23,* 406–415.

Kirk, B. Test versus academic performance in malfunctioning students. *Journal of Consulting Psychology,* 1952, *16,* 213–216.

Klausmeier, H. J. Effects of accelerating bright older elementary pupils: A follow-up. *Journal of Educational Psychology,* 1963, *54*(3), 165–171.

Klein, A. F. *Role playing in leadership training and group problem solving.* New York: Association Press, 1956.

Knickerbocker, I. Leadership: A conception and some implications. *Journal of Social Issues,* 1948, *4,* 23–40.

Koestler, A. *The act of creation.* New York: MacMillan, 1964.

Kohlberg, L., & Mayer, R. Development as the aim of education. *Harvard Educational Review,* 1972, *42*(4), 449–496.

Koplowitz, H. Higher cognitive stages. In M. Ferguson (Ed.), *Brain/Mind Bulletin,* 1978, *3*(22), p. 1.

Kowalski, C. J., & Cangemi, J. P. High school dropouts—A lost resource. *College Student Journal,* 1974, *8*(4), 71–74.

Krathwohl, D. R., Bloom, B. S., & Masia, B. B. *Taxonomy of educational objectives, handbook II: Affective domain.* New York: David McKay, 1964.

Krippner, S. The ten commandments that block creativity. *Gifted Child Quarterly,* 1967, *11*(3), 144–156.

Krippner, S., Dreistadt, R., & Hubbard, C. C. The creative person and non-ordinary reality. *Gifted Child Quarterly,* 1972, *16*(3), 203–228; 234.

Kroeber, A. *Configurations of culture growth.* Berkeley and Los Angeles: University of California Press, 1944.

Kubie, L. S. *Neurotic distortion of the creative process.* New York: Noonday, 1958.

Kubzansky, P. E. Creativity, imagery and sensory deprivation. *Acta Psychologia,* 1961, *19,* 507–508.

Kwalwasser, J., & Dykema, P. W. *Kwalwasser-Dykema music tests.* New York: Carl Fischer, 1930.

Laird, A. W. Investigative survey: Fifty states' provisions for the gifted. *Gifted Child Quarterly,* 1971, *15*(3), 205–216.

Laird, A. W., & Kowalski, C. J. Survey of 1,564 colleges and universities on courses offered in the education of the gifted. *Gifted Child Quarterly,* 1972, *16*(2), 93–111.

Land, G. *Grow or die: The unifying principle of transformation.* New York: Random House, 1973.

REFERENCES

_____. The future of education. *Journal of Creative Behavior,* 1979, *13*(2), 81–109.

Land, G., & Kenneally, C. Creativity, reality, and general systems: A personal viewpoint. *Journal of Creative Behavior,* 1977, *11*(1), 12–35.

Lane, J. B. *Imagination and personality: The multi-trait investigation of a new measure of imagery control* (Doctoral dissertation, University of Minnesota, 1974). *Dissertation Abstracts International,* 1975, *35*B, 6099. (University Microfilms No. 75-12, 105)

Langham, D. G. Genesa: Tomorrow's thinking today. *Journal of Creative Behavior,* 1974, *8*(4), 227–281.

Lawton, J. P. Effects of advance organizer lessons on children's use and understanding of the causal and logical. Unpublished manuscript, University of Wisconsin, Madison, 1976.

Lawton, J. P., & Wanska, S. K. An analytical study of the use of advance organizers in facilitating children's learning. Unpublished manuscript, University of Wisconsin, Madison, 1976.

Lehman, P. R. *Tests and measurements in music.* Englewood Cliffs, N.J.: Prentice-Hall, 1968.

Leonard, G., & Lindauer, M. S. Aesthetic participation and imagery arousal. *Perceptual and Motor Skills,* 1973, *36,* 977–978.

Lindauer, M. S. The sensory attributes and functions of imagery and imagery evoking stimuli. In P. W. Sheehan (Ed.), *The function and nature of imagery.* New York: Academic Press, 1972.

Lipman-Blumen, J., & Leavitt, H. J. Vicarious and direct achievement patterns in adulthood. *The Counseling Psychologist,* 1976, *6,* 26–32.

Littman, R. A. Motives, history and causes. In M. R. Jones (Ed.), *Nebraska Symposium on Motivation.* Lincoln: University of Nebraska Press, 1958.

Lowenfeld, V., & Brittain, W. L. *Creative and mental growth.* New York: Macmillan, 1964.

Lum, M. K. A comparison of underachieving and overachieving female college students. *Journal of Educational Psychology,* 1960, *51*(3), 109–114.

Lyon, H. C., Jr. Education of the gifted and talented. *Exceptional Children,* 1976, *43*(3), 166–168.

_____. A continuing account. *National/State Leadership Training Institute on the Gifted and the Talented Bulletin,* 1979, *6*(11), 2.

MacKinnon, D. W. Personality correlates of creativity. In M. J. Ashner & C. E. Bish (Eds.), *Productive thinking in education.* Washington, D.C.: National Education Association, 1968.

_____. Creativity and transliminal experience. *Journal of Creative Behavior,* 1971, *5*(4), 227–241.

_____. *In search of human effectiveness.* Buffalo, N.Y.: Creative Education Foundation, 1978.

Maker, J. C. *Training teachers for the gifted and talented: A comparison of models.* Reston, Va.: Council for Exceptional Children, 1976.

_____. Providing programs for the gifted handicapped. Reston, Va.: *Council for Exceptional Children,* 1977.

Maltzman, I., Bogartz, W., & Breger, L. A procedure for increasing word association, originality and its transfer effects. *Journal of Experimental Psychology,* 1958, *56,* 392–398.

Mann, R. D. A review of the relationships between personality and performance in small groups. *Psychological Bulletin,* 1959, *56,* 241–270.

Mansfield, R. S., Busse, T. V., & Krepelka, E. J. The effectiveness of creativity training. *Review of Educational Research,* 1978, *48*(4), 517–536.

Marks, D. F. Visual imagery differences and eye movements in the recall of pictures. *Perception and Psychophysics,* 1973, *14,* 407–412.

Marland, S. P., Jr. *Education of the gifted and talented: Report to the Congress of the United States,* (2 vols.) Washington, D.C.: U.S. Government Printing Office, 1972. (a)

————. The responsibilities, activities, and plans of the U.S. government for the education of the academically above-average. *Intellect,* 1972, *101,* 16–19. (b)

Martinson, R. A. *Educational programs for gifted pupils.* Sacramento: California State Department of Education, 1961.

————. *The identification of the gifted and talented.* Los Angeles, Calif.: National/State Leadership Training Institute on the Gifted and Talented, 1974.

Maslow, A. H. *Motivation and personality.* New York: Harper, 1954.

————. Creativity in self-actualizing people. In H. H. Anderson (Ed.), *Creativity and its cultivation.* New York: Harper, 1959.

————. *Toward a psychology of being* (2nd ed.). Princeton, N.J.: D. Van Nostrand, 1968.

————. *Motivation and personality* (2nd ed.). New York: Harper & Row, 1970.

McClelland, D. C., Atkinson, J. W., Clark, R. A., & Lowell, E. L. *The achievement motive.* New York: Appleton-Century-Crofts, 1953.

McCloy, C. H., & Young, N. D. Tests and measurements in health and physical education. *American Journal of Psychology,* 1958, *71*(1), 164–174.

McGrath, J. E., & Altman, I. *Small group research: A synthesis and critique of the field.* New York: Holt, Rinehart & Winston, 1966.

McGuire, C., Hindsman, E., King, F. J., & Jennings, E. Dimensions of talented behavior. *Educational and Psychological Measurement,* 1961, *21*(1), 3–38.

McIntyre, P. M. Dynamics and treatment of the passive-aggressive underachiever. *American Journal of Psychotherapy,* 1964, *18*(1), 95–107.

McKellar, P. *Imagination and thinking.* New York: Basic Books, 1957.

————. Autonomy, imagery, and dissociation. *Journal of Mental Imagery,* 1977, *1*(1), 93–108.

McNemar, Q. Lost: Our intelligence? Why? *American Psychologist,* 1964, *18,* 871–882.

Mednick, S. A. *Remote Associates Test.* Boston, Mass.: Houghton Mifflin, 1959.

————. The associative basis of the creative process. *Psychological Review,* 1962, *69,* 220–232.

Mednick, S. A., & Mednick, M. T. *Remote associates test: Examiner's manual.* Boston, Mass.: Houghton Mifflin, 1967.

Mednick, M. T., Mednick, S. A., & Mednick, E. V. Incubation of creative performance and specific associative priming. *Journal of Abnormal and Social Psychology,* 1964, *69*(1), 84–88.

Meeker, M. N. Creative experiences for the educationally and neurologically handicapped who are gifted. *Gifted Child Quarterly,* 1967, *11*(2), 160-164.

———. Differential syndromes of giftedness and curriculum planning. A four-year follow-up. *Journal of Special Education,* 1968, *2*(2), 185-196.

———. *The structure of intellect: Its interpretation and uses.* Columbus, Ohio: Charles E. Merrill, 1969.

———. *Identifying gifted Navajo children in reservations—interim report from SOI Institute.* El Segundo, Calif.: SOI Institute, 1977.

———. Nondiscriminatory testing procedures to assess giftedness in black, Chicano, Navajo, and Anglo children. In A. Y. Baldwin, G. H. Gear, & L. J. Lucito (Eds.), *Educational planning for the gifted.* Reston, Va.: Council for Exceptional Children, 1978.

———. IEPs: Diagnosing and matching curriculum to cognitive patterns. In *Developing IEPs for the gifted/talented.* Los Angeles, Calif.: National/State Leadership Training Institute on the Gifted and Talented, 1979. (a)

———. *Using SOI test results: A teacher's guide.* El Segundo, Calif.: SOI Institute, 1979. (b)

Meeker, M. N., Sexton, K., & Richardson, M. O. *SOI abilities workbooks.* Los Angeles, Calif.: Loyola-Marymount University, 1970.

Mercer, J. R., & Lewis, J. F. Using the system of multicultural pluralistic assessment (SOMPA) to identify the gifted minority child. In A. Y. Baldwin, G. H. Gear, & L. J. Lucito (Eds.), *Educational planning for the gifted.* Reston, Va.: Council for Exceptional Children, 1978.

Merenda, P. F. (Review of the *Stanford achievement test.*) *Journal of Educational Measurement,* 1965, *2*(2), 247-251.

Merry, F. Summer classes for gifted children. *Educational Method,* 1935, *14*, 388-390.

Miles, C. C. Crucial factors in the life history of talent. In E. P. Torrance (Ed.), *Talent and education.* Minneapolis: University of Minnesota Press, 1960.

Miller, L. P. (Ed.). *The testing of black students: A symposium.* Englewood Cliffs, N.J.: Prentice-Hall, 1974.

Moreno, J. L. *Psychodrama: First volume.* Beacon, N.Y.: Beacon House, 1946.

———. Psychodramatic production techniques. *Group Psychotherapy,* 1952, *4*, 243-273.

Moreno, J. L., & Moreno, Z. T. *Psychodrama: Third volume.* Beacon, N.Y.: Beacon House, 1969.

Morse, J. A., & Bruch, C. B. Gifted women: More issues than answers. *Educational Horizons,* 1970, 49, 25-32.

Mowry, H. W. *Leadership evaluation and development scale.* Psychological Services, 1964/1965.

Mursell, J. L. Measuring musical ability and achievement. *Journal of Educational Research,* 1932, *25*, 116-126.

Myers, I. B. *The Myers-Briggs type indicator.* Princeton, N.J.: Educational Testing Service, 1962.

Myers, R. E., & Torrance, E. P. *Invitations to thinking and doing.* Boston, Mass.: Ginn, 1964.

———. *Can you imagine?* Boston, Mass.: Ginn, 1965. (a)

———. *Invitations to speaking and writing creatively.* Boston, Mass.: Ginn, 1965. (b)

———. *For those who wonder.* Boston, Mass.: Ginn, 1966. (a)

———. *Plots, puzzles, and ploys.* Boston, Mass.: Ginn, 1966. (b)

———. *Stretch.* Minneapolis, Minn.: Perceptive Publishing, 1968.

Nathan, C. N. Parental involvement. In A. H. Passow (Ed.), *The gifted and the talented: Their education and development.* Chicago: University of Chicago Press, 1979. (78th Yearbook of the NSSE.)

Neivert, S. *Identification of students with science potential.* Unpublished doctoral dissertation, Columbia University, 1955.

Newland, T. E. *The gifted in socio-educational perspective.* Englewood Cliffs, N.J.: Prentice-Hall, 1976.

N/S Leadership Training Institute G/T. Masters and Ph.D. programs in gifted education or programs with emphasis in gifted education. *National/State Leadership Training Institute on the Gifted and the Talented Bulletin,* 1976, *3*(8), (insert).

Oden, M. H. *The fulfillment of promise: 40-year follow-up of the Terman gifted group.* Stanford, Calif.: Stanford University Press, 1968.

Olson, M. Right or left hemisphere processing in the gifted. *Gifted Child Quarterly,* 1977, *21*(1), 116–121.

Olson, W. C. *Child development* (2nd ed.). Boston, Mass.: D. C. Heath, 1959.

Olton, R. M. Experimental studies of incubation: Searching for the elusive. *Journal of Creative Behavior,* 1979, *13*(1), 9–22.

Ornstein, R. *The psychology of consciousness.* New York: Freeman, 1972.

Osborn, A. F. Developments in creative education. In S. J. Parnes & H. F. Harding (Eds.), *A source book for creative thinking.* New York: Charles Scribner's, 1962.

———. *Applied imagination.* New York: Charles Scribner's, 1963.

Otis, A. S., & Lennon, R. T. *Otis-Lennon mental ability test.* New York: Harcourt Brace Jovanovich, 1967.

Owens, W. A. Age and mental abilities: A longitudinal study. *Genetic Psychology Monograph,* 1953, *48,* 3–54.

Paivio, A. *Imagery and verbal processes.* New York: Holt, Rinehart & Winston, 1971.

Parnes, S. J. (Comp.). *Compendium no. 1 of research on creative imagination.* Buffalo, N.Y.: Creative Education Foundation, 1958.

———. (Comp.). *Compendium no. 2 of research on creative imagination.* Buffalo, N.Y.: Creative Education Foundation, 1960.

———. *Creative behavior guidebook.* New York: Charles Scribner's, 1967. (a)

———. *Creative behavior workbook.* New York: Charles Scribner's, 1967. (b)

———. CPSI—a program for balanced growth. *Journal of Creative Behavior,* 1975, *9*(1), 23–29.

Parnes, S. J., & Biondi, A. M. Creative behavior: A delicate balance. *Journal of Creative Behavior,* 1975, *9*(3), 149–158.

Parnes, S. J., & Meadows, A. Effects of "brainstorming" instructions on creative problem solving by trained and untrained subjects. *Journal of Educational Psychology,* 1959, *50*(4), 171–176.

Parnes, S. J., & Noller, R. B. *Toward supersanity: Channeled freedom.* Buffalo, N.Y.: D.O.K., 1973.

Parnes, S. J., Noller, R. B., & Biondi, A. M. *Creative actionbook* (Rev. ed. of *Creative behavior workbook*). New York: Charles Scribner's, 1977. (a)

──────. *Guide to creative actionbook* (Rev. ed. of *Creative behavior guidebook*). New York: Charles Scribner's, 1977. (b)

Passow, A. H. Are we short changing the gifted? *School Executive,* 1955, *75,* 54–57.

──────. Identifying and counseling the gifted college students. *Journal of Higher Education,* 1957, *28,* 21–29.

──────. Enrichment of education for the gifted. In N. B. Henry (Ed.), Education for the gifted. Chicago: University of Chicago Press, 1958. (57th Yearbook of NSSE)

──────. A look around and a look ahead. In A. H. Passow (Ed.), *The gifted and the talented: Their education and development.* Chicago: University of Chicago Press, 1979. (78th Yearbook of the NSSE)

Passow, A. H. Goldberg, M. L., Tannenbaum, A., & French, W. *Planning for talented youth.* New York: Bureau of Publications, Teachers College, Columbia University, 1955.

Patrick, C. *What is creative thinking?* New York: Philosophical Library, 1955.

Pegnato, C. W. *An evaluation of various initial methods of selecting intellectually gifted children at the junior high school level.* Unpublished doctoral dissertation, Pennsylvania State University, 1955.

Pegnato, C. W., & Birch, J. W. Locating gifted children in junior high schools: A comparison of methods. *Exceptional Children,* 1959, *25,* 300–304.

Pepinsky, P. Study of productive nonconformity. *Gifted Child Quarterly,* 1960, *4*(3), 81–85.

Perkins, H. V. Classroom behavior and underachievement. *American Educational Research Journal,* 1965, *2,* 1–12.

Perrone, P. A., Karshner, W. W., & Male, R. A. *Career development of talented persons.* Unpublished manuscript, Guidance Institute for Talented Students, University of Wisconsin, Madison, 1979.

Perrone, P., & Pulvino, C. J. New direction in the guidance of gifted and talented. *Gifted Child Quarterly,* 1977, *20*(3), 326–339.

Perry, W. G., Jr. *Forms of intellectual and ethical development in the college years.* New York: Holt, Rinehart & Winston, 1970.

Pezzulo, T. R., Thorsen, E. E., & Madus, G. F. The heritability of Jensen's level I and II and divergent thinking. *American Educational Research Journal* 1972, *9,* 539–546.

Phil J. L., Jr., *Statistical thinking.* San Francisco, Calif.: W. H. Freeman, 1973.

Piaget, J. *The pyschology of intelligence.* London: Routledge & Kegan Paul, 1950.

──────. *Six psychological studies.* New York: Random House, 1967.

Pierce, J. V., & Bowman, P. H. Motivation patterns of superior high school students. In *The gifted student* (Cooperative Research Monograph No. 2). Washington, D.C.: U.S. Government Printing Office, 1960.

Polak, F. L. *The image of the future.* New York: Elsevier, 1973.

Pressy, S. L. *Educational acceleration: appraisal and basic problems* (Bureau of Educational Research Monographs, No. 31). Columbus, Ohio: College of Education, Ohio State University, 1949.

Prince, G. M. The operational mechanism of synectics. *Journal of Creative Behavior,* 1968, *2*(1), 1–13.

_____. The mindspring theory. *Journal of Creative Behavior,* 1975, *9*(3), 159–181.

Pringle, M. L. K. *Able misfits: A study of educational and behavioral difficulties of 103 very intelligent children (IQs 120–200).* London: Longmans, 1970.

Raph, J. B., Goldberg, M. L., & Passow, A. H. *Bright underachievers.* New York: Bureau of Publications, Teachers College, Columbia University, 1966.

Raven, J. C. *Raven's progressive matrices test.* London: H. K. Lewis, 1947.

Redl, F., & Wattenberg, W. W. *Mental hygiene in teaching* (2nd ed.) New York: Harcourt, Brace & World, 1959.

Renzulli, J. S. *New directions in creativity.* New York: Harper & Row, 1973.

_____. *A guidebook for evaluating programs for the gifted and talented.* Los Angeles, Calif.: National/State Leadership Training Institute on the Gifted and Talented, 1975.

_____. Instructional management systems: A model for organizing and developing in-service training workshops. *Gifted Child Quarterly,* 1977, *21*(2), 186–194. (a)

_____. *The interest-a-lyzer.* Mansfield Center, Conn.: Creative Learning Press, 1977. (b)

_____. The enrichment triad model: A guide for developing defensible programs for the gifted. In J. C. Gowan, J. Khatena, & E. P. Torrance (Eds.), *Educating the ablest* (2nd ed.). Itasca, Ill.: F. E. Peacock, 1979. (a)

_____. *What makes giftedness?* Los Angeles, Calif.: National/State Leadership Training Institute on the Gifted and Talented, 1979. (b)

_____. Will the gifted movement be alive and well in 1990? *Gifted Child Quarterly,* 1980, *24*(1), 3–9.

Renzulli, J. S., & Smith, L. H. *The compactor.* Mansfield Center, Conn.: Creative Learning Press, 1978. (a)

_____. *The learning style inventory: A measure of student preference for instructional techniques.* Mansfield Center, Conn.: Creative Learning Press, 1978. (b)

_____. *The strength-a-lyzer.* Mansfield Center, Conn.: Creative Learning Press, 1978. (c)

_____. Issues and procedures in evaluating programs. In A. H. Passow (Ed.), *The gifted and the talented: Their education and development.* Chicago: University of Chicago Press, 1979. (78th Yearbook of the NSSE) (a)

_____. A practical model for designing individualized education programs (IEPs) for gifted and talented students. In *Developing IEPs for the gifted/talented.* Los Angeles, Calif.: National/State Leadership Training Institute on the Gifted and Talented, 1979. (b)

Renzulli, J. S., & Ward, V. S. *Diagnostic and evaluation scale for differential education for the gifted.* Storrs, Conn.: Bureau of Educational Research, University of Connecticut, 1969.

Rhodes, M. An analysis of creativity. *Phi Delta Kappan,* 1961, *42*(7), 305–310.

Ribot, T. *Essay on the creative imagination.* London, Kagan & Paul, 1906.

Richardson, A. *Mental imagery.* New York: Springer Publishing, 1969.

Richmond, B. O. *Creativity in monozygotic and dizygotic twins.* Paper presented at the meeting of the American Personnel and Guidance Association, Detroit, Mich., April 1968.

Riessman, F. *The culturally deprived child.* New York: Harper & Row, 1962.

Rimm, S., & Davis, G. A. GIFT: An instrument for the identification of creativity. *Journal of Creative Behavior,* 1976, *10*(3), 178-182.

———. Five years of international research with GIFT: An instrument for the identification of creativity. *Journal of Creative Behavior,* 1980, *14*(1), 35-46.

Ripple, R. E. A controlled experiment in acceleration from the second to the fourth grade. *Gifted Child Quarterly,* 1961, *5*(4), 119-120.

Roe, A. Personal problems in science. In C. W. Taylor & F. Barron (Eds.), *Scientific creativity: Its recognition and development.* New York: John Wiley, 1963.

Rogers, C. R. *On becoming a person: A therapist's view of psychotherapy.* Boston, Mass.: Houghton Mifflin, 1967.

———. The facilitation of significant learning. In R. C. Sprinthall & N. A. Sprinthall (Eds.), *Educational psychology: Selected readings.* New York: D. Van Nostrand, 1969.

Rogers, D. (Ed.). *Issues in adolescent psychology.* New York: Appleton-Century-Crofts, 1969.

Rosen, B. C., & d'Andrade, R. The psychosocial origins of achievement motivation. *Sociometry,* 1959, *22,* 185-195; 215-218.

Rossman, J. *The psychology of the inventor* (Rev. ed.). Washington, D.C.: Inventors, 1931.

Roth, R. M., & Meyersburg, A. H. The non-achievement syndrome. *Personnel and Guidance Journal,* 1963, *61*(6), 535-540.

Rothney, J. W. M., & Koopman, N. Guidance of the gifted. In N. B. Henry (Ed.), *Education for the gifted.* Chicago, Ill.: University of Chicago Press, 1957. (57th Yearbook of the NSSE)

Roweton, W. E. *Creativity: A review of theory and research.* Buffalo, N.Y.: Creative Education Foundation, 1973. (Occasional paper No. 7)

Royce, J. The psychology of invention. *Psychological Review,* 1898, *5,* 113-144.

Runner, K. *A theory of persons: Runner studies of attitude patterns.* San Diego, Calif.: Runner Associates, 1973.

Runner, K., & Runner, H. *Manual of interpretation for the interview form III of the Runner studies of attitude patterns.* Golden, Colo.: Runner Associates, 1965.

Runions, T. The mentor academy program: Educating the gifted/talented for the 80's. *Gifted Child Quarterly,* 1980, *4*(3), 152-157.

Russell, J. D. *Modular instruction.* Minneapolis, Minn.: Burgess, 1974.

Samples, B. Learning with the whole brain. *Human Behavior,* 1975, *53,* 17-23.

Samuda, R. J. *Psychological testing of American minorities: Issues and consequences.* New York: Dodd, Mead, 1975.

Saphier, J. D. The relation of perceptual-motor skills to learning and school success. *Journal of Learning Disabilities,* 1973, *6*(9), 56-65.

Schaefer, C. E. *Biographical inventory: Creativity.* San Diego, Calif.: Educational and Industrial Testing Services, 1970.

———. *Becoming somebody.* Buffalo, N.Y.: D.O.K., 1971.

———. The importance of measuring metaphorical thinking in children. *Gifted Child Quarterly,* 1975, *19*(2), 140-148.

Schaefer, C. E., & Anastasi, A. A biographical inventory for identifying creativity in adolescent boys. *Journal of Applied Psychology,* 1968, *52,* 42-48.

Schmeidler, G. R. Visual imagery correlated to a measure of creativity. *Journal of Consulting Psychology*, 1965, *29*, 78-80.

Scriven, M. The methodology of evaluation. In R. W. Tyler, R. M. Gagne, & M. Scriven (Eds.), *Perspectives of curriculum evaluation*. Chicago: Rand McNally, 1967.

Seashore, C. E. *The psychology of musical talent*. Morristown, N.J.: Silver Burdett, 1919.

———. *Psychology of music*. New York: McGraw-Hill, 1938.

Seashore, C. E., Lewis, D., & Saetveit, J. G. *Seashore measures of musical talents*. New York: Psychological Corporation, 1960.

Segal, D., & Raskin, E. *Multiple aptitude tests*. Monterey, Calif.: California Test Bureau, 1959.

Shaw, M. C. *Attitudes and child rearing practices of the parents of bright academic underachievers*. (U.S. Public Health Services Research Project M-2843.) Washington, D.C.: U.S. Government Printing Office, 1960.

Sheehan, P. W. A shortened form of "Betts' questionnaire upon mental imagery." *Journal of Clinical Psychology*, 1967, *23*, 386-389.

———. Hypnosis and the manifestations of imagination. In E. Fromm & R. E. Shor (Eds.), *Hypnosis: Research developments and perspectives*. New York: Aldine Atherton, 1972.

Sheikh, A. Mental images: Ghosts of sensations? *Journal of Mental Imagery*, 1977, *1*(1), 1-4.

Shepherd, J. Black lab power. *Saturday Review*, *55* (August 5, 1972), 32-39.

Shock, N. W. Gerontology. *Annual Review of Psychology*, 1951, *2*, 353-370.

Shockley, W. Dysgenics, geneticity, raceology: A challenge to the intellectual responsibility of educators. *Phi Delta Kappan*, 1972, *53*(5), 297-307.

Silberman, C. *Crisis in the classroom*. New York: Random House, 1970.

Simmons, W. L. Human intelligence: The psychological view. *The Science Teacher*, 1968, *35*(6), 18-20.

Simonton, D. K. The eminent genius in history: The critical role of creative development. *Gifted Child Quarterly*, 1978, *22*(2), 187-195.

Simpson, E. J. *The classification of educational objectives: Psychomotor domain*. Urbana: University of Illinois Press, 1966.

Simpson, J. Developmental process theory as applied to mature women. *Gifted Child Quarterly*, 1977, *21*(3), 359-371.

Simpson, R. M. Creative imagination. *American Journal of Psychology*, 1922, *33*(2), 234-243.

Singer, B. D. The future-focused role-image. In A. Toffler (Ed.), *Learning for tomorrow*. New York: Random House, 1974.

Singer, J. L., & Antrobus, J. S. *Imaginal process inventory*. New York: Authors, 1966.

———. *Imaginal process inventory* (Rev. ed.). New York: Authors, 1970.

Sisk, D. *Teaching gifted children*. (ESEA Title V South Carolina.) (Prepared for the South Carolina State Department of Education.) Unpublished manuscript, South Carolina, 1976.

———. Gifted and talented: Three year perspective. *National/State Leadership Training Institute on the Gifted and the Talented Bulletin*, 1979. *6*(7), 2; 7.

_____. Issues and future in gifted education. *Gifted Child Quarterly,* 1980, *24*(1), 29–36.

Spearman, C. *The abilities of man: Their nature and measurement.* New York: MacMillan, 1927.

_____. *Creative mind.* London: Cambridge University Press, 1930.

Sperry, R. W. Messages from the laboratory. *Engineering and Science,* January 1974.

Stanley, J. C. Intellectual precocity. In J. C. Stanley, D. P. Keating, & L. H. Fox (Eds.), *Mathematical talent: Discovery, description, and development.* Baltimore, Md.: The Johns Hopkins University Press, 1974.

_____. *Educational non-acceleration: An international tragedy.* Address to the 2nd world Conference on Gifted and Talented Children, University Center, University of San Francisco, California, August 1977. (a)

_____. Rationale of the study of mathematically precocious youth (SMPY) during its first five years of promoting educational acceleration. In J. C. Stanley, W. C. George, & C. H. Solano (Eds.), *The gifted and the creative: A fifty-year perspective.* Baltimore: Md.: The Johns Hopkins University Press, 1977. (b)

_____. The study and facilitation of talent for mathematics. In A. H. Parson (Ed.), *The gifted and the talented: Their education and development.* Chicago: University of Chicago Press, 1979. (78th Yearbook of the NSSE)

Stanley, J. C., George, W. C., & Solano, C. H. (Eds.). *The gifted and the creative: A fifty-year perspective.* Baltimore, Md.: The Johns Hopkins University Press, 1977.

Stanley, J. C., Keating, D. P., & Fox, L. H. (Eds.). *Mathematical talent: Discovery, description, and development.* Baltimore, Md.: The Johns Hopkins University Press, 1974.

Starkweather, E. K. Creativity research instruments designed for use with preschool children. *Journal of Creative Behavior,* 1971, *5*(4), 245–255.

Steele, J. M. *Dimensions of the class activities.* Unpublished manuscript, Center for Instructional Research and Curriculum Evaluation, University of Illinois, Urbana, 1969.

Stogdill, R. M. Personal factors associated with leadership: A survey of the literature. *Journal of Psychology,* 1948, *25,* 35–71.

_____. Individual behavior and group achievement. New York: Oxford University Press, 1959.

_____. *Handbook of leadership: A survey of theory and research.* New York: Free Press, 1974.

Stoney, B. *Enid Blyton: A biography.* London: Hodder & Stoughton, 1974.

Stott, L. H., & Ball, R. S. *Evaluation of infant and preschool mental tests.* Detroit, Mich.: Merrill-Palmer, 1963.

Strang, R. *Guideposts for teachers of gifted children.* New York: Bureau of Publications, Teachers College, Columbia University, 1958.

_____. *Helping your gifted child.* New York: Dutton, 1960.

Strodtbeck, F. Implication of the study of family interaction for the prediction of achievement. *Child Study,* 1958, *35,* 14–18.

Strom, R. D. The dropout problem in relation to family affect and effect. In E. P.

Torrance & R. D. Strom (Eds.), *Mental health and achievement: Increasing potential and reducing school dropout*. New York: John Wiley, 1967.

Sullivan, H. S. *The interpersonal theory of psychiatry*. New York: W. W. Norton, 1953.

Sullivan, E. T., Clark, W. W., & Tiegs, E. W. *California test of mental maturity* (Rev. ed.). New York: McGraw-Hill, 1963.

Sward, K. Jewish musicality in America. *Journal of Applied Psychology*, 1933, *17*, 675–712.

Tannenbaum, A. J. *Adolescents' attitudes toward academic brilliance*. Unpublished doctoral dissertation, Columbia University, 1960.

Taylor, C. W., (Ed.). *The 1957 University of Utah research conference on the identification of creative talent*. Salt Lake City: University of Utah Press, 1958.

————, (Ed.). *The 3rd (1959) University of Utah research conference on the identification of creative scientific talent*. Salt Lake City: University of Utah Press, 1959.

————. The highest talent potentials of man. *Gifted Child Quarterly*, 1969, *13*(1), 9–30.

————. How many types of giftedness can your program tolerate? *Journal of Creative Behavior*, 1978, *12*(1), 39–51.

Taylor, C. W., & Ellison, R. L. *Manual for alpha biographical inventory*. Salt Lake City: Institute for Behavioral Research in Creativity, 1966.

————. Biographical predictors of scientific performance. *Science*, 1967, *155*, 1075–1080.

Taylor, I. A. *A theory of creative transactualization: A systematic approach to creativity with implications for creative leadership*. Buffalo, N.Y.: Creative Education Foundation, 1972. (Occasional paper No. 8)

Terman, L. M. *The measurement of intelligence*. Boston, Mass.: Houghton Mifflin, 1916.

————. *Intelligence of school children*. Boston, Mass.: Houghton Mifflin, 1919.

————. *Mental and physical traits of a thousand gifted children: Genetic studies of genius* (Vol. 1). Stanford, Calif.: Stanford University Press, 1925.

————. Scientists and nonscientists in a group of 800 gifted men. *Psychological Monographs*, 1954, *68*, 1–41.

Terman, L. M., & Merrill, M. A. *Measuring intelligence*. Boston, Mass.: Houghton Mifflin, 1937.

————. *Stanford-Binet intelligence scale: A manual for the third revision, form L-M*. Boston, Mass.: Houghton Mifflin, 1960.

Terman, L. M., & Oden, M. H. *The gifted child grows up: Twenty-five years' follow-up of a superior group: Genetic studies of genius* (Vol. 4). Stanford, Calif.: Stanford University Press, 1947.

————. *The gifted group at mid-life: Genetic studies of genius* (Vol. 5). Stanford, Calif.: Stanford University Press, 1959.

Theodore, A. *The professional woman*. Cambridge, Mass.: Schenkman, 1971.

Thorndike, R. L. Some methodological issues in the study of creativity. In A. Anastasi (Ed.), *Testing problems in perspective*. Washington, D.C.: American Council on Education, 1966.

Thurstone, L. L. *The nature of intelligence*. New York: Harcourt, Brace, 1924.

————. *Primary mental abilities*. Chicago: University of Chicago Press, 1938.

452

Toffler, A. (Ed.), *Learning for tomorrow*. New York: Random House, 1974.

Torda, C. Some observations on the creative process. *Perceptual and Motor Skills,* 1970, *31,* 107–126.

Torrance, E. P. *Preliminary manual for personal-social motivation inventory.* Unpublished manuscript, University of Minnesota, 1958.

_____. *Guiding creative talent.* Englewood Cliffs, N.J.: Prentice-Hall, 1962. (a)

_____. Non-test ways of identifying the creatively gifted. *Gifted Child Quarterly,* 1962, *6*(3), 71–75. (b)

_____. *Education of the creative potential.* Minneapolis: University of Minnesota Press, 1963.

_____. *Constructive behavior: Stress, personality, and mental health.* Englewood Cliffs, N.J.: Prentice-Hall, 1965. (a)

_____. *Gifted children in the classroom.* New York: Macmillan, 1965. (b)

_____. *Rewarding creative behavior.* Englewood Cliffs, N.J.: Prentice-Hall, 1965. (c)

_____. *Torrance tests of creative thinking: Norms-technical manual* (Research ed.). Princeton, N.J.: Personnel Press, 1966.

_____. Helping gifted children through mental health concepts. *Gifted Child Quarterly,* 1967, *11*(1), 3–7. (a)

_____. *Understanding the fourth grade slump in creative thinking.* (Final Report on Cooperative Research Project No. 994, Office of Education). Unpublished manuscript, University of Georgia, 1967. (b)

_____. A longitudinal examination of the fourth grade slump in creativity. *Gifted Child Quarterly,* 1968, *12*(4), 195–199.

_____. Broadening concepts of giftedness in the 70's. *Gifted Child Quarterly,* 1970, *14*(4), 199–208.

_____. Are the Torrance tests of creative thinking biased against or in favor of disadvantaged groups? *Gifted Child Quarterly,* 1971, *15*(2), 75–80.

_____. Can we teach children to think creatively? *Journal of Creative Behavior,* 1972 *6*(2), 114–143. (a)

_____. Predictive validity of the *Torrance tests of creative thinking. Journal of Creative Behavior,* 1972, *6*(4), 236–252. (b)

_____. Tendency to produce unusual visual perspective as a predictor of creative achievement. *Perceptual and Motor Skills,* 1972, *34,* 911–915. (c)

_____. Non-test indicators of creative talent among disadvantaged children. *Gifted Child Quarterly,* 1973, *17*(1), 3–9.

_____. Differences are not deficits. *Teachers College Record,* 1974, *75,* 472–487. (a)

_____. *Torrance tests of creative thinking: Norms-technical manual.* Lexington, Mass.: Personnel Press, 1974. (b)

_____. Assessing children, teachers and parents against the ideal child criterion. *Gifted Child Quarterly,* 1975, *19*(2), 130–139. (a)

_____. Motivation and creativity. In E. P. Torrance & W. White (Eds.), *Issues and advances in educational psychology* (2nd ed.). Itasca, Ill.: F. E. Peacock, 1975. (b)

_____. Sociodrama as a creative problem-solving approach to studying the future. *Journal of Creative Behavior,* 1975, *9*(3), 182–195. (c)

_____. Future careers for gifted and talented students. *Gifted Child Quarterly,* 1976, *20*(2), 142–156. (a)

_____. *Sociodrama in career education.* (Pre-service Teacher Training in Career Educa-
tion Project.) Unpublished manuscript, College of Education, University of Georgia,
1976. (b)

_____. Creatively gifted and disadvantaged gifted. In J. C. Stanley, W. C. George, & C.
H. Solana (Eds.), *The gifted and the creative: A fifty year perspective.* Baltimore,
Md.: The Johns Hopkins University Press, 1977. (a)

_____. *Discovery and nurturance of giftedness in the culturally different.* Reston, Va.:
Council for Exceptional Children, 1977. (b)

_____. *Senario in the year 2002.* Keynote address presented at the *24th National
Association for Gifted Children Annual Convention,* San Diego, Calif., October
1977. (c)

_____. Dare we hope again? *Gifted Child Quarterly,* 1978, *22*(3), 292–312. (a)

_____. Letter to John C. Gowan. *Gifted Child Quarterly,* 1978, *22*(2), 175–176. (b)

_____. An instructional model for enhancing incubation. *Journal of Creative Behavior,*
1979, *13*(1), 23–35. (a)

_____. *The search for satori and creativity.* Buffalo, N.Y.: Creative Education Founda-
tion, 1979. (b)

_____. Unique needs of the creative child and adult. In A. H. Passow (Ed.), *The gifted
and the talented: Their education and development.* Chicago: University of Chicago
Press, 1979. (78th Yearbook of the NSSE) (c)

Torrance, E. P., & Ball, O. E. *Streamlined scoring and interpretation guide and norms
manual for figural form A, Torrance tests of creative thinking (4th revision).* Unpublished manuscript, University of Georgia, 1980.

Torrance, E. P., & Gibbs, M. S. *Norms-technical, administration, and scoring manual:
Thinking creatively in action and movement.* Unpublished manuscript, University of
Georgia, 1979.

Torrance, E. P., & Hall, L. K. Assessing the further reaches of creative potential. *Journal
of Creative Behavior,* 1980, *14*(1), 1–19.

Torrance, E. P., & Horng, R. *Scoring guide: Future problem-solving program.* Unpublished manuscript, University of Georgia, 1978.

Torrance, E. P., & Khatena, J. Originality of imagery in identifying creative talent in
music. *Gifted Child Quarterly,* 1969, *13*(1), 3–8.

Torrance, E. P., Khatena, J., & Cunnington, B. F. *Thinking creatively with sounds and
words,* Lexington, Mass.: Personnel Press, 1973.

Torrance, E. P., & Myers, R. E. *Creative learning and teaching.* New York: Dodd,
Mead, 1970.

Torrance, E. P., Reynolds, C. R., Ball, O. E., & Riegel, T. R. *Revised norms-technical
manual for your style of learning and thinking.* Unpublished manuscript, University
of Georgia, 1978.

Torsi, L. Woman's scientific creativity. *Impact of Science on Society,* 1975, *25,* 105–
114.

Treffinger, D. J. Teaching for self-directed learning; A priority for the talented and gifted.
Gifted Child Quarterly, 1975, *19*(1), 46–59.

_____. Individualized education program plans for gifted and talented, and creative
students. In *Developing IEPs for the gifted/talented.* Los Angeles, Calif.: National/
State Leadership Training Institute on the Gifted and Talented, 1979.

Treffinger, D. J., & Poggio, J. P. Needed research on the measurement of creativity. *Journal of Creative Behavior,* 1972, *6*(4), 253-267.

Turnbull, W. W. Achievement test scores in perspective. *Educational Testing Service Annual Report,* 1978, pp. 2-4.

Underwood, B. *Experimental Psychology.* New York: Appleton-Century-Crofts, 1949.

Upton, A. *Creative analysis.* New York: Dutton, 1961.

Vantour, J. A. Discovering and motivating the artistically gifted LD child. *Teaching Exceptional Children,* 1976, *8*(2), 92-96.

Vargiu, J. Creativity: The purposeful imagination. *Synthesis,* 1977, 3-4; 17-53.

Vaughan, M. M. Music as model and metaphor in the cultivation and measurement of creative behavior in children (Doctoral dissertation, University of Georgia, 1971). *Dissertation Abstracts International,* 1971, *32,* 5833A. (University Microfilms, 1969, No. 72-11,056)

Vernon, P. E. *The structure of human abilities.* New York: John Wiley, 1951.

_____. *Intelligence and attainment tests.* New York: Philosophical Library, 1960.

Vygotsky, L. The problem of age-periodization in child development. *Human Development,* 1974, *17,* 24-40.

Walberg, H. L. Physics, femininity and creativity. *Developmental Psychology,* 1969, *1*(1), 47-54.

Walkup, L. E. Detecting creativity: Some practical approaches. *Journal of Creative Behavior,* 1971, *5*(2), 88-93.

Wallach, M. A. (Review of the *Torrance tests of creative thinking.*) *American Research Journal,* 1968, *5,* 272-281.

_____. Creativity. In P. H. Mussen (Ed.), *Carmichael's manual of child psychology.* New York: John Wiley, 1970.

Wallach, M. A., & Kogan, N. *Modes of thinking in young children.* New York: Holt, Rinehart & Winston, 1965.

Wallach, M. A., & Wing, C. W. *The talented student: A validation of the creativity-intelligence distinction.* New York: Holt, Rinehart & Winston, 1969.

Wallas, G. *The art of thought.* London: C. A. Watts, 1926.

Walz, G. R., Smith, R. L., & Benjamin, L. A. *A comprehensive view of career development.* Washington, D.C.: APGA Press, 1974.

Ward, V. S. *Educating the gifted.* Columbus, Ohio: Charles E. Merrill, 1961.

_____. The governor's school of North Carolina. In A. H. Passon (Ed.), *The gifted and the talented: Their education and development.* Chicago: University of Chicago Press, 1979. (78th Yearbook of the NSSE)

Webster's New World Dictionary of the American Language (College ed.). New York: World, 1962.

Wechsler, D. *The measurement of adult intelligence.* Baltimore, Md.: Williams & Wilkins, 1939.

_____. Intellectual development and psychological maturity. *Child Development,* 1950, *21*(1), 45-50.

_____. *Manual for the Wechsler adult intelligence scale.* New York: Psychological Corporation, 1955.

_____. *The measurement and appraisal of adult intelligence.* (4th ed.). Baltimore, Md.: Williams & Wilkins, 1966.

REFERENCES

_____. *Manual for Wechsler preschool and primary scale.* New York: Psychological corporation, 1967.

_____. *Manual: Wechsler intelligence scale for children* (Rev. ed.). New York: Psychological Corporation, 1974.

Weinstein, J., & Altschuler, A. *Levels of self-knowledge.* Unpublished manuscript, University of Massachusetts, n.d.

Weisberg, P. S., & Springer, K. J. Environmental factors in creative function. *Archives of General Psychiatry,* 1961, *5,* 554–564.

_____. *Perspectives in individualized instruction.* Itasca, Ill.: F. E. Peacock, 1971. (b)

Weisgerber, R. A. *Developmental efforts in individualized instruction.* Itasca, Ill.: F. E. Peacock, 1971. (a)

Westfall, F. W. *Selected variables in the achievement or non-achievement of the academically talented high school student.* Unpublished doctoral dissertation, University of Southern California, 1958.

Whimbey, A., & Whimbey, L. S. *Intelligence can be taught.* New York: Dutton, 1975.

White, L. A. Genius: Its causes and incidence. In L. A. White (Ed.), *The science of culture: A study of man and civilization.* New York: Farrar, Straus, 1949.

White, W. W. Motivation reconsidered: The concept of competence. *Psychological Review,* 1959, *66,* 297–333.

White, K., Sheehan, P. W., & Ashton, R. Imagery assessment: A survey of self-report measures. *Journal of Mental Imagery,* 1977, *1*(1), 145–169.

Whitmore, J. R. *Giftedness, conflict, and underachievement.* Boston, Mass.: Allyn & Bacon, 1980.

Willard, A. Counseling the gifted. *Focus on Guidance,* 1976, *9*(1), 1–11.

Williams, F. E. Models for encouraging creativity in the classroom. *Educational Technology Magazine,* 1969, *9,* 7–13.

_____. *Classroom ideas for encouraging thinking and feeling.* Buffalo, N.Y.: D.O.K., 1970.

_____. Assessing pupil-teacher behaviors related to a cognitive-affective teaching model. *Journal of Research and Development in Education,* 1971, *4*(3), 14–22. (a)

_____. "How do you really feel about yourself?" In F. E. Williams, *Total creativity program for elementary school teachers.* Englewood Cliffs, N.J.: Educational Technology Publications, 1971. (b)

_____. *A total creativity program.* Englewood Cliffs, N.J.: Educational Technology Publications, 1972.

_____. Williams strategies orchestrating Renzulli's triad. *Gifted, creative and talented magazine,* 1979, *9,* 2–10.

Williams, R. L. *Black awareness sentence completion test.* Unpublished manuscript, St. Louis Center for Black Studies, Washington University, 1972. (a)

_____. *The BITCH–100: A culture-specific test.* Paper presented at the meeting of the American Psychological Association, Honolulu, September, 1972. (b)

_____. *Manual of directions: Black intelligence test of cultural homogeneity.* Unpublished manuscript, St. Louis Center for Black Studies, Washington University, 1972. (c)

_____. *Themes concerning blacks.* Unpublished manuscript, St. Louis Center for Black Studies, Washington, University, 1972. (d)

456

Williams, T. M., & Fleming, J. W. Methodological study of the relationship between associative fluency and intelligence. *Developmental Psychology,* 1969, *1*(2), 155–162.

Wilson, E. *Axel's castle; A study of the imaginative literature of 1870 to 1930.* New York: Charles Scribner's, 1931.

Wilson, F. T. Inservice and undergraduate preparation of the gifted. *Educational Administration and Supervision,* 1957, *43,* 295–301.

Wilson, R. C., & Morrow, W. R. School and career adjustment of bright high-achieving and underachieving high school boys. *Journal of Genetic Psychology,* 1962, *101,* 91–103.

Wilson, B., & Wilson, M. Visual narrative and the artistically gifted. *Gifted Child Quarterly,* 1976, *20*(4), 432–447.

Wing, H. D. *Standardized tests of musical intelligence.* England: National Foundation for Educational Research, 1939.

————. *Standardized tests of musical intelligence* (Rev. ed.). Slough, England: National Foundation for Educational Research, 1961.

Witt, G. The life enrichment activity program: A continuing program for creative, disadvantaged children. *Journal of Research and Development in Education,* 1971, *4*(3), 67–73.

Witty, P. A. (Ed.). *The gifted child.* Boston, Mass.: D.C. Health, 1951.

Wolleat, P. L. Guiding the career development of gifted females. In N. Colangelo & R. T. Zaffrann (Eds.), *New voices in counseling the gifted.* Dubuque, Iowa: Kendall/Hunt, 1979.

Yablonsky, L. Future-projection technique. In I. A. Greenberg (Ed.), *Psychodrama: Theory and Therapy.* New York: Behavioral Publications, 1974.

Yamamoto, K. Evaluation of some creativity measures in a high school with peer nominations as criteria. *Journal of Psychology,* 1964, *58,* 285–293.

Youtz, R. P. Psychological foundations of "applied imagination." In S. J. Parnes & H. F. Harding (Eds.), *A source book for creative thinking.* New York: Charles Scribner's, 1962.

Zettel, J. State provisions for educating the gifted and talented. In A. H. Passow (Ed.), *The gifted and the talented: Their education and development.* Chicago: University of Chicago Press, 1979. (78th Yearbook of the NSSE)

Zaffrann, R. T., & Colangelo, N., Counseling with gifted and talented students. *Gifted Child Quarterly,* 1977, *20*(3), 305–320.

AUTHOR INDEX

Foulds, G. A., 144
Fox, D. G., 8
Fox, L. H., 8, 155, 259, 325, 326, 332, 334
Fraiser, M. M., 238-239
Frankel, E., 218
French, J. L., 223, 224-225, 364, 387
French, W., 58
Freud, S., 50, 148
Frierson, E. C., 215
Fuchigami, R. Y., 238-239, 246, 250

Gage, N. L., 237
Gallagher, J. J., 12, 18, 35, 214, 215, 216, 218,
  224-225, 240, 256, 258, 320, 323, 324, 325,
  332, 356, 357, 360, 381, 391, 393, 416
Galton, F., 12, 35, 165
Gardner, E. F., 73, 142, 408
Garrett, H. E. A., 145, 408
Gear, G. H., 226
George, W. C., 7, 256
Gerencser, S., 338
Gerken, K. C., 225
Gessell, A., 5
Getzels, J. W., 8, 9, 12, 18, 19, 22, 23, 31, 213
Ghiselin, B., 106, 109, 113
Gibb, C. A., 56, 85
Gibbs, M. S., 76, 100
Giese, D. L., 252
Ginsberg, E., 203
Glasser, R., 307
Goddard, H. H., 39, 237
Gold, M. J., 173, 199, 202, 298, 307, 308, 320,
  323, 325, 365, 381
Goldberg, M. J., 8, 219
Goldberg, M. L., 58, 218, 220, 225, 298
Goolsby, T. M., 242
Gordon, E., 58, 92
Gordon, R., 113, 116, 119, 136
Gordon, W. J. J., 10, 119, 123, 205, 276, 282
Gostin, L., 215-216
Gough, H. C., 76
Gowan, J. C., 3, 5, 6, 7, 8, 11, 12, 16, 50, 56, 105,
  107, 108, 116, 139, 149, 150, 151, 152, 153,
  154, 155, 156-157, 158-159, 162, 165, 167,
  174, 175, 179, 180, 188, 201, 202-203, 213,
  214, 215, 219, 224, 226, 228, 229, 232-233,
  234, 235, 238, 256, 257, 263, 268, 272, 273,
  293, 307, 322, 323, 325, 335, 356, 364, 381,
  384, 392, 403, 407, 409, 411, 416, 426
Granzow, K. R., 218

Gray, C. E., 8, 165
Green, 223
Green, E. E., 118
Green, S., 118
Gruber, H. E., 155
Guilford, J. P., 4, 5, 8, 9, 10, 12, 18, 36, 39, 45,
  48, 49, 50, 52, 60, 75, 78, 79, 92, 94, 99, 120,
  128, 142, 144, 145, 146, 165, 176, 177, 213,
  226, 255, 265, 266, 267, 276, 293, 294-298,
  301, 401, 402, 407

Hall, G. S., 5, 77
Hall, L. K., 302
Hanaford, T., 130, 365
Hanard, S. R., 118
Harman, W. W., 118
Hass, R. B., 205
Hassan, P., 22
Havighurst, R. J., 154, 229, 256, 298, 325
Hebb, D. O., 145
Hebeler, J. R., 203
Hedbring, C., 316
Hencley, S. P., 290
Hendricks, M., 78
Henry, N. B., 36
Hiest, P., 76
Hildreth, G. H., 173, 174, 362
Hindsman, E., 213
Hirsch, S. P., 320
Hoepfner, R., 9, 78
Hollingsworth, L. S., 3, 35, 86, 172
Holt, J., 307
Holt, R. R., 7, 132
Horner, M. S., 230
Horng, R., 77
House, R. J., 56
Houtz, J. C., 77
Hoyt, K. B., 203
Hubbard, C. C., 118
Hunsicker, P., 99
Hunt, J. McV., 145, 298, 299, 301

Ickes, W., 231
Ingas, E., 307

Jackson, D. M., 327, 351, 356, 357, 359
Jackson, P. W., 8, 9, 12, 18, 19, 22, 23, 31, 213
Jaensch, E. R., 409
Jahoda, M., 183
James, L. R., 8

James, W., 165
Jastrow, J., 5
Jaynes, J., 106
Jencks, C., 243
Jennings, E., 213
Jensen, A. R., 243
Jensen, D. W., 13, 171-172
Johnson, D. M., 176
Johnson, P. G., 3
Johnson, R. A., 119, 120, 130, 131, 139
Jones, H. E., 144
Joyce, B., 246

Kamin, L. J., 243
Karnes, F. A., 265
Karnes, M. B., 215-216, 226
Karshner, W. W., 203, 204, 413
Keating, D., 7
Keating, D. P., 8, 155, 259
Kekulé von Stradnitz, F., 113
Kelley, T. L., 73, 142, 408
Kenmare, D., 172
Kenneally, C., 159-162
Khatena, J., 4, 8, 10, 12, 29, 52, 72, 75, 76, 81,
    82, 83, 84, 92, 93, 97, 101, 105, 106, 108, 111,
    112, 113, 114, 115, 119, 120, 121, 126, 127,
    128, 129, 130, 131, 133, 134, 137, 138, 142,
    147, 148, 150, 155, 165, 174, 177, 179, 180,
    188-189, 190, 213, 244, 245, 265, 292, 322,
    357, 358, 359, 360, 362, 365, 392, 402, 407,
    408, 409
Kimball, B., 215
King, F. J., 213
Kinney, L., 240
Klausmeier, H. J., 258
Klein, A. F., 205
Knickerbocker, I., 56
Koestler, A., 113
Kogan, N., 9, 20-21, 22, 52, 75
Kohlberg, L., 148, 232-233
Koopman, N., 188
Koplowitz, H., 155
Kowalski, C. J., 223-224, 356, 365
Krathwohl, D. R., 267, 272
Krepelka, E. J., 264
Krippner, S., 12, 118
Kroeber, A., 165, 166
Kubie, L. S., 12
Kuhlman, F., 5
Kwalsasser, J., 58, 92

Laird, A. W., 356, 357, 358, 359, 364, 365
Land, G., 113, 159-162, 176, 179, 281, 293, 294,
    301, 411, 426
Lane, J. B., 120
Langham, D. G., 158
Lawton, J. P., 155
Layden, M., 231
Leavitt, H. J., 231
Lehman, P. R., 58, 91
Lennon, R. T., 69
Leonard, G., 118, 133
Lewis, D., 58, 92
Lewis, J. F., 243
Lindauer, M. S., 118, 132, 133
Lipman-Blumen, J., 231
Littman, R. A., 298
Lowell, E. L., 221, 230
Lowenfeld, V., 59
Lucito, L. J., 226
Lum, M. K., 218
Lyon, H. C., 351, 353

McClelland, D. C., 221, 230
McCloy, C. H., 61
McCoy, G. F., 215-216
McDougall, W., 5
McGrath, J. E., 56
McGuire, C., 213
McIntyre, P. M., 214, 215, 216
McKellar, P., 136
McKim, R. H., 118
MacKin, E. F., 203
MacKinnon, D. W., 5, 12, 76, 128, 288
McNemar, Q., 19
Madden, R., 73, 142, 408
Maker, J. C., 226, 365, 385-386, 387, 391, 392,
    393, 394
Male, R. A., 203, 204, 413
Maltzman, I., 121, 128
Mangum, G. L., 203
Mann, R. D., 56
Mansfield, R. S., 264
Marks, D. R., 120
Marland, S. P., Jr., 9, 37, 350, 351, 387
Martinson, R. A., 68, 174, 387
Masia, B. B., 267, 272
Maslow, A. H., 50, 120, 148, 204, 300, 301
Mayer, R., 148, 232-233
Meadows, A., 121
Mednick, E. V., 109, 128

Mednick, M. T., 76, 109, 128-129
Mednick, S. A., 76, 109, 121, 128-129
Meeker, M. N., 8, 10, 165, 225, 243, 246, 263, 267-269, 270, 271, 272, 287, 308, 314-318, 327
Mercer, J. R., 243
Merenda, P. F., 74
Merrill, M. A., 39
Merry, F., 335
Meyersburg, A. H., 219
Miles, C. C., 17
Miller, L. P., 243
Mirman, B., 337
Mirman, N., 337
Mogar, R. E., 118
Moreno, J. L., 192, 205, 207, 288
Moreno, Z. T., 205
Morrow, W. R., 218
Morse, J. A., 229, 230, 231
Moseley, N., 36
Mowry, H. W., 85
Mursell, J. L., 91
Myers, R. E., 10, 165, 180, 182, 183, 192, 264, 288-289, 302, 384

Nathan, C. N., 362
Nelson, S., 231
Newland, T. E., 22, 35, 36, 214, 258, 298, 324, 356
Noller, R. B., 10, 120, 279

Oden, M. H., 2, 3, 5, 7, 11, 13, 14, 15, 16, 17, 143, 144, 172, 182, 228, 384
Olson, M., 106
Olson, W. C., 143
Olton, R. M., 264, 276
Ornstein, R., 106
Osborn, A. F., 4, 10, 77, 120, 121, 126, 205, 264, 276, 277, 279
Otis, A. S., 69
Owens, W. A., 143, 144

Paivio, A., 117, 118, 120, 406
Parnes, S. J., 10, 50, 77, 120, 121, 126, 205, 264, 276, 279-282, 285
Parsons, D. E., 273
Passow, A. H., 8, 58, 174, 218, 219, 220, 225, 298, 325, 355, 416
Patrick, C., 109
Pedro, J. D., 231
Pegnato, C. W., 8, 68

Pepinsky, P., 191
Perkins, H. V., 218-219
Perrone, P., 175
Perrone, P. A., 203, 204, 413
Perry, W. G., Jr., 232, 235
Piaget, J., 148, 149, 151, 154, 175, 272-273
Picasso, P., 116
Pierce, J. V., 216, 230
Poe, E. A., 114
Poggio, J. P., 8, 9
Poincaré, H., 109
Polak, F. L., 303
Pressey, S. L., 258
Prince, G. M., 10, 276, 282, 283-285
Pringle, M. L. K., 226-227
Pulvino, C. J., 175

Raph, J. B., 218, 220, 225, 298
Raskin, E., 98
Raven, J. C., 144, 243
Redl, F., 196
Reiff, G. G., 99
Renzulli, J. S., 10, 37, 165, 246, 260-263, 264, 265, 267, 273, 301, 302, 307, 308, 311-314, 330, 342, 343-346, 394-395, 416
Reynolds, C. R., 76, 165
Rhine, W. R., 5
Rhodes, M., 52, 128
Ribot, T., 51
Rice, R. W., 57
Richardson, A., 112, 117, 118, 119, 139, 406
Richardson, M. O., 10, 268, 270, 271, 316
Riegel, T. R., 76, 165
Riessman, R., 240
Rimm, S., 76
Ringenbach, S., 77
Ripple, R. E., 258
Roe, A., 83, 128
Rogers, D., 10, 229
Rosenkrantz, P. S., 230
Rossman, J., 120, 276, 277, 278, 301
Roth, R. M., 219
Rothney, J. W. M., 188
Roweton, W. E., 50, 51
Royce, J., 120
Rubenzer, R., 316
Rudman, H. C., 73, 142, 408
Runions, T., 309, 320-321
Runner, H., 76
Runner, K., 76

SUBJECT INDEX

characteristics, 24-26
coping with stress and, 194
developmental aspects, 10-11
developmental stage theory and, 176
development of measuring, 8, 9
education and, 179
elaboration and, 53, 59
flexibility and, 52-53, 59
fluency and, 52, 59
Freudian, 50-51
general systems and, 161-162
Henmon-Nelson tests of mental ability
    and, 19
humanistic psychology and, 5-7
identification of, 75-84
    divergent-production abilities, 77-79
    *Khatena-Torrance Creative Perception
        Inventory*, 83-84
    *Thinking Creatively with Sounds and
        Words*, 81-82
    Torrance Tests of Creative Thinking, 78,
        79-81
intelligence and, 8, 17-24
    personality traits and, 20-21
measurement, 9
    refinement of, 401-403
    validation of, 19, 22
mental health and, 50
periodic developmental stage and, 149, 151
personality and, 50
potential of, 2
preconscious and, 156-158
sociocultural environment and, 163-167
    guidance and, 178, 179-181
Something About Myself and, 126
theory of, 50-54
    creative-thinking abilities, 53-54, 77-81
    definition of, 51-52, 53-54
    divergent-production abilities, 48, 52-53,
        77-79
    Gowan's rational-psychedelic continuum,
        50-51
    Roweton's classification, 51
    thinking abilities, fourth-grade slump in,
        146-148, 408
training programs for, *see* Process approach
visual and performing arts, 59
    see also Development; Visual and
        performing arts ability
Creativity-based imagination and, 112
Creativity movement: humanistic psychology

and, 5-7
    structure of intellect and, 4, 5
Creativity Tests for Children, 78, 92
    art ability and, 94
Creativogenic society, 166, 180, 410, 425
Criterion-related validity, 70
Cultural diversity, 413-415, 425
    Chicago Non-Verbal Examination and, 243
    Creative Binet and, 243
    identification and, 240-245
        intelligence quotient (IQ) and, 236-238,
            240-242
    see also Underachievement
Culturally disadvantaged children, talents of, 9
Culture: creative development and, 163-167
    genius and, 165-167, 176, 179-181
Cupertino (California) Experimental Program
    for Gifted Underachievers, 221-223
Curriculum: college courses:
    on gifted, 365-376, 378-379, 387-389
    for teachers of gifted, 390-391
    individualizing education and, 322-324
    innovation in, 416-418
    science and, 323
    social studies and, 323

Deaf children, original verbal images by, 119,
    120, 130-131, 139
Decision-making, coping with, 195-196
Definition: of giftedness, 34-37, 64, 398-399, 424
    theory of creativity, 51-52, 53-54
    see also Identification
Delivery system: acceleration and, 340
    of projects, *see* Special projects
    school-within-a-school arrangement, 334
    see also In-service teacher preparation
Demonstration centers, 392-393
Developing Divergent Modes of Thinking in
    Mentally Gifted Minors (MGM), 327,
    328-329, 330
Development, 142-143, 408-411
    as continuous, 143-148
    discontinuity in, 177-178
        acceleration *vs.* escalation, 155
        escalation and, 151-152, 153, 154
        periodic developmental stages, 149-155,
            162
        preconscious in, 154, 155-158
    dysplasia, 409
    fourth-grade slump in creative thinking,
        177, 179, 409

Erikson-Piaget-Gowan Periodic Developmental Stage Chart, 149-155
Escalation, 11, 176, 263
  vs. acceleration, 155, 262-263
  developmental stages and, 151-152, 153, 154
  see also Educational facilitation
Ethnic groups, cultural diversity and, *see* Underachievement
Evaluation: of special projects, *see* Special projects
  structure of intellect and, 48, 49
  of teacher of gifted, 386. *See also* Teachers
Evaluative thinking, coping with stress and, 194-195
Executive High School Internship Program, 320
Exemplary Program, 328-329

Facilities, educational, 410-411. *See also specific institutions*
Factor analysis, 7, 44-45
  multivariate theories of intelligence and, *see* Intelligence
Failure: avoiding, underachievement and, 221
  coping with, 187-188, 197
Family: underachievement and, 215-217, 221
  women's affiliation to, 235
Fantasy analogy, 123-124, 126
  synectics and, 283
Federal Government, *see* Support agents
Feedback, guidance and, 179
Feed forward, 294
Figural abilities, art ability and, 94
Figural content, structure of intellect and, 48, 49
Figures of speech, 124-125
  in analogies, 125-127
Flanders Interaction Analysis Systems, 343
Flexibility, creativity and, 52-53, 59
Fluency, creativity and, 52, 59
Foreign languages, cultural diversity and, *see* Underachievement
Form Board Test, 76
Four-School Enrichment Program, 328-329, 330, 333
Fourth-grade slump in creative thinking abilities, 146-148, 177, 179, 292, 409
Freudian creativity, 50-51
Futuristic Learners Program, 332

General systems, *see* Development
Generic learning, 9-10

Genetic Studies of Genius, 12-17, 413
Genius: characteristics, 172
  culture and, 165-167
  guidance and, 176, 179-181
  education and, 165
  problems of, 172. *See also* Guidance
  vocational achievement and, 11, 172
Gifted Child Quarterly, 174, 323, 327, 355, 362, 363, 377, 392, 408, 422, 423
Gifted, Creative and Talented, 363
Giftedness, definition, 34-37, 64, 398-399, 424. *See also* Identification
Gifted and Talented Program, 328-329
Gifted and Talented Program Group, 350, 351
GIFTS Career Development Model, 203-205
Gifts for Youth Projects Program, 353
Girls, *see* Underachievement; Women
Gordon Test of Visual Imagery Control, 119, 136, 137, 138
Gough Adjective Check List, 76
Government assistance, *see* Support agents
Governor's School, 334, 335-336
Gowan-Erikson-Piaget model of developmental stages, guidance and, 176-178
Gowan-Piaget-Erikson periodic developmental stage, underachievement and, 217
Gowan's developmental stage theory, 162-163
Gowan's rational-psychedelic continuum theory of creativity, 50-51
Grade skipping, 257-258. *See also* Acceleration
Group, stress: accepting decision of, 198
  encouraging support from, 198
Group Inventory for Finding Creative Talent, 76
Growth, 142-143
  guidance and, 178
  transformation theory and, 159, 161, 178-179
  see also Development
Guidance, 411-413
  academic, 198-201, 412
    elementary school, 199-200
    secondary school, 200-201
    tests for, 98
  career, 201-208, 412-413
    gifted women and, 229-232
    GIFTS career development model, 203-205
    sociodrama and, 205-208, 413
    tests for, 98
  creative development: developmental stage theory and, 173, 175, 176-178

Maturation, 142-143. *See also* Development
Measurement: convergent-discrimination
    validation and, 9
  creativity, 8, 9
    refinement, 401-403
    validation of, 19, 22
  culturally disadvantaged and, 9
  of dimensionality, 9
  humanistic psychology and, 5
  of imagination imagery, 119-120
Measures of Musical Ability, 92
Meier Aesthetic Perception Test, 95
Meier Art Judgment Test, 95
Memory: coping with stress and, 193
  structure of intellect and, 48, 49
Mental age (MA): definition, 40
  increase of, 7
  intelligence quotient and, 41-43
Mental Health, 182-183
  creativity and, 50
  stress and, *see* Guidance
  Mentor Academy Program, 320-321
Mentor facilitation, 308, 319-322
Metaphor, 125, 126
  synectics and, 283
Metropolitan Achievement Test, 73
Mindspring, 283, 285-286
Minority group, cultural diversity and, *see*
    Underachievement
Mirman School for the Gifted, The, 334,
  336-337
Motivation, 255, 298-303, 418
  needs and, 300, 301-302
  problem-solving and, 301
  self-image and, 303
  see also Achievement motivation
Multifactor theory, of intelligence, 47-49
Multiple Aptitude Tests, 98
Multiple Talent Evaluation, cultural diversity
  and, 243
Multitalent model, 8-9
Multivariate approach, to intelligence, 44-49
Music ability, *see* Visual and performing arts
  ability
Musical Aptitude Profile, 92
Myers-Briggs Type Indicator, 76
Myers-Torrance Workbooks, 264

National Association for Gifted Children,
  363, 422
National Center for Educational Research and

Development, 351
National Defense Education Act (NDEA), 4, 349
National Endowment for the Arts and
  Humanities, 353
National Education Association (NEA), 421
National Education Association (NEA) Invita-
  tional Conference on the Academically
  Talented Pupil, 4
National Society for the Study of Education
  (NSSE) Yearbook on Individualized
  Education, 308
National/State Leadership Training Institute
  (N/S LTI), 350, 351, 353, 354-355, 392,
  421, 422
National/State Leadership Training Institute
  Gifted and Talented Bulletin
  (N/S LTI-G/T Bulletin), 362
The Nature of Human Intelligence, 78
Need: denial of and coping with stress, 197-198
  motivation and, 300, 301-302
Need hierarchy, motivation and, 301
Nondrug-induced hallucination imagery, 118
Nurturance, 306
  future visions of, 416-418
  see also Individualizing education; Special
    projects; Support agents
Nurture, 415-418
  Khatena-Torrance Creative Perception
    Inventory and, 245
  see also Educational facilitation; Environ-
    ment, Underachievement

Occupations, gifted women, 228-232. *See also*
  Guidance
Ocular pursuit, 61. *See also* Psychomotor
  ability
Office of the Gifted and Talented, 349,
  351-354, 361
Omnibus Personality Inventory, 76
Onomatopoeia and Images, 81-82, 407
  fourth-grade slump and, 147, 148
  imagery and, 108
  problem-solving and, 292
  see also Thinking Creatively with Sounds
    and Words
Organization for Gifted, parents and, 362-363
Originality: autonomy and imagery, 136-138
  creativity and, 53
Original verbal imagery, *see* Imagination
Osborn-Parnes creative problem-solving
  approach, 277, 279-282

478

general, *see* Development
leadership and, 88
structure of intellect and, 49
transformation model, 294
    problem-solving and, 277, 293, 294
see also Process approach
Systems stage, 155

Talcott Mountain Science Center in Governor's
    Honors Programs, 200
Talented, definition, 36
Talented and gifted students, 328-329, 331
Target Game, 76
Taxonomy of Education Objectives, 343
Teachers, preparation of: colleges offering
    courses on gifted, 365-376, 378-379,
    387-389
    curricula, 390-391
    preservice preparation, 389-391
    for gifted program, 426
    for gifted progress, 364-395, 423-424
    in-service, 391
        demonstration projects as centers, 392-393
        instructional management system (IMS),
        394-395
        service centers, 393-395
        states and, 377, 380
        summer institutes, 391-392
        technical assistance development system,
        393-394
    need for, 364-365
    states and, 359
    teacher qualities and, 381-387
see also Education; Schools
"Teachers Are Gifted Too!," 331
*Teaching Gifted Children To Use Creative
    Imagination Imagery*, 140, 408
Technical Assistance Development System,
    393-394
Terman Concept Mastery Test, gifted children
    selected from, 13, 15, 16
Test of General Ability, cultural diversity and, 243
Testing model, intellect model and, 4
Themes Concerning Blacks, 243
Thinking: lateral, 286-287
    vertical, 286
Thinking abilities: creative, 53-54, 77-81
    fourth-grade slump in, 146-148, 408
Thinking Course for Juniors, 287
Thinking Creatively in Action and Movement,
    76, 100

Thinking Creatively with Sounds and Words,
    81-82, 92, 402, 407
    cultural diversity and, 244
    Onomatopoeia and Images: analogy and, 120
        imagery and, 120
        original verbal images and, 126, 127, 128,
        129, 130, 131, 135, 137, 138
    Sounds and Images: analogy and, 120
        imagery and, 120
        original verbal image and, 126, 127, 128,
        129, 130, 131, 135
*Thinking Creatively with Sounds and Words:
    Norms-Technical Manual:* imagery
    and, 108
    problem-solving and, 292
Time press, originality, analogy production
    and, 128-130. *See also* Stress
Torrance Tests of Creative Thinking, 8, 9, 78,
    79-81, 128, 402
    art ability and, 94-95
    creative achievement and, 28
    cultural diversity and, 243, 244-245
    development and, 147
    developmental patterns of creativity and, 11
    fourth-grade slump in creative thinking
        abilities and, 146
    limitations, 22
    predictive validity of, 27-29
        long-range prediction, 27-29
        short-range prediction, 27
    training procedures and, 264
Total Creativity Program, 273
*Total Creativity Program for Elementary
    School Teachers*, 330
Training procedures, creative thinking, *see*
    Process approach
Transformation: art ability, 94
    leadership and, 88
    structure of intellect and, 49
Transformation model, *see* Systems
Transformation theory (Land's), 159-162, 276, 410
    guidance and, 178-179
Transposition, original verbal images and,
    121-122
Two-factor theory of intelligence, 45

Underachievement, 414
    avoiding failure and, 221
    causes of, 214-215
    cultural diversity and, 236-253
        curriculum and methods, 246